Encyclopedia of
Major League Baseball Clubs

ENCYCLOPEDIA OF

Major League Baseball Clubs

VOLUME II | THE AMERICAN LEAGUE

Edited by Steven A. Riess

Greenwood Press
Westport, Connecticut • London

Library of Congress Cataloging-in-Publication Data

Encyclopedia of Major League Baseball clubs / edited by Steven A. Riess.
    p. cm.
  Includes bibliographical references and index.
  ISBN 0–313–32991–5 (set : alk. paper) – ISBN 0–313–32992–3 (v. I : alk. paper).
– ISBN 0–313–32993–1 (v. II : alk. paper).
  1. Baseball teams—United States—History—Encyclopedias. 2. Major League
Baseball (Organization)—History—Encyclopedias. I. Riess, Steven A.
GV875.A1E52   2006
796.357'640973—dc22   2006015368

British Library Cataloguing in Publication Data is available.

Library of Congress Catalog Card Number: 2006015368
ISBN: 0–313–32991–5 (set)
     0–313–32992–3 (vol. I)
     0–313–32993–1 (vol. II)

First published in 2006

Greenwood Press, 88 Post Road West, Westport, CT 06881
An imprint of Greenwood Publishing Group, Inc.
www.greenwood.com

Printed in the United States of America

∞™

The paper used in this book complies with the
Permanent Paper Standard issued by the
National Information Standards Organization (Z39.48–1984).

10 9 8 7 6 5 4 3 2 1

Contents

THE AMERICAN LEAGUE, VOLUME II

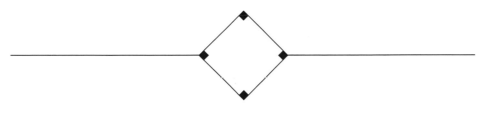

American League

Baltimore Orioles

William A. Borst

Had Charles Dickens been writing about baseball instead of the French Revolution, he could have substituted St. Louis and Baltimore for London and Paris in his novel *A Tale of Two Cities*. Both cities have enjoyed a storied past that has contributed scores of memories and traditions to baseball's unique history.

St. Louis's baseball history dates back to just after the Civil War. The city had early entries in the National Association of Professional Base Ball Players, the National League, and the Union League before finally establishing its baseball roots with the American Association in 1881. Tavern owner Chris Von der Ahe, a German immigrant with a keen business sense, was the first entrepreneur to realize that baseball fans got thirsty while watching a game in the summer sun.

Von der Ahe owned the Brown Stockings in the AA from 1882 to 1891. While his team consistently won on the field, the AA's demise in 1891 prompted him to join the NL as part of a 12-team circuit. Before the turn of the century the Brown Stockings changed the color of their hose and their name to the St. Louis Cardinals.

THE BROWNS' FIRST OWNERS

After the American League's maiden season in 1901, its founder, Ban Johnson, was convinced his AL could compete with the NL in its major cities. He recruited a new set of owners for his last-place Milwaukee Brewers, which with Detroit were the only teams from the minor Western League to have made the transition into the AL. Financial wizard Ralph T. Orthwein's syndicate purchased the Brewers from Milwaukee businessmen Henry and Matthew Killea with the intention of transferring the franchise to St. Louis, then the nation's fourth-largest city.

The St. Louis Browns, who took their name from the former St. Louis Brown Stockings of the AA, began play in 1902. They were an important part of the St. Louis sports scene during the first half of the twentieth century. Though they finished in the AL first division a mere 12 times, the players endeared themselves to a city whose baseball passions were not satisfied by just one team. For 52 seasons the Browns did everything they could to win on the field for their baseball public but usually failed, giving rise to the anonymous old adage that St. Louis was "first in shoes, first in booze, and last in the American League." The shoes were represented by the Brown Shoe Company, while the booze was Anheuser-Busch, the large beer manufacturer.

Of baseball's original 16 teams, the Browns had the worst composite record, compiling a dismal record of 3,414–4,465 (.433). The team's only pennant came in 1944 during World War II. Even then the Browns' achievement was denigrated by the derisive claim that war conditions had so watered down the competing talent that even the Browns could win a pennant. Little known to most baseball fans was that for many years the Browns were the best team in St. Louis.

Owner Orthwein naturally gravitated to Sportsman's Park, on Grand and Dodier, the former home of the Double-A Brown Stockings. Von der Ahe had turned his ballpark into a racetrack after a disagreement with his partner Al Spink of the *Sporting News*. Though seriously run-down, it was much easier to renovate an old ballpark than build a new one on short notice.

The Browns began building their roster by raiding their city rivals, the Cardinals, of their best players, including future Hall of Famers shortstop Bobby Wallace (inducted in 1953) and outfielder Jesse Burkett (inducted in 1946). The Browns lured Wallace away from the Cardinals with a five-year no-trade contract worth $32,000, including a $6,500 signing bonus, making Wallace the highest-paid player in the majors at the time. This underhanded act left a bad taste in the mouths of most St. Louisans. Orthwein's reign was short-lived, and he sold his stock in the club to carriage maker Robert Hedges in 1903 for $35,000. Burkett's highest annual salary was $5,300.

The Browns opened their maiden season on April 12, 1902, on a positive note by defeating the Cleveland Blues 5–2 before 8,000 fans. They finished the year in second place with a record of 78–58, just five games behind the Philadelphia Athletics. The Browns' best club during their first decade, in 1908, was in a four-team race until near end of their season. This was largely due to eccentric lefty pitcher Rube Waddell, who came to the Browns after he had worn out his welcome in Philadelphia. The Athletics' owner and longtime manager, the usually patient Connie Mack, had exhausted all his patience for the southpaw's erratic antics. On impulse, Waddell often left the team to go fishing, lead a parade, or just sit under a tree. He won 19 games for the fourth-place Browns.

After the 1908 season, Hedges erected a double deck made from concrete and steel that stretched from first to third with pavilions adjacent to the grandstand and the bleachers in the outfield. He also introduced steel and concrete to his structure, greatly adding to its longevity. The Browns opened in their new park in 1909, but it did not help their play on the field. Their lackluster performance that year put them in seventh place for the first of 12 times in franchise history.

In 1910 manager "Peach Pie" O'Connor tarnished the team image by participating in a scheme to deny that year's batting title to the widely despised Ty Cobb of the Detroit Tigers. The schedule called for Cleveland to finish the season with the Browns. O'Connor, who had succeeded the Browns' original manager, Jimmy McAleer, instructed rookie third baseman Red Corriden to play deep. This allowed Cleveland second baseman Nap Lajoie, the only player with a mathematical chance of catching Cobb, who tripled in his first at-bat, to bunt seven times for easy hits. Both O'Connor and third-base coach Harry Howell visited the press box to lobby the official scorer on Lajoie's behalf. They were banished from MLB for impugning the game's integrity.

THE BALL YEARS

After the Browns' sixth-place finish in 1915, Hedges sold the team to ice magnate Philip DeCatesby Ball, a former minor-league catcher, for $425,000, making Hedges a nearly $400,000 profit. Ball had recently owned the rival St. Louis Terriers of the recently defunct Federal League. He brought new enthusiasm, organization, and, more importantly, money to the Browns. Ball also signed 11 members of his Terriers squad to play for the Browns, including future Hall of Fame pitcher Eddie Plank (inducted in 1946) and outfield mainstay Johnny Tobin. Ball's reign (1916–33) is considered the golden era of St. Louis Browns' history. Under Ball's ownership the Browns fielded their best teams and their best players, and were regular members of the first division. Unfortunately, Ball would later make three disastrous decisions that hastened the decline and eventual departure of the team from St. Louis after the 1953 season.

The first was allowing the Cardinals to continue to play in St. Louis. After a second straight dismal season in 1919, the crosstown rival Redbirds were in dire straits and were forced to vacate their stadium, Robison Field, which was a firetrap. On bended knee, Cardinals owner Sam Breadon asked Ball to allow his team to play at Sportsman's Park and become his tenants. Ball could have easily forced the Cardinals out of St. Louis, but his magnanimity got the better of him. For a modest rental of between $20,000 and $25,000 a year, the Cardinals henceforth played their home games in Sportsman's Park.

Ball's second failure was to alienate Branch Rickey, the man who invented the farm-team system. After an arm injury ended his catching career, followed by a law degree at the University of Michigan, where he coached the baseball team, Rickey took a front-office job with the Browns. Near the end of the 1913 season, Rickey replaced George Stovall as manager. Rickey had already shown signs of his visionary genius and could have done for the Browns what he would later do for the Cardinals and the Brooklyn Dodgers. Unfortunately, there was room for only one ego in the Browns' offices, and Ball's was it. After a couple of years of not getting along with Ball, Rickey moved across the hall to work for Breadon's Cardinals in 1919, when he returned to baseball after serving in the army during World War I. Breadon was wise to allow Rickey the freedom to demonstrate his organizational genius, which would revolutionize the game. Rickey used the revenue gained from the sale of Robison Field to the St. Louis Board of Education to develop the farm system that sent a parade of future stars to the Cardinals' roster.

The third was hubris. In 1925, Ball remodeled and renovated his park at a cost of $500,000, and Ball boldly predicted there would be a World Series in Sportsman's Park in 1926. Ball extended the double-deck grandstand Hedges had erected into the left- and right-field corners and put a roof on the right-field pavilion. This raised the Browns' per-game capacity from 18,500 to just over 30,500. The rehab also extended the dimensions from 315 feet to 320 feet in right field and from 340 feet to 355 feet in left field while leaving centerfield at 430 feet. But Ball's bold prediction was only partly correct. There was a World Series in St. Louis, but it was hosted by the Cardinals, not the Browns. After their thrilling upset of the Yankees in seven games, St. Louis fans traded in their brown for cardinal red.

A WINNING FORMULA? THE TEENS

The first element in the Browns' winning formula was the acquisition in 1915 of left-handed pitcher George Sisler. Branch Rickey, who had been his coach at Michigan University, was instrumental in signing him. Sisler, who would prove much more potent in the batter's box than on the mound (his major-league record was 5–6), would ultimately be the most outstanding star in the team's small galaxy. In 15 major-league seasons, 12 with the Browns, he batted .340 and led the AL four times in stolen bases.

After his shift to first base in 1917, Sisler hit .353 to finish second in the AL behind perennial batting champion Ty Cobb. In 1917 the seventh-place Browns won only 57 games, but two pitchers threw no-hitters, Ernie Koob and Bob Groom on May 5 and 6 against the Chicago White Sox. (Groom's was in the nightcap of a doubleheader, so the games were not in succession.)

Following America's entry into World War I, MLB shortened the 1918 season by a month. Regulars Bull Rumler, Yale Sloan, and Bill Fincher and the newly acquired Urban Shocker traded their flannels for government issue. While the Browns were fifth in the standings, they did finish first in one category. As a patriotic gesture, AL president Ban Johnson promoted a drilling competition between each of his AL teams. Using bats instead of rifles, the players marched around the diamond and performed close-order drills before some of their games. The Browns "soldiers" were voted as the "most military" of the AL teams and were awarded a $500 first-place prize.

THE ROARING TWENTIES

In 1920 the Browns reentered the first division after an absence of 12 years, batting a remarkable .308. The revamped Browns gave some indication of what was to come; over the first seven years of the decade, the club earned an average of $133,500. Urban Shocker recorded 20 victories while Sisler won the first of his two batting titles with an incredible .407 average. He set a major-league record, which stood until 2004, with 257 hits. His 19 home runs were second only to Babe Ruth's 54.

In 1922 baseball was more exciting than ever before. MLB teams combined for a record 1,055 homers, when just five years before they had only hit 339. The big difference in production has been attributed to a combination of the livelier ball in 1920 and the banning of such trick pitches as the spit, shine, coffee, and mud ball. The 1922 season also stands out as the pinnacle of the Browns' achievement on the field. While the Browns had a stellar pitching staff, led by Urban Shocker, hitting was the team's strong suit. The team hit a collective .313, surpassed in AL history only by the 1921 Detroit Tigers' .316. Sisler hit an incredible .420 to lead all AL hitters and was MVP.

The Browns had an outstanding outfield, each of which hit .300 or better for three consecutive seasons. Ken Williams, whose 39 homers and 155 RBIs had dethroned Babe Ruth for AL leadership in both categories, led this superlative trio. A quiet man from Grants Pass, Oregon, Williams also stole 37 bases, which gave him the distinction of being the first (albeit unheralded) member of the prestigious 30-30 club. Over his 14-year career, he batted a potent .319. He hit 196 homers, and finished in the top four from 1921 through 1927.

George Sisler, 1915. Courtesy of the Baseball Hall of Fame.

"Baby Doll" Jacobson, a lifetime .311 hitter, roamed center field, while expert bunter Johnny Tobin, who hit .309 for his career, manned right field. Jacobson's colorful nickname was a throwback to his days with Mobile in the Southern Association. Whenever he came to bat, the band played "Oh You Beautiful Doll."

The Browns had boosters called "the Pennant Rooters" who supported the team with a frenzied passion in stark contrast to the more blasé demeanor of Cardinal fans. On September 5 they presented each member of the team with a gold watch in premature recognition of the team's first pennant. Sisler told the fans that during a secret meeting the players had vowed not to lose another game the rest of the season. The Rooters gave out horns, cowbells, and other noisemakers to cheer the team down the pennant stretch.

The race was all but decided in mid-September. Sisler was nearing the end of a 41-game hitting streak that would set the AL standard, but his tender shoulder made his play painfully erratic. He amassed just a pair of hits in the crucial three-game home series with the Yankees. In front of 30,000 screaming fans, the Browns split the first two games, leaving the Browns just a half game back. With a 2–1 lead going into the ninth inning in the rubber game, Whitey Witt, who had been hit in the head by a beer bottle in the first game, stroked a bases-loaded single off Shocker to rally the Yankees to victory. Even though they finished a game behind the Yankees, their 93 victories rank as the best in franchise history. The club drew an all-time team record attendance of 712,918 and a profit of $260,498.

The Browns averaged nearly 77 wins for the next three seasons, until their stars started to fade. In 1927 the Yankees won the first 21 of the season's 22 games with the Browns. After the Browns' seventh-place finish, under manager Dan Howley (59–94), 50 1/2 games behind the Yankees, Ball cleaned house with a vengeance. The team's aging superstars departed as Sisler was traded to Washington and Williams joined the Boston Red Sox.

A vastly improved pitching staff led by Alvin "General" Crowder resulted in third place in 1928. Crowder compiled an amazing 21–5 record, while Sam Gray went 20–12. Ernie Nevers, who would set the all-time record by scoring 40 points in an NFL game for the Chicago Cardinals in 1929, finished his short-lived three-year major-league career with the Browns, the most significant note in which was the fact that he had surrendered 2 of Babe Ruth's 60 home runs in 1927. Newcomer Heinie Manush hit .378, only a single point behind AL leader Goose Goslin of the Senators.

Ball's close friendship with AL president Ban Johnson put him at constant odds with Commissioner Kenesaw Mountain Landis. The epicenter of his biggest dispute with Landis was over oft-injured minor-league outfielder Fred Bennett. The Browns put Bennett on waivers in 1930 but quickly removed him once the Pirates expressed interest. Bennett protested to Landis that he was being unfairly prevented from playing in the majors. The case went to court, and all sides lost. Judge Walter C. Lindley ruled that there was nothing inherently wrong with major-league teams owning minor-league players. The Browns were forced to put Bennett on their roster or declare him a free agent. Bennett never played another game in the major leagues. Landis finally lost all patience with the Browns' irascible owner. He petitioned the other owners to discourage his continual litigation against Landis's office. On the sage advice of business manager Bob Quinn, Ball reluctantly dropped his appeal to the Supreme Court.

In 1933 the Browns hit rock bottom in the heart of the depression, finishing last for the first time since 1913. While the players earned just $140,789, the second lowest in MLB, Ball lost $33,559 because only 88,113 fans attended games, on top of the nearly $300,000 he had lost in the three previous years. In August the cantankerous Rogers Hornsby became the team's third manager.

Ball's untimely death in 1933 left the organization in chaos. The team had consistently lost money since 1926, with only one year in the black since then. The bulk of his estate, including 87 percent of the team, went to his widow, Harriet, and their two children. Ball's attorneys, Louis B. Von Weise and Ellen M. Jacoby, both baseball neophytes, held the estate, including the team, in trust. Rumors persisted that Harry Sinclair, the oil magnate involved in the Teapot Dome scandal, was interested in buying the team. The trustees unwisely decided to run the Browns themselves, with every intention of restoring the franchise to profitability. They steadfastly maintained a hold on the purse strings, resolutely refusing to dip into Ball's personal estate to pay their bills, much to Hornsby's displeasure.

One of the most despised men in baseball, Hornsby's only good decision in 1934 was acquiring pitcher Bobo Newsom from Los Angeles of the Pacific Coast League, whom he had managed with the Cubs. Newsom personified the ill fortunes of the team when he took a 1–1 no-hitter into the 10th inning, only to lose the game 2–1.

Hornsby tolerated no interference from the trustees as he attempted to run the franchise into the ground. He started a fire sale to make ends meet, including sending the peripatetic Newsom to Washington in 1935. The seventh-place Browns lost 44 of their 76 home games, before only 80,927 fans, their lowest attendance figure in franchise history and the lowest in modern MLB history.

After the end of the 1935 season, Von Weise asked Branch Rickey of the Cardinals for assistance in finding a buyer for the team. Rickey delegated this task to his able lieutenant Bill DeWitt. Over dinner one night DeWitt learned that insurance executive Donald Barnes, the president of the American Investment Company, was interested in purchasing the beleaguered Browns. Barnes formed a syndicate, which paid $325,000 for the team. Sportsman's Park remained the property of the local Dodier Realty Company until 1946. For the first time in their history, the Browns were the tenants and not the landlord. The Cardinals continued under their old agreement with the trustees. The financially astute Rickey collected a $40,000 finder's fee.

THE BARNES YEARS

While Donald Barnes was a baseball novice, he knew a good deal about business. A native Chicagoan, Barnes had built his insurance company on borrowed money into a $250 million enterprise by the time he moved to St. Louis. He instituted an era of the small stockholder by selling shares in the franchise to the public at five dollars a share. These shares provided a necessary financial lift that kept the team afloat during the closing days of the depression. They remained on the books until Baltimore Orioles owner Edward Bennett Williams redeemed them for $40 apiece in 1981.

The best player to don a Browns uniform in the 1930s was infielder Harlond Clift. After breaking in with the Browns in 1934, Clift spent nine productive seasons with the team, and drove in 118 runs in 1937 and 1938, with 63 homers those two years. In 1936 attendance picked up to 93,267. Hornsby stood pat with what was left of his lineup for another seventh-place finish.

Barnes tried to enhance the team's image with the creation of a new team emblem. The winning entry in a fan contest was an opaque figure of King Louis IX of France atop his mighty steed. It would remain the team's emblem until 1952 when Bill Veeck unveiled "Louie," an impish figure that blended the mystery of a leprechaun with the playfulness of an elf, a fitting logo for their final seasons in St. Louis.

The team's new logo did not help their performance on the field. The 1937 Browns were one of the most inept teams in baseball history, losing 108 games. Hornsby's penchant for gambling prompted Barnes to resort to wiretapping and hiring a private detective to control his erratic manager, who was replaced halfway through the season by Jim Bottomley. The Browns used 21 different pitchers before the season was over, and for the first time none had 10 wins. Surprisingly, attendance increased to 123,121. Under constant financial pressure, Barnes went to the city's business leaders and secured 10 pledges of over $5,000 apiece to tide the team over during the nation's difficult economic times.

The 1939 season ranks as the worst in Browns history. During Fred Haney's first full year at the helm, the team lost 111 games, surpassing the 1910 team's bellwether for futility. Home attendance increased to over 130,000, however, even though the team won a mere 13 games at their own park.

THE WAR YEARS

With the winds of war blowing, Barnes kept his focus on the business at hand. The first-ever Browns night game on May 24, 1940, drew 24,827. Fans saw Eldon Auker lose to Bob Feller and the Cleveland Indians 3–2. The team was floundering when Barnes hired the cerebral Luke Sewell to manage the club in mid-1941. A dedicated student of pitching, Sewell had been a catcher who often advised Senators manager Joe Cronin during games.

The grind of financial pressures ate away at Barnes's hope of success in St. Louis. He quietly made plans to shift the team to Los Angeles, which would have been a move of historic proportions. Barnes rightfully proclaimed that there were not enough fans in St. Louis to support two teams. Barnes's old friend Philip K. Wrigley, owner of the Chicago Cubs, agreed to sell Barnes his rights to Los Angeles and move his Hollywood Stars to Long Beach. Cardinals owner Breadon agreed to pay Barnes $350,000 to leave St. Louis. The fear of losing the entire team in a plane crash prompted Barnes to make arrangements with TWA president Jack Frye to fly two players on each of the 12 daily flights between Chicago to Los Angeles.

Barnes was poised to receive the approval of AL owners to relocate his club to California at their December 8, 1941, meeting in Chicago. The Japanese attack on Pearl Harbor on December 7 and America's subsequent entry into the war prevented the Browns from relocating, permanently altering the team's future. The Pacific Coast transfer now impossible, Barnes turned to his stockholders for the necessary capital to stay solvent. Ice magnate Richard Muckerman provided $300,000, for which he was named club vice president.

After Pearl Harbor, owners were fearful that their game would be shut down. Recognizing the countless benefits that baseball provided for millions of Americans, President Franklin Roosevelt's "Green Light letter" eased their fears about a baseball shutdown during the coming war.

The Browns' third-place finish in 1942 gave promise of a more successful future. Two players in particular gave the team a boost. Power-hitting rookie Vern Stephens and George McQuinn, who anchored the infield at first base, were integral parts of the winning formula. McQuinn's skills were comparable to Browns legend George Sisler. His model baseball glove became an immediate best seller and was used by future president George H. W. Bush when he played first base for Yale University during the 1947–48 seasons. In 1942 the Browns made $80,455, their biggest profit since 1926, and only the third year they did not lose money since 1929.

Nine out of 10 major leaguers active during the 1941 season traded their flannels for Uncle Sam's olive drab during the war years. Teams struggled to fill their rosters with able players who were ineligible for military service so they could compete on the field. By 1944 the Browns had assembled a crew of talented 4-Fs, work-deferred, older, and married players who amassed 89 wins and captured the franchise's first and only pennant in team history.

A MOMENT IN THE SUN

Major-league teams were prevented from holding spring-training camps in the warm South to prepare for the upcoming 1943 campaign, and were instead forced to make do in the colder climes of New York, Indiana, Missouri, and Illinois. With railways overtaxed from carrying troops and war material, Landis and director of the Office of Defense Transportation Joseph B. Eastman agreed in January 1943 that clubs would restrict their springtime travel, and announced the imposition of the Landis-Eastman Line. The Landis-Eastman Line decree prohibited major-league teams from enjoying the southerly climates of any location south of the Mason-Dixon Line or west of the Mississippi River. This policy of austerity existed until the end of the war.

So for the next three seasons, all major-league teams trained near their hometowns. The Browns erected their camp 30 miles north, on the Missouri side of the Mississippi River in a small college town named Cape Girardeau. The city's fairgrounds had an indoor arena that the Browns were able to convert into a dirt field, so the inclement chilly weather never bothered them. This publicity device paid huge dividends for the Browns in 1944.

Thanks to the stellar pitching of 32-year-old rookie Sigmund Jakucki, Jack Kramer, and Steve Sundra, the Browns reeled off nine consecutive wins to start the season, shattering the prior record of seven in a row set by the 1933 Yankees. The team's most important season came down to a crucial end-of-the-year series against the Yankees, who were out of the pennant race. The Browns trailed the Detroit Tigers by a full game with only four home games remaining. Sweeping a doubleheader, the Browns' Kramer won his 17th game of the season, while Nelson Potter won his 19th on a 1–0 shutout. With the Tigers splitting their doubleheader against the Senators, the Browns moved up one game in the standings and into a tie for first place. Both teams won their next game. In the final game of the season, Dutch Leonard of the Senators defeated the Tigers 4–1. With the heavy-drinking Jakucki on the mound, the Browns won the game and the AL pennant on the strength of a pair of two-run homers by part-time player Chet Laabs, as the Browns avenged their 1922 disappointment with a 5–2 victory. Posting an 89–65 record, that year the club was second in the AL in pitching and runs scored, despite a dismal .252 team batting average, second lowest in the league.

The Browns' World Series opponent was the local rival Cardinals, who had cruised to their third conservative pennant. The Cardinals' roster had been hurt by players departing for military service, but the nucleus of their champion teams was basically intact. They still had Stan Musial, NL MVP Marty Marion, Mort and Walker Cooper, and third baseman Whitey Kurowski.

The Browns won the first game 2–1 behind Denny Galehouse, with McQuinn's two-run homer marring the expert pitching of right-hander Mort Cooper, who allowed just two hits. Nelson Potter's misplay of a bunt by Cardinals pitcher Max Lanier led to the Browns' 10th-inning loss in the second game. The Browns won the third game easily by a score of 6–2 behind Jack Kramer, but it was the team's high-water mark, as the Cardinals combined timely hitting with the pinpoint control of Cooper, Hal Lanier, Harry Brecheen, and Ted Wilks to sweep the remaining three games.

The Browns had high hopes for the 1945 season, which was remarkable for the presence of Pete Gray, who had lost his right arm above the elbow in a childhood accident. Born Pete Wyshner in 1915, Gray led the Southern Association with a .333 mark with 68 stolen bases in 1944, garnering the SA's MVP award. With the Browns, however, he hit only .218 and was blamed by most his teammates for their failure to repeat as AL champions. They regarded his presence as a publicity stunt designed to win more fan support than games. Vern Stephens led the third-place Browns and the AL in home runs with 34, making him the first Brown to do so since Ken Williams in 1922. In August a weary Donald Barnes sold his 31 percent interest in the team to partner Robert Muckerman.

POSTWAR CHANGES

Richard Muckerman had been involved with the Browns since 1939, when he bought his first shares of stock. In 1942, during the club's reorganization, he increased his share to a quarter of all outstanding stock. Muckerman also bought back Sportsman's Park from the Dodier Realty Company in 1946, and that year saw the Browns attract 526,435 fans, more than the 508,644 that came during the pennant-winning season of 1944. This was the Browns' fourth-largest attendance and the most since 1922. Unfortunately, the timing could not have been worse for Muckerman and the Browns. The end of the war and the return of players from the military in 1946 brought imbalance back to professional baseball, and the Browns fell back to seventh place. The team released Gray, who returned to his native Nanticoke, Pennsylvania, where he lived in bitterness until his death in 2003.

Postwar inflation and the need to build a new ballpark for their farm club, the San Antonio Missions, eroded the slim profits the team had garnered during the war. The Browns seldom had any money in the bank, hardly surprising since from 1926 through 1943 they had the lowest attendance in the AL. In 1944 the Browns made a profit of $285,034. With that sole exception, since Ball's death in 1933 the team stayed just a few steps ahead of its creditors. This forced the Browns into the harmful position of having to sell its best players to pay the bills. Predictably, attendance declined, translating into less revenue and more debts, forcing yet another round of player sales.

Muckerman's second season witnessed the racial integration of MLB, which had fought the use of African American players for several generations. In the wake of Cleveland's signing of Larry Doby, the major sportswriters in the East opined that St. Louis was too southern a city to tolerate a black player. The Browns defied the conventional wisdom when in 1947 they signed Willard Brown and Henry Thompson from the Kansas City Monarchs and took out a 30-day option on Piper Davis of the Birmingham Black Barons.

The motives for the Browns' experiment in integration seemed mixed. Muckerman thought adding black players to the roster would increase the team's sagging attendance. General manager Bill DeWitt added, "It seems in order that this large Negro population should have some representation on their city's ball team," which author Jules Tygiel wrote in his *Baseball's Great Experi-*

ment was "a revolutionary concept amidst the cobwebbed conservatism of the baseball hierarchy."

Unfortunately, integration did nothing for the Browns, who ended in last place. Thompson hit a modest .256 in 27 games, while Brown had just 12 hits in his 67 at bats, including an inside-the-park home run, the first home run by a black player in the AL.

THE DEWITT YEARS

Even though the Browns improved two notches in the standings in 1948, Muckerman was forced to sell the team to baseball executive Bill DeWitt and his older brother, impresario Charley DeWitt, for $1 million on February 2, 1949. Both had enjoyed a long history with the Browns in the front office and were confident that they could swim against the financial currents that had swamped their last two predecessors. Charley, affectionately known as "the Senator," provided the charm, while his brother Bill, as the new president, provided the brainpower in running the club. Their fraternal dynamic produced another seventh-place finish. Rookie outfielder Roy Sievers compiled a solid .306 batting average to win the AL Rookie of the Year Award, making him the last Browns player to win a major award.

DeWitt hired psychologist David Tracy in a bid to improve his players' performance on the field. Tracy employed hypnosis and other relaxation techniques without any apparent success. DeWitt probably would have been better off with better players who were better paid. The team in 1950 had a payroll of $234,125, slightly more than half of the AL average of $441,297. On June 8, 1950, in what might be termed the second Boston Massacre, the Browns were outscored 29–4 in Fenway Park, with the Red Sox banging out 28 hits.

DR. VEECK'S ELIXIR

A sea of red ink forced the DeWitts to sell to the self-styled "savior of the St. Louis Browns," Bill Veeck, in 1951. He was the front man in a 16-member syndicate that included meatpackers Lester Armour and Philip Swift. The fans were betting on the riverboat swagger of the Chicago entrepreneur to save their team.

Veeck came to St. Louis after winning the World Series with Cleveland in 1948 and then selling his stock to insurance executive Ellis Ryan in November 1949. The game's most aggressive promoter saw St. Louis as another sick franchise that would respond favorably to "Dr. Veeck's" patented elixir. Veeck was well aware that his experimental medicine would only work if he could force the Cardinals, whose owner, Fred Saigh, was caught in the tangled web of a tax scandal and was facing prison, to leave town.

Even before Veeck moved in, it was apparent that the team's health was in serious jeopardy. St. Louis mayor Joe Darst and former mayor Aloys P. Kaufman formed a committee to keep the team in St. Louis. One loyal backer, Norman Handel, a former clothing executive, formed the St. Louis Browns Booster Club, which had over 5,000 members. Inexplicably, Veeck failed to enlist their support. This clearly indicated that he had no intention of a long-term stay in St. Louis.

Veeck used every promotional gimmick in his hustler's handbook to capture the public's imagination. He sponsored jazz bands, Bat Days, and Grandstand Manager's Night. He hired clowns and acrobats, providing a bread and-circus atmosphere that made the crowds forget his team was not the Yankees. He worked with the tireless dedication of a public performer animated by the smell of the greasepaint and the celebratory adulation of a hungry crowd.

Veeck's most infamous stunt came from the pages of a James Thurber short story, "You Could Look It Up." On August 19, 1951, in the home half of the first inning of the nightcap of a doubleheader with the Detroit Tigers, Veeck sent three-foot seven-inch Eddie Gaedel to pinch-hit for reserve outfielder Frank Saucier. When Detroit manager Red Rolfe and umpire Ed Hurley stopped play, Browns manager Zack Taylor quickly produced the midget's legitimate contract.

As the crowd watched intently, the diminutive Gaedel strode to the plate, lustily swinging a bat more suitable for an eight-year-old. After milking the at bat for its attendant fanfare, Gaedel walked on four pitches against Tigers lefty Bob Cain. Regular outfielder Jim Delsing came on to run for him. AL president Will Harridge quickly (though temporarily) banished Gaedel's appearance from the record book. Veeck earned the enmity of the entire AL.

The team was in turmoil by June. Veeck flew up to Boston on June 9 to personally fire Rogers Hornsby, the team's manager. The players were so thankful for Veeck's removal of the tyrannical Hornsby that they had a silver tray made in his honor. Marty Marion, former Cardinals shortstop and then a Browns coach, became their last manager. The high point of Veeck's first season was Ned Garver's outstanding 20–12 record. He became the only pitcher to win 20 games for a last-place team that lost 100 games. His .305 batting average also led the team.

The Browns improved dramatically at the gate during the 1952 season. Attendance jumped 76 percent to 518,796, the team's fifth highest ever. Veeck's promotional gimmicks were bringing in the fans and his plan to resurrect Browns baseball was working—that is, until Anheuser-Busch bought the Cardinals and Sportsman's Park in 1953.

Veeck was a gambler but not a fool. With the cross-fingered sincerity of a seasoned politician, Veeck had promised the St. Louis fans in 1951 that he had no intention of ever leaving St. Louis. Realizing his gamble was about to fail, Veeck played his ace in the hole, a quick move to Milwaukee. However, Lou Perini of the Boston Braves exercised his territorial rights, trumping Veeck. Veeck then looked to Baltimore, whose mayor, Tom D'Alesandro, had expressed great interest. Any decision to move required the unanimous approval of his fellow AL owners, owners who were embarrassed by Veeck and his antics. They patiently bided their time, hoping to force the always cash-poor Veeck out of the game.

THE FINAL SEASON

The advent of the 1953 season found the country in a time of both great uncertainty and unlimited promise. The Korean War, which would claim over 50,000 American lives, was a costly stalemate. Television, which would impact baseball's fortunes beyond all imagination, was already making its presence felt. In St. Louis the Browns were televised on Channel 5, KSD-TV.

The 1953 season opened on a note of optimism despite the inner turmoil besetting the club's ownership. Manager Marion fielded a reconstructed team that included such veterans as outfielders Don Lenhardt and Vic Wertz, Bobby Young at second, and promising rookie Billy Hunter at shortstop. The real problem was the pitching staff. Former Cardinals great Harry "the Cat" Brecheen anchored a staff that included veteran Virgil Trucks and rookies Bob Turley and Don Larsen.

When word of Veeck's intentions of moving the franchise leaked out, most long-term fans boycotted the team. Veeck was hung in effigy. Veeck's financial uncertainty worked on the players, as losing became standard fare, especially before the home crowds. With attendance declining to 297,238, the team lost 20 home games in a row, still the major-league record. The home highlight was a chilly May 6 night game against the Philadelphia Athletics when rookie Alva "Bobo" Holloman pitched a no-hitter in his first start, a feat last accomplished in 1892. Just 2,473 loyal fans attended his historic performance. By the end of the season Holloman was out of MLB.

On June 16, with the team riding another losing streak, this time a franchise record of 14 straight losses, the Browns were in Yankee Stadium to play the front-running Yankees, who had a streak of 18 straight victories. Satchel Paige was brilliant in relief of Duane Pillette as the Browns beat the Yankees 3–1, snapping both teams' streaks. The old-timer was the team's closer and appeared in 57 games. Marion had been so frustrated by the team's problems that he allowed sportswriter Milton Richman to pick out his starting lineup. Marion even donned a glove and made a rare appearance at third base.

September 27, 1953, would be the last game the team would play as the Browns. In the third inning, first baseman Ed Mickelson hit a double that scored Johnny Groth from second base. Few of the 3,174 fans in attendance realized that it was the last run scored by the Browns. The game went to extra innings, and in the top of the 12th, the White Sox scored a run to win 2–1, giving the Browns 100 losses for the eighth and final time. Fittingly, the umpires ran out of new baseballs. The public-address announcer asked the few remaining fans to return any balls that left the playing field. The ball in play before the last out had a dirty brownish hue, reminiscent of the days when the spitball, coffeeball, and other doctored balls were legal.

VEECK AS IN WRECK

The AL made it clear that any sale of the Browns would have to exclude Veeck. A local fan group tried to prevent the sale, but it was to no avail. Veeck agreed to sell his 80 percent of the stock for $2.45 million to Clarence Miles and a consortium of Baltimore businessmen, spearheaded by mayor Tom D'Alesandro. Surviving St. Louis Browns fans still regard Veeck's memory with the same cold contempt that Brooklyn fans reserved for Walter O'Malley after he moved their beloved Dodgers to Los Angeles.

D'Alesandro and Miles made for an odd couple. The mayor was the son of an immigrant laborer who had risen from the streets of Baltimore's Little Italy, where he still lived. He was a doer who had overseen the opening of the city's Friendship Airport and presided over the expansion of Memorial Stadium. The mayor numbered presidents and congressmen among his intimates. His daughter Nancy Pelosi would become House minority leader during George W. Bush's administration.

Miles was a patrician lawyer who joined the mayor not because he loved baseball, like D'Alesandro, but because he thought baseball was good for the city. Baltimore faced some stiff competition from other cities as well as the obstinacy of some AL owners, especially the Yankees' Del Webb. Their syndicate included such prominent business leaders as Zanvyl Krieger, president of the Gunther Brewing Company; Jerry Hoffberger, president of the National Brewing Company; investment specialist Joseph Iglehart; and real-estate executive James Keelty. Their financial clout, along with the expansion of the stadium, had already helped Baltimore lure an NFL franchise. This made Baltimore the best possible venue for the struggling Browns.

BALTIMORE'S BASEBALL LEGACY

Baltimore had a rich baseball history. Named after Maryland's state bird, the Orioles had been a member of the American Association between 1882 and 1891, and then jumped leagues and played in the 12-team NL from 1892 until 1899. In 1901 Baltimore became a charter member of the upstart AL, but only lasted two seasons. The team was decimated in 1902 when manager John J. McGraw jumped to the New York Giants along with several of his top players. When the Boston Somersets defeated the Orioles on September 19, 1902, in old Oriole Park, it marked the end of AL baseball on the banks of the Chesapeake Bay for more than a half century.

Baseball impresario Jack Dunn and his family kept baseball enthusiasm alive in Baltimore until the purchase of the Browns in 1953. A former major-league pitcher, Dunn switched to Baltimore in 1907 after having managed Providence in the Eastern League. Baltimore had joined the EL, moving to the International League the following season. As the owner and manager he built the most successful minor-league franchise in history. He found and developed players such as Lefty Grove, Jack Bentley, and Babe Ruth. Stiff competition from the Baltimore Terrapins of the upstart Federal League (1914–15) prompted Dunn to sell many of his top stars to the majors, including Babe Ruth to the Red Sox, and move to Richmond and become the Climbers.

The Terrapins were the only FL franchise that came close to making a profit during the gloomy days of 1915. When the Feds' owners failed to tell the Terrapins of their deal to insure that Phil Ball of the St. Louis Terriers and the owners of the Chicago Whales would get major-league franchises, the Terrapins sued in federal court. Their suit culminated in the 1922 Supreme Court *Baltimore Federal League v. Organized Baseball* decision in which Justice Oliver Wendell Holmes argued that baseball was not subject to the nation's antitrust statutes.

After returning to Baltimore in 1919, Dunn's Orioles won seven consecutive IL pennants (1919–25). Dunn succumbed to a heart attack in 1928. His widow, and later Dunn's grandson, Jack Dunn III, whose father had predeceased both his parents, continued the family ownership and management of the franchise until MLB returned to Baltimore in 1954. The Orioles paid Dunn $350,000 for the team's name and territorial rights.

THE OLD AND THE NEW

The Dunn family had operated the 14,000-seat Oriole Park, the wooden bandbox home of the Orioles of the International League, since 1915, except for their four-year hiatus in Virginia. After it burned down for a second time in 1944, they found an old football stadium, Municipal Stadium, that proved to be quite serviceable for both sports. Ten years later Baltimore's latest entry in the AL arrived at the Camden Yard railroad station and rode up Charles Street in a convoy of open convertibles to their new home on 33rd Street, renamed Memorial Stadium.

The Dunns enlarged its capacity, which eventually reached 52,137. The stadium's dimensions were a symmetrical 309 feet down the lines, and to the power alleys the distance was a cavernous 390 feet. Dead center was 410 feet. The stadium's upper deck was unique in that it did not have any roof. When the stadium first opened it had hedges running around the center-field barrier. Later a seven-foot-high wire fence was installed in right center all the way over to left center.

Stadiums often reflect the culture in which they are built, particularly the cuisine of the home city. Baltimore was no exception. Memorial Stadium had beneath its stands a cornucopia of vendors that sold submarine sandwiches and seafood delicacies, especially crab cakes, which many said surpassed all other baseball food.

The new stadium, new uniforms, and new management did not translate into more victories, as the "old Browns" stumbled home with the same 54–100 record they had had in their final season in St. Louis. However, the Orioles drew over a million fans to Memorial Stadium. After losing their inaugural game on April 13 in Detroit 3–0, the Orioles hit a positive note, defeating the Chicago White Sox 3–1 in their first home game on April 15, 1954. "Bullet Bob" Turley pitched a seven-hitter before a crowd of 46,354 that included Vice President Richard M. Nixon, who threw out the first ball. "Old Scrap Iron," catcher Clint Courtney, hit the team's first home run. Six days later Turley fanned 14 in losing the first night game in Memorial Stadium by a score of 2–1. Turley's 185 strikeouts led the AL in 1954, the only Oriole to ever do that. After the season the Orioles engaged in what may have been the biggest trade in baseball history, shipping six players to the Yankees, including Turley, pitcher Don Larsen, and infielder Billy Hunter, in return for 10 players, including Gene Woodling, Gus Triandos, Willie Miranda, and Harry Byrd. The trade helped the Yankees but did little for the Orioles. In 1955, with Paul Richards at the helm, the Orioles continued to struggle, finishing in seventh place (57–97). The following season they improved to sixth place and a 69–85 mark. By 1957 the team finally reached the .500 plateau, with a record of 76–76.

In 1958 Lee MacPhail, son of longtime baseball magnate Larry MacPhail, became Orioles general manager. In 1958 and 1959 the team struggled through a pair of sixth-place finishes. However, under MacPhail the Orioles sowed the seeds of future success by developing a highly productive farm system. They did a great job scouting, signing, and developing major-league talent, particularly pitching. As president and general manager from 1960 to 1965, MacPhail laid the foundation for the team's soon-to-come dominant years. Between 1960 and 1963 chief scouts Jim Russo and Arthur Ehlers signed up "the Kiddie Corps," led by teenage phenoms Milt Pappas and Jerry Walker. The twenty-something arms of Chuck Estrada, Steve Barber, and Jack Fisher portended a bright future on the Orioles' mound.

In 1960 the Orioles made a great leap forward, propelled by a 15-game winning streak in September that led them to an 89–65 record and a second-place finish. The club was carried by its terrific pitching, led by Estrada's 18 victories. The entire staff led the AL with a 3.52 ERA. The following season, with the team winning consistently, Richards moved on, returning home to Houston late in the season to head up the newly created Houston Colt .45s. Lum Harris replaced him as manager and the team finished in third, with its best record ever up until then at 95–67. Twenty-three-year-old Steve Barber won 18 games, and the pitchers repeated as ERA leaders (3.22).

In 1962 the Orioles' pitching collapsed and the team dropped to seventh place under new manager Billy Hitchcock (77–85). An important addition that year was soft-throwing Dave McNally, arguably the best left-hander in team history. McNally would go on to win 181 games as an Oriole over 13 seasons. After an improvement to fourth place in 1963, new manager Hank Bauer led the Orioles to first place in September 1964, only to slip to third at the end of the season, finishing one game behind Chicago and two behind New York. The Orioles maintained their consistency with another third-place finish (94–68) in 1965, led by the outstanding hurlers, who posted a league best 2.98 ERA. By then pitching was completely dominant in the majors. The average ERA for the entire AL was just 3.46. The club had a notable addition that year, 19-year-old Jim Palmer, who would prove to be the best of "the Baby Birds."

One of MacPhail's last acquisitions before leaving Baltimore to join the commissioner's staff was his best, Frank Robinson. Robinson came to the Orioles from Cincinnati in 1966 in exchange for pitcher Milt Pappas and two other players. Robinson immediately assumed the team's leadership on and off the field. He led the team to the 1966 AL pennant and a 97–63 record, and won the Triple Crown with a .316 batting average, 122 RBIs, and 49 home runs. The AL MVP also led the league in slugging percentage, runs, and total bases. The club led the AL in hitting, but was only fourth best in pitching.

In the World Series, the Dodgers, even with aces Sandy Koufax and Don Drysdale, were outscored 13–2 in the Orioles' four-game sweep, which included shutouts by Jim Palmer, Claude Osteen, and Dave McNally. The Dodgers scratched out a mere 14 hits over the four-game series. Robinson was voted the Series MVP. Already the Orioles had surpassed the entire postseason history of the St. Louis Browns.

THE HEYDAY OF JERRY HOFFBERGER

Jerry Hoffberger was a minor figure in the Orioles' first decade in Baltimore, but in 1965, when a conflict in ownership of CBS stock forced senior partners Joe Iglehart and Zanvyl Krieger to sell their shares, Hoffberger jumped at the opportunity to become the primary partner in the Orioles' ownership. He was an avid fan who sat behind the dugout and cheered like a regular fan. The scion of one of Baltimore's most influential families, Hoffberger was 46 years old when he assumed control of the team. His father, Charles, was a lawyer who built the city's first low-cost housing during the depression.

Before Hoffberger took charge the Orioles were less popular than their football rivals, the Colts. Hoffberger brought a new enthusiasm to marketing the team during his 14-year tenure, which included some of the most turbulent and also some of the most successful in the club's history. Hoffberger gave the team a stature that rivaled the Colts, and instituted modern business principles and organized the front office so that it would function more smoothly.

Hoffberger made his greatest contribution by easing the transition of Frank Robinson from Cincinnati to Baltimore. When Jackie Robinson broke the game's minor-league color barrier in 1946, the toughest city he had played in outside of Miami or Daytona was Baltimore. Citizens of the city exhibited a deep-seated racial bias that made Robinson and his wife feel unwanted. Hoffberger stepped in and made certain that the Robinsons could find suitable housing and a tolerable level of social acceptance.

The Orioles fell badly the year after the championship, slipping down to seventh place (76–85). The following year the team improved at midseason to 43–37, but that was not good enough for Hoffberger. Manager Hank Bauer's failure to pass the Detroit Tigers cost him his job in July. General manager Harry Dalton replaced Bauer with St. Louis native Earl Weaver, himself a product of the Orioles' farm system, albeit a product who never played a major-league game. He was an irascible, umpire-baiting bandy rooster who liked to poke the peak of his cap into the faces of the many umpires he pestered. His aggressive behavior led to four suspensions and nearly 100 ejections over his 18-season career. While managers such as Billy Martin played "inside baseball," scratching for runs with sacrifice bunts, squeeze plays, and stolen bases, Weaver preferred to play long ball and wait for the three-run homer.

That winter the team owners, led by Hoffberger, dropped a bombshell when they fired Commissioner William Eckert. During his short tenure, "the Unknown Soldier," as he was disparagingly called, was indecisive and had a poor public image. Bowie Kuhn, a Wall Street attorney with a physical stature that prompted immediate respect, soon replaced him. Kuhn presided over MLB's move to division play. Baseball divided its leagues into two six-team divisions. The change revitalized pennant races, which had grown stagnant under the old system.

The fiery Weaver directed the Orioles to 109 victories and a 19-game margin over second-place Detroit during the 1969 regular season, and then a sweep of the Minnesota Twins in the initial AL Championship Series. The lowered mound seemed to favor the Orioles, who had a lineup loaded with sluggers, four of whom hit over 20 homers that year. Led by sluggers Boog Powell and Frank Robinson, the Orioles scored 200 runs more than they had the previous season. The Orioles' defense was spectacular, committing just 101 errors for an awesome .984 fielding percentage. The lowered mound did not seem to hurt their pitching staff, going from an AL-leading 2.66 in 1968 to an AL-leading 2.83 in 1969. Mike Cuellar (23–11) tied Detroit's Denny McLain for the Cy Young Award. In 1982 baseball historian Donald Honig ranked the 1969 Orioles as one of the 10 best teams of all time. The 1969 club had six All-Stars and personified "the Oriole Way," which emphasized fundamentals and carefully measured development of youngsters in the minor league.

As good as the Orioles were, they stumbled against the upstart "Miracle Mets" in the World Series. After Baltimore defeated New York's ace, Tom Seaver, in the first game 4–1, they could not overcome the Mets' superlative pitching and timely hitting, or the otherworldly fielding of center fielder Tommie Agee. The deciding fifth game was highlighted by a replay of the infamous shoe-polish incident of the 1957 series between the Yankees and the Braves when Cleon Jones was awarded first base after Mets manager Gil Hodges noticed a black mark on the ball. Donn Clendenon followed with a clutch home run.

The Orioles won 108 games in 1970 with the AL's best pitching and hitting, led by McNally (24 wins), Cuellar (24), and Palmer (20). The Orioles again swept the Minnesota Twins in the ALCS, and then proceeded to take the World Series from the Cincinnati Reds in five games. Brooks Robinson electrified the baseball world with his spectacular play at third base and timely hitting (.429) to earn the Series MVP Award.

Jim Palmer hurls a pitch against the Philadelphia Phillies during his ninth World Series appearance, 1983. © AP / Wide World Photos

The Orioles made it to the World Series for the third consecutive season in 1971, and again had the league's best hitting and pitching. They amassed 101 victories, including the final 11 games of the season, making it three straight years with at least 100 wins. The three-year total of 318 wins marked the team's apex. McNally led the staff with 21 wins, as Palmer, newcomer Pat Dobson, and Cuellar joined him with 20 wins apiece. They swept Oakland in the ALCS and won the first two games of the World Series against the high-flying Pirates, led by Roberto Clemente. The home team won every game until the tension-filled seventh game, which Pittsburgh won 2–1, spoiling the Orioles' outstanding season.

Before the 1972 season, general manager Frank Dalton resigned to take a similar position with the California Angels. Executive vice president Frank Cashen became director of player personnel and traded the aging Frank Robinson to the Dodgers for pitching prospect Doyle Alexander. Palmer's 20 wins and 2.07 ERA were the only bright spots in the team's third-place finish.

The Orioles returned to the top of the Eastern Division in 1973 (97–65), sparked by Jim Palmer's 22–9 record and AL-leading 2.40 ERA. On June 16, he retired the first 25 Texas Rangers before catcher Ken Suarez broke up his perfect game with one-out single. Palmer finished with a two-hit, 9–1 victory. The team's leading hitter was former Chicago Cub Tommy Davis, the team's first designated hitter. The DH had been created to modernize the game and increase the offense. But the Orioles failed to get past the defending world champion Oakland A's, who won the ALCS in five games.

In 1974 Baltimore repeated as division champs. With a month to play, they were in fourth place, eight games behind Boston. But in the final month, the

Orioles won 28 of 34 to edge the revitalized Yankees. Weaver drove his team like a relentless jockey down the stretch, which included 15 one-run victories. Ross Grimsley, a classic left-hander acquired from Cincinnati, was the difference. His 18 wins more than made up for Palmer's uncharacteristic 7–12 season. But Oakland continued its postseason mastery of the Orioles in the ALCS. The Orioles managed just one run in the final three games of their four-game series.

The big news in 1975 was not the Orioles' second-place finish or Palmer's Cy Young Award season (23–11, 2.09 ERA) but the free-agency suits of pitchers Andy Messersmith and former Oriole Dave McNally. Arbitrator Peter Seitz ruled for the players, opening the free-agency gates and spawning a new era in baseball labor relations.

One year later, the Orioles came in second (88–74) and Palmer won his second Cy Young Award (22–13, 2.51 ERA). In a multiplayer deal, the Orioles acquired slugger Reggie Jackson and pitcher Ken Holtzman from Oakland in exchange for Don Baylor and pitcher Mike Torrez. Jackson's stay in Baltimore was brief. He lobbied from the start for a chance to play for the Yankees for fame and fortune. His home run total slipped to just 27, but he led the league in slugging percentage with a .502 mark.

By 1977 free agency and Yankees owner George Steinbrenner's unbridled determination to secure the best team money could buy made it extremely difficult for the more business minded Orioles to compete. The Orioles still won 97 games, finishing just two and half games behind New York. Eddie Murray became the AL's first Rookie of the Year to play as DH. The following season Murray moved to first base, where he won three straight Gold Glove Awards and became a steady cog in the Orioles' defense, which contributed significantly to their success in the 1970s and 1980s.

The 1977 season marked the end of the legendary career of Brooks Robinson. Discovered on a church-league sandlot, the native Arkansan had made steady progress since his 1955 debut. He played the hot corner for 23 seasons with a style and grace that was unparalleled for its time. He won the Gold Glove 16 times and for 15 straight seasons was the AL's starting third baseman in the All-Star Game. Robinson was inducted into the Baseball Hall of Fame in 1983.

The Orioles won 90 games in 1978 yet finished in fourth, but rebounded in 1979 to win the AL East at 102–52. They were led by the pitching staff, whose ERA of 3.26 was more than half a run better than any other team. Cy Young Award winner Mike Flannigan led the way with a sterling 23–9 record and 3.08 ERA, propelling the Orioles to another World Series appearance after defeating the Angels in the ALCS three games to two. Unfortunately, Willie Stargell rallied the Pirates from a three-games-to-one deficit to frustrate the Orioles' dream of another championship.

WILLIAMS AND A SEA OF RED INK

From the moment that Hoffberger, whose teams had won five pennants and two World Series, sold the Orioles to Edward Bennett Williams in 1979 for $11 million, the low-budget stability that had marked his ownership vanished. The team shed its stingy demeanor as a waterfall of new talent bathed its finances in red ink. The problem remained how to balance financial solvency and still compete on the field. A graduate of Holy Cross College, Williams was a pillar of the Washington community. His legal career included such clients as Jimmy Hoffa, Frank Costello, and Joe McCarthy. Though he was an outstanding lawyer and a great intellect, as an owner he was just a rung above a dilettante.

In 1980 Scott McGregor and Cy Young Award winner Steve Stone (25–7) led the Orioles to another 100-win season, yet they finished three games behind the Yankees. The 1981 season was one of the most convoluted in baseball history. The owners and the Players Association reached an impasse that resulted in a full one-third of the schedule being lost to a labor strike. When play resumed, the owners devised a split-season format often found in the minor leagues in a heedless effort to salvage the semblance of a competitive season. The winners from each half of the season met in a playoff at the end of the season. The Orioles finished second overall in the AL East at 59–46.

In 1982 Weaver announced his retirement effective after the season, and turned in his finest hour as the team's manager, coaxing Eddie Murray, Palmer, and 1981's AL Rookie of the Year Cal Ripken Jr. into the thick of the pennant race. Murray had a great all-around season with a .316 average, 32 home runs, and 110 RBIs. Weaver moved six-foot-four Ripken from third to short, almost immediately making him the tallest regular shortstop in history, an honor formerly held by the six-foot-three Orioles fielding great Mark Belanger. Over the course of his lengthy career Ripken redefined the shortstop position with his range, powerful arm, and consistent stroke at the plate. Weaver had the Orioles positioned three games behind division-leading Milwaukee with the final four games of the season to be played by them. Baltimore swept the first three games to deadlock the race. But in the deciding game Don Sutton defeated Palmer 10–2, backed by Robin Yount's pair of two-run home runs.

Because of a series of nagging injuries to many of its key players in 1983, rookie manager Joe Altobelli masterminded a platoon system that mixed well with the MVP heroics of Ripken, who batted .318 with 211 hits to win their division (98–64) by six games over Detroit. The club led the AL in homers and was second overall in hitting and pitching. Rookie pitcher Mike Boddicker baffled AL hitters with his "foshball," winning 16 of his 24 decisions. The White Sox took the first game of the ALCS, but then Boddicker shut out the Pale Hose, and the Orioles took three straight. In the World Series the Orioles dropped the first game and then swept the next four to win the title. The 25-year-old Boddicker provided the pitching spark in game two with a three-hit, 4–1 victory over a Philadelphia team so overburdened with aging veterans that they called them "the Wheeze Kids." The Orioles captured their first World Series since 1970. Unheralded catcher Rick Dempsey batted .385 and became the third Oriole to win a Series MVP Award.

The Orioles' unimpressive fifth-place finish (87–75) in 1984 marked Jim Palmer's 19th and last season in MLB. His pitching success was unparalleled in Orioles history. He won 20 or more games eight times, was the AL's Cy Young Award winner three times, and was a six-time All-Star. He went 268–152 in his career with an ERA of 2.68, and regularly pitched over 300 innings.

Winter baseball, personal conditioning, and a strong will to win enabled him to overcome a multitude of real or imagined physical ailments. On the mound his high kick and superior athleticism made him a four-time Gold Glove winner. Palmer's love-hate relationship with manager Earl Weaver seemed to be more for dramatic effect than from any deep-seated feeling. In 1990 he was inducted into the Hall of Fame.

In 1985 MLB's labor unrest resurfaced when the Players Association staged a two-day walkout that jeopardized the entire season. Less than a third into the 1985 season, Altobelli received his walking papers. Earl Weaver was coaxed from his short-lived retirement only to find the AL East had moved ahead of the Orioles. The club finished at 83–78, fourth in its division. Then, in 1986, Weaver suffered through the only losing season in his career (73–89), ending in seventh place. Weaver retired for good after the season. The team's most successful manager was elected to the Hall of Fame in 1996.

Longtime Baltimore coach Cal Ripken Sr. replaced the tired Weaver, but the next season was equally dreadful (67–95), good only for sixth place. On September 14, 1987, with the team in the midst of a losing rout, Ripken Sr. caved in to front-office pressure and replaced Ripken Jr. with infielder Ron Washington, which ended his streak of playing 8,243 consecutive innings over 908 games.

A DARK NIGHT

Even the great teams sometimes suffer through a dark night of the soul. The 1988 season proved to be the darkest moment in team history and tested the true mettle of the team's adoring fans like "Wild Bill" Hagy, a hairy, beer-swigging cabbie who danced on the dugout roof when the occasion seized him. He was the Orioles' self-appointed cheerleader and was more entertaining than the horde of escapees from a puppet menagerie who have plagued baseball since the San Diego Chicken first flapped his feathers in the 1970s.

The Orioles opened the season with a 12–0 shellacking at the hands of the Milwaukee Brewers with Hagy in attendance. The team's downward spiral reached its nadir as it lost the following 20 games to set a new record for April futility. Hagy had nothing in his personal repertoire that could produce a victory. A banner in center field raised the mathematical horror of 0–162.

Management showed little patience with Ripken Sr., firing him just six games into the disastrous season. Frank Robinson, who had rejoined the club in 1986 as a coach, was installed as the new manager. Robinson had been the first black manager in MLB in 1975 with Cleveland, but he had no magic potion. The Orioles finished with a .335 winning percentage (55–107) the worst in franchise history since the lowly Browns' .279 (43–111) of 1939.

Early in the season, when the Orioles were 1–23, hopes were revitalized when Governor William Schaefer announced that team owner Williams and the Maryland Stadium Authority had agreed on a long-term lease for a new downtown ballpark to be built for the 1992 season. Williams himself never attended another game, succumbing to cancer on August 13, 1988.

A LEVERAGED BUYOUT

Much changed before the start of the 1989 season. Williams's estate sold the Orioles for $70 million to Eli Jacobs, a New York investment specialist, in a leveraged buyout. He had borrowed the entire purchase price. His minority investors were team president Larry Lucchino, Williams's protégé in sports and law, and former Peace Corps director Sargent Shriver.

In December the Orioles traded star Eddie Murray, who had been feuding with the media, the front office, and even the fans, to the Dodgers for three unheralded players. In his very consistent 12 years with the team, Murray hit .295 with 2,021 hits and 303 homers. The owners, while keeping a low payroll, paid themselves enough to cover their interest payments to Citicorp. It was a terrific investment, because after the opening of Camden Yards, the Orioles became a virtual gold mine, netting $20 million a year.

Sporting new uniforms and a reformed attitude, the Orioles spent nearly three months of the 1989 season in first place. They combined timely hitting, especially that of reserve catcher and DH Mickey Tettleton, who hit 26 home runs, and improved defense with an inspired pitching staff, led by the resurgence of Jeff Ballard to give the Blue Jays a run for their money, but Toronto rebounded from a horrible start to pass the Birds by two games in September. Robinson was named AL Manager of the Year.

Spring training in 1990 was delayed for 32 days as the owners and players radiated ominous warnings of a dispute that would nearly tear the game apart four years later. The season's opener was pushed back to April 9 after a tenuous agreement was reached. The Orioles collapsed to fifth place (76–85). At this time, the Orioles payroll was $8.1 million, and the franchise was worth an estimated $200 million, tied for second in MLB.

The 1991 season marked the Orioles' final season on 33rd Street. Ripken had a career year by hitting .323 with 210 hits, 34 homers, and 144 RBIs. He swept the All-Star and AL MVPs, was Major League Player of the Year, and even won the All-Star Home Run Derby. Mike Flanagan pitched the last inning of the last game at Memorial Stadium. Robinson was fired after 37 games, replaced by Johnny Oates, and the team ended up back in fifth place.

A BRICK AND MORTAR TRIBUTE

The throwback or retro concept, which evolved over four years, was unveiled on Opening Day in 1992. The Kansas City architectural team of Hellmuth, Obata, and Kassabaum (HOK) designed a magnificent $110 million stadium in the midst of an old railroad yard that captured the city's historic beauty amid a tower of modernity that paid tribute to modern comfort and style. HOK received its direction and input from the Orioles and the state of Maryland, which owns and operates through the Maryland Stadium Authority. Oriole Park at Camden Yards, with a capacity of 48,876 (including standing room), blended the urban development of Baltimore's new architecture with a nostalgic asymmetry and natural grass. It stood proud and tall as a brick and mortar tribute to baseball's glorious past.

In a single gesture it obliterated a half century of insipid stadium designs and ugly architecture that characterized the tasteless cookie-cutter stadiums in St. Louis, Cincinnati, and Pittsburgh. The uneven outfield with a high wall and hand-operated scoreboard was a salute to Ebbets Field, Wrigley Field, and Fenway Park. In the right-field background, the B&O Railroad warehouse rises like a giant tribute to simpler times. "The Yard" sported red brick walls, high arches, cast-iron gates, and 1890s Baltimore Baseball Club logos emblazoned at the end of every row. The park was a true marriage of baseball nostalgia and modern innovation, such as a drainage system that kept the field in pristine condition. The stadium was located only 12 minutes from the birthplace of Baltimore's most famous baseball player, Babe Ruth. The fans flocked 48,000 at a time, because no game respects its past better than baseball. The Orioles, inspired by the new field, improved to 89–73 (third place).

Only the Toronto Blue Jays, who drew over 4 million fans from 1991 to 1993, surpassed the Orioles during this period. Since the Yard's opening, the Orioles have averaged over 3.3 million fans a year, a significant improvement over the 2.5 million of the last season at Memorial Stadium. The completion of the field helped drive the Orioles' value, which had fallen from $200 million in 1990 to $129 million in 1993, up to $164 million one year later, second highest in MLB to the Yankees. It peaked at $351 million in 1998.

THE STREAK

In 1993 Ripken drew 162 games closer to Gehrig as the Orioles engaged in a donnybrook with most of their division. The team's anticlimactic third-place finish paled by comparison with Ripken's everyday contributions. His 1,735 consecutive games put Gehrig's 2,130 streak well within his reach. The following season, Ripken played in only 112 games because of the baseball strike. The club moved up to second place (63–49).

Before the start of the 1995 season, the owners threatened to employ replacement players, but Orioles owner Peter Angelos, a labor attorney, swore he would never use such scabs. Opening Day was pushed back for three weeks, shortening the season to 144 games. On September 6 Ripken passed Lou Gehrig to

Cal Ripkin during a game against the Kansas City Royals, 1996. © AP / Wide World Photos

establish the new mark of 2,131 consecutive games before a packed house and a global television audience. But the club, under rookie manager Phil Regan, dropped to third (71–73).

In 1996 baseball did its best to lure the fans back to the game. The advent of the towering home run had worked miracles in the aftermath of the Black Sox scandal of 1919. Not coincidentally, baseballs started flying out of major-league parks at an alarming rate. The 30 teams combined for a resounding 4,962 home runs, shattering the old record by more than 500. Under yet another new manager, former Orioles second baseman Davey Johnson, Baltimore set a new major-league record with 257 home runs, 17 more than the former record of the 1961 Yankees. Unlikely slugger Brady Anderson's 50 home runs led a phalanx of seven Orioles with over 20 home runs, which propelled the Orioles to the wild card (88–74).

Regrettably, the Orioles' newfound power was not enough to overcome the strength and pitching of their New York nemesis. After defeating Cleveland in the AL Divisional Series three games to one, the Orioles' luck ran out in the opening game of the ALCS. Jeffrey Maier, a hooky-playing 12-year-old from Old

Tappan, New Jersey, interfered with a Derek Jeter fly ball destined for the waiting hands of Orioles right fielder Tony Tarasco. The umpire inexplicably ruled it a home run, tying the score at four. The Orioles never fully recovered from the blown call, dropping the series in five games.

The next season the Orioles went wire to wire as the division leader (94–64), led by the stellar pitching of Scott Erickson, Jimmy Key, and Mike Mussina, to finish two games ahead of the Yankees, who earned the wild-card slot. Ripken returned to third base in favor of Mike Bordick. This time Cleveland frustrated the Orioles' run to another World Series in the six-game ALCS.

In 1998, the Yankees made a shambles of the race, finishing with an amazing 114 victories, breaking the former AL record of 111 set by the 1954 Cleveland Indians. The Birds had the highest payroll, but the best they could manage was a fourth-place finish under the new manager, former pitching coach Ray Miller. Cal Ripken voluntarily ended his streak at 2,533 on the last day of the season. Sharing the human-interest spotlight was Eric Davis, who rebounded from colon cancer to hit .327 with 28 home runs.

In 1999 the team remained mired in fourth place as Ripken played in only 85 games due to unprecedented chronic injuries. The following season the Orioles began a rebuilding program that maintained their fourth-place status quo under rookie manager Mike Hargrove. Ripken had another injury-ridden season, which limited him to just 83 games. Free-agent slugger Albert Belle rarely appeared, as he was suffering from what became a career-ending hip injury. Three seasons later, the Orioles were still paying him $12,449,999.

The 2001 season served as Cal Ripken's personal farewell tour. Ripken celebrations overshadowed the play on the field. When the Orioles ran on the field for their Cal Ripken Day, first baseman Jeff Conine tossed an infield warm-up ball into the outfield grass toward Ripken, who had to turn his back to the field to retrieve it. When he turned around, his current team had been replaced with the surviving members of his 1981 rookie team. It was a magnificent moment of baseball reverence and sentimentality. The only position left unoccupied was shortstop, for Mark Belanger had died on October 6, 1998. As a crowning touch, white-haired Earl Weaver walked up to home plate with his lineup card. The regular season ended on October 6 with the customary fourth-place finish (63–98). That year *Forbes* estimated the team made $3.2 million (compared to MLB's reported loss of $5.347 million). The profit would have been larger, except the club had to pay out $1.46 million for revenue sharing, and the team only made $21 million in local media money despite being located in the third-largest metropolitan area, after New York and Los Angeles.

Ripken's retirement cost the Orioles more than the loss of a perennial All-Star. For 20 seasons he had provided the baseball community with a shinning example of character and fortitude that provided a necessary antidote to the sordid affairs of many of the game's leading players. He symbolized the hardworking American man, who always showed up, never complained, and gave his best. This was a huge contrast to the pampered, overpaid professional athletes that sports fans were becoming accustomed to. Years after he left the team, Ripken continues to give back to the Baltimore community. His foundation built a small version of Camden Yard at his Aberdeen baseball complex, which hosts the nation's finest youth-baseball facility.

CHAIRMAN ANGELOS

Chairman Peter Angelos, who purchased the team from Jacobs for $170 million in 1993, had to deal with the prospects of a rival team in the Washington-Virginia area that would have seriously jeopardized his fan base. On a more grievous note, he called on MLB to ban the use of ephedrine, a stimulant often used by athletes to lose weight. It was reputed to have played a large role in the premature death of Orioles pitcher Steve Bechler during spring training in 2003. The new season marked the 50th anniversary of the franchise's final season in St. Louis. As part of interleague play, the Orioles visited St. Louis to play the Cardinals the weekend of June 6. Several former Browns players from the 1953 team, including Roy Sievers and Don Larsen, were introduced on the field before Friday's night game at Busch Stadium. The Saturday game was a "throwback game" that witnessed the "Browns" and Cardinals dressed in polyester replicas of the regalia of the 1944 teams. The Orioles won the game behind the strong pitching of Sidney Ponson, 8–3. The team limped home in fourth place (71–91) for the sixth year in a row.

In the hope that there was magic in the Yankees' uniform, the Orioles turned to Yankees first-base coach Lee Mazzilli for 2004. At the start of the season, *Forbes* rated the team as worth $296 million, 12th in MLB. The rookie manager took over an upstart team that had high hopes for improving itself in the free-agent market. Jim Beattie, the team's executive vice president for baseball operations, thought their chances of solidifying the team would give "the Italian Stallion" a prime opportunity to return the Orioles to their fruitful days. A 12-game losing streak in August ruined any hopes for the playoffs. Mazzilli rallied his team to a third-place finish with a 79–83 mark.

In 2005, the Orioles started out all ablaze, but Sammy Sosa and Sidney Ponson flopped. Sam Perlozzo became the interim manager, replacing a clueless Mazzilli, and was hired full-time after the season. In September slugger Rafael Palmeiro, who had reached 3,000 hits and 500 home runs in an Orioles uniform, "retired" early because of a positive steroid test and contradictions in his congressional testimony earlier in the year. The Orioles finished in fifth place with a 74–88 mark, 21 games behind New York and Boston.

A FINAL REVIEW

In this modern tale of two cities, the contrast between the history of the St. Louis Browns and that of the Baltimore Orioles is striking. During their 52 seasons the Browns were "the worst of times," winning only one pennant. In their 51 seasons the Orioles enjoyed "the best of times," playing in the postseason nine times and appearing in six World Series, winning three of them. Of all the premier players in MLB history, George Sisler is the only Browns player who stood above his peers. The list of premier Baltimore players is too long to list.

The unwise business decisions of dilettante owner Philip Ball and the decline of the two-team city hastened the Browns' transfer to Baltimore. With only the Cardinals in town, St. Louis has become one of the most successful franchises in history. The Browns' move to Baltimore was good not only for the franchise but also for MLB. Baltimore had an enjoyable taste of major-league baseball in the early days of the AL. Given a second chance, it has proven to be a reservoir of baseball prosperity and energy. The franchise flourished in ways that that it never could have in St. Louis.

The pivotal question for the future of the Orioles concerns their ability to sustain their thriving prosperity. Demographic pressures and the strategic business needs of MLB have beckoned the owners to move the Montreal Expos into nearby Washington, DC, as the new Washington Nationals. Can the Orioles survive this new threat to their longevity, or will it go the way of its St. Louis predecessor? That is the remaining question that only the future will answer.

NOTABLE ACHIEVEMENTS

Most Valuable Players

Year	Name	Position
1964	Brooks Robinson	3B
1966	Frank Robinson	OF
1970	Boog Powell	1B
1983	Cal Ripken Jr.	SS
1991	Cal Ripken Jr.	SS

Cy Young Winners

Year	Name	Position
1969	Mike Cuellar	LHP
1973	Jim Palmer	RHP
1975	Jim Palmer	RHP
1976	Jim Palmer	RHP
1979	Mike Flanagan	LHP
1980	Steve Stone	RHP

Rookies of the Year

Year	Name	Position
1949	Roy Sievers	OF
1960	Ron Hansen	SS
1965	Curt Blefary	OF
1973	Al Bumbry	OF

1977	Eddie Murray	1B
1982	Cal Ripken Jr.	SS
1989	Gregg Olson	P

Batting Champions

Year	Name	#
1906	George Stone	.358
1920	George Sisler	.407
1922	George Sisler	.420
1966	Frank Robinson	.316

Home-Run Champions

Year	Name	#
1922	Ken Williams	39
1945	Vern Stephens	24
1966	Frank Robinson	49
1981	Eddie Murray	22

ERA Champions

Year	Name	#
1959	Hoyt Wilhelm	2.19
1973	Jim Palmer	2.40
1975	Jim Palmer	2.09
1984	Mike Boddicker	2.79

Strikeout Champions

Year	Name	#
1922	Urban Shocker	149
1954	Bob Turley	185

No-Hitters

Name	Date
Earl Hamilton	08/30/1912
Ernie Koob	05/05/1917
Bob Groom	05/06/1917
Bobo Holloman	05/06/1953
Hoyt Wilhelm	09/20/1958
Tom Phoebus	04/27/1968
Jim Palmer	08/13/1969

POSTSEASON APPEARANCES

AL East Division Titles

Year	Record	Manager
1969	109–53	Earl Weaver
1970	108–54	Earl Weaver
1971	101–57	Earl Weaver
1973	97–65	Earl Weaver
1974	91–71	Earl Weaver
1979	102–57	Earl Weaver
1983	98–64	Joe Altobelli
1997	98–64	Davey Johnson

AL Wild Cards

Year	Record	Manager
1996	88–74	Davey Johnson

AL Pennants

Year	Record	Manager
1944	89–65	Luke Sewell
1966	97–63	Hank Bauer
1969	109–53	Earl Weaver
1970	108–54	Earl Weaver
1971	101–57	Earl Weaver
1979	102–57	Earl Weaver
1983	98–64	Joe Altobelli

World Championships

Year	Opponent	MVP
1966	Los Angeles	Frank Robinson
1970	Cincinnati	Brooks Robinson
1983	Philadelphia	Rick Dempsey

MANAGERS

2005–	Sam Perlozzo
2004–2005	Lee Mazzilli
2000–2003	Mike Hargrove
1998–1999	Ray Miller
1996–1997	Davey Johnson

1995	Phil Regan
1991–1994	Johnny Oates
1988–1991	Frank Robinson
1987–1988	Carl Ripken Sr.
1985–1986	Earl Weaver
1985	Carl Ripken Sr.
1983–1985	Joe Altobelli
1968–1982	Earl Weaver
1964–1968	Hank Bauer
1962–1963	Billy Hitchcock
1961	Lum Harris
1955–1961	Marty Marion
1954	Jimmie Dykes
1952–1953	Marty Marion
1952	Rogers Hornsby
1948–1951	Zach Taylor
1947	Muddy Ruel
1946	Zack Taylor
1942–1946	Luke Sewell
1939–1941	Fred Haney
1938	Ski Melillo
1938	Gabby Street
1937	Jim Bottomley
1933–1937	Rogers Hornsby
1933	Allen Sothoron
1930–1933	Bill Killefer
1927–1929	Don Howley
1924–1926	George Sisler
1923	Jimmy Austin
1921–1923	Lee Fohl
1918–1920	Jimmy Burke
1918	Jimmy Austin
1916–1918	Fielder Jones
1913–1915	Branch Rickey
1913	Jimmy Austin
1912–1913	George Stovall
1911–1912	Bobby Wallace
1910	Jack O'Connor
1902–1909	Jimmy McAleer
1901	Hugh Duffy (Milwaukee)

Team Records by Individual Players

Batting Leaders

	Single Season			Career		
	Name		Year	Name		Plate Appearances
Batting average	George Sisler	.420	1922	George Sisler	.344	7,269
On-base %	George Sisler	.467	1922	Ken Williams	.403	4,668
Slugging %	Goose Goslin	.652	1930	Ken Williams	.558	4,668
OPS	Goose Goslin	1.082	1920	Ken Williams	.961	4,668
Games	Brooks Robinson	163	1961	Cal Ripken	3,001	12,883
At bats	B. J. Surhoff	673	1999	Cal Ripken	11,551	12,883
Runs	Harlon Clift	145	1936	Cal Ripken	1,647	12,883
Hits	George Sisler	257	1920	Cal Ripken	3,184	12,883
Total bases	George Sisler	399	1920	Cal Ripken	5,168	12,883
Doubles	Beau Bell	51	1937	Cal Ripken	603	12,883
Triples	George Stone	20	1906	George Sisler	145	7,269
Home runs	Brooks Anderson	50	1996	Cal Ripken	431	12,883
RBIs	Ken Williams	155	1922	Cal Ripken	1,695	12,883
Walks	Lu Blue	126	1929	Cal Ripken	1,129	12,883
Strikeouts	Mickey Tettleton	160	1990	Cal Ripken	1,308	12,883
Stolen bases	Luis Aparicio	57	1964	George Sisler	351	7,269
Extra-base hits	Brady Anderson	92	1996	Cal Ripken	1,078	12,883
Times on base	George Sisler	305	1920	Cal Ripken	4,379	12,883

Pitching Leaders

	Single Season			Career		
	Name		Year	Name		Innings Pitched
ERA	Barney Pelty	1.59	1906	Harry Howell	2.06	1,580.7
Wins	Urban Shocker	27	1921	Jim Palmer	268	3,948
Won-loss%	Alvin Crowder	.808	1928	Mike Mussina	.645	2,009.7
Hits/9 IP	Dave McNally	5.77	1968	Stu Miller	6.90	502
Walks/9 IP	Scott McGregor	1.19	1979	Dick Hall	1.47	770
Strikeouts	Rube Waddell	232	1908	Arthur Rhodes	837	622.3
Strikeouts/9 IP	Mike Mussina	8.73	1997	Jim Palmer	2,212	3,948
Games	Tippy Martinez	76	1982	Jim Palmer	558	3,948
Saves	Randy Myers	45	1997	Greg Olson	160	350.3
Innings	Urban Shocker	348	1922	Jim Palmer	3,948	3,948
Starts	Bobo Newsom	40	1938	Jim Palmer	521	3,948

(Continued)

Pitching Leaders (continued)

| | Single Season | | | Career | | |
	Name		Year	Name		Innings Pitched
Complete games	Jack Powell	36	1902	Jim Palmer	211	3,948
Shutouts	Tim. Palmer	10	1975	Tim Palmer	53	3,948

Source: Drawn from data in "Baltimore Orioles Batting Leaders (seasonal and career)." http://baseball-reference.com/teams/BAL/leaders_bat.shtml; "Baltimore Orioles Pitching Leaders (seasonal and career)." http:// baseball-reference.com/teams/BAL/leaders_pitch.shtml.

BIBLIOGRAPHY

Barney, Rex, with Norman Macht. *Rex Barney's Orioles' Memories, 1969–1994.* Woodbury, CT: Goodwood Press, 1994.

Borst, Bill. *The Best of Seasons: The 1944 St. Louis Browns and St. Louis Cardinals.* Jefferson, NC: McFarland, 1995.

———. *Still Last in the American League: The St. Louis Browns Revisited.* West Bloomfield, MI: Altwerger and Mandel, 1992.

Eisenberg, John. *From 33rd Street to Camden Yards: An Oral History of the Baltimore Orioles.* New York: McGraw-Hill, 2001.

Eskanazi, Gerald. *Bill Veeck: A Baseball Legend.* New York: McGraw-Hill, 1988.

Garver, Ned. *Touching All the Bases.* Dunkirk, MD: Pepperpot Productions, 2003.

Godin, Roger. *The 1922 St. Louis Browns: Best of the American League's Worst.* Jefferson, NC: McFarland, 1991.

Golenbock, Peter. *The Spirit of St. Louis: A History of the Cardinals and Browns.* New York: Spike, 2000.

Gutman, Bill. *Cal Ripken: Baseball's Iron Man.* Brookfield, CT: Millbrook Press, 1998.

Kashatus, William C. *One-Armed Wonder: Pete Gray.* Jefferson, NC: McFarland, 1995.

Mead, William B. *Even the Browns.* Chicago: Contemporary Books, 1978. Reprinted as *Baseball Goes to War.* New York: Farragut Publishing, 1985.

Miller, James E. *The Baseball Business: Pursuing Pennants and Profits in Baltimore.* Chapel Hill: University of North Carolina Press, 1990.

Nichols, Fred. *The Final Season: The 1953 St. Louis Browns.* St. Louis: St. Louis Browns Historical Society, 1991.

Patterson, Ted. *The Baltimore Orioles: 40 Years of Magic From 33rd St. to Camden Yards.* Dallas: Taylor Publishing, 1995.

Pluto, Terry. *The Earl of Baltimore: The Story of Earl Weaver, Baltimore Orioles Manager.* Piscataway, NJ: New Century Publishers, 1982.

Tygiel, Jules. *Baseball's Great Experiment: Jackie Robinson and His Legacy.* New York: Vintage Books, 1984.

Veeck, Bill, with Ed Linn. *Veeck—as in Wreck.* New York: G. P. Putnam, 1962.

Wolff, Rick. *Brooks Robinson.* New York: Chelsea House, 1991.

18

Boston Red Sox

Robert K. Barney and David E. Barney

Fred Hale Sr. was born in New Sharon, Maine, on December 1, 1890. By the time he was a teenager, similar to many New England boys, he had developed a fascination, indeed a passion, for the new professional baseball club in Boston, the so-called Boston Americans, a short time later to become the storied Red Sox. In 1903 he thrilled to their victory over Pittsburgh in what passed for baseball's first-ever World Series. Over the next decade and a half, Hale witnessed five more Red Sox World Series victories, the last of which occurred in 1918, an achievement he would live the greater part of a century to see repeated. In October 2004, at 113 years of age, Fred Hale, the world's oldest man, thrilled once again to a Red Sox World Series win, a feat he had waited exactly 86 years to behold. Less than a month following an improbable Red Sox demolishment of the hated Yankees for the American League championship, followed by a four-game sweep of the Cardinals in the World Series, Fred Hale, 12 days short of his 114th birthday, passed away peacefully in his sleep, content in the euphoric realization that all was well at last in the Red Sox Nation.

IN THE BEGINNING

Major-league baseball has long been an indelible part of Boston and Greater New England life, as eternally embedded in household culture as broiled haddock on Friday nights and baked beans and brown bread on Saturday nights. The Boston Red Stockings were a charter member of the National Association of Professional Base Ball Players league founded in 1871, and moved into the National League of Professional Clubs in 1876, when they were known as the Red Caps. In 1900, the energetic, effervescent, and scheming Ban Johnson modified and expanded the Western League into the American League. Essentially a Johnson crusade to challenge the NL head-to-head, the AL sported franchises moved from minor-league western cities (Kansas City, Indianapolis, and Minneapolis) to Baltimore, Washington, and Philadelphia. A Boston franchise was not a part of Johnson's original plans, but even before the highly successful inaugural season of the AL unfolded in 1900, he learned that the American Association might locate a franchise in "the best baseball town in the country" to challenge the Boston Beaneaters for the affections of the city's baseball faithful. Johnson quickly abandoned his scheme for an AL team in Buffalo; enlisted the financial backing of Cleveland's Charles Somers, a millionaire shipper of coal and lumber on the Great Lakes; and offered him controlling ownership of an AL Boston franchise. Johnson then sent emissary Connie Mack, a Massachusetts native and former major leaguer, scurrying off to Beantown to survey real estate for a ballpark. In just two days in January 1900 the hugely popular Mack found the first home for Johnson's Boston experiment, a site then conveniently situated adjacent to, and owned by, the Boston Elevated Railroad. Formerly used by traveling carnivals and Buffalo Bill's Wild West Shows, a new $35,000 ballpark, affectionately known as the Huntington Avenue Grounds, rose in time for the April 1901 inaugural Boston Americans season. Three months previous, a *Boston Post* headline trumpeted, "Rival Baseball Nine for Boston."

Across town, the Beaneaters seethed. "I can see only one termination for this state of things," thundered their owner, Arthur Soden, to a reporter. "The newcomers will have to surrender." The Americans did not surrender, and inveigled three key Boston Nationals to switch teams. A $4,000 contract lured the peerless Jimmy Collins to play third base and manage the team in 1901, and his good friends Chick Stahl and Buck Freeman followed suit. Collins solved much of the problem of pitching by luring Denton True "Cy" Young from St. Louis. At the time, Young, 35 years old and destined to be the winningest pitcher in major-league history, was slightly more than halfway along toward his eventual career mark of 511 victories. His record of 33 wins against 10 defeats in his first year in Boston was worth every penny of his $3,500 salary. On May 8, Boston's Americans opened their home season at the Huntington Grounds following a season-opening road trip that produced a 5–5 record. The new spacious, elegant field seated 9,000, plus standing room for a few thousand more in roped-off areas at the perimeters of the outfield. The multitude assembled on that auspicious day witnessed Cy Young defeat Philadelphia 12–4. The Americans, playing eye-catching ball for the remainder of the 1901 season, achieved a close second-place finish to Chicago, gaining instant credibility.

In its first season, the AL declared its parity with the NL, demanded recognition as an equal circuit, and pushed ahead in its quest for nationwide public attention. It drew 1,683,584 spectators, against the NL's 1,920,031. The following year the Boston Somersets, as journalists nicknamed the team, drew

348,567 fans to their home games, finishing in third place, six and a half games behind Philadelphia's A's. More importantly, the 1902 spectator total for the AL was 2,206,457, surpassing the NL by more than 300,000 fans. The NL recognized the junior circuit as a bona fide brother major league in January 1903, just in time for the upcoming season. The two leagues reached consensus, recognized each other as being equal but separate, adopted identical playing rules, and agreed to respect each other's rights with regard to player contracts. When peace was achieved, Charles Somers sold his controlling interest in the Boston Americans, as the team was still known to the fans, to Ban Johnson's handpicked crony, Henry Killilea. Both leagues drew almost 2.5 million spectators. However, in Boston and Chicago, which had competing franchises, the AL clubs outdrew their crosstown rivals by more than two to one. With peace in place, the roots of a historic rivalry germinated, one that captivates the attention of sports fans across America every October: the World Series.

The 1903 season produced the first pennant for Boston's newly nicknamed Pilgrims (91–47) by a whopping 14 1/2 games. Led by the pitching of Cy Young, who led the AL with 28 wins, and Long Tom Hughes and Bill Dineen, who also topped 20 wins, and the hitting of Patsy Dougherty, Chick Stahl, and Buck Freeman, who won the league home-run and RBI titles, Boston clinched the flag on September 17, one day before Pittsburgh accomplished the same feat in the NL. A postseason meeting between the two pennant winners was a natural, a "world's series," the press exclaimed. Owners of the two clubs, salivating at the prospect of bulging cash tills from such an event, agreed to play a best-of-nine series to declare a "champion of the world." Pittsburgh presented formidable talent. The incomparable Honus Wagner dominated the field at shortstop. Player-manager Fred Clarke, Ginger Beaumont, and Tommy Leach led the hitting. Pitchers Sam Leever and Deacon Phillippe won 25 and 24 games, respectively, during the regular season. Though Young lost the series opener in Pittsburgh, he recovered magnificently, and together with Dineen turned the tide in favor of the Americans. Boston won the series, five games to three. Though not sanctioned by either the AL or NL, in effect baseball history's first World Series was recorded, and the Pilgrims emerged as the champions. In the face of a mediocre Beaneaters team across town, the Pilgrims commenced to gain fan attendance, and following that would rapidly eclipse their rivals by a fourfold margin.

After owning the club for one season, and despite seeing 30-foot "American League Champions" and "World Champions" banners hoisted on the center-field flagpole of the Huntington Avenue Grounds on Opening Day, Killilea, in agreement from Johnson, sold the club in April 1904 to General Charles Taylor, owner-publisher of the *Boston Globe*. The most serious of other bidders was John "Honey Fitz" Fitzgerald, grandfather of John Fitzgerald Kennedy, 35th president of the United States. But Honey Fitz was problematic because he was Irish Catholic, was as pugnacious as Johnson, and controlled a powerful political base that would subsequently elect him mayor of Boston. He might have been entirely too difficult for Johnson to manipulate. Taylor represented a more comfortable option. The general, in an act of indulgence, bestowed the club's presidency on his son, John I. Taylor. The spoiled, high-living, incompetent young Taylor ran talent through the system so rapidly that scorecard printers often had to work frantically to keep pace with developments. As ineffectual as Taylor was, however, he did make one lasting contribution—he conceived the storied name "Red Sox." In December 1906, before escaping the rigors of a New England winter for sunny California, he met with Wright and Ditson Sporting Goods representatives to discuss new club uniforms for the coming season. At the completion of the 1906 season, the crosstown Nationals abandoned their traditional red stockings in favor of blue. Hence, Taylor announced that his team's new home uniforms would be white with bright scarlet stockings, and the team's nickname, henceforth, would be the Red Sox.

"BOSTON'S TEAM," FENWAY PARK, AND THE CURSE OF THE BAMBINO

The 1904 edition of the Pilgrims repeated their 1903 championship, winning the pennant by a game and a half over the New York Highlanders. The pitching was outstanding. Young, Dineen, and Jesse Tannehill all won over 20 games, and the staff had a 2.12 ERA to lead the league. The nation clamored for a reenactment of the previous year's World Series, but neither manager John J. McGraw nor John T. Brush, owner of the pennant-winning New York Giants, supported a World Series. Brush's Giants locked up the NL pennant race by midsummer and soon brashly announced there would be no postseason play for his club. He feared that the rival Highlanders would win the AL pennant and force a showdown that might well endanger his team's popularity in New York. When Boston finally prevailed over New York on the next-to-last day of the season, Brush remained adamant. McGraw did not want to play the series because of his loathing of Johnson stemming from his tenure as Baltimore Orioles (AL) manager in 1902. The Red Sox claimed the world championship by default. Oddly enough, Brush chaired an interleague commission during the off-season that, in fact, resolved to institute an official World Series commencing with the 1905 season.

A period of quiescence prevailed for the Red Sox from 1905 to 1911. The team got older and won far fewer games, and the scatterbrained decision making and presidential leadership of young Taylor decimated the ranks of tried-and-true players and kept those that remained in a constant state of turmoil. For much of the period the team was reduced to the second division of the AL. But one bright spot emerged; against the dwindling popularity of the local NL club, now known as the Doves, the Red Sox solidly established themselves as "Boston's team." Despite modifications to accommodate some 14,000 spectators by dint of adding bleachers in the outfield and enlarging the grandstands and pavilions flanking the infield and the right- and left-field foul lines, the Red

Sox were clearly outgrowing their playing precinct on Huntington Avenue. In 1909, for instance, they drew 668,965 fans—the most until 1940!

In 1911, General Taylor divested himself of a large chunk of his baseball interests, selling half his ownership to James McAleer, a Johnson crony and manager of the Washington Senators, and Robert McRoy, Johnson's secretary. McAleer was installed as club president. Taylor expanded his interests beyond simply baseball and newspaper publishing by becoming a developer and landlord of what would become one of the most celebrated baseball parks in all the land—storied Fenway Park.

The Sox needed a larger, fire-resistant ballpark to house all its fans. Most grandstands had been built of wood, and as a result there were several ballpark fires early in the century. But beginning in 1909, major-league teams had moved to building steel and concrete parks. Aside from the limited capacity of the Huntington Grounds and accelerating insurance rates, another motivation was that the 10-year lease on the site was expiring. General Taylor created a new initiative, connected to his major shareholder interest in the Fenway Realty Company. The Fenway, affectionately dubbed "the Fens," was a tract of once unsightly and evil-smelling mudflat land reclaimed and rejuvenated into public parkland in the 1880s by landscape architect Frederick Lewis Olmsted, thereby providing Boston with a municipal park emulating his earlier Central Park achievement in New York. By 1911, nearby Kenmore Square was in its developmental infancy, with no real identity and no trolley line extended toward it. A new baseball park would solve the identity problem and provide investors with profitable opportunities in real-estate and urban-railroad development. Using the greater portion of his proceeds from his sale of Red Sox stock, General Taylor and his partners paid the Fenway Realty Company $300,000 for the site of the new Fenway Park. Construction began in the summer of 1911 and the foundations were completed by the end of November. By then the expanse of infield and outfield had been layered with six inches of loam and bushels of grass seed, the ensuing results of which moved Irish Bostonians to extol the field's aura as being "green as the flag of the Gael." Early in the New Year the infield grandstands were completed and construction of the roof began. The right- and left-field-line grandstands, made entirely of wood, followed rapidly. On April 9, 1912, the field was dedicated. The day featured an exhibition game between the Red Sox and Harvard attended by 3,000 fans, enveloped by the snowflakes of a late spring storm, who witnessed a 2–0 Sox victory.

James McLaughlin, the park's architect, had a complex task with the owner's misshapen real estate. McLaughlin faced several design problems, particularly Taylor's order to retain the orientation of the old Huntington Avenue Grounds to the sun with respect to the location of home plate to left field (Among Bostonians the saying goes that the sun rises in the east and sets in the eyes of the right fielder. Harry Hooper was the first outfielder to wear sunglasses). This meant, of course, that the left-field foul pole had to be located due north of home plate, which placed the extremity of left field hard against Lansdowne

Street, a little over 300 feet from home plate. The constraint invoked by Lands-downe did not pose the problem it would later, since few batters of the so-called dead-ball era hit the ball that far. But the die was cast, and perhaps it's a good thing that problem was not originally envisioned, because it would have necessitated the purchase of the Lansdowne Street property and produced a symmetrical configuration of the park. The high left-field wooden wall 315 feet down the line, in essence the future Green Monster; the park's tricky carom angles in the left- and right-field corners; and the vast expanse to center and right fields made defensive play a nightmare at times even for the best outfielders of the day. From home plate to the far corner of center field was a monstrous 550 feet. At the same time, the original emerald green decor of the park's interior became the delight of the Boston Irish. The new Fenway Park showcased some features that soon became commonplace in other major-league stadiums—a parking area for automobiles, a wire screen in front of the stands behind home plate, and an electric scoreboard. The park accommodated 15,000 reserved seats and 13,000 bleacher seats, just about doubling the seating capacity of the old Huntington Grounds. Fenway Park is now the oldest of all major-league venues, and the most picturesque in an age when new park construction struggles to balance grotesque urban design with an embodiment of the old and bygone.

Tris Speaker's baseball card, 1911. Courtesy of the Library of Congress

If the new Fenway Park was greeted with awe and acclaim by Boston fans in 1912, then the ensuing season provided equal bliss. A budding young outfield that eventually became legendary was in place as the 1912 season opened. Duffy Lewis in left field, Tris Speaker in center, and Harry Hooper in right were mainstays in Red Sox success. They were one of the stellar defensive outfields in the history of the game, and each was a dangerous batter, especially the peerless Speaker, who led the AL in hitting (.383), and won the Chalmers Most Valuable Player Award. On a team that stressed speed and defense, pitching, of course, was crucial. And in 1912 the Red Sox boasted one of the best staffs in all baseball. The storied Cy Young was no longer in Boston, having been dealt to Cleveland in 1909 in yet another of the incompetent John I. Taylor's trades. "Smoky" Joe Wood, who won 34 games and struck out 258, headed the staff. Wood's "smoke-ball" was so fast that the famous Walter Johnson was led to pose the rhetorical question "Can I throw harder than Joe Wood? Listen my friend, there's no man alive that can throw harder than 'Smoky' Joe Wood." Complementing Wood was Hugh Bedient and Buck O'Brien, each of whom won 20 games. Their catcher was Bill Carrigan. Jake Stahl, who had come out of retirement from his banking job in Chicago, managed the team.

The season-opening debut of Fenway Park was scheduled for April 17, but it was rained out, as were the three following games. Finally, sunshine prevailed, the field dried out, and on April 20 the Red Sox hosted the New York Highlanders. Bleacher tickets were 50 cents, and reserved seats sold by scalpers went as high as five dollars. Mayor Honey Fitz threw out the first ball, and 24,000 fans enthused to a 7–6 Sox come-from-behind victory. By the time the season came to an end a trifle over five months later, the Red Sox had compiled a new AL won-lost season record, 105–47. The World Series opened in the Polo Grounds in New York against John McGraw's Giants, led by Christy Mathewson, Rube Marquard, Fred Merkle, Buck Herzog, and Fred Snodgrass. The series went the full seven games before the Red Sox finally prevailed. Game seven was played in Fenway Park. The game went into extra innings, tied 1–1. The Giants took the lead in the top of the 10th, and with Mathewson on the mound, felt sure of the title. However, in the bottom of the frame center fielder Fred Snodgrass dropped an easy fly ball, which led to a two-run rally, and the Sox took the game 3–2. They were once again world champions. A raucous celebration parade was held the next day, led by Mayor Fitzgerald.

On the eve of World War I, Boston was a city that showcased social, economic, and cultural features that made it the envy of most American cities. In stride with America's early twentieth-century Progressive Era, institutions of higher learning and special schools addressing people's disabilities mushroomed, prompting the city toward becoming known throughout the world as "the Athens of the West." The rise of Irish American political power in the city featured two of the most historic of all Boston mayors before or since: the popular John "Honey Fitz" Fitzgerald and his successor, the irrepressible James Michael Curley. Civic pride in its two major-league baseball nines was pronounced, especially the Red Sox.

The Red Sox began the 1913 season with one of the highest payrolls in the big leagues. The high expectations for the season were dashed in spring training when Joe Wood sprained an ankle. He never recovered sufficiently to regain his normal form, limping through half the season before retiring altogether in late July with a badly sprained thumb that had never healed. In fact, Wood won only 24 games over the remainder of his career. Wood's troubles were reflective of many Red Sox players that season; only the incomparable outfield of Lewis, Speaker, and Hooper played to potential. Jake Stahl was fired as manager in July, succeeded by longtime Sox catcher Bill "Rough" Carrigan, a move that delighted the club's huge Irish American following. Carrigan was tough but fair, a superb handler of pitchers, impartial to favoritism, and a tenacious competitor. Commanding respect from every Red Sox player, Carrigan spent the remainder of the 1913 season trying to rebuild and rejuvenate the Red Sox, who barely mustered a .500 record, finishing fourth, 15 1/2 games behind Philadelphia's Athletics. Nevertheless, McAleer's appointment of Carrigan paid huge dividends over the next few years.

Several changes greeted the 1914 Red Sox season. League president Ban Johnson, angered at McAleer's firing of Jake Stahl and doubly irritated by what he perceived as the increasing independence of the Boston owner, orchestrated a secret campaign to oust him in favor of a more malleable soul. He found such a man in Joseph L. Lannin. Quebec-born but Boston-reared, Lannin arrived in Boston as an impoverished youth, pursued the American dream in Horatio Alger–like fashion, and became a wealthy man in a relatively short time, mainly from real-estate dealings. Lannin was also a baseball fanatic, a minor shareholder in the Boston Braves, and an individual who longed to own a major-league team, if not in Boston then elsewhere. When Johnson approached him about buying the Red Sox, Lannin was already well along in a deal to buy the Philadelphia Phillies. With Johnson's blessing and encouragement, Lannin abandoned his Philadelphia quest, sold his small interest in the Braves, and paid $200,000 for McAleer's half of the Red Sox. A few months later, in May 1914, Lannin bought out General Taylor and became sole owner. Lannin gave Carrigan full control of baseball operations. Carrigan's first order of business was to keep Tris Speaker on the team. Speaker, Ty Cobb, and Walter Johnson were the premier AL players of the era, and were seriously recruited by the rival Federal League. Though few players ended up jumping to the Feds, the cost in player salaries to organized baseball was devastating. For instance, to retain the services of Tris Speaker, Lannin was forced to ante up a two-year, $36,000 contract, the largest in baseball history, doubling the outfielder's previous contract. As good a manager and developer of talent as Carrigan was, the Red Sox were no match for Connie Mack's powerful Athletics in 1914. But before the season ended, and with the Red Sox out of the pennant race by late July, an event transpired that was destined to create one of the major bits of anguish in Red Sox history—the first chapter in the saga known as "the Curse of the Bambino."

Unlike in Boston, where the Federal League was either scorned or looked upon with amusement, the upstart rival league went head-to-head with major-league teams in such traditional baseball markets as St. Louis, Chicago, and Brooklyn. In Baltimore the attendance figures of the International League's Orioles faltered badly in the face of the competition provided by the Federal League's Terrapins, housed in a stadium located just across the street from the Orioles' ballpark. An age-old solution reared its head: Orioles owner Jack Dunn was forced to sell prized players to stave off bankruptcy. In just three days, Dunn decimated his ball club. News of the impending Orioles fire sale reached Lannin in nearby Washington, where the Red Sox were in town for a series with the Senators. Lannin rushed to Baltimore to be first in line when the sale opened. For a reported $25,000, Lannin bought the contracts of Orioles pitcher Ernie Shore, catcher Ben Egan, and a 19-year-old baby-faced left-handed pitcher of some promise, the player whose name would later become known as no other in the history of baseball—the immortal George Herman "Babe" Ruth.

Ruth arrived in Boston on July 11, 1914, but his debut was inauspicious. He started that afternoon against last-place Cleveland, leaving the game after seven innings with the score tied, having yielded eight hits and three runs. Carrigan handled Ruth carefully, grooming him for a regular spot on the pitching staff of the Red Sox future. To smooth out the rough spots in Ruth's delivery, as well as to try and bring a small measure of maturity to an obviously cocky, naive, egotistical, foul-mouthed, and devil-may-care youth, Carrigan sent him to Providence in the International League, the top Red Sox minor-league franchise. There he won an astounding 22 games in leading the Grays to the league championship. Decades later, an aged and long-retired Harry Hooper—who, with Duffy Lewis and Tris Speaker, formed what some baseball historians have labeled as the most gifted Red Sox outfield combination in the club's history—gave an interview to noted baseball chronicler Lawrence Ritter, in which Hooper recalled his impressions of Ruth when the Babe arrived in Boston: "He was a left-handed pitcher then and a good one. He had never been anywhere, didn't know anything about manners or how to behave among people—just a big overgrown ape . . . You know I saw it all happen, from beginning to end. But sometimes I can't believe what I saw . . . a man transformed from a human being into something pretty close to a god. If somebody had predicted that back on the Red Sox in 1914, he would have been thrown into a lunatic asylum."

While Carrigan was assembling the future Red Sox pitching staff and making other personnel moves to guarantee success in 1915, the crosstown Boston Braves put a serious dent in the Red Sox's wide margin of popularity. Mired in last place at the end of June, the Braves reeled off 52 wins in 60 games in July, August, and early September to eventually win the NL pennant. Further, the so-called Miracle Braves flabbergasted the baseball world by sweeping past Mack's thought-to-be-invincible Athletics to win the World Series. The Braves' South End Grounds was old and ramshackle, woefully small, and completely inadequate for accommodating a Boston baseball community suddenly gone mad over its NL entry. In an act of baseball camaraderie as well as business acumen, Lannin leased Fenway Park to the Braves for their stretch run to the 1914 pennant and World Series home games. The arrangement continued through much of the following season until Braves Field, featuring a mammoth playing area and the largest spectator accommodation in MLB, was completed near the banks of the Charles River, roughly a mile northwest of Fenway Park.

Things boded well for the Red Sox in 1915. Lannin and Carrigan had assembled what the press referred to as "the million dollar pitching staff," a term used figuratively to describe Eddie Shore, George Foster, Dutch Leonard, Ray Collins, Carl Mays, and Ruth. Together with its superb outfield, defensive infield stars Jack Barry and Everett Scott, and his own services as catcher at appropriate times, Carrigan's aggregation raised the hope of Bostonians for a repeat of the glorious 1912 season. Most of Boston was gratified. On September 20, as the Red Sox battled Detroit and Ty Cobb for the championship, a crowd of 37,528 occupied every nook and cranny of the ballpark, setting a record as the largest ever to watch baseball in Fenway Park. The Red Sox won the pennant by two and a half games over the Tigers. The team won 101 games and lost 50. Five pitchers won 15 or more games, including Ruth, who won 18 games and batted .315. For the World Series against Philadelphia's Phillies, Lannin engaged the new Braves Field, which could seat 10,000 more fans than Fenway. The Red Sox triumphed by four games to one, reaping rich financial rewards at the gate. Inexplicably, Carrigan, surrogate father, psychologist, master motivator, and drill sergeant to Ruth, kept him out of the series. But he wasn't needed, as Ernie Shore, Dutch Leonard, and Rube Foster, who all pitched complete games and limited the Phillies to a batting average of .182, took the series. Boston and New England rejoiced.

With the demise of the upstart Federal League after the 1915 season, the salary leverage that players enjoyed from the existence of a competing market disappeared. Lannin attempted to cut Red Sox salaries to pre–Federal League levels, offering Tris Speaker $9,000, or half his wages in 1915. When Speaker balked, Lannin sold him to Cleveland for the largest sum ever up to that time, $50,000, plus two players. Boston fans seethed. Despite Speaker's absence, a still-intact pitching staff, solid defense, and speed in the outfield and on the bases led to another pennant in 1916. Ruth won 23 games, posted a league-leading 1.75 ERA, and beat Walter Johnson four times. The Sox finished two games ahead of Detroit and Chicago, its nearest contenders. Brooklyn's Dodgers were the opponents in the World Series following; Lannin once again engaged Braves Field for Red Sox home games. The Red Sox won the opener, 6–5. Ruth pitched the second game, which went 14 innings before the Red Sox prevailed, 2–1. In the flush of victory, an elated Ruth grabbed Carrigan in a congratulatory bear hug, boasting, "I told you I could take care of those National League sons of bitches." The Dodgers won game three in Brooklyn, but the Red Sox won game four, returned to Boston on Columbus Day, and concluded the series, winning the final game 4–1. Two consecutive World Series championships! Only the Cubs and Athletics had ever achieved that feat. The celebration was short-lived. Only 33, Carrigan retired from baseball and returned to his home in Maine to become a rural banker. The quiet but at times fiery Carrigan had proven to be a master manager of players often at odds with each other over religion, politics, and, of course, egos. And, for Babe Ruth, Carrigan may well have been the difference between a career ended prematurely by immaturity and gross behavior and one that ultimately endeared the Bambino to legions of baseball fans, though hardly his managers.

Less than a month after his club's 1916 World Series championship, Joe Lannin sold the Red Sox. His three years of ownership were marked by declining health, constant run-ins with league president Ban Johnson, and disenchantment with the politics of MLB. He had, however, made a reported $400,000. One offer came from a consortium of local Bostonians and Hibernians, headed by Honey Fitz's son-in-law, Joseph Kennedy. However, the successful buyer was Harry Harrison Frazee, destined to become one of the most infamous and scorned names in Boston baseball history. The purchase price was $675,000, which included ownership of Fenway Park, a property that Lannin had finally pried away from the Taylor family and the Fenway Realty Company.

A midwesterner from Illinois, Frazee had long been involved in the theater, first as a ticket taker, then as a theater manager, then as a booking agent, and finally as a producer of shows, many of which, starting in 1904, were smash hits. A lifelong baseball fan, he also sponsored sporting extravaganzas, including a 1913 tour by boxer Jim Jeffries, the 1915 Jack Johnson–Jess Willard heavyweight title fight in Havana, and various minor-league barnstorming tours. By 1916, Frazee was a well-established millionaire with business interests in real estate and stock brokerage. MLB, though, gave "Handsome Harry" a measure of public celebrity.

Frazee's Red Sox began the 1917 season with most of the same team that had won the World Series a year earlier. With a month and a half to go they were in the thick of the pennant race, but faded badly and finished nine games behind the pennant-winning White Sox. For much of the season, two Red Sox figures were surrounded by continual turmoil—Frazee, in arguments with Ban Johnson and an increasingly alienated Boston press, and Babe Ruth, whose conduct under player-manager Jack Barry grew more and more erratic as the season progressed. Frazee thought Johnson incompetent and schemed incessantly to oust him as AL czar. Johnson, in turn, in accord with many members of the Boston press, scorned Frazee as greedy, devious, and corrupt, and alluded obliquely to his being Jewish (which he was not), an aspersion that never sat well in Boston, with its largely Irish population. Ruth had a brilliant season, with 24 wins, second in the league, and an ERA of 2.01. However, Ruth proceeded through the season in bizarre fashion; his on-field swagger and foul mouth earned him a nine-day suspension in midseason and a $100 fine. Away from the ballpark, his drinking and whoring began to construct the legendary antiestablishment persona that would capture the awe and imagination of the entire baseball world in the 1920s and 1930s. But by the time of the World Series, Americans had more on their mind than baseball matters: the first doughboys were fighting in trenches, and the Selective Service Act, enacted the previous April, was already beginning to take its toll on playing rosters. To top it all off, America was on the verge of going dry with the passage of the 18th Amendment in the Senate, and the prohibition of sales of alcohol appeared imminent.

Despite all this, Frazee promised Boston a championship in 1918, and he delivered. In a deal $10,000 richer than the Speaker sale, Frazee brought premier Philadelphia A's catcher Wally Schang, pitcher Joe Bush, and outfielder Amos Strunk to Boston for $60,000 and two second-line players. Hardly had the new year commenced when Frazee was at it again with the A's, this time acquiring an all-purpose player of supreme magnitude, the redoubtable Stuffy McInnis. When manager Barry was inducted into the service, Frazee secured Ed Barrow, former Tigers skipper and president of the Eastern League, to replace him. The ensuing pennant race was beset by a mass exodus of players leaving for the armed forces or, especially, for defense jobs, since the federal government had ruled that MLB was a nonessential activity. In a last-minute concession to an argument proposed by Frazee and a coalition of MLB club owners that baseball was good for the nation's morale, an abbreviated season was arranged, with the World Series taking place in early September. Nonetheless, the public was none too enthused by professional ballplayers who remained out of the war effort. Attendance at Fenway Park took a 50 percent hit. The Red Sox won the pennant by two and half games over Cleveland's Indians, led by their outstanding pitching. Carl Mays won 21 games, while Ruth pitched and played the outfield, winning 13 games and losing 7 while batting .300 and hitting 11 home runs, almost 11 percent of the league's total output. The Cubs, who furnished the World Series competition, were beaten four games to one. The 1918 Series was not without incident. Ruth set a World Series record, reaching 29 2/3 consecutive innings of scoreless pitching, a mark that remained intact until broken by the Yankees' Whitey Ford in 1961. The players, who had previously been granted 60 percent of the gate proceeds for the first four Series games, were confronted by a new formula for distributing the pot. The players' share was decreased to 55 percent of the total pot for the first four games, and participants only shared 60 percent of that total—the remainder went to players on teams that finished second, third, and fourth place in both leagues during the season. This meant that each Series player's share was reduced by almost three-quarters of what it had been. Clearly, labor had been compromised in favor of club ownership and league management. Enraged, the players threatened to strike and refused to take the field for game four. In the face of a demeaning and personally humiliating plea by Ban Johnson, together with rising unrest in the grandstands from the spectators, the players relented. In the end, each Red Sox player pocketed $1,102.51 as his winner's share, while each Cub received a little more than half that, $671.09, the smallest World Series players'-share payout in the history of the game.

Frazee continued to have a festering animosity and acrimonious relationship with Ban Johnson, and schemed for Johnson's demise as both AL president and chairman of the three-man board that served as baseball's National Commission. Frazee's grand plan envisioned a commissioner of MLB, an idea that actually materialized scarcely two years later following the infamous Black Sox scandal. On the other hand, Johnson hated Frazee more than any other owner. Handsome Harry's ego, lifestyle, wealth, success, and general demeanor rankled the powerful founder of the AL.

Frazee found himself often frozen out of the trade market by Johnson-backed AL clubs, and was reduced to mainly dealing with Chicago and especially New York. Despite the general press disenchantment with Frazee's numerous deals, most of his trades can be evaluated as having been good for Boston, at least on paper. At the end of 1918 he sent Shore and Lewis to the Yankees for four players, including pitcher Ray Caldwell, and $15,000. During the season he traded the enigmatic pitcher Carl Mays, who had walked out on the team, to the Yankees for two pitchers and $40,000. Then in 1920 he sent four players to the Yankees, including rookie Waite Hoyt, a future Hall of Famer, in return for four players, including the excellent infielder Del Pratt and catcher Muddy Ruel, who went on to have a 19-year major-league career. There were several other trades with the Yankees in the future, including a huge trade in late 1921, in which the Sox secured star shortstop Roger Peckinpaugh, aging spitballer Jack Quinn, and young pitcher Rip Collins for the superb Sox shortstop Everett Scott and the team's best pitchers, "Sad Sam" Jones and "Bullet Joe" Bush.

Frazee's most famous transaction was his sale of Babe Ruth. Before the 1919 season, Ruth demanded, for his double-duty performance in 1918, a doubling of his contracted salary of $7,500. "No raise, I don't play," threatened Ruth. In response to this ultimatum, Frazee lectured the Boston press. "If Ruth doesn't want to work for the Red Sox . . . we can make an advantageous trade." There was no trade, and Frazee negotiated a three-year, $30,000 contract with Ruth. The Sox commenced the 1919 season with high hopes. Ruth, rarely pitching, played the outfield and compiled batting statistics that amply signaled the career that lay before him. He broke the major-league record for home runs with 29, batted .322, and drove in a league-leading 122 runs. Despite his lofty batting statistics, Ruth was a disruptive force on the team. His continual salary demands, boisterous conduct, bizarre drinking and womanizing, and disintegrating physical fitness, which gave every indication of a short career, reduced the Red Sox to a badly fractured team unit. Not surprisingly, it showed in the standings. Boston finished a distant sixth, 20 1/2 games behind the White Sox. Frazee was faced with a decision—keep the cancerous Ruth and reap the consequences, or trade him for the best deal possible. Frazee elected the latter, except that the deal he eventually made with the Yankees in December 1919 returned no players to the Red Sox. It was cash only—$100,000, $25,000 of it up front and the balance in three $25,000 notes payable at one-year intervals at six percent interest—by far the biggest dollar deal to that time. He also got a $350,000 loan, used to pay off the mortgage on the ballpark. (He did not make the trade, as the conventional wisdom claimed, to pay off his theater debts.) Boston's press, consistently vitriolic over the years in its criticism of Frazee, was divided on the issue of trading Ruth. The sensationalist tabloid *Evening American* and *Herald* scolded Frazee unmercifully. The *Post* remained neutral. The *Globe* and *Evening Transcript* generally supported the move, citing Ruth's disruptiveness to team cohesion. As much as Red Sox fans adored the team's star players, an even greater priority remained the prospect of team success.

COMETH AND STAYETH THE DOLDRUMS

The 1920 season opened auspiciously for the Red Sox. After two months of play they led the Yanks in the standings. But injuries set in and the team faltered badly, finishing fifth—better, though, than the previous year *with* Babe Ruth. The Yankees finished third behind the Indians and White Sox. But Ruth, to the delight of Frazee scorners, had a terrific year, clouting an electrifying 54 home runs and driving in 137 runs. The era of the Yankees' "Sultan of Swat" had commenced in spectacular fashion. Following the season the now-infamous Black Sox scandal erupted. Frazee blamed Johnson for doing nothing about a consistently growing gambling climate surrounding MLB, a climate in which the seeds of player acquiescence to gamblers' overtures were planted. In rapid manner the espousers of a commissioner system for baseball, led by Frazee, were victorious, and Kenesaw Mountain Landis was named to the post. Ban Johnson, though he remained president of the AL, lost much of his wide-reaching influence.

With dismal seasons in both 1921 (fifth) and 1922 (eighth), it remained only for Harry Frazee to sell his Boston ball club and escape the accelerating wrath that he experienced daily from Boston newspapers and fans in the Hub City. Attendance at Fenway Park dwindled to 275,000 in 1921 and 259,000 in 1922, and they were last in the AL from 1921 through 1925. To make matters worse for local fans, the Braves, since their miracle feat of 1914, had become perennial lower-division NL finishers. The aura of big-league baseball sank to an all-time low in Boston. Only semipro twilight baseball seemed to capture the fancy of local fans.

On August 1, 1923, with the Sox mired in last place in the AL standings, Frazee's stubborn resistance to sell the team finally crumbled. Bob Quinn, business manager of the St. Louis Browns, goaded in the background by a Ban Johnson eager to rid the game of his archenemy, gathered a group of investors and asked Frazee to name his price, which was $1.15 million. They accepted it. Frazee left the Red Sox after turning a profit in each of his seven years of ownership. He was an astute businessman in the worlds of both theater and sports, and when he died in 1929, he left an estate valued at close to $1.3 million.

Red Sox fortunes under the leadership of Quinn deteriorated to an excruciating level for the Fenway Faithful in Boston. In fact, the number of Fenway Faithful shrank alarmingly during owner Quinn's one-decade stewardship of the Red Sox. During those 10 years (1923–32) the Red Sox finished last each year but 1924, when the club moved up to seventh. During this time, the team made a profit only once, $7,764 in 1930, and lost a total of $182,693. Abominable seasons that hovered between 42 and 58 wins shrank fan support drastically. Only 182,150 passed through the turnstiles in 1932.

In 1926, a fire in the left-field grandstands of Fenway Park reduced the once-proud edifice to an unsightly, derelict-appearing structure. The charred remains were removed, but no reconstruction followed as Quinn was dead broke, up to his ear in debt. The Red Sox were a sorry picture, the laughing-stock of the AL, the dumping ground for the league's least talented players. Managers came and went under the increasingly desperate Quinn, six of them in 10 years: Frank Chance, Lee Fohl, Bill Carrigan (enticed from Maine), Heinie Wagner, Shano Collins, and Marty McManus. The crash of the stock market in 1929 and subsequent depression jarred Quinn to his last resorts. The Red Sox must be sold. On the downside was the fact that the club owned a derelict ballpark, a horrible pool of playing personnel, a drastically decreased fan base, and an organizational infrastructure in disarray. Under normal circumstances this debilitating picture alone would have led Quinn to entertain even the most preposterous offers for his ball club. But there was a redeeming feature of value—the land upon which Fenway Park rested, which even during the depression was worth well over $1 million. Quinn found the angel he needed in Tom Yawkey.

Yawkey, destined to own and lead the Boston Red Sox for almost half a century, was hardly 30 years of age when he bought the team and the ballpark for $1.2 million in the spring of 1933. Born to Augusta and Thomas J. Austin in February 1903, young Tom's father died from pneumonia seven months later. Three years later his mother consigned him to her brother, William Hoover Yawkey, the wealthy, high- and hard-living son of American lumber baron William Clyburn Yawkey. Bill Yawkey, who inherited most of his father's $20 million estate, purchased the Detroit Tigers in 1904 for the bargain-basement price of $50,000, a deal that his father was on the brink of consummating at the time of his death. Three-year-old Thomas was adopted by his uncle Bill and took the Yawkey family name. A bachelor until 1910 and a habitual traveler, Uncle Bill was away from home for long periods, leaving young Tom in the care and embrace of housekeepers. Tom's mother and uncle both died before he was 18, when he went off to Yale. Tom inherited a trust fund worth $7 million when he turned 30 in 1933, and lost little time in pursuing his longtime interest in baseball. When the financially beleaguered Quinn put the decrepit Red Sox on the market, Yawkey stood ready to respond. A lot of his wealth was spent on the team, which lost $1.5 million between 1933 and 1940.

Yawkey's checkbook went into action right away in a quest to invigorate the playing roster. He hired Eddie Collins as general manager, and after the end of the 1933 season, they fired holdover manager Marty McManus, replacing him with Bucky Harris of the Detroit Tigers. Yawkey, though well intentioned, was naive about baseball business matters, which was not lost on his fellow AL owners. In one five-day period, Yawkey spent some $200,000 on new ballplayers, including unproven minor leaguers, over-the-hill veterans, and onetime stars gone sour. AL owners gloated. Even so, the 1933 Red Sox won 20 games more than the team did in 1932, the club's most dismal season to this very day. That July, Yawkey inherited another $3 million from his aunt, much of which went to rehabilitate Fenway Park.

When Yawkey acquired the Red Sox, Fenway Park was in shambles and decay. Little maintenance had taken place over the prior decade, making it unpleasant and unsafe. The unrepaired damage from the fire added to the generally repugnant atmosphere. Yawkey spent $1.5 million to rebuild the structure, and not just renovate it. Before the 1934 season opened the park was transformed to the basic outline of the current facility. Down came practically everything except the girder foundations for the grandstands. Up went new stands, all the way to the right- and left-field foul poles, as well as a huge bleacher section from dead center field to the right-field corner. New steel girders supporting the roof were added to the infield grandstands, making it possible in the future to add a second deck. Additional box seats were added in front of the infield stands. A new press box took shape. The playing field was scraped bare and 8,000 cubic feet of new sod was installed. An army of 750 skilled union workers were employed, making it the second-biggest construction project in depression-era Boston, second only to the Mystic River Bridge over the Charles River The finished product increased seating capacity to 38,000. It sported a formidable left-field wall, 37 feet high, built to accommodate a huge new electric scoreboard and three huge advertising signs. Much later, the signature wall became known as "the Green Monster," after the "Dartmouth Green" paint color that bathed the entire interior of Fenway Park. When the new Fenway Park opened on the first day of the 1935 season, nearly 33,000 fans made their way into Yawkey's palace.

Yawkey was not reticent about buying talent. His most prodigious deal during the remainder of the 1930s was his acquisition of baseball's best pitcher, the indomitable Philadelphia Athletics left-hander Robert Moses Grove, for whom he paid $125,000. Grove, fast approaching his twilight years, nursed a sore arm for much of his Boston career. Still, during his eight-year tenure with the Sox he won 55 games in Fenway Park, including his 300th, the last of his storied career. Throughout his four decades of Red Sox ownership, Yawkey proved to be a ballplayer's perfect boss. He paid well, related personally to his players, and maintained a generally relaxed and friendly atmosphere in which ownership, management, and labor functioned. The 1934 Sox improved to .500 for the season, and attendance rose to 600,000, a figure that remained static for the remainder of the decade. Following the end of the season Yawkey got busy in the player market. He sent Harris packing and inveigled the Senators' Clark Griffith to part with his son-in-law, player-manager Joe Cronin, for the princely sum of $250,000. Despite high hopes and parting with another $300,000, Yawkey's 1935 "Millionaires," or "Gold Sox," as they were dubbed, barely topped .500, winning 78 and losing 75. Despite slipping to 74–80 in 1936, the Sox gave signs of significant improvement. Yawkey acquired Jimmy Foxx from Philadelphia, a player with almost Ruthian performance statistics. Foxx led the team to a record of 80–72 in 1937, finishing fifth, and in 1938 (88–61) they finished second to the Yankees. Foxx was astounding, especially at home games at Fenway, where he hit .405, bashed 35 home runs, batted in 104, and had a Ruthian slugging percentage of .887. Foxx won the MVP Award with 50 homers and a league-leading .349 batting average and .704 slugging percentage. The entire squad hit .299. Teams began to recognize that the Red Sox were hard to beat at home; Boston fans rallied to the team as it rose in the standings. But Yawkey's inflated checkbook invariably dictated a philosophy of acquiring players through purchase or trade, many of them in the retiring years of their careers. Few teams in the major leagues spent less on their farm system than the Red Sox. The long-term impact finally became apparent to Yawkey and Collins, prompting them to focus more attention on identifying and developing talent in the minor leagues. Their first dividend was future Hall of Famer Bobby Doerr, who became a Sox fixture at second base for over a decade. The second dividend arrived in the elongated frame of Ted Williams, widely acknowledged as the greatest hitter in the history of baseball.

Undated photo of Ted Williams. Courtesy of the Baseball Hall of Fame

THE SPLENDID SPLINTER

In the autumn of 1936 the *Sporting News* made its first-ever notation of the player, who, for almost the next three decades, would capture more print in the storied baseball periodical than any other major leaguer of his time. Ted Williams, sometimes referred to as "the Kid" or "Teddy Ballgame," but more aptly called "the Splendid Splinter," had the greatest impact on the Boston Red Sox of any player in the long and distinguished history of the franchise. The *Sporting News* described the 17-year-old pitcher and outfielder of the Double-A Pacific Coast League as "a gangly high school fly chaser" who showed promise. The Red Sox brought Williams to spring training in 1938 and assigned him to Minneapolis of the Triple-A American Association for further seasoning. The precocious and temperamental Williams, though supremely confident of his abilities, masked his insecurity, like Ruth, with cockiness. But unlike the Babe, he would not erode his God-given natural talents by drinking and carousing. In Minneapolis he hit .366, with 42 home runs and 142 RBIs, which assured him a place in the Red Sox outfield for the 1939 season. Williams's rookie AL season was punctuated by a .327 batting average (second on the team to Foxx's .360), 31 home runs, and a league-leading 145 RBIs. His fielding was a bit less awesome. Though he demonstrated a strong throwing arm, he committed 19 errors in right field, and his lack of speed afoot compromised him from effectively patrolling Fenway's spacious right field, the largest and most difficult sun field of any AL ballpark. The Sox again finished a distant second to the Yankees.

For the 1940 season the Red Sox youth movement unveiled a solid-hitting, ball-hawking outfielder in the person of bespectacled Dominic DiMaggio, younger brother of superb Yankees star Joe DiMaggio, whom he equaled in almost every way except power. Williams was moved to left field, where he very rapidly mastered playing the imposing wall and the tricky carom angles of the flagpole corner. Williams was never as adept in the field as at bat, but nevertheless, he developed into a far better than average defensive player. The Sox finished the season at 82–72, nine games behind the pennant-winning Detroit Tigers. Williams, by any standard but his own, piled up impressive statistics: a .344 average, 23 home runs, and 113 RBIs. He led the league with 134 runs and an on-base percentage of .442. Whenever he failed, either in the field or at bat, he often indulged in temper tantrums. Spectators, sensing in the young star a severe case of "rabbit ears," often rode him unmercifully from bleacher and grandstand alike. He badly overreacted to press criticism. His long and meritorious career in Boston was punctuated by a rancorous relationship with the press and a dismissing, aloof demeanor with his mostly adoring public.

In 1941 the Red Sox finished at 84–70, a habit-forming second to the Yankees, backed by the league's leading offense, which included three men with over 100 RBIs. The team earned a profit of $57,342, its first year in the black since 1930. Williams had a remarkable season, batting .406, which was somewhat overshadowed by Joe DiMaggio's 56-game hitting streak. Williams's signature accomplishment ended in dramatic fashion when he went six for eight in a season-ending doubleheader with Philadelphia, lifting his final batting average to .406. He narrowly missed winning the coveted Triple Crown, leading the league in home runs (37) and finishing barely behind Joe DiMaggio in RBIs (125 to 120). He also led the league in on-base percentage (.553), runs (135), and slugging (.735). Williams was the first batter since the Giants' Bill Terry (.401) in 1930 to reach the .400 mark, and was the closest of anyone to do it since, when he hit .388 in 1957, until George Brett hit .390 in 1980.

Scarcely two months after the 1941 season, the Japanese attack on Pearl Harbor occurred, bringing America into World War II. Commissioner Landis offered to cancel the 1942 season if it was in the interest of national priorities, but President Franklin Roosevelt, borrowing from the nation's World War I experience, requested that the baseball season be played. Americans needed an outlet from the tensions and sacrifices endured during the great national war effort. In the end, few major-league players remained out of the armed forces, including the heart of the Red Sox lineup. Williams, after an initial deferral due to his dependent mother, enlisted in the Naval Air Corps and entered active duty after the 1942 season. Though the Sox finished second yet again (93–59), Williams was once again sensational, winning the Triple Crown by batting .356, hitting 36 homers, and batting in 137 runs. Similar to other teams limping along on star-depleted rosters, the Red Sox labored through the next three seasons (seventh in 1943, fourth in 1944, and seventh again in 1945) as Williams spent the war years stateside in Pensacola, Florida, training to be a flight instructor. Williams loved flying almost as much as hitting and fishing.

High expectations for Red Sox success abounded in the postwar period. The team was very well paid. The 1945 team had a payroll of $511,000, tops in the majors, which rose to $561,000 in 1950, second only to the Yankees. The stars were back from military service, and new young talent had been assembled. The pitching staff, long in disarray, was formidable. Williams and DiMaggio anchored the outfield. Jim Tabor at third base, Doerr at second, Johnny Pesky at short, and Rudy York at first base were all All-Star infielders. Pitchers Tex Hughson, Joe Dobson, Mickey Harris, and Dave "Boo" Ferris formed the core of the pitching staff. The team led the AL in offense, with three 100-RBI men, and in defense, with the fewest errors. Williams was MVP, batting .342, and led the league with a slugging percentage of .667 and 142 runs scored. The Sox locked up the 1946 AL pennant by September 13, and season attendance more than doubled, reaching an all-time high of 1.4 million. After losing an average of $82,621 from 1942 to 1945, the team made $405,133 that season, and an average of $117,000 from 1946 through 1950. The St. Louis Cardinals, winners of the NL pennant following a dramatic playoff series with the Brooklyn Dodgers, were the Red Sox's opponents in their first World Series appearance since 1918. And it was in that series that the first of several bizarre World Series circumstances occurred, leading to a gut-wrenching ending that denied a championship and magnified the Curse of the Bambino. In the seventh and deciding game, with the score tied 3–3 with two outs in the ninth inning and Enos Slaughter on first base for the Cardinals, Terry Moore looped a hit-and-run single to short left center. Slaughter, running on the pitch, rounded second and, never hesitating, turned third base and headed for home. Expecting Slaughter to stop at third base, Leon Culberson lackadaisically relayed the ball back to Pesky. The second baseman, shocked at seeing a streaking Slaughter well on his way to home plate, hesitated, then threw desperately but futilely to try and cut down the winning run. Slaughter scored easily. Although most of the blame belonged to the unfortunate Culberson (subbing for an injured DiMaggio in center field), Pesky's role became etched in legend as "Pesky held the ball," a soliloquy in Boston baseball lore equal to and every bit as sad as Ernest Lawrence Thayer's classic phrase "Mighty Casey has struck out." The Red Sox threatened in the bottom of the ninth, but strange and highly debatable managing decisions by Cronin ultimately ensured defeat. Such grotesque circumstances would reoccur for the Red Sox in each of their next three World Series appearances, defeats that formed a pantheon of tragic memories for all New Englanders.

The disappointment of 1946 carried over into the following year, when a third-place finish behind New York and Detroit was only salvaged by another vintage Williams performance—a second Triple Crown (.343 average, 32 home runs, 117 RBIs). Astonishingly, Williams lost the AL MVP distinction to Joe DiMaggio, who had batted only .315 but led the Yankees to the pennant and a World Series championship. In 1948 the Sox had a new manager, the veteran Joe McCarthy. The team had its usual complement of strong batting, with three men driving in at least 111 runs. The team won the final two games of the season to put itself into a tie with Cleveland for the pennant. This historic event in club history forced a one-game playoff, played in Fenway Park. Meanwhile, across town at Braves Field, Boston's NL entry was celebrating its first pennant since 1914. A "streetcar" World Series loomed, but Lou Boudreau's Indians took care of the Red Sox in handy fashion, 8–3, and went on to defeat the Braves in the Series, four games to two. McCarthy's pitching strategy for the climactic one-game playoff was denounced vehemently in every Boston newspaper. The 1948 nightmare finale was virtually repeated one year later. The last day of the season found the Red Sox and Yankees tied for first place with identical records (96–57), with the deciding contest in New York. After the Yankees prevailed, 5–3, angry rebukes of McCarthy's managerial decisions stirred not only the ire of the press and Red Sox fans, but also the frustrated players.

Three months into the 1950 season, the increasingly depressed and driven-to-drink "Marse" Joe McCarthy resigned, replaced by former Tigers manager Steve O'Neill. O'Neill lasted but two seasons before being succeeded by Lou Boudreau, who was replaced by Pinky Higgins in 1955; Higgins lasted until 1959. Yawkey spent lavishly for top talent either developed in the minor leagues or purchased from other clubs. He had coddled and spoiled his players with bonuses and above-market salaries. Yawkey built his team a model ballpark, still a hallowed cathedral of unique quality. The product was a perennial bridesmaid to Yankee superiority and an average fourth-place finish.

The Korean War broke out less than a week after McCarthy left. The United States mobilized for war in the next six months, and thousands of young men were inducted into the armed forces. At the start of the 1952 season, Williams, a member of the Marine Reserve, was called up. He eventually flew 39 combat and reconnaissance missions behind enemy lines. On one mission, his F-9 Panther jet fighter was hit by small-arms fire, disabling his radio, crippling his landing gear, and setting the aircraft on fire, but he was able to land it before it went up in flames. In July 1953, Williams was mustered out of the service for medical reasons; after a short hospital stay he reported back to the Red Sox. Commenting on Williams's statistics for the remainder of the season, particularly his .407 batting average, one sports scribe was moved to declare that the Splendid Splinter had "set spring training back ten years."

The 1950s were underscored by a continuation of prior campaigns in which the Sox finished behind the now-hated Yankees, who won every AL pennant of the decade except in 1954 and 1959 and six World Series championships. Boston fans came to Fenway Park in the 1950s more to see Ted Williams in the twilight years of his magnificent and at times tempestuous career than to witness the (mis)fortunes of the Red Sox, underscoring that for the first time in Sox history, the mystique of a single player seemed more important than that of the franchise itself. His hitting remained majestic. However, his on-field conduct, particularly when booed for defensive misplays, often elicited juvenile gestures, such as giving a derisive crowd the finger or a spitting tantrum. On September 27, 1960, before a sparse Fenway gathering of less than 5,000 fans, Williams made his last career plate appearance, and homered for the 521st time in his career. John Updike captured the essence of that dramatic moment in Red Sox history in an elegiac essay written for the *New Yorker* in 1960: "Williams ran around the square of bases like a feather caught in a vortex at the center of our beseeching screaming. He ran as he always ran out home runs, hurriedly, unsmiling, head down, as if our praise were a storm of rain to get out of. He didn't tip his cap. Though we thumped, wept, and chanted 'We want Ted' for minutes after he hid in the dugout, he did not come back. Our noise for some seconds passed beyond excitement into a kind of immense open anguish, a wailing, a cry to be saved. But immortality is nontransferable. The papers said that the other players, and even the umpires on the field, begged him to come out and acknowledge us in some way, but he refused. Gods do not answer letters." During his 20-year career, the greatest Red Sox player of them all had 2,654 hits, 1,829 RBIs, and a batting average of .344.

"GET THOSE NIGGERS OFF THE FIELD": RED SOX INTEGRATION

The Boston Red Sox were the last major-league ball club to embrace what Jules Tygiel has called "Baseball's Great Experiment." The Red Sox had no African American in its lineup until 1959, a full dozen years after Jackie Robinson broke the color line. Boston had long been a national leader in educational and social rights for the physically and mentally afflicted, as well as a hotbed center of pre–Civil War sentiment for the abolition of slavery and enhancement of the lives of black Americans. Why, then, did baseball segregation continue in "the cradle of American liberty"?

The answer was embedded in the character of Red Sox leadership—in the mentality and intolerant dispositions of owner Tom Yawkey and general manager Eddie Collins. In the mid-1930s, when the issue of Negro players in the major leagues became extensively covered in the black press, Boston's baseball officials were queried by local black columnist Mabrey "Doc" Kountz on the question "Why not in Boston?" They shrugged their shoulders, made a weak apology, and nodded toward the front office. Yawkey continually rejected requests to meet with Kountz to discuss integration. In the early spring of 1945 Boston City Council member Isadore Muchnick, who was Jewish, took up the crusade for integration. Muchnick threatened to block the annual renewal of permission for Sunday baseball. "I cannot understand," he wrote, "how baseball . . . can continue a pre-Civil War attitude toward American citizens because of the color of their skin." The Red Sox brass bowed to the pressure and invited Jackie Robinson, Marvin Williams, and Sam Jethroe to Fenway Park to demonstrate their talents. Lodged between Muchnick and Wendell Smith, editor of the *Pittsburgh Courier* and one of black America's most fiery crusaders for the integration of MLB, a somber Joe Cronin watched as the ballplayers repeatedly tattooed the left-field wall in batting displays and demonstrated great speed afoot. Collins was nowhere to be seen. According to legend, as the three players prepared to leave the field, a voice boomed out from the top of the grandstand near the entrance to the club's offices: "Get those niggers off the field!" None of the invitees ever heard from the Red Sox. According to some historians, the fraudulent tryout and the continuing segregation of the Red Sox stands as the franchise's greatest error.

Throughout the 1950s, while other clubs were actively identifying and signing black talent the likes of Satchel Paige, Hank Aaron, Larry Doby, Monte Irvin, Willie Mays, Don Newcombe, and scores more, the Red Sox stuck to their tradition. In 1953 they signed infielder Elijah "Pumpsie" Green, who was buried in the minors for six seasons. "The Red Sox will bring up a Negro when he meets our standards," exclaimed a defiant Tom Yawkey. Even more vitriolic was manager Pinky Higgins, who reported pontificated, "They'll be no niggers on this ball club as long as I have anything to say about it." In early July 1959, with the Red Sox wallowing in last place, Higgins was fired, and Billy Jurges replaced him. On July 21 Pumpsie Green was called up from the Triple-A Minneapolis Millers. The following morning the *Boston Traveler* reported, "The accusation of discrimination by the Red Sox was silenced last night." Green's call-up had finally broken the mold. A week later pitcher Earl Wilson followed.

REBIRTH AND THE RISE OF THE RED SOX NATION

Underscored by an increasingly disinterested owner, a dwindling fan base, a ballpark in alarming need of repair, and continuing charges of racism, the Red Sox reeled into the 1960s, with Pinky Higgins back as manager through 1962. An inept but nevertheless old crony, Higgins, retained in the general manager's position by patron Tom Yawkey, ensured that Red Sox purchases, trades, and player development remained well behind the integration standard demonstrated by the rest of the league. A string of near-bottom finishes in 1961 (sixth), 1962 (eighth), 1963 (seventh), and 1964 (eighth), when the team lost a record 100 games, finally raised the ire of even the normally placid Yawkey and weakened his support for Higgins, Johnny Pesky, and Billy Herman, the managers over those disastrous years. Finally, Yawkey made an intelligent baseball decision, promoting a local Irish lad who had labored in the Red Sox front office for over 15 years, performing all sorts of tasks, including, at last, the duties of assistant general manager. Dick O'Connell became general manager following the 1965 season, a campaign that turned out to be yet another Higgins- and Herman-led debacle. In 1966, O'Connell fired Herman before the season ended, and second baseman Pete Runnels guided the team as interim manager. Led by Ted Williams's heir apparent, Polish American Carl "Yaz" Yastrzemski, a hitting phenom almost as good as the Kid but far less controversial, the club produced plenty of runs, but the pitching faltered badly. The Sox finished ninth, half a game ahead of the Yankees, the first time they had bested the New Yorkers since 1948. After the season O'Connell hired Dick Williams as manager, a no-nonsense leader with NL experience. The country-club atmosphere, prevalent for decades under Yawkey, Collins, and Higgins, ceased. Black and Hispanic talent was pursued with fervor—George Scott, Reggie Smith, Jose Tartabull, Joey Foy, Jose Santiago, and John Wyatt were signed immediately, and scores more were acquired in the future. The Red Sox for the first time began to gain ground on integration.

The first dividend of O'Connell's wisdom and energy and Williams's discipline and verve occurred immediately. The Red Sox captured the AL pennant on the last day of the 1967 season by beating the Minnesota Twins 5–3. As the Sox moved through the season and upward in the league standings, the pathetic array of some 8,000 fans present on Opening Day in Fenway swelled into daily capacity crowds. Bumper stickers appeared all over New England. The Boston press became enraptured by the drama of it all. Fans in the region went crazy. Yastrzemski, who won the Triple Crown, batting .326, knocking in 121 runs, and hitting 44 home runs (tied with Harmon Killebrew of the Twins), and the MVP Award, was lionized almost at Ted Williams's level. Pitcher Jim Lonborg was irrepressible and indefatigable, winning 22 games and the Cy Young Award. While the pitching was shaky, the lineup, with Yaz, Tony Conigliaro, Rick Burleson, Rico Petrocelli, and others, helped achieve "the Impossible Dream." A long-slumbering fandom awakened. The Red Sox Nation was born!

It mattered little that the Red Sox failed to win the 1967 World Series, losing in seven games to the Cardinals, because they were back on the baseball map—that's what counted most. A weary Lonborg pitched two masterpieces for the Sox, but a well-rested Bob Gibson pitched three for the Cardinals. Their timely hitting and speed on the bases did the rest. Under a trio of managers (Dick Williams, Eddie Kasko, and Darrell Johnson) the Sox finished between second and fourth from 1968 to 1974.

In 1975, the Red Sox captured the AL East under the divisional format established in 1969. The team was still an offensive juggernaut with weak pitching, although five men won in double figures. The star was Freddie Lynn, the AL MVP, who batted .331 and led the majors in slugging percentage (.566). The club then moved on and swept the AL Championship Series in three games against the defending world champion Oakland A's. The club met Cincinnati's Big Red Machine in the World Series. In an outcome that seemed to have become habit forming, the Red Sox were once again beaten in seven dramatic games. Luis Tiant led off the series by shutting out the Reds, who came back the next day to win in the bottom of the ninth, 3–2. The Reds eventually went up three games to two. The sixth game went into the bottom of the 12th all tied up when catcher Carleton Fisk hit a dramatic homer off the left-field foul pole to win the game. Red Sox fans will forever remember Fisk trotting to first, waving his arms, trying to will the ball fair. However, the Reds took the seventh game 4–3 to capture the series.

Seven months later, Yawkey passed away from leukemia. Boston mourned his loss, particularly those of the younger generation who experienced "the birth of the Nation" and the rise of Red Sox fortunes in the late 1960s and 1970s. Forgotten were the negative aspects of his leadership, which had produced decades of mediocrity and frustration. Remembered instead were his kindly and compassionate nature and his extreme generosity to all those involved in the Red Sox enterprise.

Tom Yawkey willed ownership and control of his Red Sox to a trust, which in effect dictated that the Yawkey tradition continue, administered by his widow, Jean. She was later joined by former bullpen catcher Haywood Sullivan and clubhouse trainer Buddy LeRoux. The result was years of power struggles and controversy when what was needed was a new-age philosophy of team enterprise. The parties rapidly became disenchanted with each other, and following vitriolic proceedings in the Suffolk County Superior Court in the mid-1980s, LeRoux was bought out. Sullivan remained a partner until shortly before Jean Yawkey's death in 1992, when he was bought out for $33 million. The club presidency and chief trust administrator was now Bostonian John Harrington, a longtime front-office employee and favorite of Mrs. Yawkey's. Eight managers came and went during the last quarter of the century (Darrell Johnson, Don Zimmer, Ralph Houk, John McNamara, Joe Morgan, Butch Hobson, Kevin Kennedy, and Jimy Williams), along with several all-time Red Sox greats destined for the Hall of Fame—Dennis Eckersley, Wade Boggs, Roger Clemens, Pedro Martinez, and Nomar Garciaparra. In general, the record was good enough to bring in capacity crowds. The Sox won four Eastern Division championships and two wild-card berths, but only in 1986, under manager John McNamara, did they win the playoffs, beating the Angels four games to three to win the AL championship and advance to the World Series. The 1986 club, which earned $15.5 million, third most in MLB, was led by Roger Clemens (24–4), MVP and Cy Young Award winner; Wade Boggs, who led the AL in batting (.357); and Jim Rice, who drove in 110 runs. They faced the Mets in a memorable World Series that went seven games. The key moment of the series was in the 10th inning of game six, when the Sox were one out from the championship. However, the Mets came back from a two-run deficit when a slow ground ball rolled between first baseman Bill Buckner's legs, allowing the winning run to score. This brought back memories of Pesky in 1946, Gibson's three-hitter in game seven in 1967, and Joe Morgan's bases-loaded bloop in the ninth inning of game seven in 1975, and provided credence to the idea that some mysterious power was at work.

The 1988 squad lost the AL Championship Series in four straight to the Athletics. That year Boggs won his fourth straight batting championship (.366) and the entire team hit .291, but the pitching was suspect, with the exception of Clemens, who led the AL in strikeouts with 291. Two years later, Clemens led the club to the playoffs with a sensational 21–6 season and a fabulous ERA of 1.93, the first of three straight ERA titles. But the team was again swept by the Athletics in the ALCS. Clemens won three Cy Young Awards for Boston and 192 games in 13 years. He left the team as a free agent in 1996 because the team thought he was finished, and signed with Toronto.

The Sox had losing seasons from 1992 to 1994, which resulted in a low payroll in 1995 ($28,672,250, 19th in the majors). They bounced back that season under Kevin Kennedy, and powered by four .300 hitters, won a divisional title. But the club was promptly swept 3–0 by the Indians in the AL Divisional Series. In 1998 and 1999, the club made the playoffs as a wild card, relying heavily on Pedro Martinez, acquired in a trade from Montreal, who won 19 and 23 games respectively. In 1999 he won the Cy Young Award, leading the AL in wins, ERA (2.07), and strikeouts (313). The Sox advanced in the ALDS by three games to two over Cleveland, but lost to the Yankees in the ALCS, four games to one. Since 1999, the team payroll has been among the five highest in MLB.

The new millennium opened with a strong Red Sox showing in 2000, finishing second behind the Yankees in the Eastern Division, led by Martinez, the Cy Young winner for the third time in four years, who again led the AL in ERA (1.74) and strikeouts (284). Nomar Garciaparra, Rookie of the Year back in 1997, won his second consecutive batting crown (.372). The payroll topped $110 million, yet the team still turned a profit. Guaranteed capacity crowds, lucrative television income, exploding licensing sales, and corporate box leases generated a steady flow of dollars into the club's treasury while simultaneously elevating the franchise's estimated value to more than $600 million.

Despite that disappointment, on October 6 the Red Sox Nation celebrated the startling public disclosure that the franchise was for sale. Harrington and the Yawkey Trust, as one author termed it, were "cashing in." At the same time, with Jimy Williams managing and Dan Duquette in the general manager's chair, the club entered the costly free-agent market to acquire proven talent. The biggest addition was hitting genius Manny Ramirez, who signed for $13 million.

The Sox in 2001 charged by far the highest average admission price in the majors ($36.08). They were 2nd in regular-season gate receipts ($89.7 million), but only 15th in other revenue at Fenway, reflecting the lack of luxury seating. Boston does not have a very large population, but only five teams represented larger metropolitan areas, which helped it rank fourth in local revenues. The team was fourth in local media money ($33.4 million) with 67 games on TV and 85 on NESN, the cable network they control that televises throughout New England. Yet despite all this revenue, MLB reported that the team lost $13.7 million in 2001, the sixth-highest amount among all teams.

In 2001, Jimy Williams was fired as manager in midseason and pitching coach Joe Kerrigan took over. The season ended ingloriously (82–79) with another second-place finish. On February 27, 2002, Harrington announced that the Red Sox franchise and Fenway Park had been sold to New England Sports Ventures, a consortium headed by entrepreneurs John Henry and Tom Werner and sports executive Larry Lucchino for slightly over $700 million. General manager Duquette was summarily fired and popular bench coach Grady Little was named manager. The first season for the new owners boded well, with the team winning 11 more games, though still finishing second. Interim general manager Mike Port, Duquette's former assistant, effectively guided the front office. The Red Sox placed seven players on the All-Star team, including Ramirez (who led the AL in batting at .349), Garciaparra, catcher Jason Varitek, center fielder Johnny Damon, and Pedro Martinez, who dazzled the opposition. He finished with a record of 20–3, and led the AL in strikeouts (239) and ERA (2.26).

The new owners, at least in the opinion of most Red Sox fans, put an end to an ongoing and often vehement debate in Boston—whether to tear down historic Fenway Park and rebuild it anew in another location, or retrofit it by introducing innovative upgrades. Since the 1950s, several concepts had jeopardized the park's future, including the heresy of tearing down the Green Monster and expanding Fenway across Lansdowne Street or simply abandoning the park altogether for a more modern suburban stadium. While most New Englanders regard Fenway as a gem, the moneymakers see it more as a fish bone stuck in the throat of modernity, without 19 percent premium seating, a dome, or acres of parking. But there is plenty of green, and naughty nooks and crazy crannies, and especially the most famous wall in baseball, more cantankerous than cute but still a "lyric little bandbox of a ballpark," according to John Updike. Perhaps that lyricism moved the new ownership to commit themselves to renovation.

The most notable upgrades have been the construction of new rows of field boxes, the addition of premium-priced seating, and altering the upper contour of Fenway. In 2003, 274 "Monster seats" and 150 standing-room positions were added atop the famous left-field wall. Then a new deck was constructed with angled seating for more than 400 fans above the existing stands in the right-field corner. The best place to increase capacity is the upper-deck area behind home plate, where the .406 Club will be reconfigured, and two open-air grandstand areas will be added (the Home Plate Pavilion Club). The owners are involved in securing corporate sponsorships for areas inside the ballpark. By 2007, the capacity will be raised to 38,000, with hopes of reaching 40,000.

Regarding the field itself, little had been done to improve it since the 1930s, especially the infield, whose eight-and-a-half-inch crown was laid out in 1912. Initially it was designed to shed water rather than absorb it, but for the most part it merely moved accumulated moisture to the outfield grass, compounding the possibility of rain delays or postponements. Furthermore, the infield crown contributed to bad hops and created line-of-sight obstructions for spectators seated at field level and players and managers in the dugouts. Neither the infield nor the outfield possessed much of a drainage system. In the 2004–5 off-season, the entire playing field, 18 million pounds of dirt and grass, was dug up and trucked away. In its place was installed a new playing surface with a flat infield, where a ball bounces more predictably. In addition, a sophisticated drainage system was developed, providing the most rain-absorbent playing field of any major-league outdoor ballpark.

To the new owners, the saga of Fenway Park was one thing, the critical general manager's position another. In a controversial and risky decision, the tripartite owners named a former Lucchino protégé, 28-year-old Theo Epstein, to the general manager's position, stunning the baseball world. Epstein proved up to the task, acquiring Todd Walker from Cincinnati, David Ortiz from Minnesota, Bill Mueller from the Cubs, and Kevin Millar from the Marlins to complement the club's core players—Varitek, Garciaparra, Ramirez, Damon, and Trot Nixon. The team was an offensive juggernaut, batting a league-leading .291, with 238 homers, and scoring a run per game more than the league average. The result, if not electrifying, provided a fair measure of satisfaction to Red Sox fans. The team won 95 games, finishing behind the Yankees yet again, but won the wild-card spot. In the ALDS they came from two games down to defeat Oakland, including two victories in their last at bat. The ALCS against the Yankees went to a deciding seventh game. The Sox led 5–2 going into the eighth inning, but Pedro Martínez, exhausted and well beyond his normal 100-pitch effectiveness, was left in to pitch. Manager Grady Little had often confounded the experts during the season, relying more on his gut instinct strategically than on the statistical record of past performances. This time his instincts proved fatal to the Sox cause. By the time Little finally removed Pedro, after 123 pitches, the damage had been done, and the game was tied. The Yankees, inevitably, won with a home run by Aaron Boone in the 11th inning. Red Sox fandom rose in livid wrath, then retired to their all-too-familiar hot stoves to discuss the next season. Little paid for his gaffe and was unceremoniously fired. Former Phillies manager Terry Francona was signed to lead the Red Sox in 2004.

The 2004 season started with discord and discontent. To begin with, the Sox lost out to the Yankees for the services of superstar Alex Rodriguez. A limping and ego-injured Nomar Garciaparra was dealt to the Chicago Cubs in midseason. But the Sox did manage to ink Arizona Diamondbacks ace Curt Schilling. The team's payroll was $127,298,500, with Ramirez alone getting $25 million. The Sox vigorously contested the Yankees all year long, with 98 victories, second most in the AL. A balanced Rex Sox squad qualified for postseason play as wild-card winner. The club led the AL in hitting (Ramirez led the league with 39 homers, and he and David Ortiz each drove in over 130 runs) and were third in pitching, abetted by closer Keith Foulke's 32 saves. The Sox swept the Angels in the ALDS, 3–0, and then took on the Yankees in the ALCS. The Yanks went up three games to none, outscoring the Sox 32–16. Then, in improbable fashion, and to the absolute surprise and delight of millions of American baseball fans, the Red Sox caught fire and reeled off four straight wins to advance to the World Series, the first time any team had come back from a 3–0 deficit in postseason play. They then proceeded to sweep the

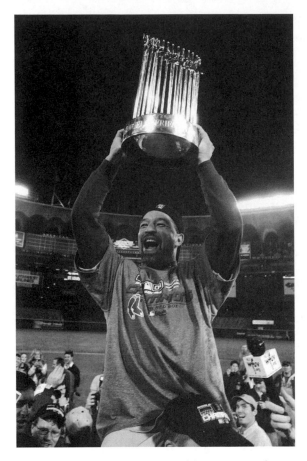

Dave Roberts hoists the World Series trophy at Busch Stadium in St. Louis, 2004. © AP / Wide World Photos

St. Louis Cardinals in the World Series. Red Sox Nation went berserk.

CODA: 2004

At the end of any other season we might have written that the end of life is always death, an existential thought, but in the "then" and "there" of Red Sox baseball it is an idea that addresses the glorious yet paradoxically tragic history of Boston's Boys of Summer. *At the end of any other season we might have written* that Fenway's flags flap once again at half-mast. After all, it is October, the cruelest month for Red Sox fans and a time of year that has perennially threatened both the nation's love of the game as well as its fanatical loyalty to the Olde Towne team, which in the lexicon of the nation's dictionary are synonymous. *At the end of any other season we might have written* that once again the Fenway Faithful had been lured to the very edge of baseball's fountain of ecstasy, tasted sweetly, for just a fleeting moment, the elixir of what could or should have been and then come away from it all with the same old familiar thirst that we've come to recognize simply as despair. *At the end of any other season we might have written* that suffering is mythical and rooted in the essence of nobility, so like the Greeks of yore, we hunkered down and endured our Sophoclean pain and rationalized that if the Sox ever did shatter the Curse of the Bambino, could our nobility endure? Along with the rest of the Red Sox Nation, we pondered that question and consoled each other winter after winter while waiting patiently for yet another season to begin, still holding fast to habit and hope and the heaven of a World Series championship.

Those were other years, other seasons, but now it is 2004 and October again, and oh the glorious contrasting aura of it all. Gone is the acrid stench of leaves burning, the ashy residue of loss. Gone are the old laments and the annual litany of "wait'll next year." Now we hear only echoic celebration, swirling sweet and golden in the crisp, autumn air of victory. The curse has run its course. Our suffering is assuaged. Amen! Hosanna! And the question has been answered: there is nobility in victory. "Yes," exclaimed the *Boston Globe*. "Hallelujah!" cried the *Providence Journal*. "Ghost Busters!" shrieked New York's *Newsday*. And rising majestically above the clamor of those headlines, above victory and nobility, above even the world-championship banner, soared something more eternal: the end of *death* is *life*, also an existential possibility.

POSTSCRIPT

The 2005 season brought Sox fans back to earth. Playing without Martinez, gone to the Mets as a free agent, and an injured Schilling, the team was very weak on the mound. The team had a terrific offense, with an AL-leading batting average of .280, and led in runs (910) for the third straight year. Ortiz and Ramirez combined for 91 homers and 292 RBIs. The Sox tied the Yankees with 95 wins, but their flaws cost them in the divisional playoffs, and they lost three straight to the White Sox.

NOTABLE ACHIEVEMENTS

Most Valuable Players

Year	Name	Position
1938	Jimmie Foxx	1B
1946	Ted Williams	OF
1949	Ted Williams	OF
1958	Jackie Jensen	OF
1967	Carl Yastrzemski	OF
1975	Fred Lynn	OF
1978	Jim Rice	OF
1986	Roger Clemens	P
1995	Mo Vaughn	1B

Cy Young Winners

Year	Name	Position
1967	Jim Lonborg	RHP
1986	Roger Clemens	RHP
1987	Roger Clemens	RHP
1991	Roger Clemens	RHP
1999	Pedro Martinez	RHP
2000	Pedro Martinez	RHP

Rookies of the Year

Year	Name	Position
1950	Walt Dropo	1B
1961	Don Schwall	P
1972	Carlton Fisk	C

| 1975 | Fred Lynn | OF |
| 1997 | Nomar Garciaparra | SS |

Batting Champions

Year	Name	#
1932	Dale Alexander	.367
1938	Jimmie Foxx	.349
1941	Ted Williams	.406
1942	Ted Williams	.356
1947	Ted Williams	.343
1948	Ted Williams	.369
1950	Billy Goodman	.354
1957	Ted Williams	.388
1958	Ted Williams	.328
1960	Pete Runnels	.320
1962	Pete Runnels	.326
1963	Carl Yastrzemski	.321
1967	Carl Yastrzemski	.326
1968	Carl Yastrzemski	.301
1979	Fred Lynn	.333
1981	Carney Lansford	.336
1983	Wade Boggs	.361
1985	Wade Boggs	.368
1986	Wade Boggs	.357
1987	Wade Boggs	.363
1988	Wade Boggs	.366
1999	Nomar Garciaparra	.357
2000	Nomar Garciaparra	.372
2002	Manny Ramirez	.349
2003	Bill Mueller	.326

Home-Run Champions

Year	Name	#
1903	Buck Freeman	13
1910	Jake Stahl	10
1912	Tris Speaker	10
1918	Babe Ruth	11
1919	Babe Ruth	29
1939	Jimmie Foxx	35
1941	Ted Williams	37
1942	Ted Williams	36
1947	Ted Williams	32
1949	Ted Williams	43

1965	Tony Conigliaro	32
1967	Carl Yastrzemski	44
1977	Jim Rice	39
1978	Jim Rice	46
1981	Dwight Evans	22
1983	Jim Rice	39
1984	Tony Armas	43
2004	Manny Ramirez	43

ERA Champions

Year	Name	#
1901	Cy Young	1.62
1914	Dutch Leonard	0.96
1915	Joe Wood	1.49
1916	Babe Ruth	1.75
1935	Lefty Grove	2.70
1936	Lefty Grove	2.81
1938	Lefty Grove	3.08
1939	Lefty Grove	2.54
1949	Mel Parnell	2.78
1972	Luis Tiant	1.91
1986	Roger Clemens	2.48
1990	Roger Clemens	1.93
1991	Roger Clemens	2.62
1992	Roger Clemens	2.41
1999	Pedro Martinez	2.07
2000	Pedro Martinez	1.74
2002	Pedro Martinez	2.26
2003	Pedro Martinez	2.22

Strikeout Champions

Year	Name	#
1901	Cy Young	158
1942	Tex Hughson	113
1967	Jim Lonborg	246
1988	Roger Clemens	291
1991	Roger Clemens	241
1996	Roger Clemens	257
1999	Pedro Martinez	313
2000	Pedro Martinez	284
2001	Hideo Nomo	220
2002	Pedro Martinez	239

No-Hitters (Italics = Perfect Game)

Name	Date
Cy Young	*05/05/1904*
Jesse Tannehill	08/17/1904
Bill Dineen	09/27/1905
Cy Young	06/30/1908
Joe Wood	07/29/1911
Rube Foster	06/21/1916
Dutch Leonard	08/30/1916
Ernie Shore	06/23/1917
Dutch Leonard	06/03/1918
Howard Ehmke	09/07/1923
Mel Parnell	07/14/1956
Earl Wilson	06/26/1962
Bill Monbouquette	08/01/1962
Dave Morehead	09/16/1965
Matt Young	04/12/1992
Hideo Nomo	04/04/2001
Derek Lowe	04/27/2002

POSTSEASON APPEARANCES

AL East Division Titles

Year	Record	Manager
1975	95–65	Darrell Johnson
1986	95–66	John McNamara
1988	89–73	John McNamara
		Joe Morgan
1990	88–74	Joe Morgan
1995	86–58	Kevin Kennedy

AL Wild Cards

Year	Record	Manager
1998	92–70	Jimy Williams
1999	94–68	Jimy Williams
2003	95–67	Grady Little
2004	98–64	Terry Francona
2005	95–67	Terry Francona

AL Pennants

Year	Record	Manager
1903	91–47	Jimmy Collins
1904	95–59	Jimmy Collins

1912	105–47	Jake Stahl
1915	101–50	Bill Carrigan
1916	91–63	Bill Carrigan
1918	71–51	Ed Barrow
1946	104–50	Joe Cronin
1967	92–70	Dick Williams
1975	95–65	Darrell Johnson
1986	95–66	John McNamara
2004	98–64	Terry Francona

World Championships

Year	Opponents	MVP
1903	Pittsburgh	Jimmy Collins
1912	New York	
1915	Philadelphia	
1916	Brooklyn	
1917	Chicago	
2004	St. Louis	Manny Ramirez

MANAGERS

2004–	Terry Francona
2002–2003	Grady Little
2001	Joe Kerrigan
1997–2001	Jimy Williams
1995–1996	Kevin Kennedy
1992–1994	Butch Hobson
1988–1991	Joe Morgan
1985–1988	John McNamara
1981–1984	Ralph Houk
1980	Johnny Pesky
1976–1980	Don Zimmer
1974–1976	Darrell Johnson
1973	Eddie Popowski
1970–1973	Eddie Kasko
1969	Eddie Popowski
1967–1969	Dick Williams
1966	Pete Runnels
1964–1966	Billy Herman
1963–1964	Johnny Pesky
1960–1962	Pinky Higgins
1960	Del Baker
1959–1960	Billy Jurges
1959	Rudy York
1955–1959	Pinky Higgins

1952–1954	Lou Boudreau
1950–1951	Steve O'Neill
1948–1950	Joe McCarthy
1935–1947	Joe Cronin
1934	Bucky Harris
1932–1933	Marty McManus
1931–1932	Shano Collins
1930	Heinie Wagner
1927–1929	Bill Carrigan
1924–1926	Lee Fohl
1923	Frank Chance
1921–1922	Hugh Duffy
1918–1920	Ed Barrow
1917	Jack Barry
1913–1916	Bill Carrigan
1912–1913	Jake Stahl
1910–1911	Patsy Donovan
1908–1909	Fred Lake
1907–1908	Deacon McGuire
1907	Bob Unglaub
1907	George Huff
1907	Cy Young
1906	Chick Stahl
1901–1906	Jimmy Collins

Team Records by Individual Players

Batting Leaders

	Single Season			Career		
	Name		Year	Name		Plate Appearances
Batting average	Ted Williams	.406	1941	Ted Williams	.344	9,791
On-base %	Ted Williams	.553	1941	Ted Williams	.482	9,791
Slugging %	Ted Williams	.735	1941	Ted Williams	.634	9,791
OPS	Ted Williams	1.287	1941	Ted Williams	1.115	9,791
Games	Jim Rice	163	1978	Carl Yastrzemski	3308	13,991
At bats	Ted Williams	684	1997	Carl Yastrzemski	1,1988	13,991
Runs	Ted Williams	150	1949	Carl Yastrzemski	1,816	13,991
Hits	Wade Boggs	240	1985	Carl Yastrzemski	3,419	13,991
Total bases	Jim Rice	406	1978	Carl Yastrzemski	5,539	13,991
Doubles	Earl Webb	67	1931	Carl Yastrzemski	646	13,991
Triples	Ttris Speaker	22	1913	Harry Hooper	130	7,330
Home runs	Jimmy Foxx	50	1938	Ted Williams	521	9,791

(Continued)

Batting Leaders (Continued)

	Single Season			Career		
	Name		**Year**	**Name**		**Plate Appearances**
RBIs	Jimmy Foxx	175	1938	Carl Yastrzemski	1,844	13,991
Walks	Ted Williams	162	1947	Ted Williams	2,021	9,791
Strikeouts	Mark Bellhorn	177	2004	Dwight Evans	1,643	10,240
Stolen bases	Tommy Harper	54	1973	Harry Hooper	300	7,330
Extra-base hits	Jimmy Foxx	92	1938	Carl Yastrzemski	1,157	13,991
Times on base	Ted Williams	358	1949	Carl Yastrzemski	5,304	13,991

Pitching Leaders

	Single Season			Career		
	Name		**Year**	**Name**		**Innings Pitched**
ERA	Leonard	0.96	1914	Joe Wood	1.99	1,418
Wins	Joe Wood	34	1912	Cy Young	192	2,728.3
Won-loss %	Bob Stanley	.882	1978	Pedro Martinez	.760	1,383.7
Hits/9 IP	Pedro Martinez	5.31	2000	Dick Radatz	6.78	557.3
Walks/9 IP	Cy Young	.69	1904	Cy Young	.99	2,728.3
Strikeouts	Pedro Martinez	313	1919	Roger Clemens	2,590	2,776
Strikeouts/ 9 IP	Pedro Martinez	13.2	1999	Pedro Martinez	10.95	1,383.7
Games	Mike Timlin	81	2005	Bob Stanley	637	1,707
Saves	Tom Gordon	46	1998	Bob Stanley	132	1,707
Innings	Cy Young	384.7	1902	Roger Clemens	2,776	2,776
Starts	Cy Young	43	1902	Roger Clemens	382	2,776
Complete games	Cy Young	41	1902	Cy Young	275	2,728.3
Shutouts	Joe Wood	10	1912	Cy Young	38	2,728.3

Source: Drawn from data in "Boston Red Sox Batting Leaders (seasonal and career)." http://baseball-reference.com/ teams/BOS/leaders_bat.shtml; "Boston Red Sox Pitching Leaders (seasonal and career)." http://baseball-reference. com/teams/BOS/leaders_pitch.shtml.

BIBLIOGRAPHY

Boswell, John, and David Fisher. *Fenway Park*. Boston: Little, Brown, 1992.

Bryant, Howard. *Shut Out: A Story of Race in Boston*. New York: Routledge, 2002.

Frommer, Harvey. *Baseball's Greatest Rivalry: The New York Yankees and Boston Red Sox*. New York: Atheneum, 1982.

Golenbock, Peter. *Fenway: An Unexpurgated History of the Boston Red Sox.* New York: G. P. Putnam's Sons, 1992.

Hirshberg, Al. *The Red Sox, the Bean and the Cod.* Boston: Waverly House, 1947.

Lieb, Frederick. *The Boston Red Sox.* New York: G. P. Putnam's Sons, 1947.

Masur, Louis P. *Autumn Glory: Baseball's First World Series.* New York: Hill and Wang, 2003.

Queenan, Joe. *True Believers: The Tragic Inner Life of Sports Fans.* New York: Henry Holt, 2003.

Riley, Dan, ed. *The Red Sox Reader.* Boston: Houghton Mifflin, 1991.

Ritter, Lawrence S. *The Glory of Their Times: The Story of the Early Days of Baseball, Told by the Men Who Played It.* New York: Macmillan, 1966.

Seidel, Michael. *Ted Williams: A Baseball Life.* Lincoln: University of Nebraska Press, 2000.

Shaughnessy, Dan. *At Fenway: Dispatches from Red Sox Nation.* New York: Crown Publishers, 1996.

———. *The Curse of the Bambino.* New York: Dutton, 1990.

Stout, Glen, and Richard A. Johnson, eds. *Red Sox Century: One Hundred Years of Red Sox Baseball.* Boston: Houghton Mifflin, 2000.

Walton, Ed. *Red Sox Triumphs and Tragedies.* New York: Stein and Day, 1980.

Chicago White Sox

Richard C. Lindberg

Founded in a turbulent period of American baseball history, haunted by the memory of the game's worst scandal and plagued by successive misfortunes collectively known as "the Comiskey Curse," the Chicago White Sox, their ownership, and their embattled fans are hunkered down and operating in a siege mentality. In an average year the team can reasonably expect 1.7 to 2 million fans passing through the turnstiles of its modernistic stadium, derided as "the Ball Mall" by an impossible-to-please Sox fandom. These attendance figures consistently place the franchise in the lower strata of major-league clubs, equal to or shade better than such small-market AL competitors as Kansas City, Minnesota, Oakland, Detroit, Tampa Bay, and Toronto.

If past history is a future indicator, the second team in Chicago is likely to confront the specter of plummeting attendance, a deafening silence from what most Sox watchers consider to be a heavily biased pro-Cubs media, and rumors of impending relocation to another city following a string of bad years of play. It is no coincidence that the venerable White Sox franchise was on the threshold of leaving Chicago on four separate occasions between 1969 and 1988 for the usual reasons of fan disinterest, media apathy, negative perceptions about a lack of adequate security in the South Side neighborhood the team plays in, and of course attendant stadium issues. Thus, it has always been incumbent upon ownership to ensure that the team *never* falls below the break-even mark, knowing that a dwindling fan base (compromised by changing ethnic and commuter demographic patterns that overtook the city of Chicago in the last 50 years) is likely to boycott the club in the difficult years, or simply walk away.

Of course, operating in a city madly obsessed with the allure of Wrigley Field and its lovable but losing National League inhabitants would present a formidable challenge to any baseball operation fighting to establish parity. In Chicago, a benign and spirited civic baseball rivalry that existed long before the Tribune Company purchased the Cubs in 1981 has lately become a grim and polarizing David-and-Goliath marketing war to bolster the South Side fan base, one that has gradually eroded with the passage of time. Poorly planned marketing decisions, bad judgment, budgetary constraints, and repeated operational blunders in the baseball organization going back decades have placed the team at a competitive disadvantage against their North Side counterparts for the undivided loyalty and affection of the Chicago baseball fan.

CHARLES COMISKEY AND THE RISE OF THE WHITE SOX

Despite the recent travails of the White Sox, the team in its earliest days under founder Charles Albert Comiskey, the venerable "Old Roman" of the Chicago sporting world, enjoyed a brief 20-year flourish of success that established them as the preeminent and arguably the most popular sporting attraction in a two-team town between 1900 and 1920. Yet since the publication of *Eight Men Out* in 1963, Eliot Asinof's quasi-fictional account of the 1919 Black Sox Scandal, a generation of revisionist authors and historians cast the White Sox founder into an unfortunate light as a miserly tightwad responsible for much of the game's accumulated ills. Comiskey became symbolic of the venality and greed of the baseball moguls and their mistreatment of players. The unflattering portrayal is a greatly exaggerated image cloaked in misconception, half-truths, and the author's labor-versus-capital political platform in which the essential facts of the Black Sox scandal became an expeditious propaganda tool to advance a particular agenda.

Charles Comiskey was for years revered as a civic leader and bold visionary well deserving of his place of honor in baseball's Hall of Fame, the victim of a greedy cabal of players. He was born in 1859 to "Honest John" Comiskey, a prominent Irish Democratic alderman from County Cork representing the immigrant communities of the Near West Side. His competitive drive and devotion to the game of baseball was solidified in 1873 after his father sent him to St. Mary's School in Kansas, where Ted Sullivan, an upperclassman with a penchant for organizing players and sandlot baseball games, mentored him. Sullivan later became Comiskey's most trusted adviser and talent scout, trolling the western minor leagues for top-flight players later acquired at auction by the White Sox.

The indefatigable Sullivan helped Comiskey got a position with a semipro outfit, the Dubuque Rabbits of Iowa's Northwestern League. Paid $125 a month, he divided his time between baseball and selling newspapers and concessions for the local railroad line that had a financial interest in the team. He subsequently moved on to play first base for the St. Louis Browns of the upstart American Association, where he revolutionized first-base play by moving off the bag, with the pitcher covering on grounders hit to the right side of the infield. Comiskey's career was given an immediate boost in 1883 when flamboyant Browns owner Chris Von der Ahe appointed him team manager. Comiskey's inspired brand of leadership and relentless determination to win at all costs left no holds barred, and led to four league championships (1885–88) and a salary of $6,200 a year. The 1886 team bested the powerful Chicago White Stockings in the forerunner of the modern-day World Series. He became known as the Old Roman because of his stoic, gladiatorial expression and posture.

In 1890, Comiskey with misgivings sided with the Brotherhood revolt of 1890 and left the Mound City to take over the reins of the Chicago Pirates of the Players' League, which played on the city's South Side in front of a makeshift

Charles Comiskey, 1900. Courtesy of the Baseball Hall of Fame

wooden grandstand at 35th and Shields. After the demise of the upstart league, Comiskey played a farewell season in St. Louis before moving on to Cincinnati for the 1892 season as player-manager. Three years later, Commy joined the Western League, a young minor league, as owner and manager of the St. Paul Saints. After the 1899 season, league president Ban Johnson realigned his circuit, renaming it the American League, and sanctioned Comiskey's request to move the Saints to Chicago, where they were reborn as the White Stockings. Organized baseball's National Agreement required the franchise respect the territorial restrictions imposed upon it by James Hart of the Chicago Colts, who forbade the interlopers from using the city's name in its publicity and written correspondence. Comiskey was also compelled to play on the South Side, south of 35th Street, an economically distressed district mostly populated by poor immigrant Irish, Poles, and Lithuanians, who freely partook of the neighborhood's saloon culture. The White Sox's arrival provided a common thread of recreation for local working-class men, in some cases ameliorating long-standing and hostile ethnic divisions.

Hart, along with the bankers, the downtown mercantile class, and certain members of the baseball fraternity, considered the South Side demographics poor for a baseball club, but Comiskey counted on his family name to help him gain support, and also his popularity with the Bridgeport Irish, who remembered his Players' League team. Comiskey was confident that the South Side

Irish and the foreign-speaking people of the stockyards district to the south and west would adopt his team as their own.

In the AL's inaugural season of 1901, the White Stockings played in an abandoned cricket and lacrosse field at 39th and Wentworth, retrofitted into a small wooden stadium known as the South Side Grounds. Once the home of the Chicago Wanderers' cricket team, the grounds were strewn with debris and litter by the time Comiskey secured a building loan from the First National Bank to build his field, which seated fewer than 5,000. Ideally situated near the Wentworth Avenue streetcar line opposite St. George's Parish, the South Side Grounds was expansive—355 feet down the lines and 450 feet to dead center. Comiskey's private office was built underneath the stands, but players had to change into their uniforms elsewhere. This sometimes precipitated fisticuffs between members of the visiting team, who had to pass though a gauntlet of heckling White Sox fans as they entered the park from an outfield gate.

Subject to the draft rules and restrictions imposed upon them by the NL, the odd assortment of veteran minor leaguers and professional castoffs like Dick Padden and "Dummy" Hoy coalesced under Comiskey's leadership. They finished first in 1900 with an 82–53 record. Their style of play that season perfectly mirrored the dead-ball era of limited offense, coupled with stellar pitching, inner defense, and abundant speed. As manager, Comiskey set the standard for the kind of club he preferred to lead. He believed that baseball in its purest form was a game of strategy played by thinking men who respected the stolen base and the hit-and-run, with a dominating pitching staff that minimized the opponent's score to less than three runs a game the surest way of winning championships. In other words, the "home run was bunk."

The Old Roman was a man of strong conviction and unwavering in his beliefs. Following the impressive debut of the AL in 1900, Ban Johnson was emboldened to move forward with a secret plan to overturn the National Agreement, declare the confederation a major league, and raid the senior circuit for their top talent. Comiskey, building on his team's artistic and financial success, spun his popularity into power and action. He endorsed the war plan and urged Johnson on, but broke with his friend and mentor on one critical issue. Johnson sought parity with the NL and believed that a balanced two-league system with a championship series played between the two circuits was in the best long-term interests of the game. However, the Old Roman was dead set against it, based on his strong enmity toward James Hart and the NL. Comiskey wanted to destroy the old league at all costs, not embrace it.

In the three-year trade war following the renunciation of the National Agreement that bound the AL to the onerous draft laws and secondary status, the White Sox owner raided the roster of his crosstown rivals, procuring Clark Griffith, a perennial 20-game winner; outfielder Sandow Mertes; and journeyman pitcher Jimmy "Nixey" Callahan with the inducement of higher salaries. Griffith, a resentful antimanagement baseball labor organizer, traversed the country in a successful effort to persuade top NL stars, including Cy Young, Nap Lajoie, and Bill Dineen, to jump to the AL. The NL was in disarray, and the White Sox owner believed monopoly was firmly in the grasp of the AL. Johnson dismissed the advice as a reflection of Comiskey's greed and shortsightedness. He advocated an equitable, negotiated peace recognizing the legitimacy of the AL as the second bona fide major league. His refusal to bend on this point cost him his friendship with Comiskey.

The conflict between Johnson and Comiskey was exacerbated by petty bickering, Johnson's tendency to rule against the White Sox in player disputes, and the egoism of two headstrong moguls, each viewing the AL as his own private fiefdom. Comiskey, with bitter recrimination toward Johnson, the NL, and particularly the crosstown Cubs, opened his checkbook and secured top-flight talent from the high minor leagues along with key veterans through the waiver lists. He built a competitive, entertaining team that won the first official AL pennant in 1901. Pitcher-manager Clark Griffith (who won 24 games), Callahan, Frank Isbell, Fielder Jones, and Roy "the Boy Wonder" Patterson captured first place on July 18 and never let go. The Sox drew 354,350 fans, and outpaced the Colts by 150,000 fans—a remarkable showing that cemented their place in the professional sporting world. In this, their golden 20-year reign, the White Sox became the league's most popular drawing card, claiming 17.1 percent of AL attendance in the league's first decade.

The ball club had their only poor season in 1903, when under new manager Nixey Callahan it came in seventh. That year they were widely called the White Sox for the first time. Callahan was replaced early in 1904 by outfielder Fielder Jones, who led the club to the pennant in 1906. Callahan did return as manager for 1912–14. Jones's "Hitless Wonders," named by *Tribune* reporter Charles Dryden for the way they managed to win with a record of 93–58 despite a league worst .230 batting average and just seven home runs, at one point won 19 straight games. The Sox faced the 116–36 Cubs in baseball's first intracity world championship, and sadly, Chicago's last. The two clubs had played in a seven-game postseason series since 1903, which continued through 1912 in years when neither club made the Series. Comiskey's team thoroughly dominated the City Series to the point of ridiculousness.

The spirited leadership of manager Fielder Allison Jones (a firebrand innovator credited with inventing the "body twist" slide), a pitching staff without peer (Ed Walsh, Doc White, Nick Altrock, and Frank Owen), and enough moxie, luck, and drive allowed the underdog Sox to upend the heavily favored Cubs four games to two. Even more hitless in the series than in the regular season, the Sox batted .198 against formidable Cubs pitching, but took the match with fine pitching and clutch hitting. Unheralded bench reserve George Rohe swatted a record four doubles in game five to thoroughly demoralize Hart's team on the eve of the clincher, won in an 8–3 rout by off-season dentist Doc White the next day. As a result of the Sox slaying Goliath, Comiskey was looked upon as a beloved mogul as he adroitly played to the press and the South Side fandom with skill and aplomb.

The glory years of the franchise, the two decades leading up to the Prohibition era, were the high-water mark in Sox fortunes. The glorious Hitless Wonders era, chiseled into White Sox folklore, ended in the thrilling 1908 pennant race that went right down to the last two days of the season before the Sox bowed to Detroit. Iron man Ed Walsh, a spitball pitcher, won 40 games with 42 complete games, 464 innings, 11 shutouts, and 269 strikeouts. Comiskey gave him a $3,500 bonus after the season. He pitched a four-hitter and struck out 15 on October 2 in a home game against Cleveland, but lost 1–0 when Addie Joss hurled a perfect game. The Hall of Famer retired in 1917 with a 1.82 ERA, the best in major-league history. Fielder Jones, the "little Napoleon" who kept his team in the thick of the race for five straight seasons, resigned after the heartbreaking setback, and the team fell into several years of mediocrity.

The personable Old Roman lavished politicians, civic leaders, reporters from the seven local newspapers, and a few close friends with a yearly all-expenses-paid fishing and hunting hegira to Mercer, Wisconsin, where his well-heeled guests and members of the White Sox Rooters Association (later known as the Woodland Bards), feasted on venison, fine wines, and more potent potables. His largesse endeared him to the media and earned the team added column inches and fan support. Comiskey's private dining area inside the ballpark was named "the Bards Room," and it was there that the press congregated in an amicable setting. The Sox faithful loved him for his jocularity, generosity, and larger-than-life persona. By comparison, the superior Cubs lacked front-office charisma and failed to court the press like Comiskey. They played in an outdated grandstand in the poor, non-English-speaking West Side. Beset by several ownership changes, the Cubs were the losers in the battle to rule the Chicago market.

The dangerously overcrowded 39th Street Grounds proved inadequate for the crush of fans that had come to see the White Sox and the off-day attraction of semiprofessional games. Plans for a new and much larger park took shape in 1903, when Comiskey revealed to the press his intention to relocate within the neighborhood and build a model ballpark. In 1908, he purchased the old Wentworth estate where his Pirates had played, four blocks north of 39th and Wentworth but still adjacent to the streetcar line, for $100,000.

On July 1, 1910, Comiskey opened his palatial two-tier $550,000 Comiskey Park, designed by architect Zachary Taylor Davis. It was baseball's third concrete and steel structure, with red bricks that helped integrate it into the local landscape. It had a huge playing field with imposing dimensions (363 feet down the lines and 420 feet to dead center). There were originally 32,000 seats, one-fourth in the bleachers selling for just 25 cents, which appealed to the fans in the surrounding working-class neighborhood. A long-term problem with the new park was that in the 1920s the dead-ball style of play faded away, dooming Comiskey Park to functional obsolescence. The park proved ill suited for big offense, as home runs were at a premium. The large capacity helped the Sox at home draw 18.2 percent of the *entire* AL attendance in the 1910s.

The White Sox were also-rans from 1909 to 1914. One significant development occurred in 1912, when Comiskey purchased controlling interest of a minor-league team in Des Moines, Iowa, to develop future talent, presaging Branch Rickey's conceptualization of baseball's modern farm system in 1926 by 14 years. Then, after the 1913 season, the Sox went on a world tour, playing 44 exhibition games against the New York Giants The goodwill junket helped pave the way for the introduction of the professional game to Japan and advanced Comiskey's name beyond national borders. After his club came in seventh in 1914, Comiskey hired Pants Rowland as manager. Then the looming threat of the Federal League and its new North Side park motivated Comiskey to loosen the purse strings, and in December 1914 he purchased second baseman Eddie Collins, the captain of the Philadelphia Athletics, AL MVP, and a mainstay of its "$100,000 infield." Collins batted .333 in 25 years in the majors and was one of the greatest second basemen in history. Comiskey also brought in rookie outfielder Happy Felsch to add to a core that included third baseman Buck Weaver, catcher Ray Schalk, and pitchers Ed Cicotte, the great knuckleballing right-hander, and young spitballing sensation Urban "Red" Faber, a 20-year White Sox mainstay and the winner of 254 games. In August 1915, he traded with the Indians for "Shoeless" Joe Jackson, the AL's second-most-feared batsman after Ty Cobb, for two undistinguished prospects and $31,500 in cash. The club improved to 93–61 and third place. In 1916, Comiskey procured Claude "Lefty" Williams from the minors to complement an improving pitching staff, and the club moved up to second, just two games behind the Red Sox in 1916. Charles "Swede" Risberg, a gritty shortstop from the Vernon club of the Pacific Coast League, arrived in time for the 1917 season.

The 1917 Sox won 100 games, the most in team history. The pennant was clinched in dramatic fashion on September 21 when Cicotte induced Babe Ruth to hit into a double play to preserve a 2–1 extra-innings victory over Boston. They were perfectly balanced, with speed, strong inner defense, and timely hitting. The team led the AL in scoring, backed by Felsch's 102 RBIs, and also had the finest pitching. Cicotte led the league with 28 wins and a 1.53 ERA. Chicago went on to complete a six-game World Series triumph against John McGraw's Giants on the strength of Faber, who won three games, including the finale in New York, sealing Chicago's last world's championship of the century.

The 1918 squad was just a shadow of the championship team, finishing in sixth place (57–67), with several players away doing war-related work. However, with the squad intact in 1919, expectations were very high, and the players responded by easily winning the pennant under first-year manager Kid Gleason with just 88 victories, finishing three and a half games ahead of the Indians. The offense, which batted just .253, led the AL in runs, but the pitching was in the middle of the pack. Cicotte had a brilliant season, with a 1.82 ERA and a league-leading 29 wins and .806 winning percentage. Jackson led the offense with a batting average of .351 and 96 RBIs.

THE BLACK SOX SCANDAL

The fix was a puzzling and multilayered event more complicated than blaming Comiskey for being a nickel-nursing despot who rewarded his players' fine effort with broken promises and a case of stale champagne. Players were unhappy with the reserve clause that limited salaries, especially after the demise of the Federal League. Widespread gambling beset the sport, and there were incidences of collegiality between athletes and gamblers that were swept under the rug. In 1917, for example, the White Sox allegedly collected a pool to reward the Detroit Tigers for laying down in back-to-back doubleheaders on September 2–3. The internal dissension among the White Sox players, beginning in 1918, had its roots in regional and cultural differences. The Eddie Collins clique of educated northerners included pitchers Red Faber and Dickie Kerr, catcher Ray Schalk, and outfielders John "Shano" Collins and Harry "Nemo" Leibold, later known in the press as "the Clean Sox" for their unwavering loyalty and dedication to the owner. The other faction included first baseman "Chick" Gandil, Risberg, Weaver, Felsch, Jackson, Cicotte, Williams, and utility man Fred McMullin. They envied Collins's $15,000 salary, which Comiskey had inherited from Philadelphia.

Cicotte's main grievance was that late in 1917, he was held back from taking his regular turn on the mound so that Comiskey could avoid paying him a $10,000 performance bonus for winning 30 games. But he got to start five games in September, winning four and losing one. Two years later, Cicotte won 29. Manager Kid Gleason rested both Williams and Cicotte from September 11 to 17 in order to audition Erskine Mayer and Bill James for the postseason, and then Cicotte was granted a two-day leave to close on the purchase of a farm. Back in the rotation on the September 19, Cicotte had three more chances to achieve the coveted mark, but failed.

The team's payroll was in line with the league. Risberg and Williams earned $3,435 and $5,524 respectively, while Cicotte's $9,075 was in the upper bracket. Weaver and Felsch pulled down $7,644 and $7,400. Jackson, at $6,299, had a legitimate grievance. First baseman Gandil, the most acrimonious of the eight and the acknowledged ringleader, was a 10-year man earning $4,500. These were very high wages by the standards of the general public. Charles Comiskey was a shrewd and sometimes petty and vindictive businessman who demanded a lot of his top players, but was more generous to his marginal, hardworking players.

The Sox were odds-on favorites to best the Redlegs, who had actually won more games, in the newly expanded nine-game World Series format. The White Sox came out of the gate flat, fueling suspicions of a fix from the opening frame. Rumors were rife, and the betting odds had mysteriously shifted. When it was over, the Redlegs had shocked the nation with a stunning five-games-to-three upset. Rookie Dickie Kerr won two games for the Pale Hose, but Cicotte lost two, and 23-game winner Williams dropped three.

Amid whispers and innuendo, the White Sox, except for Gandil, played the 1920 season and were in a position to repeat as league champions. They actually won eight more games than the year before. Jackson hit .382 and Collins .372, and four pitchers won over 20 games. In late September, a Cook County grand jury investigating an unrelated incident of bribe taking involving Chicago Cubs pitcher Claude Hendrix diverted its attention to the 1919 World Series. Jackson was subpoenaed, and without benefit of counsel, confessed to throwing games. Cicotte supported Jackson's testimony, and the stench of scandal was finally aired in public. The eight accused "Black Sox" (Cicotte, Gandil, Felsch, Jackson, McMullin, Risberg, Weaver, and Williams) were immediately suspended and the chances of a 1920 pennant blown. Subsequently, suspicions developed about some of the men not playing on the square in late August. The story was eclipsed and buried by the revelations of the World Series wrongdoing, headlining newspapers all across America on September 29. Despite these problems, the team made $155,671 in 1920, second most in the AL.

One year later, seven of the alleged conspirators were tried (McMullin, who only appeared twice as a pinch hitter, was not indicted) for perpetrating a confidence game against one Charles K. Nims, an unlucky bettor who lost $250 betting on the Sox. In the course of the trial the self-incriminating grand-jury confessions of Jackson, Cicotte, and Williams were conveniently lost (later found in the safe of Alfred Austrian, Comiskey's attorney), and the players were acquitted. But in the court of baseball justice, Kenesaw Mountain Landis, a federal judge appointed to serve as the game's high commissioner and moral arbiter, banned all eight for life.

Comiskey attempted to rebuild the shattered remnants of his team in time for the 1921 season, but without its nucleus, the team foundered. The Sox spent over $1 million on unproductive minor leaguers. In the end, the Black Sox scandal and its aftermath broke Comiskey's spirit, tenacity, and resolve. Worse, the aftershocks doomed the franchise to mediocrity and secondary status in the Windy City for decades to come. However, the team remained in the black, earning an average of $102,531 in the 1920s.

THE COMISKEY FAMILY AND THE DECLINE OF THE SOX

The White Sox had entered into a deadly 30-year losing cycle, otherwise remembered as the "wandering in the desert" years. From 1921 through 1950, there were only seven seasons on the plus side of the ledger: 1925, 1926, 1936, 1937, 1939, 1940, and 1943. In all other years, Comiskey's team was in the second division, finishing dead last in 1924, 1932, 1934, and 1948 and in seventh place six different times. Only in 1940 did the White Sox enter September in pennant contention. Not surprisingly, the team lost $66,365 a year from 1930 through 1939.

Beset by ill health and a vanquished spirit, Comiskey left day-to-day operation of the team to his lieutenant, Harry Grabiner, and only son, John Louis. Comiskey passed away from the complications of old age on October 25, 1931. He was mourned as a wise and benevolent civic leader, a true baseball pioneer victimized and driven to the grave by the cruel betrayal of a cabal of pernicious, ungrateful players. He was elected to the Hall of Fame in 1939.

Reserved in nature, Lou Comiskey continued his father's free-spending policy aimed at restoring the luster and past glories of the franchise, even as losses mounted and 1932 attendance dwindled to 233,198. That year, Lou forked over $150,000 in scarce depression-era dollars to the cash-strapped Connie Mack for slugger Al Simmons, infielder Jimmie Dykes, and George "Mule" Haas, a trio of proven AL players. The family could ill afford this expense in the heart of the depression. The yearly goal of drawing 500,000 fans a year into cavernous Comiskey Park had not been reached since 1927, when an upper deck was added to the park, whose capacity surpassed 50,000.

Journalists in the 1930s sentimentally conveyed their sincere personal regard for the White Sox to the fans, providing balanced, enthusiastic coverage of a persistently poor franchise that is absent in the modern day. Columnists Warren Brown, John Carmichael, and Arch Ward and beat reporter Irving Vaughn had come of age in the early 1900s, and were unabashed partisans. At the same time they were looking back on better days, a new fan generation was coming of age, and with each Cubs pennant achieved in "the Friendly Confines" of Wrigley Field by a galaxy of celebrity players, the colorless, punchless White Sox, playing in the stench of the stockyards, seemed bland and austere by comparison.

Sustained by shortstop Luke Appling, primarily a singles hitter; the fine pitching of Baylor University alum Ted Lyons; and an ensemble cast of bargain-basement castoffs, the Sox managed a few sanguine moments. The genial Appling, the pride of Oglethorpe University in Georgia, won the first of two batting titles in 1936 with a hefty .388 average. He had a lifetime .320 average with 2,749 hits in his 20-season Hall of Fame career. Lyons tossed a no-hitter in 1926 and posted three 20-win seasons in his 21 years that led to the Hall of Fame (260–230). Another two decades would pass before the full impact of television coverage heavily slanted in the Cubs' favor took a toll on the franchise, but the seeds were sown at a time when team fortunes were on the rise. As field manager from 1934 to 1946, Jimmie Dykes, a round little man who smoked big cigars and relentlessly baited umpires, was amusing and quotable on and off the field: "When you're winning, the beer tastes better!" Short-tempered and reputed to harbor racist sentiments, Dykes nevertheless was widely admired by his peers for making do with less.

Dykes might have done better if he had had additional working capital and a scouting system. The team was also struck by some very bad luck. Monty Stratton, a fine young pitching prospect, had posted impressive back-to-back 15-win seasons in 1937 and 1938 before blowing his leg off in a freakish off-season hunting accident.

In 1939 Lou Comiskey set in motion the first White Sox farm system, deciding that Mr. and Mrs. Roy Largent, the husband-and-wife team who scoured the South and West in their antique Model T observing high-school and college prospects, could not supply enough quality players to fuel the development pipeline. A working agreement was finalized with four Class D affiliates in the Southwestern League before Lou succumbed to heart failure at his Eagle River, Wisconsin, compound in July 1939—a month before the first night game was played in Comiskey Park. It was another in a series of unfortunate reversals coming at a moment when the team seemed to be shaking off its 20-year malaise and the sting of the Black Sox scandal. His death and the coming of war set back the rebuilding timetables by a decade.

Control of the franchise passed to his widow, Grace Reidy Comiskey, who was less interested in building up the team than acting as interim caretaker until her teenage son Chuck could take over. Grace was a stern, unbending matriarch reputed to suffer from a drinking problem and a streak of vindictiveness. She squabbled with Dykes over nickels and dimes, then insisted he resign after suffering an attack of the gallstones that had sidelined him for the start of the 1946 season. Ted Lyons, the ageless pitching marvel and a sentimental favorite of Grace and her daughter Dorothy, took over the reins of the club, but the team only got worse, reaching the nadir of its fortunes with 101 losses in 1948. Despite the disastrous play on the field, the team made $69,000 that year, nearly half of the average $126,648 profit in the period 1945–50.

The disastrous season led to a long-overdue front-office shakeup and house-cleaning. Chuck Comiskey, now in his early twenties, was promoted to the executive suite following a brief internship with a Sox minor-league affiliate in Memphis. Chuck initiated some bold strokes, hiring former Big Ten official Frank Lane as general manager. Former Sox pitcher John Rigney, Dorothy's husband, restructured the meager farm system, such as it was, while Lane dealt the hand he was given. Meanwhile John Donaldson, the first full-time African American scout, was assigned to canvass the Negro Leagues.

The Sox were outfitted in stylish new uniforms with an Old English *SOX* logo on the front, mimicking the Yankee pinstripes, in hopes of instilling a winning attitude. Lane engineered a series of ingenious trades that catapulted the Sox into the first division in 1951 with their first winning season in eight years. Fireplug second baseman Nellie Fox came over from Philadelphia in 1949 for washed-up catcher Joe Tipton and became the heart and soul of the franchise for the next 14 years. The little iron man played in 798 straight games and was a great contact hitter. He was also a great fielder who won the defensive triple crown (percentage, putouts, and assists) three times. Fox was MVP in 1959 and eventually was elected to the Hall of Fame. Other major additions were stylish lefty Billy Pierce, heir apparent to Ted Lyons, acquired from Detroit for a mere pittance prior to the 1949 season, and the charismatic Orestes "Minnie" Minoso, "the Cuban Comet," who in May 1951 broke the color line in Chicago. He energized Sox fandom, blending speed, power, and defense. The trio of talented newcomers and a renewed commitment from the front office to end years of complacency signaled to the fans that a new day had dawned on the South Side, and the fans responded to their "Go-Go" White Sox speed merchants and the left-handed slants of Pierce enthusiastically. Billy hurled 35 shutouts during his superlative 12-year White Sox career and held an important head-to-head 8–6 edge over Whitey Ford, perennial ace of the great 1950s Yankee teams.

Despite the presence of Minoso, the team did not draw well with the growing black community located directly to the east of the field. The city's African American fans had embraced the Chicago Giants of the Negro League, who played in Comiskey's vacated 39th Street Grounds from 1911 to 1949. However, they were generally apathetic toward the White Sox, and did not attend games in significant numbers until after the AL integrated in 1947. Thereafter, once the novelty wore off, blacks represented only a tiny fraction of paying ticket holders, despite noble attempts on the part of White Sox management to aggressively recruit and sign star Negro League players to contracts.

Riding the coattails of Fox, Minoso, Pierce, and company, the franchise drew a million paying customers for the first time in 1951, thereby reclaiming a share of lost market dominance in Chicago, which they held until 1967. But to sustain market success, the Sox had to win consistently, year in and year out. In 1948, WGN inaugurated live broadcasts of baseball games from Comiskey Park and Wrigley Field, with the personable Jack Brickhouse calling the action and affable sidekick Harry Creighton shilling the sponsor's beer between innings. On the radio side, courtly Bob Elson manned the booth continuously for 40 years, until 1970, when his descriptive but admittedly bland nonpartisan play-by-play style was found wanting. The Cubs, playing exclusively in the sunshine, fit perfectly into the WGN afternoon programming schedule, but the station was reluctant to sacrifice its evening fare with a menu of White Sox baseball. Thus the Cubs managed to wean a generation of baby-boom youngsters away from the South Siders, although the White Sox were far more entertaining and competitive, and a much better spectacle.

Paul Richards, "the Wizard of Waxahachie," ignited the long-abandoned running game as manager from 1951 to 1954. He taught a daring style of hit-and-run play that exploited every opponent's defensive weakness. Base thieves Jim Busby, Minnie Minoso, Jim Rivera, and later Luis Aparicio revived the forgotten art of "little ball." Aparicio arrived from Maracaibo, Venezuela, in 1956, and would spend 10 of his 16 years in the big leagues as the White Sox's everyday shortstop. Teaming with Nellie Fox, "Little Louie" provided finesse up the middle and defensive prowess that keyed the team's string of successes in the 1950s. Wedded to this "motion" style of play dictated by the contours of Comiskey Park, the White Sox finished in the first division 17 consecutive years (1951–67), an AL mark equaled or surpassed by only the Baltimore Orioles and the New York Yankees.

The Sox topped the 90-victory plateau in 1954 for the first time in 34 years, but Paul Richards bolted following a salary row with Grace, and was replaced by Marty Marion. Dorothy, at constant odds with her younger brother over tri-fling family matters, blamed Chuck for the loss. Frank Lane was out the door a year later after Chuck sided with the league when the Sox general manager was suspended for unbecoming conduct toward an umpire. Chuck's family made him the scapegoat for Lane's departure.

Grace Comiskey suffered a fatal heart attack and passed away on December 10, 1956. Having soured on the whims of her capricious son years earlier, the widow entrusted 54 percent of the team stock to daughter Dorothy, giving her control of the board of directors and voting power, which she held on to, resisting Chuck's repeated offers to buy her out. The fissure widened after Dorothy sold her shares on March 10, 1959, to baseball showman Bill Veeck, a Chicagoan who had long coveted the chance to own a Chicago team. Chuck Comiskey fought a long and futile battle to block the sale to Veeck, who became majority stockholder and gave Comiskey a ceremonial title and a do-nothing job.

In 1959 the Sox won the pennant with a veteran nucleus mostly assembled by Comiskey, who also brought in Al Lopez as manager in 1957. Comiskey angered Sox fandom by dealing Minoso to Cleveland at the end of the 1957 campaign for Early Wynn, a gritty competitor and career 300-game winner. The 1959 flag chase was a down-to-the-wire affair between the Pale Hose and the Tribe, with the Indians enjoying an early advantage before falling back. A double-play ball off the bat of Vic Power in the ninth inning of a 4–2 thriller on the shores of Lake Erie on September 22 wrapped up the first pennant in 40 years for the South Siders. The team's strength was pitching, defense, and speed (Aparicio stole 56 bases), but they batted just .250. Fox was the MVP, and Wynn, who won 22 games, became the first Sox Cy Young winner. An important factor was the late-season acquisition of Reds slugger Ted Kluszewski. In the World Series the Sox faced a veteran Los Angeles Dodgers team with considerable postseason experience, while the Sox were just happy to hoist the AL flag over Comiskey Park. The Sox running game was stifled and the bats went silent for much of the series. The disappointing six-game defeat convinced Veeck that dramatic changes in player personnel were needed if the Sox hoped to repeat as champions.

"Barnum" Bill Veeck, who made his name for the many zany stunts and fan promotions he sponsored through three ownerships, gutted the farm system in the next two years, trading away a phalanx of future 1960s stars ready to step up, including catchers Earl Battey and John Romano; outfielder Johnny Callison; infielders Norm Cash, Bubba Phillips, and Don Mincher; and utility pitchers Barry Latman and Al Worthington. Dick Donovan, a mainstay of the 1950s, was gone after 1960, only to win 20 games for the Indians in 1962. The loss of Battey, a sensitive young African American from Los Angeles, hurt the most, creating a gaping hole behind the plate. In return, the Sox received aging veterans Gene Freese, Roy Sievers, and perennial fan favorite Minnie Minoso, but what the team really needed was to get younger. By 1962, these players, and Veeck, had exited the stage, leaving the Sox with nothing left to show except a ransacked farm system, baseball's first exploding scoreboard, and the first uniforms with the players' names stitched to the backs of the home jerseys.

Ill health forced Veeck to sell his stock to Arthur C. and John Allyn in June 1961. The Allyns ran several businesses, including an oil-drilling firm and a LaSalle Street securities house. They bought the White Sox purely as an investment after Veeck thumbed his nose at Chuck Comiskey and his syndicate, which included future mayoral candidate Bernard Epton and entertainer Danny Thomas. Comiskey finally gave up and sold his 46 percent of the stock to Arthur Allyn in 1962, an untimely ending to the Comiskey dynasty.

Art Allyn proved to be obdurate, hardheaded, and impossible to deal with among the other team owners and from the player's perspective—outfielder Dave Nicholson remembered Allyn's cautious, bottom-line approach to doing things. "He was a businessman," Nicholson remembered, echoing a code-word opinion shared by many of his teammates. Still, the White Sox managed to tread water in the first division through the 1967 season. A few good trades engineered by Edwin Short, former team publicist promoted to general manager in 1961, offset his disastrous decision to release pitcher Denny McLain in 1963. The team was in the thick of things in 1964 and 1967 that went right down to the final week of the season. But in the end, the total reliance on four brilliant pitchers—Gary Peters, Joel Horlen, Hoyt Wilhelm, and Tommy John—could not overcome serious offensive deficiencies. A survey of fans in 1966 found them bored with too many 2–1, 3–2, and 1–0 outcomes The Sox played quintessential Comiskey Park dead-ball-era baseball that was out of vogue in the "swinging sixties." The fans demanded home runs and a high-scoring offense.

Growing racial tensions in the mid-1960s also hurt fan interest. One of the nation's most dangerous and crime ridden housing projects (the Robert Taylor Homes) was just a few blocks from Comiskey Park across the Dan Ryan Expressway, and there was a growing exodus from the Bridgeport neighborhood of ethnic Irish, Poles, Italians, and Lithuanians who had been among Charles Comiskey's most loyal ticket-paying customers. Bridgeport remained a tiny isolated pocket of white residents thereafter, but the sprawling South Side, extending to the Indiana state line, had changed dramatically. The public perceived the stadium's neighborhood as unsafe for suburban white fans. As a result, in 1966 attendance fell below 1 million for the first time in seven years.

The television situation was equally problematic. Executives at WGN-TV refused Sox demands to televise night home and road games. Sox ownership was left to deal as best it could with a terrible imbalance in the ratio of televised Cubs games airing in midday following the popular children's program *Bozo's Circus* versus the limited number of weekend Sox home games played in the sunshine.

Art Allyn correctly gauged that these factors were costing the Sox a generation of fans to the North Side ball club, but his ill-advised attempts to address the problems worked to the disadvantage of the team. In 1966, he submitted a preliminary rendering to Mayor Richard J. Daley and the Chicago Planning Commission seeking state and municipal assistance to build a new stadium just south of downtown Chicago along the lakefront. Daley, a lifelong Sox fan, was sympathetic, but insisted upon a multipurpose facility inclusive of the football Bears and the baseball team, envisioning it upon landfill jutting out into Lake Michigan.

Allyn threw up his hands in disgust when it was apparent there was little chance for his plan to pass muster in city hall. Next, he tried to correct the broadcast imbalance by withdrawing his agreement with WGN and committing the team to a full-season telecast on WFLD-TV, the newly inaugurated city UHF frequency. Jack Brickhouse, the dean of Windy City television baseball broadcasting, warned Allyn that he was making a dreadful mistake by pulling away from WGN. Brickhouse foresaw the coming of cable television and the "superstation" concept, but Allyn did not listen Since older televisions required the purchase of a decoder box to unscramble UHF signals, few Chicagoland households could even receive Sox broadcasts when they started on channel 32.

Meanwhile, the reenergized Cubs became competitive for the first time since World War II, and the thousands of baby-boom children growing up with day baseball piped into their living room from Wrigley Field formed the nexus of a new ticket-buying generation. The rise of the Cubs, dovetailing into the larger marketing issues plaguing the Sox in the late 1960s, soured Art Allyn on the game of baseball once his tax write-offs were exhausted. Preseason favorites to challenge for an AL pennant, the Sox instead tumbled to eighth place in 1968 with a home attendance figure barely shading 800,000, which included near sellouts from the nine "home games" played in Milwaukee. Drowning in a sea of red ink, Allyn was testing the Wisconsin market for future franchise relocation after his stadium demand was unceremoniously snubbed by Daley.

Following another losing season in 1969 and further erosion of the fan base (589,546 paid admissions that included 11 games in Milwaukee), Art opened discussions with Bud Selig, head of a Milwaukee investment group, aimed at luring the struggling franchise to the beer city. With the Sox on the verge of extinction, John W. Allyn, who was not on the best of terms with his brother Art, stepped forward at the 11th hour to buy controlling interest and rescue the team from certain demise.

Allyn realized that a winning attitude could go a long way toward healing old wounds and sweeping away misconceptions about neighborhood safety, even with the media tilting toward the Cubs. A highly motivated man of great ambition, the younger Allyn stopped Selig's scheme and recommitted full resources toward revitalizing the franchise by bringing in the sharpest young minds and an outspoken radio play-by-play man from Oakland to inject enthusiasm and a winning spirit. Allyn quietly built a foundation for the future by raiding the California Angels' minor-league system to come away with Chuck Tanner, the next Sox manager, and general manager Roland Hemond, a former farm director recognized for his exceptional player-development skill.

Before Allyn could begin to see the light of day, he had to first suffer a team record 106-game losing season in 1970, with a paltry 495,355 paid admissions. The pitiful box-office showing, the worst since the wartime 1942 season, convinced many Sox watchers that the team could no longer effectively compete for its fair market share.

Reminiscent of the 1949 rebuilding program launching the White Sox on a joyous, 17-year run in the first division, the Hemond-Tanner-Allyn combination introduced a snappy red pinstriped uniform (copying the Cincinnati Reds), 13 new faces for 1971, and Harry Caray, the audacious, opinionated former St. Louis Cardinals and Oakland Athletics broadcaster who sparked a revival of fan interest with his salty, colorful criticisms and observations. The improved Sox climbed to third place in the AL Western Division, and nearly doubled the 1970 attendance. For the moment, the chorus of complaints about the stadium and the neighborhood softened.

Hemond, a shrewd judge of talent hidden beneath a gentlemanly, almost reticent manner, engineered one of the most famous and controversial player trades of all time when he exchanged veteran southpaw Tommy John for the petulant Dick Allen, the ex-Phillies slugger. Allen related well to Chuck Tanner's gee-whiz, backslapping enthusiasm and earned MVP honors, shattering Bill Melton's two-year-old team home-run record with 37 rocketing moon shots. He led the team to an inspired second-place finish and their first winning season since 1967. Even more encouraging, the fans returned in droves, with attendance reaching 1.1 million.

Allyn was a reflective, pipe-smoking sportsman remembered as one of the unsung heroes of White Sox history. John enjoyed the camaraderie of sport and the chance to hobnob with his players. Soft-spoken and cheerfully optimistic, he did his very best to deliver a worthwhile product for the fans to enjoy without offending the sensitive egos of his players. He deserved far better than the three disappointing, injury-plagued seasons that followed and Dick Allen's sudden betrayal of his teammates in September 1974 when the enigmatic superstar walked out of the clubhouse, announcing that he was "retired" from the game, despite leading the league in home runs and basking in the admiration of hero-worshipping Chicago fans.

Without Chicago's most bankable celebrity superstar, 1975 home attendance plummeted to 770,000. In danger of missing his payroll late that season, the cash-strapped Allyn had no other choice but to put his team up on the auction block. The AL considered transferring the franchise to Seattle, where entertainer Danny Kaye had lined up an investment group to buy out Allyn and restore professional baseball to the Pacific Northwest after a five-year hiatus. The secret plan hatched in an AL star chamber was to allow Charles O. Finley to move his beleaguered Oakland A's into Comiskey Park once Kaye reached agreement with Allyn. But Allyn was not keen on the arrangement, preferring a local buyer, and Bill Veeck was waiting in the wings. Allyn accepted $10 million from Veeck, far less than the prevailing 1975 market rate he would have received from Kaye's group, but Allyn looked upon the White Sox as a cherished civic treasure, believing that his duty was to serve as team caretaker for future generations. Veeck managed to get approved by the conservative owners, though they did not relish welcoming a wooden-legged, antiestablishment carnival promoter back into their exclusive country club.

In hindsight, it would be nice to say that the Veeck years represented a panacea for the team and its fans. Barnum Bill was embraced as an ebullient, beer-guzzling, chain-smoking man of the people whose zany stunts and promotional zeal made a baseball game a total experience for fans of all ages and not just a grim and somber athletic contest. Beloved by a generation of Chicago fans who nostalgically longed for a repeat of the 1959 success in the naive belief that a casual wave of the magical Veeck wand would bring back the glory days of Nellie and Louie, they quickly found that the new owner's capital resources were stretched thin. His future promotions included Frisbee-catching dogs, beer-case-stacking competitions, cow-milking contests, belly dancers, Polish Night, and the infamous Disco Demolition Night—July 12, 1979, when 50,000 riotous teenagers swarmed the playing field, resulting in a forfeit and two decades of unending ridicule. But amid five years of bread and circuses, there was very little winning baseball to savor.

Veeck teams were a delightfully curious and weird amalgam of second-string players plucked from the league waiver lists, unwanted bargain-basement free agents, and other assorted castoffs and misfits unlikely to have made the roster of any professional ball club save one, the Chicago White Sox, where they donned baggy softball jerseys, blue clam-digger pants, and, on one ignoble occasion, *shorts*. The owner never took the game as seriously as some of his critics in the baseball establishment would have preferred, and the nightly zaniness earned the players lasting mockery from the media.

The 1976 Peter Seitz decision ushering in the era of free agency caught Bill Veeck unprepared and placed the franchise at a troublesome disadvantage. He could not afford to participate in a system of compensation that drove up the salaries of even the most marginal players. The front-office staff, the scouting system, and the minor-league operations were pared to the bone. Quality players like Richie Zisk and Oscar Gamble, who contributed to the success of the hard-hitting 1977 "South Side Hitmen," a surprising Cinderella club that rose from the ashes of a last-place finish in 1976 to challenge for division supremacy against the Kansas City Royals, a precision outfit of run-and-gun base thieves who played more like the 1950s Go-Go boys than the lumbering Sox, departed for greener pastures after only one year. The following season Larry Doby served briefly as skipper. Back in 1947 Veeck had brought him to the Indians as the second African American in the majors, and now he was the second to manage in the majors as well.

After Steve Stone, a sore-armed .500-caliber pitcher, fled to Baltimore when ownership failed to meet his 1979 salary demand, Veeck sensed that the game had passed him by and it was time to get out. It was ironic that the man who had fought the injustices of baseball's reserve clause so long and so hard should now be victimized by the players he helped set free.

Escalating player salaries was not the only reason Veeck opted out. He noted with growing alarm the diminishing levels of media coverage for the White Sox. Veeck would measure the amount of editorial and column space devoted to the Cubs versus his White Sox—two years *before* the Tribune Company acquired the NL team. Veeck dismally concluded that it was becoming impossible for his team to receive a fair shake. Veeck concluded that the number of dyed-in-the-wool South Side fans was rapidly slipping away and that the Windy City could no longer sustain two teams. As home attendance sagged in 1980, the owner took immediate steps to divest his holdings. After clandestine negotiations with Denver oil billionaire Marvin Davis fell through, Veeck tried to sell to Edward DeBartolo of Youngstown, Ohio, the builder of some of the nation's first shopping centers and suburban malls and the owner of a racetrack in Shreveport, Louisiana, and the San Francisco 49ers. Commissioner Bowie Kuhn and the lords of baseball got assurances from DeBartolo that he was committed to keeping the team in Chicago but were worried about his gambling connections. There was also a vicious whispering campaign against him that was perceived as anti-Italian bias. Anxious to win over the Chicago fans and secure some favorable PR, DeBartolo gave Veeck the necessary upfront money to sign Ron LeFlore, a blue-chip free agent. Nonetheless, DeBartolo was not admitted into the club.

A NEW REGIME TAKES OVER

The rejection of DeBartolo forced an embittered Veeck to sell the White Sox to the only serious bidder, a syndicate headed by Brooklyn-born Jerry Reinsdorf, chairman of the board and CEO of Balcor/American Express, a major investment firm. Reinsdorf and his partner, former law-school chum Eddie Einhorn, were distasteful to Veeck, who received a $19 million check on January 29, 1981. Veeck nursed a grudge up to the moment of his death in 1986. The front men were viewed as a pair of greedy New York interlopers chasing the almighty dollar, who "are not our kind of people," with implications of anti-Semitism. Sox fans were particularly incensed by the new ownership's publicly stated objective of reinventing Comiskey Park as a wholesome, family-oriented attraction, turning their backs on the blue-collar urban factory workers who symbolized the team's traditional fan base. The press was hypercritical, dubbing the pair "the Sunshine Boys" who would exit the stage "once their tax breaks ran out," recalling Art Allyn's earlier rapacity. Working-class Sox fans, many of them notorious for engaging in unchecked beer-sloshing brawls at Comiskey Park during the Veeck years, thus earning the old stadium a surly reputation as "the World's Largest Outdoor Saloon," were not the most tolerant of folk. Veeck himself fanned the flames of discontent by fending off all invitations to appear at celebratory events and old-timer reunions hosted by Reinsdorf at Comiskey Park. Instead he joined a growing cadre of youthful Cub fans sunning themselves in the left-field bleachers of Wrigley Field, holding court—very near a WGN camera, to maximize his TV exposure.

Having gotten off on the wrong foot with a skeptical Sox fan base, the new owners plunged into the free-agent market and lured away Carlton Fisk from the Boston Red Sox and Greg Luzinski from Philadelphia. On the field, at least, the ball club attained instant credibility. Only the players' strike, canceling out half of the 1981 season, prevented the season attendance record of 1.6 million set in 1977 from falling. An infusion of working capital was used to hire media strategists and marketing professionals. Einhorn, a former television executive, explored possible cable TV deals before launching Sportsvision, a pay-per-view arrangement about 10 years ahead of its time. Pulling the Sox off of the local station proved wildly unpopular with Chicago baseball fans accustomed to a full menu of free TV baseball all the time.

The Sportsvision fiasco cost the White Sox the services of announcer Harry Caray. Sensing that he was about to lose four-fifths of his TV viewing audience, Caray bolted the South Side in a huff, blasting the Sox ownership and his personal enemy, manager Tony LaRussa (the most unpopular Sox manager in at least two generations), for rank stupidity. Wisecracking sidekick Jimmy Piersall was dismissed one year later after several transgressions, notably an unprovoked physical assault against sportswriter Rob Gallas inside the clubhouse. The loss of Harry and Jimmy fed the growing rage among fans. Caray was picked up by the Chicago Cubs as heir apparent to the aging Jack Brickhouse. The Sox countered the move and brought in Ken "Hawk" Harrelson and Don Drysdale for 1982. They were polished play-by-play men and competent baseball analysts, but there was no escaping the impact of the costly Caray defection, the first of several misfires by the Reinsdorf team. Once again intrigues off the field overshadowed the steadily improving play on the diamond.

The Sox shed their insulting "Keystone Sox" identity to emerge as a serious contender in the AL Western Division with new faces acquired through trades and free agency. In 1983 Veeck holdovers Harold Baines and pitchers Britt Burns, La Marr Hoyt, and Richard Dotson, joined by newcomers Floyd Bannister, Tony Bernazard, Tom Paciorek, Jerry Koosman, Rudy Law, and Vance Law, won the West with 99 victories, the most in the majors and second-highest total in team history. It was the first major title from any of the city's major team sports since the 1963 Bears championship. La Marr Hoyt (24–10), unhittable down the stretch, grabbed Cy Young honors. Rudy Law pilfered a team record 77 bases, and Gary, Indiana, strongman Ron Kittle was named Rookie of the Year with 35 home runs. The White Sox adopted "Winning Ugly" as their rallying cry. Autumn hopes soared as the Sox crossed the 2 million threshold in home attendance for the first time. However, the pennant-starved White Sox—invincible from early July though the end of September—left their bats at home in the AL Championship Series, falling to the Baltimore Orioles in four closely fought games. Bitter and heartbreaking was the only way to describe the finale, after Orioles bench player Tito Landrum broke up a scoreless 10-inning pitcher's duel with a home run to the upper deck, connecting off of Burns's 150th pitch of the game.

The 1980s, a decade that began so promisingly, soured after the 1983 season, and only in 1985 did the Sox breach the .500 mark. Tony LaRussa was fired in 1986 following a storm of criticism over his methods and a contentious power struggle with broadcaster Ken Harrelson, who took the Sox manager to task for the team's shortfalls the year before. Harrelson stepped in as general manager for one ill-fated season, replacing Hemond, who left the organization after 16 seasons. Jim Fregosi, the new manager, was left with little material due to chronically poor draft picks. In 1985 Ozzie Guillen continued the White Sox tradition of shortstop excellence with his Rookie of the Year Award, and Tom Seaver won his 300th game in a White Sox uniform. But Seaver was traded a year later.

Attendance withered after 1984. Harry Caray, leading a chorus of soused Cub fans crooning "Take Me Out to the Ball Game" during the ceremonial seventh-inning stretch within the Friendly Confines, siphoned away a generation of fans that might have embraced the Sox, if only he had remained a South Side stalwart. As the decade wore on, neither Carlton Fisk nor Harold Baines—the only true celebrity athletes with much tenure on the team—were willing to act as public-relations spokespersons. Baines was as silent as the Sphinx, and Fisk was too proud to shill for the front office at autographing sessions, fan gatherings, or the banquet circuit. The Sox suffered from an image problem compounded by the most serious crisis since the Black Sox scandal: whether they could secure sufficient public monies for the construction of a new Comiskey Park.

BUILDING A NEW PARK TO "SAVE OUR SOX"

In December 1985, AL president Bobby Brown warned Reinsdorf about the necessity to "step up the timetables" for development of a new baseball-only facility, threatening that the "final alternative" of moving the franchise would "have to be considered" unless progress was made. The White Sox had already set their sights on a location just south of downtown, since it had become apparent that the outmoded and crumbling edifice at 35th and Shields could not be saved or renovated to satisfy the league's criteria for generating revenue.

Decades of neglect had taken their toll on Comiskey's "Baseball Palace of the World." Little had been done since 1927, when the outfield upper deck was installed. The masonry was slowly crumbling and the vertical support beams propping up the grandstands had decayed. Owners unable to afford costly infrastructure repairs made cosmetic repairs, painting the seats and the exterior walls; built exploding scoreboards; and added parking lots. The infield was carpeted with lime green Astroturf in 1969, and the first skyboxes went in after Reinsdorf took over. But the necessary behind-the-scenes improvements were largely ignored, leaving the new owners holding the bag when the aging *grande dame* of American stadiums threatened the comfort and safety of fans.

On July 8, 1986, Reinsdorf stunned the press when he announced that he would seek assistance in building a new Comiskey Park on 140 acres of empty land in suburban Addison—30 miles due west of the stadium. Reinsdorf did not convincingly explain the rationale and his timetable. He probably should have slowly leaked the details of the plan in graduated stages, allowing Sox fans some time to reconcile themselves to the idea that the old park's days were numbered. In response, ticket buyers, and a significant number of non-fans who had never attended a game in Comiskey Park, called to mind the wonderful nostalgia the old place evoked and how it would be a terrible civic tragedy to see it go. But if the old park was such a timeless architectural treasure and enduring landmark, why had so many seats gone unsold for so many years?

Although a five-year streak of winning baseball (the longest consecutive run since the 1960s), record attendance, and soaring revenues lay just over the horizon, the franchise and its browbeaten fans had to first endure four of the most miserable, anxiety-ridden seasons in team history as downstate and city politicians wrangled and postured and the front office, community activists, and historical preservationists exchanged hot words, empty rhetoric, and otherwise debated the burning question of the decade: build or move?

The front office leveraged the threat of franchise relocation to St. Petersburg, Florida, to pressure policymakers to move expeditiously, but failed to convince Addison voters, who in a nonbinding referendum on November 4, 1986, turned down by 43 votes a proposal to build a park in their city. Analysts claimed the voters were worried about traffic congestion, the spoilage of natural wetlands, and noise pollution, but knowledgeable insiders blamed local politicians for whipping up illusory fears of encroaching black crime and declining property values. Once again the race card played a dramatic role in White Sox fortunes.

In a curious twist, Sox fan Harold Washington, who had been elected Chicago's first African American mayor in 1983, declared that the "Sox aren't going anywhere," except perhaps across the street, where he envisioned a second Comiskey Park. Less than a month after the Addison setback, Washington pledged to work together with the city and the ball club to quitclaim and demolish the shabby tenement housing in South Armour Square, relocate the residents into more desirable quarters in a gentrifying neighborhood, and explore the means for public financing.

Downstaters were opposed to state support. Cardinals and Cubs fans dominated south of Kankakee, and legislators saw no political advantage in endorsing the project. In addition, community activists and self-styled urban radicals seized the opportunity to foment old racial and class divisions on the South

Side. A militant grassroots "Save Our Sox" (SOS) movement appealed to all Chicagoans to oppose the legislation, but they were duped by the activists, who cared less about baseball, the White Sox, and their stadium crisis than minority empowerment. For SOS, saving Comiskey Park at all costs was paramount, regardless of whether the White Sox chose to remain in town or not. Reinsdorf was disliked, and the public was opposed in principle to a taxpayer-financed stadium.

Meanwhile, the threat of moving to St. Petersburg grew even after four appointees were named to head the Illinois Sports Facilities Authority (ISFA), charged with overseeing the construction of new Comiskey—dependent on the legislature's willingness to fund it. Legions of disgruntled fans and Reinsdorf bashers believed the ownership was bluffing and would never abandon Chicago. But the truth was that there had to be a new park or the team was off to Florida for the 1989 season. The Illinois General Assembly took up the stadium-funding bill as their last order of business on June 30, 1988. The vote was delayed to enable the White Sox and ISFA lobbyists to marshal their forces.

It all boiled down to the persuasive abilities of Illinois governor James R. Thompson, a liberal Republican who coaxed, cajoled, and twisted arms on the floor of the chamber as the final minutes of the session ticked away. Thompson paced the aisle, whispering in the ears of key legislators and calling in the chips on old favors granted when necessary. The clock brushed past midnight as the final roll call was taken, and the funding was approved.

The second Comiskey Park was delivered within 22 months of groundbreaking, on time and under budget, on April 18, 1991. The scaled-down design cost taxpayers $119 million—$18 million *less* than the original state appropriation. The gleaming new Comiskey Park was hailed as "the wave of the future" by *Time* magazine in 1991. The old park in 1990, its last year, drew 2 million, double the prior year, because of nostalgia and an exciting pennant race. The first year of the new park saw attendance skyrocket to 2,934,154 because of the novelty of a new home and high hopes following the successful 1990 season. The huge crowds established a citywide record that held up until 2003, when the Cubs shaded the mark by 28,000. The team followed the record year by drawing over 2.5 million the next two seasons. White Sox apparel featuring a revival of the vintage 1950s Old English and black and white pinstripe configuration soared to number one in the sale of sports merchandise nationwide. During this "halo period" surrounding the opening of the modern new park, the White Sox were lumped together with the Yankees, Dodgers, Red Sox, and Cubs as baseball's elite big-market teams, benefiting from solid revenue streams, rising attendance, merchandising sales, and the ability to sign "Type A" free agents. The era of good feeling was short-lived, however, and the Sox were soon viewed by sports-marketing professionals and player agents as a small-market team just trying to get along in a large-market city.

Subsequent publicly built stadiums drew upon the fans' craving for nostalgia. Chic retro parks re-created the look and feel of the creaky dead-ball-era stadiums the baby-boom generation of ticket buyers remembered from their childhood. Careful to sidestep the mistakes made in Chicago, the next generation of new parks like Camden Yards set standards by which the new Comiskey was unfavorably judged. Its biggest design flaw, apart from the bland symmetry of the outfield walls and the unappealing blue color scheme of stadium seating, was the upper deck, perched atop two levels of private suites and pitched at a dizzying 35-degree slope. The top row was equivalent in height to a 13-story building, and the infield from that altitude looked like an ant hill. The structure itself looked to motorists on the adjacent highway like a gigantic flying saucer.

THE SECOND TEAM IN THE THIRD CITY

The team did poorly in the late 1980s, with four straight fifth places, and a seventh in 1989 (69–92). This gave the club a lot of high draft choices in baseball's annual amateur draft, and under the astute direction of general manager Larry Himes, the Sox chose wisely from a pool of vaunted college and high-school prospects. In a remarkable four-year stretch (1987–90) the top four Sox draft picks went on to make significant contributions at the major-league level. Future Cy Young winner Jack McDowell arrived from Stanford in 1987, followed a year later by Robin Ventura of Oklahoma State, arguably the most polished third baseman in team history. Burly Auburn slugger Frank Thomas, a real sleeper, was selected with the seventh pick of the first round in 1989, followed in 1990 by Miami-Dade right-hander Alex Fernandez, who was the fourth player chosen. That level of success was never duplicated by the front office before or since. The team then was operating under tight financial restrictions. The total payroll in 1988 was $5,906,952, lowest in MLB, and the Sox remained at the bottom for two more years.

On the field the fans celebrated a marvelous season in 1990 under manager Jeff Torborg. After finishing dead last the year before, the Sox continued their 20-year cycle of emerging from the abyss with an unexpected show of success on the field. This Sox unit was composed of a potent blend of talented youngsters nurtured and developed in the minor leagues. The team was embroiled in a tight division race with the Oakland A's. They won 94 games, a dramatic 25-game improvement over 1989, largely on the tired shoulders of overworked bullpen closer Bobby Thigpen, who notched 57 saves—a major-league record. The comeback season went a long way toward soothing the strained relations between the front office and the fans, and for the moment it vindicated Jerry Reinsdorf's methodical analogies of moving from point B (early rebuilding) to point A (pennant contention).

The Torborg-Himes tandem seemed to be the perfect melding of front-office wisdom and between-the-lines strategy, but their tenure was short. In what might have ranked as the greatest baseball trade for all time, Himes sent the fading Harold Baines to the Rangers on July 29, 1989, for Sammy Sosa, pitcher Wilson Alvarez, and infielder Scott Fletcher. Sosa was an extremely talented but raw player from the Dominican Republic. Himes begged the organization for a little patience, fearing that the Dominican's acclimation to the big leagues might take some time. But patience was in short supply on the South Side. Reinsdorf felt that Himes did not get along well with people and fired him on September 15, 1990. Ron Schueler, architect of the Oakland A's string of successes in the late 1980s, was brought in as the new vice president of baseball operations and general manager two months later. Reinsdorf was not a fan of Torborg, who was tied to his book of theories and statistical probability, and forced him to resign in October 1991. He hired laid-back Gene Lamont as manager. He was the first in a succession of rookie managers for the White Sox.

Building upon the Himes framework, Schueler added a veteran presence in Tim Raines, Cory Snyder, Bo Jackson, and Tim Belcher through trades or free agency. In March 1992 Schueler decided he had to fortify the offense with another veteran. Sharing the conventional wisdom that Sosa, who had an alarming strikeout ratio, was unteachable and a defensive liability, the future NL home-run king was sent to the Cubs for George Bell, a Sox killer during his years with the Toronto Blue Jays, but now reaching the tail end of his productive career. This disastrous trade helped cement the Sox's second-class stature in Chicago. Bell had a few good moments in his two-year run on the South Side, helping lead the team to a 94–68 division title in 1993, but he was quarrelsome and out of sync with manager Gene Lamont's laid-back approach. The strength of the team was its pitching, which was the best in the AL. Jack McDowell won the Cy Young Award with a league-leading 22 victories. The campaign, remembered mostly for the heroic comeback of Bo Jackson, the first major leaguer to play a full season with a replacement hip, also marked the first of two consecutive MVP Awards for Frank Thomas. "The Big Hurt" never matched Sosa's flamboyance or his ability to bond with fans. He was moody, introspective, and injury prone, and often squabbled with the front office over their refusal to renegotiate his multiyear contract. That year management began opening the purse strings, and the team had the 13th-highest payroll. By 1997 the team's payroll was 3rd in the league ($54,377,500), but in the following year it dropped to 18th ($36,840,000).

As was fast becoming their playoff custom, the Sox offense fell asleep against the victorious Toronto Blue Jays after advancing to the 1993 ALCS. On a blustery, cold October night in Comiskey Park, more than 45,000 shivering and despairing Sox fans attired in winter coats sat in muted silence as Alex Fernandez failed to contain the World Series–bound Jays. Bo Jackson went hitless for the series and Jack McDowell's ERA ballooned to 10.00. "Wait till next year" was the familiar refrain, but what happens to a contending team when next year is called off?

To this day, White Sox enthusiasts are convinced that if the final third of the 1994 season had not been canceled as the result of an acrimonious player strike, a trip to the World Series was their destiny. Instead of sipping victory champagne and throwing ticker tape, the celebrations abruptly ended on August 12 with the 67–46 White Sox holding down a slim one-game advantage over the onrushing Cleveland Indians, whose energetic young general manager John Hart provided Schueler and Reinsdorf with a perfect blueprint for building sustained success: draft the brightest young stars and lock them up with long-term contracts. The work stoppage quickly became the fodder of massive fan discontent leveled at Reinsdorf, who had become a major AL power broker, for allowing the strike to go on as long as it did. The bitter aftertaste of the strike festered in the minds of the slow-to-forgive White Sox fans. Home attendance tumbled to 1.6 million in 1995 and failed to approach the coveted 2 million mark again until 2000. Meanwhile the Chicago Bulls, Reinsdorf's other sporting venture, were winning championships on the shoulders of Michael Jordan and selling out the Chicago Stadium every night. Nonetheless, never has one man been so thoroughly vilified for his management style of a baseball team than Reinsdorf was. If it wasn't the strike that threw the fans into a frenzy, it was the stadium: the second Comiskey Park, with its half-empty stands parallel to the asphalt parking lot where the Baseball Palace of the World once towered over the tired landscape of bungalows, factories, and church parishes, became the target of their mutual disdain.

The debut of 24-hour sports talk radio in 1992 gave fans a public forum to vent their frustrations and accumulated hostility directed toward Sox ownership. They forgot that there were 25,000 close-in seats in the lower deck that were available most of the time. By 1999 Sox home attendance had slipped to 1.3 million, unsatisfactory by any standard of comparison, especially when the sixth-place Cubs surpassed 2.8 million fans.

The best way to address this imbalance was to field a contending team in the AL Central, baseball's weakest division. At the same time, Reinsdorf warned Sox fans that unless attendance improved, his ability to sign choice free agents was limited. His carrot-and-stick approach to building goodwill belied later actions, as the organization's forays into baseball's annual player sweepstakes quickly proved. The Sox were active participants, but their choice of players was often unwise. After posting the best won-lost record in the AL between 1990 and 1995 (496–409, a .548 winning percentage), the Sox unraveled in the second half of the decade, duplicating the same tired old script of one winning season wrapped around sub-.500 performance and front-office intrigue.

In November 1996 free-agent slugger Albert Belle inked a five-year, $55 million deal with Chicago, astonishing both fans and the media, who had expected the Sox to remain passive observers. But Belle hit (for him) a disappointing .274 with 30 home runs. The White Sox were three and a half games out of first on July 31 when they waved the white flag, trading three of their better pitchers for prospects. At the end of the contentious and disappointing 1997 season, when so much more had been expected of their touchy new superstar and the club ended below .500, Terry Bevington, the inept Sox rookie manager, was fired. He was replaced by taciturn Jerry Manuel, the second African American skipper in team history. Belle set a club home-run record the following year by clouting 49 dingers but proved that he was no team leader, sowing dissent in the clubhouse with antics like destroying the thermostat in the locker room after his teammates turned up the temperature without asking his permission. Then in July 1998 he was accused of domestic battery the same afternoon he was named AL Player of the Week for the second week in a row. Not surprisingly, the image-conscious Reinsdorf let Belle leave after he exercised a little-known clause in his contract allowing him to become a free agent if he was not one of the three highest-paid players in the game. Other costly free-agent acquisitions elevated hopes and fueled ticket sales in the off-season but proved useless after the opening bell rang. Jaime Navarro, a 15-game winner with the Cubs in 1996, led the AL in hits allowed and earned runs in 1997 after signing a four-year contract.

The press continued to grind away at Reinsdorf for nearly every reversal of fortune on the South Side, abetting fan antagonism toward the White Sox. Gone were the days of gentlemanly regard between the press and team moguls. Chicago sports journalism in the new millennium more closely resembles the set of *The Jerry Springer Show*. A hostile press and the shrinking demographics of the Chicago baseball market further dictate that the White Sox do not have the luxury of falling back and waiting for the farm system to bear fruit. In 2001, according to *Forbes,* the team lost $3.8 million. The Sox were 21st in gate revenue ($30,898,000) based on an attendance of 1,766,172 at $19.19 a ticket, but were 5th in TV revenue ($30.1 million).

Sox management knew that the fan base (or what was left of it) demanded a winner, or at the very least a team that can consistently surpass the .500 mark. But the team did not have the luxury of slowly rebuilding, because of competition from the Cubs. Kenny Williams, the gambling Sox general manager cut out of the Frank Lane wheel-'em-and-deal-'em mode, said he was constrained by budget considerations. The payroll in 2004 was $65,212,500, 15th in MLB. Nonetheless, he has raised the bar and fired up the hot stove in the long winter months, often trading away top minor-league prospects to the point of nearly gutting the farm system. His willingness to part with top-rated outfield prospect Jeremy Reed in June 2004 for veteran Seattle right-hander Freddy Garcia underscores the inescapable fact that the competitive stakes in Chicago have been raised.

The White Sox recognized criticism of the ballpark by conceding in 2001 that the original design was flawed and unveiling the first part of a five-year renovation plan to improve the look and feel of the park. Sixty-nine million dollars was budgeted to HKS of Dallas to design a center-field fan deck, shift the bullpens, and shave off eight rows of the upper-deck "death valley," while adding a flat roof and decorative trusses. In January 2003, stadium naming rights were sold to U.S. Cellular, a Chicago-based wireless provider, and so Comiskey Park is now known as U.S. Cellular Field, or, more colloquially, "the Cell." The infusion of cash helped fund the final and most critical stage of the makeover—the removal of the unsightly blue canopy roof and the eight rows of seating. By the start of the 2004 season, the park was dramatically transformed to better adapt to the blue-collar industrial character of the nearby neighborhood surroundings. From the exterior, the flattened roof and new translucent screens designed to repel the swirling spring and autumn winds adds an element of attractive urban functionalism to the much-maligned Cell.

Will the White Sox break the 30-year cycle of achieving success early in the decade, followed by a collapse in the second half? In 2000, they won the Central with 95 wins, the most in the AL. The new generation of offense-minded Sox led by Paul Konerko, Magglio Ordonez, Carlos Lee, Frank Thomas (143 RBIs), and Jose Valentin provided lots of firepower and thrills, but for all their success in dethroning the slipping Indians, the 2000 edition proved once again that this game is still all about pitching and defense. Manuel was selected as Manager of the Year. However, the season ended with a bitter taste as the squad was humbled by Seattle in the AL Divisional Series. The glaring shortcomings of a pitching staff whose collective ERA soared to a ghastly 4.90 made older fans long for the great Sox moundsmen of the 1950s and 1960s. They have since almost always been the bridesmaids in the lame Central Division, first to Cleveland, then to the more frustrating small-market Minnesota Twins.

Jerry Reinsdorf has been at the helm of the ship for 25 seasons, the third-longest tenure of any current owner. He is well respected among his peers in league circles as cochairman of the Equal Opportunity Committee and a four-term member of the Major League Executive Council. He effectively championed the rise of minorities with the appointments of Ken Williams as general manager and Jerry Manuel and Ozzie Guillen (in 2004) as field managers.

Reinsdorf has managed the affairs of the ball club remarkably well. He is acknowledged as the smartest moneyman in baseball, and after nearly three decades he has kept the team on firm financial footing. Recalling the many trials, tribulations, and near bankruptcies of the Allyn brothers and Bill Veeck's dime-store shopping-cart budget, the critical importance of the underdog franchise maintaining financial solvency in this volatile two-team market cannot be overstated, though it is often overlooked. Moreover, the team *has* achieved a measure of success despite the five-decade South Side pennant drought that ended in 2005. Since the dawn of free agency in 1976 (five years before the Reinsdorf syndicate took control), the White Sox are on the winning side of the ledger (2,399–2,328, ranking them 12th in all of baseball).

General manager Williams forsook the traditional Sox style of play, forsaking pitching, speed, and defense to build a ball club that lived and died with long-ball offense. His club walloped their way into baseball's record books, joining the New York Yankees as the only other major-league team to slug 200-plus home runs in five consecutive seasons. In 2004, Paul Konerko, Carlos Lee, Jose Valentin, Frank Thomas, Aaron Rowand, and the rest of the supporting cast sent 242 baseballs flying into the stands—a team record. But on the other side of the ledger, the team ERA swelled to 4.91, ranking the Sox a dismal 11th in the league. Following that season, Williams decided on a total turnaround, and restructured the team to reemphasize small ball and defense. He copied the blueprint of the low-paying Minnesota Twins, who had won three straight division titles. They demonstrated that by employing solid fundamentals without an overreliance on home runs or a marquee superstar it was possible for a small-market team to achieve success through "grinder" baseball. This was a ball club devoid of big egos, but one stocked with 25 situational players who run, hit, lay down sacrifice bunts, and prepare for their job every day in a workmanlike manner without voicing complaint.

In 2005, the front office promised to "Win or Die Trying," employing the long-absent grinder style of team play, and wash away the 88-year-old "Comiskey Curse" and the longest championship drought in AL history. Williams dipped into the free-agent market and signed combative, mentally tough catcher A. J. Pierzynski to steady the young pitching staff; outfielder Jermaine Dye to replace embittered free-agent right fielder Magglio Ordonez; and Tadahito Iguchi, a veteran second baseman with the Fukoka Daiei Hawks. However, the key acquisition was leadoff hitter Scott Podsednik, who had swiped 70 bases but batted only .244 the year before for the Milwaukee Brewers, in return for slugger Carlos Lee.

Guillen's team emphasized pitching, defense, speed, and timely hitting. The starting five of Mark Buehrle, Jon Garland, Freddy Garcia, Orlando Hernandez, and Jose Contreras were simply outstanding. If the term *perfect team play* could ever be applied to one ball club, it was the 2005 White Sox. The Sox occupied first place wire to wire for the first time in team history, building a 15 1/2 game lead in early August, making a legion of skeptics into true believers but earning little attention from the national media. The team did falter late in the season, but fended off a late-season rush by the Cleveland Indians to capture the Central Division. This helped relax the squad, which played self-assured baseball throughout the postseason.

The real litmus test was against the elite of the AL. The Boston Red Sox, old, slow, and weakened by free-agent losses, were easily swept away in the ALDS. The Los Angeles Angels, a more formidable opponent who closely mirrored the grinder style, put up a tougher fight and handed the Sox their only postseason defeat. In the Fall Classic, the Houston Astros managed to keep the games close, but White Sox pitching stifled their aging "Killer Bs" (Biggio,

Chicago White Sox players singing "Don't Stop Believin'" after winning the World Series in 2005. © AP / Wide World Photos

Bagwell, and Berkman) while the grinders came through in clutch situations in such a way that caused Sox fans to rub their eyes in astonished disbelief. A four-game sweep, and no one, least of all the South Side fandom, could believe it. "Who are these guys?" The question was asked even as the motorcade of World Champions wound its way past thousands of cheering spectators in Chicago's first downtown ticker-tape parade in many a year.

For the moment, no one dared look beyond 2005. Curses, being what they are, sometimes come back. The ominous thought was inescapable. But following this one joyous season, it was time to reflect back on the significance of the White Sox's storied past; the team's perseverance against formidable odds and its visible and enduring embodiment in the historic Bridgeport neighborhood of Chicago must never be separated from its current and future destiny, whatever that future may hold.

NOTABLE ACHIEVEMENTS

Most Valuable Players

Year	Name	Position
1959	Nellie Fox	2B
1972	Dick Allen	1B
1993	Frank Thomas	1B
1994	Frank Thomas	1B

Cy Young Winners

Year	Name	Position
1959	Early Wynn	RHP
1983	La Marr Hoyt	RHP
1993	Jack McDowell	RHP

Rookies of the Year

Year	Name	Position
1956	Luis Aparicio	SS
1963	Gary Peters	P
1966	Tommie Agee	OF
1983	Ron Kittle	OF
1985	Ozzie Guillen	SS

Batting Champions

Year	Name	#
1936	Luke Appling	.388
1943	Luke Appling	.328
1997	Frank Thomas	.347

Home-Run Champions

Year	Name	#
1971	Bill Melton	33
1972	Dick Allen	37
1974	Dick Allen	32

ERA Champions

Year	Name	#
1906	Doc White	1.52
1907	Ed Walsh	1.60
1910	Ed Walsh	1.27
1917	Eddie Cicotte	1.53
1921	Red Faber	2.48
1922	Red Faber	2.80
1941	Thornton Lee	2.37
1942	Ted Lyons	2.10
1947	Joe Haynes	2.42
1951	Saul Rogovin	2.48
1955	Billy Pierce	1.97
1960	Frank Baumann	2.67

1963	Gary Peters	2.33
1966	Gary Peters	1.98
1967	Joe Horlen	2.06

Strikeout Champions

Year	Name	#
1908	Ed Walsh	269
1909	Frank Smith	177
1911	Ed Walsh	255
1953	Billy Pierce	186
1958	Early Wynn	179
2003	Esteban Loaiza	207

No-Hitters (Italics = Perfect Game)

Name	Date
Nixey Callahan	09/20/1902
Frank Smith	09/06/1905
Frank Smith	09/20/1908
Ed Walsh	08/27/1911
Joe Benz	05/31/1914
Eddie Cicotte	04/14/1917
Charlie Robertson	*04/30/1922*
Ted Lyons	08/21/1926
Vern Kennedy	08/31/1935
Bill Dietrich	06/01/1937
Bob Keegan	08/20/1957
Joe Horlen	09/10/1967
Joe Cowley	09/19/1986
Wilson Alvarez	08/11/1991

POSTSEASON APPEARANCES

AL West Division Titles

Year	Record	Manager
1983	99–63	Tony LaRussa
1993	94–68	Gene Lamont

AL Central Division Titles

Year	Record	Manager
1994	67–46	Gene Lamont
2000	95–67	Jerry Manuel
2005	99–63	Ozzie Guillen

AL Pennants

Year	Record	Manager
1901	83–53	Clark Griffith
1906	93–58	Fielder Jones
1917	100–54	Pants Rowland
1919	88–52	Kid Gleason
1959	94–60	Al Lopez
2005	99–63	Ozzie Guillen

World Championships

Year	Opponent	MVP
1906	Chicago	
1917	New York	
2005	Houston	Jermaine Dye

MANAGERS

2004–	Ozzie Guillen
1998–2003	Jerry Manuel
1995–1997	Terry Bevington
1992–1995	Gene Lamont
1989–1991	Jeff Torborg
1986–1989	Jim Fregosi
1986	Doug Rader
1979–1986	Tony LaRussa
1979	Don Kessinger
1978	Larry Doby
1977–1978	Bob Lemon
1976	Paul Richards
1970–1975	Chuck Tanner
1970	Bill Adair
1969–1970	Don Gutterridge
1968–1969	Al Lopez
1968	Les Moss
1966–1968	Eddie Stanky
1957–1965	Al Lopez
1954–1956	Marty Marion
1951–1954	Paul Richards
1951	Red Corriden
1949–1951	Jack Onslow
1946–1948	Ted Lyons

1934–1946	Jimmie Dykes
1932–1934	Lew Fonseca
1930–1931	Donie Bush
1928–1929	Lena Blackburne
1927–1928	Ray Schalk
1924–1926	Eddie Collins
1924	Ed Walsh
1924	Johnny Evers
1919–1923	Kid Gleason
1915–1918	Pants Rowland
1912–1914	Nixey Callahan
1910–1911	Hugh Duffy
1909	Billy Sullivan
1904–1908	Fielder Jones
1903–1904	Nixey Callahan
1901–1902	Clark Griffith

Team Records by Individual Players

Batting Leaders

	Single Season			Career		
	Name		**Year**	**Name**		**Plate Appearances**
Batting average	Luke Appling	.388	1936	Joe Jackson	.340	2,797
On-base %	Frank Thomas	.487	1994	Frank Thomas	.427	8,602
Slugging %	Frank Thomas	.729	1994	Frank Thomas	.568	8,602
OPS	Frank Thomas	1.217	1994	Frank Thomas	.995	8,602
Games	Don Buford	163	1966	Luke Appling	2,422	10,243
At bats	Nellie Fox	649	1956	Luke Appling	8,856	10,243
Runs	Johnny Mostil	135	1925	Luke Appling	1,319	10,243
Hits	Eddie Collins	224	1920	Luke Appling	2,749	10,243
Total bases	Albert Belle	399	1998	Frank Thomas	3,949	8,602
Doubles	Albert Belle	48	1996	Frank Thomas	447	8,602
Triples	Joe Jackson	21	1916	Shano Collins	104	5,307
Home runs	Albert Belle	49	1998	Frank Thomas	448	8,602
RBIs	Albert Belle	152	1998	Frank Thomas	1,465	8,602
Walks	Frank Thomas	138	1991	Frank Thomas	1,466	8,602
Strikeouts	Dave Nicholson	175	1963	Frank Thomas	1,165	8,602
Stolen bases	Rudy Law	77	1983	Eddie Collins	368	7,405
Extra-base hits	Albert Belle	99	1998	Frank Thomas	906	8,602
Times on base	Frank Thomas	317	1991	Luke Appling	4,062	10,243

Pitching Leaders

	Single Season			Career		
	Name		Year	Name		Innings Pitched
ERA	Ed Walsh	1.27	1910	Ed Walsh	1.81	2,946.3
Wins	Ed Walsh	40	1908	Ted Lyons	260	4,161
Won-loss %	Sandy Consuegra	.842	1954	Lefty Williams	.648	1,156
Hits/9 IP	Ed Walsh	5.89	1910	Hoyt Wilhelm	6.19	675.7
Walks/9 IP	La Marr Hoyt	1.07	1983	Nick Altrock	1.49	1,340
Strikeouts	Ed Walsh	269	1908	Billy Pierce	1,796	2,931
Strikeouts/ 9 IP	Juan Pizarro	8.69	1961	Jason Bere	7.50	551
Games	Wilbur Wood	88	1968	Red Faber	669	4,086.7
Saves	Bobby Thigpen	57	1990	Bobby Thigpen	201	541.7
Innings	Ed Walsh	464	1908	Ted Lyons	4,161	4,161
Starts	Ed Walsh	49	1908	Ted Lyons	4,84	4,161
Complete games	Ed Walsh	42	1908	Ted Lyons	356	4,161
Shutouts	Ed Walsh	11	1908	Ed Walsh	57	2,946.3

Source: Drawn from data in "Chicago White Sox Batting Leaders (seasonal and career)." http://baseball-reference.com/ teams/CHW/leaders_bat.shtml; "Chicago White Sox Pitching Leaders (seasonal and career)." http://baseball-reference. com/teams/CHW/leaders_pitch.shtml.

BIBLIOGRAPHY

Allen, Dick, and Tim Whitaker. *Crash: The Life and Times of Dick Allen.* New York: Ticknor and Fields, 1989.

Asinof, Eliot. *Eight Men Out: The Black Sox and the 1919 World Series.* New York: Holt, Reinhart and Winston, 1963.

Axelson, Gustav. *Commy: The Life Story of Charles A. Comiskey, The Grand Old Roman of Baseball and Nineteen Years the President and Owner of the Chicago White Sox.* Chicago: Reilly and Lee, 1919.

Berke, Art. *This Date in Chicago White Sox History.* New York: Stein and Day, 1982.

Brown, Warren. *The Chicago White Sox.* New York: G. P. Putnam's Sons, 1952.

Condon, David. *The Go-Go Chicago White Sox.* New York: Coward-McCann, 1960.

Dykes, James J., and Charles Deeter, eds. *You Can't Steal First Base.* Philadelphia: Lippincott, 1967.

Gough, David, and Jim Bard. *Little Nel: The Nellie Fox Story; An Up-Close and Personal Look at Baseball's "Mighty Mite."* Alexandria, VA: D. L. Megbec Publishing, 2000.

Helpingstine, Dan. *Through Hope and Despair: A Fan's Memories of the Chicago White Sox, 1967–1997*. Highland, IN: self-published, 2001.

Lindberg, Richard. *Sox: The Complete Record of Chicago White Sox Baseball*. New York: Macmillan, 1984.

———. *Stealing First in a Two Team Town: the White Sox from Comiskey to Reinsdorf*. Champaign, IL: Sagamore Publishing, 1994.

———. *Stuck on the Sox*. Evanston, IL: Sassafras Press, 1978.

———. *The White Sox Encyclopedia*. Philadelphia: Temple University Press, 1997.

———. *Who's on Third? The Chicago White Sox Story*. South Bend, IN: Icarus Press, 1983.

Logan, Robert. *Miracle on 35th Street: Winnin' Ugly with the 1983 White Sox*. South Bend, IN: Icarus Press, 1983.

Luhrs, Victor. *The Great Baseball Mystery: The 1919 World Series*. Cranbury, NJ: A.S. Barnes, 1966.

Minoso, Minnie, with Herb Fagen. *Just Call Me Minnie: My Six Decades in Baseball*. Champaign, IL: Sagamore Publishing, 1994.

Moore, Joseph Thomas. *Pride Against Prejudice: The Biography of Larry Doby*. Westport, CT: Praeger, 1988.

Spirou, Costas, and Larry Bennett. *It's Hardly Sportin': Stadiums, Neighborhoods, and the New Chicago*. DeKalb: Northern Illinois University Press, 2003.

Stein, Irving. *The Ginger Kid: The Buck Weaver Story*. Dubuque, IA: Elysian Fields Press, 1992.

Vanderberg, Robert. *'59 Summer of the Sox*. Champaign, IL: Sports Publishing, 1999.

———. *From Lane and Fain to Zisk and Fisk*. Chicago: Chicago Review Press, 1982.

———. *Minnie and the Mick: The Go-Go White Sox Challenge the Fabled Yankee Dynasty, 1951–1964*. South Bend, IN: Diamond, 1996.

Veeck, William. *The Hustler's Handbook*. New York: Putnam Sons, 1965.

Veeck, William, and Ed Linn. *Veeck—as in Wreck*. New York: Putnam, 1962.

Ward, Arch. *The New Chicago White Sox*. Chicago: Henry Regnery, 1951.

Cleveland Indians

Philip C. Suchma

In over a century of existence, Cleveland's American League franchise (known as the Indians since the 1915 season) has ridden a roller coaster of extreme highs and lows, successes and failures. The year 2001 marked the centennial of the founding of the AL, of which Cleveland was a charter member, while 2004 marked 50 years since the Indians won a then AL record of 111 regular-season games (only to be swept by the New York Giants in the 1954 World Series) and 10 years since the opening of Jacobs Field. These anniversaries celebrated the moment in question and served as a benchmark for new eras in the team's history. The year 1954 culminated what some have called the golden era of Cleveland baseball: two AL pennants (1948 and 1954), one World Series title (1948), and numerous Hall of Fame performers on the team's rosters (names like Feller, Lemon, Boudreau, and Doby). What followed was the beginning of the franchise's decline and 40 years of baseball misery. Finally, 1994 and the opening of Jacobs Field reunited Cleveland and its baseball fans with a successful Indians franchise and a new golden era. Four decades of losing games and future stars and franchise instability gave way to two AL pennants and six playoff appearances in seven years before small-market economics caught up with the Indians. The symbolism of these events, however, tells only a portion of the story of the Cleveland Indians. Changes in ownership, issues of ballpark construction, aspects of financing and advertising, and recurring threats of franchise relocation shed light on the Indians' pattern of growth and decline that mirrors those experienced by the city of Cleveland itself.

CLEVELAND

The existence of a financially stable baseball franchise with a supportive fan base on the shores of Lake Erie was made possible by the powerful transformation the city began undergoing in the late nineteenth century as a result of the economic turn toward heavy industry and a second wave of immigration from southern and eastern Europe. Booms in Cleveland's population and industry accompanied each other as the city grew at accelerated rates during the first three decades of the twentieth century. Cleveland rose to prominence as an American center of industry and by the mid-1920s was the nation's fifth-largest city and third-largest metropolitan area, and looked to challenge Chicago as the economic and cultural capital of the Midwest and New York as the sporting capital of the America. The onset of the Great Depression stunted the city's growth and adversely changed such outlooks. Cleveland began spiraling into a decline from which some say the city is still struggling to escape. World War II and the need to produce war equipment and munitions provided a respite for Cleveland's industrial economy, but despite wartime efforts to prepare the city for postwar changes, Cleveland unsuccessfully adapted to an emerging postindustrial American economy.

The city's population in 1950 was over 900,000, but it drastically decreased in ensuing decades due to suburban sprawl, "white flight," and the relocation of jobs to the Sunbelt. Like many other midwestern and northeastern cities that had been America's chief centers of industry and culture, Cleveland transformed into a rust-belt city. In 1978 Cleveland reached its nadir when it went into default—the first major American city to do so since the depression. A brief reprieve came during the renaissance of the early 1990s with the revitalization of the downtown area, but the city's troubles continue to this day. Through it all, the Indians have sputtered along in unison with the ups and downs of the city. Taking the good with the bad, however, the Indians' baseball tradition has yielded multiple moments and characters that continue to reassert baseball's value in Cleveland's sporting culture and the team's place as a civic institution.

NEW TEAM IN A NEW LEAGUE

Cleveland served as the home to several professional baseball teams in numerous leagues during the latter half of the nineteenth century. The Forest City Baseball Club was an amalgamation of amateurs and a few professional ballplayers. In 1869 the team played the first professional game in Cleveland's history, and two years later joined the National Association of Professional Base Ball Players. The most prominent of the early professional teams was the Cleveland Spiders, who began play in 1887 and joined the National League in 1889. The Spiders played their home games in League Park starting in 1891. The park was located on Cleveland's east side at the corner of Lexington and

East 66th. Team owner and streetcar executive Frank DeHaas Robison picked this location because it intersected two of his trolley lines. Fans were dropped off 20 feet from the ballpark's entrance. The link between transportation firms and baseball was strong in the nineteenth century, with approximately 15 percent of baseball owners having ties to the transit industry. The park opened in 1891 to a sellout crowd of 9,000 fans who saw Cy Young and the Spiders beat Cincinnati. In 1895 the Spiders finished second in the regular season and qualified for the Temple Cup Series, where they defeated Baltimore four games to one to win the championship.

In subsequent seasons the Spiders' stability increasingly came into question, and declining attendance and a perceived loss of fan loyalty angered Spiders' owner Robison. In 1899 he reacted by purchasing an NL franchise in St. Louis and looked to terminate his connections to Cleveland baseball. Unable to find a buyer for the Spiders, Robison transferred the team's most talented players, including Cy Young and Jesse Burkett, to his St. Louis team (soon to be known as the Cardinals) before the 1899 season. Attendance in Cleveland suffered with the gutting of the Spiders. Only 500 fans attended the Opening Day doubleheader in 1899, and small crowds continued as the season progressed. Robison set a July 1 deadline for attendance to improve or have the remaining games played elsewhere. A few games were played in Cleveland following the deadline thanks to a small increase in attendance, but the Spiders eventually deserted the city and played the rest of season on the road. The Spiders performed terribly, winning 20 games and losing 134 in 1899. About 6,000 fans came to watch Spider home games that year. The disaster came to an end when the NL subsequently dropped the franchise along with those in Baltimore, Louisville, and Washington in an effort to shrink the league.

The loss of the Spiders left the city without professional baseball and seemed to signal an end to future hopes for a Cleveland baseball team. The opening of the Cleveland market with the NL's departure, however, provided a new opportunity that would prove most beneficial in the long run. Western League president Byron "Ban" Johnson had hoped to expand into new, larger markets and challenge the NL for major-league status. Cleveland, now an uncontested territory, joined that league in 1900. Johnson had originally sought out Cleveland banker and former Spiders secretary Davis Hawley to run the new team. He refused the offer, but introduced Johnson to clothier John F. Kilfoyl, who became team president and treasurer, and coal magnate Charles Somers, who was made vice president.

Johnson's revamped Western League existed as a minor league in 1900, during which time it took further steps toward eventual major-league status. Johnson wanted to move into the Chicago market, which was controlled by the NL, and was forced to make concessions, which included reimbursing the NL for improvements made to Cleveland's League Park by the previous owners.

Charles Somers, a millionaire by age 31, was not only the key financial figure in the franchise, but also a primary financial contributor to the young league.

The stability of the new AL and competition with the NL rested heavily on Somers's financial backing. He bankrolled Charles Comiskey's new Chicago franchise and ballpark in 1900, financed new AL franchises in Philadelphia and Boston in 1901, and financially supported the new St. Louis franchise after it moved from Milwaukee in 1902. In the process Somers contributed nearly $1 million to strengthen the new league, and more importantly, stabilized the landscape for his investment in a Cleveland team. His financial generosity guarded his investment by stabilizing the AL.

The Cleveland Blues (named for their bright blue uniforms) finished seventh among the eight teams in the AL during its inaugural season, and drew 131,380 fans in 136 games. Given the past failures of Cleveland baseball teams, most notably the Spiders and their 134-loss season, fielding a successful team and gaining a public following was essential to the new club's success. Somers and Kilfoyl were willing to spend to improve their team. When Philadelphia's Athletics (AL) and Phillies (NL) became embroiled in a legal battle over the services of star second baseman Napoleon Lajoie and pitcher William Bern-hard, the Athletics' Connie Mack transferred Lajoie and later traded Bernhard to Cleveland when it became clear that they could not play for him. Mack's actions were viewed as repayment for the financial assistance Somers gave the Athletics in their inaugural season as much as a way to spite the Phillies. Playing for the renamed Cleveland Bronchos in 1902, Bernhard posted a record of 17–5 and Lajoie batted .379 in 86 games. Attendance grew to 275,395 that season. The new second baseman quickly became the star attraction in Cleveland, and prior to the 1903 season the team was renamed the Naps in conjunction with a fan contest in the *Cleveland Press.*

The addition of Lajoie marked one of several key signings that helped cement the place of professional baseball in the city's sporting culture. Prior to the 1902 season the team signed Addie Joss from the Toledo Mud Hens of the Western Association, where he had won 25 games. After the season he was pursued by Charles Ebbets of the Brooklyn Dodgers as well as Charles Strobel, owner of the Mud Hens, who wanted to retain his star pitcher, but Cleveland offered Joss a $500 signing bonus and promised to protect him from any legal problems he might encounter from jumping leagues. In nine seasons Joss compiled a record of 160–97 with a career ERA of 1.89. But he contracted tubercular meningitis and died on April 11, 1911, at the age of 31. On May 24, a benefit game was played to raise money for Joss's widow. In a tribute to Joss's popularity among his peers, AL stars such as Walter Johnson, Ty Cobb, Frank "Home Run" Baker, and Tris Speaker played against Cleveland, and raised over $13,000. This tragedy marked the first of several deaths and injuries that would haunt the Cleveland franchise over the next century.

The popularity of baseball in Cleveland and improvements in ballpark safety and design led Somers to renovate League Park following the 1909 season, increasing seating capacity from 9,000 to 21,000. These renovations coincided with a national movement that saw construction and renovation projects modernize ballparks in many cities. A concrete and steel foundation replaced League Park's pavilion and wooden grandstands. Box seats were added in addition to the benches used for general admission. New bleachers were built along the left-field foul line, and the old wooden fence in left field was replaced by one made of 20 feet of concrete topped with 20 feet of screen. Architect Frank B. Meade of the Cleveland-based Osborn Engineering Company directed the rush job, which began soon after the season ended. The renovation project marked the beginning of Osborn Engineering's involvement with stadia and ballparks, which included the construction of Fenway Park, Yankee Stadium, and Cleveland's Municipal Stadium. Hunkin Brothers Company and Forest City Steel and Iron Company handled construction. The cost was approximately $325,000. The newly renovated League Park was a statement of the popularity and permanence of professional baseball as an integral part of a modern city across American and in Cleveland.

At the start of the 1908 season, Somers declined a trade proposal from Detroit that would have brought a young Ty Cobb to Cleveland and sent an aging Elmer Flick to the Tigers. Cobb's cantankerous demeanor was wearing thin on Detroit manager Hugh Jennings and the rest of the Tigers. Somers, not wanting to disturb his team by inserting Cobb in the locker room, declined. Cleveland finished half a game behind Detroit, which did not have to make up a rainout against Washington. Even though a Tigers loss would have impacted the final standings and sent Cleveland to the World Series, there were no league rules requiring a team to make up a rainout game. It would be another decade before Cleveland would find itself in such a pennant chase.

Over the next few years poor play, feuding, and financial problems haunted the franchise. Kilfoyl left the team for health reasons following the stressful finish to the 1908 season. Somers, always the financial power in the franchise, now stepped up to the position of president. E. S. Barnard, the Naps' traveling secretary since 1904, became the vice president and eventually was named general manager. Over the next five seasons the Naps never finished better than third (1911 and 1913) or nine and a half games back of first place (1913), and in 1914 they finished last. Nap Lajoie requested and was granted a trade following the 1914 season after feuding with the team's manager. In 13 seasons in Cleveland,

Cy Young's baseball card, 1911. Courtesy of the Library of Congress

Lajoie batted .339 and won two batting titles. Cleveland lost its star and its namesake. More importantly, Somers experienced significant financial troubles. On August 20, 1915, Cleveland traded outfielder Joe Jackson to the Chicago White Sox for a reported $31,500 and three players. Jackson batted .375 while in Cleveland, and set team records for highest season average (.408), most hits (233), and most triples (26). Somers parted with the talented "Shoeless" Joe to restore some financial solvency, but still found himself $1,750,000 in debt by 1916, victimized by bad real-estate investments, decreased coal-industry profits, and dwindling attendance in baseball. The banks issued Somers an ultimatum: sell the team or lose his coal industry and nonbaseball businesses. Somers turned to Ban Johnson, who located a buyer for the franchise with Comiskey's aid. In February 1916 Chicago businessman James Dunn and a group of investors including Johnson and Comiskey purchased the Indians for $500,000.

Lajoie's departure had left Cleveland in need of a new nickname. In 1915 the team was renamed the Indians. For decades, newspaper accounts, popular histories of the team, and the franchise's official media guide perpetuated the myth of how the franchise chose that nickname. Supposedly the team was named "Indians" after a fan submitted the name in a newspaper contest held after Lajoie's departure, to honor Louis Sockalexis, a Penobscot who played outfield with the Spiders from 1897 to 1899. In truth, Somers organized a committee of baseball writers to choose the new name. Newspaper reports from January 1915 announced that the committee had decided upon "Indians" as the new name, although it was initially given only temporary status. The baseball franchise kept the name, and it has been used since.

The sale of the Indians to Dunn injected new life into Cleveland baseball. The team remedied the loss of Joe Jackson in the outfield by trading for Boston's Tris Speaker in 1916. Speaker had batted .322 and helped lead the Red Sox to a World Series title in 1915. During the off-season he anticipated a raise. When Boston refused to give him one, Speaker demanded a trade. Ed Bang, sports editor of the *Cleveland News*, made Indians general manager Bob McRoy aware of Speaker's trade demand and told him that Red Sox owner Joe Lannin would sell any player if offered enough money. McRoy and Lannin agreed to send Speaker to Cleveland for two players and $55,000, but Speaker balked at coming to Cleveland, which he considered a bad baseball town with a bad team. Only after receiving $10,000 of the purchase price from Boston (given at the insistence of Ban Johnson) did Speaker agree to come to Cleveland. He won the AL batting title (.386) in his first season with the Indians, but the team still finished in seventh place. Over the next three seasons the Indians developed into a challenger for the AL pennant. Stanley Coveleski and Jim Bagby anchored the pitching staff while Speaker and shortstop Ray Chapman led the offense. Speaker also took over as manager midway through the 1919 season. The Indians finished second to the Chicago White Sox by three and a half games that year, but made strides in putting together a well-rounded team that would contend in 1920.

The Indians had finished second in 1918 and 1919, each time losing the AL pennant in the final week of the season. In 1920 they overcame challenges from the White Sox and New York Yankees to win the AL by two games. Bagby led the AL in wins (31) and Coveleski led the AL in strikeouts (133), while posting 24 wins. Speaker batted .388, one of six regulars to hit over .300. The Indians' offense led the AL in runs, RBIs, doubles, triples, and walks. Cleveland set a new team record for season attendance as 912,849 fans turned out in support. The celebration of Indians' first pennant was tempered by the tragic death of Ray Chapman in a game against the Yankees at the Polo Grounds. On August 16 Chapman's skull was fractured when a Carl Mays pitch hit him on the left temple. Chapman died the next day, the only major-league player to die from injuries sustained in the course of a game. Future Hall of Famer Joe Sewell took over shortstop duties, and hit .322 over the final 22 games of the 1920 season.

In its 20th season the Cleveland Indians franchise made it to the World Series, playing the Brooklyn Dodgers in the best-of-nine contest. Cleveland defeated Brooklyn five games to two, including a memorable game five in which three Indians recorded three World Series firsts: Bill Wambsganss turned the first unassisted triple play, Elmer Smith hit the first grand slam, and Jim Bagby became the first pitcher to hit a home run.

A COG IN THE "CITY OF CHAMPIONS"

Following the World Series championship of 1920, the Indians sank back into mediocrity over the next two decades. Hopes for the 1921 AL pennant were crushed when Wambsganss and Speaker suffered season-ending injuries late in the campaign. Between 1921 and 1947, the Indians finished less than 10 games back only three times, and consequently attendance hovered around 500,000 for much of that time. The Indians were also a middle-of-the-pack franchise in terms of revenue. In the exciting 1920 and 1921 seasons, the team made a total of $603,916. Then, from 1922 to 1945, the Indians surpassed $100,000-a-year profits seven times, but also lost money on seven occasions, including five of six years from 1927 to 1933. The phenomenal growth and prosperity of Cleveland through the 1920s encouraged thoughts of grandeur. Cleveland's civic leaders and sports-minded fans, despite the Indians' shortcomings, envisioned a regional and national prominence for their city. Civic leaders envisioned a new downtown of modern buildings that provided beauty and function in the Progressive tradition. Instead of an amalgamation of derelict buildings, with several civic institutions housed in rented structures, there would be a new downtown, planned by the incorporation of urban planner Daniel Burnham's Group Plan of 1903 that designed and organized public buildings and open space for leisure. All that was lacking from completing the plan was the vacant northern foot of land along the shores of Lake Erie, where City Manager William Hopkins and the Cleveland Indians hoped to build a new ballpark.

The idea of placing a stadium on the shores of Lake Erie originated nearly a decade earlier. Plans were proposed to house high-school football and other sports but were never acted on. Only when the city and the Indians joined together did the concept gain enough influence for serious consideration. Cleveland's rapid growth in the 1920s inspired civic and business leaders to push for greater urban development. League Park, located on the city's east side, was neither centrally located nor large enough to meet visions of baseball's continued popularity. Discussions between Hopkins, E. S. Barnard, and Ed Bang of the *News* between 1926 and 1927 helped determine that Cleveland would build a municipally owned stadium with the Indians being the primary tenant. Barnard had been running the Indians for Edith Dunn, Jimmy Dunn's widow, since June 1922, and was under orders to locate a buyer for the team. Barnard believed local ownership was all that was needed to make the stadium a certainty. In November 1927 a syndicate of local owners with real-estate tycoon Alva Bradley serving as president purchased the Indians for $1 million. The city then began preparations to construct the stadium on lakefront landfill.

The arguments surrounding the bond issue and construction of a municipal stadium for the Indians foreshadowed debates over ballpark, stadium, and arena construction that linger to this day. Stadium supporters argued that the facility would host a variety of sporting and nonsporting events benefiting all citizens and not just baseball fans. Bradley himself drew considerable public support for building the stadium by promising the Indians would play there, but he did not sign a lease beforehand. Opponents, who were given little coverage in the local papers, correctly feared the facility was being built by the city for the Indians and that it would never pay off the bonds, becoming a white elephant on the shores of Lake Erie. The city's black press also argued against the bond issue by pointing out that city funds should not be used as long as black ballplayers could not play in the AL. After the city council approved the idea of building a municipal stadium, residents voted on a $2.5 million bond issue to fund the construction. On November 6, 1928, nearly 60 percent approved the bond issue.

Construction was delayed by a lawsuit brought by Cleveland resident Andrew Meyer, who claimed the city did not automatically possess the rights to land created through fill. Meyer's suit also argued the stadium was being built for the Indians' benefit and was therefore not a lawful municipal act. The case went to the Ohio Supreme Court, which ruled in favor of the city government in January 1930. Legal tangles resolved, construction commenced on the proposed 80,000-seat facility. In the meantime Bradley, who had verbally agreed to gradually move Indians' home games from League Park to Municipal Stadium, wanted the new stadium to be a means of strengthening his franchise on the field and making it a bigger entertainment draw. He sought, unsuccessfully, to acquire superstars Lou Gehrig and Rogers Hornsby, which showed a desire by Indians management to build a winning franchise that would draw fans.

The $3 million Cleveland Municipal Stadium had a $500,000 cost overrun because of construction delays, effects of the Great Depression, and rising costs of materials. It opened with much fanfare and pageantry and was described as a monument to the people of Cleveland. Its first sporting event was a heavyweight boxing match between champion Max Schmeling and Willie Stribling on July 3, 1931. The Indians still had not signed a lease with the city. Despite the presence of boxing, concerts, and other large gatherings Municipal Stadium did indeed become the white elephant opponents of the bond issue feared it would become without baseball.

Beginning in June 1931 local papers reported on the ongoing negotiations between the Indians and Cleveland. City officials wanted the Indians to pay a base rent of between $80,000 and $85,000 to cover the cost of the bonds, agree to pay the city 15 percent of paid receipts over $600,000, and sign a 25-year lease to ensure the stadium's use. Bradley and the Indians counteroffered a $50,000 base rental, 15 percent of paid receipts over $750,000, and a shorter lease in case they could not draw crowds in the huge facility. One local editorial called the Indians offer "adequate but not generous" and argued that Bradley should get some leeway since he did make the Indians a "Cleveland owned" team again. Hopes the Indians would play their inaugural game in the stadium in 1931 went unrealized as the team refused to sign a lease and continued to play home games in League Park. Newly elected mayor Ray T. Miller began face-to-face negotiations with Bradley at the start of 1932. Shortly after the start of the baseball season, the two sides reached agreement on a temporary lease that gave both the Indians and the city the ability to terminate the lease after the 1932, 1933, or 1934 season.

The Indians, with the lease now signed, christened Cleveland Municipal Stadium on July 31, 1932. Mel Harder lost to Lefty Grove and the Philadelphia Athletics 1–0 in front of 80,184 fans. Bradley was excited by the huge crowd and had 32 of the Indians 54 remaining home games scheduled for Municipal Stadium. He envisioned a continuance of large crowds since downtown workers could walk from their jobs to the stadium. The splendor of the first game, however, was hardly the norm. By 1933 attendance at Municipal Stadium fell to an average of roughly 6,000 per game. Such sparse crowds seemed even smaller given the facility's cavernous size. A despondent Bradley terminated the temporary lease with the city in October 1933 and moved the Indians back to League Park on a full-time basis for 1934, 1935, and all but one game in 1936. In a letter to Mayor Miller, Bradley justified his move through a comparison of a similar number of games at Municipal Stadium and League Park over the 1932 and 1933 seasons, which showed that the Indians were losing attendance and money at the new stadium. Specifically, in 91 games at Municipal Stadium the Indians drew 529,340 fans (an average of 5,817 per game) and made $338,228.94 (an average of $3,716.80 per game). In a similar number of games at League Park the Indians drew 663,407 fans (6,960 per game) and made $487,853.89 ($5,361.03 per game). During the 1933 season, Bradley forbade radio broadcasts of Indians games out of a belief that they were partly responsible for the decline in attendance. The optimism the Cleveland owner held in his first few years of ownership gave way to the realities of a mediocre team in troubled economic market.

Several players stood out during Bradley's ownership. Outfielder Earl Averill was a skilled batter who represented the Indians in six All-Star Games, but fell out of Bradley's favor following a contract holdout after the 1936 season and was traded in 1940. He recorded over 1,000 hits and RBIs as an Indian. Hal Trosky played first base from 1933 to 1941 and was also a .300 hitter with power. Between 1929 and 1932 Wes Ferrell won 20 games each season, but was traded in 1934 while holding out. Pitcher Mel Harder was a workhorse who made four All-Star Game appearances during his 20-year career with the Indians. He won over 15 games in eight straight seasons, twice winning over 20 games in that stretch. Although these Indians stood out from their peers, many players during Bradley's ownership were unspectacular. The Indians commonly finished over 10 games behind the AL pennant winner.

While Bradley's reign as owner of the Indians failed to bring a pennant to Cleveland, it did bring arguably the greatest baseball player in the franchise's history. In 1935 scout C.C. Slapnicka signed a 16-year-old pitcher from Van Meter, Iowa, by the name of Robert Feller. Feller signed a contract with the Indians, receiving an autographed Indians baseball and a one-dollar bonus, and was assigned to Cleveland's Class D farm team in Fargo-Moorehead for the 1936 season. But he never arrived at Fargo. The signing came under the scrutiny of baseball commissioner Kenesaw Mountain Landis for violating contract rules. No player then could be signed directly out of high school or amateur ball by a major-league team because local minor-league teams were given first rights to area talent. Since Feller reported directly to Cleveland, never to Fargo or to New Orleans, where he was later "assigned," the Indians violated this rule and faced the possibility of their young prospect becoming a free agent whom many teams would eagerly sign. To make matters even more interesting, Bill Feller, Bob's father, threatened Landis and MLB with a civil suit if Bob were prevented from re-signing with the Indians. Landis's decision came down in December 1936: the Indians would pay the minor-league Des Moines Demons $7,500 in damages (the amount the Demons were set to offer Feller), but would keep the rights to Feller.

Feller's first major-league start saw him strike out 15 St. Louis Browns on August 23, 1936. He possessed a fearsome fastball that helped him become the most dominant pitcher of his era and earned him the nickname "Rapid Robert." Following his brief appearances at the end of the 1936 season, Feller joined the Indians' rotation on a full-time basis the next year. He led the AL in wins from 1939 to 1941, with a high of 27 in 1940. Feller also led the league in strikeouts from 1938 to 1941, averaging just under 252 per year during those four seasons. On April 16, 1940, he pitched a no-hitter on Opening Day against the Chicago White Sox. Five of his 12 one-hitters came before he enlisted in the

U.S. Navy the day after Pearl Harbor. Feller would spend the next four years on active duty.

In 1940, Feller and several of his teammates were linked to an attempt by the players to have manager Oscar Vitt fired. Vitt's abrasive style wore on many of the players. Their spokesman, Mel Harder, approached Bradley and suggested the Indians would be better off with a new manager. Bradley promised to look into their allegations but took no action. Word of the players' actions leaked to the local press, who labeled the players "the crybaby Indians." The Indians finished one game out of first place.

Freshly discharged from the Marine Corps, Bill Veeck, recent owner of the Milwaukee Brewers of the American Association, assembled a syndicate that sought to purchase a major-league franchise. Pittsburgh and Cleveland were targeted. He turned down the chance to purchase the Pirates for $1.6 million. Setting his sights on Cleveland, Veeck toured the city incognito for four days, talking to locals to get their thoughts on the Indians and baseball, sounding out their feelings toward the current ownership. Finding Clevelanders enthused over the Indians but disenchanted with their owners, Veeck inquired on the price of the franchise. Publicly, Bradley denied rumors of the Indians' sale. Privately, he arranged with ownership syndicate member John Sherwin Jr. to pursue it, but with instructions to not inform Bradley until it was finalized. Veeck offered $2.2 million for the club and worked the financing so he would contribute his own money, like other members of his syndicate, but maximize the potential for reward with his risk. Veeck took out a $1 million loan in the new company's name rather than in his own, and fronted $250,000 of his own money. Veeck also received $18,000, equal to 10 percent of the available stock, as a finder's fee and for putting together the additional investors. In total Veeck wound up with $268,000 worth of stock, equaling a bit more than 30 percent. The next highest stockholder owned 6 percent.

Bradley reportedly did not want sell the Indians to Veeck. He wanted an ownership group with close ties to the city, and he believed Veeck's promotional tactics would undermine baseball in Cleveland and the game in general. Nonetheless, on June 22, 1946, Veeck and his cabal of financial backers became the new owners of the Cleveland Indians. To celebrate the purchase, Veeck went to League Park to mingle with fans in various parts of the park, and watched his new investment defeat Boston 4–3. The *Cleveland Plain Dealer* celebrated the arrival of the new owner, who, while not a Cleveland native, could be expected to spend money and try harder to build a winning team.

Two weeks after Veeck purchased the Indians, team business manager Frank Kohlbecker resigned unexpectedly, apparently disapproving of Veeck's business practices. Veeck's reputation as a showman from his earlier days as owner of the Milwaukee Brewers was well known. He believed it was the team's duty to make itself attractive to its fans rather than expecting the city to blindly support a team.

Veeck followed a three-pronged plan of attack to promote baseball in Cleveland. First, he needed to ensure time spent at Municipal Stadium was entertaining and fun. Second, he stumped for the Indians to the members of any school, church, business, or bar that would listen to him. Third, he needed to put a winning team on the field. With the Indians' season half over at the time of the purchase, he went right to work promoting a sixth-place team to the entire community. Veeck reinstated Ladies' Day and invited radio stations to renew game broadcasts since there was no contract under the previous administration. He also held multiple fireworks displays after night games. One display was so loud that members of the city council wanted Cleveland to terminate the Indians' stadium lease and arrest Veeck. Mayor Thomas A. Burke dismissed the council's charges. Veeck's promotional efforts increased attendance that year, and as a gesture of thanks to Indian fans, he offered free admission to the club's final home game. When the 1946 season ended, the Indians had drawn 1,052,289 fans, a phenomenal figure since Cleveland had never drawn over 1 million fans, and had just 558,182 the year before. The team made over $375,000. Veeck accomplished this feat by moving many remaining home games to spacious Municipal Stadium and reviving interest in the Indians around Cleveland and northeast Ohio. Later promotions like Good Neighbor Night and Good Old Joe Early Day (a tribute to the average fan) continued to add excitement to a day at the stadium. In Veeck's own words, every day in Cleveland was like Mardi Gras, and every fan was a king.

Veeck was pleased with the rise in attendance in 1946, but was unhappy with the team's performance. Feller's stellar 26 wins and 348 strikeouts paced the Indians to a disappointing sixth-place finish, hobbled by a dismal offense. Veeck set out to revamp the roster before the 1947 season. Feller, shortstop Lou Boudreau, and third baseman Ken Keltner were key holdovers. Catcher Jim Hegan, pitcher Bob Lemon, and outfielders Dale Mitchell and Eddie Robinson were important young players. Veeck wanted a championship quickly, and was not content to stand pat or hope that potential would be realized. He started making trades for veteran leadership and key role players. Pitching prospect Allie Reynolds was sent to the Yankees for second baseman Joe Gordon following the 1946 season. Veeck later acquired pitcher Gene Bearden and catcher Al Lopez in trades. The most significant signing of the season, however, came in the shadow of Jackie Robinson.

During the start of the 1947 season, Jackie Robinson's Brooklyn Dodgers and the Negro Leagues' Cleveland Buckeyes received more coverage than the Indians in the city's historic black newspaper, the weekly *Cleveland Call and Post*. Veeck soon had scouts scouring the Negro Leagues looking for a quality player he could bring to the Indians and break the AL color line with. In preparation, he hired African American public-relations man Lou Jones to serve as a traveling companion and mentor for the as-yet-unchosen player. Veeck also informed Cleveland's black leaders of his intent to break the color barrier so they could prepare the black population for any and all situations. Realizing the limited opportunity in making such a move and the intense scrutiny it would be under, Veeck wanted to sign a young player with star potential. Veeck hoped that any criticism of the player would be based in prejudice, not ability, and thereby illegitimate. Even though the Cleveland Browns of the All American Football Conference had already signed African Americans Marion Motley and Bill Willis, Veeck was unsure how Cleveland's baseball fans would react to an integrated team. Cleveland was not as ethnically diverse as New York, and success was therefore uncertain. Based on his criteria, Veeck's scouts recommended the Newark Eagles' talented second baseman Larry Doby.

When Branch Rickey signed Jackie Robinson, he did not compensate the Kansas City Monarchs, his Negro League team. Veeck, on the other hand, offered Newark owner Effa Manley $10,000 for Doby's contract with an additional $5,000 if he made the team. Manley felt that Veeck's offer was low, but felt she should not obstruct the integration of MLB, so she accepted the offer. Doby made his debut with the Indians on July 5, 1947, striking out as a pinch hitter. Some teammates welcomed Doby, but others refused to shake his hand. In his first season he batted .156 in 29 games while coming off the bench. Doby's struggles on the field coincided with problems he faced while traveling. Many hotels were segregated, and opposing fans were often hostile. Veeck later concluded that Doby was probably too sensitive, or not hardened enough, to carry the weight of integrating the AL. Still, Doby emerged as a star in Cleveland. In his first full season he batted .301, hit 14 home runs, and had 66 RBIs in 121 games. This success enabled Veeck to further integrate the team, including the signing of Satchel Paige in 1948. Leroy "Satchel" Paige had long been regarded as one of baseball's most dominant pitchers, but in 1948 he was 42 years old and past his prime. Page was a noted showman because of the antics he had performed on barnstorming tours and his colorful sayings. There were many critics of his signing. However, Paige played a pivotal role in the Indians' drive to the 1948 World Series, compiling a 6–1 record and 2.48 ERA in 21 games as a spot starter and in relief.

The addition of Doby along with others after the 1946 season did not result in a pennant in 1947, but they did help the Indians improve by 12 games and finish in fourth place. Veeck's acquisitions in his first two years combined with holdovers from the Indians' roster to produce a well-rounded team that, with a little luck, could challenge for the AL pennant. Bob Lemon had been a third baseman in the Indians' farm system, but could not unseat Ken Keltner. After showing a strong arm while throwing batting practice, Lemon was converted to a pitcher in 1946 and joined the starting rotation the following year, winning 11 games. Gene Bearden, acquired from the Yankees, won only 29 games in four seasons with the Indians, but 20 of those victories came in 1948. On offense, outfielder Dale Mitchell became a consistent .300 hitter for most of his 11 seasons in Cleveland. The infield was anchored by veteran player-manager Lou Boudreau, a holdover from the Bradley era. Boudreau played a solid shortstop and was a quality hitter from 1938 to 1950. He was joined by second baseman Joe Gordon, acquired from the Yankees after the 1946 season to solidify the middle infield and providing a powerful bat in the lineup.

The year 1948 was a great one for Cleveland sports, beginning with the Cleveland Barons of the American Hockey League winning the Calder Cup championship and ending with the Cleveland Browns of the All America Football Conference winning their third straight league championship and completing an undefeated season. The Indians entered MLB record books by drawing 2,620,627 fans during the city's fabled 1948 regular season. Veeck produced a winner on the field and at the gates. His three-pronged philosophy for marketing the Indians and his belief that you build a team to win in the present and should not become infatuated with the future brought Cleveland its second pennant. Feller, Lemon, and Bearden combined for 59 victories in 1948. The team led the league in scoring. Keltner and Gordon each hit over 30 home runs, Boudreau batted .355 on his way to winning the AL MVP Award, and all three drove in over 100 runs. Mitchell batted .336, Doby .301. The Indians finished the 1948 regular season tied for first with the Boston Red Sox. For the one-game playoff in Fenway Park manager Boudreau selected Bearden to start, to the surprise of many. Bearden and the Indians defeated the Red Sox 8–3, capturing their second AL pennant in franchise history and their first in almost three decades. As the Indians prepared to play the Boston Braves in the World Series, Clevelanders reveled in their moment in the national spotlight. Local papers were able to interject news on the Indians and the forthcoming opportunity to showcase Cleveland into headlines and editorials that were otherwise dominated by the 1948 presidential election and continued Soviet maneuvers regarding Berlin. Mayor Burke called for a massive cleanup campaign in preparation for the city's presentation to visiting baseball's dignitaries, celebrities, and members of the media. Civic leaders presented the 1948 World Series as a showcase where the Indians would prove themselves as the best team in baseball while Cleveland would prove itself as the best city in America.

After fighting past the Red Sox and Yankees to win the AL pennant, the Indians faced a daunting Braves team with five .300 hitters and the pitching combination of Warren Spahn and Johnny Sain, who together won 39 games in the regular season. Indians pitching ace Feller lost 1–0 to Sain in game one in Boston. The game was marked by a controversial missed call on a pickoff attempt that eventually led to the game's only run. The Indians won the next three games behind solid pitching from Lemon and Bearden. Feller lost his second start and a chance to clinch the series in game five in Cleveland in an 11–5 drubbing by the Braves. Lemon and Bearden limited the Braves to three runs in game six in Boston, giving the Indians a 4–3 victory and Cleveland its second World Series championship. With that victory the Indians fulfilled their part in helping Cleveland's professional teams complete their champion trifecta for the year. Local sports journalists and advertisers quickly coined Cleveland "the City of Champions" in honor of its sports heroes. This new title coincided with the "Cleveland: Best Location in the Nation" slogan being used to promote the city in general. Professional sports added to a city's status within the American landscape. Not only did Cleveland know it was home of the World Series champions, but sports fans in New York, Chicago, and elsewhere also would make the connection between the city and sporting success.

Veeck believed that a new ownership group had a three-year window to produce a winning team after taking over a franchise. Two and a half years after purchasing the Indians, he had beaten this self-imposed deadline. But the excitement and fulfillment of a championship did not keep Veeck in Cleveland. Following the 1949 season, only three

Larry Doby, 1949. Courtesy of the Baseball Hall of Fame

and a half years after arriving and reviving the sleeping giant that was Cleveland as a baseball town, Veeck moved out of town. Perhaps the reason was the frustration of the 1949 season, which saw the Indians drop to third, with an 89–65 record; a feeling that the Indians would not be able to beat out the Yankees year after year in the long run; or perhaps a general feeling that the best had come and gone with the 1948 championship. Veeck insisted in his autobiography that his impending divorce with wife Eleanor and a desire to have money available for a settlement was the primary reason for the sale. He and his group sold the Indians for $2.2 million to a group headed by insurance executive Ellis Ryan. Although Veeck's stay in Cleveland was brief, it produced levels of excitement for and celebration of the Indians previously unseen. Popularity spurred profitability, especially in regards to filling Municipal Stadium. Between 1946 and 1950, the team averaged $431,842 a year, peaking at $506,000 in 1949, the year *after* the world championship. For decades after Veeck's departure, especially during the team's struggles and ownership turnover of the 1970s, Cleveland's baseball fans hoped a new Bill Veeck would arrive in town to save the Indians once again.

The 1948 World Series victory marked the beginning of the golden era of Cleveland baseball. Between 1948 and 1959 the Indians possessed dominating pitching staffs and dangerous lineups. As stars from the 1948 squad retired, were traded, or became role players, new talent was infused from the farm system or acquired via trade. Rookies Al Rosen and Luke Easter joined the Indians in 1950. Each drove in over 100 runs, and Rosen set a then record for home runs by a rookie with 37. They combined with Doby to give the Indians a powerful trio until Easter suffered a career-ending injury in 1953. Rosen batted .336 in 1953 and led the AL in runs (115), home runs (43), and RBIs (145), and was the unanimous selection as MVP. Feller was in the twilight of his career in the 1950s, but Early Wynn and Mike Garcia joined Lemon to form the "Big Three" pitching staff. Wynn was acquired from the Washington Senators in December 1948. In 10 seasons with the Indians he won 164 games, winning 20 or more in a season four times. Garcia was a product of the Indians' farm system and went on to a 12-year career in Cleveland that included two 20-win seasons and three All-Star Game appearances. From 1951 to 1956 Al Lopez managed the Indians, compiling a spectacular 570–354 win-loss record. Despite the Indians' outstanding talent, they were eclipsed by the Yankees between 1949 and 1956 every year but one. The Indians won more than 90 games in seven different seasons (coming close with 89 in 1949 and 88 in 1956) during that stretch, yet they only managed to win one more AL pennant, in 1954. The Yankees proved to be their bane, as the Indians finished second to them five times in six years between 1951 and 1956.

The 1954 season was a last hurrah for the Indians, but what a hurrah it was. Winning 111 games, they set an AL record for regular-season wins that stood until 1999. The Big Four pitching staff of Bob Lemon (23–7), Early Wynn (23–11), Mike Garcia (19–8), and Art Houtmann (15–7), who had supplanted Feller (13–3) as the fourth starter, and an offense featuring the powerful bats of Al Rosen and Larry Doby led the Indians into the World Series, where they entered as heavy favorites against the New York Giants. It took only four games, however, for the Giants to sweep the Indians. The unique configuration of the Polo Grounds arguably shifted the outcome of game one, and the momentum in the Giants favor. Dusty Rhodes's home run in the first game took advantage of the short foul lines, and Willie Mays's spectacular back-to-the-plate catch of Vic Wertz's long drive to center could only have happened in the Polo Grounds. Having again prepared for numerous visitors during the World Series, Cleveland's citizens and civic leaders were disappointed by the Indians' loss. After playing second fiddle to the Yankees for so many years, the 1954 team seemed destined for a championship. Rather than dwell on the defeat, the local media professed pride in the Indians' season and proclaimed them winners in the hearts of Clevelanders. The World Series loss, nonetheless, marked a downward shift in Indians baseball. Player movement, both trades and retirements, saw the departure of the likes of Feller and Doby, leaving the club in the care of younger players who were unable to regain pennant-winning form. Feller, a lifelong Indian, finished his Hall of Fame career with a record of 266–162, leading the league in wins six times and strikeouts seven times.

THE CURSE OF COLAVITO

Until their 2004 World Championship, Boston lamented the Curse of the Bambino. Chants of "1908" and reminders of the Billy Goat Curse continue to haunt Chicago Cubs fans. Cleveland had its own, if lesser known, curse tormenting the franchise from 1960 to 1995. Indian teammates Herb Score and Rocco Colavito were roommates on the road and the projected cornerstones of the Indians future. Score was a hard-throwing left-handed pitcher who took the AL by storm in his rookie season in 1955. He won 16 games that year and, more impressively, led the AL with 145 strikeouts, a rookie record. The following season he won 20 games, struck out 263 batters, and posted a 2.53 ERA. Score was an All-Star both seasons. Colavito, after appearing in only 5 games in 1955, played in 101 in his rookie season the following year and belted 21 home runs. The 23-year-old rookie was the Indians' major home-run threat over the next four seasons. More importantly, he represented the ethnic, working-class values many Clevelanders identified with, and emerged as the city's foremost sports idol. Colavito was a handsome, clean-living Italian American whom many of Cleveland's ethnic and working-class residents connected to and admired. Some considered him heir apparent to Joe DiMaggio. Together, Score and Colavito's presence augured a bright future for the Cleveland Indians.

The prosperous future the Indians envisioned with Score and Colavito leading the team into the next decade would not be realized. In a much-hyped series against the New York Yankees in May 1957, a line drive off the bat of Gil McDougald hit Score's eye, inflicting multiple injuries including a broken nose, swelling of the right eye, and a lacerated right eyelid. Score sat out the rest of that season, returning to spring training in 1958, but did not exhibit his prior command or velocity with his pitches. He never returned to form, and after the accident posted a 17–26 record and a 4.48 ERA with the Indians and the Chicago White Sox. The eye injury was commonly cited as the reason for the fall-off, but Score later asserted that it was arm trouble developed early in the 1958 season. Score returned to the Indians in 1964 as part of the team's television broadcasting crew. In 1968 he moved into the radio booth, where he established himself as a Cleveland institution until he retired in 1999.

The Indians lost the AL pennant to the "Go-Go" White Sox by five games in 1959, though many felt a pennant was only a matter of time, largely because Colavito had developed into one of the AL's premier power hitters, having belted 42 home runs with 111 RBIs that year. General manager Frank Lane, otherwise known as "Trader" Lane for his propensity to make deals, was unsatisfied with Colavito's performance. He previously had two separate deals in place to trade Colavito and once tried to interest the Yankees in swapping Mickey Mantle for the Cleveland slugger, all to no avail. Lane and Colavito had also butted heads during yearly contract negotiations, out of which came Colavito's contention that Lane was a liar. Lane blasted Colavito as a selfish player whose preoccupation with hitting home runs was costing the Indians games. He even inserted a clause in Colavito's contract for the 1960 season that rewarded the slugger for hitting *fewer* than 30 home runs in an attempt to increase run production through a higher batting average. The issue became a moot point when Lane shocked Colavito, the Indians and its ownership, and most especially Cleveland's baseball fans by trading the 26-year-old outfielder to Detroit for Harvey Kuenn just one day before the start of the 1960 season. The loss of Colavito drew the ire of thousands, who flooded the local press with letters of complaint and demands for Lane's firing. Similar sentiment was expressed on signs hung at Municipal Stadium during the season's first series, ironically against Detroit. The Indians went from pennant contenders in 1959 to a fourth-place finish in 1960, and finished fifth and sixth in the following two seasons. The loss of the beloved Colavito and the Indians' new misfortunes stirred speculation that the trade cursed the franchise. A generation passed with the Indians finishing better than .500 only six times and never finishing higher than fourth place, and with attendance dropping below 1 million for 18 of the next 20 years. The correlation of the two lent further credence to the validity of the Curse of Colavito.

Between 1949 and 1972 the Indians' ownership group constantly shuffled themselves. Unlike the winning Veeck years, these new groups were marked by failure on the field and at the gate. Even during the team's 111-win season in 1954, concerns about fan attendance and the Indians' financial state were already intensifying. The Indians also had 11 different managers filter in and out of the dugout from Lopez's departure in 1956 to 1972. The managerial scene took a weird turn in 1960 when Frank Lane traded manager Joe Gordon to Detroit for their manager, Jimmie Dykes. The Indians' roster was haunted by the same instability from season to season. From 1950 to 1980 the Indians traded away many promising prospects or players in their prime, including Colavito, Mickey Vernon, Early Wynn, Norm Cash, Hoyt Wilhelm, Roger Maris, Tommie Agee, Tommy John, Graig Nettles, Chris Chambliss, Luis Tiant, Pedro Guerrero, Dennis Eckersley, and Buddy Bell. Losing these high-caliber players dampened fan enthusiasm for the Indians, adding to the decline in attendance. From the 1950s into the 1970s, the constant rotation of ownership groups, managers, and players epitomized the organization's instability. It was also a period marked by threats of relocation, continued concerns about civic-minded local ownership, and hopes for a new stadium.

Ellis Ryan was the power broker in his seven-man ownership group and served as the Indians' president for three seasons. In 1952, a power struggle between Ryan and general manager Hank Greenberg led to a restructuring of ownership. The retired Detroit Tigers slugger Greenberg came to the Indians under Veeck and worked his way into both the vice president and general manager positions. Ryan's attempt to oust Greenberg was voted down by the other stockholders, and in the aftermath Ryan sold his shares in the team, netting a $250,000 profit thanks to a generous buyout. Myron Wilson Jr., an insurance executive holding only a little over three percent of team stock, was named president in his place. Wilson was a compromise candidate, chosen by Ryan and agreed upon by Greenberg and others in conjunction with Ryan selling off his shares of stock. Wilson remained in control until February 1956, when a new ownership syndicate, headed by William R. Daley and including Greenberg and Minneapolis businessman Ignatius A. O'Shaughnessy, bought the Indians for nearly $4 million. Daley, an industrialist and financial wizard, became president. The stability projected by this syndicate lasted one year before internal turmoil again hit Indians management. The team fell to sixth in the standings in 1957 and attendance declined by 140,000 from the previous year. In October 1957 Daley fired Greenberg. He argued that the fans demanded change, but was also concerned that Greenberg was organizing a group of stockholders to relocate the Indians to Minneapolis–St. Paul, a growing market benefiting from both improvements in communication and transportation and the urban decline of traditional markets in the Northeast and Midwest. The relocation of teams to Milwaukee, Los Angeles, and San Francisco in the 1950s indicated that franchises would now shift from coast to coast. Greenberg, who retained his status as a shareholder and kept a seat on the board of directors, later told the board that baseball was dead in Cleveland. He was replaced by Frank Lane, who created his own turmoil while with the Indians.

Former team president Myron Wilson passed away in August 1962. The transfer of his stock shares, although minor, initiated another restructuring of Indians' ownership determined to place it in local hands. O'Shaughnessy, from St. Paul, and several minority stockholders sold their shares in the team for $6 million to a 29-member syndicate made up of Cleveland's civic elite, and the old company was liquidated. After the restructuring of the new organization, Gabe Paul, the largest stockholder, with 20 percent, was elected president, treasurer, and general manager. Paul had previously worked for the Cincinnati Reds and Houston Colt .45s before joining the Indians after the 1961 season.

Under his direction the Indians managed to stay in Cleveland in the midst of rumors that the team was bound for Dallas, Oakland, or Seattle. The franchise continued to experience financial losses and attendance declines by staying. The Indians reportedly lost $1.2 million each of Paul's first two years at the helm. In 1964 Paul asked each stockholder to contribute additional cash for operating costs. Cleveland's population decreased by 38,758 between 1950 and 1960, and once-wealthy neighborhoods had become ghettos. The board of directors subsequently instructed Paul to study the viability of Oakland and Dallas as possible options for the team. Difficulties with the city in lease negotiations for Municipal Stadium added to the overall tensions from financial losses and possible relocation. Paul and his group concluded that Cleveland was still the best choice provided an acceptable lease could be reached. The Indians stayed in Cleveland, and even brought back Colavito in a trade that gave up good young talent (Tommy John and Tommie Agee) but revived fan interest (up from 653,293 in 1964 to 934,786 in 1965). Paul was unable to rebuild a winning franchise, and in 1966 he sold the team to minority stockholder Vernon Stouffer.

Vernon Stouffer, a frozen-food and restaurant entrepreneur and a minority stockholder since 1962, purchased the Indians for $8 million toward the end of the 1966 season. The Cleveland native was commended for his act of civic kindness in purchasing the team and saving the Indians from imminent relocation, according to the media. Stouffer wanted only Clevelanders on the board of directors to keep the team in Cleveland. Each remaining stockholder was bought out at $300 per share. Stouffer also took on responsibility for $2.5 million in team debentures. He paid for all of this with his own $5 million and a $2.5 million bank loan. Stouffer seemed an ideal, financially independent owner for the Indians. Unfortunately he lost heavily in the 1970s stock-market plunge and soon after cut expenses by reducing the farm system and scouting, which set back player development for almost two decades. Rumors of relocation continued off the field, and the franchise continued to struggle on the field. Attendance figures again began a yearly decline as fans increasingly accused Stouffer of being cheap.

The Indians' struggles and decline paralleled those of Cleveland Municipal Stadium. The lakefront stadium was not even 40 years old, but had been battered by Cleveland's winters and was outdated with the emergence of artificial turf and domed stadiums. In June 1968 Cleveland hired Charles Luckman Associates of New York City to examine the feasibility of either building a domed stadium and arena downtown or renovating Municipal Stadium with a dome. Stouffer, Art Modell of the Cleveland Browns, and Paul Bright of the Cleveland Barons all endorsed the study. Supporters of the Luckman plan hinted that a domed stadium and new arena for downtown would improve Cleveland's image. The city, however, was in no condition to aid the Indians, its owner, or any of its professional sports teams. Citizens protested using city money on a new stadium while many neighborhoods and downtown were plagued by crime and pollution, and the city's public education system was in disarray. In February 1970 Luckman concluded that neither the proposed dome and arena plan nor a renovated Municipal Stadium was economically feasible. Projections estimated that a new dome would cost the city $60.5 million and run a deficit of $3 million annually. Putting a dome on the current stadium would have cost $44 million and run a yearly deficit of $2.6 million. The media lamented the $120,000 in city, county, and state funds that paid for the study.

The 1970s were unkind to Cleveland, and likewise for the Indians, whose owners were always looking to save money. The team had an overall record of 737–866, never finishing higher than fourth in the Eastern Division or within 14 games of the division leader. It exceeded 1 million in attendance just twice. The Indians ended the 1971 season 43 games out of first place with a 60–102 record, and drew an AL low of 591,348 fans, a drop-off of 138,404 from the previous year. The team was up for sale for $9 million, which no one offered, although George Steinbrenner did submit a $6 million offer. By the season's end

Stouffer was entertaining new options to make his franchise more financially viable. In August the local media reported a proposal to share the Indians with New Orleans. The plan called for the Indians to play 30 home games in the new Louisiana Superdome to start the season. Stouffer argued that this would give the franchise $2.5 million through the transfer of 25 percent of team stock to New Orleans investors, as well as help attendance hurt by Cleveland's cold April weather. Stouffer possessed roughly 78 percent of the Indians' stock, so the sale of the proposed portion to New Orleans investors would still have left him with majority ownership.

In March 1972 native Clevelander Nick Mileti purchased the Indians from Stouffer. Mileti was a sports entrepreneur who had used syndicates to build a sporting empire including the Cavaliers, the Barons of the AHL, the Cleveland Arena, and a new suburban arena. By year's end he would also add the Crusaders of the World Hockey Association. Mileti turned to the city's civic leaders and boosters for financial backing to meet the $10 million price tag. Local businessmen Alva Bonda, Joseph Zingale, and Bruce Fine (each a member of the Cavaliers ownership syndicate) were joined by Howard Metzenbaum and Bruce's brother Marshall Fine in forming a potential ownership syndicate. Each member contributed $100,000 up front while Mileti put forth $500,000 he had borrowed. Eighty percent of the $1 million would go toward the first payment in the buyout of Stouffer, and the rest toward working capital to operate the team.

The AL owners rejected Mileti's original offer, concerned about Mileti's financial stability and cautious given the recent relocation of franchises in Seattle and Washington, DC. Brothers Dudley and C. Bingham Blossom, members of one of Cleveland's most prominent families; local attorney Richard Miller; and numerous minor partners joined the syndicate, bringing an infusion of cash. On March 22, 1972, the AL announced its approval of the sale. Mileti owned just 7.5 percent of the stock, whereas he held 51 percent of stock in his other investments. He was voted general partner and given a salary. More importantly, the public was ecstatic with the local ownership, which vowed to keep the team in town.

In 1970 the census indicated that Cleveland's inner-city population declined by 101,000 between 1960 and 1969 while its suburbs gained 241,000. As a sports businessman, Mileti wanted to capture the growing suburban market, and in the summer of 1971 he announced his hockey and basketball teams were leaving the Cleveland Arena for a new arena in Richfield, Ohio. Four million people in the metropolitan area lived within an hour's drive of that rural town. When the Indians joined Mileti's empire, Clevelanders worried he would move the Indians to Richfield too. Near the end of the 1972 season, the city canceled the Indians' stadium lease. They hoped to sign a new long-term lease in Municipal Stadium before plans for a new ballpark in Richfield would emerge. Mileti, the city, and Modell, who now controlled the Cleveland Stadium Corporation and handled all the leases, bickered privately and publicly about keeping baseball downtown, the stadium's conditions, and the strong-arm tactics used by each. In the end, Mileti and the Indians signed a new 10-year lease.

During Mileti's tenure one of the rare moments that Indians fans had reason to celebrate was Frank Robinson's arrival. Signed by the Indians in 1974, Robinson was nearing the end of a Hall of Fame career. Ted Bonda, a member of the new ownership syndicate, viewed Robinson as a future manager because he had the ability, and felt the opportunity should come in Cleveland rather than elsewhere. Secondly, he hoped to revive the team's poor attendance and diminishing drawing power among local African Americans. After the season, the Indians failed to renew manager Ken Aspromonte's contract, and on October 3 they introduced Robinson as their new manager, the first black manager in MLB history. On April 8, 1975, 56,715 fans, including Commissioner Bowie Kuhn, witnessed Robinson hit a home run in his first game as player-manager. Robinson compiled a 186–189 record in Cleveland over two and a third seasons. In 1976 the Indians finished over .500 for the first time in seven years, but overall made little improvement under Robinson. His authority over the team led to notable confrontations with several players. After pitchers Jim Perry and Gaylord Perry butted heads with Robinson early in 1975, they were traded away. Designated hitter Rico Carty, the Indians' Man of the Year in 1976, stated that Robinson lacked leadership skills at a banquet prior to the 1977 season. Carty was fined and suspended, but his comments left Robinson susceptible to growing criticism from members of the organization and the media. Fifty-seven games into the 1977 season, the Indians fired Robinson.

The onset of free agency offered a new method through which the Indians could rebuild the team. After losing out to the New York Yankees in their pursuit of pitcher Jim "Catfish" Hunter in 1975, the Indians in 1976 signed 26-year-old pitcher Wayne Garland, who had won 20 games for Baltimore, for $230,000 a year over 10 years. After hurting his arm in his first spring-training game, Garland pitched with pain that season and lost 19 games. He was diagnosed at season's end with a torn rotator cuff, from which he never fully recovered. After four more seasons the Indians released Garland, still owing him $1,150,000 in salary. The Indians' financial problems and losing ways contributed to the lack of any significant free-agent moves until 1990, when they signed first baseman Keith Hernandez to a two-year contract worth $3.5 million. Like Garland, Hernandez got injured and played only 43 games for Cleveland. At this time, the team was worth $75 million, 23rd out of 26 major-league teams. Two years later, the Indians had the lowest worth of any team in MLB ($81 million).

The celebratory beginning of Mileti's tenure as Indians owner did not last long. Like the other elements of Mileti's sporting empire, the Indians faced financial problems and floundered on the field. New ownership had not guaranteed profits, and Mileti's innovations did not increase revenue. Stockholders pushed for Mileti's removal after the 1972 season, and in August 1973 Bonda replaced Mileti as managing partner. In two years under Mileti the

Indians lost $8 million, lacked operating capital and incoming funds, and got into serious financial trouble. Some visiting clubs complained they did not received their guaranteed 20 percent share of gate receipts on time. In 1975, Bonda secured extensions on the $6 million loans Mileti's syndicate used to purchase the Indians, and sought new ownership. Concerned about the impact the Indians' financial state was having on fan attendance, Art Modell interceded and arranged for trucking magnate F. J. "Steve" O'Neill to purchase the team for $11 million in February 1978, with $5 million going toward the debt.

With Gabe Paul back as general manager, the new ownership group promised to spend on players to rebuild the franchise. But large operating deficits, including $5 million just in 1982, hampered the franchise. Steve O'Neill passed away in August 1983. His nephew Patrick took over and put the team up for sale. Finding a buyer was difficult with a reported $11.5 million in debt, especially one willing to keep the team in Cleveland. Many fans and members of the media feared the Indians would leave when Peter Bavasi was appointed team president in 1984. Bavasi had previously worked to bring a baseball franchise to the Tampa–St. Petersburg, Florida, area. These speculations were heightened when Bavasi had *Cleveland* removed from team uniforms and argued that the city was a bad baseball environment.

In 1986 real-estate developers and brothers Richard and David Jacobs purchased the Indians for $35.5 million and assumed responsibility for $12 million in loans. Hank Peters, who had previously helped build the Baltimore Orioles into pennant contenders in the late 1970s and early 1980s, was named team president and chief operating officer. In the early 1980s the Indians had surpassed the 1 million mark in attendance three times, but also dipped below 800,000 between 1983 and 1985.

The new ownership slowly rebuilt the Indians into a contender. Peters invested money in the farm system, which by the early 1990s turned out players such as Albert Belle, Jim Thome, Charles Nagy, and Manny Ramirez. Peters and John Hart, who became general manager in 1991, also brought in Omar Vizquel, Kenny Lofton, Sandy Alomar Jr., and Carlos Baerga through trades. Hart's strategy was to sign selected young players to long-term contracts to avoid inflating the payroll or losing a player to free agency. Although some money was wasted on prospects that never developed, it worked well with key players like Thome and Nagy. When the Indians moved into Jacobs Field in 1994 and experienced a new flow of income from the park, they dabbled in free agency, signing veterans Eddie Murray, Dennis Martinez, and Orel Hershiser a year later.

Hart enabled the Indians to end decades of futility. They had not finished as high as third since 1968, and had only three winning seasons in those years. The 1994 team under manager Mike Hargrove went 66–47 in the strike-shortened season, the team's best record since 1955. Then in 1995 the transactions and player development came together as the Indians won 100 regular-season games and the AL Central Division by 30 games. Cleveland was an offensive juggernaut, with five players hitting over 20 home runs. The Indians' offense led the AL in almost every category, and its pitching staff owned the lowest ERA. Belle led the AL in home runs, RBIs, runs, doubles, slugging percentage, total bases, and extra-base hits that year. The Indians made their first postseason appearance in 41 years against the Boston Red Sox in the AL Divisional Series. They swept the Red Sox in three games and then faced the Seattle Mariners in the AL Championship Series. Losers of two of their first three games, the Indians won the next three to clinch their first AL pennant since 1954. But outstanding Atlanta Braves hurlers stymied the Indians batters (.179) in the Series, which was lost 4 games to 2.

The success of the franchise on the field and at the gate temporarily gave Cleveland large-market status. Pursuing a World Series championship made the Indians accumulate an upper-echelon team payroll that ranked with the likes of the New York Yankees, Atlanta Braves, and Los Angeles Dodgers. With the city undergoing a renaissance of its own during the late 1980s and early 1990s, large-market status seemed fitting. The 1995 team payroll was just over $40 million. It would hit nearly $92 million by 2001. The surge in payroll coincided with sellout crowds at Jacobs Field. Between 1995 and 2001, Cleveland won the Central Division six times and appeared in two World Series. Following its pennant-winning 1995 season, the Indians again won the division crown with league-leading pitching and excellent hitting for average and power. Belle continued to put up big numbers with 48 homers and a league-leading 148 RBIs. But the Orioles upset the Tribe in the ALDS 3–1.

In 1997 the team fell to 87 victories as its pitching faltered. But the batting remained powerful, with a club mark of 220 homers and three 100-RBI men (Jim Thome, David Justice, and Matt Williams). Having defeated the Yankees (3–2) and the Orioles (4–2) in the ALDS and ALCS, Cleveland faced the Florida Marlins in the World Series. In the ninth inning of game seven relief pitcher Jose Mesa blew the series-clinching save, which led to an extra-innings victory for the Marlins and bitter disappointment for the Indians.

The Indians management had built a young and promising team in anticipation of the opening of Jacobs Field in 1994, which was the culmination of the city's quest for modern sporting facilities in the downtown area. Getting "the Jake" built hadn't been easy. Past dilemmas over sports facilities sullied 1980s initiatives. In 1984 Cuyahoga County voters rejected a property-tax issue to fund a $150 million domed stadium for the Indians and Cleveland Browns. But in 1987 Cleveland's Central Market and several other buildings were razed in an area that became known as the Gateway District. Redevelopment of the area included a new arena and ballpark. The Indians anticipated leaving outdated Municipal Stadium, where the weather was uncomfortable for baseball, the dimensions were too large, and there were too many empty seats. Furthermore, they felt like secondary citizens to the Browns, especially since Art Modell was their landlord. The proposed ballpark had a $375 million price tag. Funding was projected to come from a sin tax on alcohol and cigarettes in Cuyahoga County. In preparation for the countywide vote, Commissioner Fay Vincent hinted that passing the sin tax and building the new ballpark was needed to keep the Indians in Cleveland. Clevelanders rejected the tax but the rest of the county did not, passing it by a 1.2 percent margin in May 1990. HOK Sport, the designers of Oriole Ballpark at Camden Yards in Baltimore, designed Cleveland's ballpark to capture the intimacy of historic ballparks and mirror the city's industrial feel in its appearance, including light towers designed to mimic smokestacks. The retro-ballpark design also ensured that the facility would not have the multipurpose options of the stadiums and domes built in the 1960s, 1970s, and 1980s. New ballparks in Denver, Arlington, Pittsburgh, Cincinnati, San Francisco, and Seattle followed in the same pattern as those in Baltimore and Cleveland. The Indians signed a 20-year lease to play in Jacobs Field, and Richard Jacobs paid $13.9 million for naming rights. The 42,400-seat park opened on April 4, 1994, with the Indians defeating the Mariners 4–3 in 11 innings. By then the team's value had surpassed $100 million, moving the franchise to 12th in worth. Four years later the team was worth $359 million, second only to the Yankees. The success of the team and the popularity of Jacobs Field resulted in a sellout streak of 455 consecutive games between 1995 and 2001.

The Indians were one of the most successful franchises in baseball at the end of the century. In 1998 Manny Ramirez had 145 RBIs, leading the club to the ALDS, where they beat the Red Sox in four games, and then on to the ALCS, where the Yankees took the last three games to win 4–2. Ramirez did even better in 1999, with 165 RBIs and a .333 batting average. The Tribe lost the ALDS to Boston in five games, however.

Many observers felt the team's fairy tale was coming to an end, as the Cleveland area suffered a recession in the late 1990s. The cash surplus accompanying the new ballpark and the novelty of a pennant contender withered as a result, and the Indians returned to their mid- or small-market economic standing. Having seen his franchise experience an era of unparalleled success and playoff appearances, Richard Jacobs (the sole owner after the passing of his brother in 1992) announced his intent to sell the franchise in May 1999. To many it was a case of getting out while the getting was good. He sold the Indians to Lawrence Dolan for $323 million. Dolan was a Cleveland native, multimillionaire lawyer, and businessman who also held stock in his brother's Cablevision Systems Corporation. Dolan believed in responsible spending, and in 2002 he trimmed $15 million off the $91 million payroll. Fan favorites Thome, Ramirez, and pitcher Bartolo Colon were traded for younger, less costly prospects or were allowed to leave through free agency.

Cleveland and Cuyahoga County were also caught in a backlash of new economic realities when dealing with their contribution to the Indians' rise to prominence: the economic benefits to the area promised by the development of Jacobs Field and the Gateway Project had not appeared. The public wound up paying 70 percent of the cost to build Jacobs Field and Gund Arena rather than the promised 50 percent. As of 2000, the city and county used higher taxes to pay for the $125 million cost overruns. Furthermore, people of modest means were priced out of attending games as ticket prices rose in an attempt to generate more revenue.

In 2001, *Forbes* estimated the Indians were worth $360 million. According to MLB, the Tribe was one of only 11 teams to make a profit from its baseball operations, although their share of revenue sharing resulted in an $11.4 million loss (which *Forbes* downgraded to $3.6 million). The team made $137,841,000 in local revenues, compared to the MLB average of $94 million, which was fourth highest on a per-capita basis. Two major local revenue streams were local media, at $21.1 million the second highest in MLB on a per-capita basis, and other operating revenue at $45.3 million, comprised of concessions, parking, and luxury seating, fourth highest in the big leagues.

In 2000 the squad fell to second in the division and missed the playoffs despite record-setting defense from the great middle-infield combo of Roberto Alomar and Omar Vizquel. The club returned to first in 2001, led by three 100-RBI men: Alomar, Thome (124), and outfielder Juan Gonzales (140). The Tribe lost the ALDS in five to the Seattle club that set a league record of 116 wins. In 2002 the Indians faltered and finished with a losing record. Third-year manager Charley Manuel was let go in midyear for Joel Skinner. Then, under Eric Wedge, the team had its worst season in years (68–94). In 2004, the Indians were back on the verge of returning to contention after winning 80 games and briefly challenging for first place in the Central Division in midseason. General manager Mark Shapiro's five-year plan of building around pitching, strengthening the farm system, and trading veterans for young talent was firmly in place. Like Hart, he signed young talent like catcher Victor Martinez and pitcher C.C. Sabathia, each an All-Star in 2004, designated hitter Travis Hafner, to multiyear deals. The Indians remained cautious and cost conscious in approaching free agency, but for 2005 they did add free-agent hurler Kevin Millwood. Nonetheless, the total payroll was just $48 million, 26th in MLB. In 2005 the team struggled for a third of the season, but then went 76–46 the rest of the way. They led the wild-card race in the last week of the season, but then lost five of their last six games. The late-season run provoked a guarded return of fans to Jacobs Field. Attendance surpassed 2 million despite local competition for sports dollars and the depressed economy.

Like so many seasons before, fans and the local media were left to cautiously mutter, "Wait till next year." Cleveland's baseball future, like its team, remains a question of potential. Whether it will be fulfilled or not remains to be seen. With no World Series championship since 1948 and no professional sports championship of any sort since 1964, Cleveland anxiously hopes that this potential develops sooner rather than later.

NOTABLE ACHIEVEMENTS

Most Valuable Players

Year	Name	Position
1948	Lou Boudreau	SS
1953	Al Rosen	3B

Cy Young Winners

Year	Name	Position
1972	Gaylord Perry	RHP

Rookies of the Year

Year	Name	Position
1955	Herb Score	P
1971	Chris Chambliss	1B
1980	Joe Charboneau	OF
1990	Sandy Alomar Jr.	C

Batting Champions

Year	Name	#
1903	Nap Lajoie	.344
1904	Nap Lajoie	.376
1905	Elmer Flick	.306
1916	Tris Speaker	.386
1929	Lew Fonseca	.369
1944	Lou Boudreau	.327
1954	Bobby Avila	.341

Home-Run Champions

Year	Name	#
1915	Braggo Roth	7
1950	Al Rosen	37
1952	Larry Doby	32
1953	Al Rosen	43
1954	Larry Doby	32
1959	Rocky Colavito	42
1995	Albert Belle	50

ERA Champions

Year	Name	#
1903	Earl Moore	1.74
1904	Addie Joss	1.59
1908	Addie Joss	1.16
1911	Vean Gregg	1.80
1923	Stan Coveleski	2.76
1933	Monte Pearson	2.33
1940	Bob Feller	2.61
1948	Gene Bearden	2.43
1950	Early Wynn	3.20
1954	Mike Garcia	2.64
1965	Sam McDowell	2.18
1968	Luis Tiant	1.60
1982	Rick Sutcliffe	2.96
2005	Kevin Millwood	2.86

Strikeout Champions

Year	Name	#
1920	Stan Coveleski	133
1938	Bob Feller	240
1939	Bob Feller	246
1941	Bob Feller	260
1943	Allie Reynolds	151
1946	Bob Feller	348
1947	Bob Feller	196
1948	Bob Feller	164
1950	Bob Lemon	170
1955	Herb Score	245
1956	Herb Score	263
1957	Early Wynn	184
1965	Sam McDowell	325
1966	Sam McDowell	225
1968	Sam McDowell	283
1969	Sam McDowell	279
1970	Sam McDowell	304
1980	Len Barker	187
1981	Len Barker	127

No-Hitters (Italics = Perfect Game)

Name	Date
Bob Rhoads	09/18/1908
Addie Joss	10/02/1908
Addie Joss	*04/20/1910*
Ray Caldwell	09/10/1919
Wes Ferrell	04/29/1931
Bob Feller	04/16/1940
Bob Feller	04/30/1946
Don Black	07/10/1947
Bob Lemon	06/30/1948
Bob Feller	07/01/1951
Sonny Siebert	06/10/1966
Dick Bosman	07/19/1974
Dennis Eckersley	05/30/1977
Len Barker	*05/15/1981*

POSTSEASON APPEARANCES

AL Central Division Titles

Year	Record	Manager
1995	100–44	Mike Hargrove
1996	99–62	Mike Hargrove
1997	86–75	Mike Hargrove
1998	89–73	Mike Hargrove
1999	97–65	Mike Hargrove
2001	91–71	Chuck Manuel

AL Pennants

Year	Record	Manager
1920	98–56	Tris Speaker
1948	97–58	Lou Boudreau
1954	111–43	Al Lopez
1995	100–44	Mike Hargrove
1997	86–75	Mike Hargrove

World Championships

Year	Opponent
1920	Brooklyn
1948	Boston

MANAGERS

2003–	Eric Wedge
2002	Joel Skinner
2000–2002	Charlie Manual
1991–1999	Mike Hargrove
1990–1991	John McNamara
1989	John Hart
1987–1989	Doc Edwards
1983–1987	Pat Corrales
1983	Mike Ferraro
1979–1982	Dave Garcia
1977–1979	Jeff Torborg
1975–1977	Frank Robinson
1972–1974	Ken Aspromonte
1971	Johnny Lipon
1968–1971	Alvin Dark
1967	Joe Adcock
1966	George Strickland
1964–1966	Birdie Tebbetts
1964	George Strickland
1963–1964	Birdie Tebbetts
1962	Mel Harder
1962	Mel McGaha
1961	Mel Harder
1960–1961	Jimmie Dykes
1960	Jo-Jo White
1958–1960	Joe Gordon
1958	Bobby Bragan
1957	Kirby Farrell
1951–1956	Al Lopez
1942–1950	Lou Boudreau
1941	Roger Peckinpaugh
1938–1940	Ossie Vitt
1935–1937	Steve O'Neill
1933–1935	Walter Johnson
1933	Bibb Falk
1928–1933	Roger Peckinpaugh
1927	Jack McCallister
1919–1926	Tris Speaker
1915–1919	Lee Fohl
1912–1915	Joe Birmingham
1912	Harry Davis
1911	George Stovall

1909–1911	Deacon McGuire
1906–1909	Nap Lajoie
1905	Bill Bradley
1905	Nap Lajoie
1902–1904	Bill Armour
1901	Jimmie McAleer

Team Records by Individual Players

Batting Leaders

	Single Season			Career		
	Name		Year	Name		Plate Appearances
Batting average	Joe Jackson	.408	1911	Joe Jackson	.374	2,852
On-base %	Tris Speaker	.483	1920	Tris Speaker	.444	6,628
Slugging %	Albert Belle	.714	1994	Manny Ramirez	.592	4,095
OPS	Manny Ramirez	1.154	2000	Manny Ramirez	.998	4,095
Games	Leon Wagner	163	1964	Terry Turner	1,619	6,515
At bats	Joe Carter	63	1986	Nap Lajoie	6,034	6,695
Runs	Earl Averill	140	1931	Earl Averill	1,154	6,708
Hits	Joe Jackson	233	1911	Nap Lajoie	2,046	6,695
Total bases	Hal Trosky	405	1936	Earl Averill	3,200	6,708
Doubles	George Burns	64	1926	Tris Speaker	486	6,628
Triples	Joe Jackson	26	1912	Earl Averill	121	6,708
Home runs	Jim Thome	52	2002	Jim Thome	334	5,723
RBIs	Manny Ramirez	165	1999	Earl Averill	1,084	6,708
Walks	Jim Thome	127	1999	Jim Thome	997	5,723
Strikeouts	Jim Thome	185	2001	Jim Thome	1,377	5,723
Stolen bases	Kenny Lofton	75	1996	Kenny Lofton	450	5,570
Extra-base hits	Albert Belle	103	1995	Earl Averill	724	6,708
Times on base	Tris Speaker	316	1920	Tris Speaker	2,864	6,628

Pitching Leaders

	Single Season			Career		
	Name		Year	Name		Innings Pitched
ERA	Addie Joss	1.16	1908	Addie Joss	1.89	2,327
Wins	Jim Bagby	31	1920	Bob Feller	266	3,827
Won-loss %	Johnny Allen	.938	1937	Vern Gregg	.667	898.3
Hits/9 IP	Luis Tiant	5.3	1968	Herb Score	6.17	714.3
Walks/9 IP	Addie Joss	0.83	1908	Red Donahue	1.40	551.3
Strikeouts	Bob Feller	348	1946	Bob Feller	2.581	3,827
Strikeouts/ 9 IP	Sam Mcdowell	10.71	1965	Herb Score	9.35	714.3

(Continued)

Pitching Leaders   (Continued)

| | Single Season | | | Career | | |
	Name		Year	Name		Innings Pitched
Innings	Bob Feller	371.3	1946	Bob Feller	3,827	3,827
Starts	George Uhle	44	1923	Bob Feller	484	3,827
Complete games	Bob Feller	36	1946	Bob Feller	279	3,827
Shutouts	Bob Feller	10	1946	Addie Joss	45	2,327

Source: Drawn from data in "Cleveland Indians Batting Leaders (seasonal and career)." http://baseball-reference.com/ teams/CLE/leaders_bat.shtml; "Cleveland Indians Pitching Leaders (seasonal and career)." http://baseball-reference. com/teams/CLE/leaders_pitch.shtml.

BIBLIOGRAPHY

Eckhouse, Morris, ed. *All-Star Baseball in Cleveland*. Cleveland, OH: Society for American Baseball Research, 1997.

Fleitz, David L. *Louis Sockalexis: The First Cleveland Indian*. Jefferson, NC: McFarland, 2002.

Grabowski, John J. *Sports in Cleveland: An Illustrated History*. Bloomington: Indiana University Press, 1992.

Hendrick, J. Thomas. *Misfits! Baseball's Worst Team Ever*. Cleveland, OH: Pocol Press, 1991.

Jednick, Peter. *Cleveland: Where the East Coast Meets the Midwest*. Cleveland, OH: n.p., 1980.

Lewis, Franklin. *The Cleveland Indians*. New York: G. P. Putnam's Sons, 1949.

Longert, Scott. *Addie Joss: King of the Pitchers*. Cleveland, OH: Society for American Baseball Research, 1998.

Overmyer, James. *Effa Manley and the Newark Eagles*. Metuchen, NJ: Scarecrow Press, 1993.

Miller, Carol Poh, and Robert A. Wheeler. *Cleveland: A Concise History, 1796–1996*. 2nd ed. Bloomington: Indiana University Press, 1997.

Pluto, Terry. *The Curse of Rocky Colavito: A Loving Look at a Thirty-Year Slump*. New York: Simon and Schuster, 1994.

Porter, Philip W. *Cleveland: Confused City on a Seesaw*. Columbus: Ohio State University Press, 1976.

Quirk, James, and Rodney D. Fort. *Pay Dirt: The Business of Professional Team Sports*. Princeton, NJ: Princeton University Press, 1997.

Riess, Steven A. *Touching Base: Professional Baseball and American Culture in the Progressive Era*. Rev. ed. Urbana: University of Illinois Press, 1999.

Rosentraub, Mark S. *Major League Losers: The Real Cost of Sports and Who's Paying for It*. New York: Basic Books, 1997.

Schneider, Russell. *The Cleveland Indians Encyclopedia*. Philadelphia: Temple University Press, 1996.

Seymour, Harold. *Baseball: The Early Years*. New York: Oxford University Press, 1960.

———. *Baseball: The Golden Age*. New York: Oxford University Press, 1971.

Sickels, John. *Bob Feller: Ace of the Greatest Generation*. Washington, DC: Brasseys, 2004.

Staurowsky, Ellen J. "Sockalexis and the Making of the Myth at the Core of Cleveland's 'Indian' Image." In *Team Spirits: The Native American Mascot Controversy*, ed. C. Richard King and Charles Frueling, 82–106. Lincoln: University of Nebraska Press, 2001.

Suchma, Philip C. "From the Best of Times to the Worst Times: Professional Sport and Urban Decline in a Tale of Two Clevelands, 1945–1978." PhD diss., Ohio State University, 2005.

———. "The Selling of Cleveland Municipal Stadium: The Linking of Progressive Era Ideals with the Emerging Consumer Culture." *Sport History Review* 31 (November 2000): 100–19.

Veeck, Bill, with Ed Linn. *Veeck—As in Wreck*. Chicago: University of Chicago Press, 2001.

Voigt, David Quentin. *American Baseball, Vol. 1: From Gentlemen's Sport to the Commissioner System*: University of Oklahoma Press, 1966.

Voigt, David Quentin. *American Baseball, Vol. 2: From the Commissioners to Continental Expansion*. Norman: University of Oklahoma Press, 1970.

White, G. Edward. *Creating the National Pastime: Baseball Transforms Itself, 1903–1953*. Princeton, NJ: Princeton University Press, 1996.

Detroit Tigers

Steven A. Riess

The Detroit Tigers, one of the original American League teams, and the only that has always had a downtown ballpark, has had an extremely loyal following for most of its existence. Perhaps more than any other team, it has long been identified with its working-class fans. The Tigers have had their share of great players and outstanding teams, with stable ownership, but the glory years were a long time ago.

Detroit's first professional team was the Hollinger Nine, which lost its first game on May 12, 1879, by a score of 7–1 to the Troy, New York, team of the National League in front of 1,500 paying customers at multipurpose Recreation Park. The city of 120,000 secured a National League franchise two years later for $20,000. The Wolverines, operated by Mayor William G. Thompson and his associates, grossed $35,000 and made a $12,440 profit in 1881, but struggled on the field. Thompson sold out two years later to businessman Joseph H. March, who in turn sold the squad in 1885 to Frederick K. Stearns, whose father had a pharmaceutical business. Stearns added Buffalo's "Big Four" infield of Dan Brouthers, Hardy Richardson, Jack Rowe, and Deacon White for $8,000, resulting in a second-place finish in 1886. The Wolverines captured the pennant a year later with a record 969 runs (8 per game), and defeated the St. Louis Browns of the American Association 11 games to 4 for the world's championship. In 1888, Stearns resigned as president to run the family business and was replaced by Charles W. Smith, a business partner of future reform mayor Hazen Pingree. The new owners lost $58,000, sold off the squad, and gave up the franchise.

In 1889 and 1890, the city had a team in the International Association, then none until 1894, when it landed a team in the new Western League, operated by businessman George A. Vanderbeck. He had owned the Los Angeles team in the California League until he was kicked out after the 1892 season for bickering with other owners and organizing a postseason series without permission. The team played at 3,500-seat League Park, just outside the eastern city limits, near the Belle Isle Bridge, a 10-minute walk from city hall and accessed by three trolley lines. The club was known as the Creams (because they were "the cream of the league"), but in 1895 the press began calling them the Tigers, possibly after the Detroit Light Guard, the city's leading military and social organization, nicknamed the Tigers.

In 1896, after two profitable seasons, Vanderbeck moved to the larger 3.3-acre site of the Western Market, home of a former hay market, lumber mill, and dog pound at Michigan and Trumbull ("the corner"), seven minutes from city hall. He built an L-shaped grandstand with a peaked roof. The 5,000-seat park was named for Charley Bennett, star catcher of the Wolverines, who had lost a leg and a foot in a train accident.

THE COMING OF THE AMERICAN LEAGUE

In 1900, the Western League was renamed the American League, and the teams in St. Paul and Grand Rapids moved to Chicago and Cleveland. Vanderbeck sold the team, because of alimony problems, on March 6 for $12,000 to James D. Burns, the son of a pioneer Irish brick manufacturer. Burns was a star amateur boxer and wrestler who ran a saloon next door to the Majestic Building, the city's tallest edifice, which was popular among the sporting crowd, politicians, and journalists, and also the Cadillac AC, a famous boxing arena. He backed world-champion pugilists middleweight Tommy Ryan and heavyweight Tommy Burns. Burns was heavily into Democratic politics, and in 1905 he was elected Wayne County sheriff.

Burns kept on manager George Stallings, despite his reputation for lacking discipline. The team came in fourth in the pennant race and second in attendance. Working-class fans had a hard time attending games because of the late starting time and the absence of Sunday baseball. The Sabbatarian opposition included Mayor William C. Maybury, a leader in the Episcopal Church across the street from the ballpark. The Tigers had previously played a few Sunday games at suburban locations, which drew well. Burns scheduled Sunday games at suburban Burns Park, which he built on family property at Springwells Township by the western boundary of Detroit.

On October 14, the AL proclaimed itself a major league. The league moved out of Indianapolis, Kansas City, Buffalo, and Minneapolis and expanded into the east with teams in Boston, Baltimore, Philadelphia, and Washington. Detroit was the smallest city in the AL, with a population of 285,704, one-third foreign born. Burns was owner of record, but AL president Ban Johnson kept

51 percent of the stock in his own name. The team played at Bennett Park, whose 8,500-seat capacity was the smallest in the majors. Its dimensions were 308 feet to left field, 390 feet to center, and 324 feet to right, although the deepest part, in left center, was 420 feet. Detroit's first major-league game since 1888, on April 25, was attended by a city record crowd of 10,023. Milwaukee took a 13–4 lead into the ninth, and thousands of disappointed Tiger fans left early. But the Tigers staged a phenomenal rally, scoring 10 runs in the ninth to win. The Tigers finished the season in third place (74–61), and Burns made a $35,000 profit, based on an attendance of 259,430. However, management was in disarray because Stallings, a minor stockholder, and Burns did not get along. Then, when Johnson heard that Burns was allegedly cooking the books, he forced them both out. On November 14, 1901, Burns sold the team to a syndicate headed by Samuel F. Angus, who was in the railroad and insurance businesses.

In 1902 the team fell to seventh place and attendance dropped by 27 percent. There were problems with rowdy players and misbehaving fans, especially on Sundays, when many spectators were drunk before they got to the ballpark. A free-for-all at one Sunday game followed the third ejection of a player in three days, and Sunday ball was halted until 1907. Manager Frank Dwyer was fired and replaced by pitcher Win Mercer, an inveterate gambler who committed suicide while on a West Coast exhibition tour. Ed Barrow, who doubled as general manager, took his place. In 1903, when Detroit was the only Western League city still in the AL, the junior circuit merged with the NL. The agreement allowed the Tigers to keep its two latest NL signees, "Wahoo" Sam Crawford of the Cincinnati Reds and pitcher "Wild" Bill Donovan of the Brooklyn Superbas. Crawford batted .332, second in the AL, with a then major-league record 25 triples. He still holds the career marks for the most inside-the-park homers (51) and triples (309).

Johnson wanted a stronger hand in Detroit than Angus, whose primary business was failing. His bookkeeper, Frank Navin, a night-school law graduate whose brother was the city's Republican boss, orchestrated the sale for $50,000 to William H. Yawkey, the 28-year-old heir to a $10 million lumber fortune. Navin got 10 percent as a finder's fee, and Yawkey, who considered the team his personal toy, left Navin in charge.

In 1904 Barrow made several important deals, securing shortstop Charley O'Leary; third baseman Bill Coughlin, a future team captain; and left fielder Matty McIntyre, laying the groundwork for future great Tiger teams. However, the team was floundering in seventh place (62–90), and he was fired.

THE ERA OF TY COBB

The new manager in 1905 was Bill Armour, who had led the Cleveland Blues to three straight winning campaigns. The team brought in two new players, outfielder Ty Cobb, one of the first southerners in the majors, and daffy second baseman Herman "Germany" Schaefer. Schaefer was best known for stealing first base when on second, with another runner at third, hoping to draw a throw and enable his teammate to score.

Cobb was just 18 when he joined the Tigers at the end of August. He was extremely talented and physically imposing, a little over six feet tall and 180 pounds. Cobb was obsessed by a thirst to succeed and haunted by his mother's murder of his father. A keen student of the game, Cobb used a 34-inch-long bat that weighed 38–40 ounces and batted with his hands spread apart. He was a great base runner who swiped home a record 54 times, and on occasion stole second, third, and home in the same inning.

Cobb soon became the best player in the majors, and the most hated, with no friends on the team; McIntyre once did not talk to Cobb for two years. He was a loner, a racist, and had a terrible temper. He tried to intimidate opponents, though he did not sharpen his spikes, as was often alleged. He was involved in several violent episodes, beginning in spring training of 1906, when he attacked a black groundskeeper and his wife.

The 1905 team improved markedly to third (79–74), but faltered at the box office, drawing just 193,384, worst in the AL. Detroit was not yet an established baseball town. The next year the team fell to sixth (71–78), and attendance dropped to a mere 174,043, lowest in team history. Cobb led the team with a batting average of .320, 35 points higher than anyone else, and earned a 60 percent raise to $2,400. The low attendance was not only attributed to the poor play, but also competition from 50-foot-high wildcat bleachers located beyond the left-center-field fence that drew up to 400 lower-class young men at a cost of 10 cents. After the 1907 season, Navin put up a large canvas to try to block their view, with little success.

In 1907 Armour was supplanted by Hugh Jennings, a former star with the Baltimore Orioles, then managing Baltimore's minor-league team. The Tigers improved to 92–58 and took the 1907 pennant over the Philadelphia A's, led by 25-game winners Bill Donovan and Ed Killian and the majors' best team batting average (.266). Cobb won his first batting championship (.350), as well as leading the league in RBIs (119), hits (212), total bases (283), and stolen bases (49). They faced the Chicago Cubs, who had won 107 games, in the World Series. In game one, the Tigers led in the ninth, but with two out, the tying run scored when Del Howard struck out but was safe on a passed ball. The game ended in a 3–3 tie, called after 12 innings. The Cubs then went on to win the next four contests, giving up just three runs. Only 7,370 attended the final game in Detroit. Nonetheless, the players were amply rewarded for the series, earning $1,946 each. The players' share of the postseason receipts was nearly $22,000, and then Yawkey donated his $15,000 portion to the team as well. Navin had previously been lent $20,000 by Yawkey to buy a half interest in the team, and he used a portion of his $50,000 profits to repay Yawkey. Yawkey resigned as president, replaced by Navin, but remained a major stockholder until his death in 1919.

The substantial profits came because attendance (297,079) had risen by 40 percent, partly due to the resumption of Sunday baseball. A stumbling block was Navin's longtime feud with businessman Frank H. Croul, a future police commissioner. Some years earlier, when Navin worked as a bookmaker, Croul tried to make a $500 wager on a 3–1 favorite, but Navin would not accept the bet, saying it was given too late. Croul told the Tigers executive that he would not interfere with Sunday ball if Navin paid up, and Navin wrote out a $1,500 check that Croul's attorney gave to charity. The first Sunday game at Bennett Park was played on August 18, with 9,635 in attendance, including the mayor, police chief, and sheriff. The Tigers trounced the New York Highlanders 13–6. After the season Navin bought the factory behind right field and expanded the park's capacity.

In 1908, Cobb and Crawford received raises to $4,000, and Cobb also had a bonus clause calling for another $800 if he hit .300. The Tigers reached first place by Memorial Day, and remained on top for most of the summer. The race heated up in late September. Starting the last day of the season, the Tigers were up by a half game over Chicago and Cleveland. They clinched the title that day with a 7–0 victory in Chicago, ending the closest three-team pennant race in major-league history, up by half a game over Cleveland, who had played one more game, with Chicago a game and a half back. Attendance in the expanded park zoomed to 436,199, third best in the AL. Cobb led the league in batting (.324), slugging (.475), RBIs (101), hits (188), and total bases (276). McIntyre topped the AL in runs scored (105), and Crawford led with seven homers. The pitching dropped off, but knuckleballing rookie lefty Ed Summers went 24–12 with a 1.64 ERA.

The World Series opponents were again the Cubs. In Detroit the Tigers led game one 6–5 in the ninth, but the Cubs came back with five to steal the game. The next day was Sunday, and the series moved to Chicago. The Cubs got six runs in the eighth inning off Donovan and won 6–1. The following day, the Tigers won their first game against the Cubs in two years, 8–3. But the Cubs came back in game four in Detroit, blanking the Tigers 3–0 behind Three Finger Brown. Only 6,210 turned out for the fifth and final game, with Orval Overall shutting out the Tigers 2–0 in just 85 minutes. This was the poorest-attended game in World Series history. The low attendance in Detroit, and Navin's decision not to add his share into the players' pockets, resulted in their share dropping to $871.

The Tigers continued to play great baseball in 1909, winning an AL record 98 games, including 57 at home, still a team record. George Mullin won 29 to lead the majors. He had a terrific career in Detroit, winning 209 games in 12 seasons, including a no-hitter in 1912. The Tiger batsmen, tops in the AL (.267), were led again by Cobb, who led the league in batting (.377), homers (9), and RBIs (107), an achievement later known as the Triple Crown. He also led the league in hits (216), stolen bases (76), and total bases (296). The team drew a record 490,490 attendance, which encouraged Navin to raise Bennett's capacity to 13,000.

The Tigers advanced to play the Pirates in the World Series. Fans were excited by the anticipated match between baseball's two star players, Cobb and shortstop Honus Wagner of the Pirates. The teams split the first six games, but the Tigers were trounced in the finale at home, 8–0, and lost the World Series. Wagner hit .333, had six steals, and fielded brilliantly, outshining Cobb, who had his third straight disappointing Series performance, batting just .231. The total attendance set a World Series record, but the crowds at Pittsburgh's new Forbes Field were about one-third larger than at Bennett. Each Tiger got $1,273.50. After the season, McIntyre led several Tigers to Cuba on an exhibition tour, and won just 4 out of 12 games against local teams bolstered by black American ringers.

In 1910 Cobb signed a three-year contract at $9,000 a year, second only to Honus Wagner. The Tigers could not keep up with the A's, ending a distant third, 18 games off the pace. In the batting race, Cobb elected to sit out the last two games with a seemingly insurmountable lead over Napoleon Lajoie, who played a doubleheader on the last day of the season. Cobb was so hated by Browns manager Jack O'Connor that he tried to help Lajoie take the batting crown. O'Connor told rookie third baseman John "Red" Corriden to play on the outfield grass for his safety against Lajoie's famed lined shots. Lajoie tripled his first time up, and then bunted successfully seven times, going eight for nine. The press reported conflicting statistics, but the AL declared Cobb the winner, .3849 to Lajoie's .3841. Statisticians have since readjusted Cobb's mark to .383.

The Tigers traveled to Cuba after the season for a series of exhibitions and went 7–4–1. Cobb batted .370 in five games, but was outhit by three black Americans playing for local teams. Cobb promised to never again play against blacks.

In 1911 the Tigers went 86–65, second to the Athletics. The entire team hit a robust .292, second best in the AL. Crawford hit .378, his all-time high, with 115 RBIs, while Cobb was sensational, batting .420 with 248 hits, 147 runs, and 144 RBIs. He also led the league in doubles, triples, slugging, and stolen bases, and hit in an AL record 40 straight games. The Base Ball Writers Association of America chose him as AL MVP, for which he was awarded another Chalmers automobile. The team was beset by growing dissension and a near revolt against Jennings, who irritated them with his sarcastic criticism, failure to discipline Cobb when he got out of line, and questionable decisions with his pitching staff.

Increased fan interest in booming Detroit, whose population reached 465,766 in 1910 and would double to 993,678 by 1920, when it was the fourth-largest city in the United States, encouraged Navin to rebuild. In 1912 his Tigers moved into a $300,000 concrete, single-decked, 23,000-seat ballpark. Navin Field was nearly twice the size of Bennett Park. The field was symmetrical, 365 feet in right field, 400 feet to center, and 340 feet in left.

It had a 125-foot flagpole in center field, the tallest structure in fair territory inside any major-league ballpark, and a giant scoreboard in left field that reported out-of-town games. On Opening Day, April 20, 24,382 filled the park, including fans who stood in the roped-off outfield. They were entertained by a 6–5 extra-innings Tiger victory over Cleveland.

The pitching and the supporting cast collapsed that season, and the Tigers finished with their worst record since Cobb joined the club (69–84). Cobb, though, was spectacular, leading the AL in batting (.410), hits (227), and slugging (.586). The team's on-field struggles were reflected by a nearly 20 percent drop in home attendance, very unusual at a new ballpark. Yet the season was still very profitable, mainly because of the Tigers' share of out-of-town games—*Sporting Life* estimated that Cobb was such a big gate attraction that his presence was worth an additional $30,000 on the road—and such sources of revenue as the fees paid by Western Union ($17,000 in 1913) to telegraph results to poolrooms and saloons. By the end of the season, Navin had made $365,000 from his team, which was reportedly worth $650,000.

Cobb's temper got the better of him on May 15 in New York, when he was ragged by a fan sitting near the bench. After the third inning Cobb jumped into the stands and began beating up the fan, Claude Lueker, a former printing-press operator who had lost a hand and three fingers in an accident at work. Cobb was thrown out of the game and suspended indefinitely by the league. After he missed one game, his teammates, surprisingly, rallied behind him, telegraphing AL president Ban Johnson that they would not play until his reinstatement. On May 18 at Shibe Park, the Tigers fielded a team comprised of 12 Philadelphia semipros and college students at $10 each, except the pitcher, who got $50 for his efforts in a 24–2 debacle. The regular players returned for the next game, receiving a fine of $100. Cobb got off with a 10-day suspension and a $50 fine.

The team stagnated in sixth place in 1913 with the worst pitching in the AL. Cobb, who had held out to get a $12,000 contract, again led in batting at .390, and was second in slugging. One year later the Tigers were one of the highest-paid teams because Cobb ($15,000), Crawford ($7,500), and shortstop Donie Bush got big raises to prevent them from jumping to the rival Federal League. Navin raised box seats to $1.25 and grandstand seats to 75 cents and $1 to help pay for the raises, but kept the pavilion (50 cents) and bleacher (25 cents) prices low, very affordable for Henry Ford's employees, who were earning $5 a day. The team began rebuilding, and even though Cobb missed nearly two months of the season because of a cracked rib from a pitched ball and then a broken thumb from a fight with a butcher he felt had insulted his wife, the Tigers rose to third place (80–73).

The Tigers fended off Federal League recruiters by offering generous raises. Cobb was upped to $20,000 for three years, making him the highest-paid player

Ty Cobb, Detroit, and Joe Jackson, Cleveland, standing alongside each other, 1913. Courtesy of the Library of Congress

in baseball. The Tigers in 1915 were led by their outfield of Cobb, Crawford, and Bobbie Veach and the pitching of Harry Coveleski (22–13) and George "Hooks" Dauss (24–13), ending with a record of 100–54. They finished two and a half games behind the Red Sox, and were the first team with 100 victories to not win a pennant. Cobb had another remarkable season, leading the AL with a .369 batting average as well as in hits (208), runs (144), and stolen bases (96, a record that lasted until 1962, though he was also thrown out a record 38 times). His outfield mates tied for the AL lead in RBIs with 112, and Cobb was third with 99. The team made about $64,000, one of only two clubs to finish in the black as MLB struggled against the Federal League.

The Feds went out of business after the season, which resulted in many reduced salaries, except for those like Cobb with long-term salaries. His salary was one-fifth of the entire team payroll. In 1916 Harry Heilmann broke into the starting lineup, replacing the aging Crawford, who had lost his speed. The club was in a virtual tie with the Red Sox in mid-September, but their hopes were killed when the Sox swept a three-game series in Navin Field. The Tigers finished third, four games out. Cobb lost the batting crown for the first time since 1910, though he cranked out 200 hits for the sixth straight year and led the majors in steals (68) and runs scored (113). Tigers' stockholders enjoyed a banner season, with profits of $126,000, double that of 1915.

The optimism that greeted the 1917 season faded as the Tigers started out poorly, and they were in last place in late May. The team ended up in fourth (78–75), despite a league-leading .259 batting average. Crawford's distinguished career came to an end after 19 years, with a lifetime batting average of .309 and 2,964 hits. Cobb regained the AL batting title at .383, some 30 points ahead of anyone else; led the majors with 55 steals; and led the AL in base hits (225), doubles (44), triples (24), total bases (336), and slugging (.571). The Tigers continued in the black, earning $50,000.

Wartime restrictions in 1918 hindered baseball. The season was cut to 140 games. Extended workdays and the absence of star players who avoided the draft by getting jobs in defense industries hurt attendance. The Tigers had a dismal season, ending in seventh place (55–71), and lost about $30,000. Cobb again led the AL with a .382 mark, 100 points higher than any teammate. Cobb volunteered for the military, despite his deferred status as a father, and served overseas as a captain in the Chemical Warfare Service.

In 1919 rosters were cut back to 21 for the 140-game season, which started two weeks later than usual. A big addition was Dutch Leonard, purchased from New York for $15,000, which helped give the Tigers a solid pitching staff along with Howard Ehmke, George "Hooks" Dauss, and Bernie Boland. The team fell off the pace in September and came in fourth, one spot out of World Series money. The exciting pennant race enabled the Tigers to lead the AL in attendance for the first time (643,805), earning the stockholders $110,000. Cobb led the majors in batting (.384) and hits (191). Veach had a very strong year, batting .355 and leading the league in doubles (45) and triples (17), and was second to Ruth in RBIs.

In 1920 the nature of play began to change dramatically as offense became emphasized. The balls carried a lot farther, all pitches that adulterated baseballs were barred, and only clean balls were used. Furthermore, players were emulating the power and prowess of Babe Ruth instead of the hard work, guile, and meticulousness of Cobb, who resented the changes. The Tigers that year were dreadful, ending in seventh, 37 games out of first. There was dissension all season between Jennings, now a heavy drinker, and his players, especially the pitchers. Cobb was injured twice and played just 112 games, batting .334. During the season Yawkey sold his stock to auto-industry tycoons John Kelsey and Walter Briggs for $500,000. Briggs was a self-made man who made a fortune in the trim- and paint-shop business, employing 40,000 workers, and had become a fixture in the city's social elite.

Jennings resigned as manager after the season, after 14 years and 1,311 victories. Navin and his new partners, after a lot of cajoling, convinced the wealthy Cobb to become player-manager, despite his own misgivings. On December 18, 1920, Cobb signed a contract to manage the Tigers for one year for $35,000, a salary second only to John J. McGraw of the Giants. Cobb's signing was well received by the fans, and, surprisingly, by his teammates. Cobb was hired because he *was* the Detroit Tigers, even though he lacked a manager's temperament. He was moody; easily frustrated; a harsh, unrelenting critic; and a hot-tempered man.

Cobb stressed fundamentals in spring training, especially bunting, base stealing, and the hit-and-run, even though he had a very slow team. He warned against fraternizing with opponents, yet gave his players freedom off the field. Cobb often platooned players, and did well instructing batting, but was not a good handler of pitchers. He was on bad terms with several players, especially

Heilmann. Late in the season he got so irate at umpire Billy Evans's calls that he followed him into the umpire's dressing room. They had what was reputedly one of the bloodiest fights in baseball history. Cobb was briefly suspended from play, but allowed to manage.

The team ended in sixth place, with 10 more victories than in 1920. Heilmann edged Cobb for the batting crown by five points with a mark of .394, earning him a 67 percent raise to $12,000. The entire team batted .316, an all-time league record, while the three starting outfielders drove in 368 runs, the most ever by an AL outfield. But the team was sixth in defense and giving up runs.

In 1922, the season started inauspiciously on April 30 when White Sox rookie Charlie Robertson pitched a perfect game against Detroit. The Tigers finished in third (79–75) as the team again batted over .300, but the only reliable hurler was Herman Pillette, with 19 wins. Cobb batted .401, second only to George Sisler's spectacular .420. The fans came out in droves, as attendance reached 861,206, second only to the Yankees. Cobb directly benefited because he got 10 cents for every ticket sold over 700,000.

Cobb brashly predicted a pennant in 1923. The fans were ready for the season, since 36,000 attended Opening Day, and then a Sunday game on May 13 against Ruth and the Yankees drew 40,884. The team, as expected, did a great job at bat, and collectively hit .300, led by Heilmann, who led the league with .403, while Cobb .hit 340 and rookie Heinie Manush, who platooned in the outfield, hit .334. But the team had the second-highest ERA (4.09) in the AL, and the defense made the fewest double plays in the majors. The team ended up in second to the Yankees, 16 games off the pace. Over the course of the season, over 900,000 Tiger fans came out to support their team, second only to the attendance at the new Yankee Stadium. The Tigers were then considered among the four richest teams in MLB.

The fan interest convinced Navin to double-deck the grandstand, raising capacity in 1924 to 30,000, with an accompanying 25-cent rise in ticket prices. His Tigers tried to make a race of it, and led the league in batting (.298), but only hit 35 homers and had inadequate pitching and too many injuries, and came in third, drawing a record 1 million fans. The long-standing feud between Cobb and the Yankees, especially Ruth, blew up in Detroit on June 13. Cobb was very jealous of Ruth, who tested his value system, which stressed family and traditional morality; challenged the old game of inside baseball; and threatened his stature as the best player in the game. The Yankees were ahead 10–6 in the ninth when pitcher Bert Cole threw at Ruth's head. After Ruth fouled out, he told Bob Meusel, who was up next, that Cobb had signaled the pitcher to throw at him too. When the first pitch hit Meusel in the ribs; he ran out to the mound, and both teams went at it. Umpire Billy Evans had the police take the Yankees to their dressing room and forfeited the game to New York.

In 1925, Cobb made $50,000, equal to AL president Johnson. On May 4, Cobb told reporters in St. Louis that he was mad that the press saw him as the antithesis of Ruth. "I'll show you something today. I'm going for home runs." The following day Cobb had six straight hits, including three homers and a double, setting an AL record of 16 total bases. One day later, he hit two more homers, plus a single, for nine straight hits. No one had hit five homers in two games since 1884. By the end of the season, the press was applauding him as a model, disciplined athlete, unlike Ruth, hospitalized purportedly because of overeating and fined $5,000 by Miller Huggins for insubordination. The team came in fourth, with Cobb at 38 batting .378 while Heilmann hit a league-leading .393. The offense was stellar, batting .304, but the pitchers had a very high 4.61 ERA.

By 1926, Detroiters were getting tired of Cobb, who baited umpires and seemed to overmanage, especially since the team came in sixth, despite a winning record (79–75). Manush won the batting championship with a .378 average; the other outfielders, Bob Fothergill and Heilmann, both hit .367; and rookie second baseman Charlie Gehringer batted .277 in the first of his 17 seasons with the Tigers, and became known as "the Mechanical Man" for his reliability. Cobb cut back on his play, though he was still frisky enough to steal home plate on July 3, and retired as manager after the season. He amassed 4,189 hits in his career, 3,900 with the Tigers, batting .366 with 11 batting championships, and stole a record 892 bases. He led in slugging eight times, on-base percentage seven times, hits eight times, runs five times, total bases six times, and stolen bases six times, and was an original inductee into the Baseball Hall of Fame in 1936.

On December 21, Dutch Leonard charged Cobb and Tris Speaker, who had just retired as Indians manager, with having tried to fix a game in late 1919. Leonard claimed that at a meeting with them and outfielder Joe Wood, Speaker had pointed out that since his Indians had already clinched second, the next day's game was meaningless for them, but vital for the Tigers, fighting with New York for third place and World Series money. Leonard claimed they agreed to bet $5,500 on the game. The Tigers won 9–5, in a game that took just 66 minutes. Leonard produced letters from Cobb and Wood that seemed to confirm his story. Leonard admitted a grudge against Cobb and Speaker, who he thought had helped push him out of baseball.

Subsequently, Swede Risberg, the Black Sox shortstop, claimed that the 1917 Sox had contributed $1,100 to the Tigers to throw doubleheaders in Chicago on September 2 and 3, and that near the end of the 1919 season, the Sox had not tried their hardest in late-season games with the Tigers. Fellow Black Sox outfielder Happy Felsch confirmed that story. Landis interviewed 34 players from the 1917 teams. They claimed the money was a reward to the Tigers for beating the Red Sox in 12 of 21 games, which was often done back then. Landis exonerated Cobb and Speaker. Cobb returned to the diamond with the Philadelphia A's, who gave him the highest salary in MLB.

George Moriarty, the old Tigers hurler, replaced Cobb as manager in 1927 and took the team to a fourth-place finish (82–71). The team continued to hit well, led by Heilmann's .398, his fourth batting title in alternating years. The highlight was an unassisted triple play on May 31 by first baseman Johnny Neun, the fourth in baseball history. Tiger games were broadcast for the first time on WWJ, with the hope that it would promote attendance. Edwin "Ty" Tyson was the voice of the Tigers through 1942. In 1934 WXYZ paid the Tigers $25,000 to broadcast over the new Michigan Radio Network. Their show featured Heilmann, whose storytelling captivated the fans.

The club repeated in fourth in 1928, but with a dismal 68–86 record, and attendance dropped by almost 300,000, producing a loss of $85,150, most to then in team history. Only 404 attended the September 25 game with the Red Sox. Moriarty was replaced by Bucky Harris, but the team remained mediocre. The club skidded to sixth place in 1929 (70–84), while continuing to pound the ball, leading the AL in batting (.299) and runs (926), but dead last in pitching (4.96 ERA). The crowds returned, nearly doubling to 869,318. Twenty-six-year-old rookie Dale "Moose" Alexander, a six-foot three-inch, 215-pound farm boy, hit .343 with 137 RBIs and 25 homers (a Tigers record), and tied for the AL lead in hits with 215. He hit .331 in six seasons, but was a butcher at first base.

The Tigers' poor play, finishing fifth three times between 1930 and 1933 and seventh in 1931, and the collapse of the auto industry during the depression, which pushed 220,000 out of work, hurt the Tigers at the box office. In 1933 attendance was down to 320,972, the lowest since 1907, and losses were nearly $85,000. Navin tried to cut three straight years of losses by barring radio broadcasts on weekends and holidays and adding such promotions as footraces and milking contests.

THE ERA OF HANK GREENBERG

In 1933 a promising rookie, Hank Greenberg, joined the Tigers, along with lefty Schoolboy Rowe, a recent Arkansas high-school graduate. Greenberg, at six feet four inches and 215 pounds, was a highly sought-after high-school ballplayer from the Bronx whom the Tigers signed in September 1929 for $6,000 and another $3,000 when he left NYU and reported to the Tigers. He became a starter in August, and hit .301 with 87 RBIs in 117 games.

After the season, the Tigers took advantage of Connie Mack's financial woes to bolster their squad. Mack started selling off his star players. He sold superstar catcher Mickey Cochrane for $100,000 to the Tigers, who made him player-manager.

Cochrane's tough leadership led the team to a remarkable turnaround. Predicted to finish in the middle of the pack, the Tigers won the pennant handily with 101 victories, leading the AL in offense and defense and second in pitching. The entire team, including six starters, batted .300. The infielders drove in 462 runs, including 139 for Greenberg and 127 for Gehringer. Cochrane, who hit .320, was MVP. Gehringer led the AL in hits (214) and runs scored (134), and Greenberg led the AL with a near record 63 doubles. The pitching improved dramatically, with Tommy Bridges emerging as a star with 21 wins. Submariner

Eldon Auker went 15–7, and Schoolboy Rowe won 24, including 16 straight, tying a league record. Attendance rose to 919,161, tops in the AL. The success of the team reputedly built up the city's self-confidence in its fight against the depression.

Greenberg was embraced by Jewish Detroiters, beset by the anti-Semitism of Henry Ford and Royal Oak radio priest Father Charles Coughlin, as a hero. Greenberg was uncertain about playing on Rosh Hashanah, but played and hit two homers, enabling the Tigers to beat Boston 2–1. He did not play on Yom Kippur, by which time the Tigers had virtually clinched the pennant. Greenberg encountered a lot of anti-Semitism, but refused to turn the other check. Following a game in 1938 when one of the White Sox on the bench called him a "yellow Jew son of a bitch," he went into the Sox clubhouse. According to Eldon Auker, Greenberg called them out, "'The guy that called me a yellow son of a bitch get on his feet and come up here and call it to my face.' Not a guy moved. He was damn lucky, because Hank would have killed him. Hank was a tough guy."

The World Series against the Cardinals was partly sponsored by Ford Motor Company, which put $100,000 into the player's pool. Dizzy Dean won game one in Detroit before 42,505 raucous fans, 8–3, as the Tigers infield committed five errors. The Bengals won game two 3–2 in 12 innings with Rowe pitching a complete game, and then two of three in St. Louis. But they lost game six in Detroit 4–3, and then in the seventh game, before 40,902 home fans, were routed 11–0.

In 1935 the confident and hungry Tigers led the pennant race most of the season, finishing with a record of 93–58, outscoring the opposition 919–665. The Tigers again led the AL in batting (.290), and averaged a half run more than their rivals per game; made just 126 errors (.979), 25 fewer than anyone else; and had a staff ERA (4.38) that led the league. Auker had a league-leading .720 winning percentage, while Bridges (163) and Rowe (140) were first and second in strikeouts. Greenberg, who was already earning $15,000, had 110 RBIs at the All-Star break, yet was not selected for the All-Star Game. Greenberg was selected as MVP and led the league in RBIs (170, 51 more then Lou Gehrig, who was second), total bases (389), and extra-base hits (98), and tied for most homers (36) with Jimmy Foxx.

The first game of the 1935 World Series in Detroit against the Cubs drew a record 47,391, but fans went home disappointed, as the Tigers were shut out 3–0 by Lon Warneke. Game two started with the temperature at 48 degrees, the coldest for a Series game since 1907, when the same two teams had played in a snowstorm. The Tigers won 8–3, but Greenberg, who had homered earlier, broke his wrist in a play at home plate. The series moved to Wrigley Field, where the Tigers captured the next two games. The Cubs stayed alive in the fifth game, winning 3–1. The Tigers closed out the series in Detroit with a 4–3 victory, as Goose Goslin drove in Cochrane from second base with a single in the bottom of the ninth. Detroiters reveled in the victory and covered downtown with ticker tape and confetti. The club earned a record $521,202 in the championship year of 1935, and declared $200,000 in dividends. Overall, in the 1930s the Tigers made $1,345,531, not bad for the depression.

That fall, Navin had a heart attack while horseback riding and died. Only then did the players learn that Briggs was a silent partner. Briggs had a reputation as a paternalistic and generous owner, who mainly used baseball to serve his city. He never took a salary and reinvested his profits back in the team. Briggs purchased Navin's share for $1 million, $100,000 over the team's book value, and then spent another $1 million fixing up the park, expanding the second deck into right field and raising the capacity to 36,000. Before the 1938 season he spent about $1 million to double-deck the left-field stands and the center-field bleachers, expanding capacity to 52,416, and renamed the stadium for himself.

In 1936 the Tigers purchased the great Al Simmons from the White Sox for $75,000. Confident of a three-peat, the team was hindered by injuries, including Greenberg, who broke his wrist and missed nearly the whole season. Cochrane suffered a nervous breakdown in June and was replaced for several weeks by coach Del Baker. The team batted .300, second best in the AL, led by Gehringer (.354) and outfielder Gee Walker (.353). Gehringer amassed 227 hits, including a league-leading 60 doubles, and four players, led by Goslin, had 100 or more RBIs. But the pitching was subpar, with only Tommy Bridges (23–11), who led the AL with 175 strikeouts, and Rowe (19–11) having solid seasons. The Tigers finished a distant second to the Yankees.

In 1937 the Tigers fell to fourth despite batting a league-leading .291, with four men amassing over 200 hits. Gehringer won the batting title (.371) and MVP Award, and Greenberg drove in 183 runs, one short of the AL record. Rudy York was a big addition behind the plate, batting .307 with 35 homers (including a record 18 in August) and 103 RBIs. But the pitching was among the worst in the AL. Cochrane was beaned on June 25, which ended his playing days, and thereafter he became a less effective manager.

In 1938, Greenberg, a notorious pull hitter, hit 58 home runs. He enjoyed hitting in Briggs Stadium, where batters had a good background and the power alley in left center was just 365 feet. Greenberg had 46 homers by the end of August, six days ahead of Ruth's pace. His race to beat Ruth dominated fan interest because the Yankees had made a shambles of the pennant race. He had 58 with five games to go, but did not homer again. He felt he had a fair chance to beat the record, and that pitchers did not pitch around him out of respect for Babe Ruth or because of anti-Semitism. Despite his brilliant season, he had to fight with Briggs to raise his $35,000 salary by $5,000.

That season, Cochrane, who was making $45,000 as manager and vice president, would often get phone calls from the tyrannical Briggs, complaining about his work with the pitching staff. Cochrane was also second-guessed by the fans, sportswriters, and even his own players. Cochrane was fired on August 6, replaced by third-base coach Del Baker.

The Tigers fell to fifth in 1939 under Baker. One year later, he shifted York, a poor catcher but a powerful hitter, to first base. Greenberg was told to play left field or face a salary cut, agreeing only after getting a $10,000 bonus. One year later, Greenberg led the Tigers to the pennant, hitting a career high of .340, which tied him for the team lead with outfielder Barney McCoskey. He led the league in homers (41), slugging (.670), doubles (50), total bases (384), and RBIs (150), and was voted MVP, the first player so honored at two different positions. The pitching was average, except for Bobo Newsom, who went 21–5, but the strong offense, which led the league in runs and batting (.286), made up for it. Rudy York had 33 homers and 134 RBIs. The key stretch came in late September when the team won 15 of its last 21 games, with Greenberg hitting .429, with 37 RBIs and 33 runs. The late-season batting surge was probably helped by Tommy Bridges, who had started using a telescopic lens from a new rifle to read the opposing catcher's signals from a seat in the upper deck.

In the World Series, the Tigers continued to steal signals at home, but not in Cincinnati, fearful that a detected spy would be beaten up. But once Reds starting catcher Ernie Lombardi got hurt and was replaced by Jimmy Wilson, his signals were given so low that the Tigers in the dugout could see them. The veteran Tigers were favored in the series, and took game one at Crosley Field 7–2, but lost game two 5–3. The teams split the next two games in Detroit, and the Tigers took game five 8–0 behind Newsom's three-hitter. But back in Cincinnati, Bucky Walters shut out the Tigers 4–0 even though the Tigers knew every pitch that was coming. Paul Derringer beat Newsom in the final game, working on one day's rest, 2–1 to take the series.

The Tigers squad was severely weakened in 1941 when Greenberg was drafted. He was honorably discharged on December 5, but enlisted in the Army Air Corps after Pearl Harbor, the first major leaguer to sign up. The Tigers slumped to fourth (75–79). Newsom fell to 12–20, was cut from $34,000 to $12,500, and refused to sign. He was subsequently sold to Washington and led the league in strikeouts.

In 1942 and 1943, the team came in fifth, reliant on the pitching staff, which in 1943 had an ERA of 3.00. Dizzy Trout was 20–12 with a 2.48 ERA and tied for the league lead with five shutouts. The team should have done better, since it led the AL in batting and was third in run production, but they committed 171 errors, second highest in the AL. York had 34 homers, 118 RBIs, and 301 total bases, and rookie outfielder Dick Wakefield hit .316 with 200 hits. Wakefield had been signed off the University of Michigan campus for a record $52,000 bonus and automobile. He batted .293 in seven years with Detroit. Another promising youngster was 22-year-old Hal Newhouser, a local boy who had joined the Tigers four years earlier, straight off the sandlots. Hal was exempt from the draft with a heart murmur.

The Tigers sold a lot of tickets during the war. In 1943 they drew over 600,000, second best in the AL, which reflected the city's large population of war-related industrial workers looking for inexpensive entertainment. The team tried to start games around 5 P.M. to entertain defense-plant workers, but the natural lighting was inadequate. Briggs Stadium also hosted Negro League ball games aimed at a black population that doubled to 300,000 during the war.

In 1944, the Tigers led the pennant race by a game going into the final weekend, then were tied starting play on Sunday. But they lost to last-place Washington and finished second, one game behind the St. Louis Browns. The team led the AL in attendance (923,176) and in pitching with the fabulous tandem of Trout (27–14) and MVP Newhouser (29–9), the only 20-game winners in the AL. They went one-two in innings pitched (352.3 and 312.3), ERA (2.12 and 2.22), complete games (33 and 25), and shutouts (7 and 6). Newhouser led in strikeouts (187), with Trout second (144).

Greenberg was the first major leaguer to return from the military in 1945, joining the Tigers on July 1, when they were just a game out of first place. He homered that day in front of 55,000 fans. On the final day of the season, the Tigers were in first by one game over the Senators, playing a doubleheader against the third-place Browns, needing a victory to clinch the pennant. The Browns were up 4–3 in the ninth, but Greenberg hit a grand slam to win the game and take the pennant. Greenberg hit .311 in 78 games, but did not have enough at bats to qualify for the batting title. The team was second in runs scored and second in ERA (2.99), led by Newhouser, who won the pitching triple crown (25–9 with a 1.81 ERA and 212 strikeouts) and MVP Award. The team again led the AL in attendance.

The World Series against the Cubs began in Detroit, where three games drew an average of over 54,000 fans. The rest of the games were scheduled for Chicago because of travel restrictions. Hank Borowy surprised the Tigers and Newhouser by beating them 9–0 in the opening game, but the Tigers came back to win game two, 4–1, with a Greenberg homer. Claude Passeau pitched a one-hitter to beat the Tigers 3–0, but the Tigers bounced back, taking the next two games at Wrigley, 4–1 and 8–4. In game six, the Tigers were down 7–3, but tied it up in the eighth, highlighted by a Greenberg home run. But the Cubs won in the 12th when a ball hit to left struck the head of a sprinkler system and bounced over Greenberg's head, letting a runner on second score the winning run. Game seven proved to be a cakewalk, as the Tigers scored five runs in the first, the key hit a bases-loaded double by Paul Richards, and won 9–3. The Tigers got over $8,000 for the winner's share, a record at the time.

After the season York was traded to Boston, and Greenberg returned to first base at his prewar salary of $55,000, plus a $20,000 bonus, which made him the highest-paid player in MLB, second in history only to Babe Ruth. The Tigers won 92 games, 4 games more than the year before, but finished 10 back of the high-flying Boston Red Sox. Greenberg batted under .300 for the first time in his career (.277), yet led the AL in homers (44) and RBIs (127). Newhouser proved to critics that he was not just a war-era pitcher by leading the AL for the third straight time in wins and the second straight time in ERA (1.94). Attendance in the first postwar season soared to 1,722,590, one-third higher than the year before. Since 1934, the Tigers had led the AL in attendance six times and were second five times. From 1920 through 1945, the Tigers earned at least $100,000 in 21 seasons, second only to the Yankees. Detroit after the war was at the height of its economic power, with the auto industry booming and workers making a lot of overtime money. Downtown was bustling with commerce during the day and entertainment at night. The Tigers' average attendance from 1946 to 1950 was 1.6 million, more than even the Yankees. The average profit between 1934 and 1945 was $151,016, which then from 1946 to 1950 rose to $213,009. Seventy-five percent of the earnings came from the box office.

The 1947 season opened without Hank Greenberg, who was unceremoniously traded to the lowly Pirates for $10,000. This was an odd send-off for the current home-run champion, longtime Detroit favorite, and future Hall of Famer. A New York paper had inaccurately implied that Greenberg wanted to play for the Yankees, which the local papers, probably egged on by Briggs, picked up on.

Attendance dropped that season by 300,000, partly due to the loss of Greenberg. However, Briggs Stadium was the scene of the largest crowd in Detroit history when 58,369 attended a Sunday doubleheader on July 20 against the hated Yankees. The Tigers came in second to the Yankees. Newhouser fell off to 17–17, but led the league in complete games and was second in strikeouts. Young third baseman George Kell, who hit .320, was the only dependable hitter on the team.

Televised TV began in Detroit on June 3, 1947, when there were only about 2,000 TVs in the city, mainly in bars and hotel lobbies, with Ty Tyson as the broadcaster. It produced little revenue at first, but by 1952, local TV was bringing in $320,000. WWJ televised about one-third of the home games in the 1950s, mostly with Van Patrick reporting the games and anecdotal Dizzy Trout, with his malapropisms, doing the color. In 1959 George Kell replaced Patrick, and one year later Ernie Harwell was added. They would both call Tiger games for over 30 years, Harwell exclusively on the radio in 1965. In 1960 the Tigers televised 42 day games, including 24 on Saturdays, and had the highest rating of any team in MLB. In 1965 local TV brought in $12 million. The Tigers made another $300,000 from WJR, its radio outlet, equal to its share of national TV.

On June 15, 1948, the Tigers introduced night baseball, the last team in the majors other than the Cubs to install lights. Briggs wanted baseball to be played only in daylight, but his son, Walter "Spike" Briggs Jr., pushed for the change. The 14 night games in 1948 averaged about 45,000 in attendance, which reflected the team's working-class fandom. Evening attendance declined once the novelty wore off, but still averaged about 30,000 in the 1950s, well above the league average.

YEARS OF MEDIOCRITY

The Tigers were competitive through 1950. Former Yankees third baseman Red Rolfe took over as skipper in 1948, and the team came in fifth (78–76) followed by a strong fourth in 1949 (86–67), when first baseman Vic Wertz had 133 RBIs and the team drew nearly 2 million. In 1950 the team did have a great season with 95 wins, just three games behind first-place New York. Kell hit .340 and led the league in doubles (56) and hits (218). But the Tigers fell to fifth in 1951 (73–81) and then into the cellar in 1952 for the first time (50–104). The only highlights that year were Virgil Trucks's two no-hitters. The team went through six different manager and five general managers in the 1950s, and never finished closer than 17 games from first place, a poor showing compared to the NFL Lions and NHL Red Wings, who won seven championships between them.

In 1953 Fred Hutchinson took over as manager in midseason as the team went 60–94 and came in sixth. The batting was solid (.266), led by Rookie of the Year shortstop Harvey Kuenn, who had 209 hits, but the pitching was the worst in the AL, with a 5.25 ERA. That season marked the first appearance of 18-year-old phenom Al Kaline, who joined the Tigers right off the Baltimore sandlots. The right fielder played 22 years with the Tigers, appeared in 18 All-Star Games, hit .297 with 3,007 hits, and earned 10 Gold Gloves. He specialized in robbing batters of home runs, especially at Yankee Stadium. Attendance dropped to under 900,000 for the first time since 1943. The Tigers finished fifth from 1954 through 1956, though the number of victories increased from 68 to 79 and then 82. In 1955, Kaline, at age 20, became the youngest batting champion (.340) since Cobb. The following year the Tigers led the league in batting (.279), while Frank Lary won a league-leading 21 games and Billy Hoeft won 20. Lary became known as "the Yankee Killer" after going 13–1 against them over two years. He led the AL three times in innings pitched and complete games. The staff also included Jim Bunning, a future Hall of Famer, who from 1955 through 1963 won 118 games and threw a no-hitter.

The team's ownership then was totally reconfigured. Walter Briggs died in 1952, and Spike became team president, but his father's holdings were put into trust. When the heirs could not come to an agreement, the probate court ordered the team sold to the highest bidder. In 1956 the team was purchased for $5.5 million by a syndicate headed by Fred A. Knorr, owner of WKMH, which had broadcast Tiger games since 1952, and John Fetzer, a pioneer in communications who served as the U.S. censor for radio during World War II. Afterward Fetzer helped design national broadcast policies and codes of ethics and then built up a statewide network on radio and TV. Knorr became president and Spike became executive vice president and general manager. One year later, Knorr, a friend of Spike's, resigned in favor of businessman Harvey Hansen. Spike was forced out and replaced as general manager by John McHale, a former Tigers first baseman.

The Tigers fell into a period of extreme mediocrity, going 78–76, 77–77, and 76–78 between 1957 and 1959. When the 1959 team started out at 2–15, manager Bill Norman was sacked and replaced by veteran manager Jimmie Dykes, whose team at one point was within half a game of first place. The outfield was outstanding: Kuenn led the AL in batting (.353), Kaline was second, and Charlie Maxwell hit 31 homers. He was especially outstanding on Sundays, when he hit 12 home runs, including 4 straight in a doubleheader at Yankee Stadium.

The mediocre play resulted in attendance of about a million, slightly above the league average but a marked decline from the late 1940s. Daytime attendance was down to 11,088, about one-third of evening events. The team tried to change this by reinstating Ladies' Day, selling women tickets for 50 cents. The promotion had been stopped in 1944 when male fans complained about women at the park. On the other hand, in 1957 the new owners raised prices for box seats to $3 (from $2.50) and reserve seats to $2 (from $1.75). General admission at $1.25 and bleachers at 75 cents were still very affordable.

The Tigers were the second-to-last team to integrate, even though Detroit had a black population of 303,721 in 1950. Walter Briggs always opposed integration, and the Tigers in 1953 were the last team to sign a black minor leaguer, a year after his death. The African American community chastised Tigers management as racist while warmly welcoming visiting black players like Larry Doby and Luke Easter of the Indians. Finally, on June 6, 1958, the Tigers brought up Ozzie Virgil, a native of the Dominican Republic who had grown up in New York City, to be their first player of color. However, as far as the local black community was concerned, Virgil was not a "Negro," and integration did not occur until the following year, when the Tigers signed veteran Larry Doby.

THE ERA OF JOHN FETZER

In 1960 John Fetzer became the largest stockholder, and a year later, the sole stockholder. He was highly regarded by the other owners, and was responsible for negotiating the first national TV contract in 1965. While not looking to make money, from 1961 to 1980 the capital invested in the Tigers appreciated 8.3 percent annually. Bill DeWitt, the new team president, made several big deals with the Indians, especially the trade of Kuenn, who had hit .314 in eight seasons, for slugger Rocky Colavito, who at 26 already had 129 homers. Rocky was a great gate attraction because of his power and matinee-idol good looks. He homered in his first at bat at Tiger Stadium and finished with 35, the most by a Tiger since 1945. However, the Tigers fell to sixth place, due to a dismal .239 batting average. DeWitt traded Dykes to Cleveland for their manager, Joe Gordon, the first midseason trade of field managers in baseball history. The team also renamed the ballpark Tiger Stadium, following a long-standing request by Spike Briggs.

The 1961 Tigers improved enormously over the dismal 1960 squad under new manager Bob Scheffing, winning 30 more games. His squad finished at 101–61, a new franchise record, but the Yankees, with 109 victories and the Mantle-Maris home-run race, garnered the most headlines. The Tigers led the AL in batting (.266) and runs (841). First baseman Norm Cash, who later admitted using a corked bat, led the majors with a .361 batting average, and Kaline was second (.324). Colavito had 45 homers and 140 RBIs, while Frank Lary went 23–9 and led the AL with 22 complete games.

In 1962 the Tigers fell back to 85–75 and fourth place, hurt by a shoulder injury to Kaline and the team's poor batting (.248), eighth in the AL. Cash alone dropped over 100 points, down to .243. But there was a lot of power, and the squad set a team record of 209 homers to lead the AL. Cash had 39 and Colavito 37, and Colavito led the league in total bases. Stylish lefty Hank Aguirre (16–9) led the majors with a sizzling 2.21 ERA.

The team fell further in 1963 to sixth place. Scheffing was fired after 60 games, and Bunning and Colavito were traded after the season. The roster did have several future stars who were products of the rebuilt farm system, including Mickey Lolich, a lefty who won 207 games in 13 years; catcher Mickey Freehan, a former Michigan football end, who made 11 All-Star teams in 15 years; and Willie Horton, a product of the city's housing projects, the team's first black star, who hit 262 homers in 15 years with the club. In 1964 the team improved to fourth (85–77). The Tigers batted .253, which in an era of great pitching was second in the AL. The team repeated in fourth place the following year, and finished third in 1966.

The Tigers stepped up in 1967 under manager Mayo Smith to win 91 and make second place. Their .243 batting average was second in the AL, and Earl Wilson went 22–11 to pace the staff. Four teams were within one and a half games of first with two days to go. The Tigers played two doubleheaders against the Angels, splitting the first and then taking the first game of the second, leaving them a half game behind Boston. But they lost the nightcap 8–5 and missed out on a playoff. Afterward hundreds of fans rioted at the ballpark, destroying seats and other property.

The city had already suffered through the riotous summer of 1967. On July 23, the Detroit riots broke out during a game against the Yankees, and smoke from the riot scene was visible inside the ballpark. Players were sent home after the game and Willie Horton pleaded with his townsfolk to cool it. The four-day riot resulted in 43 deaths and the looting of 1,700 stores, the most violent riot in American history. The game on July 25 was canceled, and then the next two games were moved to Baltimore.

THE YEAR OF THE TIGER

The Tigers came back in 1968 primed to make up for their disappointing finish in 1967. The Tigers lost on Opening Day, but then won nine straight, and were on their way to a record 103 victories and the AL pennant. They led the AL in attendance, surpassing 2 million for the first time. In an era of great pitching, the team was led by 24-year-old Denny McLain, who went 31–6 (the first 30-game winner since 1934) with a 1.96 ERA and 280 strikeouts, and led the league with 336 innings and 28 complete games. He won both the Cy

Young and MVP Awards. The entire team had an ERA of 2.71. The team batted .235, third in the league; scored the most runs (4.09 per game); and hit the most homers (185, 52 more than anyone else), led by Horton's 36.

In game one of the World Series against the Cardinals in St. Louis, Bob Gibson struck out 17 Tigers, a Series record, to win 9–8, but Lolich won the next game, 8–1. When the series switched to Detroit, the Cards took the next two games, and led 3–2 going into the seventh inning of game five, but Kaline singled with the bases loaded to give the Tigers the lead, and they won 5–3. Then, back in St. Louis, McLain led them to a 13–1 rout, and in the final game Lolich bested Gibson as the Tigers scored four times in the seventh to win 4–1. Lolich won three starts and was Series MVP. Journalists originally claimed that the team's success played a big role in healing the city's wounds, but in hindsight, it was no more than a respite.

THE ERA OF DIVISIONAL PLAY

In 1969 the Tigers were placed in the Eastern Division of the AL. The team tailed off, with 90 victories and a second-place finish. McLain went 24–9; led the league in wins, innings pitched (325), and shutouts (9); and shared the Cy Young Award with Mike Cuellar of Baltimore. The club fell to fourth place in 1970, finishing with a losing record (79–83). McLain's personal world was unraveling, and he was suspended three times: first for his alleged involvement in a bookmaking scheme in 1967, when he had a mysterious foot injury and missed several key games; then for throwing buckets of water on sportswriters; and then for carrying a gun. He got into just 14 games in 1970, going 3–5, and was packed off to the Senators in a multiplayer trade that brought Joe Coleman, Aurelio Rodriguez, and Eddie Brinkman.

Billy Martin was hired to manage the team in 1971, and he turned things around, coming in second (91–71). The Tigers led the league in homers and were second in runs scored, but key were the performances of Mickey Lolich, who went 25–14 and pitched an incredible 376 innings, and Joe Coleman, 20–9, who threw 286 frames.

The Tigers were in the heart of the pennant race in 1972 despite a very weak offense because the pitchers had an ERA of 2.96, fifth in the AL. Lolich and Coleman carried the team with 41 wins between them, abetted by Woody Fryman, who won 10 games in half the season. The team had a superb defense and committed just 96 errors (.984 fielding percentage), best in the AL, led by Eddie Brinkman at short, who had 72 straight errorless games, and Aurelio Rodriguez at third. The Tigers finished the season at home in a series against the first-place Red Sox, down by just a half game. The Tigers took the next two games for their 85th and 86th wins and clinched the division. The Tigers then faced the powerful Oakland Athletics for the pennant. The A's took the first two games in Oakland, and then the Tigers won twice at home. The A's took the exciting finale, 2–1, and advanced to the World Series. In 1973 the team won

Al Kaline during a game in 1970. © AP / Wide World Photos

85 games, but the Billy Martin mystique blew up, and he was fired late in the season for his inability to discipline himself. Martin had a major problem with alcohol, and the players felt he was paranoid and a manipulator.

The Tigers were a great attraction from 1968 through 1973, after the 1967 riot. They averaged 1.7 million fans, and were annually first or second in the AL. This reflected the quality of the team and its fan support. The spectators were increasingly suburbanites, who found that going to games helped them maintain a sense of being Detroiters. They had excellent access to the field via the vast highway system built in the 1950s, and were apparently not afraid of the neighborhood or the city. There was a problem with traffic, and in 1958 the team shifted starting times to 1:30 compared to 3:30 in the past to avoid rush hour, which made attending games harder for industrial workers on regular shifts. The suburbanites' main problem was parking. The Tigers had no lot, but there were 6,000 private spots near the park, along with rented-out front lawns. In the 1970s people would park on city streets and pay a youth to "watch" the car.

Attendance began to decline in 1974, the year Ralph Houk, former Yankees manager, took over. His team came in sixth and last in the AL East in 1974 (72–90), with the poorest pitching in the entire league, and then things got worse. The Tigers lost 102 games, including 19 in a row, in 1975, and then won only 74 games each of the next two years. The Tigers did not finish in the first division again until 1983. The decline was also due to the decline of the rust-belt city. Detroit's population peaked at 2 million in the early 1950s, and then began to decline as white residents moved out of the city, attracted by cheap homes, improved highway travel, and fear of blacks, who in 1970 comprised 44 percent of the city's population. This led to a shift in the tax base, the migration of downtown institutions like departments stores to the suburbs, and a decline in urban services, including mass transit and police.

They city began to be perceived, correctly, as increasingly dangerous (for instance, the interstate highway inside the city had to be protected by the state police), and was known as "the Murder City," which deterred suburban fans. White fans were not replaced by black fans, who were put off by the team's racist reputation.

The team was slightly better than average from 1978 to 1980, winning 86, 85, and 84 games, but finishing in fifth each year in the powerful Eastern Division. Les Moss took over in 1979, supplanted one-third of the way into the season in favor of the legendary Sparky Anderson. The team's competitiveness was limited by a reticence to enter into free agency, ostensibly because of costs. They signed one, shortstop Tito Fuentes, between 1976 and 1979. The Tigers could have afforded to enter the bidding. In 1979 their salaries were 24th out of 26 teams. Yet the following year the team's net earnings were $2 million, followed by $900,000 in 1982. Fetzer made an average of $2.1 million between 1961 and 1981, half of the profit coming from nonbaseball operations, including rent from the Detroit Lions. The avoidance of free agency symbolized the old-fashioned ways of the management, which did not keep up with the times, avoiding promotional events and skimping on scouting, which resulted in the production of few major-league prospects.

The team did have a few notable performers in the 1970s, including Detroiter Ron LeFlore, who was paroled from Jackson State Prison to play baseball. He averaged 49 steals a year from 1974 to 1979 and hit .300 three times, while Rusty Staub, the primary designated hitter, averaged 106 RBIs between 1976 and 1978. The most refreshing performer was Mark "the Bird" Fidrych, a 21-year-old rookie in 1976, who started the All-Star Game and went 19–9, leading the AL with a 2.34 ERA. Earning just $16,000, his starts attracted 60 percent of the Tigers' home audience and accounted for $1 million of the team's revenues. But injuries led to his premature demise.

THE PIZZA BOYS

In 1981 the players went on strike and got little sympathy from struggling blue-collar workers, who did not empathize with athletes who averaged nearly $200,000 a year. In the split season of 1981, the Tigers finished fourth in the first half of the season and second in the second half, with an overall record of 60–49. In 1982, Anderson led the team to its fifth straight winning year, but still only finished fourth in the tough AL East. Finally, in 1983, the city had a contender, coming in a strong second (92–70), led by Jack Morris, who won 20 games, and Dan Petry, who won 19; the sparkling keystone combination of Alan Trammell and Lou Whitaker, who hit .319 and .320 respectively; and catcher Lance Parrish, who drove in 114 and hit 27 homers. Trammell and Whitaker eventually set a record for the longest careers as shortstop and second base teammates (1977–95). Whitaker hit .276 with 2,369 hits in 19 seasons, and Trammell hit .285 with 2,365 hits in 20 seasons.

After the season Fetzer sold the team in a highly leveraged deal for $53 million, 10 times what the team had cost back in 1956, to Tom Monaghan, the founder and owner of Domino's Pizza. Monaghan was a self-made man worth nearly $500 million who spared himself few extravagances, including a collection of over 100 antique cars. He was originally perceived as a white knight, but according to Tigers historian Richard Bak, he was "a socially inept public figure and no friend of the city." Monaghan owned the team for nine years and never lost money. His biggest source of new revenue was from the media. Detroit had the seventh-largest TV market in America, and in the mid-1980s the Tigers had the highest ratings of any team. The money made from radio and local, national, and cable TV rose from $14.4 million in 1987 to $24.9 million in 1991.

Before the 1984 campaign, Anderson promised the city the best Tigers team of all time, and he may have been right. General manager Bill Lajoie, who replaced Campbell, promoted to team president, made important trades to bolster the squad, sending John Wockenfuss and Glenn Wilson to the Phillies for much-needed lefty reliever Willie Hernandez and first baseman Dave Bergman. He also spent $800,000 outbidding 20 teams for the services of slugger Darrell Evans, the team's first important free agent. The average Tiger salary jumped from 17th ($263,899) to 10th ($371,332). The team won 104 games, was in first place from day one, and took the division by 15 games. The Tigers were a scoring machine, leading the AL in homers and runs scored. Parrish and Kirk Gibson combined for 60 homers and 189 RBIs. The pitching staff led the AL in ERA for the first time in 40 years. Five pitchers won 10 or more games, led by Morris (19–11), Petry (18–8), and Milt Wilcox (17–8). Hernandez was outstanding, going 9–3 with 32 saves in 80 games, and won the Cy Young and MVP Awards. Sparky Anderson was selected Manager of the Year. Fans came out in droves—2.7 million, still the team record. The Tigers made $7.8 million that year, second in all of baseball.

The Tigers played Kansas City for the pennant and swept them in three games, moving on to the World Series against the San Diego Padres. The teams split two games on the West Coast, and then the Tigers took three straight at home to take the series. The heroes were MVP Alan Trammell, with nine hits, and local boy Gibson, a former football star at Michigan State, who hit two homers and drove in seven. He was an extremely intense athlete, who had hit 27 homers and stolen 19 bases during the regular season. Local fans responded by rioting, which was picked up by national TV and reinforced Detroit's negative image.

In 1985, the Tigers failed to defend their crown, winning 20 fewer games and falling to third place, despite hitting 202 home runs. Evans hit 40 to lead the AL, the first Tiger to do so since Greenberg in 1946. Gibson had 39 homers, 97 RBIs, and 30 steals. He was rewarded with a $4 million contract for three years, making him the first million-dollar Tigers player. The Tigers came in third again in 1986. Jack Morris went 21–8, led the AL with eight shutouts, and gained a $1.85 million contract in arbitration.

In 1987, the divisional race came down to the final weekend in Toronto, with the Tigers down by one game. They swept the series to capture the division, with Detroiter Frank Tanana winning the final game 1–0. Morris won 21 games and got support from a late-season pickup, the veteran Doyle Alexander, who won nine straight. The offense was led by Trammell, who batted cleanup and hit .343 with 28 homers and 105 RBIs, and newcomer catcher Matt Nokes, who hit 32 homers. The team led the majors with 225 home runs and 896 runs, the most in baseball in 34 years. The Tigers, who won 98, the most in the majors, were expected to roll over the Minnesota Twins, but lost the first two games in the Metrodome. Detroit salvaged game three at home, but lost the next two and were eliminated. After the season the Tigers lost several key players, most notably Gibson, when an arbitrator ruled that the owners had conspired to restrict the opportunities of free agents. The Tigers' share of the collusion settlement was $10.8 million, including $1,786,666 to Parrish. Morris stayed with the Tigers until 1991, winning 198 games over 14 seasons.

In 1988, with the second-highest payroll in MLB, nearly $16 million, the club came in second with 88 wins, but one year later the club collapsed to seventh and just 59 victories due to the worst pitching and batting in the AL. But the Tigers bounded back in 1990 with 20 more wins, and moved up to third place. The Tigers led the league in homers in 1990 behind first baseman Cecil Fielder and his 51 homers. Fielder was a run-making machine, leading the majors in RBIs from 1990 through 1992, averaging over 129 a year. The team was first or second in the majors in both homers and runs from 1990 through 1993, with a high of 899 in 1992. The price, however, was a league record in strikeouts (1,185) in 1991, led by Rob Deer's 175.

On January 8, 1990, Campbell was promoted to chairman and CEO to make way for Monaghan's old friend, Bo Schembechler, former University of Michigan head football coach. His tenure was a total disaster. Late in 1990, WWJ fired the popular Ernie Harwell, a Hall of Fame announcer, and the public blamed Schembechler. Another problem was the status of Tiger Stadium, which had been antiquated by the 1960s, and its foundation was crumbling. In 1972 the Tigers and the Lions failed to get a bond issue passed for a $126 million domed stadium. Five years later Fetzer sold the park to the city for one dollar. The city rehabbed the edifice for $18.1 million and gave the Tigers a 30-year lease. The city was desperate to turn things around, but the quality of life in Detroit continued to decline. Fifty thousand jobs were lost between 1978 and 1988, helping push the black middle class out of the city, which had a black majority since 1973.

Schembechler and Monaghan wanted a new publicly financed stadium, but the fans wanted renovations. They liked that Tiger Stadium had the most bleacher seats in MLB, and did not care about the 10,000 obstructed seats because the seating area was so close to the field. Fans organized the 11,000-member Tiger Stadium Fan Club. The club got the field listed in the National Register of Historic Places, produced their own renovation study, and in 1992 supported a successful ballot initiative to prevent city funds from being used for a new stadium.

In 1992 Monaghan overextended himself financially, and his bankers forced him to sell the Tigers for $85 million to Mike Ilitch, owner of Little Caesar's Pizza, leaving a net profit of $40 million from the ball club. Ilitch, whose total worth in 2004 was $750 million, was a local boy and a legitimate civic booster. He moved his corporate headquarters downtown, operated the Red Wings and the Olympia Arena, and spent a lot of money renovating downtown recreational facilities. He seemed to do all the right things, bringing back Harwell and Gibson, spending $8 million renovating the ballpark, and creating a fun atmosphere at the ballyard. At first he opened his deep pockets to rebuild the team, but he passed the expense on to the fans. A family of four paid $103.45 for the full baseball experience, which rose in 2000 to $165, fourth highest in the majors. Ilitch established a premium seating area called the Tiger Den for the corporate crowd, creating a class division antithetical to the Tigers' tradition.

The 1992 squad had the worst pitching in the AL and came in sixth (75–87). The next year the team came in fourth with a winning record (85–77), the last Tiger team do so. It had a strong offense, but some of the poorest pitching in the major leagues. One year later, MLB established its three-division format and assigned the Tigers to the tough East. In the shortened strike season, the Tigers ended in last place. They were last in attendance in the AL and lost an estimated $5.4 million, the first losing season since 1941.

In the 1990s, according to historian Patrick Harrigan, "the club became separate from the city, and the wider metropolitan community divorced itself from the city." By 1990, the city's population, down to 1 million, was 80 percent African American, and while there was a lot of poverty, many could afford a game. The household income of $16,403 was among the highest of any city, reflected by their presence at the more expensive Pistons games. The low African American attendance in Detroit was hardly unique, but occurred across the country. The team did not ardently try to reach out to the community. When combined with mediocre teams, the result was that the Tigers were no better than 11th out of 14 AL teams in attendance from 1989 through 1998. In the 1990s the team averaged about 1.5 million in attendance, 25 percent below the AL norm. In the next few years, the Tigers finished as high as seventh in attendance only once after 1987. Detroit is no longer one of the top baseball towns.

Ilitch's investment dropped in value by $16 million in the two years after he bought the team. The team was still out of touch with its fans and with young players, who, if they could, avoided the Tigers. Ilitch's money was wasted on unproductive free agents. Harrigan also blamed public-relations flaps, a more critical media, an alienating mayor, and downtown violence in America's murder capital.

Following losing seasons in 1994 and 1995 (when the Tigers had the eighth-highest payroll in MLB), Anderson retired after 18 years in Detroit with a winning percentage of .516. He was replaced by Buddy Bell, burdened with a 40 percent cut in payroll (23rd in MLB) and a team comprised of inexperienced players and retreads. They went 53–109, and were last in the AL in batting (setting a record for strikeouts with 1,268), fielding, and ERA. The team's 6.38 ERA was the second worst in baseball history. Attendance was a dismal 1.2 million, half of whom were no-shows. The 1997 payroll was just $16.3 million, second lowest in MLB, but the team improved to third place in the AL East (79–83), the highest team finish since 1991. The Tigers since 1997 have ranked on average 21st out of 30 clubs in salaries. Bell was replaced late in 1998 by Larry Parrish, and then by Phil Garner in 2000.

In 1995 a deal was completed with the city for a new 25-acre park a few blocks east of Woodward Avenue and south of I-75, in an area of boarded-up buildings. The municipality's goal was to help revitalize downtown in conjunction with the creation of new museums and General Motors' purchase of the Renaissance Center for its world headquarters. The proposal to use $115 million in public funding, with Ilitch paying the balance, was approved one year later by 81 percent of Wayne County voters, especially since a lion's share of the cost would be borne by tourists paying new hotel and car-rental taxes and money from Indian casino revenue.

The park is owned by the Stadium Authority, which has leased it to the Tigers for 35 years. The team pays most of the projected $6.5 million operating costs and gets all concessions revenue from baseball events. It was designed as a 40,120-seat retro park, similar to Camden Yards, with three decks, 65 luxury boxes, 5,200 club seats, and 4,500 parking spaces. In 2000, ticket prices were the fourth highest in MLB. The field includes such old-fashioned touches as brick and steel construction and asymmetrical dimensions. Its new features included a sunken playing field, rides for children, a huge concourse, a "Walking Hall of Fame," the largest scoreboards in the United States, and a great view of downtown. It is the hub for a growing entertainment industry in its vicinity. Comerica, a locally based financial-services company, bought the naming rights for $66 million over 30 years.

The opening of Comerica Park bumped up attendance by 20 percent to 2.4 million, but the team has not reached 2 million since then. Garner was ignominiously cashiered after six games in 2002 and replaced by Luis Pujols, and the team won just 55 games. Former star shortstop Alan Trammell took the reigns in 2003, and the young team was abysmal, going 43–119, one of the all-time worst records in MLB history. The experience gained that season and the addition of free agent Pudge Rodriguez helped the Tigers improve to 72–90 in 2004, giving long-suffering Tigers fans hope for the future. But there was no improvement in 2005, and Trammell was fired. Despite the poor play on the field, the Tigers in 2005 were worth $239 million, a handsome return on Ilitch's original investment.

Throughout the Tigers' history, they have had a strong fan base, and the team itself has nearly always been an important Detroit institution, one that especially appealed to blue-collar workers. In good times and bad, it has typically stood for the finest qualities with which Detroiters identify. But what was once a booming city has deteriorated dramatically because of suburbanization and the weakening of the auto industry. Safety is a big concern when your hometown is rated in 2005 as the most dangerous city in America. The franchise's financial success depends on the continuing identification of suburbanites with their hometown team, but management has had a hard time securing the talent to bring back the fans.

NOTABLE ACHIEVEMENTS

Most Valuable Players

Year	Name	Position
1934	Mickey Cochrane	C
1935	Hank Greenberg	1B
1937	Charlie Gehringer	2B
1940	Hank Greenberg	OF
1944	Hal Newhouser	P
1945	Hal Newhouser	P
1968	Denny McLain	P
1984	Willie Hernandez	P

Cy Young Winners

Year	Name	Position
1968	Denny McLain	RHP
1969	Denny McLain	RHP
1984	Willie Hernandez	RHP

Rookies of the Year

Year	Name	Position
1953	Harvey Kuenn	SS
1976	Mark Fidrych	P
1978	Lou Whitaker	2B

Batting Champions

Year	Name	#
1907	Ty Cobb	.350
1908	Ty Cobb	.324
1909	Ty Cobb	.377
1910	Ty Cobb	.383

1911	Ty Cobb	.420
1912	Ty Cobb	.410
1913	Ty Cobb	.390
1914	Ty Cobb	.368
1915	Ty Cobb	.369
1917	Ty Cobb	.383
1918	Ty Cobb	.382
1919	Ty Cobb	.384
1921	Harry Heilmann	.394
1923	Harry Heilmann	.403
1925	Harry Heilmann	.393
1926	Heinie Manush	.378
1927	Harry Heilmann	.398
1937	Charlie Gehringer	.371
1949	George Kell	.343
1955	Al Kaline	.340
1959	Harvey Kuenn	.353
1961	Norm Cash	.361

Home-Run Champions

Year	Name	#
1908	Sam Crawford	7
1909	Ty Cobb	9
1935	Hank Greenberg	36
1938	Hank Greenberg	58
1940	Hank Greenberg	41
1943	Rudy York	34
1946	Hank Greenberg	44
1985	Darrell Evans	40
1990	Cecil Fielder	51
1991	Cecil Fielder	44

ERA Champions

Year	Name	#
1902	Ed Siever	1.91
1944	Dizzy Trout	2.12
1945	Hal Newhouser	1.81
1946	Hal Newhouser	1.94
1962	Hank Aguirre	2.21
1976	Mark Fidrych	2.34

Strikeout Champions

Year	Name	#
1935	Tommy Bridges	163
1936	Tommy Bridges	175
1944	Hal Newhouser	187
1945	Hal Newhouser	212
1949	Virgil Trucks	153
1959	Jim Bunning	201
1960	Jim Bunning	201
1971	Mickey Lolich	308
1983	Jack Morris	232

No-Hitters

Name	Date
George Mullin	07/04/1912
Virgil Trucks	05/15/1952
Virgil Trucks	08/25/1952
Jim Bunning	07/20/1958
Jack Morris	04/07/1984

POSTSEASON APPEARANCES

AL East Division Titles

Year	Record	Manager
1972	86–70	Billy Martin
1984	104–58	Sparky Anderson
1987	98–64	Sparky Anderson

AL Pennants

Year	Record	Manager
1907	92–58	Hughie Jennings
1908	90–63	Hughie Jennings
1909	98–54	Hughie Jennings
1934	101–53	Mickey Cochrane
1935	93–58	Mickey Cochrane
1940	90–64	Del Baker
1945	88–65	Steve O'Neill
1968	103–59	Mayo Smith
1984	104–58	Sparky Anderson

World Championships

Year	Opponent	MVP
1935	Chicago	
1945	Chicago	
1968	St. Louis	Mickey Lolich
1984	San Diego	Alan Trammell

MANAGERS

2006	Jim Leyland
2003–2005	Alan Trammell
2002	Luis Pujols
2000–2002	Phil Garner
1998–1999	Larry Parrish
1996–1998	Buddy Bell
1979–1995	Sparky Anderson
1979	Dick Tracewski
1979	Less Moss
1974–1978	Ralph Houk
1973	Joe Schultz
1971–1973	Billy Martin
1967–1970	Mayo Smith
1966	Frank Skaff
1966	Bob Swift
1965	Chuck Dressen
1965	Bob Swift
1963–1964	Chuck Dressen
1961–1963	Bob Scheffing
1960	Joe Gordon
1960	Billy Hitchcock
1959–1960	Jimmie Dykes
1958–1959	Bill Norman
1957–1958	Jack Tighe
1955–1956	Bucky Harris
1952–1954	Fred Hutchinson
1949–1952	Red Rolfe
1943–1948	Steve O'Neill
1938–1942	Del Baker
1938	Mickey Cochrane
1937	Cy Perkins
1937	Del Baker
1937	Mickey Cochrane

1936	Del Baker
1934–1936	Mickey Cochrane
1933	Del Baker
1929–1933	Bucky Harris
1927–1928	George Moriarty
1921–1926	Ty Cobb
1907–1920	Hughie Jennings
1905–1906	Bill Armour
1904	Bobby Lowe
1903–1904	Ed Barrow
1902	Frank Dwyer
1901	George Stallings

Team Records by Individual Players

Batting Leaders

	Single Season			Career		
	Name		Year	Name		Plate Appearances
Batting average	Ty Cobb	.420	1911	Ty Cobb	.368	12,105
On-base %	Norm Cash	.487	1961	Ty Cobb	.434	12,105
Slugging %	Hank Greenberg	.683	1938	Hank Greenberg	.616	5,586
OPS	Norm Cash	1.148	1961	Hank Greenberg	1.028	5,586
Games	Rockey Colavito	163	1961	Al Kaline	2,834	11,597
At bats	Harvey Kuenn	679	1953	Ty Cobb	10,591	12,105
Runs	Ty Cobb	147	1911	Ty Cobb	2,088	12,105
Hits	Ty Cobb	248	1911	Ty Cobb	3,900	12,105
Total bases	Hank Greenberg	397	1937	Ty Cobb	5,466	12,105
Doubles	Hank Greenberg	63	1934	Ty Cobb	665	12,105
Triples	Sam Crawford	26	1914	Ty Cobb	284	12,105
Home runs	Hank Greenberg	58	1938	Al Kaline	399	11,597
Strikeouts	Cecil Fielder	182	1990	Lou Whitaker	1,099	9,967
Stolen bases	Ty Cobb	96	1915	Ty Cobb	865	12,105
Extra-base hits	Hank Greenberg	103	1937	Ty Cobb	1,060	12,105
Times on base	Ty Cobb	336	1915	Ty Cobb	5,133	12,105

Pitching Leaders

	Single Season			Career		
	Name		Year	Name		Innings Pitched
ERA	Summers	1.64	1908	Harry Coveleski	2.34	1,023.3
Wins	Denny McLain	31	1968	Hooks Dauss	222	3,390.7
Won-loss %	Bill Donovan	.862	1907	Denny McLain	.654	1,593
Hits/9 IP	Jeff Robinson	6.33	1988	Denny McLain	7.46	1,593
Walks/9 IP	Fred Hutchinson	1.29	1951	Don Mossi	1.75	929.7
Strikeouts	Mickey Lolich	308	1971	Mickey Lolich	2,679	3,361.7
Strikeouts/9 IP	Mickey Lolich	8.69	1969	John Hiller	7.51	1,242
Games	Mike Myers	88	1997	John Hiller	546	1,242
Saves	Todd Jones	42	2000	Mike Henneman	154	669.7
Innings	George Mullin	382.3	1904	George Mullin	3,394	3,394
Starts	Mickey Lolich	45	1971	Mickey Lolich	459	3,361.7
Complete games	George Mullin	42	1904	George Mullin	336	3,394
Shutouts	Denny McLain	9	1969	Mickey Lolich	39	3,361.7

Source: Drawn from data in "Detroit Tigers Batting Leaders (seasonal and career)." http://baseball-reference.com/teams/DET/leaders_bat.shtml; "Detroit Tigers Pitching Leaders (seasonal and career)." http://baseball-reference.com/teams/DET/leaders_pitch.shtml.

BIBLIOGRAPHY

Alexander, Charles C. *Ty Cobb*. New York: Oxford University Press, 1984.

Anderson, William. "From the Ballpark to the Battlefield . . . and Back!! The Detroit Tigers during World War II." *Michigan History* 79 (September–October 1995): 10–18.

———. "They Caught Lightning! The 1968 Detroit Tigers." *Michigan History* 77 (September–October 1993): 17–21.

Bak, Richard. *A Place for Summer: A Narrative History of Tiger Stadium*. Detroit: Wayne State University Press, 1998.

Baulch, Vivian M., and Patricia Zacharias. "The Day the Tigers Finally Integrated." *Detroit News*. http://info.detnews.com/history/story/index.cfm?id=53&category=sports.

Bingay, Malcolm. *Detroit Is My Own Home Team*. Indianapolis: Bobbs-Merrill, 1946.

Cantor, George. *The Tigers of '68: Baseball's Last Real Champions.* Dallas: Taylor, 1997.

Harrigan, Patrick. J. *The Detroit Tigers: Club and Community, 1945–1995.* Toronto: University of Toronto Press, 1997.

Hawkins, Jim, and Dan Ewald. *Detroit Tigers Encyclopedia.* Toronto: Sports Publishing, 2003.

Jordan, David M. *A Tiger in His Time: Hal Newhouser and the Burden of Wartime Baseball.* South Bend, IN: Diamond, 1990.

Kaline, Al, and Dan Eward. *John Fetzer: On a Handshake; The Times and Triumphs of a Tiger Owner.* Detroit: Wayne State University Press, 2000.

Lam, Tina. "Celebration Marks End of Long Road." *Detroit Free Press,* April 11, 2000.

Okkonen, Marc. "The 1950 Detroit Tigers." *The National Pastime* 15 (1995): 154–56.

Selko, Jamie. "Harry Who? The Story of Harry Heilmann's Four Batting Titles." *The National Pastime* 15 (1995): 45–50.

Stanton, Tom. *The Final Season: Fathers, Sons, and One Last Season in a Classic American Ballpark.* New York: St. Martin's Press, 2001.

Kansas City Royals

Myles Schrag

The Kansas City Royals were the shrewdest, most innovative, and most successful franchise of the first expansion era. In their first 17 seasons they won a World Series, two American League pennants, and seven AL Western Division titles, and were in serious playoff contention within five years. However, the Royals struggled mightily to adapt to the new economic realities of the 1990s. While the team's deceased founder long vowed that the team would never be relocated, the Royals are now the poster child of small-market franchises, and suffer economically for it.

EWING KAUFFMAN: THE ANTI-FINLEY

Almost from the moment on October 18, 1967, that Charles O. Finley finally made good on his perpetual threat to move his Athletics, Kansas City baseball fans could not have asked for, let alone receive, a better benefactor. Ewing Kauffman was the anti-Finley. Whereas Finley had threatened moves to Dallas–Fort Worth, Louisville, Atlanta, Milwaukee, and Seattle in the seven years since he had bought the A's in December 1960, Kauffman readily admitted his decision to buy a baseball team was made largely because he wanted Kansas City to have one. Whereas Finley craved headlines and was known for well-publicized antics, Kauffman was an efficient, bright businessman that stayed in the background and put baseball operations in the hands of baseball men. He had started a pharmaceutical company, Marion Laboratories, in his Kansas City basement back in 1950 and turned it into a billion-dollar company by the time he sold it in 1989.

Kauffman was not even much of a baseball fan, but he had great loyalty to his city and craved a new business challenge at the time that civic leaders asked for his support in bringing a new baseball team to Kansas City. When Kauffman was officially awarded the franchise by AL president Joe Cronin on January 11, 1968, Kauffman distinguished himself from Finley in no uncertain terms: "In my lifetime, this team will never be moved. If there is a financial loss, I can stand it. But I hope we can develop a successful organization."

At the AL meeting in late 1967, Finley asked his fellow owners for permission to move to Oakland the next season, but only got five of nine votes. After a short break, another vote was taken. The Yankees changed their vote to a yes, giving Finley the necessary two-thirds. Kansas City was promised an expansion team no later than 1971 as consolation. Missouri senator Stuart Symington and others in the Kansas City delegation weren't so easily appeased. The influential Symington chastised Cronin, threatening to revoke baseball's antitrust exemption, and demanded action sooner than 1971. While Kansas City had grown tired of Finley long ago, local leaders wanted to keep professional baseball, which had arrived in 1955. The city's voters had approved in June 1967 a $42 million bond issue for the construction of a state-of-the-art baseball/football sports complex. It needed another tenant besides the defending AFL champion Chiefs. The city's representatives knew the AL had no desire to go through the hassles of litigation that the NL had two years earlier when Milwaukee had unsuccessfully sued to keep the Braves. Cronin managed to convince enough team representatives to reconsider their options. After midnight, the AL and Kansas City had agreed on granting an 11th franchise for the 1969 season.

Kauffman outbid three other local proposals to get the promised expansion team with a $5.3 million purchase price, but he had proved his ownership mettle even before the January 1968 announcement. At a chamber-of-commerce luncheon in Kansas City concerning the need to mount a financial effort for the new franchise, Kauffman raised his hand and said he would be willing to put in $1 million to the cause. When legendary Kansas City Star sports editor Ernie Mehl and businessman Earl Smith visited Kauffman in the weeks leading up to the AL owners meeting to tell him nobody else had come forward to join a consortium to purchase the team, he quickly obtained letters of credit for $4 million and $6 million to demonstrate he could afford it.

Once Kauffman had won the franchise, Cedric Tallis was his first major hire. Most recently vice president of the California Angels, Tallis would be Kauffman's executive vice president. Tallis picked Lou Gorman, Baltimore's director of minor-league clubs, to be director of player development, and longtime scout Charlie Metro to be director of player personnel. The team name was a nod to the American Royal parade and pageant held annually to celebrate Kansas City's livestock industry. Kauffman's board of directors included many local leaders, including the Star's Mehl.

The experienced Joe Gordon was chosen as field manager on September 9, five weeks before the expansion draft. In the draft, the organization proved sincere in its claims to want to build steadily with youth rather than rely on veterans. The highlight of the Royals' inaugural 69–93 campaign (fourth out of six teams in the newly formed AL Western Division) was Lou Piniella's Rookie of the Year Award. Piniella was a steal Tallis engineered from the Seattle Pilots prior to the 1969 season for Steve Whitaker and John Gelnar. Some expansion draftees became Tallis's trade bait for the future. Tallis's patience in building a strong farm system and his shrewd dealings soon made the Royals one of the most feared teams in the AL.

THE BASEBALL ACADEMY

The hallmark of that farm system was a Kauffman brainstorm known as the Royals' Baseball Academy. Kauffman felt that he needed to find an edge over his more established opponents by developing players more efficiently than traditional means. He had already hired more coaches at the minor-league level than other major-league teams, but the $1.5 million academy was a significant undertaking that showcased Kauffman's entrepreneurial spirit and creative problem solving. The academy, which opened in Sarasota, Florida, in August 1970, attempted to use science, technology, and better training methods to develop baseball skills in nonbaseball players that showcased athletic abilities. Kauffman sought athletes overlooked by the baseball-scouting establishment, figuring someone with the right temperament and talent could be taught baseball skills.

Longtime scout Syd Thrift became director of the academy, and put together a staff of baseball coaches, former players, a strength coach, a trainer, a track coach (former Olympic distance runner Wes Santee), two ophthalmologists, a physiologist, and a psychologist . This crew became the first concerted effort to measure, evaluate, and improve baseball players and the way that baseball is played. Academy teams played in the rookie Gulf Coast League. Players lived on campus at least 10 months a year and were required to take courses at Manatee Junior College.

The academy's legacy is mixed. Thrift and Kauffman wanted it to continue despite its annual $700,000 cost. Other key figures saw it as competition for resources that could be used in more traditional player development. Thrift resigned in 1972 out of frustration, and while Kauffman wanted to give the academy more time, he admitted the financial commitment was considerable. Teams fully stocked by academy players only played three seasons, 1971–73.

On the positive side, the instruction players received there was highly regarded, particularly the emphasis on smart and aggressive baserunning that became a hallmark of the dominant Royals teams of the late 1970s. Two of the three teams that consisted solely of academy players finished in first place or tied for first place in the Gulf Coast League, and all three squads led the league in stolen bases. Most importantly, some graduates moved up in the Royals' farm system, most notably Frank White, who joined the big-league squad in

June 1973 and manned second base for much of the next 18 years. White was a Kansas City native, having grown up within walking distance of Municipal Stadium. Because his high school didn't offer baseball, he had only played in summer leagues as a teen and wasn't scouted. When Royals manager Jack McKeon wanted to bring him up to the major-league team, White recalled that some in the organization were not pleased because they felt it would only encourage Kauffman to keep the academy funded.

Whether the academy only served as a bizarre, expensive baseball experiment or was a precursor to more advanced scientific and psychological testing of ballplayers that would become commonplace years later, 14 graduates eventually reached the majors. Without it, White would have kept working at a Kansas City sheet-metal company rather than become the best defensive second baseman of his era and MVP of the 1980 AL Championship Series. Interestingly, Kauffman's vow to listen to his baseball men in making baseball decisions eventually doomed the academy.

BUILDING A CONTENDER

The Royals had their first winning season in only their third year, under manager Bob Lemon in 1971, but were only a shadow of the A's, who won consecutive World Series crowns from 1972 to 1974. Kansas City was a model expansion franchise with its quick ascent, but it was unclear if the Royals would ever surpass the A's to reach the postseason. "Trader Tallis" gave the Royals that opportunity with many shrewd trades in the Royals' early years. Indeed, by the time the free-agency era opened in 1976, the Royals' patient approach to building a contender had developed a lineup that would be in place for many successful campaigns to come, while Finley's A's would soon be dismantled. It could easily be argued that until after the 1981 season, no trade the Royals had made in franchise history was a complete bust. Tallis made a number of one-sided deals in favor of the Royals. He obtained Amos Otis from the Mets in December 1969, who became a three-time Gold Glove center fielder and a crowd favorite when the team was still seeking an identity. Seven months later he obtained Cookie Rojas, a steady second baseman for the Cardinals, who held down the position until White was ready to take over full time in 1976. In December he obtained the spunky five-foot four-inch shortstop Freddy Patek from Pittsburgh, who contributed to a strong defensive presence up the middle. Burly John Mayberry came from the Astros in December 1971 and provided the Royals' biggest home-run threat during their championship years. Finally, Hal McRae, a hard-nosed competitor, came from the Reds in December 1972. He started as an outfielder and later emerged as the first designated-hitting star.

The Royals' pitching, by contrast, was mostly homegrown. Paul Splittorff, the first player originally signed by the Royals to make the big-league squad, became the team's first 20-game winner in 1973. Steve Busby tossed no-hitters in 1973 and 1974. Larry Gura, who was acquired from the Yankees in May 1976, and Dennis Leonard grew into two of the AL's most consistent starters.

Led by these players, the Royals fielded a scrappy team that could generate hits, take extra bases, and consistently force opposing bats to put the ball in play against a defense that regularly turned them into outs. This was especially important when Royals Stadium opened in 1973 as part of the Harry S. Truman Sports Complex next door to football-only Arrowhead Stadium. The team was tailor-made for the cavernous, artificial-turf-laden ballpark, where I-70 speeds past beyond left field, a regal 12-story-high scoreboard in the shape of a Royals crown is a trademark beyond center field, and a beautiful water spectacular arcs just out of the right fielder's reach as the largest privately funded fountain in the world.

GEORGE BRETT

While the Royals were motoring to an 88–74 record and second-place finish in 1973, George Brett was a stubborn but talented young third baseman struggling to get on base. The Royals' 1971 second-round draft pick was ready to give up on his career when Royals batting coach Charley Lau took him under his wing. He struggled as a rookie to adjust to big-league pitching until Lau taught him to change his mechanics, including letting his left hand off the bat at the conclusion of his swing. Brett developed a sweet swing, and became one of the AL's most consistent batsmen. He is the only player to win batting titles in three decades, plus get 3,000 hits, 300 home runs, 600 doubles, 100 triples, and 200 stolen bases. He was the 1980 AL MVP and the 1985 ALCS MVP. He was elected to 13 All-Star teams and was a first-ballot Hall of Famer, with 98 percent of the votes cast, in 1999.

One of the most memorable moments in Brett's career was the 1983 pine-tar incident, which showed Brett at his spit-fired best. Umpire Tim McClelland disallowed his go-ahead ninth-inning two-run home run off Yankees fireballer Rich "Goose" Gossage for having pine tar on his bat above the prescribed 18-inch limit. After circling the bases and waiting for the ruling in the dugout, he sprinted to home plate to confront McClelland in a moment of great drama. AL president Lee MacPhail allowed the homer on appeal, citing the "spirit of the rules," and the remaining inning of the game was played weeks later with the Royals leading, and they won, 5–4.

Other memorable images were his pennant-clinching three-run homer off Gossage in game three of the 1980 ALCS; his doff of the helmet at second base as his average soared over .400 for the first time on August 17, 1980; his penchant for challenging outfielders by taking the extra base; and his constant jabbering with players and umpires. These moments all showcased a baseball player that loved his job and was committed to his team.

Most importantly, he never left Kansas City. The free-agency era had not yet blossomed to the point where he got offers too good to refuse, so he was willing

George Brett singles off California Angels Tim Fortugno to collect his 3,000th career hit, 1992. © AP / Wide World Photos

to stay put in his adopted hometown. This was a true blessing for the Royals. As a result of the new economics of the game, the young stars that the Royals later developed were destined to maximize their salaries on the open market. Brett will likely forever remain the only player ever inducted into the Hall of Fame as a Royal.

Brett's career coincides with the Royals' rise and fall as a franchise. When Brett emerged from Triple-A Omaha for good early in the 1974 season, the fledgling Royals fought with the A's for the AL West housed in a classy year-old stadium perfectly suited for their skills. As Brett rose to stardom, the Royals locked horns with the Yankees for supremacy in the AL, a rivalry that took five years to finally tilt in the Royals' favor. As Brett matured as a player, the franchise dealt with a shocking drug scandal and emerged as a World Series champion. By the time of his retirement after the 1993 season, the prospect of labor strife in 1994 was becoming clear, and the developing economics of the game would prove disastrous for small-market teams.

RIVALRY WITH THE YANKEES

Kansas City's first serious run at an AL West title occurred in 1973, when McKeon's squad took over first place in August before settling in behind the

A's. In 1975 McKeon was let go with the club at 50–46, and then White Herzog came in to go 41–25, a harbinger of the future. In 1976 Brett and company finally overcame their perpetual runner-up status to Oakland in convincing fashion with a 90–72 record. Yet there was drama up until the season's final game, as Brett, McRae, and Minnesota's Rod Carew battled for the batting crown at Royals Stadium. McRae led Brett by .00005 points heading into the last game. Carew was eliminated from the title chase in the course of the game, leaving McRae and Brett both two for three heading into the ninth inning. Brett lofted a fly ball to Twins left fielder Steve Brye, but Brye misplayed the ball, and Brett circled the bases for an inside-the-park homer, finishing at .333. McRae grounded out, knowing that he had lost the batting title. As McRae, who is black, headed to the dugout, he acknowledged the fans' standing ovation with a tip of his helmet, then flipped off the Twins dugout, suggesting manager Gene Mauch conspired to assure a white man would win the award. Benches emptied and accusations flew, but by the next day the Royals were laughing about the incident, preparing for the AL East champion Yankees.

The Royals' first postseason appearance was heart-wrenching. In the deciding game five, Brett's three-run homer in the top of the eighth inning tied the game 6–6 until Chris Chambliss sent Mark Littell's first pitch in the bottom of the ninth over the right-field wall to clinch the pennant. The Royals hoped to erase that memory in 1977 after a 102–60 campaign that remains the franchise record. The team took control of the division with a 16-game September winning streak. The pitchers had the best ERA in the AL (3.52), and Dennis Leonard won 20 games. Unfortunately, a three-run ninth inning by the Yankees in game five allowed them to dash Kansas City's hopes once again. In the following season the speedy team reached its height with a league-leading 216 stolen bases. The 1978 ALCS featured the same two teams again, and New York won it again in four games, overcoming Brett's three solo home runs in game three against Catfish Hunter.

Herzog was fired after the Royals lost the 1979 division title to California and was replaced by Jim Frey. Fueled by outstanding seasons by Brett and his .390 batting average, speedy Willie Wilson and his 230 hits, and young relief specialist Dan Quisenberry and his 33 saves, and a third straight season of leading the league in steals, Frey's squad sealed the 1980 division title early (97–65). They swept the Yankees in the playoffs to finally gain the upper hand against their hated rivals. However, the Royals' first pennant winner failed to deliver a world championship. The dominating season fell apart in six games to the Philadelphia Phillies. Wilson struck out 12 times, Quisenberry was shelled, and Brett had to leave game two because of hemorrhoids that required surgery prior to game three. He dealt with the incessant media questions with humor—famously commenting that the event would go down in the "anals of history"—but his woes certainly helped create a disappointing end to an otherwise stellar summer in Kansas City.

THE I-70 SERIES

The misfortune and poor performances suffered by the Royals in their initial World Series appearance were a distant memory by the time they returned to the Fall Classic in 1985. The team lived a charmed life throughout that postseason as the Royals constantly flirted with elimination only to emerge as champions. To reach that point, however, Kansas City had endured a difficult five years, almost from the moment Wilson whiffed to end the 1980 World Series. The Royals made the Western Division playoff series in 1981 with a mediocre 50–53 record only because of the ill-conceived split-season format necessitated by the player's strike. Oakland took the division in a three-game sweep. Frey was fired and replaced by Dick Howser midway through the 1981 campaign. Throughout these years, the Royals were a solid gate attraction. The Royals drew 2.2 million every year from 1978 to 1982 except for the strike-shortened 1981 season, and beginning back in 1975 were no worse than fourth in AL attendance.

In the summer of 1983, four Royals were implicated in the league-wide drug scandal that rocked the sport. Wilson, Jerry Martin, Vida Blue, and Willie Aikens pleaded guilty to charges of soliciting cocaine and received prison time, and only Wilson ever returned to the team. The ordeal stunned the organization and its fans. Kansas City's successful teams had always been considered rather sterile compared to the headline-generating characters in Oakland and New York, which suited the Midwest temperament just fine. The involvement of four Royals in a scandal of that magnitude shook that assumption to its core.

The Royals won the AL West in 1984 with Wilson patrolling center field again, but succumbed quickly to Detroit in the ALCS. After the season, Kauffman confronted Brett about the need to stay healthy. Brett had missed considerable playing time with injuries during each of the previous five seasons, including only 104 games in 1984. He responded to the challenge by rededicating himself to working out in the off-season. In 1985, he played in 155 games, batting .335 with 112 RBIs and 30 homers. He won his first Gold Glove and placing second in AL MVP voting.

General manager John Schuerholz, stung by his trades for veterans Martin and Blue after he first took the job in 1981, made a brilliant move by trading for seasoned catcher Jim Sundberg just before the 1985 season opened. Sundberg proved invaluable working with a talented young pitching staff led by Bret Saberhagen, the Cy Young winner (20–6). Kansas City finished 91–71. The pitching carried the team, whose run productivity was second worst in the AL. The Royals faced the Toronto Blue Jays in the ALCS, which was now a best-of-seven series. They lost the first two games before storming back behind Brett's two-home-run performance in game three. Then, down three games to one, Danny Jackson came through with a shutout to give the Royals' hope. The Royals took the final two games to take the pennant.

The Royals were underdogs to World Series foe St. Louis, their cross-state rivals, who had posted a baseball-best 101 wins. They used a formula of excellent pitching, defense, and speed concocted by none other than Herzog. While the national audience to the first all-prime-time Series might have been put off by the lack of a marquee market, the 1985 World Series was a huge happening for Missouri.

Pitching, not surprisingly, dominated. Kansas City pitchers gave up just 13 runs and the formidable Cardinal offense batted just .185 over seven games. Saberhagen won the Series MVP Award with two wins and a 0.50 ERA. The defining moment came in the bottom of the ninth inning of game six. The Royals trailed in the series three games to two and St. Louis led the game 1–0 with young relief ace Todd Worrell entering. During the season the Cards had won all 88 games in which they had led in the ninth. Pinch hitter Jorge Orta led off with a weak grounder to first baseman Jack Clark. Worrell and Clark's throw easily beat Orta to the bag, but umpire Don Denkinger signaled Orta was safe. Clark then failed to catch Steve Balboni's foul pop-up, and the big first baseman then responded with a bloop single. With one out, the runners advanced on a passed ball. McRae was promptly walked to load the bases. Pinch-hitting journeyman Dane Iorg then smashed a single to bring home the Royals' only two runs. The finale was a complete anomaly. Darryl Motley's two-run homer in the second inning set off an 11–0 rout against John Tudor, who had given up just one run in 15 innings in his two prior wins in the series. The Royals were only the second expansion team to win the World Series.

Fans in St. Louis will never forgive Denkinger's fateful call, but in Kansas City the comeback is recalled fondly. The Royals became the first team ever to lose games one and two at home and come back to win the World Series. They also became only the fifth team to ever overcome a 3–1 series deficit. However, the Royals were unable to build on their momentum. Tragedy, unfulfilled potential, and looming economic problems ensured the Royals' next generation would pale considerably to its first.

BAD BREAKS, NEW REALITIES

Howser's opportunity to bask in the team's first championship was cut far too short. Two days after he managed the AL to victory in the 1986 All-Star Game, he was diagnosed with a brain tumor and missed the rest of the season, in which the team had a losing record. He hoped to rejoin the team in 1987, but his condition did not improve. Howser died on June 17, 1987, and two weeks later his uniform number 10 was retired.

At the same time the Royals family was dealing with Howser's illness and death, on-field excitement came back in the form of Bo Jackson, the Heisman Trophy–winning Auburn tailback, who was also highly regarded as a baseball player. The Royals plucked him out of the amateur draft and then managed to persuade him to forgo a football career. Immediately, the Bo buzz indicated

Bo Jackson in a game against the California Angeles, 1989. © AP / Wide World Photos

a great future for the Royals. Jackson's short stint in the minors was followed by a home run in his first major-league at bat in September 1986. His first full season in Kansas City resulted in a lot of strikeouts, mammoth home runs, and rocket throws from left field. It culminated with his announcement that he would play football in the off-season for the Los Angeles Raiders. For three more years the excitement he generated whenever he stepped to the plate—which included winning the 1989 All-Star Game MVP trophy—never resulted in consistent production. When he injured his hip in 1990 while playing with the Raiders, the Royals released him, and his professional athletic career ended soon afterward.

By then the Royals were clearly a team in transition. They bounced back from the difficult 1986 campaign with winning seasons five out of the next seven years, but no postseason appearances. An ailing Kauffman died on August 1, 1993, and Brett retired after the season. That dual loss of leadership has yet to be regained, although Brett has remained in the front office since his retirement.

The economics of baseball were changing, as local broadcast revenue provided a means for large-market teams to make money that did not have to be shared with other teams. For small-market teams like the Royals, who had always relied on a far-flung regional fan base, that source of income was much less substantial. As the 1994 labor negotiations moved ominously forward, the owners cited the Royals as an example of a team that could not compete under the current economic system. The players went on strike on August 12, 1994.

Much has been said about how the players' strike of 1994–95 was fatal to the Montreal Expos, the class of the NL and stocked with young stars, but the Royals were similarly harmed. They were surging in the AL West standings with a 14-game winning streak that ended the week before the strike. They lost a chance for large attendances down the stretch and, like all teams, encountered considerable anger from their fans when games resumed.

Worse, the Royals were operating without an owner. Kauffman had tried for years to find a successor that would keep the team in town, and even tried to give the team to the city, but AL owners blocked that action. Instead Kauffman set up the Greater Kansas City Community Foundation and Affiliated Trusts to own and operate the club for up to six years, or until a local buyer could be found, and to ensure local charities would benefit from the eventual sale. Afterward the Royals would be sold to the highest bidder.

The foundation put the Royals up for sale in September 1997 for $75 million, requiring potential buyers to raise at least half of their money from local investors and keep the team in town. Miles Prentice headed up a group that sought to buy the team, and the foundation accepted its bid. However, MLB did not, citing too many investors and a concern that the group was undercapitalized. Ultimately, David Glass, CEO and president of Wal-Mart and the chairman of the Royals' board since September 1993, bought the team in May 2000 for $96 million.

The damage wrought by almost seven years of ownerless limbo cannot be overstated. The Royals had to deal with the aftermath of the strike without a clear budget or direction. Their farm teams, long considered some of the most impressive in baseball, were neglected. Management went after fading stars in hopes of a quick fix and dumped payroll, to the dismay of fans. In April 1995, with the taint of the strike still thick in the air, the Royals traded the 1994 Cy Young Award winner, David Cone (16–5, 2.94 ERA), to Toronto for Chris Stynes, David Sinnes, and Tony Medrano. That clunker was the warning shot for a dismal decade to come and a sure sign to fans that the labor war had not helped the Royals compete. In 1996 and 1997, the Royals finished in last place in their division for the first time. Even their beautiful stadium, renamed after Kauffman shortly after his death, was an ironic problem in this economic puzzle. While the stadium boom swept the country, prompting new revenue streams for owners who got cities to fund significant portions of proposed ballparks, "the K" had stood the test of time. Its construction foresaw the single-sport venues some 20 years before other stadiums were lauded for that feature. It was still a beautiful place for a ballgame, especially after the turf was replaced by natural grass in 1995. There was no chance voters would approve a new downtown stadium, especially when there was no owner to lobby for it. In an odd twist, the assets the Royals had going for them almost since their inception—dedicated, stable leadership; a commitment to their farm system; and a universally admired ballpark—all were working against them at a critical juncture.

Angry fans symbolically expressed their displeasure over baseball's economic structure on April 30, 1999, when the world champion Yankees were in town.

A local radio station organized a walkout. Some 3,000 fans left Kauffman Stadium en masse in the middle of the game, wearing shirts that read "$hare the Wealth" and littering the field with fake $100 bills.

THE GLASS YEARS

In 2003 the Royals had their first winning season in eight years.

Despite staying in contention for the AL Central title almost to the season's final week under 2003 Manager of the Year Tony Pena, new ownership has not resulted in a clear direction for the Royals. Glass and general manager Allard Baird have received decidedly mixed reviews since that purchase. Exciting young stars like Johnny Damon, Jermaine Dye, and Carlos Beltran ripened and then were traded before they could become free agents. Baird's infrequent trips to acquire established names, most notably Chuck Knoblauch and Juan Gonzalez, have been disasters. The team followed up its surprise 2003 campaign with a 58–104 mark in 2004 and a laughable 2005 campaign that resulted in a franchise worst 56–106 record and a 19-game losing streak that fell just 2 short of that ignominious AL record. In a case of miserable timing, the 20th-anniversary celebration of the World Series championship and Saberhagen's induction into the team hall of fame were scheduled for two consecutive nights during the skid— and rain postponed both of those much-anticipated bright spots! Buddy Bell was hired to replace Pena after he resigned abruptly early in the 2005 season. Bell will rely on a crop of talented young pitchers led by Zack Greinke to try and right the course. The number two overall pick in the 2005 amateur draft, third baseman Alex Gordon, was signed in the last week of that dismal Royals' season, providing a glimmer of hope for an offense that was absent that summer.

The Royals' continuous stumble from baseball's elite has been tough for Kansas City fans long accustomed to a winner, but Glass's investment is still in good shape. *Forbes* magazine estimated the Royals' franchise value at $187 million in 2005, 27th among baseball's 30 franchises, but it represents a hearty 95 percent increase over Glass's purchase price five years earlier. Glass admitted that the Royals made $3 million in 2004, but added that they had lost $27 million since he bought the team.

Kauffman's vow to keep the team in his town nearly 40 years ago still rings true, but the requirement to keep the Royals in Kansas City created turmoil during a difficult transition. Meanwhile, the fan base has stagnated. Despite consistently being among the smallest media markets and population centers, the Royals used to be able to count on decent attendance. From 1973 to 1990, they were always in the top half of the AL in attendance, and attracted more than 1.8 million fans every nonstrike year from 1977 to 1993. Since the 1994–95 strike, the Royals haven't cracked that barrier and have not been better than 10th best in attendance among 14 AL clubs. The inconsistency and disappointment of the more recent Royals seems likely to continue rather than a return to the glory days, when the Royals were the class of the expansion field.

NOTABLE ACHIEVEMENTS

Most Valuable Players

Year	Name	Position
1980	George Brett	3B

Cy Young Winners

Year	Name	Position
1985	Bret Saberhagen	RHP
1989	Bret Saberhagen	RHP
1994	David Cone	RHP

Rookies of the Year

Year	Name	Position
1969	Lou Piniella	OF
1994	Bob Hamelin	DH
1999	Carlos Beltran	OF
2003	Angel Berroa	SS

Batting Champions

Year	Name	#
1976	George Brett	.333
1980	George Brett	.390
1982	Willie Wilson	.332
1990	George Brett	.329

ERA Champions

Year	Name	#
1989	Bret Saberhagen	2.16
1993	Kevin Appier	2.56

No-Hitters

Name	Date
Steve Busby	04/27/1973
Steve Busby	06/19/1974
Jim Colborn	05/14/1977
Bret Saberhagen	08/26/1991

POSTSEASON APPEARANCES

AL West Division Titles

Year	Record	Manager
1976	90–72	Whitey Herzog
1977	102–60	Whitey Herzog
1978	92–70	Whitey Herzog
1980	97–65	Jim Frey
1981	50–53	Jim Frey
		Dick Howser
1984	84–78	Dick Howser
1985	91–71	Dick Howser

AL Pennants

Year	Record	Manager
1980	97–65	Jim Frey
1985	91–71	Dick Howser

World Championships

Year	Opponent	MVP
1985	St. Louis	Bret Saberhagen

MANAGERS

2005–	Buddy Bell
2002–2005	Tony Pena
2002	John Mizerock
1997–2002	Tony Muser
1995–1997	Bob Boone
1991–1994	Hal McRae
1991	Bob Schaefer
1987–1991	John Wathan
1987	Billy Gardner
1986	Mike Ferraro
1981–1986	Dick Howser
1980–1981	Jim Frey
1975–1979	Whitey Herzog
1973–1975	Jack McKeon
1970–1972	Bob Lemon
1970	Charley Metro
1969	Joe Gordon

Team Records by Individual Players

Batting Leaders	Single Season			Career	
	Name		Year	Name		Plate Appearances
	Name		Year	Name		
Batting average	George Brett	.390	1980	George Brett	.305	11,624
On-base %	George Brett	.454	1980	Kevin Seitzer	.380	3,163
Slugging %	George Brett	.664	1980	Danny Tartabull	.518	2,684
OPS	George Brett	1.118	1980	Danny Tartabull	.894	2,684
Games	Al Cowens	162	1977	George Brett	2,707	11,624
At bats	Willie Wilson	705	1980	George Brett	10,349	11,624
Runs	Johnny Damon	136	2000	George Brett	1,583	11,624
Hits	Willie Wilson	230	1980	George Brett	3,154	11,624
Total bases	George Brett	363	1979	George Brett	5,044	11,624
Doubles	Hal McRae	54	1977	George Brett	665	11,624
Triples	Willie Wilson	21	1985	George Brett	137	11,624
Home runs	Steve Balboni	36	1985	George Brett	317	11,624
RBIs	Mike Sweeney	144	2000	George Brett	1,595	11,624
Walks	John Mayberry	122	1973	George Brett	1,096	11,624
Strikeouts	Bo Jackson	172	1989	Frank White	1,035	8,467
Stolen bases	Willie Wilson	83	1979	Wwillie Wilson	612	7,302
Extra-base hits	Hal McRae	86	1977	George Brett	1,119	11,624
Times on base	Mike Sweeney	292	2000	George Brett	4,283	11,624

Pitching Leaders	Single Season			Career	
	Name		Year	Name		Innings Pitches
	Name		Year	Name		
ERA	Roger Nelson	2.08	1972	Dan Quisenberry	2.55	920.3
Wins	Brett Saberhagen	23	1989	Paul Splittorff	166	2,254.7
Won-loss %	Larry Gura	.800	1978	Fitzmorris	.593	1,098
Hits/9 IP	Roger Nelson	6.23	1972	Jeff Montgomery	8.05	849.3
Walks/9 IP	Doug Bird	1.41	1976	Dan Quisenberry	1.36	920.3
Strikeouts	Dennis Leonard	244	1977	Kevin Appier	1,458	1,843.7
Strikeouts/9 IP	Kevin Appier	8.82	1996	Tom Gordon	7.82	1,149.7
Games	Dan Quisenberry	84	1985	Jeff Montgomery	686	849.3
Saves	Jeff Montgomery	45	1993	Jeff Montgomery	304	849.3
Innings	Dennis Leonard	294.7	1978	Paul Splittorff	2,254.7	2,254.7
Starts	Dennis Leonard	40	1978	Paul Splittorff	392	2,254.7
Complete games	Dennis Leonard	21	1977	Dennis Leonard	103	2,187
Shutouts	Roger Nelson	6	1972	Dennis Leonard	23	2,187

Source: Drawn from data in "Kansas City Royals Batting Leaders (seasonal and career)." http://baseball-reference.com/teams/KCR/leaders_bat.shtml; "Kansas City Royals Pitching Leaders (seasonal and career)." http://baseball-reference.com/teams/KCR/staff.shtml.

BIBLIOGRAPHY

Barzilla, Scott. *The State of Baseball Management: Decision-Making in the Best and Worst Teams, 1993–2003.* Jefferson, NC: McFarland, 2004.

Baseball-Reference.com. "Kansas City Royals Attendance, Stadium and Park Factors." http://www.baseball-reference.com/teams/KCR/attend.shtml.

Dutton, Bob. "Glass Confirms Royals Profited Last Year." *Kansas City Star,* May 3, 2005, http://www.baseballthinkfactory.org/files/newsstand/archives/2005/05P300/.

Eckhouse, Morris A. "Kansas City Royals: Building a Champion from Scratch in America's Heartland." In *Encyclopedia of Major League Baseball Team Histories: American League,* ed. Peter C. Bjarkman. Westport, CT: Meckler, 1991.

Flanagan, Jeffrey. "Glass Was Warned He Would Be Vilified about Payroll." *Kansas City Star,* May 4, 2005, D2.

Koppett, Leonard. *Koppett's Concise History of Major League Baseball.* Philadelphia: Temple University Press, 1998.

Launius, Roger D. *Seasons in the Sun: The Story of Big League Baseball in Missouri.* Columbia: University of Missouri Press, 2002.

Morgan, Anne. *Prescription for Success: The Life and Values of Ewing Marion Kauffman.* Kansas City, MO: Andrews McMeel, 1995.

Peterson, John E. *The Kansas City Athletics: A Baseball History, 1954–1967.* Jefferson, NC: McFarland, 2003.

Puerzer, Richard. "The Kansas City Royals' Baseball Academy." *The National Pastime* 24 (2004): 3–14.

23

Los Angeles Angels of Anaheim

Joel S. Franks

The exciting 2002 World Series witnessed the Anaheim Angels ending a four-decade-long drought in which the franchise had failed to ever win a world championship. From the time the franchise first joined MLB as the Los Angeles Angels in 1961 until the team beat the San Francisco Giants in that Fall Classic, it had often been the subject of ridicule and neglect. During those years, the team has had its share of interesting and frequently talented ballplayers, managers, and coaches, but none as interesting as owner Gene Autry.

RUDOLPH'S BALL CLUB

Major-league baseball came to Los Angeles in 1958, though it had had high-quality minor-league ball from the turn of the century with the Pacific Coast League. The PCL had one and often two franchises in the Los Angeles area, including the Angels, taken over in the 1920s by Philip Wrigley of the Chicago Cubs. He built near downtown a second Wrigley Field, a smaller but no less beautiful version than the one in Chicago. The Angels became one of the most stable PCL franchises, drawing well and winning its share of pennants. Nevertheless, the Angels had to usually share the spotlight with other Los Angeles–based franchises, mainly the Hollywood Stars, playing out of Gilmore Field in West Hollywood.

Wrigley sold his share of the Angels and Wrigley Field to Walter O'Malley in 1957 to smooth the Dodgers' transition. The Angels and the Stars disappeared as PCL franchises, and at least some Los Angelenos celebrated that their city had at last gone big-league. MLB hoped that the plague of major-league franchise movements would end. But Clark Griffith, owner of the Washington Senators, was eyeing Minneapolis, and MLB was challenged by the probability of a third major league, the Continental League, locating a franchise there, as well as in such cities as Houston, Dallas, and New York City. Launching a preemptive strike, MLB allowed Clark Griffith to move his franchise to Minnesota and granted National League franchises in New York City and Houston.

Moving the Senators out of Washington, DC, was a touchy issue because there was concern that powerful congressmen might respond by eliminating baseball's antitrust exemption. Consequently, MLB placed an American League expansion franchise in Washington, DC, to start play in 1961, and to keep an even number of teams, also granted a franchise to Los Angeles.

Los Angeles in the 1960s was a metropolitan behemoth with a relatively prosperous and diverse economy. The city's population was 2,479,015, and Los Angeles County had 6,039,834 residents. The city had no clearly identified urban center, but had plenty of middle- and upper-class neighborhoods connected by freeways. Moreover, as Dodgers owner Walter O'Malley was finding out, a major-league team could draw baseball fans from Long Beach, Riverside, Orange Country, and even Santa Barbara and San Diego. The AL magnates anticipated that these fans were not satisfied with just watching visiting NL stars like as Mays, Aaron, and Clemente, but also wanted to see AL greats such as Mantle, Maris, and Kaline.

An ownership group headed by Gene Autry took over the new Los Angeles franchise. Autry had gained fame and considerable wealth as a singing cowboy in countless B movies in the 1930s and 1940, and then along with Roy Rogers and Hopalong Cassidy thrilled baby boomers on TV. Moreover, millions heard his voice over the radio around Christmastime singing the ever-popular "Rudolph the Red-Nosed Reindeer," as well as all sorts of renditions of his composition "Here Comes Santa Claus." Few Americans symbolized the wholesome 1950s better than Gene Autry.

By 1960 Autry no longer performed, but because of sound investments, he ranked for years on the *Forbes* list of the 400 wealthiest Americans. In 1952 he bought Los Angeles radio station KMPC, and eventually built a media empire through Golden West Broadcasters, which possessed several radio and television stations in Southern California and the West. Autry's key partner was Robert Reynolds, a former football star at Stanford and KMPC executive, who was the Angels president from 1961 to 1974.

THE LOS ANGELES YEARS

In 1961, Autry's Angels became the third major-league franchise to play on the Pacific Coast. However, right from the start the team played in the shadow of O'Malley's Dodgers, who had carved out a firm identity in Southern California. After a disappointing first season in Los Angeles in 1958, the Dodgers won the 1959 World Series with a team that excelled in pitching, speed, and defense. Nothing served the Dodgers better in Los Angeles than Vin Scully, whose voice echoed through thousands of transistor radios in the mammoth Los Angeles Coliseum and thousands more portable and car radios heard on beaches, porches, and freeways. Finally, O'Malley had done a good job of gaining Hollywood support. Movie stars such as Frank Sinatra, Doris Day, Cary Grant, and Bing Crosby regularly attended games and lent a glamorous sheen to Dodgers.

Making matters worse for Autry's Angels was that Southern Californians did not have to watch and listen to baseball games to have a good time from April to October. They had plenty of indoor and outdoor recreational and leisure activities to divert them from major-league baseball. They could golf, play tennis, shop, barbecue, attend Little League games, lounge by their swimming pools, or just drive someplace—anyplace.

Autry picked baseball men for his management team who had considerable experience in Pacific Coast baseball and new major-league markets. General manager Fred Haney had managed the Hollywood Stars and led the Milwaukee Braves to the world championship in 1957. The field manager was Bill Rigney, who had previously managed the Giants when they moved west. In the expansion draft, the Angels got to purchase, for $75,000 apiece, players already deemed as expendable by their old clubs. The Angels' first choice in the expansion draft was gifted but wild Yankees pitcher Eli Grba. There were a few stars, presumed over the hill, including veteran first baseman Ted Kluszewski, who was one of the NL's most feared hitters when he played for the Cincinnati Reds, but injuries and age had reduced his effectiveness. The Angels also picked up Steve Bilko, who had slugged over 50 homers in one season for the old Los Angeles Angels, and the quick, diminutive outfielder Albie Pearson, former Rookie of the Year with the Washington Senators. Another former PCL standout, Pearson had fallen on hard times since and was drafted from the Baltimore Orioles. Outfielder Bob Cerv once hit 38 homers for the Kansas City Athletics, but could no longer break into the Yankees' formidable lineup. In April 1961, the Angels also acquired former Yankee Ryne Duren, a flamethrowing relief pitcher who, like Grba, too infrequently found the strike zone. Acquired after the season started, Leon Wagner was an NL castoff who had showed some promise for the San Francisco Giants.

The Angels played their home games in comfy Wrigley Field, a better place to watch a ball game than the spacious Los Angeles Coliseum. But the Dodgers pulled in up to 90,000 people, while Wrigley Field could fit only about 20,000. Moreover, there was not a great deal to excite Angel fans, although they finished a surprising 8th in the 10-team league, ahead of the expansion Washington Senators and the Kansas City Athletics. The Angels finished just a half game behind the Minnesota Twins, and higher than any other major-league expansion team in its first year. The presence of both the Angels and the Senators in the AL also helped generate a little more excitement in a year easily dominated by the Yankees by diluting the talent pool of pitchers. This contributed to an explosion of homers and high batting averages in the junior circuit in 1961.

The Angels drew only around 600,000 to Wrigley Field in 1961—far less than the 1 million that used to mark a franchise's success and much less than the 1.8 million the Dodgers drew in their first year in Los Angeles in 1958. The Coliseum, which was a poor fit for baseball, became available in 1962 because the Dodgers moved to their own new park. Instead, Reynolds opted, reluctantly, to play in Dodger Stadium where O'Malley wanted an exorbitant rent.

In 1962 the Angels amazed many by staying in the pennant race for much of the season. When the dust settled, the Angels were third place, a remarkable finish for a major-league team in its second year. The Angels' offense was led by Leon Wagner and Lee Thomas. Its pitching staff featured a talented young right-hander, Dean Chance, and Bo Belinsky, a colorful, egotistical southpaw, who in early May pitched the first no-hitter in the franchise's history over the Baltimore Orioles. The erratic Belinsky won 10 out of 21 decisions in 1962, initiating a three-year stint as the Angels' one-man publicity mill, which included a very public relationship with Hollywood blonde bombshell Mamie Van Doren. The Angels' strong performance helped draw 1 million fans. But despite fine play from individual performers such as Dean Chance (Cy Young winner in 1964, 20–9, 1.65 ERA), Fred Newman, Albie Pearson, and Jim Fregosi, the Angels slipped back into mediocrity from 1963 to 1965, and fans stayed away.

ORANGE COUNTY TO THE RESCUE

In the early 1960s, Orange County was best known as the home of Disneyland and a large area of political conservatism, or simply Los Angeles south. Local businessmen were tired of tourists thinking that Disneyland was in Los Angeles and wanted the county to possess its own identity. Disneyland had aided somewhat in this endeavor, but attracting a major-league baseball club to the county would help even more.

Modern major-league franchises had hitherto been located in major cities. Autry broke the mold by moving the Angels to Anaheim, the home of Disneyland and a suburb of Los Angeles. All Southern California had benefited from the economic prosperity fostered by World War II and then the cold war. Government defense contracts meant more jobs for assemblers, technicians, drafters, engineers, and scientists. Military personnel stationed in El Toro in Santa Ana and other parts of Southern California were drawn to the possibility of relocating there permanently. The GI Bill encouraged housing and highway construction, as well as the expansion of educational facilities.

Orange County's population grew dramatically like other suburban postwar Sunbelt areas, with plenty of land for defense plants, supermarkets, department stores, single-family homes, schools, and freeways. It especially offered prospective white residents an opportunity to move away from people of color in Los Angeles.

Orange County attracted Walt Disney. Admitting to a distaste for urban amusement parks that drew culturally diverse working- and middle-class Americans, Disney wanted to construct a profitable theme park to evoke a world beyond Coney Island—a world without the painful reminders of class, race, and ethnicity. He wanted his park close to major freeways linking it to Southern California's population centers, but well isolated from surrounding neighborhoods populated with folks one did not see in his movies unless they posed as contented slaves telling young viewers Joel Chandler Harris tales about Brer Rabbit and Brer Bear and singing "Zippidy Do Da," or in his TV show *Disneyland*, which started in 1954.

Anaheim served his needs. It was largely inhabited by middle-class whites whose civic leaders enthused about filling Disney's every whim. It was near completed or projected freeways and possessed acres and acres of orange groves that could be transformed into a Magic Kingdom and parking lots. The coming of Disneyland in 1955 helped Anaheim boom. It grew from 14,556 people in 1950 to 146,000 15 years later.

In 1964, the Angels broke ground on former farmland for Anaheim Stadium, better known as "the Big A," in recognition of the large A observable from the Orange Freeway that marked the stadium's site. The city paid for the $24 million baseball-only facility, which was constructed by the Del E. Webb Company. Civic leaders in Anaheim and the surrounding communities believed that they had effectively differentiated Orange County from Los Angeles, and thereby rendered it big-league, but Autry was less certain. He did not rename the club the Anaheim Angels, but rather the California Angels, which stuck for over 30 years.

The Angels played their first major-league game in Anaheim on April 19, 1966, before a crowd of 31,660. The team drew over 1.4 million that year. The team was mired in mediocrity for the next several years, despite the presence of several fine ballplayers. From 1966 to 1977, the Angels only finished above .500 twice—1967 and 1970. Moreover, after a fine 1967 season in which the Angels were 10 games over .500, the team plummeted to 67–96, 36 games out of first place. Rigney managed through early 1969.

Angel fans could find comfort in the fact that the Angels were not bereft of talent. Shortstop Jim Fregosi, a fan favorite, played for the Angels from 1961 to 1971. Outfielder Alex Johnson batted .329 in 1971 and won the AL batting crown. Hall of Fame outfielder Frank Robinson swatted 30 homers for the Halos in 1973. Speedy outfielder Mickey Rivers stole 70 bases in 1975. Outfielder Bobby Bonds gave the Angels speed and power in 1977. Rudy May was a solid pitcher for the Angels in the late 1960s and early 1970s. Left-hander Clyde Wright in 1970 and the talented Andy Messersmith in 1971 both won 20 games. Left-hander Frank Tanana emerged as one of the best young talents in big-league baseball in the mid-1970s, with three All-Star appearances. In 1975 he led the league in strikeouts (269), and two years later he led in ERA (2.54).

The biggest star on the Angels for much of the 1970s was fastballer Nolan Ryan. Acquired from the New York Mets for the popular Jim Fregosi, the hard-throwing right-hander joined the Angels in 1972. In 1973, he became the fifth major-league pitcher to hurl two no-hitters in a single season, followed by a third no-hitter in 1974. The next year, Ryan hurled his fourth no-hitter in front of just 8,000 spectators. Ryan made his last pitch for the Angels in 1979, after achieving two 20-win seasons for the Halos and leading the AL in strikeouts seven of eight seasons. His overall Angels record of 138–121 was achieved with inferior teams that had winning records only in 1978 and 1979.

During the 1970s, the managers came and went with great rapidity. They started with Lefty Phillips, Del Rice, Bobby Winkles, and Whitey Herzog. Dick Williams was hired in the middle of 1974, following his great three years at Oakland, but could not replicate his winning ways. He was fired in 1976, replaced by Norm Sherry, Dave Garcia, and then Jim Fregosi, who joined up one-third of the way into the 1978 season. By then, free agency had significantly impacted major-league baseball. The Angels, with Autry's deep pockets, seemed better prepared than most clubs to take advantage. Autry signed some terrific players, including outfielders Don Baylor, Joe Rudi, and Lyman Bostock and infielder Bobby Grich. Before then, Autry had a hard time hiring a manager to take the Angels to the top. Bill Rigney had been fired in the midst of the 1969 season. The relatively youthful Jim Fregosi led the team in 1978 to its first winning season since 1970, and second place in the AL West. The pitching staff was solid, with left-hander Frank Tanana winning 18 games. However, the season was marred by the late-season murder of Lyman Bostock, gunned down while a car passenger in Gary, Indiana. Bostock was in his first year with the Angels, and in four major-league seasons had batted .313.

In 1979, Autry's Angels captured the AL West (88–74), their first major-league title of any kind, and drew over 2 million for the first time. Fans witnessed potent bats (the team led the league in offense) and effective pitching. Baylor slugged his way into an MVP season with a league-leading 139 RBIs. He was backed by Bobby Grich (101 RBIs), young catcher Brian Downing (.326), and Rod Carew (.318), one of the best hitters in the AL, acquired via a trade from Minnesota. As for the pitching, Ryan was his usual overpowering self, with 223 strikeouts, while Tanana supplied clutch performances despite an injured left arm that had diminished his speed and transformed him into a southpaw craftsman. However, they were defeated in the AL Championship Series by Earl Weaver's Baltimore Orioles in four games.

Despite the relative success enjoyed by Autry's Angels in 1979, Doug Pappas, the late statistical expert, was not impressed. Analyzing the Angels' payroll from 1977 to 1979, he argued that compared to teams such as Kansas City and the Chicago White Sox, Autry was paying players a great deal and getting disappointing on-field results. In 1977, Autry spent $2,415,050 on his Angels' payroll and got 77 wins, while the Chicago White Sox won 90 games with a $1,630,500 payroll. Two years later, when California won 88 games, their payroll had climbed to $3,767,792. However, the Kansas City Royals won 85 games with a payroll of just $1,976,324, a little over half of the Angels.

YEARS OF HEARTBREAK

During the 1980s, the Angels flirted with greatness but more often found heartbreaking defeat. Autry could not hold on to Ryan, who in 1980 signed a free-agent contract with the Houston Astros. Autry kept such high-priced talent as Baylor, Carew, and Grich. In 1981 he traded for Fred Lynn from the Boston Red Sox and added to the mix Reggie Jackson, signed away from Steinbrenner's New York Yankees in time for the 1982 season. The Angels replaced the Ryan-led pitching staff with such solid hurlers as 20-year-old Mike Witt in 1981 and the venerable Tommy John in late 1982.

The 1980 season was a total disaster, as the team fell off to 65–95. Early in the 1981 season, Gene Mauch took over for Jim Fregosi, and the team went 51–59 in the split season. Considered one of baseball's cleverest managers, Mauch's reputation was tainted by the 1964 collapse of the Phillies. This time, however, Mauch's Angels won the Western Division race as Reggie Jackson had one of his very best seasons in a colorful career, slugging 39 home runs and knocking in 101 runs. Five Angels had 20 or more homers, and the pitchers had the second-best ERA in the league. After putting together a 93–69 record, the Angels faced the potent Milwaukee Brewers in the ALCS for the pennant. In the best-of-five series, the Angels won the first two and seemed poised to give Autry his coveted World Series team, but they lost the next three games and were eliminated. Many Angel fans faulted Mauch's pitching moves, and once again he faced demons unleashed by a championship almost won.

Mauch resigned before the start of the 1983 season, perhaps stung by the criticism of his handling of the 1982 ALCS. His replacement was the solid John McNamara, whose Angels were at best second-rate. In 1983 the team plummeted to 70–92 record, but improved to .500 in 1984. Then, when the Red Sox hired McNamara away from the Angels, a perhaps-grateful Autry rehired Mauch for the 1985 season. His Angels in the mid-1980s were a veteran club, and perhaps a little too old. Still, the Angels had a steady and strong right-hander in Mike Witt, who had pitched a perfect game in 1984; a future Hall of Famer in Don Sutton; and a top reliever in Donnie Moore. There was speed with Gary Pettis and solid position players and hitters such as third baseman Doug DeCinces, catcher Bob Boone, and DH Brian Downing, and the ever-reliable Grich. The 1985 squad showed promise, winning 90 games and finished a game behind Kansas City in the AL West race.

In 1986, the Angels added rookie sensation Wally Joyner, and Anaheim Stadium became known as "Wally's World." The Angels took the 1986 Western Division title (92–70) and moved on to face the Red Sox in the AL playoffs. The team featured a balanced offense, led by Joyner, with a .290 batting average and 100 RBIs, and DeCinces, who at $1.2 million was the highest-paid player on the team. The pitching staff featured solid performances from the 41-year-old Don Sutton (15–11, 3.74, ERA), Kirk McCaskill (17–10, 3.36 ERA), and Mike Witt (18–10, 2.84 ERA). In the best-of-seven ALCS, the Angels went up three games to one. In game five at the Big A, the Angels had a three-run lead going into the top of the ninth inning. Baylor hit a two-run homer. After two were out, Lucas came in to pitch and hit his batter. Then Mauch brought in reliever Donnie Moore, who had shut down the opposition effectively all year. With thousands of Angel fans on their feet, Moore had two strikes on outfielder Dave Henderson, who launched a two-run homer to take the lead. The Angels tied the score in the bottom of the frame. However, the Red Sox scored again off Moore in the 11th to win the game. The Red Sox swept by the Angels in the next two games and went on to the World Series. Moore never recovered from the debacle, and three years later committed suicide.

For the next several years, the Angels were consistent losers, depending on veterans, some of whom were over the hill. Gene Mauch's last year with the Angels ended with a disappointing 78–84 record in 1987. Two years later the team showed a lot of improvement under Doug Rader, finishing third in the division with a 91–61 record. The team was carried by a terrific pitching staff, led by curveballing 38-year-old Bert Blyleven (17–5, 1.73 ERA).

While Autry's Angels achieved occasional triumphs in the AL West, Doug Pappas's statistical analysis reveals that the singing cowboy continued to overspend on a generally mediocre ball club. When the Angels won the West in 1982 with a 93–69 record, they had the highest payroll in the major leagues—$10,917,284. Kansas City came in second in the West at a cost of just $6,288,548. In 1983, the Angels' payroll of $9,935,324 was the highest in the AL West, but the team won only 70 games while the division champion Chicago White Sox won 99 games with a $7,171,192 payroll. In 1987, the Angels and the Texas Rangers both won 75 games. The Angels' payroll was $12,985,489, while the Rangers' was only half as costly—$6,342,718. In 1992, when the Angels were second to the division-winning Oakland Athletics in players' salaries, the Angels won just 72 games with a $33,529,344 payroll, $6 million more than second-place Minnesota.

By the early 1990s, Gene Autry and his wife, Jackie, who had become very involved in running the Angels, had soured on spending so much money on their beloved franchise. The team was operating at such losses that the Autrys had to borrow $40 million from Wells Fargo. There was thought that the Angels might have to declare bankruptcy or relocate the team. In 1993, having concluded they could spend a lot less and not do much worse in the standings, the Angels had the lowest payroll in the Western Division, $27,230,334. They ended with a 71–91 record, virtually the same as 1992, but $6 million cheaper. In the strike-shortened 1994 season, the Angels' payroll remained the lowest in the division at $20,691,000, $7 million less than the next highest, the Seattle Mariners, who won only two more games. Then, in the strike-delayed 1995 season, Marcel Lachemann led the Angels to a division lead for most of the season, only to fall into a tie (78–66) with Seattle. The Mariners then trounced the Angels in a playoff, 9–1. The Halos had five men hit over 20 homers and had the league's best outfield in Garret Anderson (.321), Tim Salmon (.330), and Jim Edmonds (.290). Lee Smith had 37 saves.

THE DISNEY YEARS

Thankfully for Orange County's baseball fans, the Walt Disney Company bought 25 percent and management control of the Angels in 1996 from the aging Autry, who did not want to entirely cut his financial and emotional ties to the Angels. Disney was not just satisfied to run a couple of theme parks and turn out movies and television shows, but sought to broaden its holdings in the media and entertainment industries. Locally, it was frustrated with its inability to control economic development around Disneyland. While Disney envisioned its Anaheim theme park as a place that would stand above time and place, the real world surrounded Disneyland with a vengeance. There was traffic congestion, motels, bars, and gift shops. Fast-food restaurants sprouted up and prostitutes set up business along Harbor Boulevard, the main street leading to Disneyland. Orange Country political and business interests did not want to just attract wholesome families to their region, but also more hedonistic tourists and conventioneers.

By adding local sports franchises, Disney could expand its economic base and also gain greater control over Orange County's economic future. In the early 1990s, Disney acquired ownership of an NHL expansion team located in Anaheim. The company had just made a popular movie about a youth hockey team called *The Mighty Ducks*, and to the dismay of traditional NHL fans and the delight of local hockey novices, the new team also became known as the Mighty Ducks. Disney could now merchandise Mighty Duck T-shirts.

Purchasing a controlling interest of the Angels went along with a Disney strategy that soon set its sights on ABC and ESPN. It also followed Disney's production of the movie *Angels in the Outfield*, a pleasant remake of a 1950s hit, in which the Pittsburgh Pirates became an NL powerhouse through divine intervention. The 1994 remake targeted the California Angels, although home scenes were shot at the Oakland Coliseum.

In 1997 the franchise became known as the Anaheim Angels. At long last, Orange County, with the help of Michael Eisner, had become big-league. Disney helped finance a renovation of the Big A, turning it into a baseball-only facility following the NFL Rams' move to St. Louis. The region's primary utility company, Edison International Corporation, paid $50 million to rename the park Edison International Field for 20 years.

In 1998, Gene Autry died without ever seeing his beloved Angels in the World Series, the team finishing for the second straight year in second place. The Disney Corporation bought out the Autry family's share of the Angels. Their main free-agency signing was Boston's slugging first baseman Mo Vaughn to provide much-needed punch. He earned $18.3 million in the 1999–2000 seasons and hit a total of 69 homers and drove in 225 runs. But otherwise, the offense was moribund in 1999, 13th out of 14 in run production, and the club fell to 70–92.

Former Dodgers catcher Mike Scioscia was signed as Angels manager in 2000, and finished with a winning record despite weak starting pitching. The team clouted 236 homers, led by Troy Glaus (47), and four players had over 100 RBIs. Hard-throwing Troy Percival had 32 saves. He, like Anderson, Darrin Erstad, Edmonds, Salmon, and Glaus, were all products of the team's farm system.

The club faltered in 2001, but in 2002, bolstered by a reliable pitching staff, excellent defense, and the highest batting average in the AL, the Angels won 99 games, coming in second in the West and gaining a wild-card berth in the playoffs. Lefty Jerrod Washburn went 18–6 and Percival saved 40 games. Edison International Field, meanwhile, became a hell for baseball traditionalists as Angel fans were cued by "the Rally Monkey" on Edison's big screen to bang thunder sticks together whenever the home team needed runs. The Angels upset the Yankees in four games and then the Minnesota Twins in five. In both series, the Angels lost the first game and seemed on the ropes before coming back to dump the opposition.

The 2002 World Series brought together two West Coast wild-card teams. The match with the upstart San Francisco Giants turned into one of the finest Series in recent memory. This time, destiny was on the side of the Angels. Going into the middle of game six, it looked like the Giants were about to win the championship. They were leading the Angels 5–0 going into the seventh inning when a three-run homer by Scott Spezio narrowed the gap. As thousands of thunder sticks were beating together, the Angels rallied for three more runs in the eighth off of hapless Giants relievers to pull out a 6–5 victory and force a deciding seventh game. Rookie John Lackey pitched a near-flawless game, and with strong relief support, the Angels took game seven 4–1 to capture the World Series.

Garret Anderson, who hit the game winning ball, runs with the World Series Championship trophy, 2002. © AP / Wide World Photos

THE MAGIC KINGDOM SHRINKS (A BIT)

By the time the Angels won the World Series, the Disney Corporation recognized it had overextended itself by getting into professional sports. Owning the Angels garnered goodwill, but running a major-league franchise was not the best way for it to make money. Arizona advertising mogul Arturo Moreno bought the Angels after the 2002 season for $186 million. The first Mexican American to own a major-league baseball team, Moreno had previously owned shares of the Arizona Diamondbacks and the NBA's Phoenix Suns. Among his first popular actions was lowering the price of the $8.50 beer.

The 2003 season was a disappointment as the Angels dropped to a 75–87 record, 19 games behind the Western Division champion Oakland Athletics. Injuries to Glaus and Erstad did not help, and the starting pitching declined. The relief corps headed by closer Troy Percival remained effective, and outfielder Garret Anderson continued to provide a reliable bat, following his 123 RBIs in 2002 with 116 a year later.

During the off-season, Moreno won the bidding war for Vladimir Guerrero, a talented outfielder who had battered NL hurlers as a Montreal Expo. Guerrero furnished the 2004 Angels with 39 home runs, a .337 batting average, and 126 RBIs. Jose Guillen, a much-traveled outfielder, knocked in 104 runs. The team led the AL in batting (.281), but was only seventh in run production. Free-agent right-hander Bartolo Colon led the starters with 18 wins, albeit with an ERA of over 5.00. These additions helped the team fight off the Oakland Athletics to win the AL West with a 90–72 record. However, Mike Scioscia's widely respected managing could not keep the Angels from getting swept by the Boston Red Sox in the AL Division Series.

In the process, the Angels have put together one of the best-paid teams in the major leagues. In 2004, only the Yankees and the Red Sox had higher payrolls. With a $100 million payroll, the Angels even outspent their often overly generous neighbors—the Los Angeles Dodgers, who paid out about $92 million on their NL West champions. While the Angels might be finally emerging from the shadow cast by the Dodgers on Southern California baseball, the financial ledger does not seem to bear that out. As of 2004, *Fortune* estimated that the Dodgers were the 4th-most-valuable franchise in MLB, while the Angels ranked 20th. Still, at the end of the 2004 season, the Angels possess an entertaining ball club, blending hustling overachievers with the superbly talented Vladimir Guerrero—a recipe for winning seasons and hopefully large, enthusiastic crowds cramming into their ballpark, now called Angel Stadium.

Renamed the Los Angeles Angels of Anaheim, the 2005 squad had a terrific season,

Vladimir Guerrero in a game against the Seattle Mariners, 2004. © AP / Wide World Photos

Mike Scioscia's team, led by Bartolo Colon's 21 wins, fought off a second-half surge by the Oakland Athletics and won the AL West. In the ALDS, the Angels subdued the Yankees in the decisive fifth game but fell in five games to the White Sox's magnificent starting pitching in the ALCS. The entertaining Angels blend hustling overachievers with the superbly talented Vladimir Guerrero—a recipe for winning seasons and hopefully large, enthusiastic crowds cramming into Angel Stadium.

NOTABLE ACHIEVEMENTS

Most Valuable Players

Year	Name	Position
1979	Don Baylor	OF
2004	Vladimir Guerrero	OF

Cy Young Winners

Year	Name	Position
1964	Dean Chance	RHP
2005	Bartolo Colon	RHP

Batting Champions

Year	Name	#
1970	Alex Johnson	.329

Home-Run Champions

Year	Name	#
1981	Bobby Grich	22
1982	Reggie Jackson	39
2000	Troy Glaus	47

ERA Champions

Year	Name	#
1964	Dean Chance	1.65
1977	Frank Tanana	2.54

Strikeout Champions

Year	Name	#
1972	Nolan Ryan	329
1973	Nolan Ryan	383
1974	Nolan Ryan	367
1975	Frank Tanana	269
1976	Nolan Ryan	327
1977	Nolan Ryan	341
1978	Nolan Ryan	260
1979	Nolan Ryan	223

No-Hitters (Italics = Perfect Game)

Name	Date
Bo Belinsky	05/05/1962
Clyde Wright	07/03/1970
Nolan Ryan	05/15/1973
Nolan Ryan	07/15/1973
Nolan Ryan	09/28/1974
Nolan Ryan	06/01/1975
Mike Witt	*09/30/1984*

POSTSEASON APPEARANCES

AL West Division Titles

Year	Record	Manager
1979	88–74	Jim Fregosi
1982	93–69	Gene Mauch
1986	92–70	Gene Mauch
2004	92–70	Mike Scioscia

AL Wild Card

Year	Record	Manager
2002	99–63	Mike Scioscia

AL Pennants

Year	Record	Manager
2002	99–63	Mike Scioscia

World Championships

Year	Opponent	MVP
2002	San Francisco	Troy Glaus

MANAGERS

2000–	Mike Scioscia
1999	Joe Maddon
1997–1999	Terry Collins
1996	John McNamara
1994–1996	Marcel Lachemann
1993–1994	Buck Rodgers
1992	John Wathan
1991–1992	Buck Rodgers
1989–1991	Doug Rader
1988	Moose Stubing
1988	Cookie Rojas
1985–1987	Gene Mauch
1983–1984	John McNamara
1981–1982	Gene Mauch
1978–1981	Jim Fregosi
1977–1978	Dave Garcia
1976–1977	Norm Sherry
1974–1976	Dick Williams
1974	Whitey Herzog
1973–1974	Bobby Winkles
1972	Del Rice
1969–1971	Lefty Phillips
1961–1969	Bill Rigney

Team Records by Individual Players

Batting Leaders

	Single Season			Career		
	Name		Year	Name		Plate Appearances
Batting average	Darin Erstad	.355	2000	Rod Carew	.314	3,570
On-base %	Jason Thompson	.439	1980	Rod Carew	.393	3,570
Slugging %	Troy Glaus	.604	2000	Tim Salmon	.500	6,795
OPS	Tim Salmon	1.024	1995	Tim Salmon	.886	6,795
Games	Sandy Alomar	162	1970	Brian Dowling	1,661	6,912
At bats	Sandy Alomar	689	1971	Garret Anderson	6,472	6,849

(Continued)

Batting Leaders   (Continued)

	Single Season			Career	Plate Appearances
	Name		Year	Name	
Runs	Vladimir Guerrero	124	2004	Tim Salmon	956	6,795
Hits	Darin Erstad	240	2000	Garret Anderson	1,929	6,849
Total bases	Darin Erstad	366	2000	Garret Anderson	3,062	6,849
Doubles	Garret Anderson	56	2002	Garret Anderson	403	6,849
Triples	Chone Figgins	17	2004	Jim Fregosi	70	5,944
Home runs	Troy Glaus	47	2000	Tim Salmon	290	6,795
RBIs	Don Baylor	139	1979	Garret Anderson	1,043	6,849
Walks	Tony Philips	113	1995	Tim Salmon	941	6,795
Strikeouts	Mo Vaughn	181	2000	Tim Salmon	1,316	6,795
Stolen bases	Mickey Rivers	70	1975	Gary Pettis	186	2,156
Extra-base hits	Garret Anderson	88	2002	Garret Anderson	656	6,849
Times on base	Darin Erstad	305	2000	Tim Salmon	2,623	6,795

Pitching Leaders

	Single Season			Career	Innings Pitched
	Name		Year	Name	
ERA	Dean Chance	1.65	1964	Andy Messersmith 2.78	972.3
Wins	Clyde Wright	22	1970	Chuck Finley	165	2,675
Won-loss %	Bert Blyleven	.773	1989	Jarrod Washburn	.568	1,153.3
Hits/9 IP	Nolan Ryan	5.26	1972	Troy Percival	6.03	5,86.7
Walks/9 IP	Paul Byrd	1.23	2005	Bert Blyleven	1.74	508
Strikeouts	Nolan Ryan	383	1973	Nolan Ryan	2,416	2,181.3
Strikeouts/9 IP	Nolan Ryan	10.57	1973	Troy Percival	10.43	586.7
Games	Scot Shields	78	2005	Troy Percival	579	586.7
Saves	Bryan Harvey	46	1991	Troy Percival	316	586.7
Innings	Nolan Ryan	332.7	1974	Chuck Finley	2,675	2,675
Starts	Nolan Ryan	41	1974	Chuck Finley	379	2,675
Complete games	Nolan Ryan	26	1973	Nolan Ryan	156	2,181.3
Shutouts	Dean Chance	11	1974	Nolan Ryan	40	2,182.3

Source: "Los Angeles Angels of Anaheim Batting Leaders (seasonal and career)." http://baseball-reference.com/teams/ANA/leaders_bat.shtml; "Los Angeles Angels of Anaheim Pitching Leaders (seasonal and career)." http://baseball-reference.com/teams/ANA/leaders_pitch.shtml.

BIBLIOGRAPHY

Alexander, Charles, C. *Our Game: An American Baseball History*. New York: Henry Holt, 1991.

The Baseball Page. "Anaheim Angels." http://www.thebaseballpage.com/present/fp/al/ana.htm.

Baseball Prospectus. http://www.baseballprospectus.com/.

Davis, Mike. *City of Quartz*. New York: Vintage Books, 1992.

Los Angeles Angels of Anaheim official Web site. "Angels History." http://anaheim.angels.mlb.com/NASApp/mlb/ana/history/ana_history_timeline.jsp.

Newhan, Ross. *Anaheim Angels: A Complete History*. New York: Hyperion, 2000.

Rader, Benjamin. *Baseball: A History of America's Game*. Urbana: University of Illinois Press, 1992.

Sullivan, Neil J. *The Dodgers Move West*. New York: Oxford University Press, 1987.

Tygiel, Jules. *Past Time: Baseball as History*. New York: Oxford University Press, 2000.

Wescott, John. *Anaheim: City of Dreams*. Chatsworth, CA: Windsor Publication, 1990.

Minnesota Twins

Kristin M. Anderson and Christopher W. Kimball

At the dawn of the 2005 season, Major League Baseball returned to Washington, DC, with the arrival of the former Montreal Expos. This gave the city its third MLB franchise. This chapter examines the history of the first of those teams, the current Minnesota Twins, which traces its history back through the Washington Senators, one of the original members of the American League, into the mid-nineteenth-century origins of the game on the East Coast.

While both the Senators and the Twins have been famous for their lack of success—"First in war, first in peace, and last in the American League" is the signal joke about Washington baseball—the century-long history of the teams includes some significant successes, including World Series wins in 1924, 1987, and 1991; league championships in 1925, 1933, and 1965; AL Western Division championships in 1969 and 1970; and AL Central Division championships in 2002, 2003, and 2004.

The franchise has shared several characteristics with many other teams, such as troubles with facilities development, but also more distinctive ones, including decades-long ownership by a single family and an enterprise often running on the financial margins. With the team's 1961 move from the East Coast to the Midwest, its story became intertwined with the westward movement of existing franchises as well as expansion in MLB. This also represented a shift from an urban to a suburban setting, followed by a subsequent move near the central business district. In two different cities, then, the Senators-Twins franchise provides strong ties to the beginnings of professional baseball in the nineteenth century, demonstrates the growth and development of the game in an urban center in the East followed by its flight move to the homogeneous Midwest, and illustrates recent struggles as a small-market team in an outmoded facility. The story demonstrates the possibility of triumph and success, if only occasionally, under difficult circumstances.

EARLY BASEBALL IN WASHINGTON, DC

The Senators' prehistory in Washington goes back to the earliest years of professional baseball, following a typical pattern reflecting league instability, peripatetic use of ballparks and fields, and episodes of unreliable management and ownership. As in many cities, these years saw the emergence of one or two dominant teams. One of the prominent 1850s clubs was the Nationals, founded in 1859 by government clerks, whose name was later taken up by the city's AL team (until 1957), and reinvented for the new NL team in 2005.

Washington played a part in early intercity matches. The Brooklyn Atlantics and the Philadelphia Athletics visited Washington in 1865 to play local teams and demonstrate their superior skill, having recently competed in the season's championship. More significant, perhaps, were the 1867 western travels of the Nationals to compete against eight teams in cities as far west as St. Louis and as far north as Chicago. There they played a Rockford team, led by young pitching star A. G. Spalding, that beat the Nationals for their only loss on the tour.

The city's role as national capital meant that baseball received a seal of approval when government officials attended games. Abraham Lincoln is supposed to have watched games there in 1862, and Andrew Johnson was said to have watched the Nationals play in the intercity tournament of 1865. Some early teams played at the White Lot, on what is now the Ellipse, bringing baseball into the backyard of the White House. In 1897, President William McKinley was invited to throw out the first ball at the beginning of the season. The presidential tradition became formalized as an annual event in the early twentieth century, enduring even when there was no team in Washington.

The location and establishment of playing fields in Washington reflected broader trends in ballpark design and function. Early teams played in various parks around the city at a time when identifying and using open areas was relatively easy. Longtime Washington baseball entrepreneur Mike Scanlon is credited with the building of the city's first formal ballpark in 1870—an enclosed space with permanent seating, allowing the club owners to charge admission. This assisted clubs to generate revenue to pay professional players.

As standards for playing space and seating capacity increased, new facilities were constructed to meet these demands. For instance, Capitol Park was constructed in 1886, at the site of Union Station. It seated about 6,000 people in a huge facility that was 400 feet by 800 feet. Such capacious facilities could not be sustained for long on valuable core city real estate, and the Capitol Grounds were replaced in the early 1890s by National League Park in northwest Washington.

As spectator capacity increased and the size of the city grew, attention was paid to transit issues. In contrast to other cities, where transit companies invested in ballparks along or at the end of their lines, thereby bringing traffic, in Washington the transit company brought the lines to the ballpark. At Capitol Park in the late 1880s, temporary rails were laid for each game so that the city's horse cars could get fans to and from the grounds.

Available space and convenient transportation were only two of the location-related issues facing Washington teams. As elsewhere, Washington club owners pushed against legal prohibitions forbidding Sunday games. In 1890, for example, the Nationals played a Sunday game in Alexandria to avoid the blue laws in Washington. They later returned to the site to play again, hoping that a previously lucky location would bring much-needed fortune to the team. This was one illegal game too many for local authorities, and the confrontation with law enforcement played out as it often did in other cities, with fans harassing the police and stealthy escapes of team officials attempting to avoid arrest.

Typical of many late nineteenth-century teams, special promotions were devised to attract female fans to the ballparks. Washington's best-known example of this was a Ladies' Day scheduled to coincide with the pitching appearances of the handsome Win Mercer in 1897, capitalizing on his particular appeal to Washington's women fans. The intent was to increase the fan base and encourage better behavior in the grandstand. Over 1,000 women attended the game. Unfortunately, Mercer was thrown out of the game arguing a call with the umpire. The female fans harassed the umpire for the remainder of the game. Afterward, many rushed the field to attack the umpire with their parasols.

One of the prominent characteristics of baseball's late nineteenth-century evolution was the rationalizing and professionalizing of the game, including the development of teams with paid players that joined leagues that helped schedule and coordinate games and regulate the process of player acquisition. Washington's teams, especially the Olympics and the Nationals, appeared on the league landscape quite early, and yet both teams demonstrated the instability in league affiliation common in this period. These problems were due not only to shakiness in the leagues themselves, but also to an early-established tradition of perennially bad play that made Washington teams especially vulnerable to shifting league membership.

In 1871, the Washington Olympics played in the National Association of Professional Base Ball Players, going 15–15, but dropped out the next year after nine games. The Washington Nationals joined the NA in 1872, lost all 11 games, and dropped out, while the Washington Blue Legs came in seventh (8–31) in 1873. A new Nationals entry in 1875 finished a dismal ninth (5–23). In 1884 the city had a team in the Union Association called the Nationals, which finished seventh (47–65), while the Statesmen played in the American Association, and fared even worse, coming in last (12–51).

There was no Washington entry in the National League until 1886. The Nationals were very weak, coming in last three seasons out of four, and won less than one-third of their games. They were replaced in 1889 by the Cincinnati Reds, who transferred in from the American Association. In 1892, when the NL expanded from 8 to 12 teams, Washington was again included. Owners George and Earl Wagner of Philadelphia became the first in a famous sequence of notoriously stingy owners. They traded players for financial gain rather than for the good of the team, which guaranteed losing seasons and made them very unpopular with the fans. Their failure was acknowledged by the NL, which bought them out prior to the 1900 season when it reduced itself to an eight-team league, also cutting Cleveland, Louisville, and Baltimore.

THE RISE OF THE WASHINGTON SENATORS

In 1900 Washington had a team in the new American League, which was a reconstituted form of the old minor Western League. One year later the AL proclaimed itself a major league. The Washington franchise was ostensibly owned by Detroit hotelier Fred Postal and managed by Jimmy Manning, owner of the Kansas City minor-league club. In fact, AL president Ban Johnson owned the team. The Senators in 1901 drew 161,661 fans—a respectable number—to the new American League Ballpark, located near Capitol Hill in northeast Washington, but finished a less-than-respectable sixth place. Their first season set the tone for much of the team's subsequent history. In the off-season, they signed four players from the NL's Philadelphia Phillies, including superstar Ed Delahanty, who hit .376 (second in the AL) and led the league with a .590 slugging percentage. But despite the new additions, the team again finished sixth, though attendance rose to 188,158. The following season, the team collapsed, finishing last, and attendance dropped by a third. Delahanty died accidentally on a road trip in a drunken fall off a railroad bridge at the Canadian border.

The team returned to the old National Park in 1904, taking with them some of the stands from American League Park. Then, just to confuse everyone, or perhaps in honor of the transplanted stands, the Senators renamed their new home American League Park! The stadium was located at the junctions of Georgia Avenue and Seventh, W, and U Streets, Northwest, a site used for baseball from 1891 until 1961, and today the site of Howard University Hospital. Since the owners failed to acquire all of the adjoining property, when the park was rebuilt in 1911 after a fire it featured a V-shaped projection in right center field where the wall wound around five houses and a tree. The dimensions were a spacious 421 feet, 400 feet, and 399 feet from left to right.

In 1904, Ban Johnson sold the team to a local syndicate led by Thomas C. Noyes, owner of the *Washington Evening Star*, inspiring hope for the franchise's fortunes. The ownership change, however, did nothing for the team's on-field performance as they finished 38–113 (.252), their worst record so far. In early 1905, Noyes took on the role of team president and exercised a greater hand in management. His presence portended several changes and provided some stability over his 15-year tenure. The team changed its official nickname to the Nationals, though "Senators" was the name that stuck with the public. Noyes also began investing more heavily in new players, but the team's performance showed little improvement. In 1906, for example, the team's struggles continued as it finished seventh, at one point losing three doubleheaders in three days.

Joe Cantillon was appointed manager for the next season, having previously managed the Minneapolis Millers of the American Association. He guided the Senators over the next three years, finishing last twice and seventh once. His most significant action was acquiring a young Idahoan pitcher, Walter Johnson, the cornerstone of the franchise and one of the greatest pitchers of all time. Johnson signed for a $100 bonus, train fare, and a big-league salary of $350 a month. He lost his debut in August 1907 and finished the season with a 5–9 record on a last-place team (49–102).

Johnson began to establish his dominance one year later, when he pitched three shutouts in four days against the New York Highlanders. The season was also noteworthy for catcher Gabby Street's successful catch of a ball dropped from the top of the Washington Monument. Previous efforts had been blocked by the police, but this time the stunt was officially sanctioned. The episode signified that baseball had become an acceptable form of entertainment. The following year saw the Senators back in the cellar (42–110), leading to Cantillon's dismissal and replacement by Jimmy McAleer.

In 1910 the Senators started what became a fixture on Opening Day when President William Howard Taft threw out the first pitch. Previous presidents had thrown out the first ball, but now it became an annual ritual. Less well remembered was that Secretary of State Charles Bennett was hit by a line drive that day. The remainder of the season followed another tradition, as the club finished seventh, despite Johnson's 25 victories.

On March 17, 1911, the ballpark's wooden stands burned to the ground, a not-infrequent occurrence in that era. Noyes accepted the accident with good grace, even though the $15,000 insurance payment came nowhere near the estimated rebuilding expenses of $125,000. Taking a tremendous gamble, Noyes and his board of directors borrowed $100,000 from a local bank and immediately set about to build a fire-resistant structure fabricated with steel and concrete. The prominent Cleveland firm of Osborn Engineering, considered "the national pastime's foremost architectural player," designed and constructed the new park. Osborn specialized in constructing temporary stands, which made them an attractive partner for teams seeking to recover from fires and other disasters. The company also built Cleveland's League Park (1910), the Polo Grounds (1911), Navin Field (1912), Braves Field (1915), and Yankee Stadium (1923). The new ballpark was designed to resemble Forbes Field and Shibe

Park—but with a smaller capacity. A double-decked grandstand surrounded the infield; a single-decked, covered grandstand extended out to the foul poles; and there were bleachers in the outfield. The field's dimensions were an asymmetrical 407 feet, 421 feet, and 328 feet. The structure was not completed until the summer, but enough was finished by Opening Day to allow President Taft and 11,000 fans to inaugurate the new American League Park on April 12, 1911. Unfortunately the new grounds had a troubled history, and later became known as "the Rodney Dangerfield" of ballparks.

Clark Calvin Griffith, an old friend of Cantillon, became the team's field manager after the 1911 season, and he went on to become the dominant figure in the franchise's history. Griffith was an outstanding pitcher who went 237–146 in his 20 major-league seasons. In 1901, he became the player-manager of the AL's Chicago White Sox. Griffith then moved on to manage the New York Highlanders (1903–8) and the Cincinnati Reds (1909–11). He borrowed funds to secure a 10 percent interest in the Reds. Overall, he managed for 20 straight seasons in the majors. Griffith was elected to the Hall of Fame in 1946.

In his first year in Washington, Griffith led the team to a second-place finish with 91 wins, 27 more than the year before. Johnson was sensational in 1912, going 33–12, with a league-leading 1.39 ERA and 303 strikeouts. The next year, when the club again came in second, Johnson went 36–7, with a league-leading 1.14 ERA, 336 innings pitched, 243 strikeouts, and 29 complete games. He achieved the pitching triple crown and was league MVP. In 1914, the team slipped to third place and then found itself competing with the new Federal League to retain Johnson's services. In December, the Big Train signed a two-year, $40,000 contract with the Chicago Whales, but he backed out of it and stayed with the Senators. Over the next three years, the team sank back to fourth, seventh, and fifth. This was accompanied by falling attendance, and the board of directors was forced to borrow money to keep operating.

When the United States got into World War I, the team played a significant role in persuading the Woodrow Wilson administration that baseball was an important contributor to the home front. The Senators drilled before games, gave soldiers free tickets, and urged fans to buy war bonds. Griffith established a "Bat and Ball Fund" to send baseball equipment to the American troops in Europe. Griffith later claimed that Franklin Roosevelt's decision to allow MLB to continue playing during World War II was based on the sport's support for the war effort of 1917–18. Griffith's political acumen also extended to other matters. He provided free tickets to clergy, partly to head off opposition to Sunday baseball. In the war-shortened 1918 season, the Senators advanced to third behind MVP Johnson, who went 23–13 and again won the pitching triple crown, but they fell to seventh the following year.

In 1920, Griffith turned to his more well-heeled fellow owners for an infusion of cash, but was turned down. So, with the backing of Philadelphia grain merchant William Richardson, Griffith bought 40 percent of the team's stock for less than $100,000, mortgaging personal property in order to make the purchase. The cash-strapped Griffith became president of the club while continuing as manager that season.

The new ownership thoroughly renovated the ballpark and renamed it Griffith Stadium. The ballpark could not expand outward to new land, but did expand upward, much like contemporary central business districts. By 1920, the single-decked stands were double-decked, with a higher roofline and a steeper pitch than in the main grandstand. The changing roofline defined the ballpark as a place that had been cobbled together, not something carefully integrated by a master design. Seating was increased to 13,000 (still the smallest in the AL), a new concrete and steel stand was constructed along the left-field line, the clubhouses were renovated, and the playing field was resodded.

This unattractive appearance matched the state of a franchise that was always near financial ruin. A weak financial base with minimal initial capitalization was aggravated by limited operating revenues. The team's finances led to more weakness on the field and a revolving door in leadership, with a new manager each year between 1921 and 1924. But the leadership vacuum was about to change, and for a brief period, the financial situation also improved.

THE GLORY YEARS, 1924–33

In 1924, 27 year old Bucky Harris became the Senators' field manager and led them to the pennant, going 92–62, a 17-game improvement over 1923. The team led the AL in pitching with a team ERA of 3.34. Johnson went 23–7 and won his third pitching triple crown. Goose Goslin batted .344 and led the AL in RBIs (129), while Sam Rice batted .334 and led the league in hits (216). In their first World Series appearance, the Senators defeated John McGraw's New York Giants four games to three, taking the deciding game in the 12th inning. Walter Johnson won game seven in relief, after having lost his two series starts. The series was a sensation in Washington. Each of the four home games drew more than 30,000 people, with the first two drawing more than 35,000. The big crowd was accommodated by temporary seats in center field. Game one marked the first time that a president and first lady, the Coolidges, attended a World Series opener. The games were broadcast by WRC, the city's first radio station. The season was a financial boon for the team as it turned a profit of $231,037. The following year, Griffith and his family moved into a substantial home near Washington's Embassy Row, reflecting his improved financial situation.

Expectations and fan interest were high in 1925. Attendance jumped from 584,310 in 1924 to 817,199, a team record until 1946. All Senators road games were broadcast on WRC. The fans were not disappointed, as the Senators won the league championship by eight and a half games, with a record of 96–55. The entire team batted .303, led by Rice at .350 and Goslin at .334, while shortstop Roger Peckinpaugh was MVP. The pitching was again the best in the AL, with a 3.70 ERA. Stan Coveleski and Johnson both won 20. Coveleski's 2.84 ERA led the AL, as did Firpo Marberry's 15 saves. In the World Series against the

Pittsburgh Pirates, the Senators took a 3–1 lead, led by two Johnson victories. But the Pirates fought back and forced a game seven, which was played in dreadful weather, and probably should have been postponed. The Senators took the lead in the eighth inning on a Peckinpaugh homer. But Johnson failed to hold the lead in the bottom of the frame. The Pirates staged a two-out rally, tallying the winning runs in a 9–7 game after a Peckinpaugh error.

In 1926 the short run of pennants ended, as the Senators finished fourth. While the Senators led the league in hitting (.292), their pitchers, including the great Johnson (15–16), struggled. The following season started poorly when in spring training Johnson was hit by a pitch and broke his leg. He only pitched in 18 games, but the team still finished third. On August 2 the team celebrated Johnson's 20th anniversary with the franchise and gave him the gate receipts from the game.

This event marked the beginning of the end for Walter Johnson. In 1928, he contracted influenza and was forced to retire. The team was also hurt when star outfielder Goose Goslin injured his arm. The team finished fourth, and manager Bucky Harris was fired at season's end. Johnson pitched 21 seasons for the Senators, going 417–340 and earning election with the first group of players to the Hall of Fame in 1936. His winning percentage of .599 was sensational for a franchise that finished seventh or eighth seven times during his career. He often had little support from his teammates, getting shut out 65 times, including 27 1–0 losses. He primarily threw fastballs of nearly 100 miles per hour, probably about 10 miles per hour faster than other top pitchers, and his record for lifetime strikeouts lasted for 56 years. After retiring from the diamond, Johnson managed the Newark minor-league club.

In 1929 Johnson was brought back as manager. He led the club to a fifth-place finish in 1929, but they rose to second in 1930 with 94 wins, more than the 1924 champion team. The squad batted .302, second in the league, led by outfielder Heinie Manush's .362. The pitching led the AL, with five hurlers winning over 15 games. In 1931, the team won 92 games, also more than the 1924 champions, but they finished third. They finished third again in 1932 with 93 wins. Despite this fine record (.570 winning percentage), Johnson was subsequently fired, replaced by 26-year-old shortstop-manager Joe Cronin, the youngest manager in major-league history. Not incidentally, the change saved Griffith some $17,500.

In general, the team remained successful on and off the field in the 1920s and 1930s. By 1932, it had finished in the first division 9 of the last 10 years. During the 1920s the team averaged an annual profit of $121,000, including $408,746 in the exciting 1925 pennant-winning season. For the first time in years, the team lost money in 1931, and in 1932 they lost $76,634. This probably contributed to Johnson's firing, though the Great Depression undoubtedly contributed to lower revenues.

The Senators made their third, and last, World Series appearance in 1933 after winning the pennant (99–53), seven games ahead of the Yankees. The squad led the AL in batting (.284), headed by Cronin, who drove in 118 runs, and Manush, whose 221 hits put him first in the AL. The defense led the league, and the pitching was near the top, led by 20-game winners Earl Whitehill and Alvin Crowder. The New York Giants, however, defeated the Senators in five games in the Series. Game three in Washington was attended by 27,727 people, including President Franklin Delano Roosevelt. The team nearly broke even that year, the only AL franchise that did not lose a lot of money.

LAST IN THE AMERICAN LEAGUE: DEPRESSION AND WAR, 1934–45

At this point, the Senators seemed to be a relatively healthy franchise, with three World Series appearances in 10 years and the resources needed to acquire a competitive team. But the team could not repeat the success of the 1920s and early 1930s, and instead struggled for years to come. Furthermore, as they were located in the smallest city in the AL, the Senators suffered at the gate as well as on the field.

In 1934, the team was hampered by injuries to several key players and fell to seventh place. Cronin was sold to Boston at the end of the season for a record $225,000, perhaps because of his marriage to Mildred Robertson, Griffith's secretary and niece. Griffith reportedly believed it would be easier for Cronin to escape talk of nepotism if he played in another city, even though Griffith's employment loyalty to family members was well known. Besides that, Cronin was so outstanding that nepotism was really not at issue. In any event, it was unusual for Griffith to sell a star player in his prime. Cronin, who signed a five-year, $50,000 contract with the Red Sox, remained loyal to the Senators, and years later, when serving as AL president, assisted with the team's move to Minnesota.

Bucky Harris returned as manager in 1935, continuing Griffith's tradition of hiring only former players and managers to skipper the club. Unlike his first tour of duty, however, Harris led the club to many poor finishes, bouncing between fifth and seventh, with only one first-division finish before 1942. The 1935 team had excellent hitting, with second baseman Buddy Myer leading the AL in batting (.349), but the pitching was among the league's worst. Myer played 17 years in the majors, nearly all in Washington, and had a lifetime .303 batting average. The team's weak farm system began to hurt the Senators, who did not have enough good young players to bring up to the parent club who could contribute to the team's on-field success. To make up for that deficit, the Senators recruited Cuban players who were white or could pass for white, as they had done as far back as 1913. Griffith himself had led the way in recruiting Cubans in 1911 when he had managed the Reds. This openness is ironic given the team's difficulties with race issues in the future. Joe Cambria, a sometime minor-league owner and longtime scout, brought Cuban players to the United States to play in the Senators' organization. A few made the major leagues, and many others found positions in the minor leagues.

In 1935, Calvin Griffith was appointed secretary-treasurer of the Senators' minor-league Chattanooga franchise. Born Calvin Robertson, he grew up poor in Montreal and moved to Washington at age 11 to live with his uncle Clark. Though never formally adopted, Calvin took the Griffith name, as did younger sister Thelma. Calvin Griffith was just one of many family members who would be part of the team's management, and he would be the one groomed to replace his father.

Despite the difficult years of the depression, the Senators made a little money ($27,509) in the 1930s. In 1941, Clark Griffith put lights on his stadium at a cost of nearly $250,000, half of which was a loan from the league, so the Senators could play night games. He had originally opposed night games, but was persuaded by improved attendance and quickly became a leading advocate when he saw how much more money could be made.

Harris resigned after finishing in seventh place in 1942, and was replaced by yet another former player, coach Ossie Bluege. Calvin Griffith was called to Washington from Chattanooga to become director of concessions. He was quickly elevated to a vice presidency and began representing the team at league meetings.

The Senators made a huge improvement in 1943 by finishing second, their best season in a decade, but future high hopes were dashed when they finished last one year later. The team, like others, was hurt by military call-ups, but also by the departure of Cuban players when they learned they would be eligible for the military draft. Despite all the team's struggles and the joke about being "first in war, first in peace, and last in the American League," 1944 was actually the first time that a Griffith-owned team had finished at the bottom of the AL.

In 1945, the team rebounded with an excellent season, coming in second by just a game and a half. The team had the best pitching in the AL (2.92 ERA), led by 20-game winner Roger Wolff; he and Dutch Leonard each had a 2.12 ERA. Some observers argued that the team might have won but for business considerations. Griffith had not expected to contend, and so he scheduled several doubleheaders to free up Sundays for rental to the Washington Redskins. As a result, the pitching staff was overworked. That year the team made $222,473, a very healthy profit that equaled the combined earnings of the prior five years.

DECLINE AND FALL, 1945–60

Following World War II, major-league baseball was transformed by many social and economic pressures. The two-league, 16-team, 10-city major-league arrangement that had endured for half a century was replaced by a newer, less stable arrangement of franchises, leagues, and ballparks. The changing pattern was directly connected to economic and demographic changes in MLB's northern and midwestern urban strongholds, which suffered from white flight, middle-class suburbanization, and the physical decay of the inner cities.

Cities became poorer, infrastructure deteriorated, and the racial profile of cities changed. Baseball teams, like many other businesses and retail establishments, recognized the need to respond, especially as their old ballparks were deteriorating and were located in less desirable neighborhoods.

Major-league teams in the 1950s recognized these trends and considered their options. They did not get very involved in urban renewal or redevelopment in their hometowns, but rather started considering new and better markets. Cities with multiple teams—Boston, St. Louis, Philadelphia, and New York—soon found themselves with only one team. The Senators were not in a two-team city, but the migration of other teams in the 1950s had a profound impact on the Senators' fortunes.

Survey research helped owners and suitors approach potential new locations with some precision. For example, in 1953 the city of Minneapolis hired Market Facts Inc. of Chicago to evaluate its ability to host a profitable big-league franchise. The study found that "baseball attendance can be predicted on five key facts: the so-called natural trading area, that is, the health of the regional economy; team standing, or how much it wins; the closeness of the league's pennant race, or how balanced the competition in a league is; spectacular or colorful players on a team, that is, stars; and skillful promotion, that is, the creative marketing of the franchise; and other variables." The Washington Senators measured up in none of those categories.

In 1946 the team finished fourth and drew more than a million fans, both false promises. Mickey Vernon led the AL with a .353 batting average, and repeated seven years later, batting .337. In 1947 and 1948, the team stumbled to seventh place under manager Joe Kuhel, yet another former Senators player, and 1949 was even poorer, as the team finished last for only the second time in the Griffith era, going 50–104, the worst mark since 1909. The Senators earned over $1 million during the first three years after the war, but then went into the red.

Griffith took heavy criticism for bad trades and not developing young players, and faced a challenge to his ownership. A young Detroit Tigers employee, John Jachym, purchased 40 percent of the team's shares from the heirs of William Richardson, Griffith's original partner. While Richardson had been inactive, Jachym wanted to be very involved in the team's operations. Fearing that Jachym might get majority ownership, Griffith ignored the intruder, refusing him a seat on the team's board. To placate fans whose discontent might lead them to support Jachym, Griffith again turned to Bucky Harris as his field manager.

Harris led the team to a fifth-place finish in 1950, and a frustrated Jachym sold his shares to local insurance executive H. Gabriel Murphy, an old friend of Griffith's. Murphy then sold Griffith enough shares to give him a majority interest in exchange for a "first purchase" option on Griffith's shares. Murphy was welcomed as a savior, though his relationship with the Griffith family would sour later.

While Griffith's hold over the team remained secure, its on-field performance was dismal. Throughout the 1950s the team was deeply mired in the second division, especially from 1955 to 1959, when the Senators finished seventh once and eighth four times. The team failed to keep up with changes in player development. While other teams relied heavily on farm systems to develop future talent, the Senators owned only three franchises, in Charlotte, Chattanooga, and Orlando, and had no working agreements with other clubs. In addition, the club was one of the last to integrate. In September 1954, Cuban outfielder Carlos Paula became the first person of color to play for the Senators, and he started the following season. In 1957, veteran African American hurler Joe Black joined the team, but only pitched 12 innings.

This situation reflected the simple, even old-fashioned, state of the Washington franchise. One writer labeled the team the "country store" of MLB, a metaphor often used to describe the last decades of Griffith control. Besides lagging in player development, the team also lacked a modern administration. Griffith operated as general manager, chief scout, public-relations officer, and player developer, positions that other clubs delegated to different men. Griffith, however, liked to note that the team was one of the few that made money and remained debt free. Clark Griffith died in 1955, leaving a majority stake in the Senators to Calvin and Thelma, who could not sell their shares without the other's permission. They inherited a team with only $25,000 in the bank, and heavily reliant on concessions and rent—for example, the seven or eight games a year played at Griffith Stadium by the Redskins—to turn a profit. Calvin Griffith considered himself a baseball expert, and even as owner was active in game and player management. However, he was not universally admired for his judgment. For instance, noted baseball executive Gabe Paul described Calvin as "baseball dumb."

Griffith took over the Senators operation just when the urban crisis of the postwar era and the economic and geographic expansion of the United States were spurring franchise shifts. In 1954, the St. Louis Browns moved to Baltimore to become the Orioles, which put an AL rival just north of Washington and cost the Senators needed advertising revenue from Baltimore-based breweries, a sign of economic troubles to come. The Griffiths began getting relocation offers from other cities. A Louisville group presented plans for a 50,000-seat ballpark and a guarantee of 1 million fans annually for three years. Los Angeles, Houston, Dallas, Toronto, and Minneapolis were other possibilities. As a result, Griffith began thinking of moving, if only to press Washington to build a new stadium, and in 1956 tentative plans were announced to move to the West Coast. An advertisement in the 1957 season-opening supplement of the *Washington Post* begged for fan support, suggesting that the franchise's future was in grave danger: "There are at least three other cities waiting on the sidelines 'smacking their lips over this juicy plum.' Are we going to let them have it? I say No! No—a thousand times NO!" By 1958, negotiations were underway with the twin cities of Minneapolis and St. Paul, whose combined population was larger than Washington's and who had no nearby team with which to share the metropolitan market, an important criterion for future success.

When word of these offers got out, Griffith vigorously denied any interest in them in order to head off fan discontent. Griffith promised the fans that the team would stay in Washington forever. Griffith discovered that he lacked support for moving from fellow owners, afraid that Congress would be angry over losing Washington's team and would revoke MLB's antitrust exemption. This pattern of denial while listening to offers, as well as difficulties negotiating the political world, would harm the team's reputation in the future and would help shape negative images of Calvin Griffith.

To stimulate attendance, Griffith introduced some popular innovations. Clark Griffith had long resisted selling alcohol in the ballpark, but in 1957 Calvin opened up a beer garden. The ballpark was also modified to promote more offense by moving in the fences by about 30 feet, changing the dimensions to 408, 438, and 380 feet. This change helped slugger Roy Sievers, whose home-run output jumped from 29 to 42 in 1957, with 38 home runs the following year. He drove in over 100 runs in four seasons.

Despite this adjustment, the deteriorating state of Griffith Stadium was one of the main reasons for Griffith's interest in moving. The neighboring Orioles used this to their advantage. With the opening of Baltimore's Memorial Stadium for major league baseball in 1954, the Orioles began to take prospects to Griffith Stadium to contrast their new home with the Senators' drab ballpark. While its location along the streetcar line remained important, there were only 200 parking spaces next to the ballpark, a critical shortage in the new era of the suburban auto-driving commuter. The neighborhood became increasingly African American, a troubling fact for the owner and white fans. Attendance began to fall under 500,000, and few season tickets were sold. As the smallest city in the AL, Washington increasingly lacked the population base needed to keep attendance up. Many fans came only to see the visiting teams. Following Clark Griffith's death, the family, faced with a large inheritance tax bill, sold the stadium to Howard University for $1.5 million, more than half of which went to pay the tax.

In 1959, some 615,372 fans watched the Senators finish in last place. The one bright spot was the maturation of bonus-baby third baseman Harmon Killebrew, who in his first five seasons had only played 113 games. But the 23-year-old had a breakout season in 1959 with a league-leading 42 homers. Despite Killebrew's on-field heroics, city officials became increasingly unsympathetic to the Griffith family's weak finances. City officials, like the press and the fans, tended to discount Griffith's claims of poverty, though the city did drop its $12,000 annual fee for police protection. In general, though, Griffith fought with politicians over stadium issues, and his effort to secure a new ballpark made little headway. He opposed Congress over the possible site in northeast Washington, favoring a site in the more prosperous south and west regions. He also resisted a proposed new municipal stadium that would house both the Senators and the Redskins since he would lose the Redskins as tenants, thereby foregoing crucial revenues necessary to supplement the baseball team's balance sheet. Although the Senators had the lowest attendance in the AL for the sixth straight year, attendance rose to 743,404 in 1960; by then, however, Calvin Griffith was anxious to leave Washington.

READY AND WAITING: THE TWIN CITIES LURE MAJOR LEAGUE BASEBALL

In the mid-nineteenth century, baseball had established a foothold in the Twin Cities of St. Paul and Minneapolis, whose centers were about nine miles apart along the Mississippi River at the head of navigation (St. Paul) and at a large waterfall (Minneapolis). Each city established and maintained its independent identity, including the fielding of separate professional baseball teams. The cities grew into contiguous municipalities at the core of a single metropolitan region, but did not merge, and residents tended to exaggerate their differences. This made for a competitive environment for the development of professional baseball, and remains a factor in debates about new stadiums and sports facilities.

The emergence of professional baseball teams occurred after the Civil War. St. Paul had a team in the Union Association in 1884, which lasted just eight games. Minneapolis and St. Paul both had teams in the Western League, known by the late nineteenth century as the Minneapolis Millers and the St. Paul Saints.

After a few years in the Western League, including four when Charles Comiskey owned and managed the Saints, the league reorganized itself as the American League. Comiskey took the Saints to Chicago after the 1899 season, where they became the White Stockings, and Minneapolis was left without a league affiliation. Both cities joined the minor-league American Association on its founding in 1902, and each fielded a team until the 1961 season, when the Senators arrived.

The first wooden ballparks in the Twin Cities were located in or near their central business districts until the mid-1890s, when they were replaced by larger grounds well outside of the city centers, along the streetcar system at the junctions of major lines. They were used for many purposes, including high-school and college baseball and football games. Both cities hosted barnstorming teams and African American teams: the St. Paul Colored Gophers and the Minneapolis Keystones. Minneapolis's Nicollet Park and St. Paul's Lexington Park were remodeled in the 1910s, the latter because of a fire, using modern ferroconcrete construction. These grounds were not replaced until the mid-1950s, when each city built a new facility to help it attract a major-league franchise.

The intercity competition of the Millers and Saints helped build up an unusually fervent interest in baseball. Most municipal services were and remain separate in the Twin Cities, but a single transit company provided an integrated, metropolitan-wide system that extended for nearly 50 miles across the area, with amusement parks at each terminus. This network allowed easy access to both ballparks. On holidays such as Memorial Day, the Fourth of July, and Labor Day, the streetcars would carry thousands of fans from one ballpark to the other.

The presence of multiple competing morning and evening newspapers in each city gave readers plenty of opportunity to follow local and major-league baseball. Once the clubs were no longer independently owned—the Saints became part of the farm system of the Dodgers, and the Millers were affiliated with the Giants (and later the Red Sox)—fans got to see future stars such as Ted Williams, Willie Mays, and Roy Campanella on their way up, and players such as Rube Waddell, Monte Irvin, and Joe Hauser as they moved toward retirement.

While Washington struggled to retain the Senators, civic leaders in Minneapolis and St. Paul worked hard to bring them—or any other team—to the Twin Cities. Their combined populations placed the metropolitan area among the largest urban places in the 1950 census, but population, economic success, and other markers of accomplishment were not enough. The Twin Cities, like other growing urban areas outside the East, were anxious to acquire the trappings of established urban life to prove their stature. Having a major-league baseball team would show that they were a major metropolitan area.

At first, Minneapolis and St. Paul attempted to cooperate in attracting a team, jointly investigating cities with struggling squads or multiple teams. However, their inability to cooperate was demonstrated in the debate over a new ballpark. The existing parks were aging stylistically, functionally antiquated, located in areas not amenable to automobile traffic, not large enough, and not able to be sufficiently expanded for major-league crowds. The two cities competed for control of the process and the positioning of the new ballpark. This makes the eventual move of the Senators to the Twin Cities area even more remarkable, as the full influence, power, and direction of the metropolitan area was not entirely behind the project until 1959. Only after both cities had built stadiums to attract baseball were overtures made to end the enmity over the hosting of MLB.

Each city's proposed solution was as different as the cities themselves. St. Paul's plan used the existing infrastructure and transportation and embraced the urban environment. In 1957 the city of St. Paul built a new stadium within the city limits in an industrial area near existing highway and rail routes, equidistant from the two downtowns, and close to the area's only zoo and the immensely popular and widely familiar State Fair Grounds.

Minneapolis's stadium plan was in sharp contrast to St. Paul's. Local boosters were not obligated to use city land like their neighbor, and instead cooperated with the village of Bloomington, adjacent to Minneapolis's south side, in acquiring a spacious 163-acre site identified earlier in a St. Paul–funded stadium study. The location provided an opportunity for newness and space at a time when people were concerned about urban decay and congestion. Metropolitan

Stadium was constructed at the same time as the nearby Southdale Shopping Center, the nation's first enclosed mall. The triple-decked Met opened in 1956 and served as the home of the Millers of the American Association.

The illusion created by the site, a former working farm, was that it was open space, a significant commodity in postwar suburbia. While many suburban developments put houses in close proximity, having one's own yard (even if terribly small) was an important part of the suburban mystique. The stadium's location satisfied this, as did the view from its upper decks, displaying both suburban development and agricultural land. The location and view reinforced the notion of baseball's pastoral and bucolic setting, increasingly difficult to achieve in the old urban parks.

Suburban facilities like Met Stadium were no longer determined by their environment, like the old urban ballparks, designed in an age of mass transit and confined to limited and sometimes oddly shaped space. Instead, the suburban structures shaped and transformed the land they occupied. Furthermore, the open land provided a large blank canvas upon which the architect could create a perfect modernist vision, without the messy distractions of an established built environment. Following modernist principles of avoiding historic quotation and ornament in favor of revealing structure and materials, Met Stadium was a massive steel-frame facility, inviting frequent comparisons to Erector Set construction.

Metropolitan Stadium's design not only focused on the building but also included acres of parking for thousands of cars, and was close to major new superhighways. The Interstate Highway Act of 1956, reflecting changes already underway, furthered suburban developments and their accompanying car culture: shopping malls, drive-in restaurants, and even tailgating at sports events. It was precisely at this time that the Twin Cities' extensive and well-developed 60-year-old streetcar system was bought out and dismantled in favor of highways and buses, ending an era of sophisticated and useful public transportation. There was little need to plan a stadium that would take mass transit into account, because the car was now king.

There was a lot of competition for the few teams considering relocating, and it would take more than a suitable ballpark to secure a major-league franchise. A small group of men backed by the Minneapolis Chamber of Commerce, an organization that promoted economic success and civic pride, led the quest for a major-league team. Their decade-long struggle to land a team was summed up by the expression (made famous by Hubert Humphrey) that without major-league sports, the Twin Cities would simply be a "cold Omaha." To avoid that fate, and achieve other, more positive outcomes, the chamber-of-commerce group worked tirelessly to secure a big-league baseball team.

Charles Johnson, a senior sports editor from the *Minneapolis Star and Tribune,* was one of the leaders of the committee, which reflected how important a close connection to the press was to the effort to attract MLB. The mutually beneficial relationship between the media and professional sports came up again a generation later when the *Star and Tribune* owner played a key role in the construction and location of the Metrodome, which opened in 1982 adjacent to its downtown headquarters.

The committee contacted the Cleveland Indians, the Philadelphia Athletics, the St. Louis Browns, and the New York Giants, whose owner, Horace Stoneham, also owned the Minneapolis Millers and had watched the progress of stadium planning from the inside. Stoneham had expressed an interest in moving west, and even purchased land in a Minneapolis suburb in anticipation of a new stadium. When Stoneham announced his decision to move to San Francisco for the 1958 season, the committee expressed surprise and disbelief at Stoneham's decision, not yet understanding that owners were playing cities off against each other to get the best deal.

The efforts to get a team soon took a new route. Chamber of Commerce member Wheelock Whitney joined Branch Rickey's campaign to create the Continental League, a rival major league. Whitney's alliance with Rickey coincided with the chamber's efforts to woo the existing leagues, creating additional pressure on the owners to address expansion. Whether Rickey ever intended to form a new league or simply hoped to force MLB to expand the number of franchises is less important than the recognition of aggressive local endeavors to get a team.

City boosters first considered the possibility of the Senators moving to the Twin Cities back in the early 1950s, and President Jerry Moore of the Chamber of Commerce, a leader in the sports-recruitment committee, made a number of trips to Washington to court the Griffith family. In 1958 Griffith brought his team to Met Stadium for an exhibition game with the Philadelphia Phillies, and received a generous $10,000 fee. Griffith remained in the area for a few days and was heavily wooed by local leaders seeking his franchise.

The Minneapolis promoters made the relocation as appealing as possible. They guaranteed Griffith more than 750,000 attendees per year for the first three years, moving expenses of approximately $250,000, payment of $225,000 to the Red Sox and the Dodgers for the territorial rights of their local farm clubs in the American Association, and financial backing from area banks. Griffith was also promised broadcast contracts in the range of $600,000, far beyond what he was getting in Washington. The new and recently expanded $8.5 million Met Stadium was an important enticement, especially with over 14,000 parking spaces and access to the developing freeway system. In addition, Griffith was able to negotiate a lucrative concessions deal that gave him 90 percent of concessions revenue for every event at the Met. Having been the sole recipient of concessions revenue in Washington, he understood the value of this income stream.

Although Griffith was concerned about the competition from Minnesotans' summer fascination with boating, fishing, and cabin life, he was persuaded of the value of a potential fan base that covered six states and a couple of Canadian provinces—with little or no professional sports competition.

The possibility of drawing fans from a wide area was a great advantage, as were the broadcast revenues from a large geographical territory.

Calvin Griffith's decision to move the club became public on the morning of October 26, 1960, at the annual league meeting when the owners were discussing expansion. Griffith requested permission for the Senators to be moved to Minneapolis–St. Paul. The meeting was going to place an expansion team in Los Angeles, and he recommended the other new team could replace his club in Washington, satisfying the concerns of local fans and alleviating the owners' political concerns with Congress. After Calvin's request was rejected by a two-vote margin, he complained to his fellow magnates that he was now "finished" in baseball because his desire to leave would become public and he would be forced out of the game by discontented Senators fans. Following some informal discussions, his proposal was reconsidered after the lunch break, and was approved 5–3. Once Baltimore owner Joseph Iglehart realized the impact of the action, he asked to change his vote, but AL president Cronin rejected the request, saying that the Senators were in Minnesota now.

A HONEYMOON: THE TWINS IN MINNESOTA IN THE 1960S

In many ways, the 1960s were the most successful decade in the history of the Senators-Twins franchise, and certainly the best for Calvin Griffith. The team had a fresh start in a new location, with significant community and financial backing, fan support, and goodwill toward the team and its owners. The team went on to have winning seasons, division championships, and a pennant. When this generally positive environment changed in the early 1970s, Griffith looked back to the 1960s as a honeymoon. Unfortunately for Griffith, his new Twins did not function in an unchanging vacuum. While the decade brought a favorable transition in the team's fortunes and outlook, it also brought changes in how the sport was run detrimental to the Griffith's family-led operation. The club continued to operate under an old model while new and successful ways of running teams emerged and developed.

Griffith began his new venture on a relatively strong financial footing, and the prospect of strong attendance figures seemed to ensure the team's initial financial success in Minnesota. Promises of 750,000 fans a year seemed amazing to a team that had played to relatively small crowds during many losing seasons, including six consecutive years with the lowest attendance in the AL and a Griffith Stadium record-low crowd of 460 fans on September 7, 1954. Attendance in the 1960s far exceeded the guarantee, with the Twins drawing over a million fans every year, sometimes leading the AL in season attendance. It was an astonishing change of fortune for the Griffith family.

Met Stadium's capacious seating facilitated drawing large crowds. Griffith Stadium's capacity in the 1950s was below 30,000, and although Met Stadium opened in 1956 with 18,200 seats, local boosters immediately began a second funding project to bring the stadium capacity to major league standards, at about 45,000 seats. Later additions were made to satisfy the requirements of the expansion Minnesota Vikings of the NFL, whose capacity wishes were similar, but with different requirements for seating configuration.

When the 1961 season began, the old Washington team had a new identity. They were now the Minnesota Twins. The choice of name was significant, relating to location, forging a regional identity, and establishing a new naming pattern followed elsewhere. Named for both of the home cities, the Twins sported a *TC* on their caps and developed an emblem showing two ballplayers—each representing one of the two local cities—shaking hands over the Mississippi River. The team name represented a reconciliation of the separate interests that had divided Minneapolis and St. Paul in their attempts to land a franchise.

In this spirit of reconciliation, the team's location could hardly be the name of a single city. Instead, the Twins' home was Minnesota, just like the new Vikings, and both teams represented the state instead of the metropolitan area. The large territory that had so appealed to Griffith was reflected in his geographic moniker. All of the area's future franchises—the NHL North Stars and Wild, and the NBA Timberwolves—would adopt the state, rather than a city, as their identity. The practice has become widely copied in MLB with the Colorado Rockies, Texas Rangers, Arizona Diamondbacks, and Florida Marlins, helping clubs entice a broad base of fans to associate themselves with the teams and forge a regional, rather than urban, identity.

The Twins finished seventh in 1961 (70–90), but drew over a million fans, a big improvement from the attendance in Washington. Manager Cookie Lavagetto, who sported a losing .414 winning percentage in four and a half seasons at the helm, was replaced in midyear by Sam Mele, who turned the team around. The 1962 and 1963 teams produced nearly identical winning records of 91–71 and 91–70, the squad's best mark in nearly two decades. Harmon Killebrew hit a total of 93 homers during those two years. In 1963 the Twins led the AL in batting and homers (225) and had strong pitching, led by 20-game winner Camilo Pascual. Behind the plate, Earl Battey, a four-time All-Star, was a stalwart. The fans were delighted by the novelty of the team and its early success.

The club struggled in 1964 and finished sixth. The main bright spot was young outfielder Tony Oliva, Rookie of the Year, who led the AL in batting (.323), runs (109), hits (217), doubles (43), and total bases (374). The following season was a complete turnaround. The Twins hosted the All-Star Game at Met Stadium, bringing national attention to the Twin Cities, their stadium, and their team, which had placed seven men on the AL squad. The Twins won the pennant (102–60) by seven games with the best offense in the AL and sound pitching, though they did have the worst defense in the league. Shortstop Zoilo Versalles led the AL in runs (126), doubles (45), and total bases (308) and was elected MVP. The sensational Oliva repeated as AL batting champ (.321). Pitchers Mudcat Grant (21–7) and Jim Kaat (18–11) had successful seasons.

Fan support was outstanding, reaching 1.46 million, the most in the AL. The Twins played the Dodgers in their first World Series since 1933. They took the first two games at Metropolitan Stadium, but faltered and lost in seven games. They could not match up with Sandy Koufax, who shut them out in games five and seven, giving up just seven hits.

The team's new life in Minnesota was not free of the echoes of the past. Calvin Griffith was unable to attend the pennant-clinching game in Washington because he was worried that process servers would find him in the city, serving papers on yet another lawsuit filed by the team's minority shareholders, who continued to object to the Senators' departure from the capital. Griffith watched the game on television from his box at Met Stadium while the Vikings played on the field below.

The club finished second in 1966 to a strong Baltimore club. Kaat had a splendid season and was selected as *The Sporting News* Pitcher of the Year. He led the AL with 25 wins, 304.7 innings, and 19 complete games. Kaat pitched 25 seasons in the majors, 15 of them with the Senators and Twins, and won 283 games (190 for the Griffith franchise). He was the finest fielding pitcher of his era, taking 14 Golden Gloves (1962–77). In 1967, the Twins started slowly, and after going 15–15, Mele was replaced by Cal Ermer. Then the club went on a roll, winning a total of 91 games and finishing one game out of first place. Killebrew had 44 homers for his fourth championship, and young Dean Chance won 20 games. The exciting season drew a then-record attendance of nearly 1.5 million. The team slipped badly in 1968, finishing in seventh place. The next season marked the first year of divisional play. They were placed in the Western Division because of Griffith's influence with the owners, and made a huge turnaround under new manager Billy Martin, who had worked for the organization as a minor-league manager in Denver and as the Twins' third-base coach. They captured the division with a stellar mark of 97–65. The team had the most productive offense in the league and very strong pitching. Killebrew was MVP, leading the league in homers (49), RBIs (140), and walks (145). But the Twins were no match for the juggernaut Baltimore Orioles, winners of 109 games, and were swept in three games in the AL Championship Series.

After the season, fan support for the Twins was shaken when the popular Billy Martin was fired for some significant behavior issues, most notably his bar fight with pitcher Dave Boswell, and for ignoring Calvin Griffith. Martin's firing was very unpopular with some local sportswriters, who actively encouraged discontent with Griffith's leadership. Martin was replaced by the very experienced Bill Rigney. The Twins repeated as division champs (98–64) in 1970, led by Cy Young Award winner Jim Perry (24–12) and a strong pitching staff, and the league's highest batting average. Killebrew and Oliva both had over 100 RBIs. But the postseason was a repeat of the year before, as the Orioles again swept the Twins to capture the pennant.

Thereafter less successful teams were on the horizon, and the fans' goodwill was stretched. A big part of the problem was that the front office continued to employ an increasingly anachronistic approach to ownership and management. It was still a family-run operation, with Griffith's siblings, cousins, and in-laws working for the team. This sense of family was often extended to former players who worked in the minor-league system. Personal relationships complicated or compromised professional decisions. Generational differences between Calvin and his son, Clark II, were symptomatic of the many changes underway. Where Calvin had been tutored by his uncle/adopted father, Clark received an Ivy League education. Clark was interested in being innovative and wanted to employ modern marketing techniques that were foreign to his father. The conflict between traditional management and modernization became increasingly personal.

Calvin Griffith was not only unaccustomed to new management methods, but insisted on mixing front-office work with managerial decisions on the field. His ability to identify baseball talent kept him far more involved in player decisions than the new breed of businessmen now owning teams. While investors who owned professional sports franchises delegated on-field responsibilities to baseball professionals and front office tasks to trained specialists, Griffith stayed involved at all levels of the operation. This was probably wise for the baseball aspects, his strong suit. However, he insufficiently delegated business and executive authority, retaining a mom-and-pop approach that weakened the team.

Griffith's hands-on involvement made him and the team vulnerable when unpopular decisions were made, especially in baseball operations, leaving no insulating layers of management to absorb the wrath of fans and sportswriters. A series of unpopular decisions—like firing Billy Martin—eroded public confidence. Losing records in the early 1970s compounded the loss of fan support. Although increasingly unpopular in the Twin Cities, Griffith's experience made him influential in the AL, and he used that influence to establish the designated hitter, in part because he had excellent older hitters whose defensive skills had eroded. While Griffith's and the Twins' images suffered, the Minnesota Vikings became regional fan favorites because of their on-field performance, the image of their stars, and the rising popularity of professional football.

The changing situation in MLB, particularly the rising power of the players' union, which Griffith opposed, had a big impact on the Twins. Griffith's long history in the game and his tutelage at the knee of his uncle, whose history in organized baseball stretched back into the nineteenth century, meant that Griffith, perhaps more than other owners, saw the changes in baseball in the 1960s and 1970s as radical. Griffith was generally cash poor. Unable to buy high-cost players, he had relied on scouting to identify talent and on the farm system to develop it. The investment often paid off in fine young, low-cost athletes. However, Griffith could only look ahead to losing the talent he had cultivated due to the new trends in salary negotiation.

Griffith was uncomfortable with the changing nature of management-player relations. Griffith had always believed that the team was the crucial entity, and that players were fortunate to be associated with a team. Their ability to bargain for high salaries changed that relationship, making them a powerful economic force in their own right—not just mere employees—looking out for themselves as individuals rather than for the team as a group. As much as Griffith disliked the new salary negotiations and what they meant for his team, his finances, and his carefully trained farm-system players, Griffith was particularly annoyed at having to deal with agents. He was used to negotiating directly with his players, and the appearance of a third party was unpalatable to him.

THE 1970S AND BEYOND: CHALLENGE AND CHANGE

Although the Twins ended the 1960s in relatively good shape, having won two Western Division championships and maintained good attendance throughout the decade, significant problems lay ahead. Two of Calvin Griffith's family members and professional associates had died, Sherry Robertson and Joe Haynes. Fans remained angry about the firing of manager Billy Martin. Star players, some of whom had come with the team from Washington, were getting older. The world of baseball was changing rapidly, and Griffith was lagging behind.

Accordingly, the team's fortunes changed for the worse in the 1970s. The Twins were mediocre in the 1970s, finishing fifth in 1971, even with Oliva batting a league-leading .337. While their payroll had been the highest in the AL in the last half of the 1960s, they quickly dropped to one of the lowest-paid teams, with salaries often one-fourth or less than the highest-paid teams. The inability or unwillingness to pay for high-quality players hampered the Twins' success on the field. The club ended up in third or fourth under managers Frank Quilici, who took over in mid-1972, and then Gene Mauch, in 1976. Ownership suffered from increasingly negative public opinion.

In an era of change and protest, conservative Calvin Griffith represented the old way of doing things. Although he moved to advance the quality of play on the field, his actions failed to endear him to fans and sportswriters. One result was the team's losing over $500,000 in 1974, and then again in 1980. With stars like Harmon Killebrew aging, Griffith was forced to choose between cost and efficiency, between history and future concerns. He wanted Killebrew to retire after his 21st season and take a job with the organization. But Killebrew wanted to continue playing and sought a big raise. When it was not forthcoming, "Killer" Killebrew moved on to the Kansas City Royals for one more season. The future Hall of Famer ended his career there, with a lifetime 573 home runs and 11 All-Star appearances. Griffith's disagreement with Killebrew signaled a change in how things were done: an aging player negotiated for more money, while an aging owner remembered old ways of rewarding performance through a different path to retirement.

After Killebrew's departure, Tony Oliva assumed a leadership role, but injuries forced him to retire in 1976. After 15 years with the Twins, Oliva departed with a lifetime batting average of .304. The team's tradition of excellent batting was continued by second baseman Rod Carew, the 1967 Rookie of the Year, who won seven batting titles in his 12 years in Minnesota and made the All-Star team every year he wore a Twins jersey. The Hall of Famer's best season came in 1977, when the Twins came in fourth (87–77). Named *The Sporting News* Player of the Year and AL MVP, Carew led the major leagues with a .388 batting average, along with 239 hits and 128 runs.

Most problematic for Griffith's image was a newspaper account of a 1978 Lion's Club talk in Waseca, a small southern Minnesota town. Griffith spoke off the cuff in his characteristic less-than-eloquent English. A young journalist for the *Minneapolis Tribune* reported that Griffith told his audience that one of the reasons the team moved to Minnesota was because "you only had 15,000 blacks there," and as a group they did not attend a lot of baseball games, and because there were "good, hard-working white people here." His comments were outdated at best and openly racist at worst. Griffith's reputation in the community and with some of his players was irreparably damaged. Rod Carew left the team in 1979, saying, "I refuse to be a slave on this plantation and play for a bigot."

The Griffith family record on race was poor. Calvin admired talented "colored" players, saying, "They're the best ones." His father had welcomed the Homestead Grays to Griffith Stadium and built a special section at the ballpark for black Washingtonians to attend Senators games, but these were actions calculated to make money. It was not until 1964 that the Twins integrated their spring-training facilities, the last major-league team to do so, and then only after pressure from the press, the state government, civil rights groups, and behind-the-scenes lobbying by Earl Battey. Even his sister Thelma expressed controversial views: "The problem that we had run into in Washington was that our ballpark was in a very black district, and people were afraid of getting their tires cut up all the time and things like that, not that whites don't do the same thing. I don't mean that. But it was hard to control and we didn't have the parking facilities like [in Minnesota]."

In the early 1980s, the team struggled even more than before, and did not have a winning record until 1986. When the 1981 players' strike began, the Twins were in seventh place and drawing poorly. Griffith collected insurance payments greater than what he would have earned had the team played, something that reflected his dire financial situation. He had little incentive to settle the strike, especially since he was strongly opposed to players' rights and high-powered negotiations. The owners of more profitable clubs forced a settlement. The following year the team hit rock bottom, finishing in seventh place (60–102) under manager Billy Gardner. Yet Gardner kept his job through the start of the 1985 season.

Griffith also faced difficulties with Met Stadium. It was showing its age and needed nearly $1 million in renovations. Fixing an outmoded ballpark when stadium trends had moved in a different direction was an expenditure the cash-strapped team would not make. Also, the increasingly popular Vikings football franchise had grown tired of playing in a baseball stadium and of supporting Griffith's concessions income. They sought a bigger stadium to increase their own revenues.

The same downtown businesses and media interests that had helped bring the Senators to Minnesota now wanted a new stadium. Recent suburban growth was economically threatening to Minneapolis and St. Paul. Putting a stadium in the center of a city was perceived as a way to associate the team with its location. A TV shot of a stadium with the city's skyline behind it made a powerful statement to local and national viewers about the vitality of the city and its distinctive appearance and characteristics. A downtown facility would supposedly prevent or reverse urban decay, especially by bringing more people into the city, if only on evenings and weekends.

The design standards for the type of multipurpose stadium being considered were established in the mid-1960s with facilities like the Houston Astrodome. There were numerous attractions to enclosed stadiums. The huge investment was more easily justified if the edifice hosted many events, including sporting contests, concerts, religious rallies, and festivals. Weather was no impediment to indoor games, no small matter in the cold Minnesota climate. It was also important for teams with a geographically broad regional market. Fans were more likely to drive long distances if they knew the game would be played regardless of the weather. Guaranteed games were important for broadcasters and their revenues, and in many ways bright colors and controlled lighting made the Metrodome an ideal television studio for broadcast sports.

Local architects had toyed with domed stadium designs since the late 1960s, and in the mid-1970s serious discussions about such structures began between teams and civic leaders. Knowing it was not his best option but unable to craft an alternative plan, Griffith delayed his participation in stadium discussions, finally signing a lease in August 1980 with the Metropolitan Sports Facilities Commission. The Hubert H. Humphrey Metrodome, which cost $68 million, was designed by Skidmore, Owings, and Merrill and opened on April 3, 1982, with a capacity of 55,883. The only air-supported dome in the major leagues, it was covered by over 10 acres of Teflon-coated fiberglass.

Like other concrete doughnuts, the Metrodome was neither fussy nor ornamental in its appearance. There was no virtue in postmodern references to historic ballparks or nostalgic aspects of the urban environment. What now seems harsh represented the glorification of materials typical of the end of architecture's modernist era. Minneapolis's desire for a cost-conscious stadium encouraged this characteristic. The Metrodome was mainly a football stadium, whose design and economics favored the Vikings, whereas the Met had been built for baseball, and its revenues, especially concessions, heavily favored the Twins. The Metrodome was deliberately plain, and, as a point of pride, it was built on time and under budget. Until the Twins generated some memorable moments in the building, there was little to recommend it. The structure remains dull, uninviting, and uninteresting.

The Vikings were locked into the new edifice for 30 years, but Griffith had escape clauses. The Twins could leave if attendance fell below 1 million for three years (as it did in 1982 and 1983), or if the team had three successive years of financial losses. Griffith had been considering offers to sell the team to syndicates based in Seattle and Tampa since the mid-1970s. In fact the Tampa suitors eventually purchased Gabe Murphy's minority shares at the time of the 1984 sale to Carl Pohlad. The geographic proximity of Tampa and St. Petersburg suggested that the team might keep its nickname if it moved there.

In an effort to keep the team in the Twin Cities, one local businessman devised a massive ticket buyout in 1984 that would, in theory, generate the minimum attendance numbers required. This neither put more people into the stadium nor addressed the other part of Griffith's escape clause. In any case, the ticket scheme was unnecessary because banker and dealmaker Carl Pohlad bought the team. In 2005 Pohlad was the richest person in Minnesota and among the 100 wealthiest in the country. Nevertheless, he was considered an outsider in the Twin Cities business community, and was not especially involved in civic organizations or cultural philanthropy. He bought the Twins as an investment. Although the Twins did not have a particularly strong financial history, an entrepreneur looking at the possibilities in the higher echelon of baseball teams might consider a major-league franchise a reasonable option. Pohlad also intended to use the team as a vehicle to help him quickly become an insider in the region's power base. His motivation was very different from the Griffith family's, whose commitment was to the game of baseball and their family's place in it.

THE WORLD SERIES AND BEYOND

After a 63-year interim the franchise won the World Series a second time in 1987, and repeated four years later. Several key players had been acquired a number of years earlier by Griffith, especially as he retooled his team after its 1982 move into the Metrodome. Unable to buy expensive players in the open market, Griffith relied on his and his scouts' ability to identify talent and bring players up through the team's minor-league system. To the extent that the 1987 team represented a maturing of the young players of the early 1980s, like Kirby Puckett, it proved the strategy could work, and did not require a big payroll to win. In fact, the payroll in the years leading up to 1987 was at or near the bottom of all 26 major-league teams.

Their young manager Tom Kelly, who had taken over in the last month of 1986, going 11–12, led the Twins. The next year the team improved from 20 games under .500 to 85–77, good enough to top the AL West (although it would have placed them fifth in the AL East). The squad was, statistically speaking, one of the weaker hitting and pitching teams in the AL, but it was first in fielding. Only outfielder Kirby Puckett, who batted .332 and led the AL with 207 hits, was a 1986 All-Star. The squad took the ALCS four games to one over the Tigers, and then took the World Series in seven games over the Cardinals. The Twins won all four games at home, and pitcher Frank Viola was Series MVP. Many observers attributed the success of the team to its noisy crowd and the idiosyncratic building. The Twins knew how to play in the Metrodome, with its peculiar bounces, difficult roof, tremendously loud noises, and otherwise nontraditional and inhospitable surroundings.

The Twins improved to 91–71 in 1988, but came in second. They fell off to fifth and seventh the next two years, but then in 1991 jumped to first with 95 wins, the most in the AL. Kelly was Manager of the Year and second baseman Chuck Knoblauch was Rookie of the Year. The club had the highest batting average in the AL and very strong pitching, led by Scott Erickson (20–8) and Jack Morris (18–12). The squad took the pennant by beating Toronto 4–1 in the ALCS and then captured the World Series over the Braves in seven. Morris was Series MVP, shutting out Atlanta for 10 innings in the decisive game seven, winning 1–0. As in 1987, the home-field advantage was crucial, with the Twins again sweeping all their home games. In the era before interleague play, NL teams had no experience in the stadium and played at a disadvantage in the World Series. Then again, the Twins were perennially disadvantaged in this facility, especially in terms of revenue, so to turn the stadium to their advantage was neither unfair nor unreasonable. The Twins followed up with a second-place finish in 1992, led by Puckett, who hit .329 and led the AL in hits (210) and total bases (313). The popular Puckett had to retire after the 1995 season since glaucoma had blurred his vision. A .318 hitter in 12 seasons, Puckett was elected to the Hall of Fame in 2001.

Attendance at the new park started out poorly in 1982 (921,186, lowest in the AL), and it dropped the next season. Soon, however, attendance rebounded, reaching 1.6 million in 1984, 2.1 million in 1987, and then an all-time franchise high of just over 3 million in 1988, becoming the first AL team to reach that milestone. But thereafter the Twins only once finished in the top half of AL attendances, and since 1993 attendance has remained below 2 million. Much of this was brought on by poor performance on the field, as the Twins posted losing records from 1993 through 2000. Then, in 2001, the team made a breakthrough and moved up to second place. Kelly retired and was replaced by Ron Gardenhire.

Hampered by a football-friendly and outmoded stadium and a low-payroll and low-revenue team, and inspired by the stadium success of the Selig family in Milwaukee, Pohlad began to push for a new state-funded ballpark in 1996, getting Minneapolis and St. Paul to compete for the new ballpark. As his ultimate bargaining chip, Pohlad announced in 1997 that if a stadium were not built, he would sell the team to investors in North Carolina. Commissioner Bud Selig actively supported Pohlad, whose threatened sale turned out to be a bluff, concocted to push the community to build him a ballpark. The public distrust created by Pohlad's dissimulation has plagued every successive attempt to build a new ballpark, regardless of the funding details.

In November 2001, Selig stunningly announced that MLB planned to contract the leagues from 30 to 28 teams. The small-market, low-budget

Minnesota Twins and Montreal Expos were considered the most vulnerable targets in this plan. There are suspicions that the scheme was arranged with the cooperation of Pohlad, who had long complained that team ownership was a losing proposition. The Twins' 2000 season attendance was barely over 1 million, surpassing the major-league bottom-feeder Montreal Expos by fewer than 75,000 fans. Yet the team had made a profit, mainly from the $21 million it got from revenue sharing, $5 million more than its entire payroll. Contraction was seen as a way to solve Pohlad's problems, and it was suggested that he would receive as much as $250 million for surrendering the team.

In 2001, the Twins' local media revenue for the season was just $7.3 million, 26th in MLB. Cleveland, which had the same metropolitan population as the Twins, made three times as much money from the media. They also ranked 26th in other local operating revenue, reflecting their terrible contract with the Metrodome, and next to last in total local revenue ($31.9 million), surpassing only the lowly Montreal Expos. The team had the lowest payroll in the majors at $24.9 million, but got the most bang for the buck, finishing with a .525 winning percentage. The team made $526,000 in 2001 according to MLB, eighth best among all teams. The profit came from its revenue-sharing money ($19,089,000), which wiped out losses from the baseball operations.

If Pohlad was unenthusiastic about the team, the community more than compensated for his lack of interest. Many approaches were used to keep contraction at bay, including rallies by fans and congressional hearings, but legal avenues proved most effective. The Metropolitan Sports Facilities Commission, the state-appointed public agency charged with managing the Metrodome as well as keeping major-league sports in the state, sued the Twins over a potential breaking of their Metrodome lease. A county judge issued an injunction requiring the Twins to play there, a ruling upheld by the state supreme court despite challenges from the Twins and MLB. In the end, community support for the team has been strengthened, with attendance nearing 2 million every year since 2002.

In the years following the contraction threat the team's fortunes rose both on and off the field. Management made additional investments aimed at acquiring and retaining productive players who were fan favorites. Increasingly clever marketing focused fan attention on particular players, building loyalty to the team through well-known faces and personalities. Winning divisional championships in the weak AL Central in 2002 (after nearly doubling payroll to $40 million), 2003, and 2004 helped build fan interest and loyalty while at the same time extending the season, and revenues, into the fall. But the furthest they advanced was to the ALCS in 2002, when the Twins lost in five to the Anaheim Angels. The Yankees trounced the Twins in the 2003 and 2004 AL Divisional Series. The 2004 team had a payroll of $53,585,000, 18th in MLB, and was led by the best pitching staff in the AL, most notably Johan Santana, who won the Cy Young Award, going 20–6 with a league-leading 2.61 ERA and 265 strikeouts. Yet despite their recent success on the playing field, the team was only worth $178 million in 2004, second lowest in MLB. The team's

Johan Santana pitches against the Texas Rangers, 2005. © AP / Wide World Photos

performance in 2005 was disappointing, getting eliminated from the playoffs with two weeks left in the season. The strong pitching could not make up for the weak hitting. Yet over 2 million fans turned out, the most since 1993.

Remaining competitive with a low payroll and low revenues remains a challenge, consistent with the history of the franchise. The Twins continue to seek a new ballpark as a way to increase local revenues. The Metrodome's drawbacks, recognized even before its completion, and competition from a newer generation of ballparks have made a bad situation worse. Concessions revenues, naming rights, luxury seating, and other recent innovations are unavailable in the current building, and it remains a football stadium in which baseball is played. Nearly annual pitches for a new stadium have been made in various government forums for the past decade, not only for the Twins, but also for the Vikings and the University of Minnesota football team, all of which share the Metrodome.

In a promising proposal, Carl Pohlad in 2005 volunteered to contribute $125 million toward the cost of a $478 million roof-ready stadium to be built at the edge of downtown Minneapolis and opened by 2009. The projected site is considered less than desirable by many since it would sit next to a state-of-the-art garbage incinerator. The site is adjacent to the Target Center arena, home of the NBA Timberwolves; near a popular entertainment district; and at a transportation hub. The majority of stadium funding would come from a countywide sales tax that requires no referendum. At this writing, the project remains in the hands of the state legislature, which must approve this form of government support even if state funds are not used.

NOTABLE ACHIEVEMENTS

Most Valuable Players

Year	Name	Position
1965	Zoilo Versalles	SS
1969	Harmon Killebrew	1B/3B
1977	Rod Carew	1B

Cy Young Winners

Year	Name	Position
1970	Jim Perry	RHP
1988	Frank Viola	LHP
2004	Johan Santana	LHP

Rookies of the Year

Year	Name	Position
1958	Albie Pearson	OF
1959	Bob Allison	OF
1964	Tony Oliva	OF
1967	Rod Carew	2B
1979	John Castino	3B
1991	Chuck Knoblauch	2B
1995	Marty Cordova	OF

Batting Champions

Year	Name	#
1902	Ed Delahanty	.376
1928	Goose Goslin	.379
1935	Buddy Myer	.349
1946	Mickey Vernon	.353
1953	Mickey Vernon	.337
1964	Tony Oliva	.323
1965	Tony Oliva	.321
1969	Rod Carew	.318
1971	Tony Oliva	.337
1972	Rod Carew	.318
1973	Rod Carew	.350
1974	Rod Carew	.364
1975	Rod Carew	.359
1977	Rod Carew	.388

| 1978 | Rod Carew | .333 |
| 1989 | Kirby Puckett | .339 |

Home-Run Champions

Year	Name	#
1957	Roy Sievers	42
1959	Harmon Killebrew	42
1962	Harmon Killebrew	48
1963	Harmon Killebrew	45
1964	Harmon Killebrew	49
1967	Harmon Killebrew	44
1969	Harmon Killebrew	49

ERA Champions

Year	Name	#
1912	Walter Johnson	1.39
1913	Walter Johnson	1.09
1918	Walter Johnson	1.27
1919	Walter Johnson	1.49
1924	Walter Johnson	2.72
1925	Stan Coveleski	2.84
1928	Garland Braxton	2.51
1988	Allan Anderson	2.45
2004	Johan Santana	2.61

Strikeout Champions

Year	Name	#
1910	Walter Johnson	313
1912	Walter Johnson	303
1913	Walter Johnson	243
1914	Walter Johnson	225
1915	Walter Johnson	203
1916	Walter Johnson	228
1917	Walter Johnson	188
1918	Walter Johnson	162
1919	Walter Johnson	147
1921	Walter Johnson	143
1923	Walter Johnson	130
1924	Walter Johnson	158
1942	Bobo Newsom	113
1961	Camilo Pascual	221

1962	Camilo Pascual	206
1963	Camilo Pascual	202
1985	Bert Blyleven	206
2004	Johan Santana	265
2005	Johan Santana	238

No-Hitters

Name	Date
Walter Johnson	07/01/1920
Bobby Burke	08/08/1931
Jack Kralick	08/26/1962
Dean Chance	08/25/1967
Scott Erickson	04/27/1994
Eric Milton	09/11/1999

POSTSEASON APPEARANCES

AL West Division Titles

Year	Record	Manager
1969	97–65	Billy Martin
1970	98–64	Bill Rigney
1987	85–77	Tom Kelly
1991	95–67	Tom Kelly

AL Central Division Titles

Year	Record	Manager
2002	94–67	Ron Gardenhire
2003	90–72	Ron Gardenhire
2004	93–70	Ron Gardenhire

AL Pennants

Year	Record	Manager
1924	92–62	Bucky Harris
1925	96–55	Bucky Harris
1933	99–53	Joe Cronin
1965	102–60	Sam Mele
1987	85–77	Tom Kelly
1991	95–67	Tom Kelly

World Championships

Year	Opponent	MVP
1924	New York	
1987	St. Louis	Frank Viola
1991	Atlanta	Jack Morris

MANAGERS

2002–	Ron Gardenhire
1986–2001	Tom Kelly
1985–1986	Ray Miller
1981–1985	Billy Gardner
1980–1981	John Goryl
1976–1980	Gene Mauch
1972–1975	Frank Quilici
1970–1972	Bill Rigney
1969	Billy Martin
1967–1968	Cal Ermer
1961–1967	Sam Mele
1957–1961	Cookie Lavagetto
1955–1957	Chuck Dressen
1950–1954	Bucky Harris
1948–1949	Joe Kuhel
1943–1947	Ossie Bluege
1935–1942	Bucky Harris
1933–1934	Joe Cronin
1929–1933	Walter Johnson
1924–1928	Bucky Harris
1923	Donie Bush
1922	Clyde Milan
1921	George McBride
1912–1920	Clark Griffith
1910–1911	Jimmy McAleer
1907–1909	Joe Cantillon
1905–1906	Jake Stahl
1904	Patsy Donovan
1904	Malachi Kittridge
1902–1903	Tom Loftus
1901	Jim Manning

Team Records by Individual Players

Batting Leaders

	Single Season Name		Year	Career Name		Plate Appearances
Batting average	Rod Carew	.388	1977	Rod Carew	.334	6,980
On-base %	Buddy Myer	.454	1938	Rod Carew	.393	6,980
Slugging %	Goose Goslin	.614	1928	Harmon Killebrew	.514	9,462
OPS	Goose Goslin	1.056	1928	Harmon Killebrew	.892	9,462
Games	Cesar Tovar	164	1967	Harmon Killebrew	2,329	9462
At bats	Kirby Puckett	691	1985	Sam Rice	8,934	9,879
Runs	Chuck Knoblauch	140	1996	Sam Rice	1,466	9,879
Hits	Rod Carew	239	1977	Sam Rice	2,889	9,879
Total bases	Tony Oliva	374	1964	Harmon Killebrew	4,026	9,462
Doubles	Mickey Vernon	51	1946	Sam Rice	479	9,879
Triples	Goose Goslin	20	1925	Sam Rice	183	9,879
Home runs	Harmon Killebrew	49	1964	Harmon Killebrew	559	9,462
RBIs	Harmon Killebrew	140	1969	Harmon Killebrew	1,540	9,462
Walks	Eddie Yost	151	1956	Harmon Killebrew	1,505	9,462
Strikeouts	Bobby Darwin	145	1972	Harmon Killebrew	1,629	9,462
Stolen bases	Clyde Milan	88	1912	Clyde Milan	495	8,312
Extra-base hits	Tony Oliva	84	1964	Harmon Killebrew	860	9,462
Times on base	Eddie Yost	318	1950	Sam Rice	3,623	9,879

Pitching Leaders

	Single Season Name		Year	Career Name		Innings Pitched
ERA	Walter Johnson	1.14	1913	Walter Johnson	2.17	5,914.7
Wins	Walter Johnson	36	1913	Walter Johnson	417	5,914.7
Won-loss %	Walter Johnson	.837	1913	Johan Santana	.702	856
Hits/9 IP	Walter Johnson	6.03	1913	Dave Boswell	7.15	1,036.3
Walks/9 IP	Carols Silva	043	2005	Al Orth	1.55	677.3
Strikeouts	Walter Johnson	313	1910	Walter Johnson	3509	5,914.7
Strikeouts/9 IP	Johan Santana	10.46	2004	Johan Santana	9.47	856
Games	Mike Marshall	90	1979	Walter Johnson	802	5,914.7
Saves	Eddie Guardado	45	2002	Rick Aguilera	254	694
Innings	Walter Johnson	371.7	1914	Walter Johnson	5914.7	5,914.7
Starts	Walter Johnson	42	1910	Walter Johnson	666	5,914.7
Complete games	Walter Johnson	38	1910	Walter Johnson	531	5,914.7
Shutouts	Walter Johnson	11	1913	Walter Johnson	110	5,914.7

Source: Drawn from data in "Minnesota Twins Batting Leaders (seasonal and career)." http://baseball-reference.com/ teams/MIN/leaders_bat.shtml; "Minnesota Twins Pitching Leaders (seasonal and career)." http://baseball-reference. com/teams/MIN/leaders_pitch.shtml.

BIBLIOGRAPHY

Bealle, Morris A. *The Washington Senators: An 87-Year History of the World's Oldest Baseball Club and Most Incurable Fandom.* Washington, DC: Columbia, 1947.

Benson, Michael. *Ballparks of North America: A Comprehensive Historical Reference to Grounds, Yards, and Stadiums, 1845 to Present.* Jefferson, NC: McFarland, 1989.

Deveaux, Tom. *The Washington Senators, 1901–1971.* Jefferson, NC: McFarland, 2001.

Hoffbeck, Steven R. *Swinging for the Fences: Black Baseball in Minnesota.* St. Paul: Minnesota Historical Society, 2005.

Johnson, Charles. *History of the Metropolitan Stadium and Sports Center.* Minneapolis: privately published, 1970.

Judge, Mark Gauvreau. *Damn Senators: My Grandfather and the Story of Washington's Only World Series Championship.* San Francisco: Encounter Books, 2003.

Kerr, Jon. *Calvin: Baseball's Last Dinosaur; An Authorized Biography.* Dubuque, IA: Wm. C. Brown Publishers, 1990.

Mona, Dave, ed. *The Hubert H. Humphrey Metrodome Souvenir Book: A Pictorial History of the Twins, Vikings, Gophers, Millers, Saints—and Metrodome!* Minneapolis: MSP Publications, 1982.

Mona, Dave, and Dave Jarzyna. *Twenty-Five Seasons: The First Quarter Century of the Minnesota Twins.* Minneapolis: Mona Publications, 1986.

Povich, Shirley. *The Washington Senators.* New York: G. P. Putnam's Sons, 1954.

Snyder, Brad. *Beyond the Shadow of the Senators: The Untold Story of the Homestead Grays and the Integration of Baseball.* Chicago: Contemporary Books, 2003.

Thielman, Jim. *Cool of the Evening: The 1965 Minnesota Twins.* Minneapolis: Kirk House, 2005.

Thomas, Henry W. *Walter Johnson: Baseball's Big Train.* Lincoln: University of Nebraska Press, 1998.

Weiner, Jay. *Stadium Games: Fifty Years of Big League Greed and Bush League Boondoggles.* Minneapolis: University of Minnesota Press, 2000.

Witt, Leonard, ed. *Magic! The 1987 Twins' Enchanted Season.* Minneapolis: Star Tribune, 1987.

New York Yankees

Steven A. Riess

The Yankees are the most important and successful sports franchise in the history of North American sport. In 103 years the Yankees have won 26 world championships and 39 pennants, playing in the most storied of all ballparks. The team's record over this period was 9,074–6,876, a percentage of .569. While never the most beloved team, even their enemies have respected the Yankees for their outstanding accomplishments.

THE HIGHLANDERS

The Yankees were created in 1903, the last new major-league franchise until expansion in 1961. The franchise struggled for two decades. The team was the successor to the Baltimore Orioles, an original American League team, which had finished in fifth place in 1901. In the middle of the 1902 campaign, manager John J. McGraw left the team, following frequent fines and suspensions for attacking umpires. McGraw sold his stock to Giants owner Andrew Freedman, who signed him on July 8 to manage the Giants. Freedman arranged for the transfer of four star Orioles to the Giants and two to Cincinnati. One week later AL president Ban Johnson declared the franchise vacant, and the league took over the club, which finished in last place (50–88). Johnson planned to move the franchise to New York to certify his league's status and convince the NL to recognize the AL. Johnson stocked the team with experienced players, including ex-Baltimore star Wee Willie Keeler, who "hit 'em where they ain't" and had never hit under .333; Dave Fultz of the Athletics, who led the league in runs scored; and six men from the National League champion Pittsburgh

Pirates, including pitchers Jack Chesbro and Jess Tannehill, who had won 48 games between them. Johnson also convinced Charles Comiskey of the Chicago White Sox to let star pitcher Clark Griffith serve as the team's manager.

The politically connected Freedman used his clout to block the AL. Consequently, Johnson had to find politically connected men to break into New York. In March, the AL sold the franchise for $18,000 to a Tammany syndicate ostensibly headed by Joseph Gordon, a former deputy superintendent of buildings, but actually led by Frank Farrell and William Devery. Farrell operated the city's preeminent gambling casino and the Empire Race Track, and was a key figure in Tim Sullivan's Gambling Trust. Devery was the notorious ex-chief of police. They secured a 10-year lease for a site at 165th and Broadway for $100,000, and then spent $200,000 excavating the rocky site and $75,000 to build the spacious 16,000-seat, single-deck Hilltop Park. The team was called the Highlanders, supposedly after the British regiment the Gordon Highlanders, or the park site, which was the highest point in Manhattan. The team started the season with a 24-day road trip, the longest in team history, because the facility was still under construction. They finished at 72–62, in third place, led by Chesbro, who won 21 games. Attendance was just 211,808.

Hopes were high in 1904. The Highlanders added pitchers Jack Powell (a 15-game winner for the Browns with 33 complete games), Al Orth from the Senators, and rookie Walter Clarkson of Harvard (who signed for $4,000) along with Patsy Dougherty, an outstanding Boston outfielder who had a career batting average of .336. A tight pennant race came down to the last five games of the season with rival Boston. Chesbro won the first game in New York on a Friday, 3–2, but lost the first game of a doubleheader the next day in Boston. Cy Young took the nightcap 1–0 in a darkness-shortened game. On Monday, Chesbro started the morning game of a doubleheader, and went into the ninth inning with the score 1–1, but threw a wild pitch with a runner on third, which brought in the winning run. The Highlanders took the anticlimactic afternoon game, finishing 92–59, for second place. Chesbro went 41–12, the most wins in modern baseball history; finished 48 of 51 games; and threw 454 2/3 innings. The exciting season resulted in the doubling of attendance to 438,919.

The Highlanders were confident they would take the pennant in 1905, but struggled with the worst pitching staff in the league. The team finished 71–78, in sixth place, 21 1/2 games back of the Athletics, but reportedly made a profit of $30,000 to $40,000. Twenty-two-year-old rookie first basemen Hal Chase was a major addition. He quickly became a fan favorite, playing with exceptional skill and élan. In 1911 "Prince Hal" became the first major leaguer to star in a movie, *Hal Chase's Home Run*. He was an accomplished batter who hit over .300 four times, once led the AL in batting average, and was an outstanding first baseman. However, some critics claim he was mostly flash, setting the AL record for errors at first base with 285 in 10 seasons.

The team made a marked turnabout in 1906, going 90–61. Orth won 27 games, Chesbro bounced back with 24, and Chase hit .323, third best in the league. They were in a tight pennant race nearly the entire year and led the league in late September, following a 14-game winning streak. They still led with two weeks left in the season, but ended in second, three games back of the White Sox. The team was well known for its rowdy play. There was a lot of gambling on games in and around the ballpark, possibly by players, some of whom frequented the city's gambling emporiums. The first Sunday game at the park was played on April 25, an exhibition game against the Athletics attended by 15,000, which raised over $10,000 for the survivors of the San Francisco earthquake.

The Highlanders followed up with another poor season in 1907, finishing fifth (70–78), but made a $50,000 profit. When Farrell became team president in 1908 the season started out surprisingly well and the club was in first place in June, but the roof fell in, and within three weeks the Highlanders were down to seventh. They had the worst defense in the league. On June 28 catcher Branch Rickey permitted a record 13 stolen bases. Farrell interfered with the team all season and got Griffith to quit as manager. He was replaced by the unlikely choice of injured shortstop Kid Elberfeld, whom Farrell had virtually accused the year before of throwing games. Farrell made him manager so he could get some work out of him. The players hated Elberfeld because he was arrogant and hot-tempered and frequently humiliated them. His managerial record of 27–71 is the worst in Yankees history, as he guided them to a last-place finish. Angered by not being named manager, Chase led an open revolt and left the team on September 3 for Stockton of the outlaw California State League.

Former major-league player and manager George Stallings replaced Elberfeld late in the season. Stallings was Farrell's partner in the Newark (Eastern League) team, and he gave Stallings a free hand to run the team. It improved in 1909 to fifth place (74–77). Attendance reached a record and profitable 501,000. The improved play was partly attributed to sign stealing, discovered in late September. A spotter behind the outfield fence used binoculars to steal the catcher's signs, which he then signaled to batters by manipulating the crossbar on the H in a hat sign on the outfield wall. Thereafter the AL banned all tipping of signs. The team uniform was redesigned, using an interlocking NY copied from police medals.

The 1910 Highlanders were very strong, improved by the addition of outfielder Birdie Cree and rookie pitcher Russell Ford, whose emery ball enabled him to go 26–6 in 300 innings with eight shutouts and a 1.65 ERA. The team finished 88–63, 14 1/2 games behind the Athletics. Despite their fine play, the team was badly divided between veterans, who had had enough of Stallings's criticisms, and newer players, who supported him. Stallings blamed team captain Chase, responsible for calling hit-and-runs and steals, for many of the team's problems. Stallings felt that his $5,500 first baseman was fixing games to make Stallings look bad because he wanted his job. In late September Stallings told Farrell that either he or Chase had to go. When Farrell demurred, Stallings quit. Chase managed the last 14 games and then signed an $8,000 contract to manage in

1911. The Yankees and Giants, who both finished second, played a postseason series, with the winning players getting 60 percent of 90 percent of the gate in the first four games. The Giants won the series, attended by over 103,000, four games to two, led by Christy Mathewson, who won three games. The winners each got $1,100, the losers $706.

After the Polo Grounds burned down in April 1911 Farrell rented Hilltop Park to them for two months until the new field was constructed. The Highlanders hit well and stole 270 bases, but had very modest pitching and were seventh in errors, and ended in sixth place. Cree came into his own, hitting .356 with a slugging percentage of .510 and 48 stolen bases.

In 1912, the team began planning to relocate, since its lease was expiring and the site was going to be used for apartment buildings. Blueprints were drawn up for a $250,000, 40,000-seat double-decked ballpark at 225th Street, but financial troubles kept the project grounded. Money problems caused the team to sell rather than buy players, resulting in a weak team. Harry Wolverton replaced Chase as manager. Wolverton had managed Oakland in the Pacific Coast League (PCL) and had a reputation as a disciplinarian. The team had a terrible defense, and no offense after Cree broke his wrist in early July, winding up in last place (50–102), the worst season in team history. Attendance was down to 242,194. The team briefly wore pinstripes for the first time, which became permanent in 1915. At one home game Ty Cobb attacked a handicapped fan in the stands for heckling him.

In 1913 the team, rented the Polo Grounds for $60,000 per year. They became known as the Yankees, likely a patriotic designation, or because they were in the American League. Writers Mark Roth and Sam Crane first used the nickname in 1904 because it fit better into headlines. The top-hat logo was introduced in 1914, probably a reference to Uncle Sam. The new manager was Frank Chance, the tough and highly respected "Peerless Leader," who had led the Cubs to three world championships. He brought a managerial record of .667 and was paid $25,000 a year plus five percent of profits. Chance altered the roster dramatically and even experimented with Chase at second base for five games, but the club started out 9–28, including 17 straight losses. Chance blamed Chase and other openly disrespectful veterans for the poor start. Chance felt Chase was not playing his hardest, and angrily told sportswriters, "He's throwing games on me!" Chase frequently got to first base just late enough to miss accurate throws, creating errors. Two days later Chase was traded to the White Sox for two lesser players. The team ended 57–94, one game out of last place.

The Yankees improved in 1914 to 70–84 and sixth place. The team lacked chemistry, was inept on the field, and rebelled when Chance tried to discipline them. The owners did not back him up, and Devery even got into a fight with Chance when he overheard Chance complaining to sportswriters. Soon afterward Chase resigned and 23-year-old shortstop Roger Peckinpaugh became interim manager.

THE TWO COLONELS AND THE AGE OF RUTH

By 1915, the ownership was in total disarray due to the team's bad performance, poor outside investments and tensions between Devery and Farrell. The team was sold to two wealthy fans who had tried unsuccessfully to buy the Giants: C. Tillinghast Huston, a civil engineer and officer in the Spanish-American War, and beer manufacturer and Tammanyite Jacob Ruppert, a prominent figure in New York society, a member of Tammany's influential Finance Committee, and a four-term congressman. They bought the Yankees for $450,000. Despite the windfall, Farrell and Devery both died nearly penniless.

The new owners introduced a new management style of staying out of the way of their manager and general manager while investing heavily in the team to build a winner. Winning was more important to Huston and Ruppert than profits, and during the 1920s they reinvested all their substantial dividends back into the team. AL president Johnson helped the new owners hire Wild Bill Donovan, manager of Providence and International League champion, to run the team. Johnson also assisted them in obtaining new players like first baseman Wally Pipp and pitchers Ray Caldwell and Ray Fisher. The owners started taking advantage of financially struggling teams like the Athletics to acquire talented players like Bob Shawkey, who would pitch 13 years and win 168 games for the Yankees. Despite the improved roster the club finished in fifth place (69–83). Attendance was just 250,000 and the owners lost $30,000.

In 1916 Ruppert and Huston purchased the renowned "Home Run" Baker from the A's for $25,000 and paid him $24,000 over three years. Baker had led the AL in home runs from 1911 through 1914 but sat out the 1915 season in a salary dispute. Baker's presence helped the team improve to 80–74, which helped double attendance. After the United States entered World War I Huston enlisted and rose to the rank of colonel. The Yankees staged a rare Sunday game on June 17 against the Browns that drew about 30,000 spectators, and donated $10,000 from ticket sales to a reserve regiment bound for overseas duty. The team struggled that season, ending in sixth place, and Donovan was fired. Huston wanted to hire his buddy, manager Wilbert Robinson of the Superbas, but Ruppert chose Miller Huggins, the diminutive Cardinals manager who had been recommended by Ban Johnson and J. G. Taylor Spinks, publisher of the *Sporting News*. During the 1918 season, while most teams were cautious about adding players to replace men in the service or doing war-related work, the cash-rich Yankees supplemented their roster with infielder Del Pratt and outfielder Ping Bodie, their first Italian American player. The squad went 60–63 in the abbreviated campaign.

Following the war the Yankees acquired several excellent players, mainly surplus from the world champion Red Sox. They acquired quality pitchers Ernie Shore and Dutch Leonard and an excellent veteran outfielder, Duffy Lewis, in return for talented but troubled pitcher Ray Caldwell, three lesser players, and $15,000. Later that summer the Yankees got the Sox's excellent submariner

Carl Mays for pitchers Allen Russell and Bob McGraw and $40,000. Mays had not gotten along with his teammates and had become so disgusted at their poor fielding that he left the Sox during the season. Sox owner Harry Frazee traded him rather than suspending him. AL president Johnson voided the trade and suspended Mays, but the Yankees secured a court injunction that let Mays pitch. The Yankees were in the pennant race all season, ending up in third place.

After the season the Yankees went after Babe Ruth. Ruth had just hit a record 29 home runs, but his team had fallen to sixth place. The Sox had soured on Ruth, who had threatened to hold out and no longer wanted to pitch. He repeatedly broke curfew, sought to remove manager Ed Barrow, and skipped the last day of the season to play an exhibition. Furthermore, Ruth was often drunk in public, had had multiple car crashes, and was in an unhappy marriage. After the season he again whined about his salary, encouraging teammates to make similar demands. Frazee sold Ruth on December 26 to the Yankees for $25,000 in cash and three notes of $25,000 at six percent (which made the deal worth $110,000), plus a reported $350,000 loan to pay off the mortgage on Fenway Park. Some historians believe Ruppert made the deal to bolster his baseball business to counter the coming impact of Prohibition on his brewery.

The Yankees welcomed Ruth with open arms and a $20,000 bonus, anticipating he would propel them to the pennant and to larger gates because fans came out to see him swing and hit home runs. He appealed to the thousands of new fans coming out to the Polo Grounds, especially since Sunday baseball had just been legalized in New York, helping the Yankees swell their attendance in 1919 to 619,000. During the 1920s no ballplayer was as beloved for his prowess as a hitter, his lust for life, and his love of children. The press protected him, hushing up car accidents, drunken binges, and paternity suits, while playing up visits to orphanages and hospitals.

Ruth started in center field, avoiding the Polo Grounds' difficult right field with its short porch and the sun field in left. He batted fourth, but he took so many walks that they moved him to the third spot. He hit a record 54 home runs and led the AL with 137 RBIs and 158 runs scored. The Yankees ended up 95–59, but it was only good enough for third place, three games behind the champion Indians. Home attendance doubled to a major-league record of 1,289,422 (with a gate worth $860,000) and the team's best turnout until 1946. The crowds also turned out whenever Ruth and the Yankees were on the road. The club set a major-league record for profits in 1920, earning $373,862, over $75,000 more than the Giants, who were second. However, a terrible tragedy occurred on August 16 when pitcher Carl Mays threw high and tight to shortstop Ray Chapman to push him off the plate. Mays beaned Chapman, who died from his head injuries the next day.

Business manager Harry Sparrow died after the season and was replaced by Red Sox vice president Ed Barrow, who became the team's first general manager. Barrow was given carte blanche to continue building the team. He made several big deals with his old team, including a blockbuster eight-man trade that brought catcher Wally Shang and pitcher Waite Hoyt, a future Hall of Famer. The Yankees were now set to begin a brilliant era in sports history. Over the next 45 years, they won 29 pennants and 20 world championships, and led the league in attendance 80 percent of the time.

In 1921 Ruth was the second-fastest man on the team at a powerful 220 pounds, and tied for the team lead with 16 triples and 17 stolen bases. He had a sensational season with a record 59 homers (more than five teams) and led the league in slugging percentage (.846), on-base percentage (.512), runs (177), RBIs (171), and walks (145), while batting .378. Cleanup man Bob Meusel was second in the AL with 24 home runs. The pitching was the best in the AL, led by Mays with 27 victories. The Yankees were in a tight pennant race with the defending world champion Indians but took three of four in late September to edge Cleveland and win their first pennant (98–55).

The Yankees were favored over the Giants in an all–Polo Grounds World Series. The Yankees took the first two games by 3–0 scores with Mays and Hoyt pitching. In the second game Ruth stole second and third in one inning, but cut his elbow while sliding. The cut became infected. The Yankees seemed on their way to winning game three with a four-run lead in the fourth, but the Giants tied it up in their half inning and broke the game open with eight runs in the seventh to win easily, 13–5. Ruth reinjured his elbow and left the game in the eighth inning. He got two hits, including a home run in the next game, but Douglas bested Mays 4–2. Hoyt took game 5', but by then Ruth had a tube inserted into his elbow to drain his infected wound. He struck out three times and bunted for a single. Ruth sat out the rest of the series as the Giants took the next three games and the world championship.

After the season Ruth contracted to barnstorm the country with the Babe Ruth All-Stars, drawn by the potential to earn $25,000. Postseason tours by pennant-winning players had been barred since 1911, and Commissioner Kenesaw Mountain Landis directed Ruth and his teammates to cancel the tour. Ruth and two teammates ignored the commissioner and went barnstorming. Landis fined them $3,362 each, the equivalent of their World Series share, and suspended them for six weeks.

Barrow fine-tuned the roster to make it younger with more deals with the Sox. He traded team captain Peckinpaugh, veteran hurler John Quinn, and two others for shortstop Everett Scott and pitchers "Sad Sam" Jones and "Bullet Joe" Bush, who had just combined for 39 victories. Then in midseason they secured third baseman Joe Dugan to replace the aging Frank Baker. Afterward, MLB created a trading deadline. Then, one year later, the two teams concluded their last deal, which sent pitchers Herb Pennock and George Pipgras to the Yankees.

In 1922 the club was in turmoil. Huggins struggled to keep his players, especially Ruth, in line, and hired a private detective to keep an eye on them. Ruth was out of shape when he rejoined the club after his suspension. Then he got into a fight with teammate Wally Pipp, was fined for going after a fan in the stands, and was suspended for five days for confronting umpire Bill Dineen. Nonetheless, the Yankees won 94 games and took the pennant by one game over the Browns. Ruth's production was down to 35 home runs and a .315 batting average, and he was beaten out for the home-run crown by the Browns' Ken Williams, who hit 39.

The Yankees played the Giants in the World Series in the new best-of-seven format. The Yankees led in every game but lost them all except one tied game, called because of darkness even though the sun was shining bright. Ruth was curved to death, with only two hits in 17 at bats.

In 1923 the Yankees left the Polo Grounds for Yankee Stadium. Charles Stoneham had wanted them out for several years because he wanted to keep all the lucrative Sunday dates for himself and was jealous of his tenant's financial success. Stoneham figured six or seven more Sunday games were worth about $100,000, which more than offset the lost rent. Ruppert, for his part, wanted his own park to promote his own team's identity, especially after the Giants refused him a long-term lease in 1920.

Yankee Stadium was built on the old Astor estate in the West Bronx, purchased for $675,000 in 1921. The area was about to undergo an enormous boom because of the completion of the Jerome Avenue elevated subway line. Construction of the park began a year later once labor and material costs dropped. The triple-deck stadium cost nearly $2.5 million and had a seating capacity of over 60,000. The field had unusual dimensions: the foul lines were just 281 feet and 295 feet while the cavernous center-field fence was 501 feet. Reflecting its enormous size and advanced technology, it was the first baseball field referred to as a *stadium* instead of the traditional rural descriptors of *park*, *field*, or *grounds*. During the 1920s the Yankees made over $3.5 million, far more than any other team, peaking at an AL record $531,586 in 1927. They outdrew Stoneham's team in all but 2 of the next 44 seasons.

In 1923 Ruppert bought out Huston for $1.25 million. The Yankees dominated the AL, virtually leading from wire to wire, winning by 20 games. Ruth had a great year, tying for the home-run title (41), reaching base a record 379 times, and setting career marks in doubles (45) and batting average (.393). The Yankees again faced the Giants in the World Series. In game one Casey Stengel of the Giants broke up a 4–4 tie in the ninth with an inside-the-park homer. In the next game Pennock pitched a fine game and Ruth hit two home runs, leading to a 4–2 Yankees victory. Then in game three another Stengel homer was the only run of the game. But the Yankees bounced back to win the next three games and capture their first Series.

The outlook for 1924 was outstanding. Most regulars were back and the Yankees added speedy outfielder Earle Combs, who was purchased from Louisville of the American Association, where he had hit .380. The Senators, with outstanding pitching, topped the Yankees in a tight pennant race by two games. Ruth won his only batting championship at .378 and hit 46 homers to lead the league.

The following season was a total disaster. Ruth reportedly ballooned to nearly 260 pounds. After spring training he got very sick on the train back to New York and collapsed with a heavy fever. Ruth had an operation, purportedly for appendicitis, a result of his huge appetite for hot dogs, soda, and beer, and remained in the hospital for seven weeks. Ruth returned 40 games into the season with the Yankees in seventh place, where they finished the year (69–85). Ruth hit just 25 homers and batted .290, the lowest of his career. His outfield colleagues performed admirably: Bob Meusel led the AL in homers and RBIs and Combs hit .342. Ruth repeatedly defied manager Huggins, often arriving late at the ballpark on road trips. When late to a game in St. Louis on August 29, Huggins suspended Ruth and fined him $5,000. The season marked the end of Everett Scott's consecutive-game streak at 1,307. On June 2, after first baseman Wally Pipp was beaned in batting practice, he was replaced by Lou Gehrig.

In response to the bad season Ruppert opening the purse strings. The Yankees bought talented minor-league shortstops Mark Koenig and Tony Lazzeri. Lazzeri had hit an incredible 60 homers for Salt Lake City in the PCL and cost

Lou Gehrig and Babe Ruth. Courtesy of the Baseball Hall of Fame

$65,000. His presence helped promote the Yankees among Italian Americans. The Yankees were not expected to contend for the pennant, but Ruth got back into shape and helped propel them to a very fast start, including 16 straight in mid-May. They cooled off later in the season, but won the pennant over the Indians by three games. Ruth had an outstanding season, batting .372 with 47 home runs, while Gehrig hit 16, fourth best in the league.

The Yankees played the St. Louis Cardinals in the World Series. The Yankees won the first game, the Cards the next two, and the Yankees the next two. The Cards tied up the series in the sixth game under veteran Grover Cleveland Alexander, who won his second game of the series. In game seven, with the score 3–2 in favor of the Cards, Alexander was surprisingly brought back in relief in the eighth inning with the bases loaded, two out, and Lazzeri up. Lazzeri hit a shot that looked like a grand slam, but it curved foul. He then struck out. In the ninth, Alexander walked Ruth with two out, bringing up Meusel, who had two extra-base hits off Alexander the day before. But Ruth tried to steal second and was thrown out by 10 feet. This was among the worst plays ever to end a World Series.

In 1927 Ruth made $70,000, and the total payroll was a record $350,000, $100,000 more than the Giants, who were second. Still, wages comprised less than 30 percent of the team's expenditures. Most experts thought the Yankees' pitching staff was getting old and predicted the up-and-coming Athletics would win the pennant. One important new contributor was longtime journeyman minor leaguer Wilcy Moore, who had recently turned to pitching sidearm. He pitched relief at a time when relievers were mainly mop-up pitchers and went 16–1. Huggins changed his batting order. Gehrig batted cleanup and provided a lot of protection for Ruth, who got on base nearly half the time. Gehrig became a prolific RBI man and led the league with 174. The Yankees hit 158 homers, with Ruth and Gehrig accounting for 107; the Athletics were second in homers with just 56. The Yankees ran away with the pennant, clinching on September 13 on the way to 110 wins. Public attention instead focused on the home-run race between Ruth and Gehrig, and debated whether the Yankees, with their "Murderers' Row" lineup, speed, and very fine defense, were the greatest team ever. Ruth went on a tear in September with 17 home runs, and hit his 60th off Washington lefty Tom Zachary in front of just 10,000 spectators at Yankee Stadium. The New Yorkers were prohibitive favorites in the Series with the Pittsburgh Pirates, and swept them in four games.

The Yankees kept the pressure on the AL in 1928, taking 34 of their first 42 games. However, injuries and age slowed the team down. Moore could not regain his form, and the Athletics caught the Yankees in early September. However, the Bronx Bombers got hot and took the pennant with 101 victories. Ruth and Gehrig both played every game. Ruth hit 54 homers, and they tied for the RBI lead with 145. Pipgras and Hoyt both won 23 games. The Yankees again swept the Series, led by Ruth, who hit a record .625. The Babe and Gehrig together accounted for more runs and total bases than the entire Cardinals lineup.

The Yankees changed their lineup in 1929. Koenig replaced Dugan at third, second-year man Leo Durocher went from second to short, and promising rookie Bill Dickey went behind the plate. Numbers were worn on uniforms for the first time, with starters identified by their position in the batting order. The club was very strong at bat but the pitching was shaky, except for Tom Zachary, who went 12–0. The powerful Athletics outclassed the Yankees and eliminated them from the pennant race on September 14. Shortly thereafter, Huggins fell ill from a small boil under his left eye and tragically died of blood poisoning 10 days later. Coach Art Fletcher ran the team for the rest of the season, and the club ended up 88–66, 18 games out of first place. That season the Yankees started their farm system with Chambersburg of the Class D Blue Ridge League. Two years later the club bought Newark of the International League for $600,000.

Coach Bob Shawkey became the new manager in 1930. The team added rookie third baseman Ben Chapman and acquired pitcher Red Ruffing from Boston. Because of their high salaries, Koenig and Hoyt were dropped. The Yankees had a banner offensive year, leading the AL in hitting at .309 and setting a record for runs scored with 1,062, but finished third with the second-worst pitching in the league. Ruth, earning a record $80,000, hit 49 homers. Shawkey was fired and replaced by Joe McCarthy, former pennant-winning manager of the Cubs, who got a five-year contract at $30,000 a year. McCarthy was renowned as a businesslike disciplinarian who emphasized fundamentals. Joe established a dress code for road trips and required players to make an 8:30 breakfast call. The innovations did not sit well with everyone, especially Ruth, irate that he did not get the manager's job.

In 1931 the team could not compete with the Athletics. The A's won 107 games and finished 13 1/2 games ahead of the Yankees, even though Ruth and Gehrig both hit 46 homers and Gehrig led the AL in RBIs for the second straight year. The Yankees dealt with the depression by cutting salaries, including Ruth's by half. Home attendance was a healthy 1,169,230, unsurpassed until 1946. Additional revenues came from staging Negro baseball games, started the year before, and boxing shows at Yankee Stadium. The Yankees were hardly hurt by the depression, losing money only in 1932 and 1933 for a combined $130,000 loss. Overall the team made $1,139,189 between 1930 and 1939.

The Yankees regained the pennant in 1932, winning 107 games. In early June Gehrig hit four home runs at Yankee Stadium, the first modern player to achieve that feat. The Yankees played the underdog Cubs in the World Series that year. McCarthy relished it, as that team had dumped him in 1930. Yankee players were mad at the Cubs because their old teammate, Mark Koenig, a midseason pickup by the Cubs, had batted .353 and played a big role in the pennant chase, but was voted only a partial share of the World Series paycheck. The Yankees took the first two games at home, 12–6 and 5–2. Then in Chicago Ruth homered in the first inning to give the Yankees a three-run lead. But the Cubs rallied to tie the game 4–4. In the fifth inning Ruth stepped up to bat against starter Charlie Root. The Cubs' bench jockeys went after Ruth for calling them cheapskates because of the Koenig incident, and impugned Ruth's racial background. The *Chicago Tribune* reported that when the count moved to 2–2 Ruth held up two fingers; many fans thought he was pointing to center field. He homered over the center-field wall and seemed to laugh at the Cubs' dugout while running the bases. On the next pitch, Gehrig followed with a home run. The *World Telegram* headlined the event "Ruth Calls Shot," with an accompanying story, but other papers made no special mention of the event for several days. Ruth was bemused, and never denied the story. In time he embellished on it. In 1999 an amateur film was uncovered that seemed to indicate Ruth was not pointing to center field. The Yankees won the game 7–5, and romped in the finale 13–6. Gehrig led the way, hitting .529 with three homers, eight RBIs, and 19 total bases.

In 1933, when six Yankees made the first All-Star Game, the club fell to second with 91 wins. The starting lineup batted well, but not up to the previous season. Ruth, 39 years old, slipped to .301. In 1934 the Yanks faltered after Combs broke his clavicle and fractured his skull, effectively ending his career. The team won 94 games and finished second. Gehrig won the Triple Crown with a .363 batting average, 165 RBIs, and 49 home runs. Ruth left the team after the season. In his 15 years with the Yankees he hit 659 home runs, batted .349, and led the club to seven pennants and four world championships.

THE PRIDE OF THE YANKEES AND THE YANKEE CLIPPER

In 1935 Gehrig was installed as the first Yankees captain since Huggins had stripped Ruth of that title a decade earlier. George Selkirk replaced Ruth in right and hit .312 with 94 RBIs. The Yankees had the best pitching in the league, led by Lefty Gomez and Ruffing, but lacked enough offense to keep up with the Tigers. Without Ruth attendance dropped to 657,508, the lowest since 1919.

A new Yankees dynasty began one year later when the club clinched the pennant on September 10, finishing 19 1/2 games ahead of Detroit. The team batted .300 and outscored the opposition by over 300 runs. The big addition was brilliant rookie Joe DiMaggio, a five-tool prospect who hit nearly .400 for the San Francisco Seals in the PCL in 1935. DiMaggio started out in right but moved to center field in midseason. He batted .323 with 29 homers and 125 RBIs, and was one of eight Yankee All-Stars. Five teammates hit over .300, led by Dickey's .362. MVP Gehrig hit .354 with 49 homers and 152 RBIs.

The Yankees faced the Giants in the "Nickel Series," so named because a subway token cost a nickel. The Giants' great screwball pitcher Carl Hubbell won the first game at the Polo Grounds 6–1, but the Yankees came back to take the second game 18–4, with Lazzeri smacking the second grand slam in Series history. The series then moved across the Harlem River to Yankee Stadium, where the Bombers took the next two, while the Giants salvaged game five. The Yankees closed out the series in game six with seven runs in the ninth to win 13–6.

The 1937 Yankees were a run-producing machine, with three of the top four RBI men in the league, led by DiMaggio at 167 and Gehrig at 159. The pitching was outstanding, leading the AL in virtually every statistical category. Gomez won 21 and Red Ruffing 20. The team won the pennant in a rout, going 102–52, with six All-Stars. The Yankees again faced the Giants in the World Series, and took it four games to one. The Yankees won the first two at home by identical 8–1 scores, took the next at the Polo Grounds, and then lost to Hubbell, 7–3. They clinched the Fall Classic with a 4–2 win. Lazzeri hit .400 to lead the Yankees, yet was released after the season to make way for Joe Gordon, who along with Tommy Heinrich was brought up from the Yankees top minor-league team, the powerful Newark Bears.

The following season DiMaggio held out until the end of April, when he signed for $25,000. The Yankees started slowly but went 48–13 in July and August and coasted to the pennant with a record of 99–53. The season was highlighted by Monte Pearson's no-hitter, the first by a Yankee since 1923. Gehrig fell to .295 with 29 homers and 114 RBIs, but DiMaggio hit .324 and Joe Gordon and Tommy Heinrich each hit over 20 homers and 90 RBIs. In the World Series the Yankees, led by Red Ruffing, who won twice, overwhelmed the Chicago Cubs in four straight games.

Early in 1939 Ruppert died, and his two nieces shared his $7 million estate. He had recently sold Barrow 300 shares of stock and promoted him to team president. The team broadcast games on radio for a $100,000 fee. Arch MacDonald was the first voice of the Yankees, later replaced by Mel Allen. However, the big story was Lou Gehrig, "the Pride of the Yankees." Gehrig fell ill during the off-season, was diagnosed with a gallbladder ailment, struggled in spring training, and once the season started got only four hits in his first 28 at bats. On May 2, he took himself out of the lineup, ending a 2,130 consecutive-game streak. Gehrig remained with the club for a month, but his condition worsened. He was eventually diagnosed by the Mayo Clinic as suffering from amyotrophic lateral sclerosis, an incurable nervous-system disease. In his honor the Yankees staged Lou Gehrig Appreciation Day on July 4, where he delivered one of the most memorable speeches in American history: "Fans, for the past two weeks you have been reading about what a bad break I got. Yet today, I consider myself the luckiest man on the face of the earth." He died two years later.

The Yankees of 1939 may have been stronger than Murderers' Row. The team scored 967 runs and gave up merely 556. DiMaggio hit .381 with a slugging percentage of .671. All starters hit at least 10 homers, four drove in over 100 runs, and seven pitchers won 10 games or more, leading the AL in virtually all team pitching statistics. Incredibly, 10 Yankees made the All-Star team. The team went 106–45, 17 games ahead of second-place Boston The team won their fourth straight World Series, defeating the Cincinnati Reds in four straight games, making it nine straight victories in the Fall Classic. In the fourth game the Yankees scored twice in the ninth to tie the game 4–4. In the 10th inning DiMaggio singled with runners at first and third. When right fielder Irval

Goodman misplayed the ball, Charlie Keller tried to score from first. He and the ball arrived almost simultaneously, and Keller collided with catcher Ernie Lombardi. DiMaggio circled the bases before Lombardi could retrieve the ball, giving the Yankees an insurmountable three-run lead and the World Series.

Surprisingly, the 1940 team struggled, hindered by DiMaggio's wrenched knee and declining veterans. The team made a vigorous attempt to stay in the pennant race, going 21–3 during the summer, and briefly took over first place on September 11. However, they faded and ended two games behind the Tigers.

The next season the Yankees again had a rough start, going 25–22, but thereafter turned the season around, winning 41 of 47. DiMaggio struggled early on but began a hitting streak on May 15. On July 2 DiMaggio homered, surpassing Willie Keeler's all-time record of 44 straight games with at least one hit. The streak had reached 56 when he was stymied by the Indians on July 17. DiMaggio batted .407 during his streak, leading the Yankees to another pennant, clinched on September 4, the earliest in history. They went 101–53, winning by 17 games over Boston. DiMaggio hit .357 with 30 homers and 125 RBIs, edging Ted Williams, who batted .406, for MVP.

The Dodgers were the strongest NL team to face the Yankees in years. The Yankees took game one, 3–2, for their 10th straight Series win, but the Dodgers took the next, 3–2. In the next game the Yankees scored two runs in the eighth off reliever Hugh Casey and won 2–1. In the dramatic fourth game Casey, who had been pitching since the fifth inning, had the Yankees down 4–3 in the ninth with two out. Heinrich worked him to a full count and then struck out on a spitter. But the pitch fooled catcher Mickey Owens, and it rolled to the backstop, allowing Heinrich to make it to first. Carey got two strikes on each of the next four batters but retired none of them. DiMaggio and Keller both singled, tying the game. After Dickey walked on a full count, Gordon doubled to bring in three runs and take the lead. The shocked Dodgers went quietly in their half of the ninth and the Yankees won, 7–4. The series was clinched in the next game, 3–1, with Ernie "Tiny" Bonham giving up just four hits.

When World War II came the Yankees used their rich 12-team farm system to supply players or facilitate trades. The system was reduced to five by 1943, when most major-league teams were down to two or three. DiMaggio and Phil Rizzuto were both classified 3-A and played the season. The offense was down but the pitching was strong, led by Bonham, who went 21–5 and led the league in ERA. The Yankees clinched the pennant on September 14 and went on to win 103 games.

The Yankees played the Cardinals in the World Series. The Yankees took the first game at Sportsman's Park 7–4 behind surprise starter Red Ruffing. The Cards took the next four games to win the series, handing the Yankees their first postseason defeat since 1926.

In 1943 spring training was held in nearby Asbury Park, New Jersey. Several players joined the military, including Phil Rizzuto, DiMaggio, and Ruffing, but the team still included Gordon, Keller, and pitchers Bonham, Spud Chandler,

Hank Borowy, and Johnny Murphy. McCarthy relied on rookies much more than in the past, with George "Snuffy" Stirnweiss at short, Billy Johnson at third, and Johnny Lindell in right field. The pitchers held hitters to 542 runs, lowest in the league since 1920. Chandler was outstanding, with a record of 20–4 and a league-leading 1.64 ERA. New first baseman Nick Etten had 107 RBIs, Keller had 31 homers, and Dickey hit .351 while playing part-time. The team won 98 games and finished in first by 13 1/2 games. The Yankees won the Series over the Cardinals in five games, employing superior pitching led by Chandler, who won twice, including a shutout in the final game. The attendance was 618,330, tops in the AL, but the lowest for the Yankees since 1919.

By 1944, nearly all the top Yankees were serving in the military. Spring training was held in Atlantic City. McCarthy's health was failing and he was temporarily replaced by coach Art Fletcher. The Yankees compiled a record of 83–71 and finished third behind the Browns.

On January 28, 1945, Ruppert's heirs sold the team, the ballpark, and the farm system for the bargain price of $2.8 million to a syndicate led by playboy Dan Topping, son of a steel magnate, whose involvement in pro sports had begun in 1934 with his purchase of the Brooklyn Dodgers of the NFL. His partners were Del Webb, a well-connected construction magnate who had over $100 million in government contracts during the war, and Larry MacPhail, a Columbus, Ohio, businessman who had been general manager of the Cincinnati Reds, where he instituted night baseball and radio broadcasts. In 1938 MacPhail moved on to the Dodgers, and had them in the World Series in three years. MacPhail became Yankees general manager and dominated the syndicate.

McCarthy kept his modestly talented squad in contention for the first half of the 1945 season. Stirnweiss, 4-F due to ulcers, had a banner year, leading the AL in batting (.309), slugging, hits, runs, triples, and stolen bases. But in July MacPhail sold pitcher Hank Borowy, who already had 10 wins that season, to the Cubs for $97,000 without consulting his manager. McCarthy was already mad at MacPhail's criticisms and after this transaction left the team for three weeks, claiming gallbladder problems. The team finished 81–71 in fourth place. Overall, the Yankees made out well during the war era, earning an average of $129,000 from 1940 to 1945, which included a loss of $88,521 in 1943.

After the war MacPhail focused more on promotions than on building up the team. He organized a 50-game tour of the South and Midwest before the 1946 season that left his veteran team exhausted and disgruntled. More importantly, he had no relationship with McCarthy, who resigned during the season, knowing he would not be rehired. Coach Bill Dickey took over as manager, but he feuded with MacPhail and quit in September, leaving coach Johnny Neun as manager. Despite the managerial musical chairs, the club finished second to the Red Sox. Attendance nearly tripled to 2,265,512. Yankees historian Glen Stout has argued that the owners were more concerned about making money than winning, and were not concerned about the long haul. Yet they managed to do both in the postwar era, winning six world championships in seven years

(1947, 1949–53) and making a lot of money. From 1946 through 1950, the team's average profit was $603,177.

A NEW DYNASTY

MacPhail tried to reshape the franchise after the 1946 season. He made an excellent trade when he sent Joe Gordon to the Indians for pitcher Allie Reynolds, but blundered by trading Ernie Bonham, who had won 89 games with a sub-3.00 ERA, to Pittsburgh for prospect Cookie Cuccurullo, who never pitched for the Yankees. MacPhail hired Bucky Harris to manage the team. Harris came with over 20 years' major-league experience, but mainly in the second division. MacPhail tried unsuccessfully to trade DiMaggio to the Senators for AL batting champion Mickey Vernon, and in April 1947 nearly dealt him for Ted Williams. Tom Yawkey of the Red Sox backed out after sobering up. The big event at Yankee Stadium that spring was Babe Ruth Day on April 27, attended by 60,000 people. The Babe was 52, but frail from cancer, and died one year later.

The team struggled early in the season with several injuries and was below .500 in mid-May. But the Yankees regrouped and won 19 straight games early that summer. The pennant was clinched by mid-September. DiMaggio hit .315 with 20 homers and 97 RBIs and won the MVP by one vote over Ted Williams, who won the Triple Crown.

The Yankees faced a very strong Dodgers team in the first televised World Series. That year radio rights ($175,000) were nearly triple the television fees ($65,000). By comparison, the series gate was $1.7 million. The Yankees won the first two games 5–3 and 10–3, and the Dodgers came back to take the third game 9–8. In game four, journeyman pitcher Bill Bevens, 7–13 during the season, no-hit the Dodgers into the ninth inning, with the Yankees up 2–1. Bevans walked a batter, and after two outs pinch runner Al Gionfriddo stole second. Pete Reiser was intentionally walked and Eddie Miksis ran for him. Cookie Lavagetto pinch-hit for Eddie Stanky and sliced an inside fastball to the wall in right for the Dodgers' only hit of the game, driving in both runners to give the Dodgers a 3–2 win. The series went to the decisive seventh game, won by the Yanks 5–2, led by reliever Joe Page, who took over in the fifth and went the rest of the way.

After the series MacPhail sold out to Topping and Webb for $2 million. George Weiss, a longtime Yankee functionary, became general manager. He developed a great scouting system, took advantage of weaker teams to secure needed players, and was a tough contract negotiator who figured World Series shares were just a regular part of a Yankees salary. He recruited "Yankee-type" players who were large, clean cut, and handsome.

In 1948 Weiss traded catcher Aaron Robinson and some throw-ins to the White Sox for 16-game winner Ed Lopat, who won 17 for the Yankees, second to Vic Raschi's 19. Catcher Yogi Berra made the All-Star team, the first of 15 straight seasons over his 19-year Yankees career. The Yankees were in the pennant race all year but ended up in third place (94–60). The hot pennant race produced 2,373,901 in attendance, a team record that stood until 1979.

Weiss fired Bucky Harris after the season and replaced him with Casey Stengel. Stengel did not seem cut out of Yankee cloth, having had a reputation as a clown during his major-league career and amusing sportswriters with his malapropisms. He managed the hapless Dodgers and Braves for nine years before becoming a successful minor-league manager. Stengel showed his team he was the boss with twice-a-day workouts in spring training that stressed fundamentals. The club had excellent pitching with starters Raschi, Reynolds, Lopat, and Tommy Byrne, with Page in the bullpen, and a lot of depth, so Stengel avoided a set lineup. Weiss made a late-season trade to bolster the club, acquiring first baseman Johnny Mize from the Giants for $40,000. Mize was a career .323 hitter, but he was injured in his third game and was out for the season. The Yankees were one game out with two left to play when first-place Boston came to town. The Yankees were down 4–0 but rallied behind Joe Page, who pitched six and two-thirds innings of scoreless ball to defeat the Sox 5–4. The Yankees prevailed the next day to win the pennant.

The Yankees finished at 95–57 and then faced the very strong and deep Dodgers in the World Series. Reynolds pitched a two-hitter to start the series with a 1–0 victory over Don Newcombe, but then Preacher Roe topped Raschi 1–0. The third game went to the ninth tied 1–1, with Page pitching relief since the fourth. Mize hit a bases-loaded pinch-hit single to take the lead, and the Yankees won 4–3. The Yankees took the next two games 6–4 and 10–6, winning the series in five. Stengel was named Manager of the Year.

The Yankees in 1950 were in a tight pennant race with the Tigers and did not take control until late September, finishing in first place. Rizzuto was MVP, and four starting pitchers won at least 15 games. DiMaggio, who had only played 76 games in 1949, struggled so much early on that he was briefly benched, but returned to his old form and batted .301 with 122 RBIs. In the Series the Yankees faced the worn-out Phillies, who had won the pennant on the last day of the season. Raschi led off with a two-hit 1–0 shutout. Reynolds also threw a complete game, winning 2–1 on DiMaggio's homer in the 10th. The Yankees went on to sweep the series, with rookie Whitey Ford, who had gone 9–1 during just half a season, winning the clinching game.

At the start of the 1951 season DiMaggio surprised everyone by announcing his retirement after the season. But the Yankees were loaded with young talent, especially 19-year-old rookie switch-hitter Mickey Mantle, who jumped from Class C to the majors. Stengel shifted him from shortstop to the outfield, where he could take advantage of his blazing speed (he was clocked at 3.1 seconds from home to first, the fastest ever) and strong arm. Mantle started out in right field, hit around .300, and led the club in RBIs. But after a long slump he was sent down to Kansas City on July 16, returning one month later. Stengel continued to experiment with lineups, platooning Gil McDougald, the

Joe DiMaggio scores during the 1949 World Series. Courtesy of the Baseball Hall of Fame

AL Rookie of the Year, and Jerry Coleman at second and giving Bobby Brown the job at third. Late in August the Yankees got veteran pitcher Johnny Sain for the stretch from the Braves for $50,000 and prospect Lew Burdette. The big game that season was against Bob Feller and the Indians, in first place by one game, on September 16. Stengel put together an unorthodox lineup, with Mantle leading off and McDougald batting third. The Yankees won 5–1, tied for first, and never relinquished the lead, finishing 98–56. On September 28 Allie Reynolds pitched his second no-hitter of the season despite a miscue by Berra, who dropped Ted Williams's foul pop-up with two out in the ninth. But then Williams hit another pop-up that Berra corralled. Berra, who had become an excellent receiver, was named MVP, repeating in 1954 and 1955. Raschi and Lopat both won 21 games.

The Yankees faced the Giants in the World Series following their miracle playoff victory against the Dodgers. In game one at Yankee Stadium Mantle's spikes got caught on an outfield drain cover and he tore ligaments in his right knee. He thereafter had major recurring physical ailments, particularly episodes of osteomyelitis. Hank Bauer, a tough Marine veteran, replaced him in the lineup. The teams split the first four games, but in the fifth the Yankees clobbered the Giants 13–1. Behind Raschi's pitching the Yankees won the sixth and final game 4–3.

In 1952 eight players from the stellar squad made the All-Star team. The outstanding pitching staff limited the opposition to 557 runs. The Yankees finished the season 95–59, took the pennant by two games over the Indians, and faced a powerful Dodgers squad in the World Series. The teams split the first four games, and then in game five the visiting Dodgers won 6–5 in 11 innings. Back at Ebbets Field for game six, Mantle and Berra homered off Billy Loes, and the Yankees survived to win 3–2 on Raschi's second victory. In the decisive seventh game Mantle and Gene Woodling homered, giving the Yankees a 4–2 lead in the seventh inning. The Dodgers loaded the bases, and with two out reliever Bob Kuzava forced Jackie Robinson to pop up. First baseman Joe Collins lost the ball in the sun, but at the last moment second baseman Billy Martin rushed in full speed to catch the ball just above his shoes. Kuzava closed out the Dodgers and the Yankees took the series.

Mickey Charles Mantle, 1951. Courtesy of the Baseball Hall of Fame

In 1953 the Yankees had the best hitting and pitching in the AL, and finished first for the fifth straight year. The team went 99–52, which included an 18-game winning streak. Whitey Ford, now out of the army, won 18, while Lopat led the AL with a 2.43 ERA. A highlight of the season came on April 17 when Mantle, batting right-handed, hit a ball at Washington's Griffith Stadium that supposedly went 565 feet, the longest reported homer ever. The Dodgers repeated as NL champions, setting up an exciting Series rematch. The Yankees won the first two games at home and the Dodgers took the next two at Ebbets Field, including Carl Erskine's 14-strikeout effort in game three. The Yankees used four homers, including a Mantle grand slam, to win game five 11–7, and closed out the series in game six by scoring the winning run in the bottom of the ninth to prevail 4–3. Martin set a Series record with 12 hits.

In 1954 the Yankees had a brilliant season, winning 103 games, the most since 1942. But the Indians did even better, winning an incredible 111 games. The Yankees were the first team to win over 100 games and not win the pennant. The superb farm system produced three terrific first-year men, Rookie of the Year third baseman Andy Carey; first baseman Bill "Moose" Skowron, who batted .340 in part-time duty; and 20-game winner Bob Grim.

The team's pitching was depleted of its veterans with Raschi traded and Reynolds retired in 1954, so the Yankees tried to bolster their staff after the season with a blockbuster deal with the Baltimore Orioles, sending 11 men, mainly marginal prospects and aged veterans, in return for 7 players, most notably pitching prospects Bob Turley and Don Larsen and shortstop Billy Hunter, brought in to supplant the aging Rizzuto.

The Yankees did not integrate until 1955, and were among the last to do so. Back on Opening Day 1945 20 people had picketed the stadium carrying signs asking, "If We Can Pay, Why Can't We Play?" and "If We Can Stop Bullets, Why Not Balls?" One year later MacPhail wrote a secret report for MLB opposing integration because he felt it was necessary to protect the Negro Leagues. Left unspoken was an ulterior motive: he did not want to give up the over $100,000 the Yankees got by renting the stadium and their minor-league parks to black teams. In 1950 the Yankees signed their first three players of color to minor-league contracts: Elston Howard and Frank Barnes of the Kansas City Monarchs and Cuban Vic Power, probably to keep them away from competition or use as trade bait, since Weiss had no intention of bringing them up. Weiss felt blacks were less competent and would attract black spectators and thereby curtail the growing suburban white crowds. Topping had years earlier signed African American Buddy Young for his football team, but did not interfere with his general manager. First baseman Vic Power was a particularly outstanding prospect. In 1953 at Kansas City he hit .349 with 109 RBIs and 18 stolen bases. The Yankees' lame excuse was that he was a poor fielder, but he eventually earned seven Gold Gloves. In management's eyes Power's real flaws were his race, flamboyance, and popularity with white women. He was traded in late 1953 as part of an 11-man deal with the A's.

The Yankees finally integrated in 1955 by bringing up Elston Howard, who had hit .330 and was MVP with Toronto in the International League. He was a fundamentally strong catcher, but with Berra behind the plate returned to his original outfield position. Howard had the attributes the Yankees sought in a black player: light-skinned, soft-spoken, and married. Howard was generally welcomed, but he had no roommate for his first five seasons.

The Yankees opened 1955 with a 19–1 rout over the Senators. They were in a four-team pennant race for much of the season, but broke from the pack late in September with eight straight wins. Their final record was 96–58, which was a drop of seven games from the year before. They had the best pitching in the league and were second in batting. Mantle led the league with 37 homers and a .611 slugging percentage, while Ford led in wins with 18.

For the third time in four years the Yankees and Dodgers squared off in the World Series. Mantle was injured, playing in only three games. The Yankees took the first game, going with a left-handed lineup against the powerful right-hander Don Newcombe, which paid off when first baseman Joe Collins hit two homers, leading to a 6–5 victory. Lefty Tommy Byrne took the following game

4–2. The match seemed well in hand since no team had ever won the Series after losing the first two contests. But the Dodgers were tough at Ebbets Field and took three straight. The Yankees tied the series at home behind Ford's pitching. Byrne started the deciding game seven against young lefty Johnny Podres, winner of game three. The Dodgers got just five hits, but they produced two runs. In the bottom of the sixth, with McDougald on first and none out, Berra hit a shot into the left-field corner that seemed a sure extra-base hit. Left fielder Sandy Amoros, brought in late in the game as a defensive replacement, made a great grab, but only because, as a left-hander, his glove was on his right hand. After his remarkable catch he returned the ball to first base, doubling up McDougald. That was as close as the Yankees got. The Dodgers won 2–0 and were world champions for the first time.

In 1956, the 24-year-old Mantle had one of the best seasons in major-league history. He staggered the baseball community with the power of his home runs, hitting two over 500 feet on Opening Day in Washington. On May 30 he hit a home run at Yankee Stadium against Pedro Ramos that missed going over the roof by two feet, a shot estimated at 550–600 feet. Mantle not only won the Triple Crown, batting .353 with 52 homers and 130 RBIs, but led *both* leagues in these categories, as well as in slugging percentage (.705), runs (132), and total bases (376). The Yankees took the AL by nine games, leading in batting and second in pitching. This earned them a rematch with the Dodgers, led by 27-game winner Don Newcombe. The Dodgers took the first two games at home 6–3 and 13–8. In desperation Stengel brought back Ford on two days' rest. He responded with a complete-game 5–3 win. Yankee Tom Sturdivant took the next game 6–2. Stengel then went with Don Larsen, who had been KO'd by the Dodgers in the second inning of game two. Mantle had the first hit in the game, a fourth-inning homer, and the Yankees scored another run in the sixth as they managed only five hits off Sal Maglie. Larson, amazingly, threw a perfect game, ending it with a called third strike on pinch hitter Dale Mitchell. It was the first no-hitter in the World Series and the sixth perfect game in major-league history. But the Dodgers were resilient, and Clem Labine shut out the Yankees over 10 innings at Ebbets Field to hand Brooklyn a 1–0 victory that tied the series at three games apiece. In the deciding game Yankee Johnny Kucks gave up only three hits and glided to a 9–0 victory, supported by three home runs.

On February 19, 1957, the Yankees made their first of several major trades with the Kansas City Athletics, securing pitchers Art Ditmar and Bobby Shantz and infield prospect Clete Boyer for Irv Noren, Tom Morgan, and Billy Hunter. The Yankees historically had taken advantage of weaker clubs and continued the tradition with the A's, purchased after the 1954 season by Chicago businessman Arnold Johnson, who was closely tied to Topping and Weiss, having bought Yankee Stadium in 1953 and then leased it back to them. In 1955 Johnson sold the stadium to Chicago banker John Cox and moved the A's to Kansas City, where the Yankees sold him their territorial rights.

The Yankees also strengthened themselves through the farm system, bringing up second baseman Bobby Richardson and infielder and outfielder Tony Kubek, who won the Rookie of the Year Award. The Yankees took their third straight pennant, but not without some turmoil. On May 7, 1957, Indians strikeout phenom Herb Score fired a fastball that McDougald stroked right back at him, hitting him in the eye. Score did keep his eyesight, but never regained his pitching form. One week later several Yankees, including Mantle, Berra, Ford, Kucks, Martin, and their wives, celebrated Billy Martin's 29th birthday at the Copacabana nightclub. They got into an argument with customers who complained they were blocking their view and made racist comments about headliner Sammy Davis Jr. Weiss fined Mantle, Bauer, Martin, and Kucks, but mainly blamed Martin, traded two weeks later to the Athletics with Ralph Terry for outfielder Harry Simpson and reliever Ryne Duren. The trade sent a strong message to the Yankees to shape up. The squad had the best hitting and pitching in the league, with a team ERA of 3.00, led by Shantz at 2.45, and eight men made the All-Star team. Mantle was brilliant, hitting .385 until he was injured late in the season while playing golf, cutting his shin to the bone. He finished with a .365 average, 34 homers, and 94 RBIs.

The Yankees faced the formidable Milwaukee Braves, who had outstanding pitching and a powerful lineup, in the World Series. Ford beat Warren Spahn in game one 3–1, but the story of the series was former Yankee farmhand Lew Burdette, who won three games, including the second contest. The teams split the next two games, but in game five Burdette's sinker (or spitball) totally fooled the Yankees, and he won 1–0. In game six the Yankees won without Mantle, who had injured his shoulder in the fourth game and could not throw. Burdette pitched the final game on two days' rest, and again shut out the Yankees, 5–0, to win the series.

In 1958, with the Dodgers and Giants off to California, the Yankees were the only team in New York, but they made little effort to attract NL fans, who hated the arrogant Yankees. The Yankees started the season at 25–6 and coasted to the pennant, powered by the best pitching and batting in the AL, clinching on September 14. Mantle led the league in homers, runs, and total bases. Bob Turley won the Cy Young Award with a record of 21–7 while Ford had the lowest ERA, a spectacular 2.01. Nine men made the All-Star team.

The Series was a rematch with the Braves, who took the first two games in Milwaukee 4–3 and 13–5. The Yankees only got four hits in the next game back in New York, but Larsen shut out the Braves 4–0, with Bauer, hitting in his 17th straight Series game, responsible for all the runs. Spahn then put the Yankees into a huge hole, shutting them out 3–0 on two hits. No team had ever before come back from a 3–1 deficit. Braves manager Fred Haney inexplicably altered his rotation for the next game, replacing Bob Rush, who had pitched well in game three, with Burdette on three days' rest. The Yankees prevailed 7–0. Spahn then went on two days' rest and lost 4–3 in extra innings. Burdette pitched again in game seven, also on two days' rest. The Yankees broke up a thrilling tie game in the eighth with four runs and won 6–2, capturing another World Series.

The Yankees struggled badly in 1959, falling into last place on May 21 for the first time in 19 years. As a result Sturdivant, Kucks, and Jerry Lumpe were traded to Kansas City for former Yankee Ralph Terry and infielder Hector Lopez, a fine hitter but a poor fielder. The club struggled all season long, ending at 79–75 in third place, 15 games off the lead, their worst season since 1925. Even Mantle hit only .285 with 75 RBIs, and had his salary cut by $7,000.

That winter Weiss went back to Kansas City for a blockbuster trade. The A's got Larsen, Bauer, and Norm Siebern for Roger Maris and Joe DeMaestri. Maris was an outstanding fielder and strong left-handed hitter who was seen as a future star whose stroke was made for the short right-field porch in Yankee Stadium. The Yankees bolstered their defense in 1960 by putting Clete Boyer, a great fielder but weak hitter, at third and moving Lopez to left field. The club was in a tight pennant race with the defending AL champion White Sox, but the Yankees pulled away in September, going 20–7, and won the pennant by eight games. Maris batted cleanup behind Mantle and hit 39 homers, drove in 112 runs, led the league in slugging, and was named MVP.

The Yankees faced the Pirates in the World Series as prohibitive favorites. The Yankees clobbered the Pirates in the three games they won by a score of 38–3, but the Pirates narrowly won the first, fourth, and fifth games with good defense, timely hitting, and defense. In the decisive seventh game the Bombers took a 7–4 lead into the bottom of the eighth. Reliever Bobby Shantz gave up a single to Gino Cimoli, and then Bill Virdon hit a sure double-play ball to Kubek, but it took a bad hop and struck him in the neck. He had to be taken to the hospital. After Dick Groat singled, Jim Coates was brought in to pitch, and the runners were sacrificed into scoring position. Following a second out Roberto Clemente hit a grounder to Skowron, but Coates was late in covering the base. Then Hal Smith homered, giving Pittsburgh a 9–7 lead. In the ninth Richardson and Long singled, knocking out reliever Bob Friend. Harvey Haddix got Maris on a pop out but Mantle singled, making the score 9–8, with runners on first and third. Berra then hit a one-hopper to first baseman Rocky Nelson, who stepped on first for the force and started to throw to second for the game-ending double play. However, Mantle had not run to second, thinking Berra's shot would be caught. Nelson turned to throw and was stunned to see Mantle in front of him. Mantle dove back to first and avoided the tag, enabling the tying run to score from third. But in the bottom of the ninth, Ralph Terry threw one pitch to Bill Mazeroski, who parked it over the 12-foot-high left-field fence, over the 406-foot sign, to win the series. This was the first walk-off homer to ever decide a World Series.

Major changes took place after the shocking outcome. Topping and Webb began to think about selling out, and cut back on reinvesting in the team. Stengel was forced out at age 70 after winning 10 pennants and seven World Series in 12 years, a record unmatched in baseball history. Ralph Houk, a former third-string catcher, became the new skipper. Weiss, at 65, was also let go, replaced by aide Roy Hamey, former general manager in Pittsburgh and Philadelphia.

Houk inherited a very strong lineup that ran away with the pennant with 109 wins. Six men hit over 20 homers and nine made the All-Star team, leaving the Mantle-Maris home-run race the focal point of public attention. Maris, who batted third in front of Mantle, started slowly, but beginning in mid-May he hit 23 during the next 36 games. The AL season had been increased to 162 games because of expansion, and Commissioner Ford Frick, Ruth's former ghostwriter, announced that anyone requiring more than 154 games to beat the record would go into the books with an asterisk. On August 2 Mantle caught up to Maris with 40 home runs. The public and the sporting press wanted their old hero to break the record, but in mid-September Mantle developed an infected abscess in his thigh after taking a shot for a cold and hit only two more homers, finishing with 54, 128 RBIs, and a .317 batting average. Maris marched on, hitting his 59th during the 154th game, when the Yankees clinched the pennant. He hit number 60 on September 26 off Jack Fisher of Baltimore, and on the last day of the season hit 61 off Boston's Tracy Stallard in front of just 23,154. Maris led the AL in RBIs with 142 and won his second straight MVP. Other stellar performers included Howard, who batted a sparkling .348; Luis Arroyo, who saved a record 29 games; and Ford, who went 25–4 and won the Cy Young Award. "The Chairman of the Board" mystified batters with his change of speeds, curveball, and pinpoint control. Stengel had used him carefully, seldom pitching him in more than 30 games and saving him to face the opposition's ace, but Houk pitched him every fourth day, and Ford responded with 39 starts and 280 innings. The Yankees faced the Cincinnati Reds in the World Series, and even though Mantle played just two games, they dominated, winning four games to one. Ford won twice, was Series MVP, and broke Babe Ruth's record for consecutive shutout innings in the Series. The club drew an attendance of 1,747,725, the highest since 1951 and the most until 1976.

In 1962 the Yankees fell off the prior year's pace, finishing just five games over Minnesota. Mantle tore his right hamstring and pulled the ligaments behind his left knee, injuries that reflected his poor training habits, chronic joint problems, and alcoholism. He played just 123 games and had to wrap his legs before every game. Maris fell to just 33 homers and 100 RBIs and a batting average of .256. Shortstop Tom Tresh was Rookie of the Year.

The Yankees played the Giants in the Series, led by former New York hero Willie Mays. Ford won the first game but had his scoreless streak ended at 33 innings. The teams alternated victories going into the deciding seventh game. The Yankees broke a scoreless tie in the fifth, getting a run on a double play. Yankees pitcher Ralph Terry, who had won 23 games, had a two-hitter going into the bottom of the ninth when Matty Alou bunted for a single and Mays doubled with two out. Brilliant rookie Willie McCovey smoked a line drive toward right field but straight at Richardson, who caught it and saved the 1–0 game. The Yankees had won another seven-game Series.

The 1963 team had some fine new talent, including 25-year-old pitcher Stan Williams, a 14-game winner acquired from the Dodgers for Moose Skowron. Joe Pepitone was poised to take over at first base, and Jim Bouton made the starting rotation. In June Mantle caught his spikes on a chain-link fence in Baltimore and broke his foot. His roster spot was taken by stylish rookie hurler Al Downing, the team's first African American starting pitcher, who threw a two-hitter in his first start. The offense exhibited little speed or power and batted .252, which in an era of great pitching was second highest in the AL. Catcher Elston Howard batted .287 and was named AL MVP. The team's pitching was outstanding, led by Ford's 24 wins and Bouton's 21.

The Yankees, with 104 victories, had high expectations for the World Series when they faced the Dodgers, who had outstanding pitching but no offense. They were confident they could hit Koufax's fastball, but struck out 15 times in the first game to set a new Series record. Houk pitched young Downing the next day, confident he could keep the speedy Dodgers from running, but lost 4–1. The Dodgers' Drysdale pitched a 1–0 gem in the third game, and in the fourth game Koufax gave up a homer to Mantle but won 2–1, for a series sweep.

Hamey retired after the embarrassing series, with Houk promoted to general manager. He hired popular Hall of Famer Yogi Berra to manage. Berra knew baseball and was popular with the press, who enjoyed his "Yogi-isms." However, there were questions about his intellect and his ability to work with former teammates, who tried to take advantage of him, and younger players. The Yankees started the season poorly, which reflected weak preparation in spring training and the failure to bring in new blood except for pitcher Mel Stottlemyre. A turning point came on a bus ride to the airport in Chicago on August 20 following a four-game losing streak. When reserve infielder Phil Linz pulled out a harmonica and began to sing, Berra blew up and told him to stop. Linz responded, "I didn't lose the game," and kept playing. Berra then knocked the harmonica out of his hand. Linz was fined $200 but got a $20,000 endorsement from a harmonica company. Thereafter the Yankees went 22–8, abetted by new reliever Pedro Ramos, and took the pennant with 99 wins, one game over the White Sox. The team relied mainly on excellent defense and terrific starting pitching. The offense depended heavily on Mantle, who batted .303 with 35 homers and 111 RBIs despite injuries that moved him into right field. Attendance dropped for the third straight year to 1.3 million, 400,000 less than the rival Mets. Perhaps the fans had become jaded.

CBS AND THE FALL OF THE YANKEES

On August 13, 1964, CBS bought an 80 percent share of the Yankees for $11.2 million. Webb sold his remaining 10 percent a few months later, and Topping sold out in 1966. The public was uncomfortable with the new alliance between sports and TV, and the deals gave Yankee haters another reason to loathe them. CBS anticipated great synergy with the team, already earning about $2 million a year from broadcasting, hoping to feature the Bronx Bombers on its *Game of the Week* program. But it had no intention of spending money on the team.

In the 1964 World Series the Yankees were heavily favored over the youthful St. Louis Cardinals, built on speed and pitching. But in game one Ford lost 9–5, partly due to an arterial problem that slowed the blood flow to his fingers. Stottlemyre defeated Bob Gibson 8–2 in the next game. Game three was tied going into the bottom of the ninth, 1–1, when the Cards brought in star reliever Barney Schultz. He threw one pitch to leadoff hitter Mantle, which he deposited in the right-field stands to end the game. The Cards won the next two and the Yankees took the sixth game. But Gibson, the Series MVP, closed out the series with a 7–5 win. The Yankees were led by Bobby Richardson, who had a record 13 hits, and Mantle, who played with a hurt leg and hit three home runs.

Despite winning the pennant, the Yankees fired Berra. They also fired Mel Allen, the broadcast voice of the team since 1939, who had been a face for Yankee class and mystique. Berra's replacement was Cardinals manager Johnny Keane, who had just quit. Keane pushed discipline and direction, stressing fundamentals during spring training and setting a curfew. However, the veterans tuned him out. Then during the season he managed poorly, playing for one run with a team built for power. The team suffered through many injuries and was mediocre, batting a sickly .235. The team ended in sixth place at 77–85, the worst finish in 40 years. The sole bright spot was Stottlemyre, with 20 wins and 18 complete games.

When the Yankees started 1966 at 4–15, Keane was fired and Houk returned as manager. The Yankees seemed to respond to the change and went 36–29 over a two-month period in which Mantle had 18 homers and returned to center field. But Houk had lost the respect of the veterans, whom he had disparaged when negotiating contracts. The team faded to last place (10th), and the attendance of 1,124,618 was the lowest since World War II. Supporters were fed up with the poor play and were worried about the park's declining South Bronx neighborhood. When broadcaster Red Barber made fun of the poor attendance and had the TV director show the empty seats on September 21, when only 413 attended, the Yankees fired him, ending his 32-year broadcasting career.

Michael Burke became team president late that season. He was a former star football player at Penn, an Office of Strategic Services hero, and CBS's vice president for development. He brought in Lee MacPhail, former Orioles president and general manager and son of the former Yankees owner, as general manager. Maris was traded before the 1967 season to the Cardinals and Ford retired with arm trouble after losing circulation in his arm. The Hall of Famer finished with a brilliant 236–106 record (.690, fifth highest of all time). The team batted a miserable .225 and committed the most errors in the AL, finishing in ninth place (72–90).

The team did make a big improvement in 1968 to finish fifth (83–79). The offense was abysmal, even for a pitching-dominated era. Their .214 batting average was lowest in the majors. The strength of the team was on the mound, particularly Stottlemyre, 21–12 with a 2.45 ERA, while Stan Bahnsen was Rookie of the Year, going 17–12 with a 2.05 ERA. Stottlemyre won 164 games from 1964 to 1974, including 20 or more three times. Mantle hit just .237 and retired, embarrassed that his career average had fallen to .298. He played more games than any other Yankee (2,401), hit 536 homers (then 3rd best in history, currently 12th), and hit 18 homers in 12 World Series. His retirement marked the end of an era.

The squad again finished in fifth in 1969, dropping to 80–81. Only Stottlemyre, Downing, and Pepitone remained from the last pennant winners. The offense was moribund at .235 with just 94 homers, though the starting pitching was excellent, led by Stottlemyre with 20 wins. The outcome was especially embarrassing since the Mets won the World Series that season. The good pitching of Stottlemyre; Fritz Peterson, who won 20; and Bahnsen helped propel the club in 1970 to 93 victories and second place, but 15 games shy of the Orioles' division-leading pace. A huge addition was first-round draft pick Thurman Munson. The Rookie of the Year batted .302, the highest for a Yankee since 1964. But the club fell off to 82–80 the next season with mediocre offense and defense, except for Bobby Murcer's career-year .331 average, 25 homers, and 96 RBIs.

The Yankees' downward attendance spiral became a public policy issue, and there was talk of moving. The decline was attributed to mediocrity on the field, the age of the ballpark, inadequate parking, and a declining neighborhood. In 1970 Mayor John Lindsey responded to the Yankees' call for help by promising the municipality would support the team as it had the Mets, who played at the city's $25.5 million Shea Stadium. In March 1971 Lindsay announced the city would buy the stadium and lease it back on favorable terms for 30 years. The $25 million project ended up costing $97.4 million plus another $16 million for improved highway access.

MacPhail made several moves before the 1972 season, including a terrible trade with the White Sox, giving up Bahnsen for third baseman Rich McKinney, but he also traded first baseman Danny Cater to the Red Sox for much-needed reliever Sparky Lyle, who saved 35 games. The Yankees fell to fourth at 79–76, with attendance at a disturbingly low 966,328, the worst since World War II. CBS recognized their mistake in buying the club, in which they had not intended to invest money or energy. The company had lost money (as much as $1 million) in six of eight years. Broadcast revenues were down to $200,000, and the team had to pay to get on radio. CBS president William Paley decided to sell the club.

THE ERA OF GEORGE STEINBRENNER

Paley was offered, and rejected, a $14 million offer by a syndicate who wanted to move the team to the Meadowlands in nearby New Jersey. But Paley did not want the team to leave New York. Instead, on January 3, 1973, the team was sold to a syndicate that promised to stay in the city for a bargain $10 million, $3 million less than what CBS had paid, and about half the team's real value. The group was led by Cleveland shipbuilder George M. Steinbrenner III, whose personal investment was about $833,000. By 1979 he had bought 55 percent of the stock. Steinbrenner went into baseball with a win-at-all-costs mentality and was prepared to spend to achieve it. When he took over he got the city to put into the ballpark lease a clause permitting the Yankees to deduct maintenance expenses from rent. Thus in 1976, when the Yankees were back at the rebuilt stadium, they grossed $11.9 million. Under the old contract they would have paid $854,504 in rent, but the new agreement resulted in the city *owing* the Yankees $10,000. One year later, when the Yankees grossed $13.4 million, the city got just $170,681. By 2003 the rent was up to $11.4 million, but after deductions for various expenses, the Yankees paid just $5.1 million.

Steinbrenner eased Burke out as president for Gabe Paul, an experienced baseball executive, and promised to be an absentee owner. But he became involved in everything, including players' hairstyles. The team in 1973 continued to have good pitching, but the offense was moribund, and the Yankees finished fourth at 80–82. The stadium was shut down after the season for renovations, and some fans attending the final game brought wrecking tools to secure memorabilia.

When Houk resigned after the season Steinbrenner wanted to hire Dick Williams, the Oakland Athletics' skipper, but the league rejected the deal. Instead, the Yankees hired Bill Virdon. Paul began rebuilding, bringing in Lou Piniella, Elliott Maddox, Chris Chambliss, and Dick Tidrow. The Yankees played at Shea and finished second (89–73) in the Eastern Division in 1974, with the second-highest attendance in the AL. Dobson and Doc Medich each won 19 games. Steinbrenner was indicted on April 5 on 14 felony counts for illegal contributions to the 1972 Nixon presidential campaign. In August he pleaded guilty to having authorized $142,000 in illegal corporate contributions to various politicians and giving a "false and misleading explanation" about a $25,000 campaign gift. He was fined $15,000 but, surprisingly, did not get jail time. Commissioner Bowie Kuhn suspended him for two years.

The Yankees improved their lineup for 1975 by trading Bobby Murcer for Bobby Bonds, who hit 32 homers, and signing free agent and Cy Young winner Catfish Hunter to a five-year, $4.75 million contract. Hunter had just led the

A's to their third straight Series title. He was declared a free agent by an arbiter because his boss, Charles Finley, had not fulfilled an annuity clause in Hunter's contract. Hunter pitched every fourth day for the Yankees and did a brilliant job. He went 23–14, pitching 30 complete games, seven shutouts, and 328 innings, with an ERA of 2.58. But the team only went 83–77, coming in third despite outscoring the opposition by nearly 100 runs. Steinbrenner, who was running the team behind the scenes, was very disappointed in the team's performance. He changed managers on Old Timers' Day, August 1, bringing in Billy Martin. Martin was experienced, creative, aggressive, inspirational, and tough. He also provided a connection to the Yankees' golden era. Martin had worked wonders with his previous teams, getting them to play over their heads, but had a history of drinking too much, getting out of control, and being fired.

The team reshaped itself with several trades, sending Pat Dobson to Cleveland for Oscar Gamble, Bonds to California for Mickey Rivers and Ed Figueroa, and Doc Medich to Pittsburgh for Doc Ellis and rookie Willie Randolph. They combined with stars Hunter and Munson, and the invaluable third baseman Graig Nettles and first baseman Chris Chambliss. Then on June 15 pitcher Rudy May and four players were sent to Oakland for hurlers Ken Holtzman, Doyle Alexander, and Grant Jackson. The Yankees also bought star pitcher Vida Blue of the A's for $1.5 million, as Finley was breaking up his club because of concerns about spiraling salaries due to free agency and arbitration. However, the commissioner voided the sale in the best interests of baseball.

The Yankees easily took the division with 97 wins, 10 1/2 games ahead of Baltimore. The Yankees were second in offense, emphasizing speed, with 162 stolen bases, and led in defense and pitching. Hunter had a sore shoulder and won just 17, but Figueroa won 19 and Ellis 17, and Alexander and Holtzman combined for another 19. Munson was selected as MVP. The excellent play, along with the reopening of Yankee Stadium, helped nearly double attendance, and marked the first time the Yankees outdrew the Mets since 1964.

The Yankees took on the Royals, who had stolen over 200 bases and had excellent defense, in the AL Championship Series. The series was tied 2–2 going into the decisive game five. Martin sent out Figueroa with three days' rest rather than the well-rested Alexander or Holtzman, whom Martin had never wanted on the team. The Yankees led 6–3 going into the eighth, but Grant Jackson gave up a three-run homer to George Brett to tie the game. Then Chambliss, who batted .524 in the ALCS, led off the ninth inning with a home run to win the pennant. The Yankees took on Cincinnati's powerful Big Red Machine in the World Series. Munson played brilliantly, batting .529, but the Yankees were completely outclassed and handily lost all four games.

The Yankees were not discouraged, and became very active in signing more experienced talent through the new reentry draft, held to determine negotiating rights to 24 free agents. The Bombers signed former A's slugger Reggie Jackson for $2.5 million over five years. His stroke was made for the short right-field porch. Trades brought in Bucky Dent to fill a glaring need at shortstop and pitcher Mike Torrez.

Jackson was energized to be on center stage in New York City, but his teammates were not crazy about Reggie and his ego, especially after he told *Sport* magazine that "I'm the straw that stirs the drink." Team captain Munson, who already felt undercompensated and taken for granted, was especially irritated. The team's internal problems led Graig Nettles to nickname it the Bronx Zoo.

Despite fielding a nearly All-Star lineup, the Yankees struggled through mid-June. Martin and Jackson had a major argument on June 18. In the sixth inning, with the Red Sox up 7–4 and Fred Lynn on first base, Jim Rice hit a check-swing fly to short right. Jackson was playing him deep and did not break sharply for the ball, which dropped in front of him for a bloop double. As Martin jumped out of the dugout to change pitchers, he also took out Jackson for his lazy play. Their dugout harangue was captured on national TV.

The Yankees got hot in the second half of the season, feasting on weak teams. Rookie Ron Guidry became a starter and won 16 games. Rivers hit .326 and Munson .308, and Jackson had 110 RBIs, nearly half in the last 50 games. The Yankees finished the season with a 40–10 run, winning their division with a record of 100–62. Sparky Lyle, with 26 saves and 72 appearances, won the Cy Young Award. The Yankees played the Royals in the ALCS and won in five, taking the final game 5–3 with a three-run rally in the ninth inning.

The Yankees met the Dodgers in the World Series. The Yankees won the first game 4–3 with strong relief from Sparky Lyle, who came in in the 9th inning and pitched through the 12th, when the winning run scored. Catfish Hunter, out for a month, started game two but was knocked out early, and the Yankees lost. The series shifted to Dodger Stadium, where Torrez and Guidry each pitched shutouts, with the Dodgers salvaging game five. Back in New York the Dodgers were up 3–2 in the fourth when Jackson hit a two-run homer; he hit another two-run homer in the fifth, and homered again in the eighth. Yankees won 8–3 and captured the series, their first since 1962. Jackson had homered in his last at bat in game five and walked in his first appearance the next game, meaning he had hit four straight homers. "Mr. October," the Series MVP, had five homers in all, with 25 total bases, both Series records, and batted .450.

By 1978 the team was worth $25 million. Gabe Paul retired and Al Rosen, Steinbrenner's boyhood idol with the Indians, became team president, and Cedric Tallis general manager. There were a lot of problems on and off the field. Most of the starters had arm problems and Lyle was upset that the Yankees brought in the younger Goose Gossage, who had already twice led the AL in saves. Gossage ended up with a 2.01 ERA and won the Rolaids Reliever of the Year Award with 27 saves. Martin was unhappy that his pal pitching coach Art Fowler was demoted, and his relations with Jackson remained difficult. In July Munson was put into right field to ease his aching knees, making Jackson the DH, which put him into a funk. On July 17 Munson led off the 10th inning of a game with the Royals with a single. Jackson, for the first time all season, was signaled to bunt. He fouled one off, and after Martin took off the signal he bunted twice more and popped out. Martin suspended Reggie and fined him $12,500. A few days later, an inebriated Martin told reporters that George and Reggie "deserve each other. One's a born liar, and the other's convicted." Steinbrenner blew a gasket and Martin had to resign. Ironically, they had recently taped a Miller Lite commercial in which they argued about "tastes great, less filling" that ended with George telling Billy, "You're fired."

Martin was replaced by an entirely opposite personality, mellow Bob Lemon, the former great pitcher, Yankees pitching coach in 1976, and recently fired manager of the White Sox. When Lemon was hired the Yankees were 14 games behind Boston. Lemon restored the old lineup with Munson at catcher and Jackson in right field and the squad turned things around, going 48–20 for the rest of the season. On Old Timers' Day, the Yankees, bizarrely, announced that Lemon would manage through 1979 and then move up to general manager, with Martin back as skipper. The Yankees made up 10 games in the pennant race by September 7, when they staged a four-game sweep at Fenway Park known as the Boston Massacre, winning by a cumulative score of 42–9. The team had been held together that season by the pitching staff, the best in the AL, especially by 160-pound Ron Guidry, who had an excellent fastball (nicknamed "Louisiana Lightning") and a superb slider. On June 17, he struck out 18 batters to tie the then-current major-league record. He went 25–3 for the season, with a winning percentage of .893, a 1.74 ERA, and nine shutouts, all league-leading performances, and won the Cy Young Award. This may have been the finest performance ever by a Yankees pitcher.

The Yankees were up a game over the Red Sox going into the final day, but lost to the Indians 9–2, while the Sox won. A playoff was held on October 2 at Fenway with Mike Torrez of the Sox and Guidry, both starting on three days' rest. The Yankees were down 2–0 going into the seventh when Chambliss and White singled. After two outs, Dent, who had hit just .140 in his last 20 games, came up, yet Lemon let him bat because there was no one else to play short. Torrez got two quick strikes, and then Dent hit a painful foul ball off his left foot. After a five-minute wait, Dent went back into the batter's box, and propelled the next pitch over the left-field wall for a three-run homer, giving the Yankees the lead. The drama peaked in the bottom of the ninth, when Gossage gave up two runs and the Sox had the tying run on base. Jerry Remy hit a soft liner to right that Piniella lost in the sun, but he put out his glove where he guessed the ball was coming, and made the catch. Then Carl Yastrzemski came up with two out and the tying run on third, but popped up to Nettles, and the Yankees were division champs with a record of 100–63. The Yankees then defeated Kansas City in the ALCS in a competitive four-game series and moved on to the World Series.

The Series opponents were the Dodgers, who had the best batting, pitching, and defense in the NL. The Dodgers took the first two games in Los Angeles, 11–5 and 4–3. The Yankees came back in New York, 5–1, behind Guidry and spectacular play by Nettles at the hot corner. In game four the club was down

3–1 in the sixth with Munson and Jackson on base. Piniella hit a low liner to shortstop Bill Russell, who dropped it, then ran to second to force Jackson and threw to first for the double play. Jackson stopped on the baseline and purposefully stuck out his hip to deflect the throw, for what seemed intentional interference. But the umpire did not so rule, enabling Munson to score. The Yankees tied the game in the eighth on a Jackson double and won in extra innings. The fifth game was a 12–2 route in which Munson had five RBIs. Hunter closed out the series in game six by a 7–2 score. Denny Doyle, a late-season fill-in for the injured Randolph, hit a surprising .438, with 10 hits and eight RBIs, and was named Series MVP.

Despite the two straight World Series championships, the roof fell in on the Yankees, partly through bad luck, as Hunter, Figueroa, and Jim Beattie all got sore arms and Gossage tore his ligaments in a scuffle with catcher Cliff Johnson and missed half the season. But in addition, Steinbrenner poisoned the clubhouse atmosphere and allowed the organization to become dysfunctional, which discouraged free agents. Steinbrenner had no confidence in young players, trading off his best prospects, nor was he loyal to veterans like disgruntled Sparky Lyle, who was shipped off to Texas for Dave Righetti, the top minor-league pitching prospect. At midseason, when the Yankees were 34–31, Steinbrenner unceremoniously fired Lemon and brought back Billy Martin, thrilling the fans, but not the players. Then, on August 2, Munson crashed his new eight-seat Cessna while practicing landings. His death took the life out of the team. The Yankees' offense was dismal, finishing 10th in run production, although the pitching was second in the league, abetted by free agents Luis Tiant, who won 13, and Tommy John, who won 21, while Guidry won 18 with an ERA of 2.78. The Yankees' slide to 89–71, fourth in the AL East, was a better record than California's, which won the AL West. After the season, Martin got into a fight at a hotel bar with a marshmallow salesman, sending him to the hospital, and he was immediately fired. Coach Dick Howser, a former Yankees infielder, took over as manager. Steinbrenner named himself president and made former shortstop Gene Michael general manager.

The 1980 Yankees rebounded in a big way, winning 103 games, the most since 1963. Rick Cerone was secured from the Blue Jays for Chambliss to fill Munson's shoes as catcher. The Yankees had the second-best pitching and offense, led by Jackson, who had a superb season with a league-leading 41 homers and a .300 average, second only to new first baseman Bob Watson's .307, and John had 22 victories. However, the team faltered in the playoffs, losing the ALCS in three straight games to Kansas City. The key play occurred in the second game, when, down 3–2 with Randolph on first, Watson hit a double. Randolph stumbled between first and second, but coach Mike Ferraro still sent him home, and he was out. Ferraro became the scapegoat for the disappointing series, and Steinbrenner wanted him fired. Howser demurred, and so he was terminated. General manager Gene Michael became manager.

By 1981, Steinbrenner had had enough of Reggie, replacing him with free agent Dave Winfield of the Padres, who signed a 10-year contract with a base salary of $1.4 million, an annual 10 percent cost-of-living escalator, and contributions to his future charity. The contract was eventually worth $23 million. On June 12, a strike began over free-agent compensation, with the Yankees in first with a record of 34–22. After the owners caved in on August 8, Commissioner Kuhn set up a split-season plan that put teams into the playoffs if they were in first place at the break or after the second half of the season. The Yankees went through the motions in the second half, and after 26 games, Michael was fired and Lemon was brought back. They ended up 25–26, in sixth place. Other AL teams had better overall records, but the Yankees were in the playoffs. Guidry led the league with 11 wins. Winfield hit .292, and Jackson led the team in homers and RBIs, but dropped to .237. Righetti at 8–4 was Rookie of the Year. The Yankees defeated Milwaukee in the first round of the playoffs, and then swept Billy Martin's A's in the ALCS. The Yankees faced the Dodgers in the World Series, and won the first two games in New York, but lost the next three in LA, all by one run, and were clobbered back home in game six, 9–2. Winfield was a big disappointment, going 1 for 22, while reliever George Frazier lost three games, tying Lefty Williams's 1919 record for most losses in one World Series.

Steinbrenner opened his checkbook wide open after the season. The Yankees signed Cincinnati outfielders Ken Griffey and the extremely fast Dave Collins, but traded their own speedy prospect, Willie McGee. Jackson became a free agent, but never got an offer from the Yankees and moved on to the Angels. During his five seasons in New York, he hit 144 homers, with a .400 average and 8 homers in three World Series. He was a terrific attraction, and attendance went up each season, reaching a record 2.6 million in 1980.

Winfield altered his batting approach after Jackson was gone, looking for the long ball. He hit 37 homers, the most of any right-handed Yankee other than DiMaggio. But the team was on the skids, overpaying for over-the-hill free agents, making poor trades, and depleting the farm system. Lemon was fired after a 6–8 start and Michael returned, but he only lasted 86 games. He was replaced by Clyde King, the pitching coach in 1981. The team ended in fifth (79–83). Steinbrenner attracted a lot of negative attention, complaining about the ballpark and its neighborhood. He also had a falling-out with Winfield, who sued him to get $300,000 promised for his foundation.

On January 11, 1983, the Yankees rehired Billy Martin, recently fired by Oakland, for the third time, and the team improved to 91–71, good for third. There were some interesting moments. On July 4 Dave Righetti pitched the first Yankees regular-season no-hitter since 1951. Twenty days later, the Yankees were up 4–3 against Kansas City when George Brett hit a two-run homer off Gossage. However, Martin protested that Brett's bat had pine tar beyond the permitted 18 inches, and umpire Tim McClelland called Brett out. However, AL president Lee MacPhail ruled the bat should have been thrown out, the homer counted, and the game replayed. Later that season, in Toronto, when Winfield was warming up in the outfield before the fifth inning, one of his throws hit and killed a seagull. He was afterward charged with cruelty to animals, but the complaint was dropped the next day. Finally, in September, Martin was suspended for fighting umpires.

Martin was fired in December and replaced by Yogi Berra, who had managed back in 1964. Twenty-three-year-old Don "Donnie Ball" Mattingly, a 19th-round draft choice, took over at first base and became a big hero with New York fans, who respected his work ethic, great fielding, and outstanding batting. He led the league in batting in 1984 at .343 and was MVP in 1985, with 145 RBIs. Two years later he hit homers in 10 straight games. He was a six-time All-Star and nine-time Gold Glover. He played for 14 years and had a lifetime .307 batting average. The Yankees, led by Winfield and Mattingly, had a terrific offensive team and a first-rate closer in Righetti, who had 31 saves, but lacked starting pitching. The team ended up in third in its division, 87–75.

In 1985 the Yankees made a great acquisition by bringing in Rickey Henderson at a salary of nearly $1.5 million He was the Yankees' best leadoff man ever, and one of their most flamboyant players, snatching flies one-handed. He stole 80 bases and scored 146 runs. During his four and a half years in New York, he hit around .300, led the league in steals three times, and set records for leadoff home runs. The Yankees started out slowly at 6–10, and Steinbrenner pulled the plug on Berra and brought back Billy Martin. The team went 97–64, second in the division.

Managerial musical chairs continued in 1986, with Lou Piniella the new manager. The team went 90–72, again good for second. Mattingly was outstanding, batting .352 with 238 hits, the most in team history. Dennis Rasmussen was the only solid starter (18–6), but the strength of the pitching corps was Righetti, with 46 saves. The next season the team had an almost identical mark of 89–73, but fell to fourth place. A disappointed Steinbrenner sacked Piniella and went back to Martin. But early in 1988, he got into a brawl in a topless bar, and was fired for the last time. He had managed the Yankees six times, with a record of 556–385 (.591) and two World Series championships. Piniella was brought back with the Yankees at 40–28, and the team ended up at 85–76, fifth place, but only three and a half games out of first. Winfield and Jack Clark both knocked in over 100 runs, but the pitching was abysmal. Attendance was 2,627,417, a new team record.

Dallas Green was the new skipper in 1989, brought in to run a very tight ship. He got along poorly with Steinbrenner, whom he felt was a meddler. The team struggled, and after amassing a 56–65 record, Green was sacked and Bucky Dent was in. The season ended a dismal 74–87, for fifth place. Winfield missed the entire season with back surgery, and the pitching staff was even worse than the year before.

The Yankees hit rock bottom in 1990, finishing last (67–95). On May 16 Winfield was traded to California after it was revealed Steinbrenner had paid small-time crook Howard Spira $40,000 for derogatory information about Winfield's foundation. As a Yankee, Winfield had 1,300 hits, 205 homers, and 818 RBIs. Steinbrenner's unprofessional conduct resulted in a two-year suspension from Commissioner Fay Vincent. The team was a disaster, with the worst offense and defense in the league, and an especially poor pitching rotation. Dent was out after 49 games, and Stump Merrill was promoted from Triple-A to be the new manager. One game that epitomized the season was Andy Hawkins's no-hitter, which he lost 4–0. After another dismal season in 1991, in spite of salaries skyrocketing from 28 percent to 54 percent of the team's budget, Merrill was replaced by minor-league manager Buck Showalter. Given Steinbrenner's track record, no one would have predicted that the Yankees would only have two managers since 1992.

Notwithstanding the poor play, the Yankees were doing well financially, drawing nearly 1.9 million in 1991, and signed a 12-year deal with the Madison Square Garden cable system worth $50 million annually. Fans hoped that with Steinbrenner out of the picture (he would return on March 1, 1993), the team might sign some important free agents. In 1992 outfielder Danny Tartabull signed a four-year deal for $25 million, the biggest contract in team history, surpassing Mattingly, who was making $3.6 million. Tartabull batted .266 with 85 RBIs and a team-leading 26 homers. The offense was about average for the league, but the pitching was near the bottom. The team improved slightly to 78–86 for fourth place, but attendance dropped to 1.7 million, the eighth straight year the Mets outdrew them.

The front office did a terrific job in 1993, building up the team with free agents Wade Boggs at third ($2.95 million) and pitcher Jimmy Key ($4.9 million), who went 18–6, and the trade of Roberto Kelly for Paul O'Neill of the Reds, a very tough player whose swing was made for the short right-field fence. It was a veteran team, averaging 30 years of age, abetted by the new center fielder, switch-hitter Bernie Williams, a product of the Yankees' farm system. The offense was very strong, leading the league in batting average (.271) and second in homers (178). The team briefly tied for first in September, but with below-average pitching and injuries to Mattingly and Tartabull, the team ended in second, at 88–72. Attendance rose to 2.4 million, a 38 percent improvement over the prior season.

Realignment took place in 1994, dividing the AL into three divisions, with the champions and a fourth team with the best record making the playoffs. In August the season was halted by a strike caused by conflict over the salary cap, and there was no World Series. The Yankees had the best record in the AL at 70–43. The offense was outstanding, batting .290, tops in the league, led by O'Neill (.359), who led the league, and Boggs (.342). Jimmy Key was sensational, with a record of 17–4.

The following season began poorly as the strike continued into spring training. After the dispute was settled, 18 games were cut off the season. The Yankees struggled all year, with a much weaker offense and mediocre pitching. Few players came close to their 1994 performances. The Yankees traded for starting pitcher Jack McDowell and Expos star closer John Wetteland, but Key was out for the year with a torn rotator cuff. At midseason the squad secured Toronto's David Cone, about to become a free agent. He and rookie Andy Pettitte both won nine in the second half of the season, propelling the Yankees to their best September in 10 years. The team finished 79–65 and won the wild-card berth for the playoffs. They faced Western Division champion Seattle in the AL Divisional Series, winning the first two games, but lost the next four and were eliminated. Playing in his first postseason series, Mattingly hit .417 with 10 hits and six RBIs. Steinbrenner was fined $50,000 for complaining about the umpiring.

Steinbrenner took out his disappointment on his staff, pushing out general manager Michael. Five men turned down the job until Houston general manager Bob Watson, a former Yankee, took it. He was the first African American hired by the Yankees to a major front-office job. Manager Showalter was offered a new two-year contract, but was told to get a new batting coach. He refused, and he was out, replaced by a man with no connections to the Yankees, Brooklyn's own Joe Torre, a former NL star, who had managed several mediocre teams. He was considered flexible, and would operate around his players' strengths. Joe got a two-year contract, but Steinbrenner appointed a lot of the staff, including pitching coach Mel Stottlemyre.

In 1996 Mattingly was unceremoniously pushed out at first base after the Yankees traded two young pitchers to Seattle for first baseman Tino Martinez and reliever Jeff Nelson. The starting lineup was bolstered with 22-year-old Derek Jeter, a former first-round draftee at shortstop. The team was so confident in him that he was given a prestigious single-digit uniform number (2). During the season the team added Darryl Strawberry, who had started the year in independent baseball, and prior to the trading deadline sent Ruben Sierra to Detroit for highly paid ($9.2 million) right-handed slugger Cecil Fielder. The team's batting average of .288, which included four .300 hitters, was second in the league, but they were only ninth in runs scored, as Torre emphasized "small ball." Pitching was the key, and Cone was signed as a free agent along with Kenny Rogers, who replaced McDowell. When Cone had an operation to replace part of an artery in his arm, his spot in the rotation was taken by free agent "Doc" Gooden, trying to salvage his career. Gooden struggled at first, but on May 14 pitched a no-hitter, and won seven of his next eight decisions. The starters were mediocre except for Andy Pettitte, who won 21 games, but the relief corps was outstanding, with setup men Nelson and Mariano Rivera and closer Wetteland. Torre managed for short games, since any late lead was secure. The team went 70–3 when leading in the sixth inning. In September Cone bolstered the staff with his return, throwing a seven-inning no-hitter his first time out. The Yankees won 92 games and took the AL East.

The Yankees defeated the Rangers in the playoffs, three games to one, and then played wild-card winner Baltimore. In the first game at Yankee Stadium, the Yankees were down 4–2 in the eighth inning when Jeter hit a fly ball toward the right-field seats. Twelve-year-old Jeffrey Maier reached out into the playing field and grabbed the ball. The umpire mistakenly ruled it a home run, tying the game. Williams won the game in the 11th with a home run. The Orioles took the second game, but the Yankees won the next three.

The Yankees faced the defending world champion Atlanta Braves in the World Series and lost the first two games at home, 12–1 and 4–0. In Atlanta, Torre stacked the lineup with right-handed batters against Tom Glavine, and the Yankees won 5–2. Rogers pitched poorly in game four, and the Braves coasted to a seemingly insurmountable 6–0 lead. The Yankees got three in the sixth, and then in the eighth, after 99-mph closer Mark Wohlers gave up two singles, Jim Leyritz hit a slider into the left-field seats to tie the game. The Yankees scored twice in the 10th to win, Boggs driving in the go-ahead run with a bases-loaded walk. The Yankees had made up the biggest margin in Series history since 1929. In the fifth game, Pettitte, with relief help, shut out the Braves 1–0. In game six, Key took the Yankees to a 3–1 lead in the sixth, and the bullpen closed out the game. The Yankees had won the series, four games to two.

In 1997 the Yankees lost Wetteland and Key to free agency, but signed pitcher David Wells and traded several prospects and $3 million for the rights to Japanese hurler Hideki Irabu, who was a bust. The team led the AL in pitching and was second in batting, finishing with a record of 96–66, second in the East. Martinez had 44 homers and drove in 141 runs. The Yankees took on the Indians in the playoffs, and lost a hard-fought series three games to two.

After the season Steinbrenner made several adjustments, including trading Kenny Rogers for third baseman Scott Brosius and bringing in Chili Davis to DH. Watson resigned, unhappy that many changes were made without his input, and was replaced by his assistant, 31-year-old Brian Cashman. Cashman obtained Twins All-Star second baseman Chuck Knoblauch, an excellent leadoff man, for cash and several outstanding prospects. The team started the year with a $72 million payroll, which included big raises to Pettitte ($3.8 million) and Williams ($8 million) to avoid arbitration.

The team was expected to repeat, and in April went 17–6. The season was disrupted on April 13 when a support beam fell in the stadium, which was temporarily closed for repairs. One game was shifted to Shea, and a home series was switched to Detroit. By the end of June the team was 56–20, yet no player was elected to start the All-Star Game. Two months later the record stood at 94–32, and thereafter the team coasted to a final mark of 114–48 (.704), second only to the 116 victories by the Cubs in 1906. They scored 965 runs, nearly one run per game more than the league average, while giving up just 656, one per game fewer than the league average of five. Williams led the league with a .339 average. Six pitchers won 10 or more games, led by Cone (20–7) and Wells (18–4), who on May 17 pitched a perfect game. The starting staff was bolstered by the addition of 32-year-old Cuban refugee Orlando "El Duque" Hernandez, who signed a four-year, $6.6 million contract, and won 12 games in half a season. The team set an attendance record of 2.95 million.

The Yankees started the playoffs by sweeping the Rangers, with Wells and Cone pitching shutouts. The Yankees outscored the Rangers 12–1 and gave up just 13 hits. In the ALCS against the power-laden Indians, the Yankees persevered, four games to two, led by two victories by Wells. The Yankees moved on to the World Series against the San Diego Padres. Wells started game one, but was hit hard, and the Padres took a 5–2 lead into the sixth, when the Yankees scored seven runs. In game two, the Yankees had a seven-run lead after the third, and coasted behind Hernandez to a 9–3 win. Then, at Qualcomm Park, the Padres led 3–0 in the seventh when, led by two Brosius homers, the Yankees stormed back to win 5–4. The sweep was completed the next day, 3–0. The series was a success for the Yankees, but drew the lowest TV ratings in history. In all, the Yankees earned 125 wins and made some claim to be the greatest team of all time. Forbes estimated the team to be worth $425 million, 60 percent of which belonged to Steinbrenner.

The Yankees rearmed for 1999 by signing their own players, beginning with Bernie Williams, who got an $87.5 million contract for seven years. The club traded David Wells, their popular, out-of-shape, free-spirited left-hander, who had gone 27–7 in New York, with pitcher Graeme Lloyd and infielder Homer Bush to Toronto for future Hall of Famer Roger Clemens. The team started well, led by Jeter, who reached base in the first 53 games of the season. He led the league with 219 hits and reaching base 322 times, and was second in batting (.349), just ahead of Bernie Williams (.342). The team staged Yogi Berra Day on July 18, marking the end of his long estrangement from the Yankees. Afterward, David Cone threw an 88-pitch perfect game. The Yankees won 98 games to lead the AL East. Hernandez had 17 victories, and Rivera earned 45 saves and won the Rolaids Relief Award. The Yankees were a great attraction on the road and in the Bronx, where they drew a team record 3,292,736.

The Yankees slaughtered Texas in the opening round of the playoffs, winning three straight games by a total score of 15–1, and moved on to the ALCS with their hated foe, the Red Sox. The Yankees took the first two games, but were thumped in the highly anticipated Clemens-Martinez clash, 13–1. However, the Yankees won the next two contests handily, 9–2 and 6–1, to close out the Red Sox. The Yankees faced the Braves in the World Series. In game one, the Braves were up at home 1–0 in the eighth, even though Hernandez was pitching a one-hitter. But the Yankees scored four runs to win. The Yankees took game two behind Cone 7–2. In game three, at Yankee Stadium, the Braves knocked out Pettitte in the fourth and took a 5–1 lead. But three Yankee homers tied the game, and Chad Curtis homered in the bottom of the 10th to win the game. Clemens won the final 3–1, making the Yanks the first team to win the Series with back-to-back sweeps since the 1938–39 Yankees. Rivera was Series MVP. The Yankees had gone 22–3 over the past two postseasons.

The Yankees in 2000 had a huge payroll of nearly $93 million, with Williams and Cone at around $12 million and Jeter at $10 million. Ten players earned over $5 million, and another 10 were millionaires. Wages comprised over 60 percent of team expenditures for the first time since 1993 (and peaked at over 70% in 2003). The team started well, going 22–9, but the starting pitching was not reliable, and the Yankees slumped to 37–35. Several important trades were made, especially one that brought in power hitter David Justice. The Yankees had an excellent summer, and by mid-September they were well ahead at 84–59. But they slumped terribly at the end, losing 16 of the last 19 games, and were big underdogs as postseason play began against the Athletics. In the ALDS, Torre made Knoblauch a DH and sent Cone to the bullpen. The teams split the first four games, but the Yankees prevailed in the deciding fifth game in Oakland 7–5. They then met the Mariners, and prevailed in six games. The match was highlighted by Roger Clemens's 15-strikeout, one-hit shutout in game four.

This set up a subway World Series with the Mets, the first since 1956. There were a lot of ill feelings between the teams, mainly because Clemens had beaned star catcher Mike Piazza on July 8 during interleague play. The Mets appeared on their way to winning the first game with a 3–2 lead in the ninth when O'Neill fouled off 10 pitches from closer Armando Benitez to earn a walk and load the bases. Knoblauch followed with a sacrifice fly to tie the game. Then in the 12th, Jose Vizcaino singled in the winning run. In game two, Clemens broke Piazza's bat, with a large piece ending up near the pitcher's mound, which Clemens then threw at Piazza, running to first. The Yankees took a 6–0 lead into the ninth and won 6–5. The Mets took the third game, beating Hernandez, who had been 8–0 in postseason play, breaking the Yankees' streak of consecutive Series victories at 14. The Yankees came back to capture the next game 3–2 behind the strong relief work of Cone and Rivera. The fifth game was tied 2–2 going into the ninth when Al Leiter's 142nd pitch resulted in a single by Luis Sojo, driving in the go-ahead run. The Yankees scored another run, and Rivera closed out the series in the bottom of the ninth. Derek Jeter was Series MVP.

After the season, Nelson and Cone left as free agents, while Mike Mussina, who had already won 147 games for the Orioles, was added as a free agent. The payroll was $117,936,000, slightly less than the Red Sox's. Knoblauch was shifted to the outfield to make way for Alfonso Soriano at second base. The baseball season was canceled for nearly a week after 9/11, and the Yankees played out of town until September 25, when a big ceremony was held in honor of policemen and firemen killed in that tragedy The Yankees won the Eastern Division with a record of 95–65, powered by 204 home runs and pitching. Clemens went 20–3, including 16 straight wins, tying the club record, and he, Pettitte, and Mussina all struck out over 200 batters. Clemens won the Cy Young Award, and Rivera, with 50 saves, received the Rolaids Award. Yet the club was an underdog in the ALDS against the hot Athletics, with 102 wins. The A's took the two games in Oakland. The series shifted to Yankee Stadium. The key play occurred in game three with the Yankees, with only two hits in the entire game, up 1–0 late in the contest. Jeremy Giambi singled, and when Terrence Long followed with a double into the right-field corner, he tried to score when Shane Spencer threw the ball back beyond the cutoff men. However, Jeter had raced in from shortstop to help out, and caught the errant throw while running full-speed into foul territory. He tossed it backhand to Posada to tag out Giambi at the plate, saving the game. Yankees took the next two games, 9–2 and 5–3, to finish off the A's.

The underdogs then took on the Mariners, who had won a record 116 games. The Yankees, surprisingly, took the first two games in Seattle, but lost the third in New York, 13–2. In the next game, Seattle took a 1–0 lead in the top of the eighth, but Williams homered in the bottom of the frame to tie it. In the ninth, Rivera got three outs on three pitches, and then Soriano homered after a Brosius single to win the game. The next day, Pettitte, the ALCS MVP, pitched the Yankees into the World Series with a 12–3 victory.

The Yankees then faced the Arizona Diamondbacks with Curt Schilling and Randy Johnson. The Diamondbacks took the first two games in Phoenix handily, 9–1 and 4–0. Back in New York the Yankees, behind Clemens, took the third game 2–1. Schilling came back on three days' rest and left in the eighth up 3–1. Byung-Hyun Kim struck out the side in the eighth, but with one out in the ninth, O'Neill singled and Martinez homered on the next pitch, tying up the game. This was the first Series game since 1947 that a team down by two runs in the ninth had caught up. Jeter homered in the next inning to win the game. On the following day Kim tried to protect a 2–0 lead in the ninth, but gave up a double to Posada and a two-out homer to Brosius to tie the game. The Yankees won the game in the 12th when Soriano singled home Knoblauch. Back at Bank One Ballpark, Arizona took the sixth game 15–2, with a record 22 hits. The decisive seventh game featured Clemens against Schilling. The game was tied 1–1 in the eighth when Soriano homered. Rivera struck out the side in the eighth. In the ninth, Mark Grace singled softly to center. The next batter bunted, and Rivera threw it into center field. Another bunt followed. Rivera got a force-out at third, but Brosius held onto the ball and missed out on the potential double play. Tony Womack followed with a double down the right-field line, tying the game. With the infield drawn in, Luis Gonzalez hit a flare into center field to win the game and the series. The Yankees had been stymied by the Diamondback hurlers, batting only .183 and getting outscored 37–14.

In 2001, the Yankees were worth $635 million, nearly $200 million more than the Mets, the second-place team. That year regular-season game receipts were $98 million, the highest in the majors. The team had MLB's third-highest attendance and second-highest ticket price. They earned $47 million from operating revenues (concessions, parking, stadium advertising, and luxury boxes and club seats). The Yankees showed 50 games on local TV and 100 on cable, for which they were paid $56,750,000, nearly $20 million more than any other team except the Mets. Finally, the club earned $16 million from postseason play, $3 million more than the Diamondbacks, who had defeated them. After deducting expenses, the Yankees made $40,859,000 from baseball revenues. However, they had to pay $26 million in revenue sharing, leaving a net gain of $14,319,000, third highest behind Milwaukee and Seattle.

Steinbrenner made two major moves in free agency in 2002, bringing in slugger Jason Giambi to replace Tino Martinez at first and bringing back David Wells. The offense hit 223 homers and produced the most runs in the AL. Six men made the All-Star team, including Williams, who batted .333; Soriano, who led the league in hits (209), runs (128), and stolen bases (41) and was second in total bases (381); and Giambi, who had 122 RBIs and 41 homers The pitching was also strong, led by Wells with 19 wins and Mussina with 18. The result was an outstanding season, with a record of 103–58 and a team attendance record of 3,465,807. However, the pitching went south in the playoffs, and the Yankees were eliminated by the Anaheim Angels, three games to one.

In 2003, the team's payroll on Opening Day was $152,749,814, including 20 players at $1.5 million or more. The team had a superb season, finishing 101 61. Giambi had 41 homers and three Yankees had over 100 RBIs, including rookie Hideki Matsui, the "Godzilla" of Japanese baseball. Four pitchers won 15 or more games, led by Pettitte with 21, and Rivera led the AL in saves with 40. The Yankees won the ALDS 3–1 over Minnesota, followed by a memorable seven-game ALCS with the hated Red Sox. The closely matched teams split the first six games. In the deciding seventh game, the Sox had a 5–2 lead in the bottom of the eighth, but Pedro Martinez had tired. With one out Jeter doubled, Williams singled, and Matsui and Posada doubled to tie the score. Rivera came in in the ninth and pitched three innings. Then, in the bottom of the 11th, Aaron Boone hit a walk-off homer, and the Yankees were AL champions. After this drama, the Yankees seemed flat in the World Series against the Florida Marlins. After winning two of the first three games, they dropped the next three against surprisingly tough pitching for a disappointing conclusion to another exciting season.

The Yankees rearmed after the season, signing free agent Gary Sheffield, sending Jeff Weaver to the Dodgers for Kevin Brown, and securing superstar shortstop Alex Rodriguez from Texas for Soriano and other considerations. This helped propel the team's salary to $184,193,950. The Yankees took the division with 101 wins, powered by 242 homers and over 100 RBIs each from Sheffield, Matsui, and Rodriguez. The starting pitching struggled, often bailed out by Rivera, who won the Rolaids Award with 53 saves and a 1.94 ERA. The club led MLB in attendance with 3,775,292. The Yankees took the ALDS over the Twins three games to one, but faltered badly in the ALCS after winning the first three games handily. The Red Sox came back to win the next four games and capture the pennant.

The 2005 squad had a payroll of $208 million with the addition of Randy Johnson, Carl Pavano, and Jaret Wright, but suffered from an unreliable defense, little speed, and major injuries, which contributed to a patchwork pitching staff. The team struggled for most of the season, but willed themselves to 95 wins and the Eastern Division title. The team boasted a powerful lineup with 229 homers, led by Rodriguez, who had a superb season with 48 homers and 130 RBIs and won the AL MVP Award. However, he disappeared in the playoffs when most needed, and the club lost in five games to the Angels.

In the summer of 2005, plans were announced for an $800 million, 51,000-seat ballpark that will replicate the original Yankee Stadium. It will be located in the park across the street from the current site, part of a broader urban-redevelopment plan. The Yankees will pay all construction, operating, and maintenance costs. The city and state will pay an additional $220 million for parking garages and to replace the public parks where the field will be built.

The Yankees remain the outstanding professional sports franchise in North America, worth an estimated $1 billion in 2006. The club has drawn over 3 million spectators every year since 1999, including over 4 million in 2005. The organization continues to be a model of outstanding business and field management, with a newfound stability under Joe Torre. It was this success that set the Yankees apart, especially the incessant desire to continue as the best in their field. Second place is not an option.

NOTABLE ACHIEVEMENTS

Most Valuable Players

Year	Name	Position
1936	Lou Gehrig	1B
1939	Joe DiMaggio	OF
1941	Joe DiMaggio	OF
1942	Joe Gordon	2B
1943	Spud Chandler	P
1947	Joe DiMaggio	OF
1950	Phil Rizzuto	SS
1951	Yogi Berra	C
1954	Yogi Berra	C
1955	Yogi Berra	C
1956	Mickey Mantle	OF
1957	Mickey Mantle	OF
1960	Roger Maris	OF
1961	Roger Maris	OF
1962	Mickey Mantle	OF
1963	Elston Howard	C
1976	Thurman Munson	C
1985	Don Mattingly	1B
2005	Alex Rodriguez	3B

Cy Young Winners

Year	Name	Position
1958	Bob Turley	RHP
1961	Whitey Ford	LHP
1977	Sparky Lyle	LHP
1978	Ron Guidry	LHP
2001	Roger Clemens	RHP

Rookies of the Year

Year	Name	Position
1951	Gil McDougald	3B
1954	Bob Grim	P
1957	Tony Kubek	SS/OF
1962	Tom Tresh	SS/OF
1968	Stan Bahnsen	P
1970	Thurman Munson	C
1981	Dave Righetti	P
1996	Derek Jeter	SS

Batting Champions

Year	Name	#
1924	Babe Ruth	.378
1934	Lou Gehrig	.363
1939	Joe DiMaggio	.381
1940	Joe DiMaggio	.352
1945	Snuffy Stirnweiss	.309
1956	Mickey Mantle	.353
1984	Don Mattingly	.343
1994	Paul O'Neill	.359
1998	Bernie Williams	.339

Home-Run Champions

Year	Name	#
1916	Wally Pipp	12
1917	Wally Pipp	9
1920	Babe Ruth	54
1921	Babe Ruth	59
1923	Babe Ruth	41
1924	Babe Ruth	46
1925	Bob Meusel	33

1926	Babe Ruth	47
1927	Babe Ruth	60
1928	Babe Ruth	54
1929	Babe Ruth	46
1930	Babe Ruth	49
1931	Lou Gehrig	46
	Babe Ruth	46
1934	Lou Gehrig	49
1936	Lou Gehrig	49
1937	Joe DiMaggio	46
1944	Nick Etten	22
1948	Joe DiMaggio	39
1955	Mickey Mantle	37
1956	Mickey Mantle	52
1958	Mickey Mantle	42
1960	Mickey Mantle	40
1961	Roger Maris	61
1976	Graig Nettles	32
1980	Reggie Jackson	41
2005	Alex Rodriguez	48

ERA Champions

Year	Name	#
1920	Bob Shawkey	2.45
1927	Wilcy Moore	2.28
1934	Lefty Gomez	2.33
1937	Lefty Gomez	2.33
1943	Spud Chandler	1.64
1947	Spud Chandler	2.46
1952	Allie Reynolds	2.06
1953	Ed Lopat	2.42
1956	Whitey Ford	2.47
1957	Bobby Shantz	2.45
1958	Whitey Ford	2.01
1978	Ron Guidry	1.74
1979	Ron Guidry	2.78
1980	Rudy May	2.46

Strikeout Champions

Year	Name	#
1932	Red Ruffing	190
1933	Lefty Gomez	163

1934	Lefty Gomez	158
1937	Lefty Gomez	194
1951	Vic Raschi	164
1952	Allie Reynolds	160
1964	Al Downing	217

No-Hitters (Italics = Perfect Game)

Name	Date
George Mogridge	04/24/1917
Sam Jones	09/04/1923
Monte Pearson	08/27/1938
Allie Reynolds	07/12/1951
Allie Reynolds	09/28/1951
Don Larsen	*10/08/1956*
Dave Righetti	07/04/1983
Andy Hawkins	07/01/1990
Jim Abbott	09/04/1993
Dwight Gooden	05/14/1996
David Wells	*05/17/1998*
David Cone	*07/18/1999*

POSTSEASON APPEARANCES

AL East Division Titles

Year	Record	Manager
1976	97–62	Billy Martin
1977	100–62	Billy Martin
1978	100–63	Billy Martin
		Bob Lemon
1980	103–59	Dick Howser
1981	59–48	Gene Michael
		Bob Lemon
1994	70–43	Buck Showalter
1996	92–70	Joe Torre
1998	114–48	Joe Torre
1999	98–64	Joe Torre
2000	87–74	Joe Torre
2001	95–65	Joe Torre
2002	103–58	Joe Torre
2003	101–61	Joe Torre
2004	101–61	Joe Torre
2005	95–67	Joe Torre

AL Wild Cards

Year	Record	Manager
1995	79–65	Buck Showalter
1997	96–66	Joe Torre

AL Pennants

Year	Record	Manager
1921	98–55	Miller Huggins
1922	94–60	Miller Huggins
1923	98–54	Miller Huggins
1926	91–63	Miller Huggins
1927	110–44	Miller Huggins
1928	101–53	Miller Huggins
1932	107–47	Joe McCarthy
1936	102–51	Joe McCarthy
1937	102–52	Joe McCarthy
1938	99–53	Joe McCarthy
1939	106–45	Joe McCarthy
1941	101–53	Joe McCarthy
1942	103–41	Joe McCarthy
1943	98–56	Joe McCarthy
1947	97–57	Bucky Harris
1949	97–57	Casey Stengel
1950	98–56	Casey Stengel
1951	98–56	Casey Stengel
1952	95–59	Casey Stengel
1953	99–52	Casey Stengel
1955	97–57	Casey Stengel
1956	97–57	Casey Stengel
1957	98–56	Casey Stengel
1958	92–62	Casey Stengel
1960	97–57	Casey Stengel
1961	109–53	Ralph Houk
1962	96–66	Ralph Houk
1963	104–57	Ralph Houk
1964	99–63	Yogi Berra
1976	97–62	Billy Martin
1977	100–62	Billy Martin
1978	100–63	Billy Martin
		Bob Lemon
1981	59–48	Gene Michael

		Bob Lemon
1996	92–70	Joe Torre
1998	114–48	Joe Torre
1999	98–64	Joe Torre
2000	87–74	Joe Torre
2001	95–65	Joe Torre
2003	101–61	Joe Torre

World Championships

Year	Opponent	MVP
1923	New York	
1927	Pittsburgh	
1928	St. Louis	
1932	Chicago	
1936	New York	
1937	New York	
1938	Chicago	
1939	Cincinnati	
1941	Brooklyn	
1943	St. Louis	
1947	Brooklyn	
1949	Brooklyn	
1950	Philadelphia	
1951	New York	
1952	Brooklyn	
1953	Brooklyn	
1956	Brooklyn	Don Larsen
1958	Milwaukee	Bob Turley
1961	Cincinnati	Whitey Ford
1962	San Francisco	Ralph Terry
1977	Los Angeles	Reggie Jackson
1978	Los Angeles	Bucky Dent
1996	Atlanta	John Wetteland
1998	San Diego	Scott Brosius
1999	Atlanta	Mariano Rivera
2000	New York	Derek Jeter

MANAGERS

1996–	Joe Torre
1992–1995	Buck Showalter

1990–1991	Stump Merrill
1989–1990	Bucky Dent
1989	Dallas Green
1988	Lou Piniella
1988	Billy Martin
1986–1987	Lou Piniella
1985	Billy Martin
1984–1985	Yogi Berra
1983	Billy Martin
1982	Clyde King
1982	Gene Michael
1981–1982	Bob Lemon
1981	Gene Michael
1980	Dick Howser
1979	Billy Martin
1978–1979	Bob Lemon
1978	Dick Howser
1975–1978	Billy Martin
1974–1975	Bill Virdon
1966–1973	Ralph Houk
1965–1966	Johnny Keane
1964	Yogi Berra
1961–1963	Ralph Houk
1949–1960	Casey Stengel
1947–1948	Bucky Harris
1946	Johnny Neun
1946	Bill Dickey
1931–1946	Joe McCarthy
1930	Bob Shawkey
1929	Art Fletcher
1918–1929	Miller Huggins
1915–1917	Bill Donovan
1914	Roger Peckinpaugh
1913–1914	Frank Chance
1912	Harry Wolverton
1910–1911	Hal Chase
1909–1910	George Stallings
1908	Kid Elberfeld
1903–1908	Clark Griffith
1902	Wilbert Robinson (Orioles)
1901–1902	John McGraw (Orioles)

Team Records by Individual Players

Batting Leaders

	Single Season			Career	
	Name		Year	Name		Plate Appearances
Batting average	Babe Ruth	.393	1923	Babe Ruth	.349	9,197
On-base %	Babe Ruth	.545	1923	Babe Ruth	.484	9,197
Slugging %	Babe Ruth	.849	1920	Babe Ruth	.711	9,197
OPS	Babe Ruth	1.382	1920	Babe Ruth	1.195	9,197
Games	Hidcki Matsui	163	2003	Mickey Mantle	2,401	9,909
At bats	Alfonso Soriano	696	2002	Mickey Mantle	8,102	9,909
Runs	Babe Ruth	177	1921	Babe Ruth	1,960	9,197
Hits	Don Mattingly	238	1986	Lou Gehrig	2,721	9,660
Total bases	Babe Ruth	457	1921	Babe Ruth	5,131	9,197
Doubles	Don Mattingly	53	1986	Lou Gehrig	534	9,660
Triples	Earle Combs	23	1927	Lou Gehrig	163	9,660
Home runs	Roger Maris	61	1961	Babe Ruth	659	9,197
RBIs	Lou Gehrig	184	1931	Lou Gehrig	1,995	9,660
Walks	Babe Ruth	170	1923	Babe Ruth	1,852	9,197
Strikeouts	Alfonso Soriano	157	2002	Mickey Mantle	1,710	9,909
Stolen bases	Rickey Henderson	93	1988	Rickey Henderson	376	2,735
Extra-base hits	Babe Ruth	119	1921	Lou Gehrig	1,190	9,660
Times on base	Babe Ruth	379	1923	Babe Ruth	4,405	9,197

Pitching Leaders

	Single Season			Career	
	Name		Year	Name		Innings Pitched
ERA	Spud Chandler	1.64	1943	Goose Gossage	2.14	533
Wins	Jack Chesbro	41	1904	Whitey Ford	236	3,170.3
Won-loss %	Ron Guidry	.893	1978	Spud Chandler	.717	1,485
Hits/9 IP	Tommy Byrne	5.74	1949	Goose Gossage	6.59	533
Walks/9 IP	David Wells	0.85	2003	David Wells	1.47	851.7
Strikeouts	Ron Guidry	248	1978	Whitey Ford	1,956	3,170.3
Strikeouts/9 IP	David Cone	10.25	1997	David Cone	8.67	922
Games	Paul Quantrill	86	2004	Mariano Rivera	657	806.7
Saves	Mariano Rivera	53	2004	Mariano Rivera	379	806.7
Innings	Jack Chesbro	454.7	1904	Whitey Ford	3,170.3	3,170.3
Starts	Jack Chesbro	51	1904	Whitey Ford	438	3,170.3
Complete games	Jack Chesbro	48	1904	Red Ruffing	261	3,168.7
Shutouts	Ron Guidry	9	1978	Whitey Ford	45	3,170.3

Source: Drawn from data in "New York Yankees Batting Leaders (seasonal and career)." http://baseball-reference.com/teams/NYY/leaders_bat.shtml; "New York Yankees Pitching Leaders (seasonal and career)." http://baseball-reference.com/teams/NYY/leaders_pitch.shtml.

BIBLIOGRAPHY

Appel, Marty. *Now Pitching for the Yankees: Spinning the News for Mickey, Billy and George.* Toronto: Sport Classic Books, 2001.

Bagli, Charles V. "Yankees' Stadium Plans Stepping Up to the Plate." *New York Times,* June 15, 2005.

Cramer, Richard Ben. *Joe DiMaggio: The Hero's Life.* New York: Simon and Schuster, 2000.

Creamer, Robert. *Babe Ruth: The Legend Comes to Life.* New York: Simon and Schuster, 1974.

————. *Stengel: His Life and Times.* New York: Simon and Schuster, 1984.

Dewey, Donald, and Nicholas Acocella. *The Black Prince of Baseball: Hal Chase and the Mythology of the Game.* Wilmington, DE: Sport Classic Books, 2004.

Eig, Jonathan. *Luckiest Man: The Life and Times of Lou Gehrig.* New York: Simon and Schuster, 2005.

Fetter, Henry D. *Taking on the Yankees: Winning and Losing in the Business of Baseball, 1903–2003.* New York: Norton, 2003.

Fleming, Gordon H. *Murderers' Row.* New York: Morrow, 1985.

Gallagher, Mark, and Walter LeConte. *The Yankee Encyclopedia.* Champaign, IL: Sports Publishing, 2000.

Gentile, Derek. *The Complete New York Yankees: The Total Encyclopedia of the Team.* New York: Black Dog and Leventhal, 2004.

Goldman, Steven. *Forging Genius: The Making of Casey Stengel.* Dulles, VA: Potomac Books, 2005.

Golenbock, Peter. *Dynasty: The New York Yankees, 1949–1964.* Englewood Cliffs, NJ: Prentice Hall, 1975.

Hageman, William, and Warren Wilbert. *New York Yankees: Seasons of Glory.* Middle Village, NY: Jonathan David, 1999.

Halberstam, David. *Summer of '49.* New York: Morrow, 1989.

Haupert, Michael, and Kenneth Winter. "Pay Ball: Estimating the Profitability of the New York Yankees 1915–1937." *Essays in Economic and Business History: Selected Papers from the Economic and Business Historical Society* 21 (2003): 89–101.

————. "Yankee Profits and Promise: The Purchase of Babe Ruth and the Building of Yankee Stadium." In *The Cooperstown Symposium on Baseball and American Culture,* ed. William Simons. Jefferson, NC: McFarland, 2005, 197–214.

Kahn, Roger. *The Era: 1947–1957; When the Yankees, the New York Giants, and the Brooklyn Dodgers Ruled the World.* New York: Ticknor and Fields, 1993.

Kohout, Martin. *Hal Chase: The Defiant Life and Turbulent Times of Baseball's Biggest Crook.* Jefferson City, NC: McFarland, 2001.

Olney, Buster. *The Last Night of the Yankee Dynasty: The Game, the Team, and the Cost of Greatness.* New York: Ecco, 2004.

Reisler, Jim. *Babe Ruth: Launching the Legend.* New York: McGraw-Hill, 2004.

———. *Before They Were the Bombers: The New York Yankees' Early Years, 1903–1919.* Jefferson, NC: McFarland, 2002.

Riess, Steven A. *Touching Base: Professional Baseball and American Culture in the Progressive Era.* Rev. ed. Urbana: University of Illinois Press, 1999.

Robinson, Ray. *Iron Horse: Lou Gehrig in His Time.* New York: Norton, 1990.

Seidel, Michael. *Streak: Joe DiMaggio and the Summer of '41.* New York: Penguin, 1989.

Smelser, Marshall. *The Life That Ruth Built: A Biography.* New York: Quadrangle/ New York Times Book Co., 1975.

Stout, Glenn. *Yankees Century: 100 Years of New York Yankees Baseball.* Boston: Houghton Mifflin, 2002.

Sullivan, Neil J. *The Diamond in the Bronx: Yankee Stadium and the Politics of New York.* New York: Oxford University Press, 2001.

Tofel, Richard J. *A Legend in the Making: The New York Yankees in 1939.* Chicago: Ivan Dee, 2002.

Oakland Athletics

Robert F. Lewis II

In *Moneyball,* the most popular baseball book thus far in the twenty-first century, Michael Lewis analyzes the unorthodox approach that the Oakland A's, a small-market team, use to achieve competitive parity with clubs whose payroll is two to three times as great. His book centers on the major-league amateur draft of June 2002, as the A's were progressing to their third consecutive playoff appearance. Lewis, a former Wall Street broker who had achieved literary success a decade earlier with *Liar's Poker,* in an insightful probe into the financial game discovers a contrarian strategy alive and well in the national pastime. The A's relied on analyzing performance imaginatively to gain competitive advantage in the business of baseball.

Major League Baseball has compiled and increasingly revered performance statistics since Harry Chadwick, a British immigrant sportswriter, created a sustainable version of the box score in 1876. Lewis finds that the A's applied and modified *sabermetrics,* the imaginative statistical analysis that Bill James had been employing for the past quarter century. They used their analysis to supplement or supersede traditional assessments made by baseball scouts and general managers. Operating within tight budget constraints, general manager Billy Beane cut scouting expenses and redirected the savings to pay Harvard graduates to analyze the player market in order to determine what a team needed to win.

Although Lewis's label of "moneyball" represents the latest financial ploy for the A's, acquiring and spending money wisely to build competitive teams have been continuing challenges for the team since its American League inception in Philadelphia in 1901. The A's earlier versions of moneyball, herein defined as the skillful acquisition and deployment of resources to enhance competitiveness, have changed over the years. They have been forced in each of their three homes—two with competitors in the same market and the other of marginal size—to optimize what has generally been a modest revenue base compared to their competition.

THE PHILADELPHIA ATHLETICS (1901–54)

The Rise and Fall of a Dynasty, Part 1

There were several Philadelphia Athletics teams before the one headed by Connie Mack entered the newly formed American League in 1901. In 1860 U.S. Marshal James N. Kearns founded an Athletics club that quickly became the dominant team in the area, which was, like other northeastern cities, helping to develop the game. In 1865 that team signed to a $1,000 contract a left-handed second baseman named Al Reach, generally considered the first professional baseball player. Reach subsequently became owner of a prominent sporting-goods company and part owner of the National League Phillies in 1883 when the Worcester, Massachusetts, Brown Stockings franchise relocated to Philadelphia.

In 1871 another Athletics team won the first championship of the newly formed National Association of Professional Base Ball Players, the first professional baseball league. For that team in 1875 Joe Borden pitched what is regarded as the first professional no-hitter. The National Association folded after that season. An Athletics nine joined the new National League in 1876 and won the league's first game, but they lasted only one season. A fourth Athletics team joined the new American Association in 1882 and won its pennant the following year. That Athletics team died with the American Association in 1891.

In 1901, Byron Bancroft "Ban" Johnson reorganized the former minor Western League as the major American League. Bancroft chose Connie Mack to lead the new Philadelphia club. Mack had managed Milwaukee's club and named his new team the Athletics to emphasize its Philadelphia baseball legacy. Mack put up $5,000–$10,000 and received a 25 percent interest in the team while Charles W. Somers, a Cleveland coal baron, supplied $30,000, the remainder of the seed money.

Mack was born Cornelius McGillicuddy on December 22, 1862, in East Brookfield, Massachusetts, to Irish immigrants. He escaped the industrial toil of the local shoe factory by playing professional baseball. Mack was tall, and was a good-fielding but poor-hitting catcher. Starting at Meriden in the Connecticut State League in 1884, he progressed to the majors at the end of 1886 with Washington in the NL. In 1890 he jumped to Buffalo with the renegade Players' League and invested in the team, only to lose it when the league folded after one season. Returning to the NL with Pittsburgh in 1891, he became player-manager toward the end of the 1894 season, and was fired after the 1896 season despite winning records. The next year he met Johnson and joined Milwaukee as its manager.

Having retired as a player, he decided there was no need to wear a team uniform. His trademark attire consisted of a dark three-piece suit, stiff collar, straw hat, and scorecard. Not being permitted on the field out of uniform, he used the scorecard to signal his players and coaches from the dugout. During his half century as manager of the Athletics, the gentlemanly Mack became known as "the paragon of managers," "a symbol of enduring values of the national pastime," and, ultimately, "the Grand Old Man of Baseball." Arriving in Philadelphia, Mack enlisted two sportswriters, Samuel "Butch" Jones of the Associated Press and Frank Hough of the *Philadelphia Inquirer*, to locate a ballpark site. They eventually leased a vacant lot at 29th and Columbia in the Brewerytown section, constructed a 12,000-seat wooden grandstand, and called it Columbia Park, which would be home to the Athletics for the next eight years.

Jones and Hough introduced Mack to Ben Shibe, a partner of Reach's in the sporting-goods company. With encouragement from Reach, who was losing interest in his Phillies investment, and a promise from Mack, with Johnson's approval, that the AL would use Reach-manufactured baseballs, Shibe acquired a 50 percent interest in the team. Jones and Hough completed the buyout of Somers's interest and shared the remaining 25 percent. The ownership interest of sportswriters tangibly underscored a major role that sportswriters played during that era as public-relations spokespersons for sports, notably baseball, which by then had become the national pastime.

During the Progressive Era writers equated baseball with a bygone idealized American agrarian past. They focused on physical culture and youth development, relief from boring work, and assertion of civic pride and community integration to the point where baseball became a secular religion. "The arcadian, integrative, and democratic attributes of professional baseball were largely myths," asserts Steven A. Riess, in *Touching Base: Professional Baseball and American Culture in the Progressive Era*. "A substantial disparity existed between the ideology of baseball, which presented baseball in its most favorable light, and the realities of the game," he notes, but acknowledges that the public accepted the ideology as truth and responded positively. Baseball was influential in the development of urban culture.

With the financial structure in place Mack implemented an initial moneyball strategy that was virtually the antithesis of Beane's current approach. With sportswriter-partner Hough's player contacts and the seed money, he raided his NL rival, the Phillies, thereby testing whether Philadelphia, then the third-largest city in the country, could support two major-league baseball teams and who would prevail—questions that wouldn't finally be resolved until a half century later.

Philadelphia, then in what Riess calls "the industrial radial" stage of development, was a blue-collar city with heavy industry concentrations in iron, steel, coal, and the related railroad and shipbuilding businesses, as well as carpets and textiles. It was the largest city in geographic area, expanded by a growing radial network of rail lines, but generally homogeneous in population. A majority had come from Great Britain and Ireland, but there were also significant Russian Jewish and Italian elements. The African American immigration from the South was just beginning. The city's interest in sports, which had started with cricket because of the British influence, would continuously expand over the years to the present. As Rich Westcott noted, "Nothing defines the City of Philadelphia more than its passion for sports."

Unlike other major cities, Philadelphia was dominantly Republican, but like its Democratic-dominated counterparts, graft was rampant. From the first Athletics teams the Republican machine was involved in baseball. The machine generally supported it for constituent pleasure as well as tax- and license-revenue opportunities. Shibe, Mack, and the sportswriter-owners established political connections that would continue to favor the Athletics as a Republican-backed team for several decades. Although coincidental, the decline of the Athletics in Philadelphia occurred after World War II, as the political power shifted from Republicans to Democrats. Ironically, never in its history would the city name or initial appear on the uniform—it successively displayed a large *A*, an elephant, and, finally the word *Athletics* on the shirt—nor would a *P* ever appear on the cap.

Mack took advantage of an NL salary cap that limited the salaries of the better players to sign five Phillies players for the initial season. Future Hall of Famer Napoleon Lajoie was his best signing. He won the first AL Triple Crown, hitting .422 with 14 home runs and 125 RBIs. His batting average still stands as the league record.

The acquisitions helped the Athletics (or, as Mack called them, the "Ath-el-etics") finish their first year in fourth place with a 74–62 record and almost match (206,000 to 234,000) the Phillies' home attendance, despite the latter's established presence and better season record (83–57, second place). The Athletics signed three more Phillies before the 1902 season. Angered by the raids, the Phillies sued Lajoie. The state supreme court enjoined him from playing in Pennsylvania for any team but the Phillies, although it didn't require him to return to the Phillies. He and two others raided by the Athletics signed with Cleveland, which let Mack sign two of its players in apparent recompense. The Athletics laid claim as Philadelphia's favorite in 1902 when they won the AL pennant and more than doubled attendance, to 442,000, while the Phillies, beset by the player flight, fell to seventh and more than halved their attendance to 112,000. The A's would remain Philadelphia's favorite until after World War II.

Mack implemented another moneyball approach, one similar to the later Beane strategy. In addition to the normal, albeit informal, scouting that identified talent from sandlots, Mack emphasized college recruiting. At the time colleges were quickly and effectively developing organized, competitive sports programs, and baseball was more popular than football. Mack believed that the formal college-baseball program provided more valuable skills and training than the sandlots. He also believed student-athletes were both better learner-practitioners and gentlemen who could positively influence the roustabouts on a team. He required all his players to wear suits when they traveled to portray the gentlemanly image that he felt baseball needed.

Starting with future Hall of Famer Eddie Plank in 1901, he acquired 10 collegians for his roster five years later. Among them were Albert "Chief" Bender, a pitcher who was one-fourth Chippewa and a product of the Carlisle Indian School and Dickinson College; Eddie Collins, a second baseman from Columbia University; and Jack Coombs, a pitcher from Colby College. Bender and Collins would join Plank in the Hall of Fame. That strategy helped the A's win six pennants and three World Series in 13 years (1902–14) to establish its first and second dynasties. (*Dynasty* is herein defined as winning at least three pennants in four years.) The Athletics accomplished that four separate times in their history: 1911, 1913, and 1914; 1929, 1930, and 1931; 1972, 1973, and 1974; and 1988, 1989, and 1990. Only the New York Yankees have achieved dynasty status more often.

A notable complement to the college-recruiting strategy was George Edward "Rube" Waddell. Waddell pitched for Mack in Milwaukee and was probably mentally handicapped. Persuaded by Mack (and the Pinkerton detectives he sent) to join the A's from California, Waddell led them to their 1902 pennant with 24 wins, then topped that with 26 as they won again in 1905. An unfortunate late-season injury kept him out of the World Series. Waddell's occasional absences, prompted by emotional cravings for booze, women, and even fire engines, finally proved too much for the patient Mack, and he lasted only six years with the A's.

The second pennant victory in 1905 sent the A's to the World Series for the first time (there was no World Series in 1902) and inaugurated a rivalry with the New York Giants and manager John McGraw. In 1901 McGraw had called the Athletics "white elephants" (money losers) because of their NL recruiting. Responding quietly but pointedly as was his nature, Mack adopted the white elephant as a team mascot, put a likeness on the team uniform, and even purchased an elephant for the amusement of the fans. The elephant stayed on the uniform until 1928 in some form and returned in 1955, the A's first year in Kansas City. Charlie Finley replaced the elephant with a mule during his ownership, but it returned again in 1988 to inspire the A's to the first of three successive pennants, their fourth dynasty, and has since remained.

While both were successful Hall of Fame managers, McGraw and Mack were virtually opposites in appearance, personality, and style. McGraw was a short, heavy, swearing drinker-smoker, while Mack was a tall, thin, taciturn, nonswearing teetotaler. In contrast to the provocative McGraw, Mack was never ejected from a game. In management style McGraw represented the older, scientific management approach, while Mack displayed the new newer, human-relations approach. Emphasizing what is now called "small ball," McGraw employed precise strategies in contrast to the manly game of slugging and aggressive play of early baseball. His style conformed to the theory espoused by Frederick W. Taylor, the father of scientific management.

To employ his version, McGraw ran his team with an iron fist and controlled players closely on and off the field. He even monitored their eating and drinking habits to assure that they would be in winning form and to reinforce absolute discipline. Taking full accountability for results, he was the epitome of a top-down manager. His results—10 pennants and three World Series victories in 31 years with Giants—supported his approach.

In contrast, Mack, a precursor of the human-relations school, encouraged independent thought from his players as well as collaboration and cooperation between workers (players) and management (Mack and coaches). Mack directed his players with the carrot rather than the stick. As a result, Mack developed perhaps the best and certainly the longest sustained labor-management relationship in one team's history.

Mack's results compared favorably with McGraw's over their common tenure of 1902–32, when McGraw managed the Giants. Mack won nine pennants, one less than McGraw, but won five World Series, two more than McGraw, and was 2–1 in head-to-head competition. Mack finished above .500 21 times compared to McGraw's 27, largely because of the A's lower revenue base, which forced them to sell off players and spend seven consecutive years (1915–21) in the cellar before recovering.

In their 1905 inaugural World Series meeting, Mack presented McGraw with a replica of a white elephant; the Giants countered by wearing black uniforms. McGraw's Giants humbled the A's 4–1, with all five games being shutouts, three by future Hall of Famer Christy Mathewson. Only Bender's second-game shutout kept the A's from being swept when the A's scored their only runs in the series.

The A's would not win another pennant until 1910, when they went on to beat the favored Cubs, Series winners in 1907–8, 4–1 for their first world championship. The series hero was "Colby Jack" Coombs, whose 31 season victories almost matched his 35 wins in his first four years with the A's. Following Bender's three-hit victory in the opener, the next three A's wins belonged to Coombs. Only an extra-innings 4–3 victory kept the Cubs from being swept as the A's outscored them 35–15 and outhit them 56–35.

The next year Mack got revenge when the A's met the Giants again in the World Series after winning the pennant by 13 1/2 games over Detroit. In the series opener McGraw again outfitted the Giants in the black uniforms they had worn in the 1905 opener. Again Mathewson defeated the Athletics and Bender, as he had done in the 1905 finale. Despite that initial loss, the A's rebounded behind collegians Plank and Coombs to take a 2–1 lead before rain and mud postponed the series for a week. When play resumed Mack's other college pitcher, Bender, won the next game as well as the clincher in Philadelphia, 13–2. Third baseman Frank Baker acquired his nickname,

"Home Run," by hitting two crucial homers in the series to highlight his Hall of Fame career.

After a third-place finish in 1912, the A's won the pennant by six and a half games over Washington and again faced the Giants in the 1913 Series. This time Bender and Plank led the staff, while Coombs was lost for the entire season after he contracted typhoid fever. Keying the offense was the "$100,000 infield" consisting of first baseman John "Stuffy" McInnis, second baseman Collins, shortstop Jack Barry from Holy Cross, and third baseman Baker, who won the home-run and RBI titles that year. He hit .450 in the series, including a homer; Collins hit .421, including two triples; and each accounted for 8 of the A's 21 series runs as the A's prevailed 4–1. Mack used just 12 players, including only three pitchers, in the five games. Bender won two games and Plank bested Mathewson 3–1, yielding only two hits and an unearned run in the finale.

MACK, Mgr., Athletics

Manager Connie Mack's baseball card, 1910. Courtesy of the Library of Congress

In 1914 the A's won the pennant again, but the Giants finished second to the "Miracle" Boston Braves, who had been in last place as late as July 18. In the opener they shocked the A's by knocking Bender of the game for the first time in his 10 Series starts and coasting to a 7–1 win. They went on to sweep, albeit in close games: 1–0, 5–4 in 12 innings, and 3–1. This major upset prompted some rumors that A's players had thrown games because of their low salaries. In fact the A's salary costs had risen and attendance shrunk, so that they lost $60,000 in that pennant year. In response Mack abruptly cut costs by dismantling his dynasty team. As they floundered with seven consecutive last-place finishes (1915–21) local sportswriter Bugs Baer accurately quipped that for the A's "a base on balls constitutes a rally."

Mack shifted his recruiting strategy toward less expensive wholesale player tryouts and bargain hunting for also-rans. Not coincidentally, Ring Lardner's Jack O'Keefe of the contemporary popular fiction *You Know Me, Al* finished his career with the A's. A central character in one of James T. Farrell's novels wrote Mack for a job. One positive outcome of Mack's cheap recruiting approach, however, was Jimmie Dykes, who took three trolleys to Shibe Park for a tryout that launched a 22-year major-league playing career.

The Making of Shibe Park

With growing popularity and profitability, including a record 625,881 attendees supporting a second-place finish in 1907, Mack and Shibe implemented a new moneyball strategy by planning for a new, larger home to replace Columbia Park and increase revenue opportunities. Representative of baseball parks of the day, Columbia was built of wood and thus vulnerable to fire and collapse, as had befallen several such structures in the prior decade. With his engineering background Shibe sought an improved construct utilizing a recent technological advance, ferroconcrete (steel-reinforced concrete), that strengthened the building frame and made it fireproof. They broke ground in April 1908 and completed the park in time for the 1909 season opener. Riess observes that it was "the first fully modernized baseball field."

Shibe Park covered a full city block (Lehigh–Somerset, 20th–21st Streets) on the north side of Philadelphia in an Irish-dominated area called Swampoodle, a short distance from the confluence of three railroad lines. A block away from the site was the city's smallpox hospital, but the politically connected Shibe learned that it was soon to be closed before he began to acquire the property for a total cost of $67,500 through a series of clandestine transactions early in 1907. William Steele and Sons, pioneer constructors of concrete and steel buildings and many of the manufacturing facilities in Philadelphia, were named the general contractors.

The facade of the park was in the French Renaissance style, featuring a domed tower at the main (21st and Lehigh) entrances and a facade including rusticated bases, composite columns, and arched windows and vaultings, with terra-cotta casts of Shibe (at Lehigh) and Mack (at 21st) over the main entrances. The tower included an office suite for Ben's son Jack, the financial head of the A's, and, above that, Mack's "oval office." After buying tickets patrons entered a 24-foot-diameter circular lobby, by far the most elegant in baseball. Grandstand fans proceeded to a pavilion, then up a 21-foot-wide stairway to a promenade and 5,500 lower-deck and 4,500 upper-deck seats, while bleacherites followed 14-foot concourses past player dressing rooms and workrooms to their 13,000 seats, which initially sold for a quarter. The segregated grandstand-bleacher combination reinforced the A's scheme to attract upscale customers as well as to continue to appeal to the common man, with standing room for 7,000 in the wide aisles behind the bleachers and an additional space for 10,000 in a banked outfield and terraced lobby in the upper grandstand, totaling a theoretical capacity of 40,000. The field included sod transplanted from Columbia Park to preserve the team's growing baseball tradition (and to save money). Management claimed that cantilevered seats afforded unobstructed views, although steel columns impaired some. Unlike other parks, there was no advertising on the green outfield walls to distract from its "field of dreams" image. An electric scoreboard recorded who was playing and at bat.

The park was built at a cost of $301,000 plus an additional $76,000 for 1913 improvements that included covering the existing bleachers and adding unroofed stands as additional bleachers from left to center field. The park was a business investment that both reflected Shibe's entrepreneurial desire to display his wealth and business stature and to produce more revenue for the team. Historian Bruce Kuklick observes that the park's imperial and impersonal look was representative of robber-baron tastes of the time, but eliminated the intimacy of Columbia and other contemporary baseball parks. Cartoonists poked fun at Shibe Park with its long walks to seats, fan removal from the field of play, crowd crushes, and the concrete walls that precluded the "knothole gangs" of boys peeking from outside. Nevertheless, Shibe Park produced its own intimacy, enhanced by lively fan participation.

Opening Day was a sellout (23,000 seats plus 7,000 standing-room tickets), not counting the eager unticketed fans that crowded into neighborhood buildings with a view or that lined the adjacent streets, some 5,000 of whom broke through a gate into the outfield and stood behind ropes. Ceremonies included bands and speeches and Mayor John Reyburn throwing out the first ball. Plank completed the day by pitching the A's to an 8–1 victory over the Boston Red Sox. But the day had a tragic element as well. His catcher, Maurice "Doc" Powers, a practicing physician, was rushed to the hospital after the game and later died of intestinal complications attributed to a cheese sandwich he had eaten before the game.

The increased attendance, at least partially attributable to the new showcase, facilitated the emergence of the first A's dynasty. After finishing second in 1909 with record attendance of 675,000 (up from a depressed 455,000 a year earlier), the A's continued to draw well during their winning years. The Shibes made almost $350,000 between 1902 and 1913, and Mack also fared well. He received a $15,000 salary that was increased by an ownership share of the profits. Profitability, then as now in baseball, enabled the A's to pay their players well. Visibly representative of that was the $100,000 infield of McInnis, Collins, Barry, and Baker, who were the offensive core of the team.

Curiously, however, attendance in 1914, the dynasty's final pennant year, dropped to 346,541 from 571,896 in the prior year. Mack theorized that fans became bored with a repeat winner and that they were more supportive when the club simply contended. Further, he believed that player salary demands wouldn't increase if the team were merely a contender, not a winner. Baseball statistician Rob Neyer likens Mack's theory to the economic tenet of the law of diminishing marginal returns, which holds that repetitive occurrence leads to reducing yields. In that context he suggests that continued winning could lead to reduced attendance. Some of the result could also be attributable to the diminishing impact of the attraction of the new Shibe Park rather than of winning. The entry of the competing Federal League in 1914 may also have hurt attendance. Nevertheless, Mack acted aggressively on his belief, and would reaffirm it and act again, albeit more slowly, at the end of the second dynasty in 1932.

Shortly after the 1914 World Series sweep by the Boston Braves, Mack began dismantling the team. He waived the core of his pitching staff, collegians Plank,

Bender, and Coombs, and sold Collins to the Chicago White Sox, then refused to match Baker's offer from the Federal League. In defiance, Baker sat out and played semipro ball in 1915, then signed with the Yankees the following year. During the 1915 season Mack sold Barry and Herb Pennock to the Red Sox, Bob Shawkey to the Yankees, and Jack Lapp and Danny Murphy to the White Sox. While most of the players faded quickly, Baker and Collins continued their productive careers. Young pitchers Pennock, a future Hall of Famer, and Shawkey would win a combined 392 games with other teams.

The net result was that the 1915 team became the first in major-league history to fall from first to last place in one season, and attendance plummeted to 146,223, thereby affirming a continuing truism in baseball that fans don't support losers. The attendance drop may also have been influenced by the performance of the Phillies, who captured their first NL pennant. The 1916 A's, who may have been the worst team in major-league history, set a club loss record of 36–117, finishing 40 games behind the seventh-place Washington Senators and continuing what would be a seven-season run of finishing in the cellar.

Shibe Park also played a moneyball role in keeping Mack with the A's. As the dynasty leader, Mack became the recruiting target of the New York Highlanders, who were competing with the Giants for that city's attention. After the A's 1913 World Series triumph over the Giants, Mack was offered the Yankees' manager job. To counter that move, Shibe implemented a financial restructuring that benefited Mack as well as himself. First he sold Shibe Park, whose land, structure, and improvements had cost the A's almost $450,000, for $46,000 plus assumption of its $150,000 mortgage. A paper loss and a cash generator for Shibe, the transaction substantially increased the value of the A's franchise, of which Shibe was majority stockholder. It also benefited the minority stockholders, including Mack. To sweeten the deal even more Shibe loaned Mack $113,000 to buy out Hough and Jones's combined quarter share of the A's. Mack then became a half owner of the club, which now had a valuable real-estate asset, and stayed in Philadelphia.

The A's and Urban Culture

As the club's principal asset, Shibe Park was also the club's most tangible connection with Philadelphia and a historical link to the changes it would undergo during the first half of the twentieth century. Mack and many of the players chose to reside in the neighborhood of the park. Mack had lived across the street from Columbia Park when the A's played there, then moved to within seven blocks of Shibe. Despite getting an automobile as a gift from the team after the 1910 Series victory, he continued to take the trolley to work like other residents of the blue-collar community that grew around the ball park. Mack's ethnicity conformed to the neighborhood as well. "The Irish and their culture stamped the area," observes Kuklick, in noting the central presence of

St. Columbia's church and saloons such as Kilroy's, owned by Matt Kilroy, a famous nineteenth-century ballplayer, and frequented by baseball fans and players. Since in those early days the Irish were disproportionately represented throughout baseball, the neighborhood was an ethnic match for the A's.

The gentleman Mack's Athletics and the upscale Shibe Park had a reforming influence on the neighborhood despite the class segregation in the seats. Promoters of baseball argued that Shibe Park took the game off the streets and refined it in a formal setting, so that the rowdy workingmen conformed more to the behavior standards of middle-class entertainment. Conversely, the park may have popularized the working-class behaviors of informality, physical intimacy, and mixing of sexes among the middle class, thereby helping to relieve the monotony and tedium of work in industrial society. "The sport was as much the invention of industrial America as it was its antidote." And Shibe Park was a proving ground. In some sense, this reforming influence was self-fulfilling, if exaggerated. Riess observes, "The public saw baseball as an accurate reflection of contemporary society."

While the A's floundered after Mack's purge, the area around Shibe coalesced from a collection of small neighborhoods into a defined community. The Pennsylvania Railroad tracks formed a diagonal southern boundary that kept the growing black population out. Lehigh and 22nd became the hub of what locals were now calling "North Penn," which continued to be home to many ballplayers. Although thriving adjacent industries provided substantial work opportunities for the blue-collar community, the advent of Prohibition brought crime to the area.

Local religious-ethnic political differences manifested themselves in the societal issue concerning the Sunday blue laws, a collection of local ordinances and state laws in Pennsylvania that dated back to 1794. This meant the A's could not play on Sunday, potentially the best day for customers, particular the blue-collar workers that made up the majority of the neighborhood and the city. The A's tested the laws by illegally playing one Sunday game on August 22, 1926, but didn't continue because of opposition from religious groups, neighborhood residents, and eventually the county court in October. For the next seven years the A's and Phillies tried unsuccessfully to effect legislative change, even supporting Democratic blue-law-repeal candidates and threatening to build a stadium across the river in Camden, New Jersey, in order to play Sunday games.

Eventually persuaded by the opportunity to increase tax revenue during the depression, the Pennsylvania legislature passed a local option law in April 1933 that enabled Philadelphia to push through a referendum in November granting limited approval for Sunday games. Beginning with an A's-Phillies exhibition game on April 8, 1934, the teams played Sunday games between 2 and 6 P.M. They were the last major-league teams to play on Sunday. The next year the window was extended to 1–7 P.M.

The blue laws also regulated drinking and prohibited the sale of beer at Shibe Park on Sunday. Politically influenced by an unlikely alliance of temperance leaders, who generally opposed liquor, and neighborhood bar owners, who feared loss of fan business, the prohibition lasted until 1961. Mack contended that the blue laws were a major factor in the reduced revenues that caused him, beginning in 1923, to dismantle his second dynasty.

Another fan issue was the "spite fence" of 1935. From the opening of Shibe Park, houses beyond the outfield fence on 20th (right to center field) and Somerset (left to center) streets had second-story views of the ballpark. Those rooms as well as the building roofs produced income for residents. Somerset landlords lost their view and income opportunity when Shibe installed additional bleachers in 1913, but the view for those on 20th remained.

The neighborhood viewing license became an issue when the second dynasty produced bigger crowds and World Series games that inspired residents to increase viewing space by constructing stands between houses. The hard times of the depression also enhanced resident interest in acquiring income. The A's, who also needed revenue, contested resident activity through their political contacts while residents bribed officials to preserve their opportunity. The A's may also have been spurred by resident objections to the Sunday baseball initiative.

A compromise was reached whereby residents agreed not to open their business unless the A's sold out, so as not to undercut A's prices. However, one owner broke ranks by turning second-floor rooms into a permanent baseball-viewing area. After Mack began the second dynasty breakup and attendance declined, all residents opened their viewing spaces and undercut Shibe Park prices in an effort to make money. Jack Shibe retaliated after the 1934 season by adding 38 feet to the 12-foot outfield wall. Covered with corrugated tin, the extended fence became known as "the Great Tin Monster" and created challenges for outfielders because of unpredictable bounces off the uneven surface.

Night baseball became the next significant neighborhood moneyball issue. The Cincinnati Reds pioneered night baseball in 1935. Four years later the A's became the first AL team to host night baseball, which was accelerated by the Phillies, who moved to Shibe Park in 1938. Both team owners correctly projected that the costs of constructing eight 146-foot light towers and operating them would be more than offset by larger crowds and dinnertime concessions. The city zoning board complied with the building request despite strong objections from the same neighbors who had fought the spite fence. In 1939 the A's and Phillies each played nine night home games, and Mack installed a restaurant, Café Shibe, inside the park to serve dinner to patrons.

During the depression, gambling, long a problem in baseball, continued to increase at Shibe Park without curtailment by the A's. So prevalent was gambling on baseball games and boxing matches at Shibe that the lower right-field stands became locally known as "Gamblers Patch." Major-league commissioner Judge Kenesaw Mountain Landis once contended that Shibe Park gambling was the worst in baseball.

Shibe Park was also used for activities other than baseball and boxing. In order to build goodwill, they let local schools use the space for free. The most significant moneymaker was the rental to the Phillies and the football Eagles beginning in 1938. The Eagles stayed through 1957 before shifting to Franklin Field at the University of Pennsylvania. Shibe was not a football-friendly facility because of the location of fixed stands and the inadequacy of parking. Shibe also rented the facility to politicians, evangelists, and sports and other entertainment promoters. About a hundred boxing cards were staged, enhanced by Shibe's gambler-friendly environment.

Unlike many other major-league parks, however, it did not have a continuing rental relationship with Negro League teams. Eddie Gottlieb, a part owner of the Negro baseball Philadelphia Stars and later a noted basketball promoter, negotiated occasional Negro games at Shibe, which also hosted some Negro World Series games in the 1940s and some black college football games. Generally the neighborhood antipathy toward blacks kept this activity low.

For the A's and the Phillies the introduction of radio in the 1920s presented a delicate moneyball issue. Like many other teams, they initially feared that free broadcasts of games would reduce attendance. Like other two-team cities, they also tried not to compete overtly, fearful that such competition would ultimately hurt both clubs. Their first collaborative solution was to broadcast only home games, but later they liberalized the agreement to include an away game if there was no competing home game that day or if the away game occurred in a different time slot. Even when it became obvious that away broadcasts were not harmful to the other team's home attendance, the clubs were reluctant to spend the money to send broadcasters on the road. They employed "re-creation," utilizing telegraphed transmission of the action and embellishing it with theatrical commentary and local sound effects. In 1950 all games were transmitted live after franchise rights were profitably sold to a network of stations reaching a larger audience.

In 1937 Philco Radio and TV Corporation interviewed Mack on television in its factory a short distance from Shibe Park and transmitted several miles to a meeting of newspaper and magazine editors. Ten years later Mack televised the first game from Shibe Park, despite the recurring fear that television would hurt ballpark revenues. By 1950, convinced that television was another viable moneyball strategy, the A's and Phillies expanded from a simple one-camera presentation to a three-camera one.

During World War II, Kuklick observes, "Shibe Park became a center for community activity that downplayed diversity and conflict." In 1943 it hosted its first All-Star Game, the first to be held at night. Philadelphia was far enough inland to avoid military "dimout" regulations, so night baseball continued there throughout the war. To enhance its patriotic image, management began each game with "The "Star-Spangled Banner," previously only reserved for special occasions. Both the Phillies and A's admitted servicemen free and sponsored games whose profits went for servicemen's relief. They auctioned off autographed baseballs with proceeds donated to the war effort. One ball, autographed by both Connie Mack and President Roosevelt, raised $15,000 in war bonds.

Buoyed by the postwar surge in baseball popularity and a brief improvement in their play, the A's began what was to be a series of renovations to the park by spending $300,000 before the 1949 season to add additional expensive seats, replace stairways with ramps, upgrade restrooms, install water coolers, and introduce an "annunciator" that displayed the at-bat number, the ball-strike-out count, a hit-error indicator, and the score. Later they installed an organ and upgraded team dressing rooms.

Despite the continuing need for attendance, the A's did not actively seek black fans or, after Jackie Robinson broke the color line in 1947, black players to attract black fans and improve team performance. A 1951 University of Pennsylvania Wharton School study found that with weak teams and a black population that had exceeded 400,000 by the 1940s, Philadelphia was a logical target for black-player recruiting and black-fan marketing. However, as Kuklick observes, "Shibe Park was a typical place of prejudice. More than many northern cities, indeed, Philadelphia was a white baseball town." Black fans tended to come only for infrequent black exhibitions or Negro League contests. In 1902 Mack had used a Colombian, Luis "Jud" Castro, as a replacement for Lajoie, and had acquired Chief Bender in 1903 despite major-league aversion to minorities. Nevertheless, his later actions suggested that he was fundamentally against desegregating the sport.

Once the color barrier was broken, Mack hired Judy Johnson, a former Negro League All-Star third baseman with the nearby Hilldale club and future Hall of Famer, to scout black players. Mack nevertheless rejected Johnson's recommendations of Hank Aaron, whom he could have signed for $3,500, and Larry Doby and Minnie Minoso, whom he could have signed for $5,000 each. So resistant were the A's to integration that they even employed a heckler, Pete Adelis, the "loudmouth" of Shibe Park, to harass Doby, who became the first black player in the AL in 1947, from a seat behind the visitor's dugout at Shibe and on the road. Johnson contended that signing those black players might have improved club performance and revenue enough to prevent the A's departure in 1954.

It was not until September 1953 that the A's fielded a black player, pitcher Bob Trice, who also played there in 1954 and briefly the next year in Kansas City. The Phillies would not have one until 1957, 10 years after Robinson's entry. By then the North Penn neighborhood was becoming a black community. Attendance at Shibe Park declined as whites feared going there and blacks boycotted the games. "There is no doubt," asserts black historian Christopher Threshton, "that the racial chasm between black and white forced the removal of the Athletics and the relocation of the Phillies to a less threatening part of the city.

The Rise and Fall of a Dynasty, Part 2

Although starting slowly, the 1920s eventually roared for the A's. Emerging from the cellar in 1922, the year Ben Shibe died and was succeeded by sons Tom and Jack in the front office, they steadily progressed to second place in

1925. Confirming Mack's theory that contenders draw crowds, the 1925 A's drew 869,703, a record that lasted until the post–World War II boom. They continued to finish second or third until 1929, when they won the first of three consecutive pennants and the first of two straight World Series, thereby establishing a second dynasty.

Buoyed by rising attendance revenue, Mack's moneyball recruiting strategy shifted from the sandlots and also-rans to cronyism and veteran acquisitions, including some of his old stars. The former approach was more successful than the latter, perhaps because Mack's appraisal of his former players tended to be clouded by sentiment. His favorite and most productive crony was John Joseph (Jack) Dunn, owner of the Baltimore Orioles, which won seven consecutive International League pennants (1919–25) and was perhaps the most successful minor-league team ever. The International League was the only minor league that did not permit major-league teams to draft its players at a fixed price.

Like Mack, Dunn was a baseball-only businessman who believed his ballplayers should act like gentlemen for the good of the game. While Dunn obsessively wanted to win, he took advantage of the International League draft exemption to sell players to the majors at market prices in order to increase revenues. In 1914, needing cash but valuing his relationship with Mack, Dunn offered him a pitching prospect who beat the A's in an exhibition game—George Herman "Babe" Ruth—for a song. Ruth's nickname came from Oriole players who responded to Dunn's guardian relationship with the pitcher by calling him "Dunn's babe." Mack declined the offer because he was cash poor and beginning the breakup of his first dynasty.

The relationship later paid off for the A's when Mack had more money. From 1923 to 1928 Mack bought four players—two pitchers and a double-play combination—who would become instrumental in the second A's dynasty. First was second baseman Max Bishop, who came for $25,000 after the 1923 season. Next was Robert Moses "Lefty" Grove, for $100,600 (to top the $100,500 price the Red Sox received for the Ruth sale to the Yankees, but Mack paid in 10 $10,000 annual installments plus $600 interest) after the 1924 season. Shortstop Joe Foley came for $65,000 in 1927 and pitcher George Earnshaw for $70,000 in the middle of 1928.

Mack made three other purchases, all future Hall of Famers, who became critical to the second dynasty. In 1923, Mack bought outfielder Al Simmons from the minor-league Milwaukee Brewers for $50,000. From Home Run Baker, minor-league team owner and former star on the first dynasty team, he bought Jimmie Foxx for $2,500 in late 1924. Mack also purchased the entire Portland team in the Pacific Coast League in 1924 because he was so enamored of catcher Mickey Cochrane.

After second-place finishes to the Ruthian Yankees in 1927 and 1928, the A's beat New York by 18 games the next year to win the first of three consecutive pennants and establish a dynasty that has been compared to those Yankees. In contending that the 1929 A's should be favorably compared to the 1927 Yankees,

Robert "Lefty" Grove, 1925. Courtesy of the Baseball Hall of Fame

often labeled the best team in history, historian Bill Kashatus assesses the Yankees and A's over their three-peat periods of 1926–28 and 1929–31, respectively. He observes that the A's won 11 more games overall, lagged the Yankees in hitting, but outperformed them on the mound and in the field.

The 1929 A's were a very contentious team, as were those in the first dynasty and in the third in Oakland. They hated to lose and carried their competitive passion on and off the field. Mack described team leader Cochrane as Ty Cobb wearing a mask because of his aggressive play. Simmons would work himself into a rage before stepping to the plate. Dykes once threw his bat at Mack when he was lifted for a pinch hitter. When he was scheduled to pitch, Grove came to the clubhouse with a scowl, ignored teammates, and snarled at reporters. Mack's human-relations management permitted them to vent, yet enabled them focus their energy on winning.

A notable example occurred that year during a game with Cleveland. Grove, who probably ranks as the A's best-ever pitcher as well as its most irascible, was so angered at back-to-back errors by Bishop and Dykes that he berated them on the field. He then proceeded to give up home runs to the next two Indian batters. In the dugout after the inning, Mack removed Grove from the game after taking a team vote. It took Grove a week to cool off, but he won 20 games that year and led the league in ERA.

The Chicago Cubs, led by Philadelphian Joe McCarthy, were the A's opponents in the 1929 World Series. Making their first appearance since 1918, the Cubs had batted .303 during the season with a predominantly right-handed lineup led by MVP and future Hall of Famer Rogers Hornsby. Keeping it secret until game time, Mack started 35-year-old right-hander Howard Ehmke, who was at the end of his career and had won only seven games that year. Ehmke hadn't pitched for nearly a month, but was allowed to work out at home and scout the Cubs when they visited the Phillies. Mack figured that the Cubs were primed to face one the A's aces, Grove, Earnshaw, or Rube Walberg, and a victory over one them at home might give the Cubs early momentum. Ehmke responded by giving up only eight hits and an unearned run while striking out 13 (a new Series record) in leading the A's to a 3–1 victory.

The A's won the next game in Chicago behind Earnshaw and Grove, who pitched only in relief in the series, but lost the first game in Philadelphia. The Cubs jumped out to an 8–0 lead in the seventh inning of the fourth game and seemed assured of evening the count. But the A's staged the greatest comeback in Series history by scoring 10 runs off four Cubs pitchers in the bottom of the seventh before Grove came on to save victory. Critical to the rally was a fly ball that Hack Wilson lost in the sun, resulting in a three-run inside-the-park homer. The A's staged another comeback in the fifth game by scoring three runs in the ninth to clinch the championship, 3–2.

When the Great Depression hit two weeks after the A's 1929 World Series victory over the Cubs, Mack quickly reverted to his normal thrifty mode. He allegedly lost a lot of money in the market crash. Despite humanitarian gestures such as giving stadium jobs to out-of-work neighborhood families and sending leftover food to a local boys' home, for which he received Philadelphia's Outstanding Citizenship Award in 1931, he strongly resisted giving raises to his players. Having hit .329 in 1929, Dykes felt he deserved a raise, but Mack politely listened to the plea and then told him how lucky he was to be in the majors and continued his salary level for the next season. True to his conservatism, Mack typically offered one-year contracts, regardless of performance.

He reluctantly succumbed in 1930 to his two top sluggers, Foxx and Simmons, and gave them three-year contracts. Nevertheless, Foxx's annual salary ($16,667) was still less than half of his Yankees first-base counterpart, Lou Gehrig, and Simmons ($33,333) earned less than half of Yankees outfielder Ruth's $80,000. Simmons had to sit out all of spring training before Mack finally yielded minutes before the Opening Day game began. As if to reinforce his value, Simmons homered in his first at bat. That set the tone for another runaway pennant and World Series victory over the St. Louis Cardinals, who had nosed out the Cubs for the NL pennant.

After building a 2–0 series lead behind Grove and Earnshaw before sellouts (and 3,000 rooftop and second-story fans) in Philadelphia, the A's lost the next two in St. Louis. Earnshaw and Grove combined on a three-hit shutout as Jimmie Foxx's ninth-inning homer gave the A's a 2–0 victory in game five. Returning home, the A's extended the Cardinals' scoreless streak to 21 innings before Earnshaw gave up a ninth-inning run en route to a 7–1 clincher. Neither team hit over .200 in the series, but more than half of the A's hits went for extra bases as they outscored St. Louis 21–12.

The next year the Athletics became the first team to win over 100 games three seasons in a row as they bested the Yankees by 13 1/2 games for the pennant. At 31–4, Grove had his best season, but was his usual irascible self. After starting with 10 straight victories, he lost an extra-innings game in relief. He then sped home to Maryland, where he closeted himself for five days. When he returned, however, he won another 16 in a row en route to winning the AL's first MVP

Award. The stage was set for a rematch with the Cardinals, led by MVP Frankie Frisch and a new weapon, rookie John Leonard "Pepper" Martin.

Once again Grove and Earnshaw provided more than 80 percent of the pitching for the A's, but they were bested 4–3 by Cardinal aces Burleigh Grimes and Wild Bill Hallahan. After Grove coasted to a 6–2 win in the opener in St. Louis, Earnshaw held the Cardinals to two runs the next day, but Hallahan shut the A's out. The two runs were manufactured by Martin singles, stolen bases, and teammate sacrifices. Grimes outpitched Grove in game three, but Earnshaw responded with a shutout to even the series at two. Martin dominated game five in Philadelphia by driving in four runs, two with a homer, in a 5–1 Cardinals win. After the homer the Philadelphia fans gave him a five-minute ovation, uncharacteristic of the partisan faithful. Martin batted .500 for the series, accounted for 9 of the Cardinals' 19 runs, and stole five bases.

After Grove tied the series Earnshaw and Grimes squared off in the finale before a St. Louis crowd that was barely half capacity, perhaps in anticipation of losing to the highly favored A's. Despite retiring 15 in a row at one point, Earnshaw gave up four runs while the 38-year-old Grimes held the A's scoreless until the ninth, when they scored two runs with two outs and had the tying runs on for pinch hitter Max Bishop. Bishop hit a line drive off reliever Hallahan that Martin snared with a spectacular one-handed catch to win the series.

Reacting to a depression-induced 100,000 drop in 1931 attendance and consequent sportswriter speculation about another dynasty sell-off, Mack denied rumors and stuck with his team. Led by Foxx, the league's Triple Crown and MVP Award winner in the final year of his contract, but offset by relative slumps by Simmons and Cochrane, the A's finished second in 1932, 13 games behind the Yankees. Financially the A's declined further, as attendance dropped more than 200,000 to a level less than half of the 1925 peak.

A highlight of the 1932 season was Foxx's pursuit of Ruth's 60-homer season record set in 1927. Foxx hit 58 home runs, but a combination of rule changes, a new ball, stadium adjustments, and fate kept him from breaking the record. In 1927 a "one-hop homer" was permitted, that is, a hit was considered a home run if it went into the stands on one bounce. In 1930, the current ground-rule double replaced the one-hop homer. In 1931 a less lively ball was introduced to bring more balance to the game, resulting in 500 fewer major-league homers that year. Between 1927 and 1932, St. Louis, Detroit, and Cleveland erected screens above their outfield fences to keep the ball in play. Foxx hit five potential homers into the screen in St. Louis in 1932. He also hit two home runs in Detroit in a game that was canceled by rain before the requisite five innings had been played. Nevertheless, his record for right-handed batters stood until Mark McGwire, a former Oakland Athletic, hit 70 for the St. Louis Cardinals in 1998.

After the season, Foxx re-signed for slightly less money, and Mack initiated the reduction of the largest payroll in baseball by selling Dykes, outfielder George "Mule" Haas, and Simmons to the White Sox as the World Series began. Having been just told by Mack that he was keeping the team intact, Dykes was furious and vowed never to speak to Mack again. But he did, and in 1949 returned as Mack's head coach, succeeding him as manager after the 1950 season.

Dropping to third and suffering another 100,000-plus decline in attendance in 1933, despite a second straight Triple Crown and MVP year for Foxx, Mack accelerated the breakup by selling Cochrane to Detroit for $100,000 and Grove, Bishop, and Walberg to the Red Sox, where Eddie Collins was now the general manager, for $125,000. After a salary dispute he sent Earnshaw to the White Sox for $20,000. Ironically, the sales occurred as the A's were getting a repeal of the Sunday ban on games and a consequent opportunity for increased revenue. That increase, however, didn't materialize as anticipated. Despite the added incentive of lowered admission charges, they only drew 8,000 more than the prior year. The A's dropped to fifth place in 1934.

The final sell-off occurred after a 1935 last-place season with only 233,173 customers. Mack traded Foxx to the Red Sox for two journeymen and $150,000 in December, and a month later sent outfielder Doc Cramer and infielder Eric McNair to the Red Sox for two players and $75,000. In the space of two decades, the A's had built and demolished a dynasty twice. A third comparable demolition would occur after the 1972–74 Oakland dynasty years. Although the second decline was slower than that of the first dynasty, it would prove to be longer lasting. The A's would only finish in the first division twice (fourth in 1948 and 1952), and would finish last 11 times in their remaining years in Philadelphia.

As if to signify the end, on February 16, 1936, team president Tom Shibe died; a year later his brother, Jack, who had succeeded him, also died. At Ben Shibe's death, his interest had passed to his four children. The two sons had administered the business while Mack concentrated on the field. Mack assumed the presidency shortly before Jack's death and bought his interest from his widow, thereby becoming the majority stockholder in the club.

Over the next decade Mack developed a personal moneyball plan for continuing the Mack baseball tradition and dividing his interest among his heirs. He had two sons from his first marriage, Roy and Earle, both of whom were involved in the franchise, and five children from his current marriage, including one son, Connie Jr. The elder Mack assumed that Earle would succeed him on the field and Roy in the front office. He kept some shares for himself and apportioned the remainder between his wife and three sons, denying the daughters any shares. His wife wanted equal distribution among the heirs in order to shift power to the second family and the women. The Macks briefly separated in 1946–47 as a result of the dispute, but reconciled. The sons weren't on the same page either. A resultant oppositional alliance developed between the second family and the Shibe heirs, who still owned about 40 percent of the team.

The power struggle crystallized in 1950 as Connie, at 87 and in his 50th year as head of the A's, was significantly losing his mental facilities. Trades of two future Hall of Famers exemplified Mack's decline: George Kell to the Tigers in 1946 and Nellie Fox to the White Sox in 1949. Roy and Earle raised the money, principally from mortgaging Shibe Park, to buy out the other side. They also designated Dykes to replace Connie as manager after the season, but kept him in the public eye as nominal president. In 1950 the A's finished last, drew only 310,000 fans, and handily lost the crosstown competition with the Phillies, who won their first pennant since 1915.

Mack's 50-year record as manager of the Athletics was 3,582–3,814, with nine pennants, five (of eight) World Series victories, and 17 last-place finishes. Nine of his star players went to the Hall of Fame. He was elected to the Hall in 1937, the same year as McGraw, and the first time managers were admitted. In 1957, a year after his death, the Phillies changed the name of Shibe Park to Connie Mack Stadium. When Veterans Stadium replaced the park in 1970, the city put a statue of Mack waving his scorecard outside the front entrance. The statue was moved to outside the new Phillies home, Citizens Bank Park, when it opened in 2004.

Helped by acquisitions from the White Sox of Dave Philley and Gus Zernial, who won the homer and RBI crowns, and the development of Ferris Fain, who won the batting title, the A's climbed to sixth place under Dykes in 1951. Fain's second straight batting title and 24 victories from diminutive southpaw Bobby Shantz, the MVP, enabled the A's to finish fourth in 1952. When Shantz injured himself in his first 1953 start, the final slide started. The A's finished seventh and last in their final two seasons in Philadelphia. The 1954 team finished further (60 games) from first place than any team in A's history—no mean accomplishment for a club that had finished in the cellar in one-third (18 of 54) of its campaigns.

The continuing poor performances and mounting financial losses made the A's a prime candidate for purchase and/or relocation, particularly with the warring younger Macks at the helm. The major leagues had just broken its history of franchise stability after the 1952 season when the Boston Braves moved to Milwaukee, marking the first franchise relocation in the major leagues since 1903. Then, after the 1953 season, the St. Louis Browns moved to Baltimore.

Befitting their relationship, Roy and Earle Mack disagreed on what to do next with the team. In 1950 they had withstood Connie Jr. and the second Mack family's attempt to gain control, and had rebuffed a syndicate offer. In early 1954 a halfhearted, mayor-sponsored "Save the A's" ticket campaign failed. Roy could not secure enough financing to buy out his brother, who had lost interest, and his father, both of whom were reportedly willing to support an offer from Chicago businessman Arnold Johnson, who wanted to move the franchise to Kansas City.

Washington and Detroit owners opposed a move to Kansas City, the latter because of Johnson's connections with Yankee co-owners Del Webb and Dan Topping in gaining control of Automatic Canteen, a leading Chicago vending-machine company. He later developed a tax-favorable scheme for Webb and Topping to sell him Yankee Stadium and its minor-league stadium in Kansas City (and their nondepreciable land, which he sold to the Knights of Columbus and leased back), lease them back to the teams (and sublease the land), and hold a $2.9 million mortgage.

In preparing his offer for the A's, Johnson agreed to sell the Kansas City stadium to the city at cost if he moved there. Kansas City passed a bond issue to fund purchase and enlargement of the stadium on August 3, 1954, and paid Webb and Topping $100,000 to liquidate the mortgage. Johnson designated Webb's construction company to refurbish the stadium. As if recalling the Hough-Jones alliance with Mack at the beginning of the A's in Philadelphia, *Kansas City Star* sportswriter Ernest Mehl was the catalyst in getting Johnson and Kansas City officials together.

After three more months of meetings and negotiations, Johnson agreed to sell Yankee Stadium to avoid conflict of interest, and Phillies owner Bob Carpenter purchased Shibe Park (for $1.675 million) to facilitate the A's departure. After all the financial maneuvering, the net cost to Johnson, who got 52 percent of the stock, was $572,427.63. The corporation was capitalized at $1 million, including all shares. The purchase was the first Kansas City A's moneyball maneuver.

THE KANSAS CITY ATHLETICS (1955–67)

The Profitable Launch of a Loser

The move to Kansas City not only signaled a new beginning for the team, but also represented a new phase in the relationships between major-league clubs and their cities. Unlike the privately owned park in Philadelphia, the A's now leased its park from the city, thanks to Johnson's financial manipulation. Publicly owned parks would become the norm in the latter half of the century, triggered either by team relocation or threat thereof. In addition, cities often included contract concessions to lure and/or retain teams. Such was the case in the initial Kansas City deal. The city guaranteed a minimum of 1 million attendees in each of the first three seasons—a number greater than the A's had ever had in Philadelphia. In an April 9, 1955, *Saturday Evening Post* article, Arthur Mann estimated that the guarantee produced $750,000 for the team owners. Including park concessions and road receipts, which went to the club, the team stood to make about $1 million in profits in each of the first three years, or a 100 percent annual return on the investment. The city also reduced the stadium rent to $1,000 (plus $24,000 if attendance exceeded 1 million) for each of the first two years instead of $205,000 and $155,000, respectively, that the normal rental rates would have produced.

In another subtly adroit tax maneuver, Johnson chose not to utilize the Philadelphia baseball corporation, which had a $300,000 tax carryover, but instead displayed loyalty to his new home state by setting up a new Missouri corporation. This decision enabled him to take full advantage of player depreciation, a legal ploy that Bill Veeck had discovered a few years earlier. The Treasury Department had ruled that a new corporation could consider player contracts at fair market value as assets and depreciate them over five years. The total cost of the Athletics was slightly over $2 million, including the amount paid to the Macks plus outstanding debts minus proceeds from the sale of the stadium. Assuming reasonably that player contracts were $1.8 million (90%) of the new corporation's assets, that amount of income was tax-free if earned in the first five years (and it was), resulting in a tax savings of $936,000, using the 52 percent corporate tax rate at the time. Therefore, the Johnson group saved $636,000 with the new corporation instead of using the tax carryover from the Philadelphia company.

Veeck opined that Johnson really wanted to put the team in Los Angeles, but that the timing wasn't right in 1954. Therefore, Veeck assumed, Johnson would stay in Kansas City for a few years to take advantage of concessions and player depreciation before trying again. An early indication supporting Veeck's view came in 1957 when the city attempted to impose a five percent license fee on gross revenues from sporting events. When Johnson balked and threatened to move, the city didn't pass the ordinance. This confrontation evidenced an emerging general business trend where local political subdivisions were becoming more dependent upon potentially transient corporations for their economic well-being.

Because attendance was strong in the first few years, it became unlikely that AL owners could or would support another A's move. In the interim the New York Giants and Brooklyn Dodgers moved to San Francisco and Los Angeles, respectively, depriving both Johnson and the rest of the AL of those potentially lucrative markets. The A's lease expired at the end of 1959, so Johnson pushed for, and got, a short two-year extension in order to keep his options open.

Meanwhile, despite an encouraging first year, the A's would become the worst team in recent baseball history, with an aggregate record of 829–1,224. With future Hall of Fame shortstop and veteran manager Lou Boudreau at the helm, the A's finished sixth in 1955, with a 63–91 record, and played to 1,393,054 fans. In their 13 years in Kansas City the A's would never again finish that high in the standings or attendance. They would finish last or next to last in 10 of the remaining 12 seasons.

Aided by his favorable financial arrangement and player-depreciation opportunity, Johnson spent $700,000 in 1955 to purchase players. A typical Johnson-era moneyball deal sought a combination of known has-beens and unknown wannabes, often from the Yankees. For example, shortly before the end of spring training the A's bought three pitchers from New York for $400,000, including veteran Ewell Blackwell, who pitched in the opening game but was released a few weeks later. Only reliever Tom Gorman added value. During the Johnson years, the A's became a thinly disguised farm club of the New York Yankees. In his five years as owner, the A's made 16 trades involving 59 players with New York.

Critics accused Johnson of favoring his longtime associates Webb and Topping. Bill James's "win shares" analysis, which measures a player's long-term contribution to a team in comparative terms, however, suggests otherwise. Using that analysis, John E. Peterson argues that although short-term results seemed to support the criticism, the net long-term effect of the trades was more beneficial to the A's than to the Yankees. Using the James approach, even the infamous December 11, 1959, Roger Maris trade modestly favored the A's despite Maris becoming the league MVP the next two years and breaking Ruth's season home-run record. The A's had almost traded Maris to the Pittsburgh Pirates for shortstop Dick Groat, who became the NL MVP the next year. The Maris trade was also Johnson's last, because he died three months later.

The most bizarre trade was one that didn't happen. Baltimore Orioles general manager Paul Richards proposed to then A's general manager Parke Carroll on June 15, 1956, an hour before the trading deadline, that they trade entire teams. Carroll agreed but couldn't reach Johnson for approval before the deadline. They almost swapped teams again during the 1957 spring training, but then the Orioles refused to part with rookie Brooks Robinson, who would go on to a Hall of Fame career.

The farm system produced little during the Johnson years, partially because he had inherited a weak system from Philadelphia. Connie Mack's moneyball strategies had never highly valued formal scouting and a minor-league system, but had preferred trading for talent or, earlier, using crony contacts to recruit directly to the parent club. Only 11 players from the inherited system made it to the majors. The A's had the fewest players advance to the majors or Triple-A in the years 1954–60. In their first three years in Kansas City the A's only signed two bonus players, partially because of turnover in the scouting ranks. Even after 1957, when more money was available in the system, they didn't pursue top prospects. A positive exception was shortstop Dick Howser, who would become an All-Star and the *Sporting News* Rookie of the Year in 1958 and team captain in 1961.

Following Johnson's death his widow unsuccessfully tried to get on the board and maintain current ownership. The executors and minority stockholders put the club up for sale on July 3, 1960. Bidders included syndicates wanting to relocate the team to New Jersey, Minneapolis, Dallas, and Houston as well as those wanting to keep the team in Kansas City. New options for the bidders emerged a month later, however, when the major leagues announced that they each would add two teams.

A Kansas City group received conditional approval from the AL on December 5 but lacked current shareholder approval. Charles O. Finley, the Chicago insurance broker who had unsuccessfully bid for the team in Philadelphia, submitted a higher bid for Johnson's 52 percent interest. Finley had also tried unsuccessfully to buy the Tigers in 1956 and the White Sox in 1958 and 1960, and to get the Los Angeles AL expansion team in 1960. Johnson's widow withdrew her option to buy the stock, leaving Finley and the Kansas City group to compete, and Finley won.

The Kansas City group still had an option to buy the remaining 48 percent of the stock. It waived its rights after Finley indicated that if he obtained complete control he would eliminate the stadium lease's attendance clause, giving the team the option to leave if it drew less than 850,000. Finley became sole owner on February 16, 1961 at, a cost of nearly $4 million. This was a fourfold increase from the Johnson deal in 1954—and a handsome financial return for investors in a losing team.

The Not-So-Merry Finley-Go-Round—and Out

Foretelling his egotistical flamboyance as well as his duplicity, Finley ceremoniously burned a document in the mayor's office to demonstrate his commitment to the city. It was later revealed that he had burned a standard contract form, not the stadium lease, so the attendance clause remained intact. He then made 125 public appearances in the next three months to promote his A's in the community. He also spent over $400,000 in stadium improvements as a further goodwill gesture. They included a Fan-a-Gram next to the scoreboard to display messages; the addition of 1,200 bleacher seats and a picnic area beyond the left-field fence, which was moved back 30 feet; repainting the stadium; and installing new lights. Indicative of his penchant for innovation were Harvey, a mechanical rabbit that rose from the ground next to home plate to supply the umpire with new baseballs, and Blowhard, a compressed-air device that could dust off home plate as needed. These creative promotional efforts emulated Bill Veeck, who had implemented similar changes after buying the White Sox two years earlier. Finley won early acceptance by the city and its fans, which saw him as the savior of Athletics baseball.

With Veeck as a role model on the promotional side, Finley sought another on the baseball side, hiring veteran general manager Frank Lane on January 3, 1961. "Trader" Lane had built a reputation for turning around poor teams through aggressive player movement—and for creating conflicts with club ownership. He had made 241 trades involving 353 players during seven seasons (1949–55) with the White Sox. His trading helped the Cardinals move from seventh to second place in two years (1956–57) and enabled the Indians to go from sixth to second in his first two years there (1958–59). After trading the popular Rocky Colavito and dropping to fourth place in 1960, however, he became available once again. Lane made nine trades involving 36 players during his seven months with the A's before Finley fired him. There wasn't enough room for two such strong-willed men in team leadership. One notable example was when Lane traded pitcher Bud Daley to the Yankees four months after Finley publicly declared, in contrast to the Johnson-era practice, that the A's would no longer deal with New York.

As Finley would eventually demonstrate, there wasn't room for anyone but Charlie in charge of any aspect of the business. For instance, he fired minor-league director Hank Peters because he hadn't secured Finley's approval, only Lane's, to sign a prospect. Although Finley would hire more titular general managers, including Peters, in the future, he apparently thought he had learned enough from Lane in seven months to perform the baseball function well enough by himself. Eventually, in Oakland, he officially assumed the role.

His practice was the same on the business side as well. The leadership team could have only one significant player.

The honeymoon with the city and its press was short-lived, thanks in part to sportswriter Ernie Mehl, who ironically had facilitated Johnson's stadium-lease arrangement to lure the A's from Philadelphia. Mehl learned from manager Hank Bauer, who like every other Finley manager hated the boss's interference, that Finley was interested in moving the team to Dallas, which had twice the metropolitan-area population and a more lucrative radio and television audience. Mehl broke the story on August 17, 1961, and publicly revealed Finley's lease-burning charade as proof that he wanted to move the club. He accused Finley of no longer promoting the team in order to use the attendance clause as an escape route. Finley responded vindictively by staging an "Ernie Mehl Appreciation Day" between games of a Sunday, August 20, doubleheader and presented the "Poison Pen Award for 1961" to Mehl in absentia. He also tried, unsuccessfully, to get his announcers to describe the event and criticize Mehl. He replaced the announcers the next season.

MLB commissioner Ford Frick issued a statement decrying the event and called Mehl to apologize. Finley convinced the city council to send a telegram to Frick endorsing Finley. He also ordered his staff to stop making the usual travel arrangements for Kansas City sportswriters, and excluded the writers two days later from a Chicago press conference where he announced the firing of Lane. Finley did not end the feud with Mehl until Opening Day 1962, when he asked him to throw out the first ball.

Having been exposed by Mehl, Finley deleted the attendance clause from the stadium-lease contract on August 26, 1961. Relocation activity was dormant until Lamar Hunt announced on February 8, 1963, that he would move his American Football League team from Dallas to Kansas City. Finley was furious at the lease Hunt negotiated and demanded a comparable arrangement, including reimbursement for the over $400,000 he had unilaterally spent in stadium improvements. He signed a new seven-year lease with the outgoing city council that included the 850,000 attendance clause and an opportunity to recover $300,000 of his stadium-improvement costs from city-waived concessions income. However, the city counsel immediately ruled the lease invalid on a technicality. Finley responded by refusing to negotiate until after the season was over. He decided in the interim to relocate to Atlanta and tried to persuade Hunt to move there as well.

Atlanta organized a stadium authority in June and invited Finley to negotiate a 1964 move to an enlarged minor-league park until a 54,000-seat stadium could be built. The Kansas City city council offered Finley a choice of two leases on July 3, but he rejected them as not comparable to the April lease he had signed. After learning that league owners would likely not approve a move to Atlanta, he then set his sights on Oakland, which would add another West Coast team to pair with the Angels. Oakland expected to have a new stadium ready by 1965, but Finley sensed at a July league meeting that the owners wouldn't endorse any move at this time.

He nevertheless waited until December 20 to reopen lease negotiations with Kansas City, by which time he was focusing on Milwaukee, whose NL Braves were considering a move to Atlanta. When AL president Joe Cronin declared that the A's would stay in Kansas City for 1964, Finley offered a two-year lease proposal to the city, but it was rejected. So he went to Louisville and signed a two-year conditional lease without AL approval. At a January 16 meeting, the other league owners unanimously voted against Louisville and gave him until February 1 to sign a new Kansas City lease or face expulsion. He renewed negotiations on January 25, received a two-week deadline extension from the league, and went to Oakland on January 26 to resume negotiations. At February 19 and 21 league meetings, the owners rejected his request for an Oakland move and endorsed the Kansas City lease proposal. After a local group of businessmen announced on February 22 that they would seek to purchase the A's, Finley accepted terms of a four-year lease and signed it on February 28, committing the A's to Kansas City through 1967. Like role model Veeck, he was unable to gain support from other league owners for a franchise move.

While Finley was negotiating for relocation and/or better financial terms, the A's continued to perform poorly on the field, and attendance fell accordingly. In 1962, they drew 635,675, the lowest in their eight seasons. To spice things up for the next season, Finley introduced new Kelly green and Fort Knox gold uniforms (his wife's favorite colors) with player names on the backs. A year later, he would add sea-foam green and wedding-gown white to the colorful player attire. Although ridiculed by players and the press, these uniforms would set a trend away from the traditional home-white and away-gray pattern that had existed from the majors' early days.

As he had done in the business and baseball-operations areas, Finley immersed himself in scouting to learn that aspect of the business, then pared back his staff by half after two seasons. Recognizing that the A's had few very good players in the pipeline, he worked the scouting area relentlessly and participated in the signings. His moneyball strategy resembled Branch Rickey's "quality out of quantity" of 40 years earlier, only Finley was willing to pay much more money. A notable early example was the signing of 18-year-old pitcher Lew Krausse Jr., whose father had pitched and later scouted for Connie Mack. Finley paid him $125,000, the highest amount ever, and immediately started him in a June 16, 1961, game. Krausse responded with a three-hit shutout victory. Finley's demonstrated willingness to move signees up to the majors quickly enhanced his ability to sign players.

Finley's strategy was buoyed by profits from his insurance business as well as player-depreciation opportunities. Wisely anticipating the added negative financial impact of the amateur draft beginning in 1965, Finley signed 80 players for a total of $662,000 in 1964, the most ever spent by a team in one season. Included among them were Jim "Catfish" Hunter, John "Blue Moon"

Odom, Chuck Dobson, and Joe Rudi, who would all contribute significantly to the A's 1972–74 dynasty in Oakland. Complementing them were selections from the first three years (1965–67) of the amateur draft: Rick Monday, Sal Bando, Gene Tenace, Rollie Fingers, Reggie Jackson, and Vida Blue. Monday, the first ever amateur-draft selection, became the key component in a trade that brought pitcher Ken Holtzman, who won 59 regular-season and 4 World Series games for the 1972–74 A's despite Finley's having cut his salary 10 percent upon arrival. Finley's scouting strategy and eye for talent, supported by a few expert scouts, built the foundation of the dynasty from within the organization.

But the payoff wasn't imminent either on the field or in the stands, so Finley again sought to move in the final lease year of 1967. A new local sports authority recommended twin football and baseball stadiums for Kansas City in January, and a bond issue passed in June. Meanwhile, Oakland had completed its new stadium in advance of the Raiders' football season in 1966. Finley visited Oakland, Seattle, Milwaukee, and New Orleans as possible relocation sites, but quickly eliminated New Orleans because its contemplated stadium (the Superdome) wouldn't be ready until 1972. Milwaukee wanted local majority ownership, and Finley was unwilling to assume a minority position. Both Seattle and Oakland offered more promising television and radio possibilities than Kansas City. Seattle wasn't voting on a stadium bond issue until the next year, but was willing to expand a minor-league park to 25,000 in the interim. Meanwhile, the AL was considering further expansion from 10 to 12 teams.

In anticipation of an October 18 league meeting, Finley formally announced his intent to move to Oakland on October 11, giving the league three options: force the A's to stay in Kansas City, get a local group to buy the A's and give Finley an expansion franchise in Oakland, or authorize the A's move to Oakland and grant Kansas City an expansion team. Finley claimed he had lost $4 million in his seven-year tenure in Kansas City and presented a presumably biased study that favored Oakland over Seattle and Kansas City. At the meeting, the league owners approved his move to Oakland and granted expansion franchises to Kansas City and Seattle, concluding the first era in sports migration, which had started in 1952. Only the A's and the NL Braves moved twice during this period. Later, responding to political pressure, the owners accelerated the start of the 12-team league to 1969, leaving Kansas City only one year without major-league baseball. After calling Finley "one of the most disreputable characters ever to enter the American sports scene," Missouri senator Stuart Symington quipped, "Oakland is the luckiest city since Hiroshima."

THE OAKLAND ATHLETICS (1968–PRESENT)

"An Equal Opportunity Tyrant"

Local columnist Glenn Dickey identifies three problems from observing Finley and his team in Oakland: lack of staff, inability to build attendance, and promotion of self above the team. Each of those problems had surfaced in Kansas City and increased in Oakland, particularly in the later years. Having learned enough (in his mind) from Veeck, Lane, and scouts in the early Kansas City days, Finley became increasingly self-reliant. By the time he left Kansas City, he had become his own general manager.

While Finley committed to signing talent and developing them in the 1960s, he shifted his moneyball strategy to aggressive trading in the 1970s. "Trader" Finley kept churning his roster, often with recurring faces. He acquired, got rid of, and reacquired 16 players from 1970 to 1980. He also sought name talent, usually after their prime, to fill key spots, acquiring 22 former All-Stars from 1970 to 1976.

Apparently he also felt that his background in direct-mail marketing of insurance was sufficient training to enable him to attract customers to the ballpark, but his record was dismal in both cities, despite numerous (and some imaginative) promotional gimmicks. His largest promotion, however, was not for the A's, but was a 1964 Beatles children's hospital benefit concert in Kansas City that lost money. His Kansas City A's never approached the 1 million attendance mark during his seven-year tenure, while his Oakland teams only drew over 1 million twice during his 13-year ownership. The expansion Kansas City Royals almost doubled Finley's Oakland attendance during their common 12-year run (1969–80) despite the A's having the larger market and finishing higher in the first seven of those years. He would also own the local NHL Seals and the ABA Memphis Tams, but couldn't get those franchises to attract customers either.

Compounding the small staff problem was his absentee ownership position. He never relocated from Chicago either to Kansas City or to Oakland, yet he tinkered far too often. Recalling Finley's penchant for phoning, Blue later mused that it was fortunate that there weren't cell phones in the 1970s or Finley would have called his manager as he walked to the mound. In his first 10 years as A's owner he ran through 10 managers. It was not until he hired Dick Williams, perhaps his best move ever, on October 2, 1970, that some continuity came to the A's field leadership. Yet even with Williams, who led the team to its first division championship in 1971 and consecutive World Series victories the next two years, Finley crossed swords frequently. Williams quit after the 1973 world championship because he could no longer put up with Finley's intrusions.

Finley was "an equal opportunity tyrant," observes Hall of Fame researcher Bruce Markusen. When Blue claimed that Finley treated his black players like niggers, white catcher Dave Duncan responded, "He treats his non-black players like niggers, too." For example, during 1974, their third straight World Series–winning season, Finley stopped paying postage for players answering fan mail. Finley's offenses may well have aggravated feuding among a contentious group of athletes. Catcher Ray Fosse rationalized that the aggravation may have helped them be a better team on the field. Captain Bando went further to assert that the players united in their dislike for

Finley and became stronger as a team. Cohesiveness was a common characteristic among the first three dynasties. Mack was a positive unifier, Finley a negative one.

Dickey asserts that the major leagues implemented the salary-arbitration process primarily because of Finley, who had more players go to arbitration the first year than all other teams combined. Arbitration, of course, foreshadowed free agency, which was also triggered by Finley's mishandling of Hunter's contract in 1974. Those two structural changes led to his downfall as well as to an overall power shift to the players throughout baseball.

Finley also continued his virulent relations with the press in Oakland. One time he excluded Ron Bergman, a local beat writer, from team charter flights because of his statement that the A's broadcasters were competing to curry favor with Finley. Virtually every time a negative comment about the A's hit the press, Finley would respond vindictively. But if a positive comment were made, the originator became his instant friend. He also routinely withheld payment from vendors, often forcing a lower payment settlement. For Finley, it was Charlie's way or the highway. As Dickey observes, "Charles Finley was a man of many despicable qualities."

But he was also was an innovator, albeit without the class of his role model, Veeck. In addition to colored uniforms, the ball rabbit, and the plate duster, he advocated several substantive changes that were later implemented, albeit without crediting him, including night All-Star, playoff, and World Series games; the designated hitter; minor-league rehabilitation assignments for injured players; and interleague play. Not implemented were the designated runner and a three-ball, two-strike limit to speed up games. Finley also warned his fellow owners of the dire consequences of accepting arbitration and free agency, yet contributed to their implementation and became the first to suffer from them.

Ironically, when the designated-hitter idea came up for approval, Finley voted against his own idea because he wanted to package it with a designated runner. (He also didn't have a good designated-hitter candidate on the roster at the time, having just released Orlando Cepeda.) Undeterred, he created a roster spot for a designated runner, first Allan Lewis, a speedy minor leaguer with minimal overall baseball skills, then Herb Washington, a world-class sprinter who hadn't played baseball above the high-school level. Both attempts were failures.

Perhaps the most visible trademark of his Oakland regime were the mustaches worn by his dynasty team. The look started with future Hall of Famer Jackson sporting a mustache when he arrived at 1972 spring training. At Finley's direction, Williams tried to get him to shave it off, but failed. So Finley induced others to grow them in an effort to dilute Jackson's individuality. He offered $300 to any player who would grow one by Father's Day. Even the militaristic Williams joined in. Capitalizing on the look, Finley announced in May that the Father's Day game would be Mustache Day, with free admission to anyone sporting a mustache. Fingers, a 1992 Hall inductee, epitomized what would become the emblem of the A's dynasty with his elaborate waxed handlebar rendition.

Although they won eight less games than the 1971 Western Division champions, the 1972 A's repeated in the West and defeated Detroit in the AL Championship Series (inaugurated in 1969) 3–2 behind the clutch pitching of "Blue Moon" Odom, who recorded two wins and didn't allow an unearned run in the 14 innings he pitched. The first Oakland World Series pitted the A's against the favored Cincinnati Reds, who had dispatched 1971 NL champion Pittsburgh in the league playoffs. Compounding the challenge was the loss of slugger Reggie Jackson, disabled with a pulled hamstring, and key left-handed reliever Darold Knowles, who broke his thumb the last week of the season.

The series hero emerged early when backup catcher Gene Tenace, starting on a hunch by Williams, hit two home runs in the A's 3–2 opening-game victory. Tenace would hit four homers in the series, but it was his two RBIs, including the game winner in the deciding seventh-game 3–2 win, that gave Oakland its first world championship and made him the MVP. Fingers had two saves and a win, but also a loss in the fifth game that could have given the A's the series earlier.

After three-peating in the West and defeating the Orioles 3–2 for the pennant behind Catfish Hunter and Ken Holtzman, the A's battled the Mets in another seven-game World Series. Down 3–2, the A's got even as Hunter outpitched future Hall of Famer Tom Seaver, then won the deciding game 5–2 with two-run homers by Bert Campaneris and Series MVP Jackson, who accounted for 8 of the A's 21 runs. Knowles also reminded the A's what they had missed a year earlier by appearing in all seven games, not giving up a run, and recording two saves, including the clincher.

With Williams gone, Alvin Dark led the 1974 A's to their fourth West title, third pennant, and third Series championship in a row. After losing the ALCS opener to the Orioles, the A's allowed them only one run behind Holtzman, Blue, and Hunter over the final three games. Only 18 runs were scored in the four games and both teams batted under .200, but Oriole pitchers walked 22. The World Series with the Dodgers was another pitchers' battle, with only 27 runs scoring in the five games as the A's prevailed again. With a victory and two saves in four appearances, Fingers was the Series MVP.

After three straight world championships—the only time in A's history—the third dynasty began to unravel almost immediately. Hunter's grievance contended that Finley's failure to pay the premium in 1974 on a life-insurance policy that was part of his compensation voided his player contract. Peter Seitz ruled on December 13 that Finley's failure enabled Hunter to become a free agent, so the ace of the dynasty pitching staff signed a record five-year, $3.75 million contract with the Yankees. Without Hunter, the A's won the division in 1975, but were swept by Boston in the playoffs.

A few days before the 1976 season opened Finley sounded the death knell by trading Jackson, the man most identified with the A's success, to Baltimore. On June 15, he announced the sales of Rudi and Fingers to Boston for $1 million each and Blue to the Yankees for $1.5 million. All three, along with Bando, Campaneris, Tenace, and Don Baylor, acquired in the Jackson trade, were eligible for free agency after the season. MLB commissioner Bowie Kuhn voided the sales as not in the best interests of baseball. Finley sued the commissioner for restraint of trade, but was ultimately overruled in court. With the three players back in the fold, the A's finished second in the division. The seven free agents celebrated the end of the season with a champagne party, and all but Blue moved on to other clubs for 1977. As a result, the A's plummeted to last place in the division.

From Tyranny to Philanthropy

By the end of 1979, Finley knew he had to sell the team. The team finished last with an Oakland record 108 losses and a record-low attendance of 306,763, less than some minor-league teams. Moreover, his wife had sued for divorce and wouldn't take stock in the team as part of the settlement. He struck a deal with Denver oilman Marvin Davis, who wanted to move the team to Colorado. The Oakland Coliseum had an ironclad lease with the A's through 1987, however, so Finley had no choice but to renege and seek a buyer who would keep the team there. Walter Haas Jr., CEO of Levi Strauss and a friend of Bob Lurie, the San Francisco Giants' owner, was part of a local business group organized by Cornell Maier, CEO of Kaiser, to make an offer.

Finley decided he would deal only with Haas, who was reluctant because of his friendship with Lurie. Haas agreed to pursue negotiations only after his son, Wally, and son-in-law, Roy Eisenhardt, expressed enthusiasm. They closed the deal with Finley, and Roy became president in charge of operations while Wally focused on community outreach. They quickly and successfully set out to grow the previously neglected fan base to reinforce philanthropist Walter's long-standing commitment to the East Bay. "Haas was truly the last of the gentleman owners," observes Dickey, in noting how he financially and spiritually supported the team through its ups and downs while letting his operations people run the team.

Installing local icons Lon Simmons, who was elected to the Hall of Fame in 2004, and Bill King as broadcasters and Andy Dolich as marketing director, the A's built upon the respected Haas name to extend their market beyond the East Bay. In 1981, their first year, the Haas team was on target for 2 million attendance, almost twice Finley's best, before a player strike canceled one-third of the season. They actually drew over 1.3 million, 200,000 more than Finley's best, in two-thirds of the games. Admittedly, Finley's ingenious hiring of mercurial manager Billy Martin in 1980 helped the rise in attendance as well as the standings. Playing "Billy Ball," the A's won the division in 1981, but lost to the Yankees in the ALCS. As was his penchant, enhanced by his drinking problems, Martin imploded the next year as the A's slumped, and he was fired.

The new owners built up the farm system, which had been nearly eliminated by Finley in his trader phase. Unable to find an experienced general manager, they hired Sandy Alderson, a Harvard Law graduate who had represented them effectively in arbitration cases. Alderson went through a learning curve in hiring managers and securing, developing, and trading players, but emerged as a top baseball executive. He is currently executive vice president of operations in MLB. When Alderson hired Tony LaRussa, who had been a bonus baby with the Kansas City A's in 1963 and resurfaced as a utility infielder in Oakland from 1968 to 1971, to manage the A's in mid-1986, all of the managerial pieces were in place for a fourth A's dynasty.

The upgraded farm system produced three consecutive Rookies of the Year: outfielder Jose Canseco in 1986, first baseman Mark McGwire in 1987, and shortstop Walt Weiss in 1988. The first two, labeled "the Bash Brothers," would hit a combined 617 home runs over their Oakland careers. Shrewd Alderson trades brought two washed-up pitchers, Dave Stewart and Dennis Eckersley, who would become the dominant starter and closer, respectively, of the dynasty years. Eckersley, who had had a good career as a starter before succumbing to alcohol, would save 320 games for the A's and earn a ticket to the Hall of Fame. His predecessor as closer, Jay Howell, would be used as trade bait with the Dodgers to lure starter Bob Welch, who would combine with Stewart to win 125 games for the A's in their three championship seasons.

After finishing third in 1986 and 1987, the A's won three straight pennants, but only one World Series, the 1989 Bay Bridge "Earthquake Series" with the Giants.

The 1988 team set an Oakland record with 104 wins, then swept the Red Sox 4–0 (the league championship series having expanded to seven games in 1985) for the AL title as Canseco hit three homers, including one that put the A's ahead in the finale. They were heavily favored against the Dodgers, who had needed the full seven games to defeat the Mets for the NL crown, thereby idling the A's for a week. In one of the most dramatic finishes in baseball history, a hobbled Kirk Gibson hit a game-winning two-out, two-run homer off premier reliever Eckersley in the ninth inning of the series opener—and the A's never recovered. Bash Brothers Canseco and McGwire went a combined 2 for 36, both homers, and Dodgers ace Orel Hershiser allowed only one run in his two complete-game victories as Los Angeles prevailed 4–1.

The 1989 route to the Series was almost as easy, as the A's won the West by seven games and prevailed 4–1 over Toronto in the ALCS behind Stewart's two pitching victories and Rickey Henderson's explosive offense. Reacquired from the Yankees in midseason, Henderson hit two homers, walked seven times, stole eight bases, and accounted for 11 of the A's 26 runs. The San Francisco Giants also dispatched the Cubs 4–1 in the NLCS, but proved no match for the A's in the first ever Bay Bridge series. They outscored the Giants 10–1 behind Stewart and Mike Moore, signed as a free agent before the season, in the first two games in Oakland. Their juggernaut was temporarily halted, however, when an earthquake hit San Francisco minutes before game three. Delayed 10 days by the resulting damage, the A's picked up where they left off and completed the sweep as Stewart and Moore recorded the two final wins.

The pennant three-peat again proved easy with a nine-game margin in the West and a 4–0 sweep of the Red Sox for the league championship. Stewart won two, Moore one, and Cy Young winner Bob Welch one as A's pitchers

Ricky Henderson holds up the third base plate after breaking Lou Brock's all-time record for stolen bases, 1991. © AP / Wide World Photos

allowed only 4 runs while the offense plated 22. Facing the Reds, victors over the Pirates in the NLCS, the highly favored A's were shocked 7–0 in the Series opener as Stewart's six-game postseason win streak abruptly stopped. As in 1988, the A's never recovered, and the Reds swept them. Once again, the Bash Brothers collapsed, going a combined 4 for 26 with one homer and one RBI. Adding insult to injury were the two dominant wins by pitcher Jose Rijo, who the A's had traded to the Reds after the 1987 season. The A's have not returned to the Series since.

A consequence of this sustained success was the highest payroll in the majors, supported by record attendance and the Haas family's willingness to pay. The A's high-water mark of 2,900,217 in 1990 exceeded the three-year total of Finley's 1972–74 world champions. Henderson, who would set all-time major-league highs in runs, stolen bases, leadoff homers, and walks (since passed by Barry Bonds) became baseball's highest-paid player following his 1990 MVP season, only to be eclipsed quickly by several others and by Canseco in mid-1991.

From Philanthropy to Moneyball

After dropping to fourth in 1991, the A's rebounded to win the division the next year, but lost to the Toronto Blue Jays in the playoffs. Thereafter, they declined as the dynasty talent aged or departed. Walter Haas was dying and put the team on the market. Committed to keeping the A's in the area, he sold them to local residential real-estate builders Steve Schott and Ken Hofmann for $70 million, an estimated $30 million below market, on November 1, 1995. The good deal that the buyers cut foretold how they would run the team—like a tightly run business. Reversion to budgeting control was a return to the A's norm. Only the Haas regime, supplemented by brief relaxations during prior dynasties, had differed from that.

Leaving the baseball operations to Alderson, managing partner Schott devoted his attention to initiating a plan for a publicly financed, baseball-only stadium, reflecting current trends. The 1960s dual-purpose stadium, now called Network Associates, was remodeled to lure Al Davis's NFL Raiders back to Oakland in 1997. The result, including the towering east grandstand known as "Mount Davis," is a venue less conducive to baseball. In his new stadium pursuit, Schott has tried unsuccessfully to gain access to the peninsula and the more lucrative Silicon Valley market, included in the Giants' territorial rights. Unwilling to finance a stadium without public money, Schott has also not been able to convince the Oakland-area municipal leadership to cooperate. In July 2002, he negotiated a lease extension to 2007 for Network Associates, with three one-year options extending to 2010, to buy time to continue his quest.

Despite initial fan criticism that likened the new owners to Finley, Schott quickly ordered Alderson to cut payroll through trades and releases, culminating in McGwire's mid-1997 trade to the Cardinals, where LaRussa had become manager. Alderson had advised the competitive LaRussa to leave after the team sale, replaced him with Art Howe, and developed a new, long-term moneyball strategy compatible with the new ownership: invest for the longer term in scouting and development and forgo the short term. Consequently, in 1996–98, the A's finished third-fourth-fourth in the newly created four-team Western Division. In anticipation of his moving to the commissioner's office, Alderson promoted his protégé and assistant, Billy Beane, to general manager at the end of the 1997 season.

Building upon the Alderson strategy of scouting and player development, Beane, the architect of the A's current success, incorporated his modified sabermetric statistical-analysis approach. To accomplish this, Beane, a bright student-athlete who had turned down a scholarship to Stanford when he was a first-round amateur-draft choice in 1980, has employed Harvard graduates, first Paul DePodesta (later general manager of the Los Angeles Dodgers), and then David Forst.

Rather than Branch Rickey's "quality out of quantity" wholesale recruiting approach that focused primarily on the speed of teenagers, the A's look for more mature players who had learned patience at the plate, yet could hit for power. The dominant A's statistic has become OPS (on-base plus slugging percentage) because offense, Beane believes, is more important than defense in today's game. Runs, the key to victory, he reasons, depend first on reaching base, then on scoring, most easily with an extra-base hit. Players who could perform the on-base and slugging functions well, therefore, produce winning teams. Among pitchers, he prefers overall athletic ability and control over sheer speed. The traditional scouts euphemistically call his approach "performance scouting."

The older recruits are before signing, the more likely those characteristics could be substantiated, and therefore their progress toward the majors would be both quicker and more likely to succeed. Thus, the A's feel they are more likely to get a better and faster return from collegians—both position players and pitchers—on their market-limited investment. That preference recalls Connie Mack's early moneyball strategy of seeking college gentlemen players for their trained skills and mature demeanor in the early Philadelphia years.

Recognizing his limited financial resources, Beane's approach also avoids pursuit of foreign stars that aren't included in the draft. Instead, the A's nondraft concentrations are in the Caribbean and Mexico, where they sign young players for modest bonuses and spend money to school them. The A's have a successful baseball academy in the Dominican Republic that produced shortstop Miguel Tejada, who was signed by Hall of Famer Juan Marichal. Tejada was the AL MVP in 2002, then, as a free agent, signed a six-year, $72 million contract with the Orioles a year later.

Losing emerging star players, like Tejada, through free agency to wealthier teams supplies the A's with high draft choices. In the 2002 *Moneyball* amateur draft, they received three additional first-round picks as well as three "sandwich" (between the first and second round) picks for the loss of three free agents. The A's selected college players with all seven picks. Extra high-level picks not only give the A's more talent to develop for the parent club, but also additional attractive personnel to use in trades.

To complement the young recruits, Beane looks for lower-tier veteran bargains because he can't afford to compete with the high payroll teams for stars in the free-agent market. Backup catcher Scott Hatteberg signed for 2002 and was converted to replace departing free-agent first baseman Jason Giambi at less than 1/10 Giambi's annual salary with the Yankees.

Before the midseason trading deadline, Beane aggressively seeks currently needed niche players from teams out of the running and eager to sell. He often acquires the player only for that half season, particularly if he is eligible for free agency at the season's end, and therefore would generate two top draft picks. Second baseman and leadoff hitter Ray Durham, acquired in mid-2002 from the White Sox, helped the A's win the division, then signed with the Giants and generated two picks.

Beane also considers closers overpriced in the market, so he tends to trade or let his closer go to free agency after a successful year or two. Keith Foulke, the 2003 closer acquired in a White Sox trade for 2002 closer Billy Koch, went to the Red Sox after the season as a free agent and generated two top picks. Ironically, it was A's manager LaRussa, pitching coach Dave Duncan, and pitcher Eckersley who defined and modeled the current version of closer.

MONEYBALL'S QUASI DYNASTY

While Beane's teams have not created a fifth A's dynasty, they made the division playoffs four straight years (2000–2003) with payrolls only about a third as large as the highest-paying teams—and weren't eliminated from the playoffs until the next-to-last day of the 2004 season. The 2004 failure revealed what has most contributed to the prior playoff years—consistent good pitching. Although the 2004 team had a higher batting average, run production, on-base percentage, and fielding percentage than the 2003 team, the staff ERA was more than half a run higher than the prior year. Subpar performances from their "Big Three" starters (Tim Hudson, Mark Mulder, and Barry Zito), who had been instrumental in the playoff years, and an erratic bullpen, which blew 28 of 63 save opportunities, were the key detriments that led to a late-season collapse. After going 70–30 in the prior four Septembers, the A's were 14–16 in September 2004, after leading the division from early August.

The 2004 performance added to the twenty-first-century A's October record, which saw them eliminated in the first round of the 2000–2003 playoffs, although each division series went the maximum five games. At the end of those four series, the A's lost nine games, any one of which would have sent them to the league championships. Beane asserts that his strategy works well for the long season, but not necessarily for short playoff series. He defensively contends that luck plays a major role in playoffs, although critics have suggested that his lack of emphasis on small ball, including sacrifices and stolen bases, and defense have contributed to the A's failures.

Nevertheless, a "wait till next year" response was reinforced by the 2004 farm-system performance, with winning seasons for all six teams, five of which made the playoffs and two of which won championships. However, they traded away Tim Hudson and Mark Mulder, two of their Big Three pitchers, and got off to a miserable start in 2005. Then during the summer, the Athletics surged, aided by two *Moneyball* draftees, Joe Blanton and Nick Swisher, and reached first place by early September. Alas, as in 2004, the Angels surged and the A's faded, resulting in a second-place finish and their worst record since 1999.

Given the budget constraints imposed by its business-focused leadership, the competition with the Giants in a market that is only marginally sufficient for two teams, the resultant negative impact on attendance and media revenues, the lack of a new stadium in a better market, and the player fluidity caused by free agency, it is unlikely that the current strategy will produce another A's dynasty. But if success were to be redefined in financial terms, say, as wins per player salary dollar, the early twenty-first-century Beane A's would be a runaway qualifier and worthy extension of the historical legacy of Athletics moneyball. Even without a fifth dynasty, the leaders of the white elephants, from Mack to Finley to Beane, continue to haunt the ghost of John McGraw.

NOTABLE ACHIEVEMENTS

Most Valuable Players

Year	Name	Position
1931	Lefty Grove	P
1932	Jimmie Foxx	1B
1933	Jimmie Foxx	1B
1952	Bobby Shantz	P
1971	Vida Blue	P
1973	Reggie Jackson	OF
1988	Jose Canseco	OF
1990	Rickey Henderson	OF
1992	Dennis Eckersley	P
2000	Jason Giambi	1B
2002	Miguel Tejada	SS

Cy Young Winners

Year	Name	Position
1971	Vida Blue	LHP
1974	Catfish Hunter	RHP
1990	Bob Welch	RHP
1992	Dennis Eckersley	RHP
2002	Barry Zito	LHP

Rookies of the Year

Year	Name	Position
1952	Harry Byrd	P
1986	Jose Canseco	OF
1987	Mark McGwire	1B
1988	Walt Weiss	SS
1998	Ben Grieve	OF
2004	Bobby Crosby	SS

Batting Champions

Year	Name	#
1901	Nap Lajoie	.426
1930	Al Simmons	.381
1931	Al Simmons	.390
1933	Jimmie Foxx	.356
1951	Ferris Fain	.344
1952	Ferris Fain	.327

Home-Run Champions

Year	Name	#
1901	Nap Lajoie	14
1902	Socks Seybold	16
1904	Harry Davis	10
1905	Harry Davis	8
1906	Harry Davis	12
1907	Harry Davis	8
1911	Frank Baker	11
1912	Frank Baker	10
1913	Frank Baker	12
1914	Frank Baker	9
1918	Tilly Walker	11
1932	Jimmie Foxx	58
1933	Jimmie Foxx	48
1935	Jimmie Foxx	36
1951	Gus Zernial	33
1973	Reggie Jackson	32
1975	Reggie Jackson	36
1981	Tony Armas	22
1987	Mark McGwire	49
1988	Jose Canseco	42
1991	Jose Canseco	44
1996	Mark McGwire	52

ERA Champions

Year	Name	#
1905	Rube Waddell	1.48
1909	Harry Krause	1.39

1926	Lefty Grove	2.51
1929	Lefty Grove	2.81
1930	Lefty Grove	2.54
1931	Lefty Grove	2.06
1932	Lefty Grove	2.84
1970	Diego Segui	2.56
1971	Vida Blue	1.82
1974	Catfish Hunter	2.49
1981	Steve McCatty	2.32
1994	Steve Ontiveros	2.65

Strikeout Champions

Year	Name	#
1902	Rube Waddell	210
1903	Rube Waddell	302
1904	Rube Waddell	349
1905	Rube Waddell	287
1906	Rube Waddell	196
1907	Rube Waddell	232
1925	Lefty Grove	116
1926	Lefty Grove	194
1927	Lefty Grove	174
1928	Lefty Grove	183
1929	Lefty Grove	170
1930	Lefty Grove	209
1931	Lefty Grove	175

No-Hitters (Italics = Perfect Game)

Name	Date
Weldon Henley	07/22/1905
Chief Bender	05/12/1910
Joe Bush	08/26/1916
Dick Fowler	09/09/1945
Bill McCahan	09/03/1947
Catfish Hunter	*05/08/1968*
Vida Blue	09/21/1970
Mike Warren	09/29/1983
Dave Stewart	06/29/1990

POSTSEASON APPEARANCES

AL West Division Titles

Year	Record	Manager
1971	101–60	Dick Williams
1972	93–62	Dick Williams
1973	94–68	Dick Williams
1974	90–72	Alvin Dark
1975	98–64	Alvin Dark
1981	64–45	Billy Martin
1988	104–58	Tony LaRussa
1989	99–63	Tony LaRussa
1990	103–59	Tony LaRussa
1992	96–66	Tony LaRussa
2000	91–70	Art Howe
2002	103–59	Art Howe
2003	96–66	Ken Macha

AL Wild Cards

Year	Record	Manager
2001	102–60	Art Howe

AL Pennants

Year	Record	Manager
1902	83–53	Connie Mack
1905	92–56	Connie Mack
1910	102–48	Connie Mack
1911	101–50	Connie Mack
1913	96–57	Connie Mack
1914	99–53	Connie Mack
1929	104–46	Connie Mack
1930	102–52	Connie Mack
1931	107–45	Connie Mack
1972	93–62	Dick Williams
1973	94–68	Dick Williams
1974	90–72	Alvin Dark
1988	104–58	Tony LaRussa
1989	99–63	Tony LaRussa
1990	103–59	Tony LaRussa

World Championships

Year	Opponent	MVP
1910	Chicago	
1911	New York	
1913	New York	
1929	Chicago	
1930	St. Louis	
1972	Cincinnati	Gene Tenace
1973	New York	Reggie Jackson
1974	Los Angeles	Rollie Fingers
1989	San Francisco	Dave Stewart

MANAGERS

2003–	Ken Macha
1996–2002	Art Howe
1986–1995	Tony LaRussa
1986	Jeff Newman
1984–1986	Jackie Moore
1983–1984	Steve Boros
1980–1982	Billy Martin
1979	Jim Marshall
1978	Jack McKeon
1977–1978	Bobby Winkles
1977	Jack McKeon
1976	Chuck Tanner
1974–1975	Alvin Dark
1971–1973	Dick Williams
1969–1970	John McNamara
1969	Hank Bauer
1968	Bob Kennedy
1967	Luke Appling
1966–1967	Alvin Dark
1965	Heywood Sullivan
1964–1965	Mel McGaha
1963	Ed Lopat
1961–1962	Hank Bauer
1961	Joe Gordon
1960	Bob Elliott
1957–1959	Harry Craft
1955–1957	Lou Boudreau
1954	Eddie Joost
1951–1953	Jimmie Dykes
1901–1950	Connie Mack

Team Records by Individual Players

Batting Leaders

	Single Season			Career		
	Name		Year	Name		Plate Appearances
Batting average	Nap Lajoie	.426	1901	Al Simmons	.356	5,586
On-base %	Jason Giambi	.477	2001	Jimmy Foxx	.440	5,239
Slugging %	Jimmy Foxx	.749	1932	Jimmy Foxx	.640	5,239
OPS	Jimmy Foxx	1.218	1932	Jimmy Foxx	1.079	5,239
Games	Sal Bando	162	1968	Bert Campaneris	1,795	7,895
At bats	Al Simmons	670	1932	Bert Campaneris	7,180	7,895
Runs	Al Simmons	152	1930	Rickey Henderson	1,270	7,481
Hits	Al Simmons	253	1925	Bert Campaneris	1,882	7,895
Total bases	Jimmy Foxx	438	1932	Al Simmons	2,998	5,586
Doubles	Al Simmons	53	1926	Jimmy Dykes	365	6,990
Triples	Frank Baker	21	1912	Danny Murphy	102	5,676
Home runs	Jimmy Foxx	58	1932	Mark McGwire	363	5,409
RBIs	Jimmy Foxx	169	1932	Al Simmons	1,178	5,586
Walks	Eddie Joost	149	1949	Rickey Henderson	1,227	7,481
Strikeouts	Jose Canseco	175	1986	Reggie Jackson	1,226	5,430
Stolen bases	Rickey Henderson	130	1982	Rickey Henderson	867	7,481
Extra-base hits	Jimmy Foxx	100	1932	Al Simmons	655	5,586
Times on base	Jimmy Foxx	329	1932	Rickey Henderson	3,050	7,481

Pitching Leaders

	Single Season			Career		
	Name		Year	Name		Innings Pitched
ERA	Jack Coombs	1.30	1910	Rube Waddell	1.97	1,869.3
Wins	Jack Coombs	31	1910	Eddie Plank	284	3,860.7
Won-loss %	Lefty Grove	.886	1931	Lefty Grove	.712	2,401
Hits/9 IP	Cy Morgan	5.98	1909	Cy Morgan	6.86	862.7
Walks/9 IP	Catfish Hunter	1.30	1974	Dennis Eckersley	1.30	637
Strikeouts	Rube Waddell	349	1902	Eddie Plank	1,985	3,860.7
Strikeouts/9 IP	Todd Stottlemyre	8.80	1995	Dennis Eckersley	9.30	637
Games	Billy Koch	84	2002	Dennis Eckersley	525	637
Saves	Dennis Eckersley	51	1992	Dennis Eckersley	320	637
Innings	Rube Waddell	383	1904	Eddie Plank	3,860.7	3,860.7
Starts	Rube Waddell	46	1904	Eddie Plank	458	3,860.7
Complete games	Rube Waddell	39	1904	Eddie Plank	362	3,860.7
Shutouts	Jack Coombs	13	1910	Eddie Plank	59	3,860.7

Source: Drawn from data in "Oakland Athletics Batting Leaders (seasonal and career)." http://baseball-reference.com/teams/OAK/leaders_bat.shtml; "Oakland Athletics Pitching Leaders (seasonal and career)." http://baseball-reference.com/teams/OAK/leaders_pitch.shtml.

BIBLIOGRAPHY

Cagan, Joanna, and Neil deMause. *Field of Schemes: How the Great Stadium Swindle Turns Public Money into Private Profit.* Monroe, ME: Common Courage Press, 1998.

Danielson, Michael N. *Home Team: Professional Sports and the American Metropolis.* Princeton, NJ: Princeton University Press, 1997.

Dickey, Glenn. *Champions: The Story of the First Two Oakland A's Dynasties—and the Building of a Third.* Chicago: Triumph Books, 2002.

Jordan, David M. *The Athletics of Philadelphia: Connie Mack's White Elephants, 1901–1954.* Jefferson, NC: McFarland, 1999.

Kaplan, Jim. *Lefty Grove: An American Original.* Cleveland, OH: Society for American Baseball Research, 2000.

Kashatus, William C. *Connie Mack's '29 Triumph.* Jefferson, NC: McFarland, 1999.

Kuklick, Bruce. *To Every Thing a Season: Shibe Park and Urban Philadelphia, 1909–1976.* Princeton, NJ: Princeton University Press, 1991.

Lewis, Michael. *Moneyball: The Art of Winning an Unfair Game.* New York: Norton, 2003.

Markusen, Bruce. *Baseball's Last Dynasty: Charlie Finley's Oakland A's.* Indianapolis, IN: Masters Press, 1998.

Neyer, Rob, and Eddie Epstein. *Baseball Dynasties: The Greatest Teams of All Time.* New York: Norton, 2000.

Peterson, John E. *The Kansas City Athletics: A Baseball History, 1954–1967.* Jefferson, NC: McFarland, 2003.

Philadelphia Athletics Historical Society Web site. http://philadelphiaathletics.org/.

Puerzer, Richard J. "From John McGraw to Joe Torre: Industrial Management Styles Applied throughout the History of Major League Baseball." In *Baseball and American Culture: Across the Diamond,* ed. Edward J. Rielly, 137–49. New York: Haworth Press, 2003.

Riess, Steven A. *City Games: The Evolution of American Urban Society and the Rise of Sports.* Urbana: University of Illinois Press, 1989.

———. *Sport in Industrial America, 1850–1920.* American History Series. Wheeling, IL: Harlan Davidson, 1995.

———. *Touching Base: Professional Baseball and American Culture in the Progressive Era.* Rev. ed. Urbana: University of Illinois Press, 1999.

Sporting News, February 22, 1956, 16–17.

Stuart, Jeffrey Saint John. *Twilight Teams.* Gaithersburg, MD: Sark Publishing, 2000.

Thorn, John, Phil Birnbaum, Bill Deane, et al., eds. *Total Baseball: The Ultimate Baseball Encyclopedia.* 8th ed. Toronto: Sport Media, 2004.

Threshton, Christopher. *The Integration of Baseball in Philadelphia.* Jefferson, NC: McFarland, 2003.

2003 Oakland A's Media Guide. Tempe, AZ: Ben Franklin Press, 2003.

2004 Oakland A's Media Guide. Fresno, CA: Dumont Printing, 2004.

Westcott, Rich. *A Century of Philadelphia Sports.* Philadelphia: Temple University Press, 2001.

Seattle Mariners

Adam R. Hornbuckle

The Seattle Mariners played their first game on April 6, 1977, in front of 57,762 fans at the $67 million Kingdome, and promptly lost to the Anaheim Angels. The Mariners would go on to earn a reputation as the worst expansion team in the history of American professional sports over the next several years, as it failed to post a winning season until 1991. In three of their first seven seasons the Mariners lost over 100 games. Art Thiel, a sportswriter for the *Seattle Post-Intelligencer*, described the Mariners' quest to better .500 as "the slowest meandering to a winning season of any expansion team in modern American professional sports." By the mid-1990s, however, the Mariners had become a major-league powerhouse led by All-Stars Ken Griffey Jr., Randy Johnson, Edgar Martinez, and Alex Rodriguez. In 2001 the Mariners won 116 games, tying a major-league record for the most games won in a single season, but failed to win the American League pennant, losing to the New York Yankees.

THE MAJORS COME TO SEATTLE

Seattle had a long history as a minor-league baseball town, but did not get a major-league team until 1969, when it was awarded an expansion franchise, the Seattle Pilots. The team went 64–98, playing in Sick's Stadium. The team was days from bankruptcy during the 1970 spring-training season when owners and brothers Dewey and Max Soriano sold the Pilots to a Milwaukee business consortium led by Bud Selig. Selig, a prominent Milwaukee businessman and leader, wanted to bring MLB back to Milwaukee after Atlanta lured the Braves' franchise south for the 1965 season. Seattle lost the Pilots not because of a distaste for professional sports, but because the city did not possess a wealthy individual or group willing to buy the Pilots and invest the capital needed to develop a winning major-league team. Washington attorney general Slade Gorton considered his hometown "quintessentially middle class" in contrast to the slums and great concentrations of wealth dotting the eastern seaboard. For example, the two wealthiest families in Seattle, the Boeings and the Weyerhaeusers, aircraft- and forestry-industry magnates respectively, had spread their wealth generously over several generations. Only the Nordstroms, owners of the Pacific Northwest's leading upscale department store, possessed enough capital to finance a professional sports team. They had no interest in buying the Pilots, but they did bring the expansion NFL Seahawks to the Emerald City in 1976.

Exempt from antitrust laws, MLB enjoys unfettered discretion in determining who owns a franchise and where it is located. While most of MLB's location decisions have been above the board, some were improperly influenced, as occurred in Seattle. In 1973 Attorney General Gorton sued the AL for violating its own code of conduct in determining the location of baseball franchises and for not upholding its promise to field a team in Seattle. There was talk about selling the White Sox and moving the club to Seattle to block Gorton's suit. Gorton hired Bill Dwyer, an ambitious young Seattle attorney, to prosecute the case. Instead of charging the league with breach of contract and fraud in permitting the sale and relocation of the Pilots, Dwyer argued that the AL had violated its lease and other financial agreements with the city. Rather than seeking a financial settlement, Dwyer and Gorton sought to expose the owners' improprieties to a jury and, ultimately, secure another expansion team for Seattle. The case went to trial in 1976 with witness Charles O. Finley, the boisterous and ill-tempered owner of the Oakland Athletics, exposing the major-league owners' questionable business practices. Thanks to the loose-tongued Finley, the AL agreed to franchise a baseball team in Seattle for the 1977 season in exchange for the $32.5 million suit being dropped.

News of major-league baseball's return to Seattle resounded through the Puget Sound region, but the city lacked much enthusiasm for a new team, especially for one born from depositions and legal opinions. Emmett Watson, sportswriter for the *Seattle Post-Intelligencer,* remarked that the new team should have been named the Litigants instead of the Mariners. Despite the public's lack of passion, Lester Smith, a local broadcasting and recording executive, stepped forward to be part owner of the Mariners along with his friend Danny Kaye, the renowned Hollywood entertainer. Kaye provided most of the $6.5 million required to purchase and initially finance the team, but also received funds from four local businessmen interested in seeing baseball return to Seattle: jeweler Stan Golub, furniture executive Walter Schoenfeld, department-store executive Jim Walsh, and construction contractor Jim Stillwell.

Smith and Kaye owned the Mariners from 1977 to 1980, when the team won only 246 of 646 games. Total attendance at home games dropped each year, starting with an impressive 1,338,511 in 1977, but sinking to a bleak 836,204 in 1980. The drop was less from a lack of initial enthusiasm than overall fan dissatisfaction with a losing team and a bad place to watch the Mariners play ball, the sterile Kingdome. The Mariners' poor performance reflected in part management's failure to select promising young players during the 1977 expansion draft. Smith later revealed that the established owners had frozen "all the good players," limiting the Mariners and the Toronto Blue Jays, the other expansion team, to less talented players. "If I had known what was going happen," Smith remarked, "I wouldn't have touched [baseball] with a ten-foot pole." Some Mariners, however, gained recognition, such as outfielder Leon Roberts, who had 22 home runs, 92 RBIs, and a .301 batting average in 1978, and first baseman Bruce Bochte, an All-Star in 1979, who led the franchise with a .300 batting average and 78 RBIs in 1980. Former Dodger Maury Wills replaced Darrell Johnson as manager midway through 1980, but failed to lift the team. When the Mariners started the 1981 campaign 6–18 Wills was fired, to be replaced by Rene Lachemann. By the time Lachemann replaced Wills as manager, the partnership led by Smith and Kaye had disintegrated.

George Argyros, a real-estate developer from Orange County, California, bought the sagging team in January 1981 for $13.1 million. The Mariners experienced much chaos and instability under Argyros. The team had seven managers in his eight years of ownership. Dave Henderson, the Mariners' center fielder from 1981 to 1987, noted how managerial instability contributed to the team's inconsistency, because "every manager wanted to create his own identity." In 1986 the Mariners changed managers three times, moving from Chuck Cottier to Marty Martinez to Dick Williams, who remained in the position until 1988, when Jim Snyder replaced him in midseason. There were bright spots, however. In 1984 the Mariners placed fifth, Alvin Davis was named AL Rookie of the Year, with 27 homers and 116 RBIs, and teammate Mark Langston placed second in the Rookie of the Year ballot after posting a 17–10 record and a league-leading 204 strikeouts.

Argyros disrupted all of MLB when in 1987 he attempted to buy the San Diego Padres while still owning the Mariners. This violated major-league rules against tampering with another team. Commissioner Peter Ueberroth fined Argyros $10,000 and placed the Mariners in a trust for two months while allowing the offer to proceed. Although the proposed purchase fell through, Argyros held on to the Mariners despite efforts by local businessmen to purchase the team. In 1989 Argyros finally sold the team to Jeff Smulyan, a radio-broadcasting executive from Indianapolis. Argyros made more than $50 million on the sale, and for all his complaints about the unfavorable market conditions in Seattle, he made a $2 million operating profit in his final year of ownership.

THE JEFF SMULYAN ERA

During Smulyan's tenure, the Mariners enjoyed their first winning season, winning 83 and losing 79 games in 1991. Seattle had made great strides toward becoming a winning team late in the Argyros era, going 78–84 in 1987, its best record up to then. The Mariners boasted two All-Stars that year, pitcher Mark Langston, 19–13 with an ERA of 3.84, and Harold Reynolds, who stole a then team record 60 bases. In 1989 the Mariners traded Langston, who had led the AL three times in strikeouts and was the club's best pitcher, to the Montreal Expos for three pitchers, including Randy Johnson, an unknown left-hander and the tallest pitcher in major-league history at 6 feet 10 inches. By 1991 Johnson would become the Mariners' ace, going 13–10 and striking out 228 batters. Seattle brought Ken Griffey Jr. up from the minors in 1989. Griffey, Seattle's first-round draft pick in 1987, made his major-league debut in the team's first home game that season, and launched a home run on the first pitch thrown to him. In 1990 the Mariners acquired Ken Griffey Sr. from the Atlanta Braves to become the first team in major-league history to possess a father-son duo. Griffey Jr. contributed to the Mariners' 1991 winning season by posting 22 home runs, 100 RBIs, a .327 batting average, and a .527 slugging average, winning the Silver Slugger Award.

Much of the Mariners' improvement came under Jim LeFebvre, who replaced Jim Snyder as manager at the beginning of the 1989 season. The eighth manager the team's 12-year history, LeFebvr e brought a stability absent in previous years. Senior management disliked his boisterous and unrestrained personality, however—he often complained to the media about management's reluctance to increase the payroll to pay for much-needed players. Despite leading the Mariners to a winning season, Lefebvre was fired by general manager Woody Woodward. Woodward's decision to fire LeFebvre came as a surprise. The team then was secretly planning to move to Tampa by 1993, and the general manager did not want to share this information with the loose-lipped LeFebvre, especially after he "voiced his complaints about ownership and management in the media." Woodward chose to fire him rather than risk exposure of the team's secret relocation plans. However, the media learned of the plan in August 1991 when the *Seattle Times* obtained records from Smulyan's local creditor, Security Pacific Bank Washington, which revealed his intention to put the team up for sale in November and move it out of Seattle after the 1992 season.

Smulyan asked community leaders for a plan to keep the team in Seattle after his plans were discovered. By 1992 he wanted to see the team raise its revenues to 90 percent of the AL average through huge increases in ticket sales, new corporate sponsorships and advertising, and the establishment of the club's first cable-television deal. Despite this proposal, Smulyan announced he was selling the club on December 6. Smulyan had worked out a deal with Tampa business and community leaders to move the club there. Major-league owners had long been interested in establishing a team in Tampa, especially since it had already built a domed stadium. More importantly, Tampa business and community interests had promised Smulyan a ticket base of 22,000 and a cable-television package worth $12 million. This was a striking improvement, because in 1991 the team had a major-league worst $3 million TV contract. The only thing holding up the sale was a 120-day local buyers provision in the city's lease. But the campaign for a local buyer floundered, as major Seattle businesses such as Boeing and Weyerhaeuser showed no interest. In the meantime Smulyan attended the annual meeting of AL owners in Miami, Florida, where he presented his plan to move the Mariners from Seattle, a city long seen by the league as a losing proposition. Smulyan received full support from his colleagues, especially from George W. Bush, small-time oilman and managing director of the Texas Rangers, who stated, "Whatever Jeff has to do, we're behind him."

Despite the uncertainty of baseball remaining in Seattle in the early 1990s, the city's economic and social demographics started moving in baseball's favor. Businessmen with the wealth, interest, and enthusiasm to keep the Mariners in place began to emerge. During the 1980s Seattle had become a haven for entrepreneurs in the emerging computer, cellular-phone, and video-game industries. In 1978 Bill Gates and Paul Allen, graduates of Seattle's esteemed Lakeside School, moved their nascent computer-software company, Microsoft, from Albuquerque, New Mexico, to the burgeoning suburb of Bellevue. In 1986, following Microsoft's initial public stock offering, which turned Gates and Allen into billionaires, the company moved to Redmond, where by 1991 it had grown in value to $21.9 billion. In 1980 Craig McCaw, another Lakeside graduate and cable-TV entrepreneur, established Northwest Mobile Telephone in Bellevue to capture a segment of the promising cellular-phone market. Known as McCaw Cellular by the late 1980s, the company became a national force in the burgeoning cellular-phone business, with revenues of $78 million in 1986. McCaw earned $2.39 billion in its initial public stock offering. In 1980 the Japan-based video-game company Nintendo established its North American base in the suburb of Tukwila, and largely on the success of the video game *Donkey Kong*, the company's sales topped $5.3 billion by 1992.

Soon after Smulyan announced the sale of the Mariners, Slade Gorton, now a U.S. senator, again stepped up to the plate to keep baseball in Seattle. Gorton decided to pursue the possibility of a Japanese buyer, a route that he had considered taking when Argyros talked about buying the Padres while still owning the Mariners in 1987 because of the strength then of the Japanese economy and Japan's great interest in baseball. After being rebuffed by the U.S. ambassador to Japan, Gorton called on President Minouru Arakawa of Nintendo of America, asking if he would be interested in buying a baseball team. Arakawa's assistant returned Gorton's call, indicating that while Arakawa was not interested in baseball, he would meet with the senator. After meeting with Gorton, Arakawa called Hiroshi Yamauchi, his father-in-law and president of Nintendo. Yamauchi, to his son-in-law's surprise, accepted Gorton's proposal, noting that "the purchase would be a good public relations gesture," and besides, "it is always good to have a senator as a friend."

Yamauchi's willingness to commit $100 million toward the team's purchase price was more to show his gratitude to the city of Seattle and the state of Washington than because of his love of baseball. The businessmen believed he owed "something back to the community." Gorton feared a backlash from anti-Japanese sentiments, which saw Japanese investment in American business and property as a threat to the nation's economic sovereignty. He assembled a group of American partners, particularly from Seattle, who would become known as the Baseball Club of Seattle. Although Gorton did not contact him directly, Chris Larson, a lead programmer at Microsoft, who graduated from Lakeside a couple of years behind Gates and returned to Seattle to work for Microsoft in 1981, expressed the most interest in financing the Mariners' stay in Seattle. Lawson, who grew up on baseball, attended a Pilots game at age 10, and sneaked a transistor radio into class to listen to the World Series, assembled seven other Microsoft employees interested in investing in the Mariners. Gorton also gained a commitment from his friend Wayne Perry, second-in-command at McCaw Cellular, and the Baseball Club solidified its hometown base by getting Frank Shortz, the chairman and CEO of Boeing, to invest $10,000. As a representative of Seattle's established elite, Shortz's membership in the Baseball Club indicated support from key community leaders.

Despite the formation of domestic partners and backers, the potential purchase of the Mariners by a Japanese majority interest left many within major-league baseball uneasy. Baseball commissioner Fay Vincent proclaimed that baseball "has a strong policy against approving investors from outside the U.S and Canada," adding that approval of the deal "was unlikely." The conflict became headlines on the CBS evening news and in the *New York Times* the next day. Dave Anderson of the *New York Times* described baseball's position as "narrow as a bat handle." Media sources soon disclosed that the Japanese already owned minor-league teams in Vancouver, British Columbia; Birmingham, Alabama; and Visalia, California, and that MLB had nothing in its charter against foreign investment, only "a recommended policy" adopted informally a couple of years earlier.

Gorton exercised his own political muscle in contacting George W. Bush, the managing director of the Texas Rangers, the one AL owner who wasn't predisposed to hate him from his earlier history of baseball battles. Gorton convinced the younger Bush that his plan was not a plot to undermine the national pastime. He probably had discussions with George Bush Sr. on the matter too. Gorton said that he imagined "that President Bush would not want his son voting against Japanese ownership of a Major League team. He was an internationalist and Japan was one of our great allies. He would not want his son accused of xenophobia." The younger Bush took a leading role in getting his fellow owners to move forward on the purchase.

Early in June 1991, the MLB ownership committee met with members of the Baseball Club of Seattle. The committee insisted that a single individual, not a corporation, had to be the club's managing general partner. The committee was not interested in a proposal with Yamauchi in control. Yamauchi subsequently met with his partners and agreed to reduce his ownership share to 49 percent, while shifting part of his investment into the $25 million operating capital agreed to by the purchasers. To meet MLB's requirements, the Baseball Club of Seattle formed a seven-member board of American citizens, which appointed attorney James Ellis, who had led the fight to build the Kingdome, as managing general partner. Ownership was divided into classes of A and B stock that precluded Yamauchi from having majority control, even though he had 60 percent of the total investment. After Ellis agreed to contribute $250,000 of his own money to the team, the MLB ownership committee voted on June 10, 1992, to approve the sale.

Before the Baseball Club of Seattle purchase of the Mariners in 1992, the team had cycled through nine managers, each staying an average of 1.6 years, with the longest tenures held by Darrell Johnson, from 1977 to 1980, and Jim LeFebvre, from 1989 to 1991. Under Bill Plummer, the last of the Smulyan-era managers, the Mariners dipped far below .500 (64–98). In 1993, the owners hired Lou Piniella to manage the Mariners. Originally drafted by the Seattle Pilots in 1969, but traded immediately to the Kansas City Royals, Piniella had played for the Royals and the New York Yankees. After retiring from the Yankees in 1984 he served in various managerial and advisory posts with the Yankees before managing the Cincinnati Reds from 1989 to 1992. In his first year the Mariners bettered .500 for the second time in club history (82–80).

Then, in 1995, Piniella led the Mariners to the AL West title, defeating the California Angels in a title-deciding playoff game. Piniella was named Manager of the Year, and Randy Johnson won the Cy Young Award (18–2), leading the league in strikeouts (294) and ERA (2.48). DH Edgar Martinez led the league in batting (.356). The following year the Mariners set a club record of 85 wins, but finished second in the AL West behind the Texas Rangers. The team had the best offense in the league (four men had over 100 RBIs), but the pitching was weak. The team hit 245 homers, led by Griffey (49) and Jay Buhner (44). Twenty-year-old shortstop Alex Rodriguez led the AL in batting (.358), runs (141), and total bases (379). The turnout reached 2.7 million, the first time the team was not in the lower half in team attendance, and since then Seattle has been no lower than fifth. In 1997 the Mariners improved the club record to 90 wins, winning the AL West title, but lost the AL Championship Series to the Orioles in four games. The Mariners led the AL in scoring, propelled by 264 home runs, the most in major-league history. Six men had 20 or more, led by Griffey with 56. He was MVP, leading the league in slugging (.646), runs (125), total bases (393), and homers. Johnson was sensational (20–4, 2.28 ERA), and fellow starters Jeff Fassaro (16–9) and Jamie Moyer (17–5) were very strong, but the rest of the staff was dreadful, attested by a team ERA of 4.79, 11th of 14 teams.

In March 1994 King County Executive Gary Locke appointed a 28-member task force to determine the need, cost, and location of a new major-league baseball stadium. As the task force deliberated the issue, the need for a new stadium became undeniably clear when on July 19 several wooden tiles fell from the ceiling of the Kingdom before the start of a game, which was then canceled. The Mariners played their remaining 15 games on the road. The repairs cost $70 million. The stadium task force recommended public participation in financing a much-needed baseball stadium, but King County voters in September 1995 narrowly defeated a proposal to increase sales taxes to finance construction. In October the state legislature authorized a funding package that included 0.017 percent credits against state sales taxes, sales of special stadium license plates, and receipts from sports-themed lottery games. New levies were added in King County, including a 2 percent car-rental surcharge, a 0.5 percent tax on food and beverage in restaurants

Randy Johnson pitches in game 4 of the American League Division Series playoff against the Baltimore Orioles, 1997. © AP / Wide World Photos

and bars, and a ballpark admission tax of up to 5 percent. In October, the King County Council approved the funding package and established the Washington State Major League Baseball Public Facilities District (PFD) to construct, own, and operate the new ballpark at a site south of the Kingdome.

At a cost of $517.6 million, the new field became the most expensive baseball park ever built, with King County picking up $372 million (63 percent) of the cost. The edifice was designed by Seattle-based NBBJ and built by Hunt-Kiewit. Construction began in March 1997, and on June 4, 1998, naming rights for the stadium were sold to Safeco Corporation, a Seattle-based insurance company, for $1.8 million for 10 years.

The park is designed in a retro style, has a retractable roof that does not close all the way yet keeps fans protected from the elements, and has real grass. Its 46,621 seats are close to the field, and fans have great sight lines. Nearly half of the spectators are drawn from beyond the immediate Puget Sound area. The amenities include a baseball museum, a team store, and picnic and children's play areas.

The team got a sweetheart 20-year lease with the stadium management in 1996. The Mariners get to run the stadium and keep all revenue from concessions, luxury suites, and parking; they have also been booking up to 180 other events each year like parties, proms, and graduations, making as much as $8 million. The team is supposed to share 10 percent of its operating profits with the county, but only once the team's cumulative net loss, $108 million in 2005, is eliminated.

In 1998 the Mariners finished with a losing record and finished third. At the end of July they traded star pitcher Randy Johnson, who was going to become a free agent at the end of the season, to Houston for prospects Freddy Garcia, Carlos Guillen, and John Halama. The Mariners played their first game in Safeco Field on July 15, 1999, losing 3–2 to the San Diego Padres. The club again came in third in 1999. Piniella achieved a major-league milestone in becoming the 14th manager to earn both 1,000 wins as a manager and 1,000 hits as a player. After the season Griffey was traded to Cincinnati in a cost-cutting move. He was earning $8.8 million, having hit 398 homers in 11 All-Star seasons. In 2000, their first full year at Safeco Field, the Mariners returned to the playoffs as a wild-card team and swept the Chicago White Sox in the AL Divisional Series, but lost the ALCS to the New York Yankees in six games. Pitcher Kazuhiro Sasaki, the first of several successful Japanese players on the Mariners' roster, earned AL Rookie of the Year honors with 37 saves. Three men had over 100 RBIs, including Martinez with 145 to lead the AL. After the season Rodriguez became a free agent and signed with the Texas Rangers for $250 million. He was just 24, with four All-Star appearances, and had already hit 189 home runs.

In 2001 the Mariners tied the major-league record by winning 116 games, despite the absence of former superstars Johnson, Griffey, and Rodriguez. The team had the best defense and offense in the AL, stressing speed rather than power. Five pitchers won 10 or more games, led by Jamie Moyer (20–6), and were supported by Sasaki, with 45 saves. Newcomer Ichiro Suzuki was Rookie of the Year and MVP, leading the AL in batting (.350) and steals (56). Second baseman Bret Boone also had a great year, batting .331 with 37 homers and 141 RBIs. Eight men made the All-Star team. After defeating the Cleveland Indians in the ALDS in five games, the Mariners were dominated by the underdog New York Yankees and lost the ALCS in five games. Piniella was recognized as AL Manager of the Year, while general manager Pat Gillick won Executive of the Year.

In 2002, the Mariners won 93 games, second most in their history, yet came in third. Over three years they had won 300 games, the 16th club to achieve that mark. The Mariners set a franchise record for attendance of 3,540,482 in 2002, the second year in a row that the club led the AL. In 2003 Bob Melvin replaced Piniella, who resigned from Seattle after posting an 840–711 record at the team's helm to manage his hometown Tampa Bay Devil Rays. Manager Bob Melvin led the club to another 93-win season, good for second place. Boone had over 100 RBIs for the third straight year and Moyer won 21 games. The team had a meltdown the following season and won just 63, a 30-game differential from the year before. Ichiro hit .372 and had 262 hits to break the single-season hit record of 256 established by George Sisler in 1920. The Mariners replaced Melvin as manager with Mike Hargrove. The 2005 club did only marginally better, going 69–93.

Despite middling success on the field, the Mariners are financially among the most successful teams in baseball. At the start of 2005 they ranked fifth

Ichiro Suzuki singles against the Texas Rangers for his final hit of the season, 2004. © AP / Wide World Photos

among all teams with a value of $415 million, 63 times their initial $6.5 million cost, fifth in revenues ($173 million), and seventh in player costs ($84 million), less than half of total revenue. In 2004 they had an operating income of $10.8 million, 10th in the majors. Between 2000 and 2004, Seattle was first in operating profits with an average of $17 million, third in attendance at 3.3 million (fans paid an average of $24 a ticket, fifth highest in the AL), fourth in total revenues ($163 million), and fifth in media revenues ($53 million). The Mariners signed a 10-year, $250 million TV contract with Fox in 2000, surpassed only by the New York and Atlanta clubs. This small-market team, in the 20th-largest market in MLB, has made out rather well for its shareholders.

NOTABLE ACHIEVEMENTS

Most Valuable Players

Year	Name	Position
1997	Ken Griffey Jr.	OF
2001	Ichiro Suzuki	OF

Cy Young Winners

Year	Name	Position
1995	Randy Johnson	LHP

Rookies of the Year

Year	Name	Position
1984	Alvin Davis	1B
2000	Kazuhiro Sasaki	P
2001	Ichiro Suzuki	OF

Batting Champions

Year	Name	#
1992	Edgar Martinez	.343
1995	Edgar Martinez	.356
1996	Alex Rodriguez	.358
2001	Ichiro Suzuki	.350
2004	Ichiro Suzuki	.372

Home-Run Champions

Year	Name	#
1994	Ken Griffey Jr.	40
1997	Ken Griffey Jr.	56
1998	Ken Griffey Jr.	56
1999	Ken Griffey Jr.	48

ERA Champions

Year	Name	#
1995	Randy Johnson	2.48
2001	Freddy Garcia	3.05

Strikeout Champions

Year	Name	#
1982	Floyd Bannister	209
1984	Mark Langston	204
1986	Mark Langston	245
1987	Mark Langston	262
1992	Randy Johnson	241
1993	Randy Johnson	308

1994	Randy Johnson	204
1995	Randy Johnson	294

No-Hitters

Name	Date
Randy Johnson	06/02/1990
Chris Bosio	04/22/1993

POSTSEASON APPEARANCES

AL West Division Titles

Year	Record	Manager
1995	79–66	Lou Piniella
1997	90–72	Lou Piniella
2001	116–46	Lou Piniella

AL Wild Cards

Year	Record	Manager
2000	91–71	Lou Piniella

MANAGERS

2005–	Mike Hargrove
2003–2004	Bob Melvin
1993–2002	Lou Piniella
1992	Bill Plummer
1989–1991	Jim Lefebvre
1988	Dick Snyder
1986–1988	Dick Williams
1986	Marty Martinez
1984–1986	Chuck Cottier
1983–1984	Del Crandall
1981–1983	Rene Lachemann
1980–1981	Maury Wills
1977–1980	Darrell Johnson

Team Records by Individual Players

Batting Leaders

| | Single Season | | | Career | |
	Name		Year	Name		Plate Appearances
Batting average	Ichiro Suzuki	.372	2004	Ichiro Suzuki	.332	3,692
On-base %	Edgar Martinez	.479	1995	Edgar Martinez	.418	8,672
Slugging %	Ken Griffey Jr.	.674	1994	Ken Griffey Jr.	.569	6,688
OPS	Edgar Martinez	1.107	1995	Ken Griffey Jr.	.948	6,688
Games	Willie Horton/ Ruppert Jones	162	1979	Edgar Martinez	2,055	8,672
At bats	Ichiro Suzuki	704	2004	Edgar Martinez	7,213	8,672
Runs	Alex Rodriguez	141	1996	Edgar Martinez	1,219	8,672
Hits	Ichiro Suzuki	262	2004	Edgar Martinez	2,247	8,672
Total bases	Ken Griffey Jr.	393	1997	Edgar Martinez	3,718	8,672
Doubles	Alex. Rodriguez	54	1996	Edgar Martinez	514	8,672
Triples	Ichiro Suzuki	12	2005	Harold Reynolds	48	4,593
Home runs	Ken Griffey Jr.	56	1997	Ken Griffey Jr.	398	6,688
RBIs	Ken Griffey Jr.	147	1997	Edgar Martinez	1,261	8,672
Walks	Edgar Martinez	123	1996	Edgar Martinez	1,283	8,762
Strikeouts	Mike Cameron	176	2002	Jay Buhner	1,375	5,828
Stolen bases	Harold Reynolds	60	1987	Julio Cruz	290	3,068
Extra-base hits	Ken Griffey Jr.	93	1997	Edgar Martinez	838	8,672
Times on base	Ichiro Suzuki	315	2004	Edgar Martinez	3,619	8,672

Pitching Leaders

| | Single Season | | | Career | |
	Name		Year	Name		Innings Pitched
ERA	Randy Johnson	2.28	1997	Randy Johnson	3.42	1,838.3
Wins	Jamie Moyer	21	2003	Jamie Moyer	139	1,933
Won-loss %	Randy Johnson	.900	1995	Jamie Moyer	.650	1,933
Hits/9 IP	Randy Johnson	6.21	1997	Randy Johnson	6.92	1,838.3
Walks/9 IP	Jamie Moyer	1.61	1998	Jamie Moyer	2.23	1933
Strikeouts	Randy Johnson	308	1993	Randy Johnson	2,162	1,838.3
Strikeouts/9 IP	Randy Johnson	12.35	1995	Randy Johnson	10.58	1,838.3
Games	Ed Vande Berg	78	1982	Jeff Nelson	432	447.3
Saves	Kazuhiro Sasaki	45	2001	Kazuhiro Sasaki	129	223.3
Innings	Mark Langston	272	1987	Jamie Moyer	1933	1933
Starts	Mike Moore	37	1986	Jamie Moyer	298	1933
Complete games	Mike Moore	14	1985	Mike Moore	56	1457
Shutouts	Dave Fleming	4	1992	Randy Johnson	19	1836.3

Source: Drawn from data in "Seattle Mariners Batting Leaders (seasonal and career)." http://baseball-reference.com/ teams/SEA/leaders_bat.shtml; "Seattle Mariners Pitching Leaders (seasonal and career)." http://baseball-reference. com/teams/SEA/leaders_pitch.shtml.

BIBLIOGRAPHY

Dozer, Richard. "Seattle in American…Well, Almost: AL Decides to Let Seattle Try Again." *Chicago Tribune,* February 1, 1976.

Fobes, Natalie, Frank Wetzel, and John W. Ellis. *A Diamond in the Emerald City.* Seattle: Seattle Mariners, 1999.

Murphy, Victoria. "Seattle's Best-Kept Secret." *Forbes,* April 25, 2005, 86–95.

Seattle Mariners official Web site. http://seattle.mariners.mlb.com/.

Sports E-Cyclopedia. "Seattle Mariners." http://www.sportsecyclopedia.com/al/seattlems/mariners.html.

Thiel, Art. *Out of Left Field: How the Mariners Made Baseball Fly in Seattle.* Seattle: Sasquatch Books, 2003

Tampa Bay Devil Rays

Paul M. Pedersen

The Tampa Bay Devil Rays—who came into existence in 1998 as an expansion franchise—have a much longer and intriguing off-the-field history than what their on-field record might suggest. The quest to secure the area's Major League Baseball team and build its first MLB stadium is one of the most poignant examples of urban sporting rivalry. But in preceding decades there had been multiple baseball battles between Tampa Bay's two prominent cities. These previous competitions had laid the foundation for the intense battle that emerged between St. Petersburg and Tampa. The sporting rivalry between these two cities, separated by Tampa Bay, received its impetus shortly after the turn of the century when baseball teams began to migrate to warmer climates for spring training. Although St. Petersburg initiated the movement to lure baseball franchises to the west coast of Florida, the first to come, the Chicago Cubs in 1913, played in Tampa. Throughout the twentieth century, both cities built baseball complexes and competed for teams until the Tampa Bay metropolitan area established itself as the spring-training capital. Seven different teams have trained in Tampa (the Cubs, Boston Red Sox, Washington Senators, Detroit Tigers, Cincinnati Reds, Chicago White Sox, and New York Yankees) while St. Petersburg has had eight (the St. Louis Browns, Philadelphia Phillies, Boston Braves, New York Yankees, St. Louis Cardinals, New York Giants, New York Mets, and Devil Rays).

While spring training acted as a prelude for each upcoming baseball season, both cities ultimately hoped that their storied traditions as spring hosts would lead to a full-time baseball club. Promoters on both sides of the bay believed that the area's historic romance with baseball reflected the interest the region had in the sport and would be the basis of support for a permanent major-league club.

QUEST FOR A BASEBALL STADIUM

In 1976, at a time when the population of the Tampa Bay metro area consisted of over 1.1 million residents, St. Petersburg began to seriously consider the construction of a baseball stadium that would be used to obtain the first MLB franchise for Florida. Boosters and civic leaders believed that a baseball stadium and its accompanying team would be visible signs of the economic and social rejuvenation their downtown needed. For six years, the city slowly moved forward with the preliminary work of this endeavor, unimpeded and unchallenged by its rival metropolis across the bay. When Tampa entered the stadium race in 1982, it could not convince St. Petersburg to step aside. The stadium battle raged on until St. Petersburg—after a decade of planning, urban site clearing, lawsuits, political reversals, and hotly debated governmental votes—began in 1987 construction of a 43,000-seat multipurpose sports facility. By 1990, a domed stadium was completed on the western edge of downtown. During the construction process Tampa yielded St. Petersburg the rights to the region's first baseball stadium, the Florida Suncoast Dome. It was renamed the Thunderdome in 1993 after the arrival of the NHL's Tampa Bay Lightning and Tropicana Field in 1996 after Tropicana Dole Beverages signed a 30-year, $46 million naming-rights deal.

QUEST FOR A BASEBALL TEAM

The quest to bring a permanent baseball franchise to Tampa Bay involved relocation and expansion efforts that lasted a dozen years. In 1983, the Tampa Bay Baseball Group (TBBG) made a $24 million bid for Calvin Griffith's majority ownership of the Minnesota Twins. The investors eventually purchased 42 percent of the club for $11.5 million. But a last-minute ticket purchase by Minneapolis and St. Paul corporations kept Griffith from activating an escape clause that would have allowed his team's relocation to Tampa. This action forced Griffith to sell his majority share to Carl Pohlad, a leader in the local business community, for $32 million. At the behest of Commissioner Bowie Kuhn, who hinted that compliance might bring future considerations, the TBBG agreed to relinquish its minority-ownership portion for no profit to the new baseball proprietor.

Tampa Bay's second attempt to obtain a franchise came in April 1985 when the TBBG reached an agreement to buy the Oakland Athletics for $37 million. An all-night meeting, however, between Oakland mayor Lionel Wilson and A's president Roy Eisenhardt resulted in a new stadium lease, a $10 million loan for the team from the city of Oakland, and the second aborted purchase endeavor by the TBBG.

Three years later, Tampa shifted its sights to Texas, where a variety of factors forced the Rangers onto the baseball market. Although this team had consistently shown an operating profit, majority owner Eddie Chiles struck a deal with a new Tampa ownership group (MXM Corporation) to buy his club for $74 million. But the Tampa investors were eliminated when Commissioner Peter Ueberroth discouraged the deal and the team's minority owner (Ed Gaylord) decided to exercise his option to purchase Chiles's share of the Rangers.

The negotiations between Tampa and the Rangers overlapped St. Petersburg's quest to obtain the Chicago White Sox. Owners Jerry Reinsdorf and Eddie Einhorn began serious relocation plans after Chicago residents defeated a final stadium bond issue in 1987. To entice the owners, the Florida legislature approved a low-interest loan of $20 million to the White Sox, and St. Petersburg offered a rent-free lease on its as-yet uncompleted facility. But St. Petersburg lost another relocation opportunity when, in unsanctioned overtime (according to Illinois law, no legislation could be enacted after midnight at the conclusion of the legislative session) after the 1988 legislative session, the Illinois lawmakers turned off the clock, ignored the deadline, and found enough votes to grant the White Sox $150 million to build a new baseball stadium across the street from Comiskey Park.

The NL created an expansion committee that solicited more than a dozen bids for a 1991 expansion. St. Petersburg was a front-runner early on, but its ownership groups collapsed. Tampa Bay's bid began to falter and lost out to Miami's and Denver's financial and organizational packages.

The west coast of Florida launched in 1991 its sixth quest for a team when Jeff Smulyan put his struggling Seattle Mariners up for sale. A prospective St. Petersburg ownership group quickly placed an offer for the club. Seattle began to lose all hope of retaining the team until Hiroshi Yamauchi, a Japanese video-game tycoon, offered to buy the franchise. Many Americans cried out that the national pastime should not be allowed to join the many other businesses that had fallen into Far East hands. But Washington and Seattle officials threatened everything from racial-discrimination suits to antitrust legislation to persuade baseball to validate the Yamauchi offer. In July 1992, MLB approved the sale to Yamauchi in order to keep the team in Seattle.

That same year, Commissioner Fay Vincent allowed Bob Lurie of the Giants to shop for offers after Bay Area residents rejected four initiatives to tax themselves into building a fan-friendly stadium to replace the 30-year-old Candlestick Park. For the seventh time, St. Petersburg became the front-runner. The Tampa Bay Ownership Group (TBOG), led by St. Petersburg industrialist Vincent J. Naimoli, received baseball's endorsement and offered Lurie $115 million for his team. But MLB rejected the relocation offer when a local San Francisco ownership group, led by Safeway president Peter Magowan, stepped forward with a $100 million proposal.

For the next two years, Tampa Bay baseball boosters brooded over the failure to secure the Giants. By 1994, however, the promoters found renewed optimism and agreed to suspend all of their lawsuits against organized baseball when rumors began to circulate that their perseverance would be rewarded with an expansion franchise. In March 1995, the MLB Expansion Committee awarded expansion teams to Arizona and Naimoli's St. Petersburg ownership group. The members of the TBOG purchased the rights to this expansion franchise for $130 million. In an effort to show the unified sporting image of the region, the new baseball club was named, after receiving nearly 7,000 suggestions, the Tampa Bay Devil Rays. The west coast of Florida, after seven humiliating failures, found victory in its eighth quest to obtain a team. What began as a dream in 1976 became a reality in 1998 when the Devil Rays opened their inaugural season against the Detroit Tigers in Tropicana Field. Over 2.5 million fans came into the stadium to watch the expansion franchise throughout the 1998 season. But the novelty quickly wore off, and after averaging nearly 31,000 spectators per game in the inaugural year, the Devils Rays have been averaging around 15,000 in each year since, and have been last in the AL since 2001.

THE DEVELOPMENT OF THE DEVIL RAYS

MLB provided the expansion teams (the Devil Rays and Diamondbacks) of 1995 the luxury of three years to participate in three drafts, set up their organizations, and develop players. This gave the new clubs an opportunity to be successful franchises on the field soon after their April 1998 openers. This was very different from the expansion teams of 1993, which had their farm systems in place for only one year and participated in just one amateur draft before they began play. The Devil Rays took advantage of this opportunity by taking their time with the selection of a general manager, the formulation of a minor-league structure, and the drafting and signing of players.

The new general manager would shape the immediate and long-term future of professional baseball in Tampa Bay. Therefore, the Devil Rays started with a lengthy list of 27 candidates. Chuck LaMar, a 38-year-old Atlanta Braves assistant general manager, was hired in July 1995. During 10 years in professional baseball with the Reds, Pirates, and Braves, LaMar had progressed steadily as a scout, director of minor-league operations, director of scouting, and assistant general manager. He has been the only general manager in Devil Rays history.

The Devil Rays' minor-league affiliations went into operation in 1996. The first minor-league game in the organization's history occurred on June 19, when, in a rookie-ball contest, the St. Petersburg Devil Rays faced the Tampa Yankees in their Gulf Coast League season opener. The Devil Rays eventually settled on Princeton, West Virginia (the Devil Rays), for their rookie-level affiliate; Wappingers Falls, New York (the Renegades), Charleston, South Carolina (the Riverdogs), and Bakersfield, California (the Blaze), as their Class A affiliates; Orlando, Florida (the Rays), as their Double-A affiliate; and Durham, North Carolina (the Bulls), as their Triple-A affiliate.

The Devil Rays filled their early minor-league rosters with free-agent signings and draft picks. Only six months after the expansion announcement, the Devil Rays signed their first player, Adam Sisk. But Sisk, a right-handed pitcher who had spent the previous year attending junior college in Baltimore, was cut in May 1997 without pitching a game for the Devil Rays. The next newsworthy signing occurred in April 1997 when the Devil Rays won a bidding war for the rights to Rolando Arrojo. The right-handed pitcher, a Cuban defector, received a $7 million signing bonus and a minor-league contract that paid him $850 a month. Arrojo made the major-league roster for two years but was eventually traded to the Colorado Rockies in December 1999. With the first draft in the organization's history, the 1996 June amateur draft, the Devil Rays selected Paul Wilder as their first pick (29th overall). The 18-year-old high-school slugger from North Carolina signed for a $650,000 bonus but eventually left baseball without making it to the major leagues.

Expansion franchises had a unique opportunity to become competitive early on due to the opening of the free-agent market and the decision that both leagues had to contribute to the expansion-draft pool. In November 1997, with a nationwide audience watching the live broadcast from ESPN, the Devil Rays participated in the expansion draft. The Devil Rays made left-handed pitcher Tony Saunders their first pick, and then took speedy outfielder Quinton McCracken. Before the draft ended, the Devil Rays had secured either through the draft or through trades 11 players who made the original 25-man roster (Fred McGriff, Roberto Hernandez, Rich Butler, Mike Kelly, Kevin Stocker, Miguel Cairo, Bobby Smith, Esteban Yan, Mike Difelice, Bubba Trammell, and Aaron Ledesma). Throughout the team's initial years, the Devil Rays have had numerous talented and noteworthy players on their roster. This included the Opening Day lineup in 1998, which had McGriff and Wade Boggs. Since that lineup, additional newsworthy players on the rosters over the years have included Dwight Gooden, Jose Canseco, Greg Vaughn, Vinny Castilla, and Jim Morris, the teacher-turned-pitcher who made the major-league roster as a rookie relief pitcher in 1999 at the age of 35. His story was made into a book and the major motion picture *Rookie* starring Dennis Quaid.

Tampa Bay waited nearly three years after getting a team to hire a field manager. On November 7, 1997, two days after Tampa Bay officially joined the AL East, the Devil Rays hired pitching coach Larry Rothschild. He managed the Devil Rays from 1998 through the first 13 games of 2001, when Hal McRae took over. Then in 2003 the Devil Rays signed a four-year, $13 million deal with Tampa native Lou Piniella to be their field manager. Although publicized as "It's a whole new ballgame," the Devil Rays continued

Aubrey Huff hits a home run against the Chicago White Sox, 2005. © AP / Wide World Photos

to lose more games than they won, as they finished the 2003 campaign with 63 wins and another fifth place in the AL East. In the team's six years, the Devil Rays have finished higher than last place only once, and have never won more than 70 games.

After decades of being the spring-training capital, Tampa Bay continued this tradition in 1998 when the Devil Rays made a historical decision to train in their hometown. Tampa Bay was the first team since the St. Louis Cardinals and Philadelphia Athletics in 1919 to do so, as the Devil Rays took over the Cardinals' spring-training lease in St. Petersburg and used Al Lang Stadium.

Although MLB officials provided the Devil Rays and Diamondbacks with the best possible conditions to organize winning teams, only Arizona was successful, winning the World Series in 2001. The Devil Rays have struggled on the field every year. Their high-priced free-agent signings (in 2000 the team had the 10th-highest salary structure in MLB at $64.4 million) failed to live up to expectations, and their teams have been unable to compete on a regular basis with other AL teams. Two years later the salaries were cut in half, and Tampa Bay had the lowest payroll in the majors, a distinction it has easily maintained for most seasons. The Devil Rays have had trouble bringing fans to Tropicana Field because of the losing product on the field (they have finished an average of 35 1/2 games behind the AL East champion), the inability to make the dome

Carl Crawford dives for a line drive in a game against the Oakland Athletics, 2005.
© AP / Wide World Photos

a fan-friendly facility (i.e., sight lines, seating distance from field of play), the low percentage of native Tampa Bay residents (meaning many residents have established affinities to other clubs), and the car drive for Tampa fans to St. Petersburg. Devil Rays officials, however, were optimistic after an increase in attendance for the 2003 season. The hiring of Piniella injected some life into the players and fans. The team won a team record 70 games in 2004, but returned to the cellar a year later. Piniella's contract was bought out at the end of the 2005 season. The team was valued then at just $176 million, the lowest in MLB, yet its operating income was $27.2 million, compared to the league average of $4.4 million. The ownership spent little and put out a poor product, but made a very nice return. After the season, Stuart Sternberg, who made his fortune with an options-trading firm, and his five partners bought 48 percent of the team for $65 million. Sternberg became managing partner and hired 29-year-old Matt Silverman as president, and they planned to bring life to the moribund club.

MANAGERS

2006–	Joe Madden
2003–2005	Lou Piniella
2001–2002	Hal McRae
1998–2001	Larry Rothschild

Team Records by Individual Players

Batting Leaders

| | Single Season | | | Career | |
	Name		Year	Name		Plate Appearances
Batting average	Aubrey Huff	.313	2002	Fred McGriff	.291	2,399
On-base %	Fred McGriff	.405	1999	Fred McGriff	.380	2,399
Slugging %	Jose Canseco	.563	1999	Fred McGriff	.484	2,399
OPS	Fred McGriff	.957	1999	Fred McGriff	.864	2,399
Games	Aubrey Huff	162	2003	Aubrey Huff	736	3,066
At bats	Carl Crawford	644	2003	Aubrey Huff	2,798	3,066
Runs	Carl Crawford	104	2004	Aubrey Huff	374	3,066
Hits	Aubrey Huff	198	2003	Aubrey Huff	805	3,066
Total bases	Aubrey Huff	353	2003	Aubrey Huff	1,338	3,066
Doubles	Aubrey Huff	47	2003	Aubrey Huff	157	3,066
Triples	Carl Crawford	19	2004	Carl Crawford	49	2,298
Home runs	Jose Conseco	34	1999	Aubrey Huff	120	3,066
RBIs	Jorge Cantu	117	2005	Aubrey Huff	421	3,066
Walks	Fred McGriff	91	2000	Fred McGriff	305	2,399
Strikeouts	Ben Grieve	159	2001	Fred McGriff	433	2,399
Stolen bases	Carl Crawford	59	2004	Carl Crawford	169	2,298
Extra-base hits	Aubrey Huff	84	2003	Aubrey Huff	285	3,066
Times on base	Aubrey Huff	259	2003	Aubrey Huff	1,049	3,066

Pitching Leaders

| | Single Season | | | Career | |
	Name		Year	Name		Innings Pitched
ERA	Rolando Arrojo	3.56	1998	Jim Mercir	3.03	154.1
Wins	Rolando Arrojo	14	1998	Victor Zambrano	35	481.7
Won-loss %	Mark Hendrickson	.579	2005	Victor Zambrano	.565	481.7
Hits/9 IP	Victor Zambrano	7.88	2003	Jim Mecir	6.88	154.3
Walks/9 IP	Bryan Rekar	2.02	2000	Lance Carter	2.36	179.7
Strikeouts	Scott Kazmir	1714	2005	Victor Zambrano	372	481.7
Strikeouts/ 9 IP	Scott Kazmir	8.42	2005	Doug Creek	9.86	160.7
Games	Roberto Hernandez	72	1999	Esteban Yan	266	418.7
Saves	Roberto Hernandez	43	1999	Roberto Hernandez	101	218
Innings	Tanyon Sturtze	224	2002	Bryan Rekar	495.3	495.3
Starts	Tanyon Sturtze	33	2002	Ryan Rupe	83	466.7
Complete games	Joe Kennedy	5	2002	Joe Kennedy	6	448
Shutouts	Rolando Arrojo	2	1998	Rolando Arrojo	2	342.7

Source: Drawn from data in "Tampa Bay Devil Rays Batting Leaders (seasonal and career)." http://baseball-reference. com/teams/TBD/leaders_bat.shtml; "Tampa Bay Devil Rays Pitching Leaders (seasonal and career)." http://baseball-reference.com/teams/TBD/leaders_pitch.shtml.

BIBLIOGRAPHY

Andelman, Bob. *Stadium for Rent: Tampa Bay's Quest for Major League Baseball.* Jefferson, NC: McFarland, 1993.

Euchner, Charles. *Playing the Field: Why Sports Teams Move and Cities Fight to Keep Them.* Baltimore: Johns Hopkins Press, 1993.

Miller, James Edward. *The Baseball Business: Pursuing Pennants and Profits in Baltimore.* Chapel Hill: University of North Carolina Press, 1990.

Pedersen, Paul Mark. *Build It and They Will Come: The Arrival of the Tampa Bay Devil Rays.* Stuart: Florida Sports Press, 1997.

Voigt, David Quentin. *American Baseball, Vol. 2: From the Commissioners to Continental Expansion.* Norman: University of Oklahoma Press, 1970.

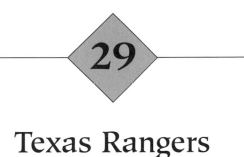

Texas Rangers

Jarrod Schenewark

The Texas Rangers lay claim to one of the worst all-time records for any of the expansion teams that have emerged since 1960. Throughout their history, the club has generated future Hall of Fame players, produced MVPs, and hired managers with some of the most recognized names in the game. Thirty-five years after its formation, the franchise experienced its first taste of postseason play, only to slip back to the bottom of its division.

EXPANSION AND A REBIRTH

The beginning of the Texas Rangers starts not in Texas but in Washington, DC. Since 1901, the nation's capital had fielded a major-league team, but by 1960, the Washington Senators were no longer of the same caliber as the team that had won three pennants and a world championship. Washington was an undesirable place for both major-league players and the team. It was a losing club with little fan support and a ballpark located in a slum, and there were rumors that owner Calvin Griffith wanted to move.

Griffith originally sought to move the team to the St. Paul–Minneapolis area, but American League owners were worried about leaving Washington and upsetting politicians who might retaliate by revoking MLB's antitrust exemption. However, on October 26, 1960, AL owners approved the Senators' move to the Twin Cities, and they became the Minnesota Twins. The owners also approved the expansion of the AL to 10 teams, with new franchises for Los Angeles and Washington. The owners believed politicians and fans alike would not be upset with the Senators' shift to Minnesota as long as there was a replacement. The city had not adequately supported a big-league franchise for years, but got a second chance solely because of its status as the national capital and the center of political power.

One month later the AL approved a 10-member Washington syndicate led by air-force general Elwood R. "Pete" Quesada, the first administrator of the FAA, which purchased the local expansion team for $1.9 million. The syndicate, known as "Senators Inc.," hired Ed Doherty, former president of the Triple-A American Association, as general manager, and former Senators star Mickey Vernon, a coach for the 1960 World Series champion Pittsburgh Pirates, as manager. The Senators participated, along with the Los Angeles Angels, in the first expansion draft. Washington choose 31 men from a list of players unprotected by the AL's eight existing clubs to be the new Senators. The first pick was left-handed pitcher Bobby Shantz of the pennant-winning New York Yankees. Shantz was a crafty veteran of 12 major-league seasons, which included one outstanding year with 24 victories, but he'd had just 5 in 1960. However, he never pitched for the Senators, being traded to the Pirates before the start of the 1961 season.

ONE, TWO, THREE STRIKES, YOU'RE OUT!

President John F. Kennedy threw out the first pitch at the franchise's first game at Griffith Stadium, attended by 26,725 fans. The Senators lost 4–3 to the Chicago White Sox, the first of many losses. The Senators, in the expanded 162-game season, lost 100 games for the first of four straight seasons. Losing is what the club did on a consistent basis. The expansion team's record bolstered the popular slogan "Washington—first in war, first in peace, and last in the American League."

As a result, between 1961 and 1971 the Washington Senators had four managers. Vernon led the team to 101 losses in 1962, playing at the year-old DC Stadium (renamed RFK Stadium in 1969), which had been built for $24 million by the DC Sports and Entertainment Commission and seated 43,500. Forty games into the 1963 season, with the Senators once again in last place, Gil Hodges replaced Vernon, and this time the Senators finished with 106 losses. Hodges led the team through the end of 1967, when the team improved to its best record to date (76–85). Two years later, Hodges led the expansion New York Mets to a World Series title.

During Hodges' tenure, the Senators obtained their first star, Frank Howard, who came in December 1964 in a multiplayer trade from the Los Angeles Dodgers. Howard stood six foot seven, weighed 255 pounds, and brought power and maturity to the club. Howard was a product of the Dodgers' farm system, 1960 NL Rookie of the Year, and helped the Dodgers win the 1963 World Series. In 1968, Howard hit 10 home runs in 20 at bats, and went on to lead the AL with 44 home runs. The manager that year was Jim Lemon, who had played for the original Senators. Lemon had hit 38 homers in Washington and was an All-Star in 1960. His team went 65–96 in his only year as a big-league manager.

BOB SHORT AND TEDDY BALLGAME

On December 3, 1968, Robert Short, the Democratic National Committee treasurer, purchased a majority interest of the Washington Senators at the winter meetings in San Francisco. Short had made millions in the trucking industry. He had previously owned the Minneapolis Lakers, purchased back in 1957. Short was instrumental in the franchise moving to the Los Angeles area three years later. In 1965, Short sold the Lakers for a profit of $5.2 million.

The new owner promptly dismissed Lemon, and in January hired Hall of Fame hitter Ted Williams, who had retired as a player in 1960. Williams received a four-year contract worth $1.5 million. Short hoped to capitalize on his famous skipper, and on Opening Day distributed facsimile versions of the pen with which he signed Williams. The "Splendid Splinter" led the club to its first winning season (86–76 record) and was selected AL Manager of the Year. Williams was instrumental in improving the team's batting. Howard batted .296 with a .574 slugging percentage, 48 home runs, 111 runs, and 111 RBIs, while outfielder Mike Epstein had a career year, hitting .278 with 30 home runs.

The team's success was short-lived, mainly because Short dealt away players against Williams's advice. The manager and fans were most infuriated by a four-player deal that sent three Senators to Detroit for Denny McLain, who had won 31 games in 1968 and 24 the following year, but fell off to 3–5 in 1970. The trade gutted the Senators infield and gave away one of the team's best pitchers, Joe Coleman, who went 20–9 the next season. McLain in one season with Washington was a dismal 10–22, and he was sent to Oakland the following year. The next three seasons were not much fun for Williams, who felt that Short traded away the ball club.

Meddling with player personnel was not Short's only fault in the eyes of Washington fans, who should have seen his agenda for the Lakers as an omen for the future of the Senators. When Short bought the club, he had refused any clause in the contract that would obligate him to keep the team in Washington, and would not improve DC Stadium. Short seemed to follow Kansas City A's owner Charley O. Finley's example of how to engender antipathy for the hometown team. Soon after taking control, Short raised the prices of all seats and converted much of the regular grandstand into reserved seats. Despite the price increase, attendance for the exciting 1969 season, a 400,000 increase over the year before, was the second highest in the 71-year history of major-league baseball in Washington. The next year he raised prices again, producing an average increase of between 50 and 100 percent on tickets over two years, and gave Washington the distinction of having the most expensive seats in baseball. Unreserved grandstand seats ran $2.25 in Washington, compared to 55 cents for the nearby Baltimore Orioles.

Short earned a miserly public image by alienating senior citizens on fixed incomes who could not afford the higher prices. He also discontinued the custom of complementary tickets for wounded and sick veterans from nearby Walter Reed Army Hospital, eliminated discount tickets for children, and refused to televise the presidential opener all three years in Washington, even though those games were sellouts. Short compounded his problems by publicly stating that Washington was a "bad baseball town." His failure to pay his stadium rent and other bills caused a series of actions that threatened the team's presence at DC Stadium. Short's response was that the team was not wanted in Washington and should be moved.

The local media criticized Short for his threats to move, his failure to pay his rent and other bills, and his trade for Denny McLain. Nonetheless, concessions were in the works to keep the team in Washington. Commissioner Bowie Kuhn and AL president Joe Cronin worked together to save the franchise for Washington. Even President Richard Nixon spoke out against the team leaving. Stadium management offered Short free rent for the first 1 million admissions, the right to name the concessionaire, operation of the concession stands during baseball and football seasons, and revenue from billboard and other stadium advertising during the baseball season. Short turned them down, labeling the deal, offered in mid-August, as too late.

TOM VANDERGRIFF AND THE TEXAS OPTION

Beginning in 1958, Mayor Tom Vandergriff of Arlington, Texas, a suburb of the Dallas–Fort Worth area, sought a major-league franchise for the region. Vandergriff failed to get an expansion club twice from the American League and once from the National League, and was unsuccessful in convincing the Kansas City and Seattle owners to relocate. Then, in 1971, Cleveland Indians president Gabe Paul and Angels owner Gene Autry informed Vandergriff of Short's financial difficulties and the possibilities of his moving his club. Vandergriff decided to pursue the Senators and set out to visit every AL spring-training camp, lobbying club owners for support of his goal of bringing the Senators to Texas. Vandergriff proposed a financial package backed by 10 area banks that would provide Short with $7.5 million in low-interest loans. Short would also receive $7.5 million over 10 years for the sale of the team's broadcast rights to the city of Arlington. Short seriously considered Vandergriff's proposal, and by the summer of 1971 had agreed to move the team to Texas. Vandergriff then stepped up his lobbying efforts, and with the cooperation of the local media, kept his endeavors confidential until the deal was done.

On September 20, the AL owners met in Boston to consider the proposed transfer. Vandergriff felt he had the nine necessary votes, but supporter Gene Autry of the Angeles took ill and had to be hospitalized. On the first vote and each vote thereafter, only eight clubs voted to approve the move, with Baltimore and Chicago in opposition. Oakland owner Charlie Finley tried to trade his vote in exchange for the Senators' best young player, Jeff Burroughs, but Short refused. With the vote deadlocked at 8–2–2 (with Finley and Autry abstaining), AL president Joe Cronin took action. He visited Autry in his Boston hospital room and got Autry's proxy, allowing Cronin to register his vote in favor of the move. Finley then followed suit, resulting in a final vote of 10–2 in favor of relocation.

Washington fans were outraged and saddened. At the final home game on September 30, many fans brought signs depicting how they felt about Bob Short and about the team. Frank Howard thrilled the crowd with a sixth-inning home run that helped the Senators to a 7–5 lead over the Yankees. But in the ninth inning, fans swarmed the field looking for souvenirs. They pulled up the grass, took the bases, and pulled lights and lettering off the scoreboards. The umpires declared the field unsafe and unplayable and forfeited the game to the Yankees. The Senators' final season in Washington was a dismal 63–96.

THE MOVE TO ARLINGTON

The franchise changed its name from the Washington Senators to the Texas Rangers. Opening Day was supposed to be April 6, 1972, but the start of the season was delayed when the Players Association voted, for the first time, to strike over the size of the owners' contribution to the players' pension fund. The team ended up starting on the road (1–3), and opened at home on Friday, April 21, before a crowd of 20,105. Before the game, the players dressed in white cowboy hats, and Ted Williams was presented cowboy boots with spikes. Frank Howard hit his 361st home run in the bottom of the first inning to help the Rangers to a 7–6 victory over the Angels. But he only hit eight more before being sold to the Detroit Tigers in August.

Following the victorious home opener, attendance problems plagued the club. Only 5,517 came the next day to witness Pete Broberg pitch the first shutout for the team. Short believed the team needed a million fans to build a championship club, with 800,000 the break-even point. But home attendance totaled only 662,974, an average of 8,840 a game.

Part of the attendance problem was the Rangers' ballpark. Originally called Turnpike Stadium, Arlington Stadium had originally been a minor-league facility built in 1965 in a natural bowl at a cost of $1.5 million, 40 feet below street level and away from residential property. A comparable ballpark at a different site would have cost $15 million. The original capacity was 10,000, expanded to 20,000 in 1970. Then, when MLB arrived, it was further increased to 35,694 (18,000 of these seats were aluminum bleachers). The new home was no oasis for either the team or the fans. A consistent wind blew from right and right center toward home plate, contributing to the Rangers' major-league low of 56 home runs. During midsummer, day-game temperatures climbed toward 120 degrees, while night games attracted swarms of insects.

The low attendance was also a product of the team's sixth-place finish (54–100). Williams resigned and was replaced by rookie manager Dorrel Norman Elvert "Whitey" Herzog. Herzog emphasized building a team, but Short was more concerned with poor attendance, which averaged about 9,000. They looked toward the June 5, 1973, baseball amateur draft as an answer to both problems. The Rangers had the first pick based on their last-place finish in 1972. Short sought to use the pick to build the team and reverse the flailing attendance. His hope rested on an 18-year-old right-hander named David Clyde, who had won all 18 starts for Houston's Westchester High School, with an ERA of 0.18. Herzog felt Clyde was a good pick, but did not know Short's plan to immediately bring the teenager to the big leagues.

Against Herzog's wishes, Clyde was given a $65,000 bonus and three weeks of publicity before he made his major-league debut. Short gambled with the young man's arm and psyche in order to produce bigger audiences and more revenue. Clyde debuted on June 27, and for the first time, the stadium was filled. The game started 15 minutes late in order to give fans caught in the unprecedented traffic jam time to arrive at the stadium. Clyde won his first game, and took a regular spot in the starting rotation. When Clyde pitched, home attendance averaged 18,187, compared to 7,546 on other days. Clyde finished the season with a 4–8 record and a 5.01 ERA. He pitched three seasons with the Rangers, but only went 7–18. They floundered in sixth place, but Herzog had a two-year contract and felt he had time to develop the team. However, four days after Short publicly praised Herzog, he fired him, bringing in Billy Martin.

BILLY BALL COMES TO TEXAS

Billy Martin was a highly successful major-league manager with two first-place finishes in four years, but the highly volatile skipper was fired by the Detroit Tigers late in the 1973 season. Short immediately scooped him up and gave him a $65,000 a year contract for three years, a new house, the use of a new car each year, and, most importantly, the last say over players (except for Clyde). Short and Martin had developed a friendship in 1969 when Martin managed the Minnesota Twins. Martin even campaigned for Short when he ran for Minnesota governor. Martin managed the Rangers for the final 33 games of 1973. The Rangers finished in sixth place with 105 losses, 20 games behind the fifth-place team. They scored the fewest runs, gave up the most runs, and made the most errors in the league. During the off-season, Martin acquired pitcher Ferguson Jenkins, the future Hall of Famer, from the Chicago Cubs for rookie phenom third baseman Bill Madlock and outfielder Vic Harris. The 31-year-old Jenkins had six straight 20-win seasons, but had fallen off to 14–16 in 1973. Martin still felt he was the kind of pitcher around which a team could be built. Martin also brought in new players from the Rangers' farm system and promised a pennant. Martin made Jim Sundberg, promoted from Class A, the starting catcher, and he earned a berth on the 1974 All-Star team. He also brought up Mike Hargrove, who hit .323 in 1974 and was named AL Rookie of the Year. Outfielder Jeff Burroughs led the AL with 118 RBIs and was selected MVP.

"Billy Ball" came to town as Martin worked on sacrifice bunts and speed to produce runs. Five players stole at least 13 bases. The Rangers finished second in runs, despite coming in 10th in homers. Jenkins went 25–12, earning the Comeback Player of the Year Award. The Rangers contended for the division title, finishing five games behind the Oakland A's, who went on to capture their third consecutive World Series title. Martin was voted AL Manager of the Year as the team improved from 57–105 to 84–76. Billy attributed the team's success to the lack of interference from the owner, general manager, and farm director. The team went into the 1975 season favored to win the pennant.

NEW OWNERSHIP DASHES HOPES

Two days before Opening Day, Bob Short sold the Rangers to a group of investors led by Bradford G. Corbett, president and CEO of Robintech, a chemical and plastic-pipe business. Corbett enjoyed being in the spotlight and actively traded and signed players. He got into a big fight with Martin over control of the team. Corbett and Martin quarreled over Clyde, who Martin wanted demoted to make room for a better pitcher. An even sharper dispute arose over the acquisition of 35-year-old outfielder Willie Davis, a favorite of Corbett's but unwanted by Martin. Davis played just 42 games before he was traded. Martin lost the authority that Short had promised him and was fired on July 21. He was promptly picked up by the Yankees. Corbett replaced Martin with Rangers coach Frank Lucchesi, and the team finished in third (79–83) and then fourth (76–86).

Before the 1977 season, Corbett hired Eddie Robinson, a former major-league first baseman, as executive vice president. The pair signed two free agents, shortstop Bert Campaneris and starting pitcher Doyle Alexander, and traded the popular Jeff Burroughs to the Atlanta Braves for five marginal players. From the farm system came the highly regarded Bump Wills, son of Maury Wills, who became the new second baseman. Veteran Lenny Randle felt he was not given a chance to compete, and bitterly complained, privately and publicly. During spring training, tension mounted between Randle and the manager. Randle brutally attacked Lucchesi, who spent seven days in the hospital with a broken cheekbone, which required plastic surgery, and bruises to his back and kidney. Randle was suspended, fined, charged with battery, and traded to the New York Mets. Lucchesi returned to the club in time for Opening Day, where the Rangers defeated the Orioles and Bump Wills made the game-winning hit.

Midway through the season, with a record of 31–31 and lagging attendance, Lucchesi was fired. He was replaced by Eddie Stanky, who had last managed the 1968 Detroit Tigers. He managed one game and resigned, to stay near his home in Alabama. Robinson tried to recruit Harmon Killebrew, who declined the job, as did interim manager and Rangers coach Connie Ryan. Finally, a week after firing Lucchesi, the Rangers hired Orioles third-base coach Billy Hunter. Even with the commotion of the preseason and the managerial changes, the team, built on speed, defense, and pitching, performed very well, and won 94 games, a franchise record until 1999. However, the Kansas City Royals finished the season with 102 wins and Texas had to settle for second, eight games behind.

Hunter led the Rangers to another winning season in 1978, making him the first manager to produce back-to-back .500-plus seasons. Despite being the manager with the most wins in Rangers history, problems between Hunter and the players led to his dismissal before the final game of the season. The off-season brought more changes, beginning with new skipper Pat Corrales, the first Mexican American major-league manager. Corbett negotiated one of the biggest trades in baseball history, a 10-player deal with the New York Yankees. The Rangers acquired renowned closer Sparky Lyle, who would record 21 saves for the club, but gave up their top pitching prospect, Dave Righetti, who amassed 224 saves with the Bronx Bombers in eight years.

In the late 1970s, Corbett's chemical and plastic-pipe business fell on hard times, which compelled him to trade or sell 10 players from the 1978 team to bring in much-needed cash. He sold John Lowenstein to Baltimore and traded fan favorite Mike Hargrove to San Diego and Reggie Cleveland to Milwaukee. Toby Harrah, a two-time All-Star and the last of the original Rangers who had come from Washington, was traded to the Cleveland Indians in return for Buddy Bell. Corrales's squad had a winning record (83–79), good for third, led by Bell, who had 200 hits and 101 RBIs.

Corbett sold the club in 1980 to Fort Worth oilman Eddie Chiles. The team took a step backward in 1980, going 76–85. One important new addition was veteran knuckleball pitcher Charlie Hough, purchased from the Los Angeles Dodgers. Hough recorded 139 wins and 1,452 strikeouts from 1980 through 1990 to become the Rangers' all-time leader. Chiles, like previous owners, brought in his own manager, replacing Corrales with Don Zimmer in 1981, and he nearly got the club into the playoffs. A strike began on June 12, just after the Rangers had lost a game to Milwaukee, 6–3, leaving them with a record of 32–22 and costing them first place. After the season resumed, they went 24–26 in the second half of the split season, and were out of the playoffs. Midway through a disastrous 1982 season (64–98), Chiles replaced Zimmer with Darrell Johnson, former managers of the Red Sox and the Mariners. Johnson was supplanted by Doug Rader, whose team continued to flounder, falling into the cellar in 1984 (69–92). After going 9–23 at the start of the 1985 season, Rader was replaced by Bobby Valentine. The Rangers were Valentine's first managerial opportunity. The team again finished last (62–99). They made a big turnaround in Valentine's first complete season, winning 87 games, led by Charlie Hough (17–10), and coming in second in the Western Division, but then fell off to sixth the next two years (75–87, 70–91). The club ended the decade with identical 83–79 marks in 1989 and 1990. After the 1988 season, when the Rangers had the second-lowest payroll in baseball ($6,008,000), the team added three key players, trading for future All-Stars Julio Franco and Rafael Palmeiro and signing free agent Nolan Ryan.

THE RYAN EXPRESS

The signing of 41-year-old Nolan Ryan, baseball's all-time strikeout king, in December 1988 was one of the team's most important acquisitions in its history. The future Hall of Fame player was upset with the Houston Astros for trying to cut his salary. Ryan wanted to continue playing near his home of Alvin, Texas, and turned down a higher offer from Angels owner Gene Autry. The expectation was that Ryan would play a year and then retire; however, he played the next five years for the Rangers, with a record of 51–39.

Ryan was impressive from the start. In 1989 he pitched two one-hitters and carried five no-hitters into the eighth inning or later. Ryan contributed to the Rangers enjoying the earliest sellout in their history on August 22, 1989. The stadium had sold out five days earlier because of anticipation of Ryan passing the 5,000-strikeout mark for his career. Six shy of the mark at the start of the game, the moment came in the fifth inning against Rickey Henderson, who on a full count swung and missed a 96-mph fastball to become Ryan's 5,000th strikeout. Ryan was the team's best pitcher, with a 16–10 record and a league-leading 301 strikeouts. He helped the team draw over 2 million fans for the first time.

Ryan began 1990 with a 4–0 record, but then went on the disabled list, suffering from muscle spasms in his lower back. In June, Ryan, the only man to throw five no-hitters, threw his sixth in a 5–0 win over the Oakland A's. Later in the season Ryan became the 20th player to win 300 games. Ryan went 13–9 and again led the league in strikeouts (232).

Nolan Ryan, baseball's all-time strike-out leader, pitches in his final season against the California Angels, 1993 © AP / Wide World Photos

Ivan Rodriguez throws to first base to complete a double play against the San Francisco Giants, 1997. © AP / Wide World Photos

May 1, 1991, was Arlington Appreciation Night at the Rangers' home field, and that night Ryan pitched his seventh career no-hitter in a 3–0 victory over Toronto. He was the oldest pitcher to throw a no-hitter. The Rangers honored Ryan on September 15, 1996, when they retired his number, 34. When Ryan went into the Hall of Fame, he was the first player to honor the Rangers by choosing to wear their hat on his plaque. The team in 1991 went 85–77, good for third place, with the league's most productive offense, including two outstanding young Latino starters, catcher Ivan "Pudge" Rodriguez and outfielder Juan Gonzalez. Julio Franco led the AL in batting at .341. But the team was hindered by the worst pitching in the league, with an ERA of 5.02. But the next year, with the team at 45–41, Valentine was fired and replaced by Toby Harrah, the former Rangers star. The club ended up at 77–85, in fourth place. Kevin Kennedy then took over, and led the team back up to second place in 1993 (86–76). Gonzalez had a huge year, leading the AL in homers (46) and slugging (.632), second in total bases (339), and fourth in RBIs (118).

GEORGE W. BUSH AND THE BALLPARK IN ARLINGTON

In April 1990, a syndicate that included George W. Bush purchased a controlling interest in the Texas Rangers for $89 million. Bush had learned that family friend Eddie Chiles was looking to sell the ball club back in October 1988 while he was helping to manage his father's presidential campaign. Bush borrowed $500,000 to buy a small stake in the team and convinced the group to make him a managing general partner. He subsequently added another $106,302 to his investment. Bush became the public face of the team, for a salary of $200,000, while fellow general partner Edward Rose assumed control of the financial side.

Bush led the team's efforts to secure a new $191 million stadium in Arlington, with funding from public and private funds. The syndicate threatened to move elsewhere unless the new park was built. In January 1991, Arlington voters approved by a two-to-one margin a half-cent sales tax in order to help service the debt acquired through the issuance of $135 million in bonds. In April the state legislature approved a bill to create the Arlington Sports Facilities Development Authority (ASFDA), a quasi-governmental entity that used the power of eminent domain to secure 13 acres of private property for the new field.

The Ballpark in Arlington opened in 1994 with a capacity of 49,178, including 122 suites. Seating by the dugouts is very close to the playing field, placed 22 feet below street level to avoid summer winds. The new stadium reflects the movement in stadium building to promote the history and nostalgia of the game, including a granite and brick facade. The stadium includes a manual scoreboard similar to the one located in historic Fenway Park, nooks and crannies like Ebbets Field, and a covered pavilion porch with pillars like at Tiger Stadium. There is a 17,000-square-foot museum with baseball artifacts from the nineteenth century to the present. Statues of Tom Vandergriff and Nolan Ryan reflect the local history of the Rangers. Arlington Stadium was torn down and converted into parking spaces. Along with a new ballpark came new uniforms, which featured red as the primary color instead of blue.

In 1994, when MLB went to a three-division format, the realignment seemed to favor the Rangers, who were placed in the weak four-team Western Division. Throughout the season Texas and the rest of the West struggled to go .500. The main highlight was the perfect game pitched by Kenny Rogers at the Ballpark. The season ended early on August 12 when the players responded to the threat of a salary cap by going on strike. When Commissioner Bud Selig canceled the season on September 14, the Rangers were standing on top of the Western Division with a dismal record of 52–62, one game better than Oakland. Despite the losing record and a shortened season, fans flocked to the new ballpark. Attendance reached an all-time high of 2,503,198, and before the strike seemed to be on track for the club to break 3 million.

Major changes were made during the off-season. Bush, having been elected governor of Texas, stepped down as general partner. Tom Grieve, the general manager for the past decade, was replaced by Baltimore assistant general manager Doug Melvin. One of his first acts was the dismissal of manager Kevin Kennedy, who had finished his two-year stint at .500 (138–138), replacing him with former major-league catcher and Baltimore Orioles manager Johnny Oates. In 1995, MLB held the All-Star Game at the Ballpark. Attendance dropped as the Rangers, like other major-league teams, continue to suffer from the fans' adverse reaction to the labor stoppage. The team averaged only 27,582 fans compared to 40,374 the year before. Oates did a fine job in 1995, producing a winning record with a modestly talented team.

The following year, Oates led the team to first place in the West and was chosen as AL Manager of the Year. Juan Gonzalez was MVP, batting .318 with 47 homers, 144 RBIs, and a slugging percentage of .643. Left fielder Rusty Greer hit .332, and he and third baseman Dean Palmer both drove in 100 or more runs.

The Rangers took the first game of the AL Divisional Series against the Yankees, but then lost the next three games, and were eliminated. Attendance rose by about one-third, the team's box office revenues increased to $25.5 million, and the value of the team was estimated at $174 million. In 1997 the team continued to hit well, with four men over .300, but the result was a disappointing third place and a losing record (77–85). Nonetheless, the team set its all-time record for attendance, 2,945,228, and increased in value by one-third to $254 million.

In June 1998 the Rangers were sold to Tom Hicks for $250 million, then the second most ever paid for a major-league franchise. Bush then held a 1.8 percent equity interest, but was also owed a 10 percent bonus if the team was sold for a profit. Consequently, Bush received $14.9 million for his $600,000 investment. That season the Rangers captured first place in the West (88–74), leading the league in hitting and second in runs, but near the bottom in pitching, though Rick Helling won 20 games and Aaron Sele won 19. Gonzalez, who was making $7.8 million, won his second MVP, batting .318, slugging .630, slamming 45 homers, and leading in RBIs (157) and doubles (50). However, in the ALDS, the Yankees swept them in three straight, and the Rangers lineup managed just one run.

In 1999, Hicks settled a long-term dispute with the ASFDA that went back to the Bush era, when the club had failed to reimburse the authority for $7.5 million owed over a court case regarding the seizure of private land for the ballpark. The Rangers agreed to a total settlement of $22.2 million to cover costs the ASFDA had incurred.

The Rangers improved to 95 wins that year and repeated their victory in the division. They had a superb offense, leading the AL in batting at .293, second overall in runs scored, and third in homers (230), but again had very weak pitching, with a team ERA of 5.07. John Wetteland did yeoman-like work as the closer with 43 saves, second in the AL. Pudge Rodriguez was MVP, batting .332 with 35 homers. His 113 RBIs was only third on the team, after Rafael Palmeiro (148) and Gonzalez (128). But all went for naught in the postseason, when the Yankees swept in three, and the Rangers again only scored one run.

The Rangers won 24 fewer games in 2000 than the year before, and ended in last place. After the season, the Rangers attempted to upgrade by overpaying to sign free-agent shortstop Alex Rodriguez, who had no other bidders. He got a record 10-year, $252 million contract. Alex hit .318 in 2001 with 135 RBIs, leading a stellar offense, but the pitching was the worst in the AL, with an ERA of 5.71. The team had the fifth-highest payroll with little to show for it on the field, and the fifth-largest deficit among all major-league teams ($24,433,000), even with $25.3 million in local media revenue, seventh among all teams. Despite these disturbing numbers, the team achieved its highest value ever at $356 million. Oates was replaced early in the season by Jerry Narron, but the team remained mired in last place (73–89), and ended up with virtually an identical mark in 2002 with the third-highest payroll in MLB ($105,726,122).

After the season catcher Pudge Rodriguez, a 10-time All-Star who had been making $9.6 million, left the team as a free agent, joining the Florida Marlins. In 2003, Alex Rodriguez led the AL in homers (47) as well as slugging (.600) and runs (124), and became the third Rangers MVP, but could not prevent the team, with the AL's worst pitching staff, from finishing with just 71 wins, 25 games behind the division winner. Nonetheless, he was traded to the New York Yankees before the start of the 2004 season for Alfonso Soriano. By 2004 the payroll had been cut in half to $55,050,417, while the value of the team dropped to $306 million, 11th highest in MLB. Despite the lower total wages, second-year skipper Buck Showalter led the club to what was thought to be another turnaround season in 2004, finishing in third place (89–73), only three games back. However, Rangers history repeated itself in 2005, and high expectations gave way to another letdown for Ranger fans. The team went 79–83, with poor pitching and outstanding hitting. Michael Young led the AL at .331, while Mark Teixeira had 43 homers and 144 RBIs, and the team had 260 homers.

For the past four decades the organization has been a model of conflict between the interests of the owners and the men on the playing field. While both are interested in winning, the return on investment is the overriding concern of the owners. The professional baseball man, whether player, coach, or manager, is a pawn in the owners' hands to do with as they please. This attitude, highlighted by the actions of the various owners of the Rangers, is what has and will continue to prevent the organization from achieving long-term excellence on the field.

NOTABLE ACHIEVEMENTS

Most Valuable Players

Year	Name	Position
1974	Jeff Burroughs	OF
1996	Juan Gonzalez	OF
1998	Juan Gonzalez	OF
1999	Ivan Rodriguez	C
2003	Alex Rodriguez	SS

Rookies of the Year

Year	Name	Position
1974	Mike Hargrove	1B

Batting Champions

Year	Name	#
1991	Julio Franco	.341

| 2004 | Michael Young | .331 |

Home-Run Champions

Year	Name	#
1968	Frank Howard	44
1970	Frank Howard	44
1992	Juan Gonzalez	43
1993	Juan Gonzalez	46
2001	Alex Rodriguez	52
2002	Alex Rodriguez	57
2003	Alex Rodriguez	47

ERA Champions

Year	Name	#
1961	Dick Donovan	2.40
1969	Dick Bosman	2.19
1983	Rick Honeycutt	2.42

Strikeout Champions

Year	Name	#
1989	Nolan Ryan	301
1990	Nolan Ryan	232

No-Hitters (Italics = Perfect Game)

Name	Date
Jim Bibby	07/30/1973
Bert Blyleven	09/22/1977
Nolan Ryan	06/11/1990
Nolan Ryan	05/01/1991
Kenny Rogers	*07/28/1994*

POSTSEASON APPEARANCES

AL West Division Titles

Year	Record	Manager
1994	52–62	Kevin Kennedy
1996	90–72	Johnny Oates

| 1998 | 88–74 | Johnny Oates |
| 1999 | 95–67 | Johnny Oates |

MANAGERS

2003–	Buck Showalter
2001–2002	Jerry Narron
1995–2001	Johnny Oates
1993–1994	Kevin Kennedy
1992	Toby Harrah
1985–1992	Bobby Valentine
1983–1985	Doug Rader
1982	Darrell Johnson
1981–1982	Don Zimmer
1978–1980	Pat Corrales
1977–1978	Billy Hunter
1977	Connie Ryan
1977	Eddie Stanky
1975–1977	Frank Lucchesi
1973–1975	Billy Martin
1973	Del Wilber
1973	Whitey Herzog
1969–1972	Ted Williams
1968	Jim Lemon
1963–1967	Gil Hodges
1963	Eddie Yost
1961–1963	Mickey Vernon

Team Records by Individual Players

Batting Leaders

| | Single Season | | | Career | | |
	Name		Year	Name		Plate Appearances
Batting average	Julio Franco	.341	1991	Al Oliver	.319	2,263
On-base %	Toby Harrah	.432	1985	Mike Hargrove	.399	3,004
Slugging %	Juan Gonzalez	.643	1996	Alex Rodriguez	.615	2,172
OPS	Rafael Palmeiro	1.050	1999	Alex Rodriguez	1.011	2,172
Games	Al Oliver	163	1980	Rafael Palmeiro	1,573	6,767
At bats	Michael Young	690	2004	Rafael Palmeiro	5,830	6,767
Runs	Alex Rodriguez	133	2001	Rafael Palmeiro	958	6,767
Hits	Michael Young	221	2005	Ivan Rodriguez	1,723	6,062

(Continued)

Batting Leaders   (Continued)

	Single Season			Career	Plate Appearances
	Name	Year	Name		
Total bases	Alex Rodriguez	393	2001	Juan Gonzalez	3,073	5,925
Doubles	Juan Gonzalez	50	1998	Ivan Rodriguez	344	6,062
Triples	Ruben Sierra	14	1989	Sierra	44	4,975
Home runs	Alex Rodriguez	57	2002	Juan Gonzalez	372	5,925
RBIs	Juan Gonzalez	157	1998	Juan Gonzalez	1,180	5,925
Walks	Frank Howard	132	1970	Rafael Palmeiro	805	6,767
Strikeouts	Pete Incaviglia	185	1986	Juan Gonzalez	1,076	5,925
Stolen bases	Bump Wills	52	1978	Bump Wills	161	2,962
Extra-base hits	Juan Gonzalez	97	1998	Juan Gonzalez	713	5,925
Times on base	Frank Howard	294	1970	Rafael Palmeiro	2,551	6,767

Pitching Leaders

	Single Season			Career	Innings Pitched
	Name	Year	Name		
ERA	Dick Bosman	2.19	1969	Gaylord Perry	3.26	827.3
Wins	Ferfie Jenkins	25	1974	Charlie Hough	139	2,308
Won-loss %	Danny Darwin	.765	1980	Kenny Rogers	.581	1,909
Hits/9 IP	Nolan Ryan	5.31	1991	Nolan Ryan	6.35	840
Walks/9 IP	Fergie Jenkins	1.23	1974	Fergie Jenkins	2.01	1,410.3
Strikeouts	Nolan Ryan	301	1989	Charlie Hough	1,452	2,308
Strikeouts/9 IP	Nolan Ryan	11.32	1989	Nolan Ryan	10.06	840
Games	Mitch Williams	85	1987	Kenny Rogers	528	1,909
Saves	Francisco Cordero	49	2004	John Wetteland	150	253
Innings	Fergie Jenkins	328.3	1974	Charlie Hough	2,308	2,308
Starts	Jim Bibby/Fergie Jenkins	41	1974	Charlie Hough	313	2,308
Complete games	Fergie Jenkins	29	1974	Charlie Hough	98	2,308
Shutouts	Bert Blyleven	6	1976	Fergie Jenkins	17	1,410.3

Source: Drawn from data in "Texas Rangers Batting Leaders (seasonal and career)." http://baseball-reference.com/ teams/TEX/leaders_bat.shtml; "Texas Rangers Pitching Leaders (seasonal and career)." http://baseball-reference. com/teams/TEX/leaders_pitch.shtml.

BIBLIOGRAPHY

Deveaux, Tom. *The Washington Senators, 1901–1971*. Jefferson, NC: 2001.

Falkner, David. *The Last Yankee: The Turbulent Life of Billy Martin*. New York: Simon and Schuster, 1992.

Farrey, Tom. "A Series of Beneficial Moves." ESPN.com, November 1, 2000. http://espn.go.com/mlb/bush/timeline.html.

Golenbock, Peter. *Wild, High, and Tight: The Life and Death of Billy Martin*. New York: St. Martin's Press, 1994.

Munsey and Suppes. "Ameriquest Field in Arlington." Ballparks. http://www.ballparks.com/baseball/american/bpkarl.htm.

Nadel, Eric. *Texas Rangers: The Authorized History*. Dallas: Taylor Publishing, 1997.

Rosentraub, Mark S., and S.R. Nunn. "Suburban City Investment in Professional Sport—Estimating Fiscal Returns of the Dallas Cowboys and Texas Rangers to Investor Communities." *American Behavioral Scientist* 21 (1978): 393–414.

Seidel, Michael. *Ted Williams: A Baseball Life*. Lincoln: University of Nebraska Press, 2000.

Shropshire, Mike. *Seasons in Hell: With Billy Martin, Whitey Herzog and "The Worst Baseball Team in History"—The 1973–1975 Texas Rangers*. New York: Donald I. Fine Books, 1996.

Whitfield, Shelby. *Kiss It Goodbye*. New York: Abelard-Schuman, 1973.

Toronto Blue Jays

Russell Field

In February 1886, star pitcher and sporting-goods magnate Albert Spalding visited Toronto and announced that the city was ready for a major-league baseball franchise. While prescient, he was 90 years early. In the intervening nine decades, Toronto's path to becoming first host to a major-league baseball team and subsequently home to back-to-back World Series champions was intimately tied to the city's emergence as English Canada's dominant financial and media center. Equally important was the vision, and deep pockets, of local and regional politicians and the business community who held dear the notion of Toronto as a world-class city.

NINETY YEARS OF BIG-LEAGUE ASPIRATIONS

A variety of bat-and-ball games were popular summer pastimes in nineteenth-century Canada. In the decades preceding Canadian confederation in 1867, cricket was the most popular organized summer sport. In the 1860s and 1870s, nationalist sentiment tended to favor the "indigenous" game of lacrosse. But by the 1880s, baseball had supplanted both as the dominant and increasingly most commercial summer game.

In 1886, a Toronto franchise entered the International League, and except for 1891–95, remained a member until the Maple Leafs folded in 1967. During the franchise's 77-year history, it won 12 pennants and two Little World Series, and listed on its roster such future Hall of Famers as Wee Willie Keeler, Carl Hubbell, and Ralph Kiner.

Toronto's major-league aspirations were first fanned by the construction of the 20,000-seat Maple Leaf Stadium in 1926. Civic interest in a major-league team quieted during the depression of the 1930s and Canada's involvement in World War II. The Maple Leafs prospered in the late 1940s and early 1950s. In the era before television and the migration of urban populations to new suburbs, the team regularly outdrew some of the major leagues' less successful clubs.

The owner of the Maple Leafs then was local businessman Jack Kent Cooke, who later gained notoriety as owner of the Los Angeles Lakers and the Washington Redskins. In the 1950s, Toronto was frequently mentioned as a possible destination for relocating major-league teams, and Cooke was involved in the plan to start a third major league, the Continental League. One of the stumbling blocks for Cooke was Toronto's lack of a major-league ballpark. By the mid-1950s, the age of Maple Leaf Stadium encouraged Cooke to seek out civic funding for a ballpark on the city's Canadian National Exhibition (CNE) grounds. However, that site was used for a football-specific facility for the Canadian Football League (CFL) Argonauts, whose owner had much stronger ties to local politicians. The importance of access to public funds and political power for sports promoters would become even more evident as Toronto's dreams of a major-league franchise were realized in the 1970s.

BIRTH OF THE BLUE JAYS

In the early 1970s, Alderman Paul Godfrey decided to pursue his dream of major-league baseball in Toronto. On the advice of baseball commissioner Bowie Kuhn, he made building a suitable stadium his first order of business (Maple Leaf Stadium had been demolished in 1968). When his 1971 plan for a publicly financed domed stadium was quashed by the opposition of taxpayer and amateur sport groups, he turned to Exhibition Stadium on the CNE grounds. Godfrey exerted considerable influence on the local sports press to support his planned renovation. In 1974, he successfully negotiated for $15 million in public funding for the project, half from the municipality and half from an interest-free provincial government loan. The result was a converted football stadium, with cool lakeside temperatures, poor sight lines, few creature comforts, and outfield bleachers that followed the football sidelines and stretched off into center field rather than wrapping around the outfield fence.

A number of different groups were interested in owning the team that would someday play in this ballpark, including one bankrolled by the owner of the city's National Hockey League franchise. The Blue Jays' eventual owners were a financially strong partnership that included Labatt, one of three breweries that dominated the Canadian marketplace, with annual sales of $500 million; R. Howard Webster, a wealthy entrepreneur whose holdings included the *Globe and Mail*; and the Canadian Imperial Bank of Commerce (CIBC), Canada's second-largest bank, with assets of $33 billion. Labatt and Webster each held a 45 percent stake and the CIBC held 10 percent, the maximum allowed by the federal Bank Act. Configurations of this partnership would control the Blue Jays until the mid-1990s, though Labatt's would be the dominant financial interest and the public face of the team. Since 1974, Labatt Breweries had decided that sports-team ownership—specifically baseball, since its main competitors were already involved in hockey and football—would help the company establish a presence in the Toronto market.

The primary strategy was to buy an existing major-league team. In January 1976, Godfrey—now chairman of Metropolitan Toronto—held a press conference to announce that the San Francisco Giants had been purchased, were to be renamed the Toronto Giants, and would begin play in the National League in time for the 1976 season. Before February was out, however, the mayor of San Francisco had obtained an injunction blocking the Giants' move, found new local owners, and convinced NL owners to oppose the move and support the city's desire to keep the club in San Francisco. It seemed, for a time, as though the Labatt-Webster-CIBC effort, along with Godfrey's desire to put a team in a ballpark renovated with public funds, had all come to naught. However, later that month, the American League owners decided to add a second expansion team along with Seattle.

The Labatt-Webster-CIBC group switched strategies. Instead of pursuing an existing franchise, they worked to become the Toronto group chosen to become the AL's 14th team. On March 29, 1976, for an expansion fee of $7 million, the league's owners offered them just such an opportunity. As spring turned to summer in 1976, fans in Toronto readied themselves for major-league baseball beginning in 1977.

TAKING FLIGHT (1977–81)

April 7, 1977. Images from that day are iconographic in the history of Toronto sport: grounds-crew members frantically sweeping snow off the artificial turf, naively battling Mother Nature; singer Anne Murray, hidden beneath a mammoth parka, rushing through "O Canada"; and the umpiring crew and team managers huddled together, as much for warmth as to exchange lineup cards. And the fans: 44,649 of them—far fewer than the number who would later claim they were there—cheering their new sports heroes and tossing in the occasional "We want beer" chant for good measure.

Work began soon after the franchise was awarded in 1976. The Metro Toronto Council approved an additional $2.8 million to complete the Exhibition Stadium renovations. Meanwhile, the team's first employee, Paul Beeston, was hired to oversee the franchise's finances. He eventually rose to the team presidency before his departure in 1997. In June 1976, Peter Bavasi was hired as the team's first president and general manager. The son of longtime Dodgers and Padres general manager Buzzie Bavasi, he assembled a front-office staff that would remain in place long after he had parted company with the Blue

Jays. Bavasi's key appointments included vice president of player personnel Pat Gillick and veteran scouts Bobby Mattick and Al LaMacchia. In September, Roy Hartsfield was named the team's first manager.

Concurrently, the club ran a contest inviting fans to suggest potential team names. The eventual choice, the Blue Jays, was on 154 of the more than 30,000 entries that proposed more than 4,000 different names. There was suggestion in the media that the team's name and Labatt's flagship beer brand (Labatt's Blue) bore a striking resemblance, and therefore offered numerous promotional opportunities. The irony was that Toronto's bylaw prohibiting the public consumption of alcohol meant that Exhibition Stadium was major-league baseball's only dry stadium.

Bavasi began stocking Hartsfield's Blue Jays at the AL expansion draft in November 1976. The first selection, Bob Bailor, hit .310 as a rookie in 1977. The remaining selections were largely anonymous to the average fan (veteran pitcher and inaugural Opening Day starter Bill Singer was perhaps the best known). Yet Toronto baseball fans found their favorites among this motley bunch, including first baseman Doug Ault (an instant hero with two home runs in the Blue Jays' 9–5 win over Chicago in the franchise's first-ever game) and infielder Dave McKay (the first Canadian-born Blue Jay). But the most enduring legacy of the expansion draft was a trio of players—pitcher Jim Clancy, catcher Ernie Whitt, and infielder Garth Iorg—who were still with the team when the franchise won its first division championship in 1985.

After averaging 55 wins in its first three seasons, the club fired Hartsfield and replaced him with scout Bobby Mattick. While there was little improvement on the field—the club finished in last place both seasons he managed the club—Mattick's skills as a teacher helped develop the young talent collecting in the farm system. This included pitcher Dave Stieb, outfielder Lloyd Moseby, and flashy shortstop Alfredo Griffin, who was named cowinner of the 1979 AL Rookie of the Year Award. By the end of 1981, the team's fifth season, the prospects were finally starting to show promise. They finished the second half of the strike-cleaved season with a mediocre yet respectable 21–27 record.

When the Blue Jays were first established, only 16 games were broadcast on television. However, they eventually captured a national media audience, and by 1981, they were benefiting from a lucrative local television contract. A regional following was built from the team's inception on radio as Telemedia Broadcast Systems carried Blue Jays games on a 28-station network. The Blue Jays attracted 1.7 million fans to Exhibition Park in their first year, then the largest attendance ever recorded by an expansion team. The club lost 108 games, yet had the AL's fourth-best attendance. The team, thanks both to novelty and a marketing plan that sold Toronto sports fans the experience of seeing major-league baseball played by visiting teams, was a financial success in its inaugural season. Attendance began to fall in subsequent years, however, as the novelty wore off and the team failed to win. From an average of 21,263 fans per game in 1977, the Blue Jays averaged only 14,247 in 1981, 11th highest in a 14-team league. As Beeston later told sportswriter Stephen Brunt, "You know the year of the strike in '81, we wouldn't have drawn a million people. We had one crowd over twenty thousand people. We won. That is why we have drawn here. We won. In '82, we started winning."

THE FARM BEARS FRUIT (1982–89)

As teams assessed the impact of 1981's two-month-long players' strike, in Toronto at least it appeared that Beeston was prophetic. If there were disgruntled customers among the Blue Jays' fan base, what brought them to the ballpark was winning baseball, which the team began to do for the first time in the 1980s.

The new era began with a changing of the guard in the front office. Gone was Bavasi, the club's first president, whose hands-on management style had worn thin after five years, replaced by Labatt's executive Peter Hardy, who divided the baseball (Gillick) and business (Beeston) operations between the two men who would lead the franchise for more than a decade. The stability of the club's ownership was also remarkable. The partnership of Labatt's (45%), R. Howard Webster (45%), and the CIBC (10%) remained intact from the franchise's inauguration in 1977 until Webster's death in 1990.

One of the final battles in the power struggle between Bavasi and Gillick was naming Mattick's replacement. Gillick's choice, and the man who eventually became the Blue Jays' third manager, was former Atlanta Braves skipper Bobby Cox. He inherited a roster in transition, as raw talents from a well-stocked farm system replaced expansion-draft castoffs. In 1983, Cox's second season, the Blue Jays finished over .500 for the first time, and treated Toronto fans to their initial, and brief, taste of a pennant race, leading the division at the All-Star break. The franchise would not finish another season under .500 until 1994, as the Blue Jays became a perennial contender in the AL's Eastern Division and one of the wealthiest clubs in baseball.

In 1985, Toronto fans found their club in a bona fide pennant race as the Jays battled the Yankees into a final weekend series between the two clubs at Exhibition Stadium. On Saturday, before a national television audience, Doyle Alexander pitched the franchise into its first postseason. The squad won 99 games with a strong offense and sparkling pitching, including a league-leading 3.31 ERA. Cox was selected AL Manager of the Year. The club came agonizingly close to the World Series, blowing a 3–1 lead in the AL Championship Series to the George Brett–led Kansas City Royals. After the season Cox resigned and was replaced by third-base coach Jimy Williams. His tenure was often stormy, as the talented club underachieved. The most disappointing season was 1987, when the Blue Jays led Detroit by three and a half games entering the season's final week. But they lost their last seven games to finish in second place with a record of 96–66. George Bell won the MVP with 134 RBIs.

The stability of the Blue Jays' lineup was a testament to the franchise's farm system. It was also a valuable marketing tool, as the faces of the

Blue Jays' success were prominent in the Toronto media and broadcast across Canadian television. The infield featured first baseman Willie Upshaw, second baseman Damaso Garcia, and Gold Glove shortstop Tony Fernandez. In the outfield was the talented young trio labeled "the best outfield in baseball": Moseby flanked by Bell in left field and 1986 AL home-run leader Jesse Barfield in right. On the mound, the rotation was anchored by Stieb, Clancy, Alexander, and young left-hander Jimmy Key.

The team's primary weakness at this time was in the bullpen. A variety of unsuccessful closers preceded the Blue Jays' first major foray into free agency. In 1984 Gillick signed Dennis Lamp, formerly of the White Sox. This was followed by the equally unsuccessful trade for Oakland's Bill Caudill. The club did not find a stopper until minor leaguer Tom Henke was called up in mid-1985.

As the Blue Jays spent little on free agents, Cox was lauded for making the most out of the talent given to him. He employed a system of platoons, most notably at catcher (Whitt and Buck Martinez) and third base (Iorg and Rance Mulliniks). In addition, led by scout Epy Guerrero, the Blue Jays were one of the first clubs to recruit Latin American players. With many hailing from the small Dominican town of San Pedro de Macoris, the Blue Jays' Latin talent included Griffin, Fernandez, Garcia, and Bell. Finally, Gillick was a pioneer in using the Rule 5 draft of nonroster players to acquire contributors such as Upshaw, Bell, Kelly Gruber, and Manny Lee.

Attendance increased as the Blue Jays improved. From the AL's 10th-highest attendance in 1982 (15,750 per game), the team climbed to 2nd in its division-winning season of 1985 and 1st in 1987 (averaging more than 34,300). The introduction of beer sales at Exhibition Stadium in 1982 did not hurt. Success on the field also translated into profits off it. By mid-1983 the team's national telecasts were regularly drawing a million viewers. The ownership benefits for Labatt's were considerably enhanced in 1984 when it became a partner in Canada's first all-sports cable network, The Sports Network (TSN). TSN carried Blue Jays games to a national audience in English Canada, and by 1986, the team's games were being carried on 54 stations by Telemedia's radio network.

SKYDOME AND SUCCESS (1989–93)

As the Blue Jays became more successful and popular, civic leaders worried over Exhibition Stadium's suitability as a major-league ballpark. Its inadequacies were never more evident than on a chilly October 1985 night when only 32,000 fans showed up for the seventh game of the ALCS. That same year, William Davis, the premier of Ontario, announced the creation of the Stadium Corporation of Ontario (Stadco), whose purpose was to build and manage a new, publicly owned, modern domed stadium. Toronto's sporting landscape was being altered by the value civic leaders placed on commercial entertainment facilities as part of a world-class city, plus the precedent set by the publicly funded renovations of Exhibition Stadium in the mid-1970s.

The original cost for SkyDome was projected at $150 million: $60 million from the province and the municipality, $20 million in debt, and $70 million from private interests. To generate the latter, Trevor Eyton—chief executive of Brascan, a holding company whose assets included Blue Jays co-owners Labatt's—created Dome Stadium Inc., which raised $5 million from each of 14 corporations, who received a variety of skybox, advertising, and supplier privileges. Located downtown—after much public debate about the best location for a stadium—SkyDome was a world apart from Exhibition Stadium. With a spectator capacity in excess of 50,000, the new stadium was best known for its retractable roof and Jumbotron scoreboard, and included a hotel with rooms overlooking the field, bars and restaurants, and a private fitness club. The cost of such modernity, however, far exceeded any original projections. By the time SkyDome opened on June 4, 1989, the cost had risen to $562.8 million (and eventually exceeded $580 million). As a result, Eyton's SkyDome investors increased their share from $70 million to $150 million. But, most troubling, SkyDome's debt reached $310 million, borne by Ontario's taxpayers. The new park was a great hit with the fans, and attendance reached 3.38 million, most in the AL.

Change was the order of the day as the Blue Jays entered a new era in their new ballpark with Beeston installed as president in 1989. In the dugout, a poor start to the 1989 season (12 wins, 24 losses) spelled the end for Williams, who became the first manager in team history to be fired midseason. His interim replacement was hitting instructor Cito Gaston, who reluctantly became the full-time manager. Gaston turned around the underachieving team (behind rookie Junior Felix, veteran Mookie Wilson, and slugger Fred McGriff, who led the AL with 36 homers), and the Blue Jays won their second AL East division title on the season's final weekend. The ALCS was anticlimactic (except for Jose Canseco becoming the first player to homer into SkyDome's upper deck) as the Jays lost in five games to Oakland.

The 1990 team failed to live up to the expectations of the large SkyDome crowds. Nevertheless, on September 2, pitcher Dave Stieb threw the first no-hitter in franchise history, after coming within an out of no-hitters in two consecutive starts in 1988 and coming within a strike of a perfect game against the Yankees on a humid night inside SkyDome in 1989. It would be the last great moment for the most talented pitcher ever produced by the Blue Jays' farm system, as Stieb suffered through two injury-plagued seasons and was out of baseball for four years before a brief comeback in 1998.

The failure of the team to realize success prompted a major rethinking of the roster in 1990. Gillick abandoned the plan to build primarily through the farm system. He began with two trades at the 1990 winter meetings. The first yielded Devon White, the best defensive outfielder in team history. The second was a blockbuster involving four All-Stars as the Jays sacrificed Fernandez and McGriff to acquire outfielder Joe Carter and second baseman Roberto Alomar. The three new players became the centerpieces of a revamped lineup that in 1991 won the team's third division championship, only to lose the ALCS to

Minnesota, four games to one. Carter was the highest-paid player in the AL at $3,791,166. However, the strength of the team was its pitching staff, which led the AL with a sizzling 3.50 ERA and 60 saves. That same season, the Blue Jays hosted the All-Star Game and became the first franchise to attract 4 million fans in a season.

The enhanced revenue afforded by SkyDome's appeal and capacity coupled with the club's postseason failures fueled subsequent moves. Gillick pursued impact free agents. In 1992, those players were pitcher Jack Morris (who became the first Blue Jay to earn $5 million in a season) and DH Dave Winfield. A year later, Winfield was replaced by Paul Molitor and Morris was joined in the rotation by Dave Stewart. Gillick also tinkered with the roster in midseason. He forfeited young prospects for the rewards of players in their prime. For the 1992 stretch drive he acquired pitcher David Cone from the Mets, and in 1993 stolen-base king Rickey Henderson arrived from Oakland (though the reacquisition of veteran shortstop Tony Fernandez had greater impact). Few stars were produced by the farm system, though setup man Mike Timlin and hard-throwing starter Juan Guzman (obtained in a minor-league trade) were two exceptions.

The team reaped the benefits of these moves in 1992 with the second-most-productive offense in the AL, which along with Jack Morris's league-leading 21 wins resulted in a fourth division title. After beating Oakland in the ALCS four games to two—the most memorable moment being a ninth-inning game-four Alomar home run off closer Dennis Eckersley—the Blue Jays moved on to face the Atlanta Braves. Toronto won its first championship in six games. The 1992 World Series was memorable for its odd moments—the minor international incident that ensued when the U.S. Marine Corps honor guard flew the Canadian flag upside down prior to game two, and the umpires, during game three, missing the third out of what would have been the second triple play in World Series history. There were highlights, however: pinch hitter Ed Sprague winning game two with a 9th-inning home run off career saves leader Jeff Reardon; White making a remarkable over-the-shoulder catch in game three; Winfield driving in the go-ahead runs in the 11th inning of game six; and Timlin fielding Otis Nixon's bunt for the series-clinching out a half inning later.

A year later, with a vastly revamped lineup, the Blue Jays were back in the World Series after dispatching the White Sox in the ALCS four games to two. Gone were Henke, Winfield, Gruber, Stieb, Key, and Cone. Duane Ward moved into the closer's spot and first baseman John Olerud blossomed. He led the AL in hitting (.363), on-base percentage, and doubles, and he, Molitor, and Alomar became the first teammates to finish one-two-three in a batting race. The 1993 team was led by its offense (which the local media nicknamed WAMCO, for White, Alomar, Molitor, Carter, and Olerud), which led the AL in batting (.279), and the defense was led by closer Duane Ward with 45 saves. The strong offense was most evident in game four of the World Series, which the Blue Jays trailed 14–9 heading into the eighth inning, only to score six runs off Philadelphia's bullpen. But the most dramatic moment of the series, the most significant highlight in franchise history, occurred in game six, when, trailing 6–5 with two runners on base and one out in the bottom of the ninth inning, Joe Carter faced erratic reliever Mitch Williams. His homer was only the second bottom-of-the-ninth home run to clinch a World Series championship (Pittsburgh's Bill Mazeroski in 1960 being the other), and it set off a national celebration.

The team's success was due in no small part to its place in baseball's economic hierarchy. The move to SkyDome, with its increased attendance and debt load paid for by others, had been a boon to team profits, which reached $17.5 million in 1989 and $14 million a year later. The Blue Jays were suddenly among the wealthiest teams in baseball. A lot of the profits were invested in the free-agent market. The Blue Jays' salary budget went from $31 million in 1991 to $45 million at the start of 1992. The Blue Jays ended 1993 with the highest payroll in baseball ($51,575,034), becoming the first team to exceed $50 million in salaries. The club still managed to break even, thanks to postseason revenues and continuing record attendance. In 1993, the Blue Jays led the AL in attendance for the fifth straight year, exceeded 4 million in paid attendance for the third straight year, and set an MLB record with an attendance of 4,057,947, or an average of 50,098 per game.

Joe Carter celebrates his game winning three-run homerun in the ninth inning of game 6 of the World Series, 1993. © AP / Wide World Photos

But attendance was not the only story. On August 19, 1990, original owner R. Howard Webster died. In accordance with the partnership agreement, his estate offered his 45 percent interest in the team to the remaining partners. Since the CIBC was limited by the Bank Act to a 10 percent share, Labatt's was the only viable internal option. In 1977, Webster's share was worth $3.15 million, but when Labatt's purchased his stock in 1991, the value had appreciated to $67.5 million. While the team benefited from what Stephen Brunt called a "lucrative local television contract," Labatt offshoots such as TSN and TV Labatt also made substantial profits.

In 1993, *Financial World* magazine ranked the Blue Jays as the third-most-valuable franchise in North American professional sport, tied with the Los Angeles Lakers and trailing only the Dallas Cowboys and New York Yankees. With an estimated franchise value of $155 million (for a team worth $7 million only 16 years earlier) and despite little presence in the U.S. media or merchandise markets, the Blue Jays were among the most successful businesses in all of professional sports.

THE POSTSTRIKE MALAISE (1994–2000)

SkyDome, when filled by fans watching a successful team, had provided the revenue for Gillick's forays into free agency. But when the Blue Jays faltered, SkyDome increasingly became a financial albatross. While not owned directly by the ball club, the stadium realized operating surpluses of $34 million and $35 million in the World Series–winning years of 1992 and 1993. Despite record attendance, thanks to interest, taxes, and depreciation, Stadco had net losses of $21.7 million and $14.2 million in those same years.

In 1991, with Ontario's economy in recession and SkyDome's debts mounting, the Stadco board recommended that the provincial government privatize the stadium. In November, an agreement was reached to sell SkyDome to Stadium Acquisitions Inc. It took until March 1994 to finalize the deal—for only $151 million—as part of which taxpayers absorbed $263 million of SkyDome's debt. Then, in November 1998, Stadium Acquisitions filed for bankruptcy protection. In the same month, the Blue Jays signed a new 10-year lease to play in the stadium. Shortly thereafter, an American firm, Sportsco International, bought SkyDome out of bankruptcy for $85 million.

Putting together a competitive team became increasingly challenging after the 1994–95 strike. While Toronto fans may not have punished the Blue Jays organization for the labor stoppage, they were less interested in paying to watch a losing team. The Blue Jays began 1994 with optimism, as the nucleus of the 1993 World Series–winning team remained intact. But injuries, especially to Ward, resulted in the team's first losing record since 1982. It was the first of four consecutive losing seasons, which, in 1997, cost Gaston, the winningest manager in team history, his job.

Off the field, Gillick—an original member of the organization—stepped down in 1994 to be replaced as general manager by assistant Gord Ash. Then Beeston left in 1997 to become MLB's president and chief operating officer. Most significantly, in 1995, Labatt's was taken over by Interbrew SA. The Belgian brewery showed little interest in Labatt's sporting assets. TSN and the CFL Argonauts were sold off, while the Blue Jays' front office anticipated the team's seemingly imminent sale.

In an attempt to remain competitive in the Toronto market—where new entertainment districts were being built, the hockey team was successful and entering a new arena, and a new basketball franchise had entered the marketplace—Ash made big splashes in putting together the team's roster. David Cone returned to the Blue Jays after the strike was settled in 1995, and Roger Clemens spent two Cy Young Award–winning seasons in Toronto (1997–98). Even the low-risk signing of Jose Canseco in 1998 paid dividends when he slugged 46 home runs. But there were also unsuccessful free-agent signings (Erik Hanson in 1996, Randy Myers in 1998), and the club found its veteran talent base disintegrating as key players, including White, Alomar, Molitor, and Al Leiter, chose not to re-sign after becoming free agents. For the first time, the Blue Jays found themselves sellers at the midseason trade deadline. Cone was dealt in 1995, only months after his return, and Guzman was traded at the deadline in 1998. High-priced veterans, notably Clemens and Pat Hentgen, were also moved in the off-season. The Blue Jays returned to their roots in the post–World Series championship years, building the roster around young prospects: first baseman Carlos Delgado, shortstop Alex Gonzalez, and outfielders Shawn Green and Shannon Stewart.

The prospects and free-agent signees, however, were unable to compete with the stronger clubs of the AL East, never finishing higher than third place. Increasing mediocrity on the field was reflected at SkyDome's turnstiles. In the post–World Series, prestrike 1994 season, the Blue Jays led the AL in attendance, averaging over 49,000 fans per game. Five years (and two fifth-, one fourth-, and two third-place finishes) later, attendance had dwindled to 26,700, 8th best in a 14-team league. With crowds dwindling, gate receipts dried up. The World Series teams had better than broken even, but losses in the millions of dollars in 1994 grew to $15 million in 1995.

ROGERS AND MONEYBALL (2000–2005)

Into this situation stepped one of Canada's largest and most visible communications companies. In 2000, Rogers Communications Inc. (RCI) purchased an 80 percent stake in the Blue Jays from Interbrew SA for $112 million, and in 2004 they acquired the remaining 20 percent. RCI operates a network of cable, satellite, and digital television pipelines, as well as Canada's largest wireless network and Internet and digital-media operations. Led by Ted Rogers, the 13th-wealthiest individual in Canada, RCI articulated a vision of sports-team ownership that emphasized branding and cross-promotional opportunities. In 2005, through direct ownership, radio- or television-broadcasting rights, or sponsorship using its local cable stations, RCI was involved with nearly every commercial sports franchise in Toronto. RCI not only owns the Blue Jays, it also operates a national all-sports television channel that broadcasts the team's games as well as the club's flagship radio station.

RCI's choice as Blue Jays' president was Paul Godfrey, the man who had lobbied for the franchise's creation in the mid-1970s. After firing Ash in 2002, Godfrey selected Oakland assistant general manager J.P. Ricciardi to head baseball operations. Charged with decreasing payroll to pre-1994 levels, Ricciardi preached the principles of what became popularly known as "moneyball"—winning with high-value, low-salary players. In less than a decade the Blue Jays went from having the AL's highest payroll to a struggling small-market club. Behind a rotating door of managers (five in seven years), the team finished in third place behind the Yankees and Red Sox for six straight years (1998–2003) before dropping into last place in 2004. The team did improve in 2005, nearly breaking even (80–82) and coming in third, rebuilding with several players from the farm system.

At the start of Ricciardi's tenure, 2002, the Blue Jays had the 11th-highest Opening Day payroll of the 30 MLB clubs, the 15th-best record, and the 6th-lowest attendance. In subsequent years, the club's attendance remained well below 25,000 per game (SkyDome's capacity is 50,516). In such an environment, the Blue Jays consistently lost money. In 2002, the team reported a loss of $69.8 million for the first nine months of the fiscal year. This came a year after the Blue Jays' operating loss of $83.3 million led MLB and was blamed on the impact the weak Canadian dollar (relative to the U.S. dollar) had on payroll costs, which have to be paid in American currency. In response, RCI advanced the baseball team $55 million in 2002 from its other operations.

The Blue Jays' shifting fortunes and RCI's convergence aspirations were also reflected in media coverage of the club. In 2002, for example, Blue Jays games were televised nationally by the Canadian Broadcasting Corporation (CBC) and regionally by both TSN and RCI's own sports station, Sportsnet. Beginning in 2003, however, CBC ceased national telecasts, and Sportsnet provided regional coverage.

In the face of dwindling attendance and a payroll budget frozen at $50–55 million, Ricciardi chose to rebuild with youth. Success came in the form of 2003 Cy Young Award winner Roy Halladay, 2002 AL Rookie of the Year Eric Hinske, and talented outfielder Vernon Wells. While future talents were being groomed in the farm system, Delgado chose not to wait for the team's fortunes to improve. After the 2004 season, the franchise's career leader in home runs and RBIs (and second in hits and games played) signed as a free agent with Florida.

Vernon Wells makes a leaping catch on a line drive by Oakland Athletics' Eric Byrnes. © AP / Wide World Photos

In February 2005, the Blue Jays' owners added SkyDome to their holdings. The stadium that had cost $580 million (with taxpayers paying over half) was purchased for only $25 million. The newly renamed Rogers Centre was fitted with new Field Turf to replace the outdated Astroturf. At the same time, RCI armed Ricciardi with $210 million to invest in salaries over three seasons. Despite these changes, over a decade removed from the back-to-back championships that helped justify the *World* in World Series, the Toronto Blue Jays are the poster child for what troubles MLB. Since baseball's 1994 work stoppage, the Blue Jays have changed owners twice and played mediocre baseball with a roller-coaster payroll in front of average-sized major-league crowds in a cavernous, outdated (yet only 16-year-old) stadium. This was all in a city that in 1991 became the first to send 4 million fans out to the ballpark, and that is too large and cosmopolitan to be "small-market."

NOTABLE ACHIEVEMENTS

Most Valuable Players

Year	Name	Position
1987	George Bell	OF

Cy Young Winners

Year	Name	Position
1996	Pat Hentgen	RHP
1997	Roger Clemens	RHP
1998	Roger Clemens	RHP
2003	Roy Halladay	RHP

Rookies of the Year

Year	Name	Position
1979	Alfredo Griffin	SS
2002	Eric Hinske	3B

Batting Champions

Year	Name	#
1993	John Olerud	.363

Home-Run Champions

Year	Name	#
1986	Jesse Barfield	40
1989	Fred McGriff	36

ERA Champions

Year	Name	#
1985	Dave Stieb	2.48
1987	Jimmy Key	2.76
1996	Juan Guzman	2.93
1997	Roger Clemens	2.05
1998	Roger Clemens	2.65

Strikeout Champions

Year	Name	#
1997	Roger Clemens	292
1998	Roger Clemens	271

No-Hitters

Name	Date
Dave Stieb	09/02/1990

POSTSEASON APPEARANCES

AL East Division Titles

Year	Record	Manager
1985	99–62	Bobby Cox
1989	89–73	Jimy Williams
		Cito Gaston
1991	91–71	Cito Gaston
1992	96–66	Cito Gaston
1993	95–67	Cito Gaston

AL Pennants

Year	Record	Manager
1992	96–66	Cito Gaston
1993	95–67	Cito Gaston

World Championships

Year	Opponent	MVP
1992	Atlanta	Pat Borders
1993	Philadelphia	Paul Molitor

TORONTO MANAGERS

2004–	John Gibbons
2002–2004	Carlos Tosca
2001–2002	Buck Martinez
1999–2000	Jim Fregosi
1998	Tim Johnson
1997	Mel Queen
1992–1997	Cito Gaston
1991	Gene Tenace
1989–1991	Cito Gaston
1986–1989	Jimy Williams
1982–1985	Bobby Cox
1980–1981	Bobby Mattick
1977–1979	Roy Hartsfield

Team Records by Individual Players

Batting Leaders

| | Single Season | | | Career | Plate |
	Name		Year	Name		Appearances
Batting average	John Olerud	.363	1993	Roberto Alomar	.307	3,105
On-base %	John Olerud	.473	1993	John Olerud	.395	3,689
Slugging %	Carlos Delgado	.664	2000	Carlos Delgado	.556	6,018
OPS	Carlos Delgado	1.134	2000	Carlos Delgado	.949	6,018
Games	Tony Fernandez	163	1986	Tony Fernandez	1,450	5,900
At bats	Tony Fernandez	687	1986	Tony Fernandez	5,335	5,900
Runs	Shawn Green	134	1999	Carlos Delgado	889	6,018
Hits	Vernon Wells	215	2003	Tony Fernandez	1,583	5,900
Total bases	Carlos Delgado	378	2000	Carlos Delgado	2,786	6,018
Doubles	Carlos Delgado	57	2000	Carlos Delgado	243	6,018
Triples	Tony Fernandez	17	1990	Tony Fernandez	72	5,900
Home runs	George Bell	47	1987	Carlos Delgado	336	6,018
RBIs	Carlos Delgado	145	2003	Carlos Delgado	1,058	6,018
Walks	Carlos Delgado	123	2000	Carlos Delgado	827	6,018
Strikeouts	Jose Canseco	159	1998	Carlos Delgado	1,242	6,018
Stolen bases	Dave Collins	60	1984	Lloyd Moseby	255	5,799
Extra-base hits	Carlos Delgado	99	2000	Carlos Delgado	690	6,018
Times on base	Carlos Delgado	334	2000	Carlos Delgado	2,362	6,018

Pitching Leaders

| | Single Season | | | Career | Innings |
	Name		Year	Name		Pitched
ERA	Roger Clemens	2.05	1997	Tom Henke	2.48	5,630
Wins	Roy Halladay	22	2003	Dave Stieb	175	2,873
Won-loss %	Juan Guzman	.824	1993	Roy Halladay	.648	1,116.3
Hits/9 IP	Roger Clemens	6.48	1998	Tom Henke	6.57	5,630
Walks/9 IP	Roy Halladay	1.08	2003	Doyle Alexander	2.06	750
Strikeouts	Roger Clemens	292	1997	Dave Stieb	1,658	2,873
Strikeouts/9 IP	Roger Clemens	10.39	1998	Tom Henke	10.29	5,630
Games	Mark Eichhorn	89	1997	Duane Ward	452	650.7
Saves	Duane Ward	45	1993	Tom Heinke	217	5,630
Innings	Dave Stieb	288.3	1982	Dave Stieb	2,873	2,873
Starts	Jim Clancy	40	1982	Dave Stieb	408	2,873
Complete games	Dave Stieb	19	1982	Dave Stieb	103	2,873
Shutouts	Dave Stieb	5	1982	Dave Stieb	30	2,873

Source: Drawn from data in "Toronto Blue Jays Batting Leaders (seasonal and career)." http://baseball-reference.com/teams/TOR/leaders_bat.shtml; "Toronto Blue Jays Pitching Leaders (seasonal and career)." http://baseball-reference.com/teams/TOR/leaders_pitch.shtml.

BIBLIOGRAPHY

Brunt, Stephen. *Diamond Dreams: 20 Years of Blue Jays Baseball.* Toronto: Viking, 1996.

Cauz, Louis. *Baseball's Back in Town.* Toronto: Controlled Media, 1977.

Humber, William. *Diamonds of the North: A Concise History of Baseball in Canada.* Toronto: Oxford University Press, 1995.

Kidd, Bruce. "Toronto's SkyDome: The World's Greatest Entertainment Centre." In *The Stadium and the City,* ed. John Bale and Olof Moen, 175–96. Keele, UK: Keele University Press, 1995.

Millson, Larry. *Ballpark Figures: The Blue Jays and the Business of Baseball.* Toronto: McClelland and Stewart, 1987.

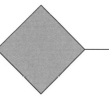

Appendix A

NATIONAL LEAGUE SEASON STANDINGS, 1876–2005

1876

Team	W	L	%
Chicago	52	14	.788
St. Louis	45	19	.703
Hartford	47	21	.691
Boston	39	31	.557
Louisville	30	36	.455
New York	21	35	.375
Philadelphia	14	45	.237
Cincinnti	9	56	.138

1877

Team	W	L	%
Boston	42	18	.700
Louisville	35	25	.583
Hartford	31	27	.534
St. Louis	28	32	.467
Chicago	26	33	.441
Cincinnati	15	42	.263

1878

Team	W	L	%
Boston	41	19	.683
Cincinnati	37	23	.617
Providence	33	27	.550
Chicago	30	30	.500
Indianapolis	24	36	.400
Milwaukee	15	45	.250
Syracuse	22	48	.314
Troy	19	56	.253

1879

Team	W	L	%
Providence	59	25	.702
Boston	54	30	.643
Buffalo	46	32	.590
Chicago	46	33	.582
Cincinnati	43	37	.538
Cleveland	27	55	.329

1880

Team	W	L	%
Chicago	67	17	.798
Providence	52	32	.619
Cleveland	47	37	.560
Troy	41	42	.494
Worcester	40	43	.482
Boston	40	44	.476
Buffalo	24	58	.293
Cincinnati	21	59	.262

1881

Team	W	L	%
Chicago	56	28	.667
Providence	47	37	.560
Buffalo	45	38	.542
Detroit	41	43	.488
Troy	39	45	.464
Boston	38	45	.458
Cleveland	36	48	.429
Worcester	32	50	.390

1882

Team	W	L	%
Chicago	55	29	.655
Providence	52	32	.619
Boston	45	39	.536
Buffalo	45	39	.536
Cleveland	42	40	.512
Detroit	42	41	.506
Troy	35	48	.422
Worcester	18	66	.214

1883

Team	W	L	%
Boston	63	35	.643
Chicago	59	39	.602
Providence	58	40	.592
Cleveland	55	42	.567
Buffalo	52	45	.536
New York	46	50	.479
Detroit	40	58	.408
Philadelphia	17	81	.173

1884

Team	W	L	%
Providence	84	28	.750
Boston	73	38	.658
Buffalo	64	47	.577
Chicago	62	50	.554
New York	62	50	.554
Philadelphia	39	73	.348
Cleveland	35	77	.312
Detroit	28	84	.250

United States Championship (3–0): Providence Grays over New York Metropolitans

1885

Team	W	L	%
Chicago	87	25	.777
New York	85	27	.759
Philadelphia	56	54	.509
Providence	53	57	.482
Boston	46	66	.411
Detroit	41	67	.380
Buffalo	38	74	.339
St. Louis	36	72	.333

Championship of America (3-3-1): Chicago White Stockings tied St. Louis Browns

1886

Team	W	L	%
Chicago	90	34	.726
Detroit	87	36	.707
New York	75	44	.630
Philadelphia	71	43	.623
Boston	56	61	.479
St. Louis	43	79	.352
Kansas City	30	91	.248
Washington	28	92	.233

World Series (4-2): St. Louis Browns over Chicago White Stockings

1887

Team	W	L	%
Detroit	79	45	.637
Philadelphia	75	48	.610
Chicago	71	50	.587
New York	68	55	.553
Boston	61	60	.504
Pittsburgh	55	69	.444
Washington	46	76	.377
Indianapolis	37	89	.294

World Series (10-5): Detroit Wolverines over St. Louis Browns

1888

Team	W	L	%
New York	84	47	.641
Chicago	77	58	.570
Philadelphia	69	61	.531
Boston	70	64	.522
Detroit	68	63	.519
Pittsburgh	66	68	.493
Indianapolis	50	85	.370
Washington	48	86	.358

World Series (6-4): New York Giants over Brooklyn Bridegrooms

1889

Team	W	L	%
New York	83	43	.659
Boston	83	45	.648
Chicago	67	65	.508
Philadelphia	63	64	.496
Pittsburgh	61	71	.462
Cleveland	61	72	.459
Indianapolis	59	75	.440
Washington	41	83	.331

World Series (6-3): New York Giants over St. Louis Browns

1890

Team	W	L	%
Brooklyn	86	43	.667
Chicago	84	53	.613
Philadelphia	78	54	.591
Cincinnati	77	55	.583
Boston	76	57	.571
New York	63	68	.481
Cleveland	44	88	.333
Pittsburgh	23	113	.169

World Series (3–3–1): Brooklyn Bridegrooms ties Louisville Colonels

1891

Team	W	L	%
Boston	87	51	.630
Chicago	82	53	.607
New York	71	61	.538
Philadelphia	68	69	.496
Cleveland	65	74	.468
Brooklyn	61	76	.445
Cincinnati	56	81	.409
Pittsburgh	55	80	.407

1892

Team	W	L	%
Boston	102	48	.680
Cleveland	93	56	.624
Brooklyn	95	59	.617
Philadelphia	87	66	.569
Cincinnati	82	68	.547
Pittsburgh	80	73	.523
Chicago	70	76	.479
New York	71	80	.470
Louisville	63	89	.414
Washington	58	93	.384
St. Louis	56	94	.373
Baltimore	46	101	.313

World Series (5-0-1): Boston Beaneaters over Cleveland Spiders

1893

Team	W	L	%
Boston	86	43	.667
Pittsburgh	81	48	.628
Cleveland	73	55	.570
Philadelphia	72	57	.558
New York	68	64	.515
Brooklyn	65	63	.508
Cincinnati	65	63	.508
Baltimore	60	70	.462
Chicago	56	71	.441
St. Louis	57	75	.432
Louisville	50	75	.400
Washington	40	89	.310

1894

Team	W	L	%
Baltimore	89	39	.695
New York	88	44	.667
Boston	83	49	.629
Philadelphia	71	57	.555
Brooklyn	70	61	.534
Cleveland	68	61	.527
Pittsburgh	65	65	.500
Chicago	57	75	.432
St. Louis	56	76	.424
Cincinnati	55	75	.423
Washington	45	87	.341
Louisville	36	94	.277

1895

Team	W	L	%
Baltimore	87	43	.669
Cleveland	84	46	.646
Philadelphia	78	53	.595
Chicago	72	58	.554
Brooklyn	71	60	.542
Boston	71	60	.542
Pittsburgh	71	61	.538
Cincinnati	66	64	.508
New York	66	65	.504
Washington	43	85	.336
St. Louis	39	92	.298
Louisville	35	96	.267

1896

Team	W	L	%
Baltimore	90	39	.698
Cleveland	80	48	.625
Cincinnati	77	50	.606
Boston	74	57	.565

1897

Team	W	L	%
Boston	93	39	.705
Baltimore	90	40	.692
New York	83	48	.634
Cincinnati	76	56	.576

1896

Team	W	L	%
Chicago	71	57	.555
Pittsburgh	66	63	.512
New York	64	67	.489
Philadelphia	62	68	.477
Brooklyn	58	73	.443
Washington	58	73	.443
St. Louis	40	90	.308
Louisville	38	93	.290

1897

Team	W	L	%
Cleveland	69	62	.527
Brooklyn	61	71	.462
Washington	61	71	.462
Pittsburgh	60	71	.458
Chicago	59	73	.447
Philadelphia	55	77	.417
Louisville	52	78	.400
St. Louis	29	102	.221

1898

Team	W	L	%
Boston	102	47	.685
Baltimore	96	53	.644
Cincinnati	92	60	.605
Chicago	85	65	.567
Cleveland	81	68	.544
Philadelphia	78	71	.523
New York	77	73	.513
Pittsburgh	72	76	.486
Louisville	70	81	.464
Brooklyn	54	91	.372
Washington	51	101	.336
St. Louis	39	111	.260

1899

Team	W	L	%
Brooklyn	101	47	.682
Boston	95	57	.625
Philadelphia	94	58	.618
Baltimore	86	62	.581
St. Louis	84	67	.556
Cincinnati	83	67	.553
Pittsburgh	76	73	.510
Chicago	75	73	.507
Louisville	75	77	.493
New York	60	90	.400
Washington	54	98	.355
Cleveland	20	134	.130

1900

Team	W	L	%
Brooklyn	82	54	.603
Pittsburgh	79	60	.568
Philadelphia	75	63	.543
Boston	66	72	.478
Chicago	65	75	.464
St. Louis	65	75	.464
Cincinnati	62	77	.446
New York	60	78	.435

1901

Team	W	L	%
Pittsburgh	90	49	.647
Philadelphia	83	57	.593
Brooklyn	79	57	.581
St. Louis	76	64	.543
Boston	69	69	.500
Chicago	53	86	.381
New York	52	85	.380
Cincinnati	52	87	.374

1902

Team	W	L	%
Pittsburgh	03	36	.741
Brooklyn	75	63	.543
Boston	73	64	.533
Cincinnati	70	70	.500
Chicago	68	69	.496
St. Louis	56	78	.418
Philadelphia	56	81	.409
New York	48	88	.353

1903

Team	W	L	%
Pittsburgh	91	49	.650
New York	84	55	.604
Chicago	82	56	.594
Cincinnati	74	65	.532
Brooklyn	70	66	.515
Boston	58	80	.420
Philadelphia	49	86	.363
St. Louis	43	94	.314

World Series (5-3): Boston Pilgrims over Pittsburgh Pirates

1904

Team	W	L	%
New York	106	47	.693
Chicago	93	60	.608
Cincinnati	88	65	.575
Pittsburgh	87	66	.569
St. Louis	75	79	.487
Brooklyn	56	97	.366
Boston	55	98	.359
Philadelphia	52	100	.342

1905

Team	W	L	%
New York	105	48	.686
Pittsburgh	96	57	.627
Chicago	92	61	.601
Philadelphia	83	69	.546
Cincinnati	79	74	.516
St. Louis	58	96	.377
Boston	51	103	.331
Brooklyn	48	104	.316

World Series (4-1): NY Giants over Philadelphia Athletics

1906

Team	W	L	%
Chicago	116	36	.763
New York	96	56	.632
Pittsburgh	93	60	.608
Philadelphia	71	82	.464
Brooklyn	66	86	.434
Cincinnati	64	87	.424
St. Louis	52	98	.347
Boston	49	102	.325

World Series (4-2): Chicago White Sox over Chicago Cubs

1907

Team	W	L	%
Chicago	107	45	.704
Pittsburgh	91	63	.591
Philadelphia	83	64	.565
New York	82	71	.536
Brooklyn	65	83	.439
Cincinnati	66	87	.431
Boston	58	90	.392
St. Louis	52	101	.340

World Series (4-0-1): Chicago Cubs over Detroit Tigers

1908

Team	W	L	%
Chicago	99	55	.643
New York	98	56	.636
Pittsburgh	98	56	.636
Philadelphia	83	71	.539
Cincinnati	73	81	.474
Boston	63	91	.409
Brooklyn	53	101	.344
St. Louis	49	105	.318

World Series (4-1): Chicago Cubs over Detroit Tigers

1909

Team	W	L	%
Pittsburgh	110	42	.724
Chicago	104	49	.680
New York	92	61	.601
Cincinnati	77	76	.503
Philadelphia	74	79	.484
Brooklyn	55	98	.359
St. Louis	54	98	.355
Boston	45	108	.294

World Series (4-3): Pittsburgh Pirates over Detroit Tigers

1910

Team	W	L	%
Chicago	104	50	.675
New York	91	63	.591
Pittsburgh	86	67	.562
Philadelphia	78	75	.510
Cincinnati	75	79	.487
Brooklyn	64	90	.416
St. Louis	63	90	.412
Boston	53	100	.346

World Series (4-1): Philadelphia Athletics over Chicago Cubs

1911

Team	W	L	%
New York	99	54	.647
Chicago	92	62	.597
Pittsburgh	85	69	.552
Philadelphia	79	73	.520
St. Louis	75	74	.503
Cincinnati	70	83	.458
Brooklyn	64	86	.427
Boston	44	107	.291

World Series (4-2): Philadelphia Athletics over New York Giants

1912

Team	W	L	%
New York	103	48	.682
Pittsburgh	93	58	.616
Chicago	91	59	.607
Cincinnati	75	78	.490
Philadelphia	73	79	.480
St. Louis	63	90	.412
Brooklyn	58	95	.379
Boston	52	101	.340

World Series (4-3-1): Boston Red Sox over New York Giants

1913

Team	W	L	%
New York	101	51	.664
Philadelphia	88	63	.583
Chicago	88	65	.575
Pittsburgh	78	71	.523
Boston	69	82	.457
Brooklyn	65	84	.436
Cincinnati	64	89	.418
St. Louis	51	99	.340

World Series (4-1): Philadelphia Athletics over New York Giants

1914

Team	W	L	%
Boston	94	59	.614
New York	84	70	.545
St. Louis	81	72	.529
Chicago	78	76	.506
Brooklyn	75	79	.487
Philadelphia	74	80	.481
Pittsburgh	69	85	.448
Cincinnati	60	94	.390

World Series (4-0): Boston Braves over Philadelphia Athletics

1915

Team	W	L	%
Philadelphia	90	62	.592
Boston	83	69	.546
Brooklyn	80	72	.526
Chicago	73	80	.477
Pittsburgh	73	81	.474
St. Louis	72	81	.471
Cincinnati	71	83	.461
New York	69	83	.454

World Series (4-1): Boston Red Sox over Philadelphia Phillies

1916

Team	W	L	%
Brooklyn	94	60	.610
Philadelphia	91	62	.595
Boston	89	63	.586
New York	86	66	.566
Chicago	67	86	.438
Pittsburgh	65	89	.422
Cincinnati	60	93	.392
St. Louis	60	93	.392

World Series (4-1): Boston Red Sox over Brooklyn Robins

1917

Team	W	L	%
New York	98	56	.636
Philadelphia	87	65	.572
St. Louis	82	70	.539
Cincinnati	78	76	.506
Chicago	74	80	.481
Boston	72	81	.471
Brooklyn	70	81	.464
Pittsburgh	51	103	.331

World Series (4-2): Chicago White Sox over New York Giants

1918

Team	W	L	%
Chicago	84	45	.651
New York	71	53	.573
Cincinnati	68	60	.531
Pittsburgh	65	60	.520
Brooklyn	57	69	.452
Philadelphia	55	68	.447
Boston	53	71	.427
St. Louis	51	78	.395

World Series (4-2): Boston Red Sox over Chicago Cubs

1919

Team	W	L	%
Cincinnati	96	44	.686
New York	87	53	.621
Chicago	75	65	.536
Pittsburgh	71	68	.511
Brooklyn	69	71	.493
Boston	57	82	.410
St. Louis	54	83	.394
Philadelphia	47	90	.343

World Series (5-3): Cincinnati Reds over Chicago White Sox

1920			
Team	**W**	**L**	**%**
Brooklyn	93	61	.604
New York	86	68	.558
Cincinnati	82	71	.536
Pittsburgh	79	75	.513
Chicago	75	79	.487
St. Louis	75	79	.487
Boston	62	90	.408
Philadelphia	62	91	.405

World Series (5-2): Cleveland indians over Brooklyn Robins

1921			
Team	**W**	**L**	**%**
New York	94	59	.614
Pittsburgh	90	63	.588
St. Louis	87	66	.569
Boston	79	74	.516
Brooklyn	77	75	.507
Cincinnati	70	83	.458
Chicago	64	89	.418
Philadelphia	51	103	.331

World Series (5-3): New York Giants over New York Yankees

1922			
Team	**W**	**L**	**%**
New York	93	61	.604
Cincinnati	86	68	.558
Pittsburgh	85	69	.552
St. Louis	85	69	.552
Chicago	80	74	.519
Brooklyn	76	78	.494
Philadelphia	57	96	.373
Boston	53	100	.346

World Series (4-0-1): New York Yankees over New York Giants

1923			
Team	**W**	**L**	**%**
New York	95	58	.621
Cincinnati	91	63	.591
Pittsburgh	87	67	.565
Chicago	83	71	.539
St. Louis	79	74	.516
Brooklyn	76	78	.494
Boston	54	100	.351
Philadelphia	50	104	.325

World Series (4-2): New York Yankees over New York Giants

1924			
Team	**W**	**L**	**%**
New York	93	60	.608
Brooklyn	92	62	.597
Pittsburgh	90	63	.588
Cincinnati	83	70	.542
Chicago	81	72	.529
St. Louis	65	89	.422
Philadelphia	55	96	.364
Boston	53	100	.346

World Series (4-3): Washington Senators over New York Giants

1925			
Team	**W**	**L**	**%**
Pittsburgh	95	58	.621
New York	86	66	.566
Cincinnati	80	73	.523
St. Louis	77	76	.503
Boston	70	83	.458
Brooklyn	68	85	.444
Philadelphia	68	85	.444
Chicago	68	86	.442

World Series (4-3): Pittsburgh Pirates over Washington Senators

1926			
Team	W	L	%
St. Louis	89	65	.578
Cincinnati	87	67	.565
Pittsburgh	84	69	.549
Chicago	82	72	.532
New York	74	77	.490
Brooklyn	71	82	.464
Boston	66	86	.434
Philadelphia	58	93	.384

World Series (4-3): St. Louis Cardinals over New York Yankees

1927			
Team	W	L	%
Pittsburgh	94	60	.610
St. Louis	92	61	.601
New York	92	62	.597
Chicago	85	68	.556
Cincinnati	75	78	.490
Brooklyn	65	88	.425
Boston	60	94	.390
Philadelphia	51	103	.331

World Series (4-0): New York Yankees over Pittsburg Pirates

1928			
Team	W	L	%
St. Louis	95	59	.617
New York	93	61	.604
Chicago	91	63	.591
Pittsburgh	85	67	.559
Cincinnati	78	74	.513
Brooklyn	77	76	.503
Boston	50	103	.327
Philadelphia	43	109	.283

World Series (4-0): New York Yankees over St. Louis Cardinals

1929			
Team	W	L	%
Chicago	98	54	.645
Pittsburgh	88	65	.575
New York	84	67	.556
St. Louis	78	74	.513
Philadelphia	71	82	.464
Brooklyn	70	83	.458
Cincinnati	66	88	.429
Boston	56	98	.364

World Series (4-1): Philadelphia Athletics over Chicago Cubs

1930			
Team	W	L	%
St. Louis	92	62	.597
Chicago	90	64	.584
New York	87	67	.565
Brooklyn	86	68	.558
Pittsburgh	80	74	.519
Boston	70	84	.455
Cincinnati	59	95	.383
Philadelphia	52	102	.338

World Series (4-2): Philadelphia Athlectics over St. Louis Cardinal

1931			
Team	W	L	%
St. Louis	101	53	.656
New York	87	65	.572
Chicago	84	70	.545
Brooklyn	79	73	.520
Pittsburgh	75	79	.487
Philadelphia	66	88	.429
Boston	64	90	.416
Cincinnati	58	96	.377

World Series (4-3): St. Louis Cardinals over Philidelphia Athletics

1932

Team	W	L	%
Chicago	90	64	.584
Pittsburgh	86	68	.558
Brooklyn	81	73	.526
Philadelphia	78	76	.506
Boston	77	77	.500
New York	72	82	.468
St. Louis	72	82	.468
Cincinnati	60	94	.390

World Series (4-0): New York Yankees over Chicago Cubs

1933

Team	W	L	%
New York	91	61	.599
Pittsburgh	87	67	.565
Chicago	86	68	.558
Boston	83	71	.539
St. Louis	82	71	.536
Brooklyn	65	88	.425
Philadelphia	60	92	.395
Cincinnati	58	94	.382

World Series (4-1): New York Giants over Washington Senators

1934

Team	W	L	%
St. Louis	95	58	.621
New York	93	60	.608
Chicago	86	65	.570
Boston	78	73	.517
Pittsburgh	74	76	.493
Brooklyn	71	81	.467
Philadelphia	56	93	.376
Cincinnati	52	99	.344

World Series (4-3): St. Louis Cardinals over Detroit Tigers

1935

Team	W	L	%
Chicago	100	54	.649
St. Louis	96	58	.623
New York	91	62	.595
Pittsburgh	86	67	.562
Brooklyn	70	83	.458
Cincinnati	68	85	.444
Philadelphia	64	89	.418
Boston	38	115	.248

World Series (4-2): Detroit Tigers over Chicago Cubs

1936

Team	W	L	%
New York	92	62	.597
Chicago	87	67	.565
St. Louis	87	67	.565
Pittsburgh	84	70	.545
Cincinnati	74	80	.481
Boston	71	83	.461
Brooklyn	67	87	.435
Philadelphia	54	100	.351

World Series (4-2): New York Yankees over New York Giants

1937

Team	W	L	%
New York	95	57	.625
Chicago	93	61	.604
Pittsburgh	86	68	.558
St. Louis	81	73	.526
Boston	79	73	.520
Brooklyn	62	91	.405
Philadelphia	61	92	.399
Cincinnati	56	98	.364

World Series (4-1): New York Yankees over New York Giants

1938

Team	W	L	%
Chicago	89	63	.586
Pittsburgh	86	64	.573
New York	83	67	.553
Cincinnati	82	68	.547
Boston	77	75	.507
St. Louis	71	80	.470
Brooklyn	69	80	.463
Philadelphia	45	105	.300

World Series (4-0): New York Yankees over Chicago Cubs

1939

Team	W	L	%
Cincinnati	97	57	.630
St. Louis	92	61	.601
Brooklyn	84	69	.549
Chicago	84	70	.545
New York	77	74	.510
Pittsburgh	68	85	.444
Boston	63	88	.417
Philadelphia	45	106	.298

World Series (4-0): New York Yankees over Cincinnati Reds

1940

Team	W	L	%
Cincinnati	100	53	.654
Brooklyn	88	65	.575
St. Louis	84	69	.549
Pittsburgh	78	76	.506
Chicago	75	79	.487
New York	72	80	.474
Boston	65	87	.428
Philadelphia	50	103	.327

World Series (4-3): Cincinnati Reds over Detroit Tigers

1941

Team	W	L	%
Brooklyn	100	54	.649
St. Louis	97	56	.634
Cincinnati	88	66	.571
Pittsburgh	81	73	.526
New York	74	79	.484
Chicago	70	84	.455
Boston	62	92	.403
Philadelphia	43	111	.279

World Series (4-1): New York Yankees over Brooklyn Dodgers

1942

Team	W	L	%
St. Louis	106	48	.688
Brooklyn	104	50	.675
New York	85	67	.559
Cincinnati	76	76	.500
Pittsburgh	66	81	.449
Chicago	68	86	.442
Boston	59	89	.399
Philadelphia	42	109	.278

World Series (4-1): St. Louis Cardinals over New York Yankees

1943

Team	W	L	%
St. Louis	105	49	.682
Cincinnati	87	67	.565
Brooklyn	81	72	.529
Pittsburgh	80	74	.519
Chicago	74	79	.484
Boston	68	85	.444
Philadelphia	64	90	.416
New York	55	98	.359

World Series (4-1): New York Yankees over St. Louis Cardinals

1944

Team	W	L	%
St. Louis	105	49	.682
Pittsburgh	90	63	.588
Cincinnati	89	65	.578
Chicago	75	79	.487
New York	67	87	.435
Boston	65	89	.422
Brooklyn	63	91	.409
Philadelphia	61	92	.399

World Series (4-2): St. Louis Cardinals over St. Louis Browns

1945

Team	W	L	%
Chicago	98	56	.636
St. Louis	95	59	.617
Brooklyn	87	67	.565
Pittsburgh	82	72	.532
New York	78	74	.513
Boston	67	85	.441
Cincinnati	61	93	.396
Philadelphia	46	108	.299

World Series (4-3): Detroit Tigers over Chicago Cubs

1946

Team	W	L	%
St. Louis	98	58	.628
Brooklyn	96	60	.615
Chicago	82	71	.536
Boston	81	72	.529
Philadelphia	69	85	.448
Cincinnati	67	87	.435
Pittsburgh	63	91	.409
New York	61	93	.396

World Series (4-3): St. Louis Cardinals over Boston Red Sox

1947

Team	W	L	%
Brooklyn	94	60	.610
St. Louis	89	65	.578
Boston	86	68	.558
New York	81	73	.526
Cincinnati	73	81	.474
Chicago	69	85	.448
Philadelphia	62	92	.403
Pittsburgh	62	92	.403

World Series (4-3): New York Yankees over Brooklyn Dodgers

1948

Team	W	L	%
Boston	91	62	.595
St. Louis	85	69	.552
Brooklyn	84	70	.545
Pittsburgh	83	71	.539
New York	78	76	.506
Philadelphia	66	88	.429
Cincinnati	64	89	.418
Chicago	64	90	.416

World Series (4-2): Cleveland Indians over Boston Braves

1949

Team	W	L	%
Brooklyn	97	57	.630
St. Louis	96	58	.623
Philadelphia	81	73	.526
Boston	75	79	.487
New York	73	81	.474
Pittsburgh	71	83	.461
Cincinnati	62	92	.403
Chicago	61	93	.396

World Series (4-1): New York Yankees over Brooklyn Dodgers

1950

Team	W	L	%
Philadelphia	91	63	.591
Brooklyn	89	65	.578
New York	86	68	.558
Boston	83	71	.539
St. Louis	78	75	.510
Cincinnati	66	87	.431
Chicago	64	89	.418
Pittsburgh	57	96	.373

World Series (4-0): New York Yankees over Philadelphia Phillies

1951

Team	W	L	%
New York	98	59	.624
Brooklyn	97	60	.618
St. Louis	81	73	.526
Boston	76	78	.494
Philadelphia	73	81	.474
Cincinnati	68	86	.442
Pittsburgh	64	90	.416
Chicago	62	92	.403

World Series (4-2): New York Yankees over New York Giants

1952

Team	W	L	%
Brooklyn	96	57	.627
New York	92	62	.597
St. Louis	88	66	.571
Philadelphia	87	67	.565
Chicago	77	77	.500
Cincinnati	69	85	.448
Boston	64	89	.418
Pittsburgh	42	112	.273

World Series (4-3): New York Yankees over Brooklyn Dodgers

1953

Team	W	L	%
Brooklyn	105	49	.682
Milwaukee	92	62	.597
Philadelphia	83	71	.539
St. Louis	83	71	.539
New York	70	84	.455
Cincinnati	68	86	.442
Chicago	65	89	.422
Pittsburgh	50	104	.325

World Series (4-2): New York Yankees over Brooklyn Dodgers

1954

Team	W	L	%
New York	97	57	.630
Brooklyn	92	62	.597
Milwaukee	89	65	.578
Philadelphia	75	79	.487
Cincinnati	74	80	.481
St. Louis	72	82	.468
Chicago	64	90	.416
Pittsburgh	53	101	.344

World Series (4-0): New York Giants over Cleveland Indians

1955

Team	W	L	%
Brooklyn	98	55	.641
Milwaukee	85	69	.552
New York	80	74	.519
Philadelphia	77	77	.500
Cincinnati	75	79	.487
Chicago	72	81	.471
St. Louis	68	86	.442
Pittsburgh	60	94	.390

World Series (4-3): Brooklyn Dodgers over New York Yankees

1956

Team	W	L	%
Brooklyn	93	61	.604
Milwaukee	92	62	.597
Cincinnati	91	63	.591
St. Louis	76	78	.494
Philadelphia	71	83	.461
New York	67	87	.435
Pittsburgh	66	88	.429
Chicago	60	94	.390

World Series (4-3): New York Yankees over Brooklyn Dodgers

1957

Team	W	L	%
Milwaukee	95	59	.617
St. Louis	87	67	.565
Brooklyn	84	70	.545
Cincinnati	80	74	.519
Philadelphia	77	77	.500
New York	69	85	.448
Chicago	62	92	.403
Pittsburgh	62	92	.403

World Series (4-3): Milwaukee Braves over New York Yankees

1958

Team	W	L	%
Milwaukee	92	62	.597
Pittsburgh	84	70	.545
San Francisco	80	74	.519
Cincinnati	76	78	.494
Chicago	72	82	.468
St. Louis	72	82	.468
Los Angeles	71	83	.461
Philadelphia	69	85	.448

World Series (4-3): New York Yankees over Milwaukee Braves

1959

Team	W	L	%
Los Angeles	88	68	.564
Milwaukee	86	70	.551
San Francisco	83	71	.539
Pittsburgh	78	76	.506
Chicago	74	80	.481
Cincinnati	74	80	.481
St. Louis	71	83	.461
Philadelphia	64	90	.416

World Series (4-2): Los Angeles Dodgers over Chicago White Sox

1960

Team	W	L	%
Pittsburgh	95	59	.617
Milwaukee	88	66	.571
St. Louis	86	68	.558
Los Angeles	82	72	.532
San Francisco	79	75	.513
Cincinnati	67	87	.435
Chicago	60	94	.390
Philadelphia	59	95	.383

World Series (4-3): Pittsburgh Pirates over New York Yankees

1961

Team	W	L	%
Cincinnati	93	61	.604
Los Angeles	89	65	.578
San Francisco	85	69	.552
Milwaukee	83	71	.539
St. Louis	80	74	.519
Pittsburgh	75	79	.487
Chicago	64	90	.416
Philadelphia	47	107	.305

World Series (4-1): New York Yankees over Cincinnati Reds

1962			
Team	**W**	**L**	**%**
San Francisco	103	62	.624
Los Angeles	102	63	.618
Cincinnati	98	64	.605
Pittsburgh	93	68	.578
Milwaukee	86	76	.531
St. Louis	84	78	.519
Philadelphia	81	80	.503
Houston	64	96	.400
Chicago	59	103	.364
New York	40	120	.250

World Series (4-3): New York Yankees over San Francisco Giants

1963			
Team	**W**	**L**	**%**
Los Angeles	99	63	.611
St. Louis	93	69	.574
San Francisco	88	74	.543
Philadelphia	87	75	.537
Cincinnati	86	76	.531
Milwaukee	84	78	.519
Chicago	82	80	.506
Pittsburgh	74	88	.457
Houston	66	96	.407
New York	51	111	.315

World Series (4-0): Los Angeles Dodgers over New York Yankees

1964			
Team	**W**	**L**	**%**
St. Louis	93	69	.574
Cincinnati	92	70	.568
Philadelphia	92	70	.568
San Francisco	90	72	.556
Milwaukee	88	74	.543
Los Angeles	80	82	.494
Pittsburgh	80	82	.494
Chicago	76	86	.469
Houston	66	96	.407
New York	53	109	.327

World Series (4-3): St. Louis Cardinals over New York Yankees

1965			
Team	**W**	**L**	**%**
Los Angeles	97	65	.599
San Francisco	95	67	.586
Pittsburgh	90	72	.556
Cincinnati	89	73	.549
Milwaukee	86	76	.531
Philadelphia	85	76	.528
St. Louis	80	81	.497
Chicago	72	90	.444
Houston	65	97	.401
New York	50	112	.309

World Series (4-3): Los Angeles Dodgers over Minnesota Twins

1966			
Team	**W**	**L**	**%**
Los Angeles	95	67	.586
San Francisco	93	68	.578
Pittsburgh	92	70	.568
Philadelphia	87	75	.537
Atlanta	85	77	.525
St. Louis	83	79	.512
Cincinnati	76	84	.475
Houston	72	90	.444
New York	66	95	.410
Chicago	59	103	.364

World Series (4-0): Baltimore Orioles over Los Angeles Dodgers

1967			
Team	**W**	**L**	**%**
St. Louis	101	60	.627
San Francisco	91	71	.562
Chicago	87	74	.540
Cincinnati	87	75	.537
Philadelphia	82	80	.506
Pittsburgh	81	81	.500
Atlanta	77	85	.475
Los Angeles	73	89	.451
Houston	69	93	.426
New York	61	101	.377

World Series (4-3): St. Louis Cardinals over Boston Red Sox

1968			
Team	**W**	**L**	**%**
St. Louis	97	65	.599
San Francisco	88	74	.543
Chicago	84	78	.519
Cincinnati	83	79	.512
Atlanta	81	81	.500
Pittsburgh	80	82	.494
Los Angeles	76	86	.469
Philadelphia	76	86	.469
New York	73	89	.451
Houston	72	90	.444

World Series (4-3): Detroit Tigers over St. Louis Cardinals

1969

East Division			
Team	W	L	%
New York	100	62	.617
Chicago	92	70	.568
Pittsburgh	88	74	.543
St. Louis	87	75	.537
Philadelphia	63	99	.389
Montreal	52	110	.321

West Division			
Team	W	L	%
Atlanta	93	69	.574
San Francisco	90	72	.556
Cincinnati	89	73	.549
Los Angeles	85	77	.525
Houston	81	81	.500
San Diego	52	110	.321

World Series (4-1): New York Mets over Baltimore Orioles

NL Championship Series (3-0): New York Mets over Atlanta Braves

1970

East Division			
Team	W	L	%
Pittsburgh	89	73	.549
Chicago	84	78	.519
New York	83	79	.512
St. Louis	76	86	.469
Philadelphia	73	88	.453
Montreal	73	89	.451

West Division			
Team	W	L	%
Cincinnati	102	60	.630
Los Angeles	87	74	.540
San Francisco	86	76	.531
Houston	79	83	.488
Atlanta	76	86	.469
San Diego	63	99	.389

World Series (4-1): Baltimore Orioles over Cincinnati Reds

NL Championship Series (3-0): Cincinnati Reds over Pittsburgh Pirates

1971

East Division			
Team	W	L	%
Pittsburgh	97	65	.599
St. Louis	90	72	.556
Chicago	83	79	.512
New York	83	79	.512
Montreal	71	90	.441
Philadelphia	67	95	.414

West Division			
Team	W	L	%
San Francisco	90	72	.556
Los Angeles	89	73	.549
Atlanta	82	80	.506
Cincinnati	79	83	.488
Houston	79	83	.488
San Diego	61	100	.379

World Series (4-3): Pittsburgh Pirates over Baltimore Orioles

NL Championship Series (3-1): Pittsburgh Pirates over San Francisco Giants

1972

East Division			
Team	W	L	%
Pittsburgh	96	59	.619
Chicago	85	70	.548
New York	83	73	.532
St. Louis	75	81	.481
Montreal	70	86	.449
Philadelphia	59	97	.378

West Division			
Team	W	L	%
Cincinnati	95	59	.617
Houston	84	69	.549
Los Angeles	85	70	.548
Atlanta	70	84	.455
San Francisco	69	86	.445
San Diego	58	95	.379

World Series (4-3): Oakland Athletics over Cincinnati Reds

NL Championship Series (3-2): Cincinnati Reds over Pittsburgh Pirates

1973

East Division			
Team	W	L	%
New York	82	79	.509
St. Louis	81	81	.500
Pittsburgh	80	82	.494
Montreal	79	83	.488
Chicago	77	84	.478
Philadelphia	71	91	.438

West Division			
Team	W	L	%
Cincinnati	99	63	.611
Los Angeles	95	66	.590
San Francisco	88	74	.543
Houston	82	80	.506
Atlanta	76	85	.472
San Diego	60	102	.370

World Series (4-3): Oakland Athletics over New York Mets

NL Championship Series (3-2): New York Mets over Cincinnati Reds

1974

East Division			
Team	W	L	%
Pittsburgh	88	74	.543
St. Louis	86	75	.534
Philadelphia	80	82	.494
Montreal	79	82	.491
New York	71	91	.438
Chicago	66	96	.407

West Division			
Team	W	L	%
Los Angeles	102	60	.630
Cincinnati	98	64	.605
Atlanta	88	74	.543
Houston	81	81	.500
San Francisco	72	90	.444
San Diego	60	102	.370

World Series (4-1): Oakland Athletics over Los Angeles Dodgers

NL Championship Series (3-1): Los Angeles Dodgers over Pittsburgh Pirates

1975

East Division				West Division			
Team	W	L	%	Team	W	L	%
Pittsburgh	92	69	.571	Cincinnati	108	54	.667
Philadelphia	86	76	.531	Los Angeles	88	74	.543
New York	82	80	.506	San Francisco	80	81	.497
St. Louis	82	80	.506	San Diego	71	91	.438
Chicago	75	87	.463	Atlanta	67	94	.416
Montreal	75	87	.463	Houston	64	97	.398

World Series (4-3): Cincinnati Reds over Boston Red Sox

NL Championship Series (3-0): Cincinnati Reds over Pittsburgh Pirates

1976

East Division				West Division			
Team	W	L	%	Team	W	L	%
Philadelphia	101	61	.623	Cincinnati	102	60	.630
Pittsburgh	92	70	.568	Los Angeles	92	70	.568
New York	86	76	.531	Houston	80	82	.494
Chicago	75	87	.463	San Francisco	74	88	.457
St. Louis	72	90	.444	San Diego	73	89	.451
Montreal	55	107	.340	Atlanta	70	92	.432

World Series (4-0): Cincinnati Reds over New York Yankees

NL Championship Series (3-0): Cincinnati Reds over Philadelphia Phillies

1977

East Division				West Division			
Team	W	L	%	Team	W	L	%
Philadelphia	101	61	.623	Los Angeles	98	64	.605
Pittsburgh	96	66	.593	Cincinnati	88	74	.543
St. Louis	83	79	.512	Houston	81	81	.500
Chicago	81	81	.500	San Francisco	75	87	.463
Montreal	75	87	.463	San Diego	69	93	.426
New York	64	98	.395	Atlanta	61	101	.377

World Series (4-2): New York Yankees over Los Angeles Dodgers

NL Championship Series (3-1): Los Anegels Dodgers over Philadelphia Phillies

1978

East Division			
Team	W	L	%
Philadelphia	90	72	.556
Pittsburgh	88	73	.547
Chicago	79	83	.488
Montreal	76	86	.469
St. Louis	69	93	.426
New York	66	96	.407

West Division			
Team	W	L	%
Los Angeles	95	67	.586
Cincinnati	92	69	.571
San Francisco	89	73	.549
San Diego	84	78	.519
Houston	74	88	.457
Atlanta	69	93	.426

World Series (4-2): New York Yankees over Los Angeles Dodgers

NL Championship Series (3-1): Los Angeles Dodgers over Philadelphia Phillies

1979

East Division			
Team	W	L	%
Pittsburgh	98	64	.605
Montreal	95	65	.594
St. Louis	86	76	.531
Philadelphia	84	78	.519
Chicago	80	82	.494
New York	63	99	.389

West Division			
Team	W	L	%
Cincinnati	90	71	.559
Houston	89	73	.549
Los Angeles	79	83	.488
San Francisco	71	91	.438
San Diego	68	93	.422
Atlanta	66	94	.412

World Series (4-3): Pittsburgh Pirates over Baltimore Orioles

NL Championship Series (3-0): Pittsburgh Pirates over Cincinnati Reds

1980

East Division			
Team	W	L	%
Philadelphia	91	71	.562
Montreal	90	72	.556
Pittsburgh	83	79	.512
St. Louis	74	88	.457
New York	67	95	.414
Chicago	64	98	.395

West Division			
Team	W	L	%
Houston	93	70	.571
Los Angeles	92	71	.564
Cincinnati	89	73	.549
Atlanta	81	80	.503
San Francisco	75	86	.466
San Diego	73	89	.451

World Series (4-2): Philadelphia Phillies over Kansas City Royals

NL Championship Series (3-2): Philadelphia Phillies over Houston Astros

1981

East Division					West Division			
Team	W	L	%		Team	W	L	%
St. Louis	59	43	.578		Cincinnati	66	42	.611
Montreal	60	48	.556		Los Angeles	63	47	.573
Philadelphia	59	48	.551		Houston	61	49	.555
Pittsburgh	46	56	.451		San Francisco	56	55	.505
New York	41	62	.398		Atlanta	50	56	.472
Chicago	38	65	.369		San Diego	41	69	.373

World Series (4-2): Los Angeles Dodgers over New York Yankees

NL Championship Series (3-2): Los Angeles Dodgers over Montreal Expos

NL Division Series (3-2): Montreal Expos over Philadelphia Phillies

NL Division Series (3-2): Los Angeles Dodgers over Houston Astros

1982

East Division					West Division			
Team	W	L	%		Team	W	L	%
St. Louis	92	70	.568		Atlanta	89	73	.549
Philadelphia	89	73	.549		Los Angeles	88	74	.543
Montreal	86	76	.531		San Francisco	87	75	.537
Pittsburgh	84	78	.519		San Diego	81	81	.500
Chicago	73	89	.451		Houston	77	85	.475
New York	65	97	.401		Cincinnati	61	101	.377

World Series (4-3): St. Louis Cardinals over Milwaukee Brewers

NL Championship Series (3-0): St. Louis Cardinals over Atlanta Braves

1983

East Division					West Division			
Team	W	L	%		Team	W	L	%
Philadelphia	90	72	.556		Los Angeles	91	71	.562
Pittsburgh	84	78	.519		Atlanta	88	74	.543
Montreal	82	80	.506		Houston	85	77	.525
St. Louis	79	83	.488		San Diego	81	81	.500
Chicago	71	91	.438		San Francisco	79	83	.488
New York	68	94	.420		Cincinnati	74	88	.457

World Series (4-1): Baltimore Orioles over Philadelphia Phillies

NL Championship Series (3-1): Philadelphia Phillies over Los Angeles Dodgers

1984

East Division					West Division			
Team	W	L	%		Team	W	L	%
Chicago	96	65	.596		San Diego	92	70	.568
New York	90	72	.556		Atlanta	80	82	.494
St. Louis	84	78	.519		Houston	80	82	.494
Philadelphia	81	81	.500		Los Angeles	79	83	.488
Montreal	78	83	.484		Cincinnati	70	92	.432
Pittsburgh	75	87	.463		San Francisco	66	96	.407

World Series (4-1): Detroit Tigers over San Diego Padres

NL Championship Series (3-2): San Diego Padres over Chicago Cubs

1985

East Division					West Division			
Team	W	L	%		Team	W	L	%
St. Louis	101	61	.623		Los Angeles	95	67	.586
New York	98	64	.605		Cincinnati	89	72	.553
Montreal	84	77	.522		Houston	83	79	.512
Chicago	77	84	.478		San Diego	83	79	.512
Philadelphia	75	87	.463		Atlanta	66	96	.407
Pittsburgh	57	104	.354		San Francisco	62	100	.383

World Series (4-3): Kansas City Royals over St. Louis Cardinals

NL Championship Series (4-2): St. Louis Cardinals over Los Angeles Dodgers

1986

East Division					West Division			
Team	W	L	%		Team	W	L	%
New York	108	54	.667		Houston	96	66	.593
Philadelphia	86	75	.534		Cincinnati	86	76	.531
St. Louis	79	82	.491		San Francisco	83	79	.512
Montreal	78	83	.484		San Diego	74	88	.457
Chicago	70	90	.438		Los Angeles	73	89	.451
Pittsburgh	64	98	.395		Atlanta	72	89	.447

World Series (4-3): New York Mets over Boston Red Sox

NL Championship Series (4-2): New York Mets over Houston Astros

1987

East Division				West Division			
Team	**W**	**L**	**%**	**Team**	**W**	**L**	**%**
St. Louis	95	67	.586	San Francisco	90	72	.556
New York	92	70	.568	Cincinnati	84	78	.519
Montreal	91	71	.562	Houston	76	86	.469
Philadelphia	80	82	.494	Los Angeles	73	89	.451
Pittsburgh	80	82	.494	Atlanta	69	92	.429
Chicago	76	85	.472	San Diego	65	97	.401

World Series (4-3): Minnesota Twins over St. Louis Cardinals

NL Championship Series (4-3): St. Louis Cardinals over San Francisco Giants

1988

East Division				West Division			
Team	**W**	**L**	**%**	**Team**	**W**	**L**	**%**
New York	100	60	.625	Los Angeles	94	67	.584
Pittsburgh	85	75	.531	Cincinnati	87	74	.540
Montreal	81	81	.500	San Diego	83	78	.516
Chicago	77	85	.475	San Francisco	83	79	.512
St. Louis	76	86	.469	Houston	82	80	.506
Philadelphia	65	96	.404	Atlanta	54	106	.338

World Series (4-1): Los Angeles Dodgers over Oakland Athletics

NL Championship Series (4-3): Los Angeles Dodgers over New York Mets

1989

East Division				West Division			
Team	**W**	**L**	**%**	**Team**	**W**	**L**	**%**
Chicago	93	69	.574	San Francisco	92	70	.568
New York	87	75	.537	San Diego	89	73	.549
St. Louis	86	76	.531	Houston	86	76	.531
Montreal	81	81	.500	Los Angeles	77	83	.481
Pittsburgh	74	88	.457	Cincinnati	75	87	.463
Philadelphia	67	95	.414	Atlanta	63	97	.394

World Series (4-0): Oakland Athletics over San Francisco Giants

NL Championship Series (4-1): San Francisco Giants over Chicago Cubs

1990

East Division				West Division			
Team	W	L	%	Team	W	L	%
Pittsburgh	95	67	.586	Cincinnati	91	71	.562
New York	91	71	.562	Los Angeles	86	76	.531
Montreal	85	77	.525	San Francisco	85	77	.525
Chicago	77	85	.475	Houston	75	87	.463
Philadelphia	77	85	.475	San Diego	75	87	.463
St. Louis	70	92	.432	Atlanta	65	97	.401

World Series (4-0): Cincinnati Reds over Oakland Athletics

NL Championship Series (4-2): Cincinnati Reds over Pittsburgh Pirates

1991

East Division				West Division			
Team	W	L	%	Team	W	L	%
Pittsburgh	98	64	.605	Atlanta	94	68	.580
St. Louis	84	78	.519	Los Angeles	93	69	.574
Chicago	77	83	.481	San Diego	84	78	.519
Philadelphia	78	84	.481	San Francisco	75	87	.463
New York	77	84	.478	Cincinnati	74	88	.457
Montreal	71	90	.441	Houston	65	97	.401

World Series (4-3): Minnesota Twins over Atlanta Braves

NL Championship Series (4-3): Atlanta Braves over Pittsburgh Pirates

1992

East Division				West Division			
Team	W	L	%	Team	W	L	%
Pittsburgh	96	66	.593	Atlanta	98	64	.605
Montreal	87	75	.537	Cincinnati	90	72	.556
St. Louis	83	79	.512	San Diego	82	80	.506
Chicago	78	84	.481	Houston	81	81	.500
New York	72	90	.444	San Francisco	72	90	.444
Philadelphia	70	92	.432	Los Angeles	63	99	.389

World Series (4-2): Toronto Blue Jays over Atlanta Braves

NL Championship Series (4-3): Atlanta Braves over Pittsburgh Pirates

1993

East Division			
Team	W	L	%
Philadelphia	97	65	.599
Montreal	94	68	.580
St. Louis	87	75	.537
Chicago	84	78	.519
Pittsburgh	75	87	.463
Florida	64	98	.395
New York	59	103	.364

West Division			
Team	W	L	%
Atlanta	104	58	.642
San Francisco	103	59	.636
Houston	85	77	.525
Los Angeles	81	81	.500
Cincinnati	73	89	.451
Colorado	67	95	.414
San Diego	61	101	.377

World Series (4-2): Toronto Blue Jays over Philadelphia Phillies

NL Championship Series (4-2): Philadelphia Phillies over Atlanta Braves

1994

East Division			
Team	W	L	%
Montreal	74	40	.649
Atlanta	68	46	.596
New York	55	58	.487
Philadelphia	54	61	.470
Florida	51	64	.443

Central			
Team	W	L	%
Cincinnati	66	48	.579
Houston	66	49	.574
Pittsburgh	53	61	.465
St. Louis	53	61	.465
Chicago	49	64	.434

West Division			
Team	W	L	%
Los Angeles	58	56	.509
San Francisco	55	60	.478
Colorado	53	64	.453
San Diego	47	70	.402

1995

East Division			
Team	W	L	%
Atlanta	90	54	.625
New York	69	75	.479
Philadelphia	69	75	.479
Florida	67	76	.469
Montreal	66	78	.458

Central			
Team	W	L	%
Cincinnati	85	59	.590
Houston	76	68	.528
Chicago	73	71	.507
St. Louis	62	81	.434
Pittsburgh	58	86	.403

West Division			
Team	W	L	%
Los Angeles	78	66	.542
Colorado	77	67	.535
San Diego	70	74	.486
San Francisco	67	77	.465

World Series (4-2): Atlanta Braves over Cleveland Indians

NL Championship Series (4-0): Atlanta Braves over Cincinnati Reds

NL Division Series (3-1): Atlanta Braves over Colorado Rockies

NL Division Series (3-0): Cincinnati Reds over Los Angeles Dodgers

1996

East Division				Central				West Division			
Team	W	L	%	Team	W	L	%	Team	W	L	%
Atlanta	96	66	.593	St. Louis	88	74	.543	San Diego	91	71	.562
Montreal	88	74	.543	Houston	82	80	.506	Los Angeles	90	72	.556
Florida	80	82	.494	Cincinnati	81	81	.500	Colorado	83	79	.512
New York	71	91	.438	Chicago	76	86	.469	San Francisco	68	94	.420
Philadelphia	67	95	.414	Pittsburgh	73	89	.451				

World Series (4-2): New York Yankees over Atlanta Braves

NL Championship Series (4-3): Atlanta Braves over St. Louis Cardinals

NL Division Series (3-0): Atlanta Braves over Los Angeles Dodgers

NL Division Series (3-0): St. Louis Cardinals over San Diego Padres

1997

East Division				Central				West Division			
Team	W	L	%	Team	W	L	%	Team	W	L	%
Atlanta	101	61	.623	Houston	84	78	.519	San Francisco	90	72	.556
Florida	92	70	.568	Pittsburgh	79	83	.488	Los Angeles	88	74	.543
New York	88	74	.543	Cincinnati	76	86	.469	Colorado	83	79	.512
Montreal	78	84	.481	St. Louis	73	89	.451	San Diego	76	86	.469
Philadelphia	68	94	.420	Chicago	68	94	.420				

World Series (4-3): Florida Marlins over Cleveland Indians

NL Championship Series (4-2): Florida Marlins over Atlanta Braves

NL Division Series (3-0): Florida Marlins over San Francisco Giants

NL Division Series (3-0): Atlanta Braves over Houston Astros

1998

East Division				Central				West Division			
Team	W	L	%	Team	W	L	%	Team	W	L	%
Atlanta	106	56	.654	Houston	102	60	.630	San Diego	98	64	.605
New York	88	74	.543	Chicago	90	73	.552	San Francisco	89	74	.546
Philadelphia	75	87	.463	St. Louis	83	79	.512	Los Angeles	83	79	.512
Montreal	65	97	.401	Cincinnati	77	85	.475	Colorado	77	85	.475
Florida	54	108	.333	Milwaukee	74	88	.457	Arizona	65	97	.401
				Pittsburgh	69	93	.426				

World Series (4-0): New York Yankees over San Diego Padres

NL Championship Series (4-2): San Diego Padres over Atlanta Braves

NL Division Series (3-0): Atlanta Braves over Chicago Cubs

NL Division Series (3-1): San Diego Padres over Houston Astros

1999

East Division				Central				West Division			
Team	W	L	%	Team	W	L	%	Team	W	L	%
Atlanta	103	59	.636	Houston	97	65	.599	Arizona	100	62	.617
New York	97	66	.595	Cincinnati	96	67	.589	San Francisco	86	76	.531
Philadelphia	77	85	.475	Pittsburgh	78	83	.484	Los Angeles	77	85	.475
Montreal	68	94	.420	St. Louis	75	86	.466	San Diego	74	88	.457
Florida	64	98	.395	Milwaukee	74	87	.460	Colorado	72	90	.444
				Chicago	67	95	.414				

World Series (4-0): New York Yankees over Atlanta Braves
NL Championship Series (4-2): Atlanta Braves over New York Mets
NL Division Series (3-1): Atlanta Braves over Houston Astros
NL Division Series (3-1): New York Mets over Arizona Diamondbacks

2000

East Division				Central				West Division			
Team	W	L	%	Team	W	L	%	Team	W	L	%
Atlanta	95	67	.586	St. Louis	95	67	.586	San Francisco	97	65	.599
New York	94	68	.580	Cincinnati	85	77	.525	Los Angeles	86	76	.531
Florida	79	82	.491	Milwaukee	73	89	.451	Arizona	85	77	.525
Montreal	67	95	.414	Houston	72	90	.444	Colorado	82	80	.506
Philadelphia	65	97	.401	Pittsburgh	69	93	.426	San Diego	76	86	.469
				Chicago	65	97	.401				

NL Championship Series (4-1): New York Mets over St. Louis Cardinals
NL Division Series (3-0): St. Louis Cardinals over Atlanta Braves
NL Division Series (3-1): New York Mets over San Francisco Giants

2001

East Division				Central				West Division			
Team	W	L	%	Team	W	L	%	Team	W	L	%
Atlanta	88	74	.543	Houston	93	69	.574	Arizona	92	70	.568
Philadelphia	86	76	.531	St. Louis	93	69	.574	San Francisco	90	72	.556
New York	82	80	.506	Chicago	88	74	.543	Los Angeles	86	76	.531
Florida	76	86	.469	Milwaukee	68	94	.420	San Diego	79	83	.488
Montreal	68	94	.420	Cincinnati	66	96	.407	Colorado	73	89	.451
				Pittsburgh	62	100	.383				

World Series (4-3): Arizona Diamondbacks over New York Yankees
NL Championship Series (4-1): Arizona Diamondbacks over Atlanta Braves
NL Division Series (3-0): Atlanta Braves over Houston Astros
NL Division Series (3-2): Arizona Diamondbacks over St. Louis Cardinals

2002

East Division				Central				West Division			
Team	W	L	%	Team	W	L	%	Team	W	L	%
Atlanta	101	59	.631	St. Louis	97	65	.599	Arizona	98	64	.605
Montreal	83	79	.512	Houston	84	78	.519	San Francisco	95	66	.590
Philadelphia	80	81	.497	Cincinnati	78	84	.481	Los Angeles	92	70	.568
Florida	79	83	.488	Pittsburgh	72	89	.447	Colorado	73	89	.451
New York	75	86	.466	Chicago	67	95	.414	San Diego	66	96	.407
				Milwaukee	56	106	.346				

World Series (4-3): Anaheim Angels over San Francisco Giants

NL Championship Series (4-1): San Fran Giants over St. Louis Cardinals

NL Division Series (3-2): San Francisco Giants over Atlanta Braves

NL Division Series (3-0): St. Louis Cardinals over Arizona Diamondbacks

2003

East Division				Central				West Division			
Team	W	L	%	Team	W	L	%	Team	W	L	%
Atlanta	101	61	.623	Chicago	88	74	.543	San Francisco	100	61	.621
Florida	91	71	.562	Houston	87	75	.537	Los Angeles	85	77	.525
Philadelphia	86	76	.531	St. Louis	85	77	.525	Arizona	84	78	.519
Montreal	83	79	.512	Pittsburgh	75	87	.463	Colorado	74	88	.457
New York	66	95	.410	Cincinnati	69	93	.426	San Diego	64	98	.395
				Milwaukee	68	94	.420				

World Series (4-2): Florida Marlins over New York Yankees

NL Championship Series (4-3): Florida Marlins over Chicago Cubs

NL Division Series (3-1): Florida Marlins over San Francisco Giants

NL Division Series (3-2): Chicago Cubs over Atlanta Braves

2004

East Division				Central				West Division			
Team	W	L	%	Team	W	L	%	Team	W	L	%
Atlanta	96	66	.593	St. Louis	105	57	.648	Los Angeles	93	69	.574
Philadelphia	86	76	.531	Houston	92	70	.568	San Francisco	91	71	.562
Florida	83	79	.512	Chicago	89	73	.549	San Diego	87	75	.537
New York	71	91	.438	Cincinnati	76	86	.469	Colorado	68	94	.420
Montreal	67	95	.414	Pittsburgh	72	89	.447	Arizona	51	111	.315
				Milwaukee	67	94	.416				

World Series (4-0): Boston Red Sox over St. Louis Cardinals

NL Championship Series (4-3): St. Louis Cardinals over Houston Astros

NL Division Series (3-1): St. Louis Cardinals over Los Angeles Dodgers

NL Division Series (3-2): Houston Astros over Atlanta Braves

2005

East Division				Central				West Division			
Team	W	L	%	Team	W	L	%	Team	W	L	%
Atlanta	90	72	.566	St. Louis	100	62	.617	San Diego	82	80	.506
Philadelphia	88	74	.543	Houston	89	73	.549	Arizona	77	85	.475
Florida	83	79	.512	Milwaukee	81	81	.549	San Francisco	75	87	.463
New York	83	79	.512	Chicago	79	83	.488	Los Angeles	71	91	.438
Washington	81	81	.500	Cincinnati	73	89	.451	Colorado	67	95	.414
				Pittsburgh	67	95	.414				

World Series (4-0): Chicago White Sox over Houston Astros

NL Championship Series (4-2): Houston Astros over St. Louis Cardinals

NL Division Series (3-0): St. Louis Cardinals over San Diego Padres

NL Division Series (3-1): Houston Astros over Atlanta Braves

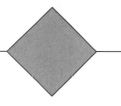

Appendix B

AMERICAN LEAGUE SEASON STANDINGS, 1901–2005

1901

Team	W	L	%
Chicago	83	53	.610
Boston	79	57	.581
Detroit	74	61	.548
Philadelphia	74	62	.544
Baltimore	68	65	.511
Washington	61	72	.459
Cleveland	54	82	.397
Milwaukee	48	89	.350

1902

Team	W	L	%
Philadelphia	83	53	.610
St. Louis	78	58	.574
Boston	77	60	.562
Chicago	74	60	.552
Cleveland	69	67	.507
Washington	61	75	.449
Detroit	52	83	.385
Baltimore	50	88	.362

1903

Team	W	L	%
Philadelphia	83	53	.610
St. Louis	78	58	.574
Boston	77	60	.562
Chicago	74	60	.552
Cleveland	69	67	.507
Washington	61	75	.449
Detroit	52	83	.385
Baltimore	50	88	.362

World Series (5-3): Boston Pilgrims over Pittsburgh Pirates

1904

Team	W	L	%
Boston	95	59	.617
New York	92	59	.609
Chicago	89	65	.578
Cleveland	86	65	.570
Philadelphia	81	70	.536
St. Louis	65	87	.428
Detroit	62	90	.408
Washington	38	113	.252

1905

Team	W	L	%
Philadelphia	92	56	.622
Chicago	92	60	.605
Detroit	79	74	.516
Boston	78	74	.513
Cleveland	76	78	.494
New York	71	78	.477
Washington	64	87	.424
St. Louis	54	99	.353

World Series (4-1): New York Giants over Philadelphia Athletics

1906

Team	W	L	%
Chicago	93	58	.616
New York	90	61	.596
Cleveland	89	64	.582
Philadelphia	78	67	.538
St. Louis	76	73	.510
Detroit	71	78	.477
Washington	55	95	.367
Boston	49	105	.318

World Series (4-2): Chicago White Sox over Chicago Cubs

1907

Team	W	L	%
Detroit	92	58	.613
Philadelphia	88	57	.607
Chicago	87	64	.576
Cleveland	85	67	.559
New York	70	78	.473
St. Louis	69	83	.454
Boston	59	90	.396
Washington	49	102	.325

World Series (4-0-1): Chicago Cubs over Detroit Tigers

1908

Team	W	L	%
Detroit	90	63	.588
Cleveland	90	64	.584
Chicago	88	64	.579
St. Louis	83	69	.546
Boston	75	79	.487
Philadelphia	68	85	.444
Washington	67	85	.441
New York	51	103	.331

World Series (4-1): Chicago Cubs over Detroit Tigers

1909

Team	W	L	%
Detroit	98	54	.645
Philadelphia	95	58	.621
Boston	88	63	.583
Chicago	78	74	.513
New York	74	77	.490
Cleveland	71	82	.464
St. Louis	61	89	.407
Washington	42	110	.276

World Series (4-3): Pittsburgh Pirates over Detroit Tigers

1910

Team	W	L	%
Philadelphia	102	48	.680
New York	88	63	.583
Detroit	86	68	.558
Boston	81	72	.529
Cleveland	71	81	.467
Chicago	68	85	.444
Washington	66	85	.437
St. Louis	47	107	.305

World Series (4-1): Philadelphia Athletics over Chicago Cubs

1911

Team	W	L	%
Philadelphia	101	50	.669
Detroit	89	65	.578
Cleveland	80	73	.523
Boston	78	75	.510
Chicago	77	74	.510
New York	76	76	.500
Washington	64	90	.416
St. Louis	45	107	.296

World Series (4-2): Philadelphia Athletics over New York Giants

1912

Team	W	L	%
Boston	105	47	.691
Washington	91	61	.599
Philadelphia	90	62	.592
Chicago	78	76	.506
Cleveland	75	78	.490
Detroit	69	84	.451
St. Louis	53	101	.344
New York	50	102	.329

World Series (4-3-1): Boston Red Sox over New York Giants

1913

Team	W	L	%
Philadelphia	96	57	.627
Washington	90	64	.584
Cleveland	86	66	.566
Boston	79	71	.527
Chicago	78	74	.513
Detroit	66	87	.431
New York	57	94	.377
St. Louis	57	96	.373

World Series (4-1): Philadelphia Athletics over New York Giants

1914

Team	W	L	%
Philadelphia	99	53	.651
Boston	91	62	.595
Washington	81	73	.526
Detroit	80	73	.523
St. Louis	71	82	.464
Chicago	70	84	.455
New York	70	84	.455
Cleveland	51	102	.333

World Series (4–0): Boston Braves over Philadelphia Athletics

1915

Team	W	L	%
Boston	101	50	.669
Detroit	100	54	.649
Chicago	93	61	.604
Washington	85	68	.556
New York	69	83	.454
St. Louis	63	91	.409
Cleveland	57	95	.375
Philadelphia	43	109	.283

World Series (4-1): Boston Red Sox over Philadelphia Phillies

1916

Team	W	L	%
Boston	91	63	.591
Chicago	89	65	.578
Detroit	87	67	.565
New York	80	74	.519
St. Louis	79	75	.513
Cleveland	77	77	.500
Washington	76	77	.497
Philadelphia	36	117	.235

World Series (4-1): Boston Red Sox over Brooklyn Robins

1917

Team	W	L	%
Chicago	100	54	.649
Boston	90	62	.592
Cleveland	88	66	.571
Detroit	78	75	.510
Washington	74	79	.484
New York	71	82	.464
St. Louis	57	97	.370
Philadelphia	55	98	.359

World Series (4-2): Chicago White Sox over New York Giants

1918

Team	W	L	%
Boston	75	51	.595
Cleveland	73	54	.575
Washington	72	56	.562
New York	60	63	.488
St. Louis	58	64	.475
Chicago	57	67	.460
Detroit	55	71	.437
Philadelphia	52	76	.406

World Series (4-2): Boston Red Sox over Chicago Cubs

1919

Team	W	L	%
Chicago	88	52	.629
Cleveland	84	55	.604
New York	80	59	.576
Detroit	80	60	.571
Boston	66	71	.482
St. Louis	67	72	.482
Washington	56	84	.400
Philadelphia	36	104	.257

World Series (5-3): Cincinnati Reds over Chicago White Sox

1920

Team	W	L	%
Cleveland	98	56	.636
Chicago	96	58	.623
New York	95	59	.617
St. Louis	76	77	.497
Boston	72	81	.471
Washington	68	84	.447
Detroit	61	93	.396
Philadelphia	48	106	.312

World Series (5-2): Cleveland Indians over Brooklyn Robins

1921

Team	W	L	%
New York	98	55	.641
Cleveland	94	60	.610
St. Louis	81	73	.526
Washington	80	73	.523
Boston	75	79	.487
Detroit	71	82	.464
Chicago	62	92	.403
Philadelphia	53	100	.346

World Series (5-3): New York Giants over New York Yankees

1922

Team	W	L	%
New York	94	60	.610
St. Louis	93	61	.604
Detroit	79	75	.513
Cleveland	78	76	.506
Chicago	77	77	.500
Washington	69	85	.448
Philadelphia	65	89	.422
Boston	61	93	.396

World Series (4-0-1): New York Giants over New York Yankees

1923

Team	W	L	%
New York	98	54	.645
Detroit	83	71	.539
Cleveland	82	71	.536
Washington	75	78	.490
St. Louis	74	78	.487
Philadelphia	69	83	.454
Chicago	69	85	.448
Boston	61	91	.401

World Series (4-2): New York Yankees over New York Giants

1924

Team	W	L	%
Washington	92	62	.597
New York	89	63	.586
Detroit	86	68	.558
St. Louis	74	78	.487
Philadelphia	71	81	.467
Cleveland	67	86	.438
Boston	67	87	.435
Chicago	66	87	.431

World Series (4-3): Washington Senators over New York Giants

1925

Team	W	L	%
Washington	96	55	.636
Philadelphia	88	64	.579
St. Louis	82	71	.536
Detroit	81	73	.526
Chicago	79	75	.513
Cleveland	70	84	.455
New York	69	85	.448
Boston	47	105	.309

World Series (4-3): Pittsburgh Pirates over Washington Senators

1926

Team	W	L	%
New York	91	63	.591
Cleveland	88	66	.571
Philadelphia	83	67	.553
Washington	81	69	.540
Chicago	81	72	.529
Detroit	79	75	.513
St. Louis	62	92	.403
Boston	46	107	.301

World Series (4-3): St. Louis Cardinals over New York Yankee

1927

Team	W	L	%
New York	110	44	.714
Philadelphia	91	63	.591
Washington	85	69	.552
Detroit	82	71	.536
Chicago	70	83	.458
Cleveland	66	87	.431
St. Louis	59	94	.386
Boston	51	103	.331

World Series (4-0): New York Yankees over Pittsburgh Pirates

1928

Team	W	L	%
New York	101	53	.656
Philadelphia	98	55	.641
St. Louis	82	72	.532
Washington	75	79	.487
Chicago	72	82	.468
Detroit	68	86	.442
Cleveland	62	92	.403
Boston	57	96	.373

World Series (4-0): New York Yankees over St. Louis Cardinals

1929			
Team	W	L	%
Philadelphia	104	46	.693
New York	88	66	.571
Cleveland	81	71	.533
St. Louis	79	73	.520
Washington	71	81	.467
Detroit	70	84	.455
Chicago	59	93	.388
Boston	58	96	.377

World Series (4-1): Philadelphia Athletics over Chicago Cubs

1930			
Team	W	L	%
Philadelphia	102	52	.662
Washington	94	60	.610
New York	86	68	.558
Cleveland	81	73	.526
Detroit	75	79	.487
St. Louis	64	90	.416
Chicago	62	92	.403
Boston	52	102	.338

World Series (4-2): Philadelphia Athletics over St. Louis Cardinals

1931			
Team	W	L	%
Philadelphia	107	45	.704
New York	94	59	.614
Washington	92	62	.597
Cleveland	78	76	.506
St. Louis	63	91	.409
Boston	62	90	.408
Detroit	61	93	.396
Chicago	56	97	.366

World Series (4-3): St. Louis Cardinals over Philadelphia Athletics

1932			
Team	W	L	%
New York	107	47	.695
Philadelphia	94	60	.610
Washington	93	61	.604
Cleveland	87	65	.572
Detroit	76	75	.503
St. Louis	63	91	.409
Chicago	49	102	.325
Boston	43	111	.279

World Series (4-0): New York Yankees over Chicago Cubs

1933			
Team	W	L	%
Washington	99	53	.651
New York	91	59	.607
Philadelphia	79	72	.523
Cleveland	75	76	.497
Detroit	75	79	.487
Chicago	67	83	.447
Boston	63	86	.423
St. Louis	55	96	.364

World Series (4-1): New York Giants over Washington Senators

1934			
Team	W	L	%
Detroit	101	53	.656
New York	94	60	.610
Cleveland	85	69	.552
Boston	76	76	.500
Philadelphia	68	82	.453
St. Louis	67	85	.441
Washington	66	86	.434
Chicago	53	99	.349

World Series (4-3): St. Louis Cardinals over Detroit Tigers

1935			
Team	W	L	%
Detroit	93	58	.616
New York	89	60	.597
Cleveland	82	71	.536
Boston	78	75	.510
Chicago	74	78	.487
Washington	67	86	.438
St. Louis	65	87	.428
Philadelphia	58	91	.389

World Series (4-2): Detroit Tigers over Chicago Cubs

1936			
Team	W	L	%
New York	102	51	.667
Detroit	83	71	.539
Chicago	81	70	.536
Washington	82	71	.536
Cleveland	80	74	.519
Boston	74	80	.481
St. Louis	57	95	.375
Philadelphia	53	100	.346

World Series (4-2): New York Yankees over New York Giants

1937			
Team	W	L	%
New York	102	52	.662
Detroit	89	65	.578
Chicago	86	68	.558
Cleveland	83	71	.539
Boston	80	72	.526
Washington	73	80	.477
Philadelphia	54	97	.358
St. Louis	46	108	.299

World Series (4-1): New York Yankees over New York Giants

1938			
Team	W	L	%
New York	99	53	.651
Boston	88	61	.591
Cleveland	86	66	.566
Detroit	84	70	.545
Washington	75	76	.497
Chicago	65	83	.439
St. Louis	55	97	.362
Philadelphia	53	99	.349

World Series (4-0): New York Yankees over Chicago Cubs

1939			
Team	W	L	%
New York	106	45	.702
Boston	89	62	.589
Cleveland	87	67	.565
Chicago	85	69	.552
Detroit	81	73	.526
Washington	65	87	.428
Philadelphia	55	97	.362
St. Louis	43	111	.279

World Series (4-0): New York Yankees over Cincinnati Reds

1940			
Team	W	L	%
Detroit	90	64	.584
Cleveland	89	65	.578
New York	88	66	.571
Boston	82	72	.532
Chicago	82	72	.532
St. Louis	67	87	.435
Washington	64	90	.416
Philadelphia	54	100	.351

World Series (4-3): Cincinnati Reds over Detroit Tigers

1941

Team	W	L	%
New York	101	53	.656
Boston	84	70	.545
Chicago	77	77	.500
Cleveland	75	79	.487
Detroit	75	79	.487
St. Louis	70	84	.455
Washington	70	84	.455
Philadelphia	64	90	.416

World Series (4-1): New YorkYankees over Brooklyn Dodgers

1942

Team	W	L	%
New York	103	51	.669
Boston	93	59	.612
St. Louis	82	69	.543
Cleveland	75	79	.487
Detroit	73	81	.474
Chicago	66	82	.446
Washington	62	89	.411
Philadelphia	55	99	.357

World Series (4-1): St. Louis Cardinals over New York Yankees

1943

Team	W	L	%
New York	98	56	.636
Washington	84	69	.549
Cleveland	82	71	.536
Chicago	82	72	.532
Detroit	78	76	.506
St. Louis	72	80	.474
Boston	68	84	.447
Philadelphia	49	105	.318

World Series (4-1): New York Yankees over St. Louis Cardinals

1944

Team	W	L	%
St. Louis	89	65	.578
Detroit	88	66	.571
New York	83	71	.539
Boston	77	77	.500
Cleveland	72	82	.468
Philadelphia	72	82	.468
Chicago	71	83	.461
Washington	64	90	.416

World Series (4-2): St. Louis Cardinals over St. Louis Browns

1945

Team	W	L	%
Detroit	88	65	.575
Washington	87	67	.565
St. Louis	81	70	.536
New York	81	71	.533
Cleveland	73	72	.503
Chicago	71	78	.477
Boston	71	83	.461
Philadelphia	52	98	.347

World Series (4-3): Detroit Tigers over Chicago Cubs

1946

Team	W	L	%
Boston	104	50	.675
Detroit	92	62	.597
New York	87	67	.565
Washington	76	78	.494
Chicago	74	80	.481
Cleveland	68	86	.442
St. Louis	66	88	.429
Philadelphia	49	105	.318

World Series (4-3): St. Louis Cardinals over Boston Red Sox

1947

Team	W	L	%
Team	W	L	%
New York	97	57	.630
Detroit	85	69	.552
Boston	83	71	.539
Cleveland	80	74	.519
Philadelphia	78	76	.506
Chicago	70	84	.455
Washington	64	90	.416
St. Louis	59	95	.383

World Series (4-3): New York Yankees over Brooklyn Dodgers

1948

Team	W	L	%
Team	W	L	%
Cleveland	97	58	.626
Boston	96	59	.619
New York	94	60	.610
Philadelphia	84	70	.545
Detroit	78	76	.506
St. Louis	59	94	.386
Washington	56	97	.366
Chicago	51	101	.336

World Series (4-2): Cleveland Indians over Boston Braves

1949

Team	W	L	%
New York	97	57	.630
Boston	96	58	.623
Cleveland	89	65	.578
Detroit	87	67	.565
Philadelphia	81	73	.526
Chicago	63	91	.409
St. Louis	53	101	.344
Washington	50	104	.325

World Series (4-1): New York Yankees over Brooklyn Dodgers

1950

Team	W	L	%
New York	98	56	.636
Detroit	95	59	.617
Boston	94	60	.610
Cleveland	92	62	.597
Washington	67	87	.435
Chicago	60	94	.390
St. Louis	58	96	.377
Philadelphia	52	102	.338

World Series (4-0): New York Yankees over Philadelphia Phillies

1951

Team	W	L	%
New York	98	56	.636
Cleveland	93	61	.604
Boston	87	67	.565
Chicago	81	73	.526
Detroit	73	81	.474
Philadelphia	70	84	.455
Washington	62	92	.403
St. Louis	52	102	.338

World Series (4-2): New York Yankees over New York Giants

1952

Team	W	L	%
New York	95	59	.617
Cleveland	93	61	.60
Chicago	81	73	.526
Philadelphia	79	75	.513
Washington	78	76	.506
Boston	76	78	.494
St. Louis	64	90	.416
Detroit	50	104	.325

World Series (4-3): New York Yankees over Brooklyn Dodgers

1953

Team	W	L	%
New York	99	52	.656
Cleveland	92	62	.597
Chicago	89	65	.578
Boston	84	69	.549
Washington	76	76	.500
Detroit	60	94	.390
Philadelphia	59	95	.383
St. Louis	54	100	.351

World Series (4-2): New York Yankees over Brooklyn Dodgers

1954

Team	W	L	%
Cleveland	111	43	.721
New York	103	51	.669
Chicago	94	60	.610
Boston	69	85	.448
Detroit	68	86	.442
Washington	66	88	.429
Baltimore	54	100	.351
Philadelphia	51	103	.331

World Series (4-0): New York Giants over Cleveland Indians

1955

Team	W	L	%
New York	96	58	.623
Cleveland	93	61	.604
Chicago	91	63	.591
Boston	84	70	.545
Detroit	79	75	.513
Kansas City	63	91	.409
Baltimore	57	97	.370
Washington	53	101	.344

World Series (4-3): BrooklynDodgers over New York Yankees

1956

Team	W	L	%
New York	97	57	.630
Cleveland	88	66	.571
Chicago	85	69	.552
Boston	84	70	.545
Detroit	82	72	.532
Baltimore	69	85	.448
Washington	59	95	.383
Kansas City	52	102	.338

World Series (4-3): New York Yankees over Brooklyn Dodgers

1957

Team	W	L	%
New York	98	56	.636
Chicago	90	64	.584
Boston	82	72	.532
Detroit	78	76	.506
Baltimore	76	76	.500
Cleveland	76	77	.497
Kansas City	59	94	.386
Washington	55	99	.357

World Series (4-3): Milwaukee Braves over New York Yankees

1958

Team	W	L	%
New York	92	62	.597
Chicago	82	72	.532
Boston	79	75	.513
Cleveland	77	76	.503
Detroit	77	77	.500
Baltimore	74	79	.484
Kansas City	73	81	.474
Washington	61	93	.396

World Series (4-3): New York Yankees over Milwaukee Braves

1959

Team	W	L	%
Chicago	94	60	.610
Cleveland	89	65	.578
New York	79	75	.513
Detroit	76	78	.494
Boston	75	79	.487
Baltimore	74	80	.481
Kansas City	66	88	.429
Washington	63	91	.409

World Series (4-2): Los Angeles Dodgers over Chicago White Sox

1960

Team	W	L	%
New York	97	57	.630
Baltimore	89	65	.578
Chicago	87	67	.565
Cleveland	76	78	.494
Washington	73	81	.474
Detroit	71	83	.461
Boston	65	89	.422
Kansas City	58	96	.377

World Series (4-3): Pittsburgh Pirates over New York Yankees

1961

Team	W	L	%
New York	109	53	.673
Detroit	101	61	.623
Baltimore	95	67	.586
Chicago	86	76	.531
Cleveland	78	83	.484
Boston	76	86	.469
Minnesota	70	90	.438
Los Angeles	70	91	.435
Kansas City	61	100	.379
Washington	61	100	.379

World Series (4-1): New York Yankees over Cincinnati Reds

1962

Team	W	L	%
New York	96	66	.593
Minnesota	91	71	.562
Los Angeles	86	76	.531
Detroit	85	76	.528
Chicago	85	77	.525
Cleveland	80	82	.494
Baltimore	77	85	.475
Boston	76	84	.475
Kansas City	72	90	.444
Washington	60	101	.373

World Series (4-3): New York Yankees over San Francisco Giants

1963

Team	W	L	%
New York	104	57	.646
Chicago	94	68	.580
Minnesota	91	70	.565
Baltimore	86	76	.531
Cleveland	79	83	.488
Detroit	79	83	.488
Boston	76	85	.472
Kansas City	73	89	.451
Los Angeles	70	91	.435
Washington	56	106	.346

World Series (4-0): Los Angeles Dodgers over New York Yankees

1964

Team	W	L	%
New York	99	63	.611
Chicago	98	64	.605
Baltimore	97	65	.599
Detroit	85	77	.525
Los Angeles	82	80	.506
Cleveland	79	83	.488
Minnesota	79	83	.488
Boston	72	90	.444
Washington	62	100	.383
Kansas City	57	105	.352

World Series (4-3): St. Louis Cardinals over New York Yankees

1965

Team	W	L	%
Minnesota	102	60	.630
Chicago	95	67	.586
Baltimore	94	68	.580
Detroit	89	73	.549
Cleveland	87	75	.537
New York	77	85	.475
California	75	87	.463
Washington	70	92	.432
Boston	62	100	.383
Kansas City	59	103	.364

World Series (4-3): Los Angeles Dodgers over Minnesota Twins

1966

Team	W	L	%
Baltimore	97	63	.606
Minnesota	89	73	.549
Detroit	88	74	.543
Chicago	83	79	.512
Cleveland	81	81	.500
California	80	82	.494
Kansas City	74	86	.462
Washington	71	88	.447
Boston	72	90	.444
New York	70	89	.440

World Series (4-0): Baltimore Orioles over Los Angeles Dodgers

1967

Team	W	L	%
Boston	92	70	.568
Detroit	91	71	.562
Minnesota	91	71	.562
Chicago	89	73	.549
California	84	77	.522
Baltimore	76	85	.472
Washington	76	85	.472
Cleveland	75	87	.463
New York	72	90	.444
Kansas City	62	99	.385

World Series (4-3): St. Louis Cardinals over Boston Red Sox

1968

Team	W	L	%
Detroit	103	59	.636
Baltimore	91	71	.562
Cleveland	86	75	.534
Boston	86	76	.531
New York	83	79	.512
Oakland	82	80	.506
Minnesota	79	83	.488
California	67	95	.414
Chicago	67	95	.414
Washington	65	96	.404

World Series (4-3): Detroit Tigers over St. Louis Cardinals

1969

East Division

Team	W	L	%
Baltimore	109	53	.673
Detroit	90	72	.556
Boston	87	75	.537
Washington	86	76	.531
New York	80	81	.497
Cleveland	62	99	.385

West Division

Team	W	L	%
Minnesota	97	65	.599
Oakland	88	74	.543
California	71	91	.438
Kansas City	69	93	.426
Chicago	68	94	.420
Seattle	64	98	.395

World Series (4-1): New York Mets over Baltimore Orioles

AL Championship Series (3-0): Baltimore Orioles over Minnesota Twins

1970

East Division			
Team	W	L	%
Baltimore	108	54	.667
New York	93	69	.574
Boston	87	75	.537
Detroit	79	83	.488
Cleveland	76	86	.469
Washington	70	92	.432

West Division			
Team	W	L	%
Minnesota	98	64	.605
Oakland	89	73	.549
California	86	76	.531
Kansas City	65	97	.401
Milwaukee	65	97	.401
Chicago	56	106	.346

World Series (4-1): Baltimore Orioles over Cincinnati Reds

AL Championship Series (3-0): Baltimore Orioles over Minnesota Twins

1971

East Division			
Team	W	L	%
Baltimore	101	57	.639
Detroit	91	71	.562
Boston	85	77	.525
New York	82	80	.506
Washington	63	96	.396
Cleveland	60	102	.370

West Division			
Team	W	L	%
Oakland	101	60	.627
Kansas City	85	76	.528
Chicago	79	83	.488
California	76	86	.469
Minnesota	74	86	.462
Milwaukee	69	92	.429

World Series (4-3): Pittsburgh Pirates over Baltimore Orioles

AL Championship Series (3-0): Baltimore Orioles over Oakland Athletics

1972

East Division			
Team	W	L	%
Detroit	86	70	.551
Boston	85	70	.548
Baltimore	80	74	.519
New York	79	76	.510
Cleveland	72	84	.462
Milwaukee	65	91	.417

West Division			
Team	W	L	%
Oakland	93	62	.600
Chicago	87	67	.565
Minnesota	77	77	.500
Kansas City	76	78	.494
California	75	80	.484
Texas	54	100	.351

World Series (4-3): Oakland Athletics over Cincinnati Reds

AL Championship Series (3-2): Oakland Athletics over Detroit Tigers

1973

East Division				West Division			
Team	W	L	%	Team	W	L	%
Baltimore	97	65	.599	Oakland	94	68	.580
Boston	89	73	.549	Kansas City	88	74	.543
Detroit	85	77	.525	Minnesota	81	81	.500
New York	80	82	.494	California	79	83	.488
Milwaukee	74	88	.457	Chicago	77	85	.475
Cleveland	71	91	.438	Texas	57	105	.352

World Series (4-3): Oakland Athletics over New York Mets

AL Championship Series (3-2): Oakland Athletics over Detroit Tigers

1974

East Division				West Division			
Team	W	L	%	Team	W	L	%
Baltimore	91	71	.562	Oakland	90	72	.556
New York	89	73	.549	Texas	84	76	.525
Boston	84	78	.519	Minnesota	82	80	.506
Cleveland	77	85	.475	Chicago	80	80	.500
Milwaukee	76	86	.469	Kansas City	77	85	.475
Detroit	72	90	.444	California	68	94	.420

World Series (4-1): Oakland Athletics over Los Angeles Dodgers

AL Championship Series (3-1): Oakland Athletics over Baltimore Orioles

1975

East Division				West Division			
Team	W	L	%	Team	W	L	%
Boston	95	65	.594	Oakland	98	64	.605
Baltimore	90	69	.566	Kansas City	91	71	.562
New York	83	77	.519	Texas	79	83	.488
Cleveland	79	80	.497	Minnesota	76	83	.478
Milwaukee	68	94	.420	Chicago	75	86	.466
Detroit	57	102	.358	California	72	89	.447

World Series (4-3): Cincinnati Reds over Boston Red Sox

AL Championship Series (3-0): Boston Red Sox over Oakland Athletics

1976

East Division					West Division			
Team	W	L	%		Team	W	L	%
New York	97	62	.610		Kansas City	90	72	.556
Baltimore	88	74	.543		Oakland	87	74	.540
Boston	83	79	.512		Minnesota	85	77	.525
Cleveland	81	78	.509		California	76	86	.469
Detroit	74	87	.460		Texas	76	86	.469
Milwaukee	66	95	.410		Chicago	64	97	.398

World Series (4-0): Cincinnati Reds over New York Yankees

AL Championship Series (3-2): New York Yankees over Kansas City Royals

1977

East Division					West Division			
Team	W	L	%		Team	W	L	%
New York	100	62	.617		Kansas City	102	60	.630
Baltimore	97	64	.602		Texas	94	68	.580
Boston	97	64	.602		Chicago	90	72	.556
Detroit	74	88	.457		Minnesota	84	77	.522
Cleveland	71	90	.441		California	74	88	.457
Milwaukee	67	95	.414		Seattle	64	98	.395
Toronto	54	107	.335		Oakland	63	98	.391

World Series (4-2): New York Yankees over Los Angeles Dodgers

AL Championship Series (3-2): New York Yankees over Kansas City Royals

1978

East Division					West Division			
Team	W	L	%		Team	W	L	%
New York	100	63	.613		Kansas City	92	70	.568
Boston	99	64	.607		California	87	75	.537
Milwaukee	93	69	.574		Texas	87	75	.537
Baltimore	90	71	.559		Minnesota	73	89	.451
Detroit	86	76	.531		Chicago	71	90	.441
Cleveland	69	90	.434		Oakland	69	93	.426
Toronto	59	102	.366		Seattle	56	104	.350

World Series (4-2): New York Yankees over Los Angeles Dodgers

AL Championship Series (3-1): New York Yankees over Kansas City Royals

1979

East Division			
Team	W	L	%
Baltimore	102	57	.642
Milwaukee	95	66	.590
Boston	91	69	.569
New York	89	71	.556
Detroit	85	76	.528
Cleveland	81	80	.503
Toronto	53	109	.327

West Division			
Team	W	L	%
California	88	74	.543
Kansas City	85	77	.525
Texas	83	79	.512
Minnesota	82	80	.506
Chicago	73	87	.456
Seattle	67	95	.414
Oakland	54	108	.333

World Series (4-3): Pittsburgh Pirates over Baltimore Orioles

AL Championship Series (3-1): Baltimore Orioles over California Angels

1980

East Division			
Team	W	L	%
New York	103	59	.636
Baltimore	100	62	.617
Milwaukee	86	76	.531
Boston	83	77	.519
Detroit	84	78	.519
Cleveland	79	81	.494
Toronto	67	95	.414

West Division			
Team	W	L	%
Kansas City	97	65	.599
Oakland	83	79	.512
Minnesota	77	84	.478
Texas	76	85	.472
Chicago	70	90	.438
California	65	95	.406
Seattle	59	103	.364

World Series (4-2): Philadelphia Phillies over Kansas City Royals

AL Championship Series (3-0): Kansas City Royals over New York Yankees

1981

East Division			
Team	W	L	%
Milwaukee	62	47	.569
Baltimore	59	46	.562
New York	59	48	.551
Detroit	60	49	.550
Boston	59	49	.546
Cleveland	52	51	.505
Toronto	37	69	.349

West Division			
Team	W	L	%
Oakland	64	45	.587
Texas	57	48	.543
Chicago	54	52	.509
Kansas City	50	53	.485
California	51	59	.464
Seattle	44	65	.404
Minnesota	41	68	.376

World Series (4-2): Los Angeles Dodgers over New York Yankees

AL Championship Series (3-0): New York Yankees over Oakland Athletics

AL Division Series (3-2): New York Yankees over Milwaukee Brewers

AL Division Series (3-0): Oakland Athletics over Kansas City Royals

1982

East Division				West Division			
Team	W	L	%	Team	W	L	%
Milwaukee	95	67	.586	California	93	69	.574
Baltimore	94	68	.580	Kansas City	90	72	.556
Boston	89	73	.549	Chicago	87	75	.537
Detroit	83	79	.512	Seattle	76	86	.469
New York	79	83	.488	Oakland	68	94	.420
Cleveland	78	84	.481	Texas	64	98	.395
Toronto	78	84	.481	Minnesota	60	102	.370

World Series (4-3): St. Louis Cardinals over Milwaukee Brewers

AL Championship Series (3-2): Milwaukee Brewers over California Angels

1983

East Division				West Division			
Team	W	L	%	Team	W	L	%
Baltimore	98	64	.605	Chicago	99	63	.611
Detroit	92	70	.568	Kansas City	79	83	.488
New York	91	71	.562	Texas	77	85	.475
Toronto	89	73	.549	Oakland	74	88	.457
Milwaukee	87	75	.537	California	70	92	.432
Boston	78	84	.481	Minnesota	70	92	.432
Cleveland	70	92	.432	Seattle	60	102	.370

World Series (4-1): Baltimore Orioles over Philadelphia Phillies

AL Championship Series (3-1): Baltimore Orioles over Chicago White Sox

1984

East Division				West Division			
Team	W	L	%	Team	W	L	%
Detroit	104	58	.642	Kansas City	84	78	.519
Toronto	89	73	.549	California	81	81	.500
New York	87	75	.537	Minnesota	81	81	.500
Boston	86	76	.531	Oakland	77	85	.475
Baltimore	85	77	.525	Chicago	74	88	.457
Cleveland	75	87	.463	Seattle	74	88	.457
Milwaukee	67	94	.416	Texas	69	92	.429

World Series (4-1): Detroit Tigers over San Diego Padres

AL Championship Series (3-0): Detroit Tigers over Kansas City Royals

1985

| East Division | | | |
Team	W	L	%
Toronto	99	62	.615
New York	97	64	.602
Detroit	84	77	.522
Baltimore	83	78	.516
Boston	81	81	.500
Milwaukee	71	90	.441
Cleveland	60	102	.370

| West Division | | | |
Team	W	L	%
Kansas City	91	71	.562
California	90	72	.556
Chicago	85	77	.525
Minnesota	77	85	.475
Oakland	77	85	.475
Seattle	74	88	.457
Texas	62	99	.385

World Series (4-3): Kansas City Royals over St. Louis Cardinals

AL Championship Series (4-3): Kansas City Royals over Toronto Blue Jays

1986

| East Division | | | |
Team	W	L	%
Boston	95	66	.590
New York	90	72	.556
Detroit	87	75	.537
Toronto	86	76	.531
Cleveland	84	78	.519
Milwaukee	77	84	.478
Baltimore	73	89	.451

| West Division | | | |
Team	W	L	%
California	92	70	.568
Texas	87	75	.537
Kansas City	76	86	.469
Oakland	76	86	.469
Chicago	72	90	.444
Minnesota	71	91	.438
Seattle	67	95	.414

World Series (4-3): New York Mets over Boston Red Sox

AL Championship Series (4-3): Boston Red Sox over California Angels

1987

| East Division | | | |
Team	W	L	%
Detroit	98	64	.605
Toronto	96	66	.593
Milwaukee	91	71	.562
New York	89	73	.549
Boston	78	84	.481
Baltimore	67	95	.414
Cleveland	61	101	.377

| West Division | | | |
Team	W	L	%
Minnesota	85	77	.52
Kansas City	83	79	.51
Oakland	81	81	.500
Seattle	78	84	.481
Chicago	77	85	.475
California	75	87	.463
Texas	75	87	.463

World Series (4-3): Minnesota Twins over St. Louis Cardinals

AL Championship Series (4-1): Minnesota Twins over Detroit Tigers

1988

East Division					West Division			
Team	W	L	%		Team	W	L	%
Boston	89	73	.549		Oakland	104	58	.642
Detroit	88	74	.543		Minnesota	91	71	.562
Milwaukee	87	75	.537		Kansas City	84	77	.522
Toronto	87	75	.537		California	75	87	.463
New York	85	76	.528		Chicago	71	90	.441
Cleveland	78	84	.481		Texas	70	91	.435
Baltimore	54	107	.335		Seattle	68	93	.422

World Series (4-1): Los Angeles Dodgers over Oakland Athletics

AL Championship Series (4-0): Oakland Athletics over Boston Red Sox

1989

East Division					West Division			
Team	W	L	%		Team	W	L	%
Toronto	89	73	.549		Oakland	99	63	.611
Baltimore	87	75	.537		Kansas City	92	70	.568
Boston	83	79	.512		California	91	71	.562
Milwaukee	81	81	.500		Texas	83	79	.512
New York	74	87	.460		Minnesota	80	82	.494
Cleveland	73	89	.451		Seattle	73	89	.451
Detroit	59	103	.364		Chicago	69	92	.429

World Series (4-0): Oakland Athletics over San Francisco Giants

AL Championship Series (4-1): Oakland Athletics over Toronto Blue Jays

1990

East Division					West Division			
Team	W	L	%		Team	W	L	%
Boston	88	74	.543		Oakland	103	59	.636
Toronto	86	76	.531		Chicago	94	68	.580
Detroit	79	83	.488		Texas	83	79	.512
Cleveland	77	85	.475		California	80	82	.494
Baltimore	76	85	.472		Seattle	77	85	.475
Milwaukee	74	88	.457		Kansas City	75	86	.466
New York	67	95	.414		Minnesota	74	88	.457

World Series (4-0): Cincinnati Reds over Oakland Athletics

AL Championship Series (4-0): Oakland Athletics over Boston Red Sox

1991

East Division					West Division			
Team	W	L	%		Team	W	L	%
Toronto	91	71	.562		Minnesota	95	67	.586
Boston	84	78	.519		Chicago	87	75	.537
Detroit	84	78	.519		Texas	85	77	.525
Milwaukee	83	79	.512		Oakland	84	78	.519
New York	71	91	.438		Seattle	83	79	.512
Baltimore	67	95	.414		Kansas City	82	80	.506
Cleveland	5	105	.352		California	81	81	.500

World Series (4-3): Minnesota Twins over Atlanta Braves

AL Championship Series (4-1): Minnesota Twins over Toronto Blue Jays

1992

East Division					West Division			
Team	W	L	%		Team	W	L	%
Toronto	96	66	.593		Oakland	96	66	.593
Milwaukee	92	70	.568		Minnesota	90	72	.556
Baltimore	89	73	.549		Chicago	86	76	.531
Cleveland	76	86	.469		Texas	77	85	.475
New York	76	86	.469		California	72	90	.444
Detroit	75	87	.463		Kansas City	72	90	.444
Boston	73	89	.451		Seattle	64	98	.395

World Series (4-2): Toronto Blue Jays over Atlanta Braves

AL Championship Series (4-2): Toronto Blue Jays over Oakland Athletics

1993

East Division					West Division			
Team	W	L	%		Team	W	L	%
Toronto	95	67	.586		Chicago	94	68	.580
New York	88	74	.543		Texas	86	76	.531
Baltimore	85	77	.525		Kansas City	84	78	.519
Detroit	85	77	.525		Seattle	82	80	.506
Boston	80	82	.494		California	71	91	.438
Cleveland	76	86	.469		Minnesota	71	91	.438
Milwaukee	69	93	.426		Oakland	68	94	.420

World Series (4-2): Toronto Blue Jays over Philadelphia Phillies

AL Championship Series (4-2): Toronto Blue Jays over Chicago White Sox

1994

East Division				Central Division				West Division			
Team	W	L	%	Team	W	L	%	Team	W	L	%
New York	70	43	.619	Chicago	67	46	.593	Texas	52	62	.456
Baltimore	63	49	.562	Cleveland	66	47	.584	Oakland	51	63	.447
Toronto	55	60	.478	Kansas City	64	51	.557	Seattle	49	63	.438
Boston	54	61	.470	Minnesota	53	60	.469	California	47	68	.409
Detroit	53	62	.461	Milwaukee	53	62	.461				

1995

East Division				Central Division				West Division			
Team	W	L	%	Team	W	L	%	Team	W	L	%
Boston	86	58	.597	Cleveland	100	44	.694	Seattle	79	66	.545
New York	79	65	.549	Kansas City	70	74	.486	California	78	67	.538
Baltimore	71	73	.493	Chicago	68	76	.472	Texas	74	70	.514
Detroit	60	84	.417	Milwaukee	65	79	.451	Oakland	67	77	.465
Toronto	56	88	.389	Minnesota	56	88	.389				

World Series (4-2): Atlanta Braves over Cleveland Indians

AL Championship Series (4-2): Cleveland Indians over Seattle Mariners

AL Division Series (3-0): Cleveland Indians over Boston Red Sox

AL Division Series (3-2): Seattle Mariners over New York Yankees

1996

East Division				Central Division				West Division			
Team	W	L	%	Team	W	L	%	Team	W	L	%
New York	92	70	.568	Cleveland	99	62	.615	Texas	90	72	.556
Baltimore	88	74	.543	Chicago	85	77	.525	Seattle	85	76	.528
Boston	85	77	.525	Milwaukee	80	82	.494	Oakland	78	84	.481
Toronto	74	88	.457	Minnesota	78	84	.481	California	70	91	.435
Detroit	53	109	.327	Kansas City	75	86	.466				

World Series (4-2): New York Yankees over Atlanta Braves

AL Championship Series (4-1): New York Yankees over Baltimore Orioles

AL Division Series (3-1): Baltimore Orioles over Cleveland Indians

AL Division Series (3-1): New York Yankees over Texas Rangers

1997

East Division					Central Division					West Division			
Team	W	L	%		Team	W	L	%		Team	W	L	%
Baltimore	98	64	.605		Cleveland	86	75	.534		Seattle	90	72	.556
New York	96	66	.593		Chicago	80	81	.497		Anaheim	84	78	.519
Detroit	79	83	.488		Milwaukee	78	83	.484		Texas	77	85	.475
Boston	78	84	.481		Minnesota	68	94	.420		Oakland	65	97	.401
Toronto	76	86	.469		Kansas City	67	94	.416					

World Series (4-3): Florida Marlins over Cleveland Indians

AL Championship Series (4-2): Cleveland Indians over Baltimore Orioles

AL Division Series (3-2): Cleveland Indians over New York Yankees

AL Division Series (3-1): Baltimore Orioles over Seattle Mariners

1998

East Division					Central Division					West Division			
Team	W	L	%		Team	W	L	%		Team	W	L	%
New York	114	48	.704		Cleveland	89	73	.549		Texas	88	74	.543
Boston	92	70	.568		Chicago	80	82	.494		Anaheim	85	77	.525
Toronto	88	74	.543		Kansas City	72	89	.447		Seattle	76	85	.472
Baltimore	79	83	.488		Minnesota	70	92	.432		Oakland	74	88	.457
Tampa Bay	63	99	.389		Detroit	65	97	.401					

World Series (4-0): New York Yankees over San Diego Padres

AL Championship Series (4-2): New York Yankees over Cleveland Indians

AL Division Series (3-1): Cleveland Indians over Boston Red Sox

AL Division Series (3-0): New York Yankees over Texas Rangers

1999

East Division					Central Division					West Division			
Team	W	L	%		Team	W	L	%		Team	W	L	%
New York	98	64	.605		Cleveland	97	65	.599		Texas	95	67	.586
Boston	94	68	.580		Chicago	75	86	.466		Oakland	87	75	.537
Toronto	84	78	.519		Detroit	69	92	.429		Seattle	79	83	.488
Baltimore	78	84	.481		Kansas City	64	97	.398		Anaheim	70	92	.432
Tampa Bay	69	93	.426		Minnesota	63	97	.394					

World Series (4-0): New York Yankees over Atlanta Braves

AL Championship Series (4-1): New York Yankees over Boston Red Sox

AL Division Series (3-2): Boston Red Sox over Cleveland Indians

AL Division Series (3-0): New York Yankees over Texas Rangers

2000

East Division				Central Division				West Division			
Team	W	L	%	Team	W	L	%	Team	W	L	%
New York	87	74	.540	Chicago	95	67	.586	Oakland	91	70	.565
Boston	85	77	.525	Cleveland	90	72	.556	Seattle	91	71	.562
Toronto	83	79	.512	Detroit	79	83	.488	Anaheim	82	80	.506
Baltimore	74	88	.457	Kansas City	77	85	.475	Texas	71	91	.438
Tampa Bay	69	92	.429	Minnesota	69	93	.426				

World Series (4-1): New York Yankees over New York Mets

AL Championship Series (4-2): New York Yankees over Seattle Mariners

AL Division Series (3-2): New York Yankees over Oakland Athletics

AL Division Series (3-0): Seattle Mariners over Chicago White Sox

2001

East Division				Central Division				West Division			
Team	W	L	%	Team	W	L	%	Team	W	L	%
New York	95	65	.594	Cleveland	91	71	.562	Seattle	116	46	.716
Boston	82	79	.509	Minnesota	85	77	.525	Oakland	102	60	.630
Toronto	80	82	.494	Chicago	83	79	.512	Anaheim	75	87	.463
Baltimore	63	98	.391	Detroit	66	96	.407	Texas	73	89	.451
Tampa Bay	62	100	.383	Kansas City	65	97	.401				

World Series (4-3): Arizona Diamondbacks over New York Yankees

AL Championship Series (4-1): New York Yankees over Seattle Mariners

AL Division Series (3-2): Seattle Mariners over Cleveland Indians

AL Division Series (3-2): New York Yankees over Oakland Athletics

2002

East Division				Central Division				West Division			
Team	W	L	%	Team	W	L	%	Team	W	L	%
New York	103	58	.640	Minnesota	94	67	.584	Oakland	103	59	.636
Boston	93	69	.574	Chicago	81	81	.500	Anaheim	99	63	.611
Toronto	78	84	.481	Cleveland	74	88	.457	Seattle	93	69	.574
Baltimore	67	95	.414	Kansas City	62	100	.383	Texas	72	90	.444
Tampa Bay	55	106	.342	Detroit	55	106	.342				

World Series (4-3): Anaheim Angels over San Francisco Giants

AL Championship Series (4-1): Anaheim Angels over Minnesota Twins

AL Division Series (3-1): Anaheim Angels over New York Yankees

AL Division Series (3-2): Minnesota Twins over Oakland Athletics

2003

East Division				Central Division				West Division			
Team	W	L	%	Team	W	L	%	Team	W	L	%
New York	101	61	.623	Minnesota	90	72	.556	Oakland	96	66	.593
Boston	95	67	.586	Chicago	86	76	.531	Seattle	93	69	.574
Toronto	86	76	.531	Kansas City	83	79	.512	Anaheim	77	85	.475
Baltimore	71	91	.438	Cleveland	68	94	.420	Texas	71	91	.438
Tampa Bay	63	99	.389	Detroit	43	.265	119				

World Series (4-2): Florida Marlins over New York Yankees

AL Championship Series (4-3): New York Yankees over Boston Red Sox

AL Division Series (3-1): New York Yankees over Minnesota Twins

AL Division Series (3-2): Boston Red Sox over Oakland Athletics

2004

East Division				Central Division				West Division			
Team	W	L	%	Team	W	L	%	Team	W	L	%
								Anaheim	92	70	.568
New York	101	61	.623	Minnesota	92	70	.568	Oakland	91	71	.562
Boston	98	64	.605	Chicago	83	79	.512	Texas	89	73	.549
Baltimore	78	84	.481	Cleveland	80	82	.494	Seattle	63	99	.389
Tampa Bay	70	91	.435	Detroit	72	90	.444				
Toronto	67	94	.416	Kansas City	58	104	.358				

World Series (4-0): Boston Red Sox over St. Louis Cardinals

AL Championship Series (4-3): Boston Red Sox over New York Yankees

AL Division Series (3-0): Boston Red Sox over Anaheim Angels

AL Division Series (3-1): New York Yankees over Minnesota Twins

2005

East Division				Central Division				West Division			
Team	W	L	%	Team	W	L	%	Team	W	L	%
New York	95	87	.586	Chicago	99	63	.611	Anaheim	95	87	.586
Boston	95	87	.586	Cleveland	93	69	.574	Oakland	88	74	.543
Toronto	80	82	.494	Minnesota	83	79	.512	Texas	79	83	.488
Baltimore	74	88	.457	Detroit	71	91	.438	Seattle	69	93	.426
Tampa Bay	67	95	.414	Kansas City	56	106	.346				

World Series (4-0): Chicago White Sox over Houston Astros

AL Championship Series (4-1): Chicago White Sox over Los Angeles Angels of Anaheim

AL Division Series (3-0): Chicago White Sox over Boston Red Sox

AL Division Series (3-2): Los Angeles Angels of Anaheim over New York Yankees

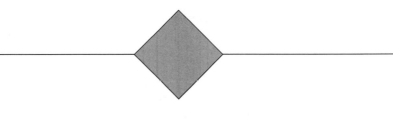

Appendix C

NATIONAL LEAGUE TEAM TOTAL ATTENDANCE, 2005–1890

Year	Arizona	Atlanta	Chicago	Cincinnati	Colorado	Florida	Houston	Los Angeles
2005	2,059,331	2,521,534	3,100,262	1,943,157	1,915,586	1,823,388	2,762,472	3,404,686
2004	2,519,560	2,327,565	3,170,154	2,287,250	2,338,069	1,723,105	3,087,872	3,488,283
2003	2,805,542	2,401,084	2,962,630	2,355,259	2,334,085	1,303,215	2,454,241	3,138,626
2002	3,198,977	2,603,484	2,693,096	1,855,787	2,737,918	813,111	2,517,357	3,131,255
2001	2,736,451	2,823,530	2,779,465	1,879,757	3,168,579	1,261,226	2,904,277	3,017,143
2000	2,942,251	3,234,304	2,789,511	2,577,371	3,149,117	1,173,389	3,056,139	2,880,242
1999	3,019,654	3,284,897	2,813,854	2,061,222	3,235,833	1,369,421	2,706,017	3,095,346
1998	3,610,290	3,360,860	2,623,194	1,793,649	3,792,683	1,750,395	2,458,451	3,089,222
1997		3,464,488	2,190,308	1,785,788	3,888,453	2,364,387	2,046,781	3,319,504
1996		2,901,242	2,219,110	1,861,428	3.891,014	1,746,767	1,975,888	3,188,454
1995		2,561,831	1,918,265	1,837,649	3,290,037	1,700,466	1,363,801	2,766,251
1994		2,539,240	1,845,208	1,897,681	4,483,350	1,937,467	1,561,136	2,279,355
1993		3,884,720	2,653,763	2,453,232	3,281,511	3,064,847	2,084,618	3,170,393
1992		3,077,400	2,126,720	2,315,946			1,211,412	2,473,266
1991		2,140,217	2,314,250	2,372,377			1,196,152	3,348,170
1990		980,129	2,243,791	2,400,892			1,310,927	3,002,396
1989		984,930	2,491,942	1,979,320			1,834,908	2,944,653
1988		848,089	2,089,034	2,072,528			1,933,505	2,980,262
1987		1,217,402	2,035,130	2,185,205			1,909,902	2,797,409
1986		1,387,181	1,859,102	1,692,432			1,734,276	3,023,208
1985		1,350,137	2,161,534	1,834,619			1,184,314	3,264,593
1984		1,724,892	2,107,655	1,275,887			1,229,862	3,134,824
1983		2,119,935	1,479,717	1,190,419			1,351,962	3,510,313
1982		1,801,985	1,249,278	1,326,528			1,558,555	3,608,881
1981		535,418	565,637	1,093,730			1,321,282	2,381,292
1980		1,048,411	1,206,776	2,022,450			2,278,217	3,249,287
1979		769,465	1,648,587	2,356,933			1,900,312	2,860,954
1978		904,494	1,525,311	2,532,497			1,126,145	3,347,845
1977		872,464	1,439,834	2,519,670			1,109,560	2,955,087
1976		818,179	1,026,217	2,629,708			886,146	2,386,301
1975		534,672	1,034,819	2,315,603			858,002	2,539,349
1974		981,085	1,015,378	2,164,307			1,090,728	2,632,474
1973		800,655	1,351,705	2,017,601			1,394,004	2,136,192
1972		752,973	1,299,163	1,611,459			1,469,247	1,860,858
1971		1,006,320	1,653,007	1,501,122			1,261,589	2,064,594
1970		1,078,848	1,642,705	1,803,568			1,253,444	1,697,142
1969		1,458,320	1,674,993	987,991			1,442,995	1,784,527
1968		1,126,540	1,043,409	733,354			1,312,887	1,581,093
1967		1,389,222	977,226	958,300			1,348,303	1,664,362
1966		1,539,801	635,891	742,958			1,872,108	2,617,029
1965		555,584	641,361	1,047,824			2,151,470	2,553,577
1964		910,911	751,647	862,466			725,773	2,228,751
1963		773,018	979,551	858,805			719,502	2,538,602
1962		766,921	609,802	982,095			924,456	2,755,184
1961		1,101,441	673,057	1,117,603				1,804,250
1960		1,497,799	809,770	663,486				2,253,887
1959		1,749,112	858,255	801,298				2,071,045

Milwaukee	New York	Philadelphia	Pittsburgh	San Diego	San Francisco	St. Louis	Washington/ Montreal
2,211,023	2,782,212	2,665,301	1,794,237	2,832,039	3,140,781	3,491,837	2,692,123
2,062,382	2,318,951	3,250,092	1,580,031	3,016,752	3,256,854	3,048,427	749,550
1,700,354	2,140,599	2,259,948	1,636,751	2,030,084	3,264,898	2,910,386	1,025,639
1,969,153	2,804,838	1,618,467	1,784,988	2,220,601	3,253,203	3,011,756	812,045
2,811,041	2,658,330	1,782,054	2,464,870	2,378,128	3,311,958	3,109,578	642,745
1,573,621	2,820,530	1,612,769	1,748,908	2,352,443	3,318,800	3,336,493	926,272
1,701,796	2,725,668	1,825,337	1,638,023	2,523,538	2,078,399	3,225,334	773,277
1,811,593	2,287,948	1,715,722	1,560,950	2,555,874	1,925,364	3,195,691	914,909
	1,766,174	1,490,638	1,657,022	2,089,333	1,690,869	2,634,014	1,497,609
	1,588,323	1,801,677	1,332,150	2,187,886	1,413,922	2,654,718	1,616,709
	1,273,183	2,043,598	905,517	1,041,805	1,241,500	1,756,727	1,309,618
	1,151,471	2,290,971	1,222,520	953,857	1,704,608	1,866,544	1,276,250
	1,873,183	3,137,674	1,650,593	1,375,432	2,606,354	2,844,977	1,641,437
	1,779,534	1,927,448	1,829,395	1,721,406	1,560,998	2,418,483	1,669,127
	2,284,484	2,050,012	2,065,302	1,804,289	1,737,478	2,448,699	934,742
	2,732,745	1,992,484	2,049,908	1,856,396	1,975,528	2,573,225	1,373,087
	2,918,710	1,861,985	1,374,141	2,009,031	2,059,701	3,080,980	1,783,533
	3,055,445	1,990,041	1,866,713	1,506,896	1,785,297	2,892,799	1,478,659
	3,034,129	2,100,110	1,161,193	1,454,061	1,917,168	3,072,122	1,850,324
	2,767,601	1,933,335	1,000,917	1,805,716	1,528,748	2,471,974	1,128,981
	2,761,601	1,830,350	735,900	2,210,352	818,697	2,637,563	1,502,494
	1,842,695	2,062,693	773,500	1,983,904	1,001,545	2,037,448	1,606,531
	1,112,774	2,128,339	1,225,916	1,539,815	1,251,530	2,317,914	2,320,651
	1,323,036	2,376,394	1,024,106	1,607,516	1,200,948	2,111,906	2,318,292
	704,244	1,638,752	541,789	519,161	632,274	1,010,247	1,534,564
	1,192,073	2,651,650	1,646,757	1,139,026	1,096,115	1,385,147	2,208,175
	788,905	2,775,011	1,435,454	1,456,967	1,456,402	1,627,256	2,102,173
	1,007,328	2,583,389	964,106	1,670,107	1,740,477	1,278,215	1,427,007
	1,066,825	2,700,070	1,237,349	1,376,269	700,056	1,659,287	1,433,757
	1,468,754	2,480,150	1,025,945	1,458,478	626,868	1,207,079	646,704
	1,730,566	1,909,233	1,270,018	1,281,747	522,919	1,695,270	908,292
	1,722,209	1,808,648	1,110,552	1,075,399	519,987	1,838,413	1,019,134
	1,912,390	1,475,934	1,319,913	611,826	834,193	1,574,046	1,246,863
	2,134,185	1,343,329	1,427,460	644,273	647,744	1,196,894	1,142,145
	2,266,680	1,511,223	1,501,132	557,513	1,106,043	1,604,671	1,290,963
	2,697,479	708,247	1,341,947	643,679	740,720	1,629,736	1,424,683
	2,175,373	519,414	769,369	512,970	873,603	1,682,783	1,212,608
	1,781,657	664,546	693,485		837,220	2,011,167	
	1,565,492	828,888	907,012		1,242,480	2,090,145	
	1,932,693	1,108,201	1,196,618		1,657,192	1,712,980	
	1,768,389	1,166,376	909,279		1,546,075	1,241,201	
	1,732,597	1,425,891	759,496		1,504,364	1,143,294	
	1,080,108	907,141	783,648		1,571,306	1,170,546	
	922,530	762,034	1,090,648		1,592,594	953,895	
		590,039	1,199,128		1,390,679	855,305	
		862,205	1,705,828		1,795,356	1,096,632	
		802,815	1,359,917		1,422,130	929,953	

Year	Arizona	Atlanta	Chicago	Cincinnati	Colorado	Florida	Houston	Los Angeles
1958		1,971,101	979,904	788,582				1,845,556
1957		2,215,404	670,629	1,070,850				1,028,258
1956		2,046,331	720,118	1,125,928				1,213,562
1955		2,005,836	875,800	693,662				1,033,589
1954		2,131,388	748,183	704,167				1,020,531
1953		1,826,397	763,658	548,086				1,163,419
1952		281,278	1,024,826	604,197				1,088,704
1951		487,475	894,415	588,268				1,282,628
1950		944,391	1,165,944	538,794				1,185,896
1949		1,081,795	1,143,139	707,782				1,633,747
1948		1,455,439	1,237,792	823,386				1,398,967
1947		1,277,361	1,364,039	899,975				1,807,526
1946		969,673	1,342,970	715,751				1,796,824
1945		374,178	1,036,386	290,070				1,059,220
1944		208,691	640,110	409,567				605,905
1943		271,289	508,247	379,122				661,739
1942		285,332	590,972	427,031				1,037,765
1941		263,680	545,159	643,513				1,214,910
1940		241,616	534,878	850,180				975,978
1939		285,994	726,663	981,443				955,668
1938		341,149	951,640	706,756				663,087
1937		385,339	895,020	411,221				482,481
1936		340,585	699,370	466,345				489,618
1935		232,754	692,604	448,247				470,517
1934		303,205	707,525	206,773				434,188
1933		517,803	594,112	218,281				526,815
1932		507,606	974,688	356,950				681,827
1931		515,005	1,086,422	263,316				753,133
1930		464,835	1,463,624	386,727				1,097,329
1929		372,351	1,485,166	295,040				731,886
1928		227,001	1,143,740	490,490				664,863
1927		288,685	1,159,168	442,164				637,230
1926		303,598	885,063	672,987				650,819
1925		313,528	622,610	464,920				659,435
1924		177,478	716,922	473,707				818,883
1923		227,802	703,705	575,063				564,666
1922		167,965	542,283	493,754				498,865
1921		318,627	410,107	311,227				613,245
1920		162,483	480,783	568,107				808,722
1919		167,401	424,430	532,501				360,721
1918		84,938	337,256	163,009				83,831
1917		174,253	360,218	269,056				221,619
1916		313,495	453,685	255,846				447,747
1915		376,283	217,058	218,878				297,766
1914		382,913	202,516	100,791				122,671
1913		208,000	419,000	258,000				347,000

Milwaukee	New York	Philadelphia	Pittsburgh	San Diego	San Francisco	St. Louis	Washington/ Montreal
		931,110	1,311,988		1,272,625	1,063,730	
		1,146,230	850,732		653,923	1,183,575	
		934,798	949,878		629,179	1,029,773	
		922,886	469,397		824,112	849,130	
		738,991	475,494		1,155,067	1,039,698	
		853,644	572,757		811,518	880,242	
		755,417	686,673		984,940	913,113	
		937,658	980,590		1,059,539	1,013,429	
		1,217,035	1,166,267		1,008,878	1,093,411	
		819,698	1,449,435		1,218,446	1,430,676	
		767,429	1,517,021		1,459,269	1,111,440	
		907,332	1,283,531		1,600,793	1,247,913	
		1,045,247	749,962		1,219,873	1,061,807	
		285,057	604,694		1,016,468	594,630	
		369,586	604,278		674,483	461,968	
		466,975	498,740		466,095	517,135	
		230,183	448,897		779,621	553,552	
		231,401	482,241		763,098	633,645	
		207,177	507,934		747,852	324,078	
		277,973	376,734		702,457	400,245	
		166,111	641,033		799,633	291,418	
		212,790	459,679		926,887	430,811	
		249,219	372,524		837,952	448,078	
		205,470	352,885		748,748	506,084	
		169,885	322,622		730,851	325,056	
		156,421	288,747		604,471	256,171	
		268,914	287,262		484,868	279,219	
		284,849	260,392		812,163	608,535	
		299,007	357,795		868,714	508,501	
		281,200	491,377		868,806	399,887	
		182,168	495,070		916,191	761,574	
		305,420	869,720		858,190	749,340	
		240,600	798,542		700,362	668,428	
		304,905	804,354		778,993	404,959	
		299,818	736,883		844,068	272,885	
		228,168	611,082		820,780	338,551	
		232,471	523,675		945,809	536,998	
		273,961	701,567		973,477	384,773	
		330,998	429,037		929,609	326,836	
		240,424	276,810		708,857	167,059	
		122,266	213,610		256,618	110,599	
		354,428	192,807		500,264	288,491	
		515,365	289,132		552,056	224,308	
		449,898	225,743		391,850	252,666	
		138,474	139,620		364,313	256,099	
		470,000	296,000		630,000	203,531	

Year	Arizona	Atlanta	Chicago	Cincinnati	Colorado	Florida	Houston	Los Angeles
1912		121,000	514,000	344,000				243,000
1911		116,000	576,000	300,000				269,000
1910		149,027	526,152	380,622				279,321
1909		195,188	633,480	424,643				321,300
1908		253,750	665,325	399,200				275,600
1907		203,221	422,550	317,500				312,500
1906		143,280	654,300	330,056				277,400
1905		150,003	509,900	313,927				227,924
1904		140,694	439,100	391,915				214,600
1903		143,155	386,205	351,680				224,670
1902		116,960	263,700	217,300				199,868
1901		146,502	205,071	205,728				198,200
1900		202,000	248,577	170,000				183,000
1899		200,384	352,130	259,536				269,641
1898		229,275	424,352	336,378				122,514
1897		334,800	327,160	336,800				220,831
1896		240,000	317,500	373,000				201,000
1895		242,000	382,300	281,000				230,000
1894		152,800	239,000	158,000				214,000
1893		193,300	223,500	194,250				235,000
1892		146,421	109,067	196,473				183,727
1891		184,472	181,431	97,500				181,477
1890		147,539	102,536	131,980				121,412

Source: Data drawn from Baseball-Reference.com, http://www.baseball-reference.com/team.

Milwaukee	New York	Philadelphia	Pittsburgh	San Diego	San Francisco	St. Louis	Washington/ Montreal
		250,000	384,000		638,000	241,759	
		416,000	432,000		675,000	447,768	
		296,597	436,586		511,785	355,668	
		303,177	534,950		783,700	299,982	
		420,660	382,444		910,000	205,129	
		341,216	319,506		538,350	185,377	
		294,680	394,877		402,850	283,770	
		317,932	369,124		552,700	292,800	
		140,771	340,615		609,826	386,750	
		151,729	326,855		579,530	226,538	
		112,066	243,826		302,875	226,417	
		234,937	251,955		297,650	379,988	
		301,913	264,000		190,000	270,000	
		388,933	251,834		121,384	373,909	
		265,414	150,900		265,414	151,700	
		290,027	165,950		390,340	136,400	
		357,025	197,000		274,000	184,000	
		474,971	188,000		240,000	170,000	
		352,773	159,000		387,000	155,000	
		293,019	184,000		290,000	195,000	
		193,731	177,205		130,566	192,442	
		217,282	128,000		210,568	60,667	
		148,366	16,064				

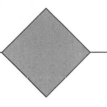

Appendix D

NATIONAL LEAGUE TEAM DAILY AVERAGE ATTENDANCE, 2005–1890

Year	Arizona	Atlanta	Chicago	Cincinnati	Colorado	Florida	Houston	Los Angeles
2005	25,423	31,519	38,753	23,989	23,944	22,792	34,530	44,489
2004	31,106	28,735	38,660	28,238	28,865	21,539	38,122	43,065
2003	34,636	29,643	36,576	29,077	28,816	16,089	30,299	38,748
2002	39,494	32,142	33,248	22,911	33,800	10,038	31,078	38,657
2001	33,783	34,858	34,314	23,207	39,097	15,765	35,855	37,249
2000	36,324	39,930	34,438	31,431	40,681	15,041	37,730	35,559
1999	37,280	40,554	34,739	25,137	42,976	17,118	33,000	38,214
1998	44,571	41,492	31,990	22,144	46,823	21,363	30,351	38,139
1997		42,771	27,041	22,047	48,006	29,190	25,269	40,982
1996		35,818	27,396	22,981	48,037	21,565	24,394	39,364
1995		35,581	26,643	25,523	47,084	23,950	18,942	38,420
1994		46,168	31,275	31,628	57,570	32,838	26,460	41,443
1993		47,960	32,363	30,287	55,350	37,838	25,736	39,141
1992		37,993	26,256	28,592			14,956	30,534
1991		26,422	27,883	29,289			14,767	41,335
1990		12,100	27,701	29,641			16,184	37,067
1989		12,467	30,765	24,436			22,377	36,354
1988		10,735	25,476	25,907			23,870	36,793
1987		15,030	25,439	26,978			23,579	34,536
1986		17,126	23,239	20,894			21,411	37,324
1985		16,668	26,686	22,650			14,621	40,304
1984		21,295	26,346	15,752			15,183	38,702
1983		26,499	18,268	14,697			16,487	43,879
1982		22,247	15,423	16,377			19,241	44,554
1981		10,708	9,752	20,254			25,907	42,523
1980		13,105	14,898	24,664			28,126	39,625
1979		9,740	20,353	29,462			23,461	35,320
1978		11,167	18,601	31,656			13,903	41,331
1977		10,771	17,776	31,107			13,698	36,483
1976		10,101	12,669	32,466			10,807	29,461
1975		6,683	12,776	28,588			10,593	31,350
1974		12,112	12,536	26,394			13,466	32,500
1973		9,885	16,896	24,909			17,210	26,373
1972		9,654	16,872	21,203			19,081	24,811
1971		12,272	20,407	18,532			15,575	25,489
1970		13,319	20,534	22,266			15,475	20,952
1969		18,004	20,427	12,197			17,815	22,031
1968		13,908	12,724	8,943			16,208	19,520
1967		17,151	11,634	11,831			16,646	20,548
1966		18,778	7,851	9,405			23,112	32,309
1965		6,859	7,727	12,936			26,561	31,526
1964		11,246	9,280	10,518			8,960	27,515
1963		9,427	12,093	10,603			8,883	31,341
1962		9,468	7,528	12,125			11,274	33,195
1961		14,304	8,629	14,514				23,432
1960		19,452	10,250	8,617				29,271
1959		22,141	11,146	10,406				26,552

Milwaukee	New York	Philadelphia	Pittsburgh	San Diego	San Francisco	St. Louis	Washington
27,296	35,217	33,316	23,003	35,400	39,259	43,647	33,651
25,462	25,462	40,125	19,750	37,244	39,718	37,635	9,369
20,992	20,992	27,901	20,207	25,063	40,307	35,931	12,662
24,311	24,311	20,231	22,312	27,415	40,163	37,182	10,025
34,704	34,704	22,001	30,430	29,360	40,888	37,922	7,935
19,427	19,427	19,911	21,591	29,043	40,973	41,191	11,435
21,272	21,272	22,535	20,223	31,155	25,659	40,317	9,547
22,365	22,365	21,182	19,271	31,554	23,770	38,972	11,295
	18,050	18,403	20,457	25,794	20,875	32,519	18,489
	16,385	22,243	16,652	27,011	17,243	32,774	19,959
	15,105	28,383	12,577	14,470	17,243	24,399	18,189
	22,650	38,183	20,041	16,734	28,410	33,331	24,543
	20,840	38,737	20,378	16,981	32,177	35,123	20,265
	22,930	23,796	22,585	21,252	19,272	29,858	20,607
	18,484	24,699	24,587	22,275	21,450	29,151	13,746
	21,641	24,599	25,308	22,918	24,389	31,768	16,952
	24,330	22,987	16,965	24,803	25,428	37,120	22,019
	23,744	24,568	23,046	18,604	22,041	35,714	18,255
	23,571	25,927	14,336	17,951	23,669	37,927	22,844
	15,813	24,167	12,357	22,293	18,873	30,518	14,112
	17,003	22,597	9,199	27,288	10,107	32,563	18,549
	19,858	25,465	9,549	24,493	12,365	25,154	19,834
	29,594	25,955	15,135	18,778	15,451	28,616	28,650
	24,133	29,338	12,643	19,846	14,827	26,073	28,621
	17,843	29,795	10,623	9,439	11,930	19,061	27,403
	22,651	32,736	20,330	14,062	13,532	17,101	27,602
	23,683	34,259	17,722	17,987	17,980	19,845	25,953
	19,770	31,505	11,903	20,619	21,487	15,780	17,838
	13,765	33,334	15,276	16,991	8,643	19,991	17,701
	12,496	30,619	12,666	18,231	7,739	14,902	8,084
	14,980	23,571	15,875	15,824	6,456	20,674	11,213
	11,799	22,329	13,711	13,277	6,420	22,696	12,739
	13,483	18,221	16,295	7,553	10,299	19,433	15,393
	7,601	17,004	18,301	8,053	8,412	15,544	14,643
	8,921	18,657	18,764	6,883	13,655	19,569	16,137
	11,527	8,853	16,365	7,947	9,145	20,120	17,809
	8,268	6,413	9,498	6,333	10,785	21,035	14,970
	21,728	8,204	8,562		10,336	24,829	
	20,070	10,361	11,198		15,152	25,804	
	23,860	13,681	14,773		20,459	21,148	
	21,566	14,580	11,089		19,087	15,323	
	21,129	17,604	9,376		18,572	14,115	
	13,335	11,199	9,675		19,399	14,451	
	11,532	9,525	13,465		19,422	11,776	
		7,565	15,573		18,061	10,965	
		11,197	21,870		23,316	14,242	
		10,292	17,661		18,469	12,077	

Year	Arizona	Atlanta	Chicago	Cincinnati	Colorado	Florida	Houston	Los Angeles
1958		25,599	12,726	10,241				23,968
1957		28,403	8,598	13,907				13,354
1956		26,576	9,001	14,622				15,761
1955		26,050	11,374	9,009				13,423
1954		27,680	9,717	9,145				13,254
1953		23,119	9,918	7,027				14,916
1952		3,653	13,309	7,847				13,609
1951		6,250	11,616	7,640				16,444
1950		11,954	14,948	7,089				15,204
1949		14,049	14,846	9,074				20,945
1948		19,151	15,869	10,693				17,935
1947		16,589	17,266	11,688				23,173
1946		12,593	17,441	9,295				22,745
1945		4,989	13,637	3,767				13,580
1944		2,676	8,207	5,251				7,869
1943		3,523	6,777	4,861				8,594
1942		4,019	7,577	5,546				13,136
1941		3,469	7,080	8,146				15,379
1940		3,222	6,946	11,041				12,049
1939		3,918	9,083	12,117				12,252
1938		4,549	12,359	9,179				8,961
1937		5,070	11,475	5,140				6,348
1936		4,311	9,083	6,136				6,198
1935		3,103	8,995	5,898				6,111
1934		4,043	9,189	2,651				5,639
1933		6,725	7,520	2,763				6,585
1932		6,592	12,658	4,636				8,741
1931		6,603	14,109	3,420				9,910
1930		6,037	18,527	5,022				14,251
1929		4,836	19,041	3,783				9,505
1928		2,987	14,854	6,288				8,635
1927		3,901	14,861	5,527				8,611
1926		3,943	11,347	8,740				8,563
1925		4,125	8,086	6,117				8,564
1924		2,335	9,191	6,233				10,635
1923		2,958	9,139	7,373				7,239
1922		2,210	7,135	6,250				6,396
1921		4,306	5,396	4,095				7,862
1920		2,196	6,244	7,378				10,368
1919		2,462	5,978	7,607				5,153
1918		1,633	4,558	2,296				1,552
1917		2,263	4,678	3,363				2,841
1916		4,019	5,743	3,366				5,740
1915		4,824	2,819	2,771				3,818
1914		4,847	2,665	1,309				1,553
1913		2,701	5,513	3,308				4,506

Milwaukee	New York	Philadelphia	Pittsburgh	San Diego	San Francisco	St. Louis	Washington
		12,092	17,039		16,528	13,815	
		14,695	11,048		8,493	15,371	
		12,140	12,178		8,171	13,202	
		11,986	6,259		10,432	11,028	
		9,474	6,175		15,198	13,503	
		10,944	7,438		10,539	11,285	
		9,940	8,918		12,791	11,859	
		12,177	12,572		13,584	12,828	
		15,603	15,146		13,275	14,387	
		10,645	18,824		15,423	18,110	
		10,098	18,963		18,952	14,434	
		11,784	16,247		21,063	16,207	
		13,401	9,615		15,843	13,613	
		3,702	7,654		13,032	7,623	
		4,678	7,460		8,993	6,000	
		5,987	6,394		6,053	6,384	
		3,111	5,830		9,869	7,097	
		3,045	6,183		9,783	8,021	
		2,622	6,772		9,840	4,209	
		3,756	4,893		9,493	5,066	
		2,215	8,218		10,954	3,598	
		2,876	5,893		12,358	5,385	
		3,195	4,902		10,743	5,819	
		2,601	4,583		9,478	6,573	
		2,393	4,136		9,745	4,222	
		2,173	3,750		7,850	3,327	
		3,492	3,780		6,297	3,534	
		3,748	3,338		10,412	7,802	
		3,883	4,647		11,282	6,604	
		3,700	6,465		11,283	5,193	
		2,429	6,429		11,899	9,891	
		3,916	11,009		11,597	9,367	
		3,166	10,108		9,215	8,461	
		3,960	10,446		10,250	5,328	
		3,945	9,570		10,962	3,544	
		3,042	7,936		10,659	4,340	
		3,019	6,714		11,972	6,974	
		3,605	9,231		12,322	4,933	
		4,299	5,500		11,620	4,300	
		3,386	3,954		10,273	2,421	
		2,145	3,009		4,582	1,515	
		4,664	2,441		6,253	3,699	
		6,524	3,707		7,078	2,951	
		5,920	2,858		5,156	3,119	
		1,775	1,813		4,554	3,242	
		6,026	3,747		7,778	2,750	

Year	Arizona	Atlanta	Chicago	Cincinnati	Colorado	Florida	Houston	Los Angeles
1912		1,532	6,590	4,468				3,197
1911		1,547	6,857	3,659				3,635
1910		1,911	6,833	4,943				3,492
1909		2,568	8,227	5,308				4,067
1908		3,253	8,530	5,184				3,579
1907		2,746	5,560	3,920				4,058
1906		1,885	8,282	4,231				3,650
1905		1,974	6,295	3,974				2,960
1904		1,781	5,629	4,961				2,824
1903		2,105	5,290	4,627				3,078
1902		1,624	3,767	3,104				2,897
1901		2,093	2,930	2,857				2,915
1900		2,845	3,405	2,361				2,577
1899		2,619	4,633	3,327				3,595
1898		3,017	5,584	4,285				1,644
1897		4,960	4,741	5,027				3,248
1896		3,636	4,811	5,828				3,023
1895		3,667	5,749	4,258				3,459
1894		2,298	3,541	2,394				3,194
1893		2,951	3,492	2,966				3,615
1892		1,927	1,484	2,535				2,326
1891		2,635	2,649	1,413				2,649
1890		2,202	1,475	1,970				1,882

Source: *Data drawn from Baseball-Reference.com, http://www.baseball-reference.com/teams/attend.shtml.*

Milwaukee	New York	Philadelphia	Pittsburgh	San Diego	San Francisco	St. Louis	Washington
		3,333	5,120		8,395	3,140	
		5,474	5,538		9,000	5,668	
		3,803	5,745		6,478	4,680	
		3,937	6,858		10,178	3,947	
		5,393	4,967		11,375	2,664	
		4,550	4,149		6,992	2,347	
		3,827	5,128		5,371	3,685	
		4,183	4,732		7,272	3,803	
		1,928	4,367		7,260	5,089	
		2,487	4,669		8,279	3,283	
		1,624	3,434		4,266	3,235	
		3,405	3,652		4,192	5,278	
		4,282	3,771		2,695	3,803	
		5,051	3,271		1,597	4,825	
		3,539	1,986		3,381	1,970	
		4,329	2,459		5,698	2,067	
		5,493	3,008		4,120	2,809	
		7,142	2,806		3,636	2,519	
		5,169	2,409		5,650	2,331	
		4,406	2,809		4,265	2,889	
		2,500	2,287		1,707	2,483	
		3,149	1,869		3,097		
		2,231	233		899		

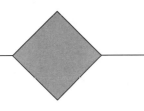

Appendix E

NATIONAL LEAGUE TEAM ATTENDANCE RANKINGS,
2005–1890

Year	Arizona	Atlanta	Chicago	Cincinnati	Colorado	Florida	Houston	Los Angeles
2005	12	10	4	13	14	15	7	1
2004	8	10	4	12	9	14	5	1
2003	5	7	3	8	9	15	6	2
2002	2	8	7	12	6	15	9	3
2001	9	6	8	13	2	15	5	4
2000	6	4	9	10	3	15	5	7
1999	5	2	6	11	1	15	8	4
1998	2	3	6	1	1	13	8	5
1997		2	6	9	1	5	8	3
1996		3	5	8	1	10	7	2
1995		3	5	6	1	8	9	2
1994		2	8	7	1	6	10	3
1993		2	7	9	1	5	10	3
1992		1	5	4			12	2
1991		6	4	2			11	1
1990		12	5	4			11	1
1989		12	4	7			9	2
1988		12	5	4			7	2
1987		11	6	4			8	3
1986		10	5	8			7	1
1985		9	5	6			10	1
1984		7	2	9			10	1
1983		4	7	11			8	1
1982		5	10	82			7	1
1981		9	11	5			4	1
1980		12	8	5			3	1
1979		11	6	3			5	1
1978		12	6	2			9	1
1977		11	5	3			9	1
1976		10	7	1			9	3
1975		11	8	2			10	1
1974		11	10	2			7	1
1973		11	7	2			6	1
1972		10	7	3			4	2
1971		11	3	7			9	2
1970		9	4	2			8	3
1969		5	4	8			6	2
1968		5	6	8			4	3
1967		4	8	7			5	2
1966		6	10	9			3	1
1965		10	9	7			2	1
1964		6	9	7			10	1
1963		9	5	7			10	1
1962		9	10	4			7	1
1961		5	7	4				1
1960		4	7	8				1
1959		2	6	7				1

Milwaukee	New York	Philadelphia	Pittsburgh	San Diego	San Francisco	St. Louis	Washington
11	6	9	16	5	3	2	8
13	11	2	15	7	3	6	16
13	11	10	14	12	1	4	16
11	5	14	13	10	1	4	16
7	10	14	11	12	1	3	16
14	8	13	12	11	2	1	16
13	7	12	14	9	10	3	16
11	9	14	15	7	10	4	16
	10	14	12	7	11	4	13
	12	9	14	6	13	4	11
	11	4	14	13	12	7	10
	12	4	13	14	9	5	11
	11	4	12	14	8	6	13
	8	6	7	9	11	3	10
	5	7	8	9	10	3	12
	2	7	6	9	8	3	10
	3	8	11	6	5	1	10
	1	6	8	10	9	3	11
	2	5	12	10	7	1	9
	2	4	12	6	9	3	11
	2	7	12	4	11	3	8
	6	3	12	5	11	4	8
	12	5	10	6	9	3	2
	9	2	12	6	11	4	3
	7	2	10	12	8	6	3
	9	2	6	10	11	7	4
	12	2	10	8	9	7	4
	10	3	11	5	4	8	7
	10	2	8	7	12	4	6
	5	2	8	4	12	6	11
	4	3	6	7	12	5	9
	5	4	6	8	12	3	9
	3	5	8	12	10	4	9
	1	6	5	12	11	8	9
	1	6	5	12	10	4	8
	1	11	7	12	10	5	6
	1	11	10	12	9	3	7
	2	10	9		7	1	
	3	10	9		6	1	
	2	8	7		5	4	
	3	6	8		4	5	
	2	4	8		3	5	
	4	6	8		2	3	
	6	8	3		2	5	
		8	3		2	6	
		6	3		2	5	
		8	4		3	5	

Year	Arizona	Atlanta	Chicago	Cincinnati	Colorado	Florida	Houston	Los Angeles
1958		1	6	8				2
1957		1	7	4				5
1956		1	7	3				2
1955		1	4	7				2
1954		1	5	7				4
1953		1	6	8				2
1952		8	2	7				1
1951		8	6	7				1
1950		7	4	8				2
1949		6	5	8				1
1948		1	5	7				4
1947		4	3	8				1
1946		6	2	8				1
1945		6	1	7				2
1944		8	2	6				3
1943		8	2	7				1
1942		7	3	6				1
1941		7	5	3				1
1940		7	4	2				1
1939		7	4	2				1
1938		6	1	3				4
1937		7	2	6				3
1936		7	2	4				3
1935		7	2	5				4
1934		6	2	7				3
1933		3	2	7				4
1932		3	1	5				2
1931		5	1	7				3
1930		5	1	6				2
1929		6	1	7				3
1928		7	1	6				4
1927		8	1	6				5
1926		7	1	4				5
1925		7	4	5				3
1924		8	4	5				2
1923		8	2	4				5
1922		8	2	6				5
1921		6	4	7				3
1920		8	4	3				2
1919		7	3	2				4
1918		6	2	4				7
1917		8	2	5				6
1916		5	3	7				4
1915		3	7	8				4
1914		1	4	8				7
1913		8	3	6				4

Milwaukee	New York	Philadelphia	Pittsburgh	San Diego	San Francisco	St. Louis	Washington
		7	3		4	5	
		3	6		8	2	
		6	5		8	4	
		3	8		6	5	
		6	8		2	3	
		4	7		5	3	
		5	6		3	4	
		5	4		2	3	
		1	3		6	5	
		7	2		4	3	
		8	2		3	6	
		7	5		2	6	
		5	7		3	4	
		8	4		3	5	
		7	4		1	5	
		6	3		5	4	
		8	5		2	4	
		8	6		2	4	
		8	5		3	6	
		8	6		3	5	
		8	5		2	7	
		8	4		1	5	
		8	6		1	5	
		8	6		1	3	
		8	5		1	4	
		8	5		1	6	
		8	6		4	7	
		6	8		2	4	
		8	7		3	4	
		8	4		2	5	
		8	5		2	3	
		7	3		2	4	
		8	2		3	6	
		8	1		2	6	
		6	3		1	7	
		7	3		1	6	
		7	4		1	3	
		8	2		1	5	
		7	5		1	6	
		6	5		1	8	
		5	3		1	8	
		3	7		1	4	
		2	6		1	8	
		1	6		2	5	
		6	5		2	3	
		2	5		1	7	

Year	Arizona	Atlanta	Chicago	Cincinnati	Colorado	Florida	Houston	Los Angeles
1912		8	2	4				6
1911		8	2	6				7
1910		8	1	4				7
1909		8	2	4				5
1908		7	2	4				6
1907		7	2	6				5
1906		8	1	4				7
1905		8	2	5				7
1904		8	2	4				6
1903		8	2	4				6
1902		7	2	5				6
1901		8	5	7				6
1900		5	4	8				7
1899		7	3	5				4
1898		5	1	2				9
1897		3	4	2				7
1896		6	3	1				8
1895		5	2	4				7
1894		9	4	7				5
1893		6	4	5				3
1892		6	1	1				4
1891		5	4	8				3
1890		2	5	3				4

Source: *Data drawn from Baseball-Reference.com, http://www.baseball-reference.com/teams/attend.shtml.*

Milwaukee	New York	Philadelphia	Pittsburgh	San Diego	San Francisco	St. Louis	Washington
		5	3		1	7	
		5	4		1	3	
		6	3		2	5	
		7	3		1	6	
		3	5		1	8	
		3	4		1	8	
		5	3		2	6	
		4	3		1	6	
		7	5		1	3	
		7	3		1	5	
		8	3		1	4	
		4	3		2	1	
		1	3		6	2	
		1	6		9	2	
		3	6		4	7	
		5	8		1	11	
		2	9		4	10	
		1	8		6	9	
		2	6		1	8	
		1	8		2	7	
		2	5		8	3	
		1	7		2		
		1	8		6		

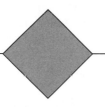

Appendix F

AMERICAN LEAGUE TEAM TOTAL ATTENDANCE, 2005–1901

Year	Baltimore	Boston	Chicago	Claveland	Detroit	Kansas City	Los Angeles
2005	2,624,804	2,813,354	2,342,834	1,973,185	2,024,505	1,371,181	3,404,686
2004	2,744,018	2,837,294	1,930,537	1,814,401	1,917,004	1,661,478	3,375,677
2003	2,454,523	2,724,165	1,939,524	1,730,002	1,368,245	1,779,895	3,061,094
2002	2,682,439	2,650,862	1,676,911	2,616,940	1,503,623	1,323,036	2,305,547
2001	3,094,841	2,625,333	1,766,172	3,175,523	1,921,305	1,536,371	2,000,919
2000	3,297,031	2,585,895	1,947,799	3,456,278	2,438,617	1,564,847	2,066,982
1999	3,433,150	2,446,162	1,338,851	3,468,456	2,026,441	1,506,068	2,253,123
1998	3,684,650	2,314,704	1,391,146	3,467,299	1,409,391	1,494,875	2,519,280
1997	3,711,132	2,226,136	1,864,782	3,404,750	1,365,157	1,517,638	1,767,330
1996	3,646,950	2,315,231	1,676,403	3,318,174	1,168,610	1,435,997	1,820,521
1995	3,098,475	2,164,410	1,609,773	2,842,745	1,180,979	1,233,530	1,748,680
1994	2,535,359	1,775,818	1,697,398	1,995,174	1,184,783	1,400,494	1,512,622
1993	3,644,965	2,422,021	2,581,091	2,177,908	1,971,421	1,934,578	2,057,460
1992	3,567,819	2,468,574	2,681,156	1,224,094	1,423,963	1,867,689	2,065,444
1991	2,552,753	2,562,435	2,934,154	1,051,863	1,641,661	2,161,537	2,416,236
1990	2,415,189	2,528,986	2,002,357	1,225,240	1,495,785	2,244,956	2,555,688
1989	2,535,208	2,510,012	1,045,651	1,285,542	1,543,656	2,477,700	2,647,291
1988	1,660,738	2,464,851	1,115,749	1,411,610	2,081,162	2,350,181	2,340,925
1987	1,835,692	2,231,551	1,208,060	1,077,898	2,061,830	2,392,471	2,696,299
1986	1,973,176	2,147,641	1,424,313	1,471,805	1,899,437	2,320,794	2,655,872
1985	2,132,387	1,786,633	1,669,888	655,181	2,286,609	2,162,717	2,567,427
1984	2,045,784	1,661,618	2,136,988	734,079	2,704,794	1,810,018	2,402,997
1983	2,042,071	1,782,285	2,132,821	768,941	1,829,636	1,963,875	2,555,016
1982	1,613,031	1,950,124	1,567,787	1,044,021	1,636,058	2,284,464	2,807,360
1981	1,024,247	1,060,379	946,651	661,395	1,149,144	1,279,403	1,441,545
1980	1,797,438	1,956,092	1,200,365	1,033,827	1,785,293	2,288,714	2,297,327
1979	1,681,009	2,353,114	1,280,702	1,011,644	1,630,929	2,261,845	2,523,575
1978	1,051,724	2,320,643	1,491,100	800,584	1,714,893	2,255,493	1,755,386
1977	1,195,769	2,074,549	1,657,135	900,365	1,359,856	1,852,603	1,432,633
1976	1,058,609	1,895,846	914,945	948,776	1,467,020	1,680,265	1,006,774
1975	1,002,157	1,748,587	750,802	977,039	1,058,836	1,151,836	1,058,163
1974	962,572	1,556,411	1,149,596	1,114,262	1,243,080	1,173,292	917,269
1973	958,667	1,481,002	1,302,527	615,107	1,724,146	1,345,341	1,058,206
1972	899,950	1,441,718	1,177,318	626,354	1,892,386	707,656	744,190
1971	1,023,037	1,678,732	833,891	591,361	1,591,073	910,784	926,373
1970	1,057,069	1,595,278	495,355	729,752	1,501,293	693,047	1,077,741
1969	1,062,069	1,833,246	589,546	619,970	1,577,481	902,414	758,388
1968	943,977	1,940,788	803,775	857,994	2,031,847		1,025,956
1967	955,053	1,727,832	985,634	662,980	1,447,143		1,317,713
1966	1,203,366	811,172	990,016	903,359	1,124,293		1,400,321
1965	781,649	652,201	1,130,519	934,786	1,029,645		566,727
1964	1,116,215	883,276	1,250,053	653,293	816,139		760,439
1963	774,343	942,642	1,158,848	562,507	821,952		821,015
1962	790,254	733,080	1,131,562	716,076	1,207,881		1,144,063
1961	951,089	850,589	1,146,019	725,547	1,600,710		603,510
1960	1,187,849	1,129,866	1,644,460	950,985	1,167,669		
1959	891,926	984,102	1,423,144	1,497,976	1,221,221		
1958	829,991	1,077,047	797,451	663,805	1,098,924		

Milwaukee	Minnesota	New York	Oakland	Seattle	Tampa Bay	Texas	Toronto
	2,013,453	4,090,440	2,109,298	2,689,529	1,124,189	2,486,925	1,977,949
	1,911,490	3,775,292	2,201,516	2,940,731	1,274,911	2,513,685	1,900,041
	1,946,011	3,465,600	2,216,596	3,268,509	1,058,695	2,513,685	1,799,458
	1,924,473	3,465,807	2,169,811	3,542,938	1,065,742	2,094,394	1,637,900
	1,782,929	3,264,907	2,133,277	3,507,326	1,298,365	2,831,021	1,915,438
	1,000,760	3,055,435	1,603,744	2,914,624	1,449,673	2,588,401	1,705,712
	1,202,829	3,292,736	1,434,610	2,916,346	1,562,827	2,771,469	2,163,464
	1,165,976	2,955,193	1,232,343	2,651,511	2,506,293	2,927,399	2,454,303
	1,411,064	2,580,325	1,264,218	3,192,237		2,945,228	2,589,297
	1,437,352	2,250,877	1,148,380	2,723,850		2,889,020	2,094,394
	1,057,667	1,705,263	1,174,310	1,643,203		1,985,910	2,352,397
	1,398,565	1,675,556	1,242,692	1,104,206		2,503,198	2,907,933
	2,048,673	2,416,942	2,035,025	2,052,638		2,244,616	4,057,947
	2,482,428	1,748,737	2,494,160	1,651,367		2,198,231	4,028,318
	2,293,842	1,863,733	2,713,493	2,147,905		2,297,720	4,001,527
	1,751,584	2,006,436	2,900,217	1,509,727		2,057,911	3,885,284
1,970,735	2,277,438	2,170,485	2,667,225	1,298,443		2,043,993	3,375,883
1,923,238	3,030,672	2,633,701	2,287,335	1,022,398		1,581,901	2,595,175
1,909,244	2,081,976	2,427,672	1,678,921	1,134,255		1,763,053	2,778,429
1,265,041	1,255,453	2,268,030	1,314,646	1,029,045		1,692,002	2,455,477
1,360,265	1,651,814	2,214,587	1,334,599	1,128,696		1,112,497	2,468,925
1,608,509	1,598,692	1,821,815	1,353,281	870,372		1,102,471	2,110,009
2,397,131	858,939	2,257,976	1,294,941	813,537		1,363,469	1,930,415
1,978,896	921,186	2,041,219	1,735,489	1,070,404		1,154,432	1,275,978
874,292	469,090	1,614,353	1,304,052	636,276		850,076	755,083
1,857,408	769,206	2,627,417	842,259	836,204		1,198,175	1,400,327
1,918,343	1,070,521	2,537,765	306,763	844,447		1,519,671	1,431,651
1,601,406	787,878	2,335,871	526,999	877,440		1,447,963	1,562,585
1,114,938	1,162,727	2,103,092	495,599	1,338,511		1,250,722	1,701,052
1,012,164	715,394	2,012,434	780,593			1,164,982	
1,213,357	737,156	1,288,048	1,075,518			1,127,924	
955,741	662,401	1,273,075	845,693			1,193,902	
1,092,158	907,499	1,262,103	1,000,763			686,085	
600,440	797,901	966,328	921,323			662,974	
731,531	940,858	1,070,771	914,993			655,156	
933,690	1,261,887	1,136,879	778,355			824,789	
677,944	1,349,328	1,067,996	778,232			918,106	
	1,143,257	1,185,666	837,466			546,661	
	1,483,547	1,259,514	726,639			770,868	
	1,259,374	1,124,648	773,929			576,260	
	1,463,258	1,213,552	528,344			560,083	
	1,207,514	1,305,638	642,478			600,106	
	1,406,652	1,308,920	762,364			535,604	
	1,433,116	1,493,574	635,675			729,775	
	1,256,723	1,747,725	683,817			597,287	
	743,404	1,627,349	774,944				
	615,372	1,552,030	963,683				
	475,288	1,428,438	925,090				

Year	Baltimore	Boston	Chicago	Claveland	Detroit	Kansas City	Los Angeles
1957	1,029,581	1,181,087	1,135,668	722,256	1,272,346		
1956	901,201	1,137,158	1,000,090	865,467	1,051,182		
1955	852,039	1,203,200	1,175,684	1,221,780	1,181,838		
1954	1,060,910	931,127	1,231,629	1,335,472	1,079,847		
1953	297,238	1,026,133	1,191,353	1,069,176	884,658		
1952	518,796	1,115,750	1,231,675	1,444,607	1,026,846		
1951	293,790	1,312,282	1,328,234	1,704,984	1,132,641		
1950	247,131	1,344,080	781,330	1,727,464	1,951,474		
1949	270,936	1,596,650	937,151	2,233,771	1,821,204		
1948	335,564	1,558,798	777,844	2,620,627	1,743,035		
1947	320,474	1,427,315	876,948	1,521,978	1,398,093		
1946	526,435	1,416,944	983,403	1,057,289	1,722,590		
1945	482,986	603,794	657,981	558,182	1,280,341		
1944	508,644	506,975	563,539	475,272	923,176		
1943	214,392	358,275	508,962	438,894	606,287		
1942	255,617	730,340	425,734	459,447	580,087		
1941	176,240	718,497	677,077	745,948	684,915		
1940	239,591	716,234	660,336	902,576	1,112,693		
1939	109,159	573,070	594,104	563,926	836,279		
1938	130,417	646,459	338,278	652,006	799,557		
1937	123,121	559,659	589,245	564,849	1,072,276		
1936	93,267	626,895	440,810	500,391	875,948		
1935	80,922	558,568	470,281	397,615	1,034,929		
1934	115,305	610,640	236,559	391,338	919,161		
1933	88,113	268,715	397,789	387,936	320,972		
1932	112,558	182,150	233,198	468,953	397,157		
1931	179,126	350,975	403,550	483,027	434,056		
1930	152,088	444,045	406,123	528,657	649,450		
1929	280,697	394,620	426,795	536,210	869,318		
1928	339,497	396,920	494,152	375,907	474,323		
1927	247,879	305,275	614,423	373,138	773,716		
1926	283,986	285,155	710,339	627,426	711,914		
1925	462,898	267,782	832,231	419,005	820,766		
1924	533,349	448,556	606,658	481,905	1,015,136		
1923	430,296	229,688	573,778	558,856	911,377		
1922	712,918	259,184	602,860	528,145	861,206		
1921	355,978	279,273	543,650	748,705	661,527		
1920	419,311	402,445	833,492	912,832	579,650		
1919	349,350	417,291	627,186	538,135	643,805		
1918	122,076	249,513	195,081	295,515	203,719		
1917	210,486	387,856	684,521	477,298	457,289		
1916	335,740	496,397	679,923	492,106	616,772		
1915	150,358	539,885	539,461	159,285	476,105		
1914	244,714	481,359	469,290	185,997	416,225		
1913	250,330	437,194	644,501	541,000	398,502		
1912	214,070	597,096	602,241	336,844	402,870		

Milwaukee	Minnesota	New York	Oakland	Seattle	Tampa Bay	Texas	Toronto
	457,079	1,497,134	901,067				
	431,647	1,491,784	1,015,154				
	425,238	1,490,138	1,393,054				
	503,542	1,475,171	304,666				
	595,594	1,537,811	362,113				
	699,457	1,629,665	627,100				
	695,167	1,950,107	465,469				
	699,697	2,081,380	309,805				
	770,745	2,283,676	816,514				
	795,254	2,373,901	945,076				
	850,758	2,178,937	911,566				
	1,027,216	2,265,512	621,793				
	652,660	881,845	462,631				
	525,235	789,995	505,322				
	574,694	618,330	376,735				
	403,493	922,011	423,487				
	415,663	964,722	528,894				
	381,241	988,975	432,145				
	339,257	859,785	395,022				
	522,694	970,916	385,357				
	397,799	998,148	430,738				
	379,525	976,913	285,173				
	255,011	657,508	233,173				
	330,074	854,682	305,847				
	437,533	728,014	297,138				
	371,396	962,320	405,500				
	492,657	912,437	627,464				
	614,474	1,169,230	721,663				
	355,506	960,148	839,176				
	378,501	1,072,132	689,756				
	528,976	1,164,015	605,529				
	551,580	1,027,675	714,508				
	817,199	697,267	869,703				
	584,310	1,053,533	531,992				
	357,406	1,007,066	534,122				
	458,552	1,026,134	425,356				
	456,069	1,230,696	344,430				
	359,260	1,289,422	287,888				
	234,096	619,164	225,209				
	182,122	282,047	177,926				
	89,682	330,294	221,432				
	177,265	469,211	184,471				
	167,332	256,035	146,223				
	243,888	359,477	346,641				
	325,831	357,551	571,896				
	350,663	242,194	517,653				

Year	Baltimore	Boston	Chicago	Claveland	Detroit	Kansas City	Los Angeles
1911	207,984	503,961	583,208	406,296	484,988		
1910	249,889	584,619	552,084	293,456	391,288		
1909	366,274	668,965	478,400	354,627	490,490		
1908	618,947	473,048	636,096	422,262	436,199		
1907	419,025	436,777	666,307	382,046	297,079		
1906	389,157	410,209	585,202	325,733	174,043		
1905	339,112	468,828	687,419	316,306	193,384		
1904	318,108	623,295	557,123	264,749	177,796		
1903	380,405	379,338	286,183	311,280	224,523		
1902	272,283	348,567	337,898	275,395	189,469		
1901	139,034	289,448	354,350	131,380	259,430		

Source: *Data drawn from Baseball-Reference.com, http://www.baseball-reference.com/teams/attend.shtml.*

Milwaukee	Minnesota	New York	Oakland	Seattle	Tampa Bay	Texas	Toronto
	244,884	302,444	605,749				
	254,591	355,857	588,905				
	205,199	501,000	674,915				
	264,252	305,500	455,062				
	221,929	350,020	625,581				
	129,903	434,700	489,129				
	252,027	309,100	554,576				
	131,744	438,919	512,294				
	128,878	211,808	422,473				
	188,158	174,606	420,078				
	161,661	141,952	206,329				

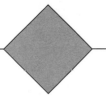

Appendix G

AMERICAN LEAGUE TEAM AVERAGE DAILY ATTENDANCE, 2005–1901

Year	Baltimore	Boston	Chicago	Cleveland	Detroit	Kansas City	Los Angeles
2005	32,404	35,166	28,923	24,664	25,306	17,356	42,033
2004	33,877	35,028	23,834	22,400	23,667	20,768	41,675
2003	30,303	33,632	23,945	21,358	16,892	22,249	37,330
2002	33,117	32,727	20,703	32,308	18,795	16,334	28,464
2001	38,686	32,412	21,805	39,694	23,720	18,968	24,703
2000	40,704	31,925	24,047	42,670	30,106	19,319	25,518
1999	42,385	30,200	16,529	42,820	25,018	18,826	27,816
1998	45,490	28,577	16,965	42,806	17,400	18,686	31,102
1997	45,816	27,483	23,022	42,034	16,854	18,970	21,553
1996	44,475	28,583	20,696	41,477	14,427	17,950	22,476
1995	43,034	30,061	22,358	39,483	16,402	17,132	24,287
1994	46,097	27,747	32,026	39,121	20,427	23,737	24,010
1993	45,000	29,901	31,865	26,888	24,339	23,884	25,401
1992	44,047	30,476	32,697	15,112	17,800	23,058	25,499
1991	31,515	31,635	36,224	12,828	20,267	26,686	29,830
1990	30,190	31,222	25,029	15,126	18,466	27,716	31,552
1989	31,299	30,988	13,071	15,871	19,057	30,589	32,683
1988	20,759	30,430	13,775	17,427	25,693	29,377	28,900
1987	22,386	27,894	14,914	13,307	25,455	29,537	33,288
1986	24,977	26,514	17,584	18,170	23,450	28,652	32,389
1985	26,326	22,057	20,616	8,089	28,230	26,375	32,499
1984	25,257	20,514	26,383	9,063	32,985	22,346	29,667
1983	25,211	22,004	26,331	9,493	22,588	23,950	31,543
1982	19,671	24,076	19,597	12,889	20,198	28,203	34,659
1981	18,623	20,007	19,319	12,248	20,894	27,221	26,695
1980	22,191	24,149	14,819	13,086	21,772	28,256	28,362
1979	21,279	29,414	16,211	12,489	20,387	27,924	31,155
1978	12,984	28,301	18,639	10,264	21,172	27,846	21,671
1977	14,763	25,932	20,458	11,116	16,788	22,872	17,687
1976	13,069	23,406	11,437	12,010	18,338	20,744	12,429
1975	13,015	21,587	9,269	12,213	13,235	14,220	13,064
1974	11,884	19,215	14,019	13,756	15,347	14,485	11,324
1973	11,835	18,284	16,081	7,594	21,286	16,609	13,064
1972	11,688	18,484	15,094	8,134	24,261	9,190	9,302
1971	13,286	20,984	10,295	7,301	19,643	11,244	11,437
1970	13,050	19,695	5,897	9,009	18,534	8,773	13,305
1969	13,112	22,633	7,278	7,654	19,475	11,005	9,363
1968	11,800	23,960	9,923	10,593	25,085		12,666
1967	12,403	21,331	12,020	8,185	17,648		15,876
1966	15,232	10,014	12,222	11,153	13,880		17,288
1965	9,894	8,052	13,957	11,400	12,712		7,084
1964	13,612	10,905	15,433	7,967	9,953		9,388
1963	9,560	11,783	14,132	6,945	10,148		10,136
1962	9,637	9,279	13,970	8,840	14,730		14,124
1961	11,599	10,373	14,148	8,957	19,521		7,360
1960	15,427	14,674	21,357	12,350	15,165		
1959	11,435	12,781	18,245	19,454	15,860		
1958	10,641	13,988	10,357	8,734	14,272		

Milwaukee	Minnesota	New York	Oakland	Seattle	Tampa Bay	Texas	Toronto
	25,168	50,499	26,040	33,619	14,052	31,480	24,724
	23,599	46,609	27,179	35,863	15,936	25,857	23,457
	24,025	42,263	27,365	40,352	13,070	29,042	22,216
	23,759	43,323	26,788	43,740	13,157	34,525	20,221
	22,011	40,811	26,337	43,300	16,029	31,956	23,359
	12,355	38,193	19,799	35,983	18,121	34,216	21,058
	14,850	40,651	17,711	36,004	19,294	36,141	26,709
	14,395	36,484	15,214	32,735	30,942	36,361	30,300
16,385	17,421	32,254	15,608	39,410		35,667	31,967
15,105	17,529	28,136	14,178	33,628		27,582	31,600
22,650	14,690	23,360	16,310	22,510		39,733	39,257
20,840	23,704	29,396	22,191	25,096		27,711	49,287
22,930	25,292	29,839	25,124	25,341		27,139	50,098
18,484	30,647	21,589	30,792	20,387		28,367	49,732
21,641	28,319	23,009	33,500	26,517		25,096	49,402
24,330	21,624	24,771	35,805	18,639		25,234	47,966
23,744	28,117	26,796	32,929	16,030		19,530	41,678
23,571	37,416	32,921	28,239	12,622		21,766	32,039
15,813	25,703	29,971	20,727	14,003		20,889	34,302
17,003	15,499	28,350	15,839	12,549		13,906	30,315
19,858	19,664	27,682	16,894	13,599		13,781	30,862
29,594	19,737	22,492	16,707	10,745		16,833	26,049
24,133	10,604	27,876	15,987	16,833		14,252	23,832
17,843	11,373	25,200	21,426	14,252		15,180	15,753
22,651	7,690	31,654	23,287	15,180		14,977	14,247
23,683	9,615	32,437	10,398	14,977		18,761	17,288
19,770	13,216	31,330	3,787	18,761		17,658	17,675
13,765	9,727	28,838	6,587	17,658		15,441	19,291
12,496	14,534	25,964	6,119	15,441		14,382	21,263
14,980	8,832	25,155	9,637	14,382		14,099	
11,799	8,990	16,513	13,278	14,099		14,924	
13,483	8,078	15,717	10,441	14,924		8,470	
7,601	11,204	15,582	12,355	8,470		8,610	
8,921	10,782	12,550	11,965	8,610		8,088	
11,527	11,910	13,219	11,296	8,088		10,183	
8,268	15,579	14,036	9,609	10,183		11,335	
	16,658	13,350	9,608	11,335		6,749	
	14,114	14,459	10,090	6,749		9,636	
	18,315	15,360	8,971	9,636		7,388	
	15,548	13,715	9,555	7,388		6,915	
	18,065	14,621	6,523	6,915		7,409	
	14,726	16,119	7,932	7,409		6,695	
	17,366	16,362	9,412	6,695		9,122	
	17,477	18,670	7,848	9,122		7,561	
	15,515	21,577	8,548	7,561			
	9,655	21,134	9,935				
	7,992	20,156	12,515				
	6,093	18,313	11,860				

Year	Baltimore	Boston	Chicago	Cleveland	Detroit	Kansas City	Los Angeles
1957	13,371	15,339	14,749	9,380	16,524		
1956	11,704	14,579	12,988	11,240	13,477		
1955	10,785	15,426	15,269	15,867	15,349		
1954	13,778	11,786	15,790	17,344	14,024		
1953	3,860	13,502	15,274	13,707	11,198		
1952	6,651	14,490	15,591	18,761	13,336		
1951	3,815	17,497	17,029	22,143	14,710		
1950	3,340	17,456	9,890	22,435	24,092		
1949	3,519	20,736	12,171	29,010	23,349		
1948	4,415	19,985	10,235	33,172	22,637		
1947	4,162	17,621	11,693	19,513	17,476		
1946	6,837	18,166	12,448	13,731	21,805		
1945	6,355	7,741	8,892	7,249	16,847		
1944	6,606	6,500	7,319	6,093	11,836		
1943	2,784	4,653	6,697	5,700	7,773		
1942	3,320	9,485	6,082	5,743	7,534		
1941	2,231	9,331	8,571	9,688	8,895		
1940	3,112	9,066	8,466	11,007	14,085		
1939	1,399	7,641	7,716	7,324	10,722		
1938	1,694	8,619	4,634	8,579	10,121		
1937	1,578	7,563	7,653	7,242	13,926		
1936	1,211	8,141	5,877	6,178	11,376		
1935	1,065	7,070	6,108	5,164	13,100		
1934	1,517	7,930	3,154	5,017	11,490		
1933	1,144	3,732	5,166	5,038	4,115		
1932	1,501	2,366	3,029	6,090	5,092		
1931	2,326	4,387	5,241	6,356	5,637		
1930	1,950	5,843	5,207	6,866	8,326		
1929	3,645	5,059	5,616	7,055	11,290		
1928	4,409	5,364	6,335	4,882	6,160		
1927	3,178	3,914	8,192	4,846	9,919		
1926	3,595	3,703	8,992	7,843	8,789		
1925	5,935	3,570	10,808	5,442	10,659		
1924	6,838	5,825	7,879	6,425	13,015		
1923	5,517	2,945	7,650	7,165	11,836		
1922	9,259	3,550	7,829	6,602	11,184		
1921	4,623	3,627	7,060	9,723	8,591		
1920	5,376	5,295	10,825	11,703	7,431		
1919	4,991	6,323	8,960	7,799	9,197		
1918	2,303	3,564	3,484	4,766	3,512		
1917	2,699	4,848	8,665	6,119	6,017		
1916	4,250	6,364	8,830	6,309	8,010		
1915	1,978	7,104	6,829	2,069	6,183		
1914	3,021	6,093	5,794	2,354	5,336		
1913	3,251	5,829	8,370	6,762	5,243		
1912	2,710	7,655	7,721	4,375	5,301		

Milwaukee	Minnesota	New York	Oakland	Seattle	Tampa Bay	Texas	Toronto
	5,936	19,443	11,702				
	5,606	19,374	13,184				
	5,523	19,352	18,330				
	6,456	18,912	3,957				
	7,941	19,972	4,642				
	8,967	21,164	8,040				
	9,147	25,001	5,892				
	8,970	27,031	4,023				
	10,010	29,278	10,604				
	10,196	30,830	12,274				
	11,049	28,298	11,687				
	13,516	29,422	7,972				
	8,367	11,603	6,008				
	6,821	10,128	6,649				
	7,562	8,030	4,769				
	5,240	11,974	5,572				
	5,329	12,368	6,869				
	4,951	13,013	6,087				
	4,406	11,166	5,198				
	6,701	12,290	5,070				
	4,972	12,635	5,452				
	4,929	12,687	3,704				
	3,312	8,885	3,239				
	4,343	11,100	4,024				
	5,757	9,707	3,910				
	4,823	12,498	5,266				
	6,236	11,850	8,366				
	7,980	15,385	9,496				
	4,558	12,469	11,340				
	4,731	13,924	8,958				
	6,696	15,117	7,864				
	7,454	13,702	10,063				
	10,753	8,826	11,295				
	7,396	13,507	7,093				
	4,524	13,251	7,122				
	5,804	13,326	5,453				
	6,001	15,778	4,473				
	4,727	16,746	3,739				
	3,251	8,482	3,217				
	2,461	4,210	2,617				
	1,121	4,404	2,914				
	2,188	5,939	2,427				
	2,092	3,122	1,976				
	3,167	4,609	4,444				
	4,177	4,767	7,525				
	4,496	3,187	6,723				

Year	Baltimore	Boston	Chicago	Cleveland	Detroit	Kansas City	Los Angeles
1911	2,666	6,631	7,477	5,277	6,381		
1910	3,163	7,308	6,988	3,668	5,017		
1909	4,636	8,920	5,906	4,606	6,288		
1908	7,935	6,143	8,155	5,414	5,592		
1907	5,513	5,600	8,434	4,659	3,760		
1906	5,120	5,327	7,408	4,123	2,231		
1905	4,293	6,089	8,383	4,108	2,545		
1904	4,078	7,695	7,143	3,394	2,251		
1903	5,434	5,419	4,088	4,206	3,454		
1902	3,730	4,909	4,693	4,237	2,828		
1901	1,986	4,195	4,991	1,904	3,706		

Source: *Data drawn from Baseball-Reference.com, http://www.baseball-reference.com/teams/attend.shtml.*

Milwaukee	Minnesota	New York	Oakland	Seattle	Tampa Bay	Texas	Toronto
	3,180	3,928	8,077				
	3,306	4,622	7,550				
	2,665	6,506	8,880				
	3,388	3,968	5,834				
	2,959	4,667	8,570				
	1,732	5,720	6,700				
	3,273	4,121	7,494				
	1,689	5,852	6,485				
	1,815	3,161	6,306				
	2,767	2,728	5,754				
	2,377	2,151	3,126				

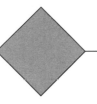

Appendix H

AMERICAN LEAGUE TEAM ATTENDANCE RANKINGS, 2005–1901

Year	Baltimore	Boston	Chicago	Cleveland	Detroit	Kansas City	Los Angeles
2005	5	3	7	12	9	13	2
2004	5	4	8	12	9	13	2
2003	5	4	9	12	13	10	3
2002	3	4	10	5	12	13	7
2001	4	6	12	3	9	13	8
2000	2	6	9	1	7	12	8
1999	2	6	13	1	9	11	7
1998	1	9	12	2	11	10	6
1997	1	7	8	2	13	10	9
1996	1	6	9	2	13	10	8
1995	1	4	9	2	11	10	6
1994	2	7	5	4	14	10	9
1993	2	4	3	7	12	13	8
1992	2	6	3	14	13	9	8
1991	5	4	2	14	12	9	6
1990	5	4	8	14	13	6	3
1989	4	5	14	13	11	6	3
1988	10	4	13	12	8	5	6
1987	9	5	12	14	7	4	2
1986	6	5	10	9	7	3	1
1985	6	7	8	14	3	5	1
1984	5	8	3	14	1	7	2
1983	5	9	4	14	8	6	1
1982	8	5	9	13	7	2	1
1981	8	6	7	12	5	2	3
1980	6	4	10	11	7	3	2
1979	6	3	10	12	7	4	2
1978	10	2	8	12	5	3	4
1977	10	2	5	13	7	3	6
1976	6	2	10	9	4	3	8
1975	9	1	11	10	7	4	8
1974	8	1	6	7	3	5	10
1973	9	2	4	12	1	3	7
1972	6	2	3	11	1	9	8
1971	3	1	9	12	2	8	6
1970	6	1	12	10	2	11	5
1969	5	1	12	11	2	7	9
1968	6	2	9	7	1		5
1967	6	1	7	10	3		4
1966	3	8	6	7	4		1
1965	6	7	3	5	4		8
1964	4	5	2	8	6		7
1963	7	4	3	9	5		6
1962	6	7	5	9	3		4
1961	5	6	4	7	2		10
1960	3	5	1	6	4		
1959	7	5	3	2	4		
1958	5	3	6	7	2		

Milwaukee	Minnesota	New York	Oakland	Seattle	Tampa Bay	Texas	Toronto
	10	1	8	4	14	6	11
	10	1	7	3	14	6	11
	8	1	6	2	14	7	11
	9	2	8	1	14	6	11
	11	2	7	1	14	5	10
	14	3	11	4	13	5	10
	14	3	12	4	10	5	8
	14	3	13	5	7	4	8
11	12	5	14	3		4	6
12	11	7	14	4		3	5
13	14	7	12	8		5	3
12	11	6	13	8		3	1
14	10	5	11	9		6	1
10	5	11	4	12		7	1
13	8	11	3	10		7	1
10	11	9	2	12		7	1
10	7	8	2	12		9	1
9	1	2	7	14		11	3
8	6	3	11	13		10	1
12	13	4	11	14		8	2
10	9	4	11	13		12	2
9	10	6	11	13		12	4
2	12	3	11	13		10	7
4	14	3	6	12		11	10
9	14	1	4	13		10	11
5	14	1	12	13		9	8
5	11	1	14	13		8	9
6	13	1	14	11		9	7
12	11	1	14	8		9	4
7	12	1	11			5	
3	12	2	6			5	
9	12	2	11			4	
6	10	5	8			11	
12	7	4	7			10	
10	5	4	5			11	
7	3	4	9			8	
10	3	4	8			6	
	4	3	8			10	
	2	5	9			8	
	2	5	9			10	
	1	2	10			9	
	3	1	9			10	
	1	2	8			10	
	2	1	10			8	
	3	1	8			9	
	8	2	7				
	8	1	6				
	8	1	4				

Year	Baltimore	Boston	Chicago	Cleveland	Detroit	Kansas City	Los Angeles
1957	5	3	4	7	2		
1956	6	2	5	7	3		
1955	7	4	6	3	5		
1954	5	6	3	2	4		
1953	8	4	2	3	5		
1952	8	4	3	2	5		
1951	8	3	4	2	5		
1950	8	4	5	3	2		
1949	8	4	5	2	3		
1948	8	4	6	1	3		
1947	8	3	5	2	4		
1946	8	3	6	4	2		
1945	6	5	3	6	1		
1944	6	7	3	8	1		
1943	8	7	4	5	2		
1942	8	2	4	5	3		
1941	8	3	5	2	4		
1940	8	4	5	3	1		
1939	8	4	3	5	2		
1938	8	3	7	4	2		
1937	8	4	3	5	1		
1936	8	3	5	4	2		
1935	8	3	4	5	1		
1934	8	3	7	4	1		
1933	8	7	3	4	5		
1932	8	7	6	2	4		
1931	8	7	6	3	5		
1930	8	6	7	5	3		
1929	8	6	5	4	3		
1928	8	5	3	6	4		
1927	8	7	3	6	2		
1926	8	7	3	5	4		
1925	6	8	2	7	4		
1924	6	8	3	7	2		
1923	6	8	3	4	2		
1922	3	8	4	5	2		
1921	6	8	4	2	3		
1920	5	6	3	2	4		
1919	6	5	2	4	1		
1918	8	3	5	1	4		
1917	7	4	1	2	3		
1916	6	3	1	4	2		
1915	7	1	2	6	3		
1914	7	1	2	8	3		
1913	8	4	1	3	5		
1912	8	2	1	6	4		

Milwaukee	Minnesota	New York	Oakland	Seattle	Tampa Bay	Texas	Toronto
	8	1	6				
	8	1	4				
	8	1	2				
	7	1	8				
	6	1	7				
	6	1	7				
	6	1	7				
	6	1	7				
	7	1	6				
	7	2	5				
	7	1	6				
	5	1	7				
	4	2	8				
	4	2	5				
	3	1	6				
	7	1	6				
	7	1	6				
	7	2	6				
	7	1	6				
	5	1	6				
	7	2	6				
	6	1	7				
	6	2	7				
	5	2	6				
	2	1	6				
	5	1	3				
	4	1	2				
	4	1	2				
	7	1	2				
	7	1	2				
	5	1	4				
	6	1	2				
	3	5	1				
	4	1	5				
	7	1	5				
	6	1	7				
	5	1	7				
	7	1	8				
	7	3	8				
	7	2	6				
	8	5	6				
	8	5	7				
	5	4	8				
	6	4	5				
	7	6	2				
	5	7	3				

Year	Baltimore	Boston	Chicago	Cleveland	Detroit	Kansas City	Los Angeles
1911	8	3	2	5	4		
1910	8	2	3	6	4		
1909	6	1	5	7	4		
1908	2	3	1	6	5		
1907	4	3	2	6	7		
1906	5	4	1	6	7		
1905	4	3	1	6	8		
1904	5	1	2	6	7		
1903	2	3	5	4	6		
1902	5	2	3	4	6		
1901	7	2	1	8	3		

Source: *Data drawn from Baseball-Reference.com, http://www.baseball-reference.com/teams/attend.shtml.*

Milwaukee	Minnesota	New York	Oakland	Seattle	Tampa Bay	Texas	Toronto
	7	6	1				
	7	5	1				
	8	3	2				
	8	7	4				
	8	5	1				
	8	3	2				
	7	5	2				
	8	4	3				
	8	7	1				
	7	8	1				
	5	6	4				

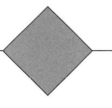

Appendix I

NATIONAL LEAGUE TEAM CONSOLIDATED PROFIT AND LOSS, 1920–56 (DOLLARS)

Year	Boston	Brooklyn	Chicago	Cincinatti	New York	Philadelphia	Pittsburgh	St. Louis
1920	($593)	$189,785	$87,969	$121,056	$296,803	$84,295	$156,052	$37,388
1921	90,393	151,604	4,959	75,450	262,950	20,977	248,807	200,151
1922	79,399	146,372	181,337	76,278	(13,540)	(7,420)	173,933	136,770
1923	(88,844)	93,092	43,970	104,176	185,754	18,424)	143,084	(13,919)
1924	(34,111)	264,070	69,924	47,029	256,786	35,852	254,203	(48,680)
1925	62,440	4,166	(20,049)	(1,000)	169,657	7,648	341,365	79,372
1926	(38,966)	135,668	134,425	136,560	218,219	15,470	286,246	359,223
1927	(60,756)	148,296	227,186	(7,806)	183,038	1118	467,046	235,455
1928	(24,042)	61,985	304,949	(23,299)	111,681	(32,358)	90,030	444,737
1929	19,587	124,060	426,874	(203,091)	160,583	24,611	147,382	50,584
1930	22,401	426,976	523,651	(17,027)	151,063	23,563	95,443	230,918
1931	(16,247)	(5,308)	179,455	(161,331)	(19,630)	38,482)	89,401	345,263
1932	14,094	(160,170)	56,799	(116,133)	(214,812)	100,176	(86,960)	(73,895)
1933	(120,597)	(48,682)	(247,667)	(56,473)	59,416	3,184	(96,275)	(80,198)
1934	(10,974)	(137,868)	(169,994)	(62,625)	101,920	13,670	(56,972)	109,229
1935	(48,625)	(148,692)	135,736	47,293	199,258	1,468	45,165	61,718
1936	(20,222)	(42,453)	60,953	105,545	301,870	21,256	37,087	68,025
1937	(13,608)	(129,140)	99,627	29,781	331,186	(16,932)	58,838	53,074
1938	(14,828)	(3,751)	32,540	157,324	28,526	(44,411)	167,100	(14,823)
1939	22,400	143,637	(21,528)	335,210	94,914	(69,250)	(40,316)	89,466
1940	7,309	125,221	(182,019)	270,240	(69,437)	(40,325)	(14,954)	68,190
1941	(61,075)	146,794	(157,846)	123,025	45,969	(60,797)	19,615	154,557
1942	(57,941)	155,451	(7,188)	4,916	54,151	(56,251)	(33,735)	63,553
1943	(41,166)	(62,719)	33,009	16,503	(248.973)	6,076	56,160	105,791
1944	(133,022)	3,923	69,660	30,611	53,489	(136,669)	111,112	146,417
1945	(137,142)	252,721	45,554	(33,224)	339,079	(202,923)	43,942	94,826
1946	39,565	412,314	510,053	192,499	(211,546)	124,563	71,799	699,093
1947	229,153	519,143	278,918	207,685	529,827	64,163	39,497	630,978
1948	238,104	543,201	141,128	163,632	(114,286)	(197,886)	66,071	608,663
1949	147,934	642,614	211,523	73,162	(88,103)	46,757	194,899	857,553
1950	(316,510)	(8,587)	(133,124)	(64,873)	(264,114)	309,579	138,220	263,202
1952	(459,099)	446,102	154,793	(68,368)	(222,344)	(118,029)	(667,263)	(89,152)
1953	637,798	290,006	(418,363)	15,518	(63,307)	(10,688)	(421,422)	(702,193)
1954	457,110	209,979	(72,014)	(24,198)	395,725	(256,306)	(198,920)	(589,382)
1955	807,395	427,195	68,684	58,145	151,113	(270,671)	(601,846)	(43,142)
1956	414,398	487,462	(159,712)	301,216	81,415	(78,063)	(47,852)	329,495

Note: *Brooklyn Dodgers and Pittsburgh Pirates profits include associated real estate companies. Boston moved to Milwaukee in 1953.*

Parentheses indicate net loss.

Source: *House. Committee on the Judiciary.* Study of Monopoly Power: Hearings Before the Subcommittee on Study of Monopoly Power, *serial no. 1, pt. 6,* Organized Baseball, *82nd Cong., 1st sess. July 3–October 24, 1951, 1600. United States, House. Committee on the Judiciary.* Organized Professional Team Sports. Hearings Before the Antitrust Subcommittee. *85th Cong., 1st sess., pt. 1, serial 8, June 17–August 8, 1957, 353.*

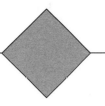

Appendix J

NATIONAL LEAGUE TEAM DIVIDENDS, 1920–56 (DOLLARS)

Year	Boston	Brooklyn	Chicago	Cincinatti	New York	Philadelphia	Pittsburg	St. Louis	Total
1920	n.a.	n.a.	0	n.a.	0	0	$17,000	0	$17.000
1921	n.a.	n.a.	$69,965	n.a.	25,000	$30,000	17,000	0	141,965
1922	0	n.a.	23,988	n.a.	$25,000	30,000	27,200	0	106,188
1923	0	$40,000	47,976	n.a.	0	0	52,000	$28,317.5	168,294
1924	0	80,000	0	n.a.	125,000	0	30,000	0	245,000
1925	0	50,000	0	n.a.	125,000	20,000	167,000	0	362,000
1926	0	100,000	100,000	n.a.	625,000	20,000	112,000	0	957,000
1927	0	225,000	100,000	n.a.	125,000	0	171,000	28,317.5	549,318
1928	0	125,000	0	0	100,000	0	95,.500	50,800	429,000
1929	0	184,000	100,000	0	125,000	0	20,000	0	471,300
1930	0	175,000	100,000	0	312,500	0	20,000	50,800	718,300
1931	0	75,000	160,000	0	0	0	20,000	101,600	366,600
1932	0	50,000	170,000	$1,122.5	100,000	0	20,000	0	341,123
1933	0	0	170,000	830	0	0	20,000	0	130,830
1934	0	0	110,000	0	100,000	0	20,000	101,520	221,520
1935	0	0	0	0	124,500	0	20,000	101,520	276,020
1936	0	0	30,000	0	305,693	0	27,550	121,824	495,067
1937	0	0	40.000	0	258,522	0	46,425	81,216	446,163
1938	0	0	60,000	0	82,257	0	114,375	0	196,632
1939	0	0	0	108,620	23,502	0	27,550	101,520	261,192
1940	0	0	0	84,770	0	0	20,000	71,064	175,834
1941	0	0	0	42,770	11,751	0	20,000	101,520	176,041
1942	0	0	0	18,770	47,004	0	20,000	20,304	106,078
1943	0	21,000	0	24,770	0	0	20,000	30,456	96,226
1944	0	0	0	30,770	0	0	52,850	30,456	114,076
1945	0	0	0	12,770	94,008	0	42,650	0	149,428
1946	0	0	0	39,770	23,502	0	10,000	71,064	194,336
1947	0	0	50,000	42,770	23,502	0	0	670,032	816,304
1948	0	49,000	80,000	36,770	70,506	0	0	0	236,276
1949	0	24,500	0	21,770	23,502	0	0	0	69,772
1950	0	99,750	0	14,270	23,502	0	16,000	0	153,522
1952	0	0	0	14,270	0	0	0	0	14,270
1953	0	0	0	14,270	0	0	0	0	14,270
1954	0	0	0	14,270	70,506	0	0	0	14,776
1955	0	0	0	30,770	47,004	0	0	0	77,774
1956	0	0	0	60,770	0	0	0	0	60,770
Total	0	0	0	625,453	3,016,761	100,000	1,246,100	1,762,331	9,188,464

n.a. = not available.

Source: *United States. Congress. House. Committee on the Judiciary.* Study of Monopoly Power: Hearings Before the Subcommittee on Study of Monopoly Power, *serial no. 1, pt. 6. Organized Baseball 82nd. Cong., 1st sess. July 30–October 24, 1951, 1601; United States. Congress, House Committee on the Judiciary.* Organized Team Sports. Hearings Before the Antitrust Subcommittee. *85th Cong., 1st sess., pt. 1, serial 8, June 17–August 8, 1957, 352.*

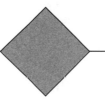

Appendix K

AMERICAN LEAGUE TEAM CONSOLIDATED PROFIT AND LOSS, 1920–56 (DOLLARS)

Year	Boston	Chicago	Cleveland	Detroit	New York	Philadelphia	St. Louis	Washington
1920	—	$155,671	$314,836	$111,762	$372,862	$63,291	$125,541	$153,608
1921	—	93,642	289,080	120,529	226,237	42,512	63,687	133,410
1922	—	111,829	65,712	239,854	294,387	64,327	260,498	75,134
1923	($37,258)	90,465	126,006	214,106	451,116	46,169	79,818	33,167
1924	(15.867)	102,216	66,188	297,369	288,616	18,994	162,850	231,037
1925	2,573	200,057	68,564	204,529	69,332	313,036	192,515	408,746
1926	(56,327)	139,613	88,091	193,703	472,123	138,646	49,954	95,573
1927	(41,321)	20,351	(73,302)	151,237	531,586	(7,710)	(709)	90,222
1928	(59,096)	100,898	(126,726)	(85,150)	293,927	88,842	(126,606)	33,106
1929	(35,053)	10,750	(22,556)	123,184	271,028	276,483	5,251	(43,935)
1930	7,674	15,473	27,952	75,348	244,734	162,542	(87,152)	56,808
1931	(71,717)	(135)	(38,482)	(42,228)	25,457	109,123	(103,084)	(28,343)
1932	(83,754)	(244,319)	(120,754)	(61553)	(31,527)	10,023	(109,872)	(76,634)
1933	(537,004)	(156,288)	(132,427)	(84,566)	(98,126)	(21,047)	(33,559)	(501)
1934	(113,819)	(208,163)	33,978	378,562	36,810	(139,174)	(54,937)	20,382
1935	(204,877)	8,802	35,708	521,202	(103,610)	(4,059)	572	18,247
1936	(229,708)	(5323)	71,465	204,709	328,322	(41,694)	(159,202)	30,019
1937	(251,894)	8,707	104,996	181,595	285,246	(1,922)	(107,998)	(85,513)
1938	(165,249)	(88,967)	147,522	115,361	365,232	(50,595)	(119,712)	94,803
1939	(106,858)	16,739	95,910	57,101	382,501	(42,940)	(124,792)	1,759
1940	(84,297)	40,790	169,292	194,320	136,548	(55,862)	27,963	56,189
1941	57,342	63,866	60,639	(6.568)	237,621	4,898	(141,842)	(11,358)
1942	28,343	(55,251)	35,775	1,966	136,567	(44,198)	80,855	42,526
1943	(31,241)	24,423	27,873	132,046	(88,521)	(28,255)	45,375	46,631
1944	(43,131)	61,295	86,803	207,043	151,043	(6,133)	285,034	90,429
1945	(30,287)	102,237	108,737	191,755	200,959	(17,026)	30,452	222,473
1946	405,133	291,262	375,679	467,283	808,866	82,709	260,225	357,414
1947	(95,109)	209,264	318,801	196,750	846,737	129,809	303,170	457,195
1948	(202,875)	69,106	499,819	255,146	516,476	233,258	156,783	261,020
1949	21,257	102,554	506,218	33,229	346,806	90,306	83,482	(18323)
1950	(100,992)	65,363	458,694	112,638	497,000	(315,921)	5,117	5117
1952	(342,014)	65,052	204,088	(26,265)	223,943	(51,437)	(329,637)	$58,471
1953	(421,276)	204,720	157,288	43,639	622,185	(102,461)	(706,998)	26,607
1954	3,086	202,897	583,283	86,465	174,876	(217,936)	643,407	48,800
1955	242,901	201,631	89,756	257,191	121,852	28,214	(86,715)	4,222
1956	122,032	141,089	(167,110)	81,591	301,483	1,657	69,307	23,218

Note: *St. Louis Browns profits include associated real estate companies.*
Parentheses indicates net loss.

Source: *United States. Congress. House. Committee on the Judiciary. Subcommittee on Study of Monopoly Power. Study of Monopoly Power: Hearings Before the Subcommittee on Study of Monopoly Power of the Committee on the Judiciary, House of Representatives, 82nd Cong., 1st sess., pt. 6.* Organized Baseball, *1601; United States. Congress. House. Committee on the Judiciary. Subcommittee on Study of Monopoly Power.* Organized Professional Team Sports. *Hearings Before the Antitrust Subcommittee. 85th Cong., 1st sess., pt. 1, serial 8, June 17–August 8, 1957, 353.*

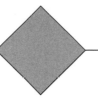

Appendix L

AMERICAN LEAGUE TEAM DIVIDENDS, 1920–56
(DOLLARS)

Year	Boston	Chicago	Cleveland	Detroit	New York	Philadelphia	St. Louis	Washington	Total
1920	n.a.	0	186,350	100,000	0	0	0	20,000	306,350
1921	n.a.	0	124,225	50,000	0	0	0	10,000	184,225
1922	0	0	0	50,000	0	100,000	240,000	20,000	410,000
1923	0	0	99,400	50,000	0	50,000	40,000	0	239,400
1924	0	0	59,640	50,000	0	50,000	40,000	80,000	279,640
1925	0	0	49,700	100,000	0	0	42,000	317,600	509,300
1926	0	0	99,400	100,000	0	50,000	0	39,500	288,900
1927	0	0	0	100,000	0	0	0	79,000	179,000
1928	0	0	0	0	0	50,000	0	19,650	69,650
1929	0	0	0	150,000	0	50,000	0	0	200,000
1930	0	0	0	50,000	0	0	0	39,300	89,300
1931	0	0	1,250	0	0	250,050	0	0	251,300
1932	0	0	250	0	0	0	0	0	250
1933	0	0	0	0	0	0	0	000	0
1934	0	0	2,500	0	0	0	0	0	2,500
1935	0	0	2,750	200,000	100,000	0	0	0	302,750
1936	0	0	18,144	200,000	420,000	0	0	19,650	657,794
1937	0	0	84,000	0	0	0	0	0	84,000
1938	0	0	60,500	0	0	0	0	38,900	99,400
1939	0	0	2,450	0	0	0	0	0	2,450
1940	0	0	20,250	0	0	0	0	19450	39,700
1941	0	37,500	20,250	0	130,000	0	0	0	187,750
1942	0	0	4,050	0	0	0	0	0	4,050
1943	0	0	20,250	0	0	0	0	19,400	39,650
1944	0	0	24,300	0	0	0	0	19,400	43,700
1945	0	0	40,500	0	0	0	0	38,800	79,300
1946	0	74,500	202,500	0	0	0	137,500	77,600	492,100
1947	0	0	0	0	0	0	0	77,600	77,600
1948	0	0	16,875	0	0	0	0	77,600	94.475
1949	0	74,500	112,500	0	0	0	0	0	225,800
1950	0	0	0	0	0	0	0	38,800	38,800
1952	0	0	0	0	0	0	0	58,200	58,200
1953	0	74,500	3,000	0	0	0	0	38,200	38,200
1954	0	0	15,000	0	0	0	0	18,925	33,925
1955	0	0	12,780	100,000	0	0	0	18,925	131,705
1956	0	7,450	0	50,000	0	0	0	0	57,450
Total	0	268,450	1,282,814	1,350,000	650,000	600,050	499,500	1,224,040	5,798,361

n.a = not available.

Source: United States. Congress. House. Committee on the Judiciary. Subcommittee on Study of Monopoly Power. Study of Monopoly Power: Hearings Before the Subcommittee on Study of Monopoly Power of the Committee on the Judiciary, House of Representatives, 82nd Cong., 1st sess., pt. 6. Organized Baseball, 1601; United States. Congress. House. Committee on the Judiciary. Subcommittee on Study of Monopoly Power. Organized Professional Team Sports. Hearings Before the Antitrust Subcommittee. 85th Cong., 1st sess., pt. 1, serial 8, June 17–August 8, 1957, 353.

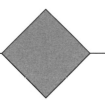

Appendix M

MAJOR LEAGUE BASEBALL TEAM SALARIES, SELECTED YEARS

Teams	1929	1933	1939	1943	1946
Boston AL	$171,260	$145,806	$227,237	$212,982	$511,025
Chicago	*200,000	*150,000	243,041	213,129	386,377
Cleveland	215,523	178,598	272,359	204,864	378,773
Detroit	185,771	138,758	297,154	172,733	504,794
New York	365,741	294,982	361,471	301,229	442,854
Philadelphia	255,231	166,533	165,258	135,405	271,925
St. Louis	200,312	140,789	159,925	186,441	221,789
Washington	231,618	187,059	165,849	192,190	356,631
Boston NL	*238,260	*218,776	171,159	138,000	322,000
Brooklyn	245,309	179,702	204,047	271,424	313,369
Chicago	310,299	266,431	292,178	251,026	348,546
Cincinnati	224,655	160,788	231,389	196,329	316,137
New York	291,368	210,645	291,448	201,661	344,635
Philadelphia	*250,000	197,503	234,141	185,624	312,312
Pittsburgh	140,422	171,322	144,255	158,008	302,471
St. Louis	219,815	197,267	192,085	195,597	313,530

Source: *House Committee on the Judiciary,* Organized Baseball, *82nd Cong., 1st Sess. (1951), 1610; Senate Committee on the Judiciary,* Organized Professional Team Sports, *85th Cong., 2nd Sess. (1958), 795–798.*

Salary information only collected for 1929, 1933, 1939, 1943, 1946 and 1950. All salaries include coaches and managers. St. Louis Browns, Brooklyn Dodgers and Pittsburgh Pirates profits include associated real estate companies. Asterisks indicate subcommittee estimates.

1950	1952	1953	1954	1955	1956
$561,482	$378,270	$425,000	$372,750	$398,000	$421,000
339,163	264,210	333500	408,000	430,630	438,090
524,229	442,930	451,000	487,050	567,000	444,520
548,913	380,230	335160	278,660	291,730	361,770
651,605	421,000	438,250	510,000	411,500	492,000
365,901	269,310	272,500	215,730	251,440	253,039
234,125	262,470	292,630	272,400	270,750	302,000
304,959	274,250	251,000	300,500	287,500	215,250
490,000	425,000	372,750	398,000	421,000	378,270
430,249	333,500	408,000	430,630	438,090	264,210
389,374	451,000	487,050	567,000	444,520	442,930
316,699	335160	278,660	291,730	361,770	380,230
444,320	438,250	510,000	411,500	492,000	421,000
460,802	272,500	215,730	251,440	253,039	269,310
363,508	292,630	272,400	270,750	302,000	262,470
495,683	251,000	300,500	287,500	215,250	274,250

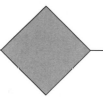

Appendix N

ESTIMATED MLB REVENUES/INCOME, FRANCHISE VALUES (IN MILLIONS), AND SALARIES, 1990–2004

Teams in 1990	Primary Revenue Sources			Revenue Total	Operating Expenses	Operating Income	Salaries	Salaries Rank	Value	Value Rank
	Gate	Media	Stadium							
Anaheim Angels	17.0	24.0	5.4	48.6	39.9	8.7	21,870,000	3	102	13
Atlanta Braves	8.0	20.0	3.2	35.4	27.6	7.8	13,328,334	23	74	24
Baltimore Orioles	18.1	22.5	5.1	47.9	38.3	9.6	10,037,084	26	200	2
Boston Red Sox	25.3	34.1	6.9	68.7	56.2	12.3	20,983,333	6	180	5
Chicago Cubs	19.7	24.2	4.2	50.3	41.1	9.2	14,496,000	21	125	9
Chicago White Sox	19.7	24.2	4.2	49.0	40.2	8.8	9,496,238	26	125	9
Cincinnati Reds	15.6	21.8	5.0	48.7	37.7	11.0	14,769,500	20	102	13
Cleveland Indians	9.9	20.0	2.6	34.8	41.6	-6.8	15,656,000	17	75	22
Detroit Tigers	12.4	22.3	1.1	38.0	32.9	5.1	18,092,238	14	84	18
Houston Astros	10.8	24.2	2.8	40.0	42.0	-2.0	18,830,000	11	92	17
Kansas City Royals	19.7	24.2	4.2	53.2	63	-9.8	23,873,745	1	122	11
Los Angeles Dodgers	22.5	29.7	10.0	64.4	56.8	7.6	21,618,704	4	200	2
Milwaukee Brewers	15.5	19.0	1.7	38.4	34.5	3.9	20,019,167	9	81	20
Minnesota Twins	13.0	19.6	3.2	38.6	38.0	0.6	15,106,000	18	81	20
Montreal Expos	10.6	20.0	2.5	35.3	28.9	6.4	16,656,388	15	74	24
New York Mets	25.2	38.3	15.4	81.1	65.3	15.8	22,418,834	2	200	2
New York Yankees	19.8	69.4	6.6	98.0	73.5	24.5	20,991,318	5	225	1
Oakland Athletics	24.6	32.3	9.9	57.9	45.5	12.4	19,987,501	10	116	12
Philadelphia Phillies	16.0	35.0	8.7	61.0	63.6	13.9	13,953,667	22	130	7
Pittsburgh Pirates	14.6	20.0	4.3	41.1	41.8	-0.7	15,656,000	16	82	19

Teams in 1990	Primary Revenue Sources			Revenue Total	Operating Expenses	Operating Income	Salaries	Salaries Rank	Value	Value Rank
	Gate	Media	Stadium							
San Diego Padres	13.5	25.1	6.4	47.2	38.7	8.5	18,588,334	12	99	16
San Francisco Giants	19.0	23.3	5.5	50.0	41.0	9.0	20,942,333	7	105	13
St. Louis Cardinals	20.8	27.4	5.4	55.8	45.3	11.5	20,923,334	8	128	8
Seattle Mariners	11.6	17.0	3.2	34	37.1	-3.1	12,841,667	24	71	26
Texas Rangers	14.7	24.6	6.6	50.3	41.2	9.1	15,104,372	19	101	15
Toronto Blue Jays	39.1	28.0	8.2	77.5	63.6	13.9	18,486,834	13	178	6
Average	17.3	26.3	6.0	51.8	42.5	7.4	19,700,279		121.3	

Source: Adapted from Baldo, Anthony, with Alexander Biesada, Holt Hackney, and Michael K. Ozanian. "Secrets of the Front Office: What America's Pro Teams Are Worth." Financial World 160 (July 9, 1991): 42–43; http://asp.usatoday.com/sports/baseball/salaries/totalpayroll.aspx?year=1990.

Teams in 1991	Primary Revenue Sources			Revenue Total	Operating Expenses	Operating Income	Salaries	Salaries Rank	Value	Value Rank
	Gate	Media	Stadium							
Los Angeles Angels	19.0	27.9	5.0	54.1	61.7	7.6	31,782,501	5	103	14
Atlanta Braves	15.4	18.9	3.8	40.3	40.8	-0.5	20,423,500	20	83	21
Baltimore Orioles	19.0	24.4	5.0	50.6	39.5	11.1	14,627,334	25	140	6
Boston Red Sox	24.5	40.5	14.3	81.5	70.8	10.7	32,767,500	3	160	4
Chicago Cubs	22.8	27.5	12.1	64.5	58.0	6.5	26,923,120	9	132	8
Chicago White Sox	27.5	25.7	19.3	78.0	60.0	18.0	16,830,437	23	140	6
Cincinnati Reds	17.1	24.4	5.3	49.0	48.8	0.2	25,369,166	10	98	16
Cleveland Indians	9.5	23.7	6.6	42.0	46.8	-4.8	18,270,000	22	77	25
Detroit Tigers	15.6	28.8	5.0	51.6	54.4	-2.8	23,736,334	13	87	19
Houston Astros	10.6	25.2	8.0	46.0	31.5	14.5	11,546,000	26	95	18

Teams in 1991	Primary Revenue Sources			Revenue Total	Operating Expenses	Operating Income	Salaries	Salaries Rank	Value	Value Rank
	Gate	Media	Stadium							
Kansas City Royals	16.9	20.5	14.0	53.6	60.8	-7.2	28,722,662	7	117	11
Los Angeles Dodgers	26.6	32.5	18.0	79.3	72.0	7.3	33,216,664	2	180	2
Milwaukee Brewers	14.2	19.4	3.0	38.8	50.2	-11.4	24,398,000	11	77	24
Minnesota Twins	18.2	20.5	3.2	44.1	48.2	-4.1	22,431,000	16	83	21
Montreal Expos	10.7	23.5	3.0	39.4	43.6	-4.2	20,813,500	19	75	26
New York Mets	22.9	50.0	16.0	91.1	70.4	20.7	32,590,002	4	170	3
New York Yankees	19.4	61.0	7.4	90.0	59.6	30.4	27,815,835	8	200	1
Oakland Athletics	25.7	27.0	10.0	64.9	66.6	-1.7	33,632,500	1	115	12
Philadelphia Phillies	15.2	23.2	7.6	48.2	43.4	4.8	20,298,332	21	115	12
Pittsburgh Pirates	16.2	21.9	5.5	45.8	49.8	-4.0	23,064,667	14	87	19
San Diego Padres	15.6	23.1	7.5	48.4	48.8	-0.4	22,585,001	15	96	17
San Francisco Giants	15.5	26.2	5.0	48.9	53.3	-4.4	30,839,333	6	99	15
St. Louis Cardinals	19.9	25.0	12.0	59.1	46.4	12.7	20,813,500	18	132	8
Seattle Mariners	15.5	22.0	5.0	44.7	41.8	1..9	16,126,834	2	79	23
Texas Rangers	19.0	25.5	14.0	61.5	47.6	13.9	22,224,500	17	123	10
Toronto Blue Jays	44.5	30.0	12.0	88.7	62.4	26.3	27,538,751	8	160	4
Average	19.1	27.6	8.8	56.1	53.0	4.9	24,207,114		116.2	

Source: *Adapted from Ozanian, Michael K., and Stephan Taub. "Big Leagues, Bad Business." Financial World 161 (July 7, 1992): 50–51; http://asp.usatoday.com/sports/baseball/salaries/totalpayroll.aspx?year=1991.*

Teams in 1992	Primary Revenue Sources			Revenue Total	Operating Expenses	Operating Income	Salaries	Salaries Rank	Value	Value Rank
	Gate	Media	Stadium							
Anaheim Angels	16.8	28.2	6.9	55.8	56.1	-0.3	33,529,854	9	106	11
Atlanta Braves	24.5	17.3	3.4	50.7	59.7	-9.0	32,975,333	11	88	21
Baltimore Orioles	30.6	25.0	21.5	83.5	49.3	34.2	20,997,667	23	130	6
Boston Red Sox	26.7	40.1	18.9	90.6	78.9	11.7	42,203,584	4	136	4
Chicago Cubs	23.1	28.0	9.4	64.0	59.8	5.1	29,740,667	15	101	15
Chicago White Sox	28.3	26.2	18.0	77.9	61.2	16.7	28,413,500	17	123	8
Cincinnati Reds	15.9	24.4	4.9	49.6	61.4	-11.8	35,203,999	7	103	12
Cleveland Indians	11.6	23.0	1.4	39.9	57.6	3.4	8,236,166	26	81	26
Detroit Tigers	14.4	28.8	3.4	50.5	53.7	-3.2	28,773,834	16	97	17
Houston Astros	10.0	24.1	5.3	43.3	31.9	11.4	13,352,000	25	87	22
Kansas City Royals	17.5	21.0	9.1	52.0	57.1	-5.1	33,643,834	8	111	9
Los Angeles Dodgers	21.8	33.0	23.0	84.2	69.5	14.7	43,788,166	2	135	5
Milwaukee Brewers	15.3	19.8	6.3	45.3	58.1	-12.8	30,253,668	13	86	25
Minnesota Twins	21.5	20.0	6.9	52.8	52.5	0.2	27,432,834	19	95	19
Montreal Expos	14.0	24.0	4.9	46.7	35.0	11.8	15,869,667	24	81	23
New York Mets	19.0	50.0	13.0	86.9	81.3	5.6	44,352,002	1	145	3
New York Yankees	21.2	61.0	6.0	94.6	69.6	25.0	35,966,834	6	160	1
Oakland Athletics	24.0	25.0	9.0	64.4	77.2	-12.8	39,957,834	5	124	7
Philadelphia Phillies	15.2	23.7	6.7	50.0	50.3	-0.3	23,804,834	21	96	18
Pittsburgh Pirates	16.5	23.3	5.9	50.1	60.0	-9.9	32,589,167	12	95	19

Teams in 1992	Primary Revenue Sources			Revenue Total	Operating Expenses	Operating Income	Salaries	Salaries Rank	Value	Value Rank
	Gate	*Media*	*Stadium*							
San Diego Padres	16.8	28.2	6.9	53.6	53.9	-0.3	27,584,167	18	103	12
San Francisco Giants	13.8	24.5	4.8	47.0	58.1	-11.1	33,126,168	10	103	12
St. Louis Cardinals	21.0	25.5	0.0	50.9	47.6	3.3	26,889,836	20	98	16
Seattle Mariners	14.3	22.0	5.2	45.4	47.8	-2.4	22,483,834	22	81	24
Texas Rangers	19.7	26.8	15.3	66.2	51.4	14.8	29,740,667	14	106	10
Toronto Blue Jays	44.4	28.0	9.9	87.7	89.0	-1.3	43,663,666	3	155	2
Average	19.8	27.6	8.8	60.9	57.6	3.4	31,319,787		108.8	

Source: *Adapted from Ozanian, Michael K. "Foul Ball."* Financial World *162 (May 25, 1993): 28; http://asp.usato-day.com/sports/baseball/salaries/totalpayroll.aspx?year=1992.*

Teams in 1993	Primary Revenue Sources			Revenue Total	Operating Expenses	Operating Income	Salaries	Salaries Rank	Value	Value Rank
	Gate	*Media*	*Stadium*							
Anaheim Angels	17.1	26.7	7.3	53.8	51.2	2.6	27,230,334	18	93	18
Atlanta Braves	35.5	35.0	5.8	79.0	80.4	-1.4	38,131,000	7	96	14
Baltimore Orioles	35.4	27.4	15.8	81.3	52.4	28.9	26,914,000	19	129	8
Boston Red Sox	26.8	38.0	9.9	77.5	70.1	7.4	37,108,583	9	141	4
Chicago Cubs	30.3	36.0	13.6	82.8	75.4	7.4	38,303,166	6	120	9
Chicago White Sox	28.1	26.2	21.8	78.8	68.1	10.7	34,598,166	13	133	6
Cincinnati Reds	18.8	25.0	6.4	52.9	57.9	-5.0	42,851,167	2	86	21
Cleveland Indians	18.8	23.7	3.1	48.8	35.5	13.3	15,717,667	26	100	13
Colorado Rockies	33.3	5.0	11.0	52.2	34.5	12.7	8,829,000	28	110	11
Detroit Tigers	18.9	30.3	4.0	55.6	61.0	-5.4	36,548,166	10	89	20
Florida Marlins	28.7	5.0	7.5	44.9	32.4	12.5	18,196,545	25	81	25

Teams in 1993	Primary Revenue Sources			Revenue Total	Operating Expenses	Operating Income	Salaries	Salaries Rank	Value	Value Rank
	Gate	Media	Stadium							
Houston Astros	19.7	26.2	11.8	60.5	53.8	6.7	28,854,500	16	85	22
Kansas City Royals	18.3	21.0	9.7	51.7	58.0	-6.3	40,102,666	4	94	17
Los Angeles Dodgers	29.9	34.0	13.1	79.7	68.6	11.1	37,833,000	8	138	5
Milwaukee Brewers	17.0	21.5	5.1	46.3	48.5	-2.2	22,948,834	23	96	14
Minnesota Twins	18.8	22.3	5.0	48.9	47.9	1.0	27,284,933	17	83	24
Montreal Expos	14.2	24.0	4.3	46.2	33.8	12.4	14,881,334	27	75	26
New York Mets	20.3	46.1	11.5	80.8	75.9	4.9	38,350,167	5	150	3
New York Yankees	30.1	63.0	11.7	107.6	894.	18.2	41,305,000	3	166	1
Oakland Athletics	20.9	27.4	9.1	60.1	60.5	-0.4	35,565,834	12	114	10
Philadelphia Phillies	24.6	28.0	5.8	61.1	60.6	0.5	24,557,333	20	96	14
Pittsburgh Pirates	14.4	23.5	2.3	43.0	38.9	4.1	23,565,667	23	79	25
San Diego Padres	14.1	25.0	5.9	47.7	30.2	17.5	24,557,333	21	85	22
San Francisco Giants	23.6	27.5	15.0	69.1	69.8	-0.7	34,567,500	14	93	18
St. Louis Cardinals	25.0	27.0	10.1	64.8	44.8	20.0	22,615,334	24	105	12
Seattle Mariners	17.0	21.0	10.0	50.7	54.7	-4.0	31,616,333	15	80	24
Texas Rangers	20.0	27.5	10.1	60.3	59.2	1.1	35,641,959	11	132	7
Toronto Blue Jays	47.8	31.6	6.3	88.4	87.1	1.3	45,747,666	1	150	2
Average	23.8	27.7	9.0	63.4	57.2	6.0	30,515,119		107	

Source: Adapted from Ozanian, Michael K. "This $11 Billion Pastime." Financial World 163 (May 10, 1994): 52; http://asp.usatoday.com/sports/baseball/salaries/totalpayroll.aspx?year=1993.

Teams in 1994	Primary Revenue Sources			Revenue Total	Operating Expenses	Operating Income	Salaries	Salaries Rank	Value	Value Rank
	Gate	Media	Stadium							
Anaheim Angels	13.0	8.7	5.7	30.0	38.7	-8.7	20,691,500	23	102	20
Atlanta Braves	29.6	16.6	7.0	55.8	61.1	-5.3	40,502,167	3	120	10
Baltimore Orioles	25.6	11.4	13.4	53.1	47.6	5.5	37,669,769	9	164	2
Boston Red Sox	22.3	18.0	7.0	49.9	49.6	0.2	36,334,084	11	143	6
Chicago Cubs	23.7	17.0	9.7	53.8	50.1	3.7	35,717,333	12	135	8
Chicago White Sox	21.1	7.2	14.6	45.5	51.3	-5.8	38,413,836	8	152	4
Cincinnati Reds	14.4	8.4	5.3	30.6	47.5	-16.8	39,826,333	7	84	21
Cleveland Indians	22.9	5.4	10.1	41.0	45.5	-4.5	28,490,167	19	103	13
Colorado Rockies	24.3	6.2	10.2	43.5	38.9	4.6	22,979,000	22	117	11
Detroit Tigers	14.3	12.5	3.7	33.0	48.7	-15.7	40,042,501	6	83	22
Florida Marlins	19.4	12.7	5.6	40.9	31.9	9.0	20,275,500	21	92	18
Houston Astros	14.5	8.0	9.1	34.3	42.6	-8.4	32,041,500	15	92	18
Kansas City Royals	14.9	5.4	9.1	31.9	49.3	-17.4	40,481,334	4	96	16
Los Angeles Dodgers	21.3	15.3	10.4	49.5	53.6	-4.1	37,194,001	10	143	6
Milwaukee Brewers	13.2	6.3	3.6	26.0	37.9	-12.0	23,375,513	22	75	26
Minnesota Twins	14.6	5.4	3.6	26.2	35.7	-9.6	27,641,500	21	80	23
Montreal Expos	10.8	7.8	4.0	25.8	29.6	-3.8	18,640,000	27	76	24
New York Mets	12.5	22.2	7.6	45.0	47.2	-2.2	29,890,324	17	134	9
New York Yankees	22.5	36.4	10.0	71.5	62.8	8.7	44,785,334	1	185	1
Oakland Athletics	14.3	13.2	6.7	36.7	47.3	-10.6	33,169,500	13	101	15

Teams in 1994	Primary Revenue Sources			Revenue Total	Operating Expenses	Operating Income	Salaries	Salaries Rank	Value	Value Rank
	Gate	Media	Stadium							
Philadelphia Phillies	21.8	10.3	6.5	41.1	44.8	-3.7	31,422,000	16	96	16
Pittsburgh Pirates	11.8	8.6	2.5	25.6	31.7	-6.1	20,265,500	26	70	28
San Diego Padres	9.0	9.0	4.4	25.0	26.6	-1.6	13,529,333	28	74	27
San Francisco Giants	17.6	10.7	12.0	43.1	53.4	-10.3	40,054,300	5	102	14
St. Louis Cardinals	18.5	10.7	7.6	39.3	43.3	-4.0	28,956,001	18	110	12
Seattle Mariners	14.6	5.4	3.6	27.4	39.5	-12.1	27,872,167	20	76	24
Texas Rangers	27.0	10.0	10.3	50.1	44.9	5.2	32,423,097	14	157	3
Toronto Blue Jays	35.4	12.9	5.6	56.4	55.0	1.4	41,937,668	2	146	5
Average	18.7	11.5	7.5	40.4	44.9	4.4	31,593,617		110.5	

Source: *Adapted from Ozanian, Michael K., with Tushen Atre, Ronald Fink, Jennifer Reingold, John Kimmelman, Andrew Osterlund, and Jeff Sklar. "Suite Deals: Why New Stadiums Are Shaking up the Pecking Order of Sports Franchises."* Financial World *164 (May 9, 1995): 46; http://asp.usatoday.com/sports/baseball/salaries/totalpayroll.aspx?year=1994.*

Teams in 1995	Primary Revenue Sources			Revenue Total	Operating Expenses	Operating Income	Salaries	Salaries Rank	Value	Value Rank
	Gate	Media	Stadium							
Anaheim Angels	15.1	12.8	9.1	39.0	42.0	-3.0	28,974,167	18	90	22
Atlanta Braves	30.9	22.1	5.6	60.7	63.6	-2.9	45,199,000	3	163	3
Baltimore Orioles	35.4	18.9	18.8	75.1	69.1	6.0	40,835,519	4	168	2
Boston Red Sox	27.1	24.2	14.7	67.9	52.5	15.4	28,672,250	19	143	7
Chicago Cubs	25.3	21.1	14.5	62.9	58.1	4.8	32,460,834	12	140	8
Chicago White Sox	20.0	16.4	17.3	55.7	63.7	-8.0	39,632,834	5	144	6
Cincinnati Reds	14.4	8.4	5.3	40.4	52.2	-11.8	37,240,667	6	99	17
Cleveland Indians	31.5	15.7	11.0	60.2	58.8	1.4	35,185,500	9	125	12

(Continued)

Teams in 1995	Primary Revenue Sources			Revenue Total	Operating Expenses	Operating Income	Salaries	Salaries Rank	Value	Value Rank
	Gate	*Media*	*Stadium*							
Colorado Rockies	35.5	15.0	17.6	70.3	58.8	11.5	31,146,135	15	133	10
Detroit Tigers	13.9	18.1	5.2	39.1	44.4	-5.3	35,862,501	8	106	15
Florida Marlins	16.4	19.0	9.5	47.8	41.0	6.8	23,670,000	25	98	18
Houston Astros	12.3	15.3	13.8	44.4	48.9	-4.5	31,624,000	14	97	19
Kansas City Royals	13.5	10.9	9.5	35.8	42.7	-6.9	27,608,834	21	80	23
Los Angeles Dodgers	26.6	24.4	18.0	70.9	58.1	12.8	30,459,001	17	147	5
Milwaukee Brewers	11.9	12.1	3.4	29.5	28.5	1.0	16,189,600	27	71	25
Minnesota Twins	11.4	14.3	2.5	30.2	27.7	2.5	24,527,500	23	74	24
Montreal Expos	11.9	12.1	3.4	29.3	22.2	7.1	12,031,000	28	68	26
New York Mets	14.1	33.6	11.2	61.5	40.7	20.8	24,301,440	24	131	11
New York Yankees	24.7	54.3	12.9	93.9	69.9	24.0	46,657,016	2	209	1
Oakland Athletics	13.6	17.0	8.7	41.2	46.1	-4.9	35,961,500	7	97	19
Philadelphia Phillies	19.8	15.9	7.7	45.3	41.9	3.4	28,580,000	20	103	16
Pittsburgh Pirates	9.2	12.2	1.5	24.9	26.6	-1.7	17,043,000	26	62	28
San Diego Padres	9.8	11.1	5.4	28.2	33.3	-5.1	25,923,334	22	67	27
San Francisco Giants	14.0	19.8	10.4	46.4	48.3	-1.9	34,931,849	10	122	13
St. Louis Cardinals	17.2	19.8	9.9	48.8	47.9	0.9	30,956,000	16	112	14
Seattle Mariners	17.2	11.6	6.0	36.7	46.5	-9.8	34,241,533	11	92	21
Texas Rangers	22.2	16.9	20.7	61.9	54.3	7.6	32,367,226	13	138	9

Teams in 1995	Primary Revenue Sources			Revenue Total	Operating Expenses	Operating Income	Salaries	Salaries Rank	Value	Value Rank
	Gate	Media	Stadium							
Toronto Blue Jays	33.1	20.7	6.7	62.5	64.1	-1.6	49,791,500	1	152	4
Average	19.6	18.4	10.2	50.4	48.3	2.1	31,502,634		115.4	

Source: Adapted from Ozanian, Michael K. "Sports: The High Stakes Game of Team Ownership." Financial World 165 (May 20, 1996): 56; http://asp.usatoday.com/sports/baseball/salaries/totalpayroll.aspx?year=1995.

Teams in 1996	Primary Revenue Sources			Revenue Total	Operating Expenses	Operating Income	Salaries	Salaries Rank	Value	Value Rank
	Gate	Media	Stadium							
Anaheim Angels	15.0	18.3	7.1	39.0	42.0	-3.0	28,974,167	18	90	22
Atlanta Braves	40.1	30.3	6.3	60.7	63.6	-2.9	45,199,000	3	163	3
Baltimore Orioles	51.0	30.6	21.4	75.1	69.1	6.0	40,835,519	4	168	2
Boston Red Sox	39.0	30.9	16.4	67.9	52.5	15.4	28,672,250	19	143	7
Chicago Cubs	28.3	29.3	16.9	62.9	58.1	4.8	32,460,834	12	140	8
Chicago White Sox	22.2	24.3	20.9	55.7	63.7	-8.0	39,632,834	5	144	6
Cincinnati Reds	14.9	21.5	7.0	40.4	52.2	-11.8	37,240,667	6	99	17
Cleveland Indians	48.0	21.6	22.9	60.2	58.8	1.4	35,185,500	9	125	12
Colorado Rockies	46.0	22.8	23.9	70.3	58.8	11.5	31,146,135	15	133	10
Detroit Tigers	12.4	24.7	5.4	39.1	44.4	-5.3	35,862,501	8	106	15
Florida Marlins	21.5	23.9	7.3	47.8	41.0	6.8	23,670,000	25	98	18
Houston Astros	21.8	22.3	14.4	44.4	48.9	-4.5	31,624,000	14	97	19
Kansas City Royals	14.5	16.5	10.2	35.8	42.7	-6.9	27,608,834	21	80	23
Los Angeles Dodgers	31.9	31.8	22.0	70.9	58.1	12.8	30,459,001	17	147	5
Milwaukee Brewers	14.9	15.1	9.7	29.5	28.5	1.0	16,189,600	27	71	25

(Continued)

Teams in 1996	Primary Revenue Sources			Revenue Total	Operating Expenses	Operating Income	Salaries	Salaries Rank	Value	Value Rank
	Gate	Media	Stadium							
Minnesota Twins	23.8	20.4	5.0	30.2	27.7	2.5	24,527,500	23	74	24
Montreal Expos	14.8	19.4	4.8	29.3	22.2	7.1	12,031,000	28	68	26
New York Mets	18.2	30.9	16.8	61.5	40.7	20.8	24,301,440	24	131	11
New York Yankees	42.6	69.8	17.5	93.9	69.9	24.0	46,657,016	2	209	1
Oakland Athletics	12.5	25.2	9.8	41.2	46.1	-4.9	35,961,500	7	97	19
Philadelphia Phillies	18.7	21.4	8.0	45.3	41.9	3.4	28,580,000	20	103	16
Pittsburgh Pirates	23.4	17.7	7.7	24.9	26.6	-1.7	17,043,000	26	62	28
San Diego Padres	21.7	16.5	12.1	28.2	33.3	-5.1	25,923,334	22	67	27
San Francisco Giants	14.3	25.5	9.6	46.4	48.3	-1.9	34,931,849	10	122	13
St. Louis Cardinals	27.3	25.7	14.9	48.8	47.9	0.9	30,956,000	16	112	14
Seattle Mariners	31.0	17.2	7.5	36.7	46.5	-9.8	34,241,533	11	92	21
Texas Rangers	35.5	24.3	25.5	61.9	54.3	7.6	32,367,226	13	138	9
Toronto Blue Jays	36.3	28.4	3.1	62.5	64.1	-1.6	49,791,500	1	152	4
Average	25.7	25.2	12.6	50.4	48.3	2.1	31,502,634		115.4	

Source: *Adapted from Tushen, Atre, and Kristine Auns, Kurt Badenhausen, Karen McAuliffe, Christopher Nikolov, and Michael K. Oznanian. "Scoreboard Evaluation."* Financial World *166 (June 17, 1997): 47; http://asp.usatoday. com/sports/baseball/salaries/totalpayroll.aspx?year=1996.*

Teams in 1997	Revenue	Operating Expenses	Operating Income	Salaries	Salaries Rank	Value	Value Rank
Anaheim Angels	62.6	72.2	-9.6	29,452,672	22	157	18
Atlanta Braves	119.6	101.4	18.2	50,488,500	5	299	5
Baltimore Orioles	134.5	115.8	18.7	54,871,399	2	362	2

Teams in 1997	Revenue	Operating Expenses	Operating Income	Salaries	Salaries Rank	Value	Value Rank
Boston Red Sox	97.6	88.5	9.1	43,232,000	12	236	9
Chicago Cubs	81.5	73.4	8.1	39,829,333	14	204	11
Chicago White Sox	82.3	86.5	-4.2	54,377,500	3	214	10
Cincinnati Reds	50.2	70.1	-19.9	46,267,000	8	136	21
Cleveland Indians	134.0	118.6	15.4	54,130,232	4	322	3
Colorado Rockies	116.6	78.3	38.3	42,870,501	13	303	4
Detroit Tigers	50.6	51.0	-0.4	16,304,500	27	137	20
Florida Marlins	88.2	93.7	-5.5	47,753,000	7	159	17
Houston Astros	68.0	65.7	2.3	32,935,000	20	190	13
Kansas City Royals	51.2	63	-11.8	31,225,000	21	108	26
Los Angeles Dodgers	94.3	93.4	0.9	43,400,000	11	236	8
Milwaukee Brewers	46.9	51.7	-4.8	21,020,332	25	127	24
Minnesota Twins	46.8	63.3	-16.5	25,747,500	23	94	27
Montreal Expos	43.6	47.3	-3.7	18,335,500	26	87	28
New York Mets	80.5	72.4	8.1	38,474,567	16	193	12
New York Yankees	144.7	123.3	21.4	59,148,877	1	362	1
Oakland Athletics	56.4	48.9	7.5	21,911,000	24	118	25
Philadelphia Phillies	57.1	54.6	2.5	35,463,500	17	131	23
Pittsburgh Pirates	49.3	41.8	7.5	9,071,666	28	38	22
San Diego Padres	57.6	64.3	-6.7	34,698,672	18	161	16
San Francisco Giants	69.8	70.0	0.2	33,469,213	19	188	14
St. Louis Cardinals	82.9	80.5	2.4	44,179,167	10	174	15
Seattle Mariners	89.8	78.4	11.4	39,667,628	15	251	7
Texas Rangers	97.6	88.5	9.1	50,112,268	6	254	6

(Continued)

Teams in 1997	Revenue	Operating Expenses	Operating Income	Salaries	Salaries Rank	Value	Value Rank
Toronto Blue Jays	67.1	87.6	-20.5	45,894,833	9	141	19
Average	79.1	76.6	2.5	48,954,882		194	

Adapted from Badenhouse, Kurt, and Christopher Nikolov, Michael Alken, and Michael K. Oza-nian. "Sports Values: More than a Game." Forbes 162 (December 14, 1998): 126;. Forbes magazine data © 2006, reprinted by permission; http://asp.usatoday.com/sports/baseball/salaries/totalpayroll. aspx?year=1997.

Teams in 1998	Revenue	Operating Expenses	Operating Income	Salaries	Salaries Rank	Value	Value Rank
Anaheim Angels	88.5	88.7	-0.2	38,537,000	17	195	18
Arizona Diamondbacks	116.3	93.8	22.5	28,936,500	23	291	6
Atlanta Braves	142.7	126.3	16.4	63,159,898	3	357	3
Baltimore Orioles	140.5	132.0	8.5	70,408,134	1	351	4
Boston Red Sox	106.9	114.5	-7.6	51,647,000	8	256	9
Chicago Cubs	93.1	101.0	-7.9	49,383,000	10	224	14
Chicago White Sox	74.1	74.3	0.2	36,840,000	18	178	19
Cincinnati Reds	54.4	55.0	0.6	21,995,000	27	163	20
Cleveland Indians	149.7	127.2	22.5	59,033,499	4	359	2
Colorado Rockies	124.6	105.1	19.5	47,433,333	13	311	5
Detroit Tigers	54.2	58.7	-4.5	22,625,000	26	152	24
Florida Marlins	69.5	78.1	-8.6	33,434,000	20	153	23
Houston Astros	82.5	86.2	-3.7	40,629,000	15	239	11
Kansas City Royals	53.5	64.4	-10.9	32,912,500	21	98	28
Los Angeles Dodgers	107.9	119.6	-11.7	47,970,000	12	270	8
Milwaukee Brewers	55.5	64.3	-8.8	32,252,583	22	155	22
Minnesota Twins	46.8	53.9	-7.1	26,182,500	24	89	29
Montreal Expos	46.5	40.9	5.6	9,202,000	30	84	30
New York Mets	99.7	14.9	-5.2	49,559,665	9	249	10

Teams in 1998	Revenue	Operating Expenses	Operating Income	Salaries	Salaries Rank	Value	Value Rank
New York Yankees	175.5	152.5	23.0	63,159,898	2	491	1
Oakland Athletics	56.7	53.4	3.3	20,063,000	28	125	27
Philadelphia Phillies	66.0	61.5	4.5	36,085,000	19	145	25
Pittsburgh Pirates	51.7	49.1	2.6	13,752,000	29	145	25
San Diego Padres	78.9	86.9	-8.0	45,368,000	14	213	16
San Francisco Giants	73.3	79.7	-6.4	40,320,835	16	213	15
St. Louis Cardinals	97.8	96.2	1.6	52,572,500	6	205	16
Seattle Mariners	81.3	89.9	-8.6	52,032,291	7	236	12
Tampa Bay Devil Rays	93.7	73.1	20.6	25,317,500	25	225	13
Texas Rangers	108.1	107.6	0.5	54,704,595	5	281	7
Toronto Blue Jays	73.4	82.9	-9.5	48,415,000	11	162	21
Average	88.8	86.9	1.9	40,465,041		220	

Adapted from Badenhausen, Kurt, and William Sicheri. "Baseball Games." Forbes 163 (May 31, 1999): 114; Forbes magazine data © 2006, reprinted by permission; http://asp.usatoday.com/sports/baseball/salaries/totalpayroll.aspx?year=1998.

Teams in 1999	Revenue	Operating Expenses	Operating Income	Salaries	Salaries Rank	Value	Value Rank
Anaheim Angels	90.7	93.2	-2.5	49,893,166	13	195	18
Arizona Diamondbacks	111.5	98.6	12.9	70,370,999	9	268	12
Atlanta Braves	155.2	137.1	18.3	75,065,000	3	388	2
Baltimore Orioles	151.7	135.2	16.5	70,818,363	8	364	4
Boston Red Sox	123.3	120.9	2.4	71,720,000	5	284	10
Chicago Cubs	105.4	107.0	-1.6	55,368,500	10	242	13
Chicago White Sox	73.8	62.1	11.7	24,550,000	24	166	21
Cincinnati Reds	49.4	54.5	-5.1	42,927,395	20	175	19

(Continued)

Teams in 1999	Revenue	Operating Expenses	Operating Income	Salaries	Salaries Rank	Value	Value Rank
Cleveland Indians	151.7	135.2	16.5	73,857,962	4	364	3
Colorado Rockies	122.2	114.3	7.9	54,392,504	12	305	7
Detroit Tigers	71.5	70.4	1.1	34,959,666	22	200	16
Florida Marlins	59.3	56.9	2.4	15,150,000	30	125	27
Houston Astros	93.3	98.8	-5.5	55,289,000	11	280	11
Kansas City Royals	62.5	56.7	5.8	16,527,000	27	122	28
Los Angeles Dodgers	120.3	141.4	-21.1	70,935,786	7	325	5
Milwaukee Brewers	60.8	75.2	-14.4	42,927,395	19	167	20
Minnesota Twins	47.7	45.2	2.2	16,355,000	29	91	29
Montreal Expos	47.1	45.2	1.9	16,363,000	28	89	30
New York Mets	125.6	126.8	-1.2	71,331,425	6	314	6
New York Yankees	195.6	178.1	17.5	88,130,709	1	548	1
Oakland Athletics	60.9	57.0	3.9	24,150,333	26	134	26
Philadelphia Phillies	68.1	65.1	3.0	30,516,500	23	150	25
Pittsburgh Pirates	57.6	57.4	0.2	24,217,666	25	161	24
San Diego Padres	78.9	87.7	-8.8	45,932,179	17	197	17
San Francisco Giants	71.9	80.9	-9.0	46,059,557	16	237	14
St. Louis Cardinals	104.5	99.1	5.4	46,248,195	15	219	15
Seattle Mariners	111.6	106.1	5.5	44,371,336	18	290	9
Tampa Bay Devil Rays	77.5	84.0	-6.5	37,812,500	21	163	22
Texas Rangers	117.5	127.0	-9.5	81,301,598	2	294	8
Toronto Blue Jays	73.7	76.5	-2.8	48,165,333	14	162	23
Average	94.3	93.3	1.0	48,190,369		233.4	

Adapted from Ozanian, Michael K. "Too Much to Lose." Forbes 165 (12 June 2000): 100; Forbes magazine data © 2006, reprinted by permission; http://asp.usatoday.com/sports/baseball/salaries/to-talpayroll.aspx?year=1999.

Teams in 2000	Revenue	Operating Expenses	Operating Income	Salaries	Salaries Rank	Value	Value Rank
Anaheim Angels	94.4	103.3	-8.9	51,266,667	19	198	21
Arizona Diamondbacks	109.1	117	-7.9	79,230,333	7	245	15
Atlanta Braves	145.5	137.8	7.7	82,732,500	4	407	3
Baltimore Orioles	124.0	121.9	2.1	83,141,198	3	335	8
Boston Red Sox	125.7	118.3	7.4	81,210,333	5	342	7
Chicago Cubs	112.4	103.3	9.1	62,129,333	12	247	14
Chicago White Sox	92.6	74.8	17.8	31,159,000	26	213	17
Cincinnati Reds	77.8	70.9	6.9	44,217,500	22	187	22
Cleveland Indians	142.9	138.7	4.2	76,508,334	8	372	5
Colorado Rockies	119.1	112.7	6.4	61,314,190	14	334	9
Detroit Tigers	120.8	108.7	12.1	61,740,167	13	290	13
Florida Marlins	67.3	60.8	6.5	19,870,000	29	128	28
Houston Astros	122.2	99.9	22.3	52,081,667	18	318	12
Kansas City Royals	72.6	68.3	4.3	23,132,500	28	138	27
Los Angeles Dodgers	131.3	148.7	-17.4	90,375,953	2	381	4
Milwaukee Brewers	69.6	71.2	-1.6	35,782,833	23	211	19
Minnesota Twins	58.0	52.2	5.8	15,654,500	30	99	29
Montreal Expos	53.9	62.0	-8.1	33,527,666	24	92	30
New York Mets	162.0	140.7	21.3	79,759,762	6	454	2
New York Yankees	192.2	170.3	21.9	92,938,260	1	645	1
Oakland Athletics	74.7	69.5	5.2	32,121,833	25	149	26
Philadelphia Phillies	79.2	80.3	-1.1	46,947,667	20	158	24
Pittsburgh Pirates	70.4	68.1	2.3	26,561,667	27	211	18
San Diego Padres	84.0	92.0	-8.0	54,971,000	16	176	23

(Continued)

Teams in 2000	Revenue	Operating Expenses	Operating Income	Salaries	Salaries Rank	Value	Value Rank
San Francisco Giants	138.8	111.4	27.4	53,541,000	17	333	10
St. Louis Cardinals	110.5	113.5	-3.0	63,093,023	11	243	16
Seattle Mariners	138.3	120.5	17.8	59,215,000	15	332	11
Tampa Bay Devil Rays	81.3	92.6	-11.3	64,407,910	10	150	25
Texas Rangers	126.5	119.1	7.4	70,785,000	9	342	6
Toronto Blue Jays	80.3	86.2	-5.9	46,363,332	21	161	23
Average	105.9	101.6	4.3	55,859,338		262.9	

Adapted from Ozanian, Michael K., and Kurt Badenhausen. "Cable Guy." Forbes 167 (April 16, 2001): 148; Forbes magazine data © 2006, reprinted by permission; http://asp.usatoday.com/sports/baseball/salaries/totalpayroll.aspx?year=2000.

Teams in 2001	Revenue	Operating Expenses	Operating Income	Salaries	Salaries Rank	Value	Value Rank
Anahim Angels	103.0	97.3	5.7	47,735,168	22	195	23
Arizona Diamondbacks	127.0	130.9	-3.9	85,247,999	8	280	14
Atlanta Braves	160.0	150.5	9.5	91,936,166	6	424	5
Baltimore Orioles	133.0	129.8	3.2	74,279,540	12	319	12
Boston Red Sox	152.0	163.4	-11.4	109,675,833	2	426	4
Chicago Cubs	131.0	123.1	7.9	64,515,833	15	287	13
Chicago White Sox	101.0	104.8	-3.8	65,628,667	14	233	20
Cincinnati Reds	87.0	82.7	4.3	48,784,000	21	204	22
Cleveland Indians	150.0	153.6	-3.6	92,660,001	5	360	7
Colorado Rockies	142.0	125.2	16.8	71,541,334	13	347	10
Detroit Tigers	114.0	101.7	12.3	49,356,167	20	262	16
Florida Marlins	81.0	79.6	1.4	35,562,500	26	137	28
Houston Astros	125.0	120.9	4.1	60,387,667	17	337	11
Kansas City Royals	85.0	82.8	2.2	35,422,500	27	152	26
Los Angeles Dodgers	143.0	172.6	-29.6	109,105,953	3	435	3

Teams in 2001	Revenue	Operating Expenses	Operating Income	Salaries	Salaries Rank	Value	Value Rank
Milwaukee Brewers	108.0	89.2	18.8	45,099,333	23	238	18
Minnesota Twins	75	71.4	3.6	24,130,000	30	127	29
Montreal Expos	63	66.4	-3.4	34,849,500	28	108	30
New York Mets	169.0	154.7	14.3	93,674,428	4	482	2
New York Yankees	215.0	196.3	18.7	112,287,143	1	730	1
Oakland Athletics	90.0	83.2	6.8	33,810,750	29	157	25
Philadelphia Phillies	94.0	91.4	2.6	41,663,833	24	231	19
Pittsburgh Pirates	108.0	98.5	9.5	57,760,833	18	242	17
San Diego Padres	92.0	86.3	5.7	38,882,833	25	207	21
San Francisco Giants	142.0	125.2	16.8	63,280,167	16	355	9
St. Louis Cardinals	123.0	128.1	-5.1	78,333,333	9	271	15
Seattle Mariners	166.0	151.9	14.1	74,720,834	11	373	6
Tampa Bay Devil Rays	92.0	98.1	-6.1	56,980,000	19	142	28
Texas Rangers	134.0	140.5	-6.5	88,633,500	7	356	8
Toronto Blue Jays	91.0	111.6	-20.6	76,895,999	10	182	24
Average	119.0	116.5	2.5	63,277,533		286.0	

Adapted from Badenhausen, Kurt, and Cecily Fluke, Leslie Kump, and Michael K. Ozaniana." Double Play." Forbes 169 (April 15, 2002): 96; Forbes magazine data © 2006, reprinted by permission; http://asp.usatoday.com/sports/baseball/salaries/totalpayroll.aspx?year=2001.

Teams in 2002	Revenue	Operating Expenses	Operating Income	Salaries	Salaries Rank	Value	Value Rank
Anaheim Angels	n.a.	n.a.	-3.7	61,721,667	15	225	21
Arizona Diamondbacks	n.a.	n.a.	-22.2	102,819,999	4	269	14
Atlanta Braves	n.a.	n.a.	-25.0	93,470,367	7	449	5
Baltimore Orioles	n.a.	n.a.	12.4	60,493,487	16	310	11

(Continued)

Teams in 2002	Revenue	Operating Expenses	Operating Income	Salaries	Salaries Rank	Value	Value Rank
Boston Red Sox	n.a.	n.a.	-2.1	108,366,060	2	488	3
Chicago Cubs	n.a.	n.a.	11.9	75,690,833	12	335	8
Chicago White Sox	n.a.	n.a.	1.2	57,052,833	18	233	17
Cincinnati Reds	n.a.	n.a.	4.9	45,050,390	23	223	22
Cleveland Indians	n.a.	n.a.	-1.0	78,909,449	9	331	9
Colorado Rockies	n.a.	n.a.	7.1	56,851,043	19	304	13
Detroit Tigers	n.a.	n.a.	-5.3	55,048,000	20	237	16
Florida Marlins	n.a.	n.a.	-14	41,979,917	25	136	29
Houston Astros	n.a.	n.a.	-0.8	63,448,417	14	327	10
Kansas City Royals	n.a.	n.a.	-11.2	47,257,000	22	153	26
Los Angeles Dodgers	n.a.	n.a.	-25.0	94,850,953	5	449	4
Milwaukee Brewers	n.a.	n.a.	-6.1	50,287,833	21	206	23
Minnesota Twins	n.a.	n.a.	0.4	40,225,000	27	148	27
Montreal Expos	n.a.	n.a.	-9.1	38,670,500	29	113	30
New York Mets	n.a.	n.a.	11.6	94,633,593	6	498	2
New York Yankees	n.a.	n.a.	16.1	125,928,583	1	849	1
Oakland Athletics	n.a.	n.a.	6.6	40,004,167	28	172	24
Philadelphia Phillies	n.a.	n.a.	-11.9	57,954,999	17	239	15
Pittsburgh Pirates	n.a.	n.a.	-1.6	42,323,599	24	224	16
San Diego Padres	n.a.	n.a.	4.6	41,425,000	26	226	19
San Francisco Giants	n.a.	n.a.	13.9	78,299,835	10	382	7
St. Louis Cardinals	n.a.	n.a.	-2.0	74,660,875	13	308	12
Seattle Mariners	n.a.	n.a.	23.3	80,282,668	8	385	8

Teams in 2002	Revenue	Operating Expenses	Operating Income	Salaries	Salaries Rank	Value	Value Rank
Tampa Bay Devil Rays	n.a.	n.a.	1.4	34,380,000	30	145	28
Texas Rangers	n.a.	n.a.	-24.5	105,726,122	3	332	9
Toronto Blue Jays	n.a.	n.a.	-23.9	76,864,333	11	166	25
Average			-1.3	67,489,258		295	

n.a. = Not available.

Adapted from Ozanian, Michael K., and Cecily J. Fluke, "Inside Pitch." Forbes 171 (April 28, 2003): 66; Forbes magazine data © 2006, reprinted by permission; http://asp.usatoday.com/sports/baseball/salaries/totalpayroll.aspx?year=2002.

Teams in 2003	Revenue	Operating Expenses	Operating Income	Salaries	Salaries Rank	Value	Value Rank
Anaheim Angels	127	132.5	-5.5	79,031,667	12	241	20
Arizona Diamondbacks	126	141.2	-15.2	80,657,000	10	276	16
Atlanta Braves	156	156.3	-0.3	106,243,667	3	374	6
Baltimore Orioles	129	119.9	9.1	73,877,500	13	296	12
Boston Red Sox	190	201.4	-11.4	99,946,500	6	533	2
Chicago Cubs	156	147.7	8.3	79,868,333	11	358	8
Chicago White Sox	124	111.2	12.8	51,010,000	22	248	18
Cincinnati Reds	123	111.3	11.7	59,355,667	17	245	19
Cleveland Indians	127	116.6	10.4	48,584,834	26	292	13
Colorado Rockies	124	130.3	-6.3	67,179,667	16	285	14
Detroit Tigers	117	116.7	0.3	49,168,000	24	235	21
Florida Marlins	101	112.6	-11.6	48,750,000	25	172	25
Houston Astros	128	129.9	-1.9	71,040,000	14	320	9
Kansas City Royals	98	91.4	6.6	40,518,000	29	171	26
Los Angeles Dodgers	154	173.1	-19.1	105,872,620	4	399	4
Milwaukee Brewers	102	96.9	5.1	40,627,000	28	174	24

(Continued)

Teams in 2003	Revenue	Operating Expenses	Operating Income	Salaries	Salaries Rank	Value	Value Rank
Minnesota Twins	81	89.3	-8.3	55,505,000	18	168	28
Montreal Expos	81	89.3	-8.3	51,948,500	20	145	30
New York Mets	158	177.3	-19.3	117,176,429	2	442	3
New York Yankees	238	264.3	-26.3	152,749,814	1	832	1
Oakland Athletics	110	98.8	11.2	50,260,834	23	186	23
Philadelphia Phillies	115	127.5	-12.5	70,780,000	15	281	15
Pittsburgh Pirates	109	109.3	-0.3	54,812,429	19	217	22
San Diego Padres	106	101.1	4.9	45,210,000	27	276	17
San Francisco Giants	153	152.3	0.7	82,852,167	9	368	7
St.Louis Cardinals	131	142.1	-11.1	83,786,666	8	314	10
Seattle Mariners	169	152	17	86,959,167	7	396	5
Tampa Bay Devil Rays	101	93.5	7.5	19,630,000	30	152	29
Texas Rangers	127	155.5	-28.5	103,491,667	5	306	11
Toronto Blue Jays	99	99	0	51,269,000	21	169	27
Average	129	130.9	-1.9	70,938,738		295	

Adapted from Vardi, Than. "Hardball." Forbes 173 (April 26, 2004): 70; Forbes magazine data © 2006, reprinted by permission; http://asp.usatoday.com/sports/baseball/salaries/totalpayroll. aspx?year=2003.

Teams in 2004	Revenue	Operating Expenses	Operating Income	Salaries	Salaries Rank	Value	Value Rank
Anaheim Angels	147	177.0	-30.0	100,534,667	3	294	16
Arizona Diamondbacks	136	154.7	-18.7	69,780,750	13	286	18
Atlanta Braves	162	146.6	15.4	90,182,500	8	382	8
Baltimore Orioles	148	114.0	34.0	51,623,333	20	341	12

Teams in 2004	Revenue	Operating Expenses	Operating Income	Salaries	Salaries Rank	Value	Value Rank
Boston Red Sox	201	238.1	-37.1	127,298,500	2	563	2
Chicago Cubs	170	158.6	11.4	90,560,000	7	398	6
Chicago White Sox	131	122.9	8.1	65,212,500	15	262	19
Cincinnati Reds	127	124.4	22.6	46,615,250	4	255	20
Cleveland Indians	139	111.8	27.2	34,319,300	27	319	15
Colorado Rockies	132	139.8	-7.8	65,445,167	14	290	17
Detroit Tigers	126	118.1	7.9	46,832,000	23	239	22
Florida Marlins	103	100.0	3.0	42,143,042	25	206	26
Houston Astros	155	146.4	9.6	75,397,000	12	357	11
Kansas City Royals	104	101.0	3.0	47,609,000	22	187	27
Los Angeles Dodgers	166	173.4	-7.4	92,902,001	6	424	4
Milwaukee Brewers	112	87.8	24.2	27,528,500	30	208	25
Minnesota Twins	102	102.5	-0.5	53,585,000	19	178	29
Montreal Expos	80	83.0	-3.0	41,197,500	26	310	16
New York Mets	180	191.1	-11.1	96,660,970	4	505	3
New York Yankees	264	301.1	-37.1	184,193,950	1	950	1
Oakland Athletics	116	100.1	5.9	59,425,667	16	185	28
Philadelphia Phillies	167	160.9	6.1	93,219,167	5	392	7
Pittsburgh Pirates	109	96.8	12.2	32,227,929	28	218	22
San Diego Padres	150	132.9	17.1	55,384,833	17	329	13
San Francisco Giants	259	252.1	6.9	82,019,166	10	381	9
St. Louis Cardinals	151	154.9	-3.9	83,228,333	9	370	10

(Continued)

Teams in 2004	Revenue	Operating Expenses	Operating Income	Salaries	Salaries Rank	Value	Value Rank
Seattle Mariners	173	162.2	10.8	81,515,834	11	415	5
Tampa Bay	110	82.8	27.2	29,556,667	29	178	29
Texas Rangers	142	139.1	2.9	55,050,417	18	326	14
Toronto Blue Jays	107	99.2	7.8	50,017,000	21	214	24
Average	142	137.6	4.4	69,042,199		332	

Adapted from Badenhausen, Kurt, and Jack Gage, Lesley Kump, Michael K. Ozanian, Maya Roney. "Baseball Team Valuations." Forbes 175 (April 25, 2005): 95; Forbes magazine data © 2006, re-printed by permission; http://asp.usatoday.com/sports/baseball/salaries/totalpayroll.aspx?year=2004.

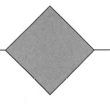

Appendix O

MAJOR LEAGUE TEAM PAYROLLS, 1987–1989, 2005–2006

Team	1987 Salaries	1988 Rank	1988 Salaries	1988 Rank
Anaheim Angels/Los Angeles Angels	11,559,593	10	10,932,388	15
Arizona Diamondbacks				
Atlanta Braves	14,771,382	2	9,967,167	18
Baltimore Orioles	12,371429	4	9,995,404	17
Boston Red Sox	11,080,695	11	15,544,592	3
Chicago Cubs	13,478,225	3	12,339,833	9
Chicago White Sox	9,849,689	19	5,906,952	26
Cincinnati Reds	9,258,848	21	8,368,833	21
Cleveland Indians	6,623,133	25	7,819,500	22
Colorado Rockies				
Detroit Tigers	10,850,643	13.2	15,597,071	2
Florida Marlins				
Houston Astros	10,153,335	17	13,454,667	7
Kansas City Royals	11,754,512	9	11,558,873	13
Los Angeles Dodgers	11,970,412	6	15,462,515	5
Milwaukee Brewers	12,216,965	5	10,932,388	16
Minnesota Twins	7,238,667	23	12,154,800	11
New York Mets	11,013,714	12	15,502,714	4
New York Yankees	15,398,047	1	18,909,152	1
Oakland Athletics	10,008,823	18	11,380,183	14
Philadelphia Phillies	11,785,445	5	12,935,500	8
Pittsburgh Pirates	10,223,945	15	7,627,500	23
San Diego Padres	9,801,052	20	9,878,168	19
San Francisco Giants	7,777,945	24	12,188,000	10
St. Louis Cardinals	10,441,639	14	14,000,000	6
Seattle Mariners	5,549,870	26	6,545,950	24
Tampa Bay				
Texas Rangers	8,101,222	22	6,008,000	25
Toronto Blue Jays	11,800,281	7	11,673,725	12

1989 Salaries	1989 Rank	2005 Salaries	2005 Rank	2006 Salaries	2006 Rank
14,713,833	11	97,725,322	4	103,625,333	3
		62,329,166	17	59,22l226	23
9,551,334	22	86,457,302	10	92,461,852	9
8,176,666	25	73,914,333	14	72,585,713	15
18,553,385	4	123,505,125	2	120,,100,524	2
10,165,500	20	87,032,933	9	94,841,167	7
7,595,561	26	75,178,000	13	102,875,667	4
11,087,000	17	61,892,583	18	59,4889,015	22
8,928,500	24	41,502,500	26	56,795,867	24
		48,155,000	24	41,133,000	28
15,099,596	10	69,092,000	15	82,302,069	14
		60,408,834	19	14,998,500	30
16,011,000	5	76,779,000	12	92,551.503	8
15,427,162	9	36,881,000	29	47,294,000	26
21,584,161	1	83,039,000	11	99,176,950	6
10,373,000	19	39,934,833	27	56,790,000	25
15,540,500	8	56,186,000	20	63,810,048	19
20,013,212	3	101,305,821	3	100,901,085	5
20,562,985	2	208,306,817	1	198,662,180	1
14,602,999	12	55,425,762	22	62,322,054	21
9,640,000	21	95,522,000	5	88,273,333	13
11,993,500	16	39,934,833	28	46,867,750	27
13,094,000	14	63,290,833	16	69,725,179	17
14,094,000	13	90,199,500	7	90,862,063	10
15,555,333	7	92,106,833	6	88,441,218	11
9,547,500	23	87,754,334	8	88,324,500	12
		29,679,067	30	35,417,967	29
10,689,500	18	55,849,000	21	65,468,130	18
16,011,000	6	45,719,500	25	71,915,000	16

Team	1987 Salaries	1988 Rank	1988 Salaries	1988 Rank
Montreal Expos/Washington Nationals	10,195,246	16	8,852,333	20
Average	10,587,491		11,366,777	

Source: USA Today, *November 5, 1987; http://asp.usatoday.com/sports/baseball/salaries/totalpay-roll.aspx?year=1988; http://asp.usatoday.com/sports/baseball/salaries/totalpayroll.aspx?year=1989; http://asp.usatoday.com/sports/baseball/salaries/totalpayroll.aspx?year=2005;* Chicago Tribune, *April 6, 2006, IV:8. The payrolls were obtained by Associated Press from management and player sources. They include salaries and pro-rated shares of signing bonuses.*

1989 Salaries	1989 Rank	2005 Salaries	2005 Rank	2006 Salaries	2006 Rank
12,305,389	15	48,581,500	23	63,267,500	20
13,496,793		73,122,958		74,262,169	

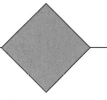

Appendix P

MAJOR LEAGUE BALLPARKS, 2006

National League

Team	Ballparks	First Game	Capacity	Dimensions (feet)		
				LF	*CF*	*RF*
Arizona Diamondbacks	Chase Field	03/31/1998	48,500	328′	402′	335′
Atlanta Braves	Turner Field	04/12/1997	50,062	335′	401′	330′
Chicago Cubs	Wrigley Field	04/23/1914	38,902	355′	400′	353′
Cincinnati Reds	Great American Ballpark	03/31/2003	42,059	328′	404′	325′
Colorado Rockies	Coors Field	04/26/1995	50,381	347′	415′	350′
Florida Marlins	Dolphins Stadium	04/05/1993	42,531	335′	410′	345′
Houston Astros	Minute Maid Park	04/07/2000	42,000	315′	435′	326′
Los Angeles Dodgers	Dodger Stadium	04/10/1962	56,000	330′	395′	330′
Milwaukee Brewers	Miller Park	04/06/2001	43,000	342′	400′	345′
New York Mets	Shea Stadium	04/17/1964	55,777	338′	410′	338′
Philadelphia Phillies	Citizens Bank Park	04/12/2004	43,500	329′	401′	330′
Pittsburgh Pirates	PNC Park	04/09/2001	38,127	325′	399′	320′
San Diego Padres	PETCO Park	04/08/2004	42,445	367′	396′	382′
San Francisco	AT&T Park	04/11/2000	40,800	335′	404′	307′
St. Louis	Busch Stadium	05/16/2006	49,625	336′	402′	335′
Washington	RFK Stadium	04/09/1962	56,500	335′	410′	335′

American League

Team	Ballparks	First Game	Capacity	Dimensions (feet)		
				LF	CF	RF
Baltimore Orioles	Oriole Park at Camden Yards	04/06/1992	48,876	333′	400′	318′
Boston Red Sox	Fenway Park	04/20/1912	36,298	310′	420′	302′
Chicago White Sox	U.S. Cellular Field	04/18/1991	44,321	347′	400′	347′
Cleveland Indians	Jacobs Field	04/04/1994	43,368	325′	405′	325′
Detroit Tigers	Comerica Park	04/11/2000	40,000	346′	422′	330′
Kansas City Royals	Kauffman Stadium	04/10/1973	40,625	330′	400′	330′
Los Angeles Angles	Angel Stadium	04/19/1966	45,050	333′	400′	333′
Minnesota Twins	Metrodome	04/06/1982	48,678	343′	408′	327′
New York Yankees	Yankee Stadium	04/18/1923	57,545	318′	408′	314′
Oakland Athletics	McAfee Coliseum	04/17/1968	43,662	330′	400′	330′
Seattle Mariners	Safeco Field	07/15/1999	47,000	331′	405′	327′
Tampa Bay Devil Rays	Tropicana Field	04/06/1998	45,200	315′	410′	322′
Texas Rangers	Ameriquest Field in Arlington	04/11/1994	49,166	332′	400′	325′
Toronto Blue Jays	Rogers Centre	06/05/1989	50,516	328′	400′	328′

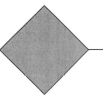

Appendix Q

MAJOR LEAGUE BALLPARKS USED BY CURRENT TEAMS, WITH NAME CHANGES

ARIZONA DIAMONDBACKS

Bank One Ballpark	1998–2004
renamed Chase Field	2005–

ATLANTA BRAVES

South End Grounds I (Boston)	1876–1882
South End Grounds II (The Grand Pavilion)	1883–1894
Congress Street Park	1894
South End Grounds III	1894–1914
Fenway Park	1914–1915, 1946
Braves Field	1915–1952
Milwaukee County Stadium	1953–1965
Atlanta–Fulton County Stadium	1966–1996
Turner Field	1997–

BALTIMORE ORIOLES

Sportsman's Park (St. Louis)	1902–1953
Memorial Stadium (Baltimore)	1954–1991
Oriole Park at Camden Yards	1992–

BOSTON RED SOX

Huntington Avenue Baseball Grounds	1901–1911
Fenway Park	1912–
Braves Field (Sundays)	1929–1932

CHICAGO CUBS

Twenty–third Street Grounds	1876–1877
Lakefront Park	1878–1884

Congress Street Park	1885–1891
South Side Park	1891–1893
West Side Park	1893–1915
Wrigley Field	1916–

CHICAGO WHITE SOX

South Side Park	1901–1910
Comiskey Park	1910–1990
County Stadium (Milwaukee)	1968–1969
New Comiskey Park	1991–2002
renamed Cellular Field	2003–

CINCINNATI REDS

Avenue Grounds	1876–1877
Bank Street Grounds	1880
Bank Street Grounds (AA)	1883–1883
Cincinnati Baseball Grounds (AA)	1884–1889
renamed League Park	1890–1902
Palace of the Fans	1902–1911
Redland Field	1912–1933
renamed Crosley Field	1934–1969
Riverfront Stadium	1970–2002
Great American Ballpark	2003–

CLEVELAND INDIANS

League Park	1901–1932, 1934–1946
Municipal Stadium	1932–1933, 1934–1946 (Sundays), 1947–1993
Jacobs Field	1994–

COLORADO ROCKIES

| Mile High Stadium | 1993–94 |
| Coors Field | 1995– |

DETROIT TIGERS

Bennett Park	1901–1911
Burns Park	1901–1909 (Sundays)
Navin Field	1912–1937
Briggs Stadium	1938–1960
Tiger Stadium	1961–1999
Comerica Park	2000–

FLORIDA MARLINS

Joe Robbie Stadium	1993–1995
renamed Pro Player Stadium	1996–2004
renamed Dolphins Stadium	2005–

HOUSTON ASTROS

Colt Stadium	1962–1964
Astrodome	1965–1999
Enron Field	2000–2002
renamed Astro Field	2002
renamed Minute Maid Park	2002–

KANSAS CITY ROYALS

Municipal Stadium	1969–1972
Royals Stadium	1973–1992
renamed Kauffman Stadium	1993–

LOS ANGELES ANGELS OF ANAHEIM

Wrigley Field	1961
Dodger Stadium	1962–1965
Anaheim Stadium	1966–1996
renamed Edison International Field	1997–2003
renamed Angel Stadium	2004–

LOS ANGELES DODGERS

Washington Park I (Brooklyn) (AA)	1884–1889
Ridgewood Park (AA)	1886–1889
Union Grounds (AA)	1889
Washington Park I	1890
Eastern Park	1891–1897
Washington Park II	1898–1912
Ebbets Field	1913–1957
Roosevelt Stadium (Jersey City)	1956–1957
Los Angeles Coliseum	1958–1961
Dodger Stadium	1962–

MILWAUKEE

County Stadium	1970–2000
Miller Park	2001–

MINNESOTA TWINS

American League Park (Washington)	1901–1910
Griffith Stadium	1911–1960
Metropolitan Stadium	1961–1981
Hubert H. Humphrey Metrodome	1982–

NEW YORK METS

Polo Grounds III	1962–1963
Shea Stadium	1964–

NEW YORK YANKEES

Hilltop Park	1903–1912
Polo Grounds III	1913–1922
Yankee Stadium	1923–1973
Shea Stadium	1974–1975
Yankee Stadium II	1976–

OAKLAND ATHLETICS

Columbia Park (Philadelphia)	1901–1908
Shibe Park	1909–1954
Municipal Stadium (Kansas City)	1955–1967
Oakland–Alameda County Coliseum	1968–1997
renamed Network Associates Coliseum	1998–2003
renamed McAfee Coliseum	2004–

PHILADELPHIA PHILLIES

Recreation Park	1883–1886
Huntington Grounds	1887–1894
University of Pennsylvania Athletic Field	1894
Baker Bowl	1895–1938
Columbia Park	1903
Shibe Park	1927, 1938–1952
renamed Connie Mack Stadium	1953–1970
Veterans Stadium	1971–2003
Citizens' Ball Park	2004–

PITTSBURGH PIRATES

Recreation Park	1887–1890
Exposition Park	1891–1909
Forbes Field	1909–1970
Three Rivers Stadium	1970–2000
PNC Park	2001–

SAN DIEGO PADRES

San Diego Stadium	1969–1979
renamed Jack Murphy Stadium	1980–1996
renamed Qualcomm Stadium	1997–2003
PETCO Park	2004–

SAN FRANCISCO GIANTS

Polo Grounds (NY)	1883–1888
St. George Grounds (Staten Island)	1889
Oakland Park (Jersey City)	1889
Polo Grounds II (Manhattan Field) (NY)	1889–1890
Polo Grounds III	1891–1910
Hilltop Park	1911
Polo Grounds IV (New York)	1911–1957
Seals Stadium (S.F.)	1958–1959
Candlestick Park	1960–1999
Pacific Bell Park	2000–2003
renamed SBC	2004–2005
renamed AT&T Park	2006–

ST. LOUIS CARDINALS

Sportsman's Park (AA)	1882–1891
Sportsman's Park	1892
New Sportsman's Park	1893–1898
renamed League Park	1899–1911
renamed Robison Field	1911–1920
Sportsman's Park	1921–1952
renamed Busch Stadium I	1953–1965
Busch Stadium II	1966–2005
Busch Stadium III	2006–

SEATTLE MARINERS

Kingdome	1977–1998
SAFECO Stadium	1999–

TAMPA BAY

Tropicana Field	1998–

TEXAS RANGERS

Griffith Stadium	1961
Robert F. Kennedy Stadium	1962–1971
Arlington Stadium	1972–1993
The Ballpark in Arlington	1994–2003
renamed Ameriquest Field in Arlington	2004–

TORONTO BLUE JAYS

Exhibition Stadium	1977–1989
Skydome	1989–2004
renamed Rogers Centre	2005–

WASHINGTON NATIONALS

Jarry Park (Montreal)	1969–1976
Olympic Stadium	1977–2004
Robert F. Kennedy Stadium (Washington)	2005–

Source: *Michael Gershman*, Diamonds: The Evolution of the Ballpark *(Boston: Houghton Mifflin, 1993)*; *Philip J. Lowry*, Lost Cathedrals: The Ultimate Celebration of all 271 Major League and Negro League Ballparks, Past and Present *(Reading, MA: Addison–Wesley, 1992)*; *Michael Benson*, Ballparks of North America: A Comprehensive Historical Reference to Baseball Grounds, Yards, and Stadiums, 1845 to Present *(Jefferson, NC: McFarland, 1989)*; *Munsey & Suppes, "Ballparks." http://www.ballparks.com/baseball/index.htm.*

Bibliography

Aaron, Hank, and Lonnie Wheeler. *I Had a Hammer: The Hank Aaron Story.* New York: HarperCollins, 1991.

Adomites, P. D. "Seattle Pilots—Milwaukee Brewers: The Bombers, the Bangers, and the Burners." In *Encyclopedia of Major League Baseball Team Histories: American League*, ed. Peter Bjarkman, 422–44. Westport, CT: Meckler, 1991.

Ahrens, Arthur R. "Chicago's City Series: Cubs versus White Sox." *Chicago History* 5 (1976–77): 243–52.

Ahrens, Art, and Eddie Gold. *The Cubs: The Complete Record of Chicago Cubs Baseball.* New York: Macmillan, 1986.

Alexander, Charles C. *Breaking the Slump: Baseball in the Depression Era.* New York: Columbia University Press, 2002.

———. *John McGraw.* New York: Penguin, 1988.

———. *Our Game: An American Baseball History.* New York: Henry Holt, 1991.

———. *Rogers Hornsby: A Biography.* New York: Henry Holt, 1996.

———. *Ty Cobb.* New York: Oxford University Press, 1984.

Allen, Dick, and Tim Whitaker. *Crash: The Life and Times of Dick Allen.* New York: Ticknor and Fields, 1989.

Allen, Maury. *After the Miracle: The 1969 Mets Twenty Years Later.* New York: Franklin Watts, 1989.

———. *The Incredible Mets.* New York: Paperback Library, 1969.

Altherr, Thomas L. *Above the Fruited Plain: Baseball in the Rocky Mountain West.* Cleveland, OH: Society for American Baseball Research, 2003.

Andelman, Bob. *Stadium for Rent: Tampa Bay's Quest for Major League Baseball.* Jefferson, NC: McFarland, 1993.

————. William B. "Sports Page Boosterism: Atlanta and Its Newspapers Accomplish the Unprecedented." *American Journalism* 17, no. 3 (2000): 89–107.

Anderson, William M. "From the Ballpark to the Battlefield . . . and Back!! The Detroit Tigers during World War II." *Michigan History* 79 (September–October 1995): 10–18.

————. "They Caught Lightning! The 1968 Detroit Tigers." *Michigan History* 77 (September–October 1993): 17–21.

Angell, Roger. "Fish Story." *New Yorker,* November 27, 1997, 79–87.

————. "The Sporting Scene: The Cool Bubble." *New Yorker,* May 14, 1966, 125–42.

Angle, Paul. *Philip K. Wrigley: A Memoir of a Modest Man.* Chicago: Rand McNally, 1975.

Anson, Adrian C. *A Ball Player's Career.* Chicago: Era Publishing, 1900.

Appel, Marty. *Now Pitching for the Yankees: Spinning the News for Mickey, Billy and George.* Toronto: Sport Classic Books, 2001.

————. *Slide, Kelly, Slide: The Wild Life and Times of Mike "King" Kelly, Baseball's First Superstar.* Lanham, MD: Scarecrow Press, 1996.

Asinof, Eliot. *Eight Men Out: The Black Sox and the 1919 World Series.* New York: Holt, Reinhart and Winston, 1963.

Avila, Eric. *Popular Culture in the Age of White Flight: Fear and Fantasy in Suburban Los Angeles.* Berkeley: University of California Press, 2004.

Axelson, Gustav. *Commy: The Life Story of Charles A. Comiskey, The Grand Old Roman of Baseball and Nineteen Years the President and Owner of the Chicago White Sox.* Chicago: Reilly and Lee, 1919.

Bak, Richard. *A Place for Summer: A Narrative History of Tiger Stadium.* Detroit: Wayne State University Press, 1998.

Barney, Rex, with Norman Macht. *Rex Barney's Orioles' Memories, 1969–1994.* Woodbury, CT: Goodwood Press, 1994.

Bartell, Dick, with Norman Macht. *Rowdy Richard: A Firsthand Account of the National League Baseball Wars of the 1930s and the Men Who Fought Them.* Ukiah, CA: North Atlantic Books, 1987.

Barzilla, Scott. *The State of Baseball Management: Decision-Making in the Best and Worst Teams, 1993–2003.* Jefferson, NC: McFarland, 2004.

The Baseball Encyclopedia: The Complete and Definitive Record of Major League Baseball. 10th ed. New York: Macmillan, 1996.

Bavasi, Buzzie, with John Strege. *Off the Record.* Chicago: Contemporary Books, 1987.

Bealle, Morris A. *The Washington Senators: An 87-Year History of the World's Oldest Baseball Club and Most Incurable Fandom.* Washington, DC: Columbia, 1947.

Benson, Michael. *Ballparks of North America: A Comprehensive Historical Reference to Grounds, Yards, and Stadiums, 1845 to Present.* Jefferson, NC: McFarland, 1989.

Berke, Art. *This Date in Chicago White Sox History*. New York: Stein and Day, 1982.

Bevis, Charlie. *Sunday Baseball: The Major Leagues' Struggle to Play Baseball on the Lord's Day, 1876–1934*. Jefferson, NC: McFarland, 2003.

Biesel, David. *Can You Name That Team?* Lanham, MD: Scarecrow Press, 1991.

Bingay, Malcolm. *Detroit Is My Own Home Team*. Indianapolis: Bobbs-Merrill, 1946.

Bjarkman, Peter C. *Baseball with a Latin Beat: A History of the Latin American Game*. Jefferson, NC: McFarland, 1994.

———, ed. *Encyclopedia of Major League Baseball Team Histories: American League*. Westport, CT: Meckler, 1991.

———, ed. *Encyclopedia of Major League Baseball Team Histories: National League*. Westport, CT: Meckler, 1991.

———. *The New York Mets Encyclopedia*. Champaign, IL: Sports Publishing, 2002.

Bodley, Hal. *The Philadelphia Phillies: The Team That Wouldn't Die*. Wilmington, DE: Serendipity Press, 1981.

Bogen, Gil. *Tinkers, Evers and Chance: A Triple Biography*. Jefferson, NC: McFarland, 2004.

Borst, Bill. *Baseball through a Knothole: A St. Louis History*. St. Louis: Krank Press, 1980.

———. *The Best of Seasons: The 1944 St. Louis Cardinals and the St. Louis Browns*. Jefferson, NC: McFarland, 1995.

———. *Still Last in the American League: The St. Louis Browns Revisited*. West Bloomfield, MI: Altwerger and Mandel, 1992.

Boswell, John, and David Fisher. *Fenway Park*. Boston: Little, Brown, 1992.

Bready, James H. *Baseball in Baltimore: The First 100 Years*. Baltimore: Johns Hopkins Press, 1998.

Briley, Ron. "The Houston Colt .45's: The Other Expansion Team of 1962." *East Texas Historical Journal* 32, no. 2 (1994): 59–74.

Broeg, Bob. *Redbirds: A Century of Cardinals' Baseball*. St. Louis: River City, 1984.

Brown, Warren. *The Chicago Cubs*. New York: G. P. Putnam's Sons, 1946.

———. *The Chicago White Sox*. New York: G. P. Putnam's Sons, 1952.

Browning, Reed. *Cy Young: A Baseball Life*. Amherst: University of Massachusetts Press, 2000.

Brunt, Stephen. *Diamond Dreams: 20 Years of Blue Jays Baseball*. Toronto: Viking, 1996.

Bryant, Howard. *Shut Out: A Story of Race in Boston*. New York: Routledge, 2002.

Buege, Bob. *Milwaukee Braves: A Baseball Eulogy*. Milwaukee, WI: Douglas American Sports Publications, 1988.

Burk, Robert F. *Much More than a Game: Players, Owners, and American Baseball since 1921*. Chapel Hill: University of North Carolina Press, 2001.

————. *Never Just a Game: Players, Owners, and American Baseball to 1920*. Chapel Hill: University of North Carolina Press, 1994.

Cagan, Joanna, and Neil deMause. *Field of Schemes: How the Great Stadium Swindle Turns Public Money into Private Profit*. Rev. ed. Monroe, ME: Common Courage Press, 1998.

Callison, John, with Austin Sletten. *The Johnny Callison Story*. New York: Vantage, 1991.

Campanella, Roy. *It's Good to Be Alive*. Boston: Little, Brown, 1959.

Cantor, George. *The Tigers of '68: Baseball's Last Real Champions*. Dallas: Taylor, 1997.

Carlson, Chuck. *True Brew: A Quarter Century with the Milwaukee Brewers*. Dallas: Taylor Publishing, 1993.

Carroll, John M. "Houston Colt .45s—Houston Astros: From Showbiz to Serious Business." In *Encyclopedia of Major League Baseball Team Histories: National League*, ed. Peter C. Bjarkman, 239–62. Westport, CT: Meckler, 1991.

Caruso, Gary. *The Braves Encyclopedia*. Philadelphia: Temple University Press, 1995.

————. *Turner Field: Rarest of Diamonds*. Marietta, GA: Longstreet Press, 2001.

Cash, Jon David. *Before They Were Cardinals: Major League Baseball in Nineteenth-Century St. Louis*. Columbia: University of Missouri Press, 2002.

Cauz, Louis. *Baseball's Back in Town*. Toronto: Controlled Media, 1977.

Cobb, Ty, and Al Stump. *My Life in Baseball: The True Record*. New York: Doubleday, 1961.

Cohen, Stanley. *A Magic Summer: The '69 Mets*. San Diego: Harcourt Brace Jovanovich, 1988.

Colangelo, Jerry, and Len Sherman. *How You Play the Game: Lessons for Life from the Billion-Dollar Business of Sports*. New York: American Management Association, 1999.

Condon, David. *The Go-Go Chicago White Sox*. New York: Coward-McCann, 1960.

Conner, Floyd, and John Snyder. *Day-by-Day in Cincinnati Reds History*. New York: Macmillan, 1983.

Cook, William A. *Pete Rose: Baseball's All-Time Hit King*. Jefferson, NC: McFarland, 2003.

Cramer, Richard Ben. *Joe DiMaggio: The Hero's Life*. New York: Simon and Schuster, 2000.

Creamer, Robert. *Babe Ruth: The Legend Comes to Life*. New York: Simon and Schuster, 1974.

————. *Baseball in '41*. New York: Penguin, 1999.

————. *Stengel: His Life and Times*. New York: Simon and Schuster, 1984.

Crepeau, Richard. *Baseball: America's Diamond Mind*. Orlando: University Presses of Florida, 1980.

Daniel, W. Harrison. *Jimmy Foxx: The Life and Times of a Baseball Hall of Famer, 1907–1967*. Jefferson, NC: McFarland, 1996.

Danielson, Michael N. *Home Team: Professional Sports and the American Metropolis*. Princeton, NJ: Princeton University Press, 1997.

Davis, Jack E. "Baseball's Reluctant Challenge: Desegregating Major League Spring Training Sites, 1961–1964." *Journal of Sport History* 19 (1992): 144–62.

Delaney, Kevin J., and Rick Eckstein. *Public Dollars, Private Stadiums: The Battle Over Building Sports Stadiums*. Piscataway, NJ: Rutgers University Press, 2003.

DeValaria, Dennis, and Jeanne Burke DeValaria. *Honus Wagner: A Biography*. New York: Henry Holt, 1995.

Deveaux, Tom. *The Washington Senators, 1901–1971*. Jefferson, NC: McFarland, 2001.

Devine, Christopher. *Harry Wright: The Father of Professional Base Ball*. Jefferson, NC: McFarland, 2003.

Dewey, Donald, and Nicholas Acocella. *The Ball Clubs*. New York: HarperPerennial, 1996.

———. *The Black Prince of Baseball: Hal Chase and the Mythology of the Game*. Wilmington, DE: Sport Classic Books, 2004.

———. *Encyclopedia of Major League Baseball Teams*. New York: HarperCollins, 1993.

———. *Total Ballclubs: The Ultimate Book of Baseball Teams*. New York: Sport Classic, 2005.

Dickey, Glenn. *Champions: The Story of the First Two Oakland A's Dynasties—and the Building of a Third*. Chicago: Triumph Books, 2002.

Di Salvatore, Bryan. *A Clever Base-Ballist: The Life and Times of John Montgomery Ward*. Baltimore: Johns Hopkins University Press, 1999.

Drysdale, Don, with Bob Verdi. *Once a Bum, Always a Dodger*. New York: St. Martin's Press, 1990.

Durocher, Leo, with Ed Linn. *Nice Guys Finish Last*. New York: Simon and Schuster, 1975.

Durso, Joseph. *Amazing: The Miracle of the Mets*. Boston: Houghton Mifflin, 1970.

Dykes, James J., and Charles Deeter, eds. *You Can't Steal First Base*. Philadelphia: Lippincott, 1967.

Eckhouse, Morris, ed. *All-Star Baseball in Cleveland*. Cleveland, OH: Society for American Baseball Research, 1997.

Eig, Jonathan. *Luckiest Man: The Life and Times of Lou Gehrig*. New York: Simon and Schuster, 2005.

Eisenberg, John. *From 33rd Street to Camden Yards: An Oral History of the Baltimore Orioles*. New York: McGraw-Hill, 2001.

Eisenrath, Mike. *The Cardinals Encyclopedia*. Philadelphia: Temple University Press, 1995.

Ellard, Harry. *Base Ball in Cincinnati: A History.* 1907. Reprint, Jefferson, NC: McFarland, 2004.

Eskanazi, Gerald. *Bill Veeck: A Baseball Legend.* New York: McGraw-Hill, 1988.

Euchner, Charles. *Playing the Field: Why Sports Teams Move and Cities Fight to Keep Them.* Baltimore: Johns Hopkins Press, 1993.

Falkner, David. *The Last Yankee: The Turbulent Life of Billy Martin.* New York: Simon and Schuster, 1992.

Federal Writers Project. *Baseball in Old Chicago.* Chicago: A.C. McClurg, 1939.

Feldman, Doug. *September Streak: The Chicago Cubs Chase the Pennant.* Jefferson, NC: McFarland, 2003.

Fetter, Henry D. *Taking on the Yankees: Winning and Losing in the Business of Baseball, 1903–2003.* New York: Norton, 2003.

Fetteroff, Robert J. "Baseball Public Relations: A Case Study of the Milwaukee Brewers (1970–1975)." Master's thesis, University of Wisconsin–Madison, 1975.

Finoli, David. *For the Good of the Country: World War II Baseball in the Major and Minor Leagues.* Jefferson, NC: McFarland, 2002.

Finoli, David, and Bill Ranier. *The Pittsburgh Pirates Encyclopedia.* Urbana, IL: Sports Publishing, 2003.

Fitzpatrick, Frank. *You Can't Lose Them All: The Year the Phillies Finally Won the Pennant.* Dallas: Taylor Trade, 2001.

Fleitz, David L. *Louis Sockalexis: The First Cleveland Indian.* Jefferson, NC: McFarland, 2002.

Fleming, Gordon H. *Murderers' Row.* New York: Morrow, 1985.

Flood, Curt, with Richard Carter. *The Way It Is.* New York: Pocket Books, 1972.

Fobes, Natalie, Frank Wetzel, and John W. Ellis. *A Diamond in the Emerald City.* Seattle: Seattle Mariners, 1999.

Fox, Larry. *Last to First: The Story of the Mets.* New York: Harper and Row, 1970.

Frommer, Harvey. *Baseball's Greatest Rivalry: The New York Yankees and Boston Red Sox.* New York: Atheneum, 1982.

Gallagher, Mark, and Walter LeConte. *The Yankee Encyclopedia.* Champaign, IL: Sports Publishing, 2000.

Garver, Ned. *Touching All the Bases.* Dunkirk, MD: Pepperpot Productions, 2003.

Gentile, Derek. *The Complete Chicago Cubs.* New York: Black Dog and Leventhal, 2002.

———. *The Complete New York Yankees: The Total Encyclopedia of the Team.* New York: Black Dog and Leventhal, 2004.

Gerlach, Larry R. "Crime and Punishment: The Marichal-Roseboro Incident." *Nine* 12, no. 2 (2004): 1–28.

Gershman, Michael. *Diamonds: The Evolution of the Ball Park.* Houghton Mifflin, 1993.

Gibson, Bob, with Phil Pepe. *From Ghetto to Glory: The Story of Bob Gibson.* New York: Popular Library, 1968.

Gilbert, Bill. *They also Served: Baseball and the Home Front, 1941–1945.* New York: Crown, 1992.

Glendzel, Glen. "Competitive Boosterism: How Milwaukee Lost the Braves." *Business History Review* 69 (1995): 530–66.

Godin, Roger. *The 1922 St. Louis Browns: Best of the American League's Worst.* Jefferson, NC: McFarland, 1991.

Gold, Eddie, and Art Ahrens. *The Golden Era Cubs, 1876–1940.* Chicago: Bonus Books, 1985.

———. *The Renewal Era Cubs, 1985–1990.* Chicago: Bonus Books, 1990.

Goldberg, Robert, and Gerald Goldberg. *Citizen Turner: The Wild Ride of an American Tycoon.* New York: Harcourt Brace, 1995.

Goldman, Steven. *Forging Genius: The Making of Casey Stengel.* Dulles, VA: Potomac Books, 2005.

Goldstein, Richard. *Spartan Seasons: How Baseball Survived the Second World War.* New York: Macmillan, 1980.

Goldstein, Warren. *Playing for Keeps: A History of Early Baseball.* Ithaca, NY: Cornell University Press, 1989.

Golenbock, Peter. *Amazin': The Miraculous History of New York's Most Beloved Baseball Team.* New York: St. Martin's Press, 2002.

———. *Bums: An Oral History of the Brooklyn Dodgers.* New York: Putnam, 1984.

———. *Dynasty: The New York Yankees, 1949–1964.* Englewood Cliffs, NJ: Prentice Hall, 1975.

———. *Fenway: An Unexpurgated History of the Boston Red Sox.* New York: G. P. Putnam's Sons, 1992.

———. *The Spirit of St. Louis: A History of the Cardinals and Browns.* New York: Spike, 2000.

——— *Wild, High, and Tight: The Life and Death of Billy Martin.* New York: St. Martin's Press, 1994.

———. *Wrigleyville.* New York: St. Martin's Press, 1999.

Gottlieb, Alan. *In the Shadow of the Rockies: An Outsider's Look inside a New Major League Baseball Team.* Niwot, CO: Roberts Rinehart Publishers, 1994.

Gough, David, and Jim Bard. *Little Nel: The Nellie Fox Story; An Up-Close and Personal Look at Baseball's "Mighty Mite."* Alexandria, VA: D. L. Megbec Publishing, 2000.

Grabowski, John J. *Sports in Cleveland: An Illustrated History.* Bloomington: Indiana University Press, 1992.

Graham, Frank. *The New York Giants: An Informal History of a Great Baseball Club.* Carbondale: Southern Illinois University Press, 2002.

Greenberg, Hank, and Ira Berkow. *Hank Greenberg: The Story of My Life.* New York: Times Books, 1989.

Gregory, Robert. *Diz: The Story of Dizzy Dean and Baseball during the Great Depression.* New York: Viking, 1992.

Gropman, Donald. *Say It Ain't So, Joe: The True Story of Shoeless Joe Jackson.* New York: Citadel Press, 2002.

Guschow, Stephen D. *The Red Stockings of Cincinnati.* Jefferson, NC: McFarland, 1998.

Gutman, Bill. *Cal Ripken: Baseball's Iron Man.* Brookfield, CT: Millbrook Press, 1998.

Hageman, William, and Warren Wilbert. *New York Yankees: Seasons of Glory.* Middle Village, NY: Jonathan David, 1999.

Halberstam, David. *October 1964.* New York: Fawcett Columbine, 1995.

———. *Summer of '49.* New York: Morrow, 1989.

———. *The Teammates.* New York: Hyperion, 2003.

Harrigan, Patrick. *The Detroit Tigers: Club and Community, 1945–1995.* Toronto: University of Toronto Press, 1997.

Haupert, Michael, and Kenneth Winter. "Pay Ball: Estimating the Profitability of the New York Yankees 1915–1937." *Essays in Economic and Business History: Selected Papers from the Economic and Business Historical Society* 21 (2003): 89–101.

———. "Yankee Profits and Promise: The Purchase of Babe Ruth and the Building of Yankee Stadium." In *The Cooperstown Symposium on Baseball and American Culture,* 2003–2004 ed. William Simons. Jefferson, NC: 2005, 197–214.

Hawkins, Jim, and Dan Ewald. *Detroit Tigers Encyclopedia.* Toronto: Sports Publishing, 2003.

Helpingstine, Dan. *Through Hope and Despair: A Fan's Memories of the Chicago White Sox, 1967–1997.* Highland, IN: self-published, 2001.

Helyar, John. *Lords of the Realm: The Real History of Baseball.* New York: Villard, 1994.

Henderson, Cary S. "Los Angeles and the Dodger War, 1957–1962." *Southern California Quarterly* 62 (1980): 261–69.

Hendrick, J. Thomas. *Misfits! Baseball's Worst Team Ever.* Cleveland, OH: Pocol Press, 1991.

Hertzel, Bob. *The Big Red Machine.* Englewood Cliffs, NJ: Prentice Hall, 1976.

Herzog, Whitey, and Kevin Horrigan. *White Rat: A Life in Baseball.* New York: Perennial Library, 1988.

Herzog, Whitey, and Jonathan Pitts. *You're Missin' a Great Game: From Casey to Ozzie, the Magic of Baseball and How to Get It Back.* New York: Simon and Schuster, 1999.

Hines, Thomas S. "Housing, Baseball and Creeping Socialism: The Battle of Chavez Ravine, Los Angeles, 1949–1959." *Journal of Urban History* 8 (1982): 123–43.

Hirshberg, Al. *The Red Sox, the Bean and the Cod.* Boston: Waverly House, 1947.

Hoffbeck, Steven R. *Swinging for the Fences: Black Baseball in Minnesota.* St. Paul: Minnesota Historical Society, 2005.

Hoffmann, Gregg. *Down in the Valley: The History of Milwaukee County Stadium; The People, the Promise, the Passion.* Milwaukee, WI: Milwaukee Brewers Baseball Club: Milwaukee Journal Sentinel, 2000.

Hofmann, Dale, and Martin J. Greenberg. *Sport$biz: An Irreverent Look at Big Business in Pro Sports.* Champaign, IL: Leisure Press, 1989.

Holtzman, Jerome. "The Cubs' Curious Experiment." *Sport*, 32 (August 1961).

Holtzman, Jerome, and George Vass. *Baseball, Chicago Style.* Chicago: Bonus Books, 2001.

———. *The Chicago Cubs Encyclopedia.* Philadelphia: Temple University Press, 1997.

Honig, Donald. *Baseball's 10 Greatest Teams.* New York: Macmillan, 1982.

———. *The Philadelphia Phillies: An Illustrated History.* New York: Simon and Schuster, 1992.

Humber, William. *Diamonds of the North: A Concise History of Baseball in Canada.* Toronto: Oxford University Press, 1995.

James, Bill. *The New Bill James Historical Baseball Abstract.* New York: Free Press, 2001.

Jennings, Kenneth M. *Balls and Strikes: The Money Game in Professional Baseball.* New York: Praeger, 1990.

Johnson, Arthur T. "Economic and Policy Implications of Hosting Sports Franchises: Lessons from Baltimore." *Urban Affairs Quarterly* 21 (1986): 411–33.

Johnson, Charles. *History of the Metropolitan Stadium and Sports Center.* Minneapolis: privately published, 1970.

Johnson, Tom L. *My Story.* Ed. Elizabeth J. Hauser. New York: B. W. Huebsch, 1913.

Jordan, David M. *The Athletics of Philadelphia: Connie Mack's White Elephants, 1901–1954.* Jefferson, NC: McFarland, 1999.

———. *Occasional Glory: The History of the Philadelphia Phillies.* Jefferson, NC: McFarland, 2002.

———. *A Tiger in His Time: Hal Newhouser and the Burden of Wartime Baseball.* South Bend, IN: Diamond, 1990.

Jordan, David M., Larry R. Gerlach, and John P. Rossi. "A Baseball Myth Exploded: Bill Veeck and the 1943 Sale of the Philadelphia Phillies." *The National Pastime* 18 (1998): 3–13.

Judge, Mark Gauvreau. *Damn Senators: My Grandfather and the Story of Washington's Only World Series Championship.* San Francisco: Encounter Books, 2003.

Kaese, Harold. *The Boston Braves, 1871–1953.* Boston: Northeastern University Press, 2004.

Kahn, Roger. *The Boys of Summer.* New York: Harper and Row, 1972.

————. *The Era: 1947–1957; When the Yankees, the New York Giants, and the Brooklyn Dodgers Ruled the World.* New York: Ticknor and Fields, 1993.

Kaline, Al, and Dan Eward. *John Fetzer: On a Handshake; The Times and Triumphs of a Tiger Owner.* Detroit: Wayne State University Press, 2000.

Kaplan, Jim. *Lefty Grove: An American Original.* Cleveland, OH: Society for American Baseball Research, 2000.

Kashatus, William C. *Connie Mack's '29 Triumph.* Jefferson, NC: McFarland, 1999.

————. "Dick Allen, the Phillies, and Racism." *Nine* 9 (2000–2001): 151–91.

————. *One-Armed Wonder: Pete Gray.* Jefferson, NC: McFarland, 1995.

Kerr, Jon. *Calvin: Baseball's Last Dinosaur; An Authorized Biography.* Dubuque, IA: Wm. C. Brown Publishers, 1990.

Kidd, Bruce. "Toronto's SkyDome: The World's Greatest Entertainment Centre." In *The Stadium and the City,* ed. John Bale and Olof Moen, 175–96. Keele, UK: Keele University Press, 1995.

Kiner, Ralph, with Danny Peary. *Baseball Forever: Reflections on Sixty Years in the Game.* Chicago: Triumph Books, 2004.

Klapisch, Bob, and John Harper. *The Worst Team Money Could Buy: The Collapse of the New York Mets.* New York: Random House, 1993.

Klapisch, Bob, and Pete Van Wieren. *The Braves: An Illustrated History of America's Team.* Atlanta: Turner Publications, 1995.

Klein, Alan M. *Baseball on the Border: A Tale of Two Laredos.* Princeton, NJ: Princeton University Press, 1997.

Kohout, Martin. *Hal Chase: The Defiant Life and Turbulent Times of Baseball's Biggest Crook.* Jefferson City, NC: McFarland, 2001.

Koppett, Leonard. *Koppett's Concise History of Major League Baseball.* Philadelphia: Temple University Press, 1998.

————. *The Man in the Dugout: Baseball's Top Managers and How They Got That Way.* Expanded ed. Philadelphia: Temple University Press, 2000.

————. *The New York Mets: The Whole Story.* New York: Macmillan, 1970.

Korr, Charles P. *The End of Baseball as We Knew It.* Urbana: University of Illinois Press, 2002.

Koufax, Sandy, with Ed Linn. *Koufax.* New York: Viking, 1966.

Kravitz, Bob. *Mile High Madness: A Year with the Colorado Rockies.* New York: Random House, 1994.

Kuhn, Bowie. *Hardball: The Education of a Baseball Commissioner.* New York: Times Books, 1987.

Kuklick, Bruce. *To Every Thing a Season: Shibe Park and Urban Philadelphia, 1909–1976.* Princeton, NJ: Princeton University Press, 1991.

Lang, Jack, and Peter Simon. *The New York Mets: Twenty-five Years of Baseball Magic.* New York: Henry Holt, 1986.

Langford, Jim. *The Game Is Never Over.* South Bend, IN: Icarus, 1982.

Launius, Roger D. *Seasons in the Sun: The Story of Big League Baseball in Missouri.* Columbia: University of Missouri Press, 2002.

Leavy, Jane. *Sandy Koufax: A Lefty's Legacy.* New York: HarperCollins, 2002.

Levine, Peter. *A. G. Spalding and the Rise of Baseball.* New York: Oxford University Press, 1985.

Lewis, Allen. *The Philadelphia Phillies: A Pictorial History.* Virginia Beach, VA: JCP Corp. of Virginia, 1983.

Lewis, Franklin. *The Cleveland Indians.* New York: G. P. Putnam's Sons, 1949.

Lewis, Michael. *Moneyball: The Art of Winning an Unfair Game.* New York: Norton, 2003.

Lichtenstein, Michael. *Ya Gotta Believe! The 40th Anniversary New York Mets Fan Book.* New York: St. Martin's Press, 2002.

Lieb, Frederick G. *The Boston Red Sox.* New York: G. P. Putnam's Sons, 1947.

———. *The Detroit Tigers.* New York: G. P. Putnam's Sons, 1946.

———. *The Pittsburgh Pirates.* New York: G. P. Putnam's Sons, 1948.

Light, Jonathan Fraser. *The Cultural Encyclopedia of Baseball.* Jefferson, NC: McFarland, 1997.

Lindberg, Richard. *Sox: The Complete Record of Chicago White Sox Baseball.* New York: Macmillan, 1984.

———. *Stealing First in a Two Team Town: The White Sox from Comiskey to Reinsdorf.* Champaign, IL: Sagamore Publishing, 1994.

———. *Stuck on the Sox.* Evanston, IL: Sassafras Press, 1978.

———. *The White Sox Encyclopedia.* Philadelphia: Temple University Press, 1997.

———. *Who's on Third? The Chicago White Sox Story.* South Bend, IN: Icarus Press, 1983.

Logan, Robert. *Miracle on 35th Street: Winnin' Ugly with the 1983 White Sox.* South Bend, IN: Icarus Press, 1983.

Longert, Scott. *Addie Joss: King of the Pitchers.* Cleveland, OH: Society for American Baseball Research, 1998.

Lowenfish, Lee. *The Imperfect Diamond: A History of Baseball's Labor Wars.* Rev. ed. New York: Da Capo, 1991.

———. "A Tale of Many Cities: The Westward Expansion of Major League Baseball in the 1950s." *Journal of the West* 17, no. 3 (1978): 71–82.

Lowry, Philip J. *Green Cathedrals: The Ultimate Celebration of All 271 Major League and Negro League Ballparks Past and Present.* Reading, MA: Addison-Wesley, 1992.

Luhrs, Victor. *The Great Baseball Mystery: The 1919 World Series.* Cranbury, NJ: A. S. Barnes, 1966.

Lyle, Sparky, and Peter Golenbock. *The Bronx Zoo.* New York: Crown, 1979.

Mack, Connie. *My Sixty-six Years in the Big Leagues.* Philadelphia: John C. Winston, 1950.

Mandel, Mike. *SF Giants: An Oral History.* N.p.: Self-published, 1979.

Markusen, Bruce. *Baseball's Last Dynasty: Charlie Finley's Oakland A's.* Indianapolis, IN: Masters Press, 1998.

Marshall, William. *Baseball's Pivotal Era, 1945–1951.* Lexington: University of Kentucky Press, 1999.

Masur, Louis P. *Autumn Glory: Baseball's First World Series.* New York: Hill and Wang, 2003.

Mays, Willie, with Lou Sahadi. *Say Hey: The Autobiography of Willie Mays.* New York: Simon and Schuster, 1988.

McCollister, John. *The Bucs! The Story of the Pittsburgh Pirates.* Lenexa, KS: Addax Publishing, 1998.

McGee, Bob. *The Greatest Ballpark Ever: Ebbets Field and the Story of the Brooklyn Dodgers.* New Brunswick, NJ: Rutgers University Press, 2005.

McGraw, John J. *My Thirty Years in Baseball.* Lincoln: University of Nebraska Press, 1995.

McKelvey, G. Richard. *The MacPhails: Baseball's First Family of the Front Office.* Jefferson, NC: McFarland, 1999.

McNeil, William F. *The Dodgers Encyclopedia.* Champaign, IL: Sports Publishing, 2003.

Mead, William B. *Baseball Goes to War.* New York: Farragut Publishing, 1985.

———. *Even the Browns: The Zany, True Story of Baseball in the Early Forties.* Chicago: Contemporary Books, 1978.

Miller, Donald C. *City of the Century: The Epic of Chicago and the Making of America.* New York: Simon and Schuster, 1996.

Miller, James Edward. *The Baseball Business: Pursuing Pennants and Profits in Baltimore.* Chapel Hill: University of North Carolina Press, 1990.

Miller, Marvin. *A Whole Different Ball Game: The Sport and Business of Baseball.* Secaucus, NJ: Carol Publishing, 1991.

Miller, Richard, and Gregory L. Rhodes. "The Life and Times of the Old Cincinnati Ballparks." *Queen City Heritage* 46, no. 2 (1988): 25–41.

Millson, Larry. *Ballpark Figures: The Blue Jays and the Business of Baseball.* Toronto: McClelland and Stewart, 1987.

Minoso, Minnie, with Herb Fagen. *Just Call Me Minnie: My Six Decades in Baseball.* Champaign, IL: Sagamore Publishing, 1994.

Mishler, Todd. *Baseball in Beertown: America's Pastime in Milwaukee.* Black Earth, WI: Prairie Oak Press, 2005.

Mona, Dave, ed. *The Hubert H. Humphrey Metrodome Souvenir Book: A Pictorial History of the Twins, Vikings, Gophers, Millers, Saints—and Metrodome!* Minneapolis: MSP Publications, 1982.

Mona, Dave, and Dave Jarzyna. *Twenty-Five Seasons: The First Quarter Century of the Minnesota Twins.* Minneapolis: Mona Publications, 1986.

Moore, Joseph Thomas. *Pride against Prejudice: The Biography of Larry Doby.* Westport, CT: Praeger, 1988.

Morgan, Anne. *Prescription for Success: The Life and Values of Ewing Marion Kauffman.* Kansas City, MO: Andrews McMeel, 1995.

Moss, Rivin, and Mark Foster. *Home Run in the Rockies: The History of Baseball in Colorado*. Denver: Publication Design, 1994.

Muskat, Carrie, comp. *Banks to Sandberg to Grace*. Chicago: Contemporary Books, 2001.

Nadel, Eric. *Texas Rangers: The Authorized History*. Dallas: Taylor Publishing, 1997.

Names, Larry D. *Bury My Heart at Wrigley Field: The History of the Chicago Cubs*. Neshkoro, WI: Sportsbook, 1990.

Nathan, Daniel. *Saying It's So: A Cultural History of the Black Sox Scandal*. Urbana: University of Illinois Press, 2002.

Neft, David S., Michael L. Neft, and Richard M. Cohen. *The Sports Encyclopedia: Baseball*. 25th ed. New York: St. Martin's Griffin, 2005.

Newhan, Ross. *Anaheim Angels: A Complete History*. New York: Hyperion, 2000.

Neyer, Rob, and Eddie Epstein. *Baseball Dynasties: The Greatest Teams of All Time*. New York: Norton, 2000.

Nichols, Fred. *The Final Season: The 1953 St. Louis Browns*. St. Louis: St. Louis Browns Historical Society, 1991.

Nichols, John. *The History of the Florida Marlins*. Mankato, MN: CreativeEducation, 1999.

Noll, Roger G., and Andrew Zimbalist. *Sports, Jobs and Taxes: The Economic Impact of Sports Teams and Facilities*. Washington, DC: Brookings Institution, 1997.

Okkonen, Marc. "The 1950 Detroit Tigers." *The National Pastime* 15 (1995): 154–56.

Okrent, Daniel. *Nine Innings*. Boston: Houghton Mifflin, 2000.

Oliphant, Thomas. *Praying for Gil Hodges: A Memoir of the 1955 World Series and One Family's Love of the Brooklyn Dodgers*. New York: St. Martin's Press, 2005.

Olney, Buster. *The Last Night of the Yankee Dynasty: The Game, the Team, and the Cost of Greatness*. New York: Ecco, 2004.

Orodenker, Richard. *The Phillies Reader*. Philadelphia: Temple University Press, 2005.

O'Toole, Andrew. *Branch Rickey in Pittsburgh*. Jefferson, NC: McFarland, 2000.

Overmyer, James. *Effa Manley and the Newark Eagles*. Metuchen, NJ: Scarecrow Press, 1993.

Page, Brian, Frederick Chambers, and Clyde Zaidins. "Into Thin Air: What's All the Fuss about Coors Field?" In *Above the Fruited Plain: Baseball in the Rocky Mountain West*, ed. Thomas L. Altherr, 53–62. Cleveland, OH: Society for American Baseball Research, 2003.

Pappas, Doug. "The Numbers." Pts. 1–8. *Baseball Prospectus*, 2001–2. http://www.baseballprospectus.com/article.php?articleid=1294.

Papucci, Nelson. *The San Diego Padres, 1969–2002: A Complete History*. San Diego: Big League Press, 2002.

Parrot, Harold. *The Lords of Baseball*. New York: Praeger, 1976.

Patterson, Ted. *The Baltimore Orioles: 40 Years of Magic from 33rd St. to Camden Yards*. Dallas: Taylor Publishing, 1995.

Pedersen, Paul Mark. *Build It and They Will Come: The Arrival of the Tampa Bay Devil Rays*. Stuart: Florida Sports Press, 1997.

Peterson, John E. *The Kansas City Athletics: A Baseball History, 1954–1967*. Jefferson, NC: McFarland, 2003.

Peterson, Richard. *The Pirates Reader*. Pittsburgh: University of Pittsburgh Press, 2003.

Pietrusza, David. *Judge and Jury: The Life and Times of Judge Kenesaw Mountain Landis*. South Bend, IN: Diamond, 1998.

———. *Lights On! The Wild Century-Long Saga of Night Baseball*. Lanham, MD: Scarecrow Press, 1997.

———. *Major Leagues: The Formation, Sometimes Absorption, and Mostly Inevitable Demise of Eighteen Professional Baseball Organizations, 1871 to Present*. Jefferson, NC: McFarland, 1991.

Plaut, David. *Chasing October: The Dodgers-Giants Pennant Race of 1962*. South Bend, IN: Diamond, 1994.

Pluto, Terry. *The Curse of Rocky Colavito: A Loving Look at a Thirty-Year Slump*. New York: Simon and Schuster, 1994.

———. *The Earl of Baltimore: The Story of Earl Weaver, Baltimore Orioles Manager*. Piscataway, NJ: New Century Publishers, 1982.

Porter, David L. "San Diego Padres: The Saga of Big Mac and Trader Jack." In *Encyclopedia of Major League Baseball Team Histories: National League*, ed. Peter C. Bjarkman, 465–512. Westport, CT: Meckler, 1991.

Porter, David, and Joe Naiman. *The Padres Encyclopedia*. Champaign, IL: Sports Publishing, 2002.

Post, Paul V. "Origins of the Montreal Expos." *Baseball Research Journal* 22 (1993): 107–10.

Povich, Shirley. *The Washington Senators*. New York: G. P. Putnam's Sons, 1954.

Prince, Carl. *Brooklyn's Dodgers: The Bums, the Borough, and the Best of Baseball, 1947–1957*. New York: Oxford University Press, 1996.

Puerzer, Richard J. "From John McGraw to Joe Torre: Industrial Management Styles Applied throughout the History of Major League Baseball." In *Baseball and American Culture: Across the Diamond*, ed. Edward J. Rielly, 137–49. New York: Haworth Press, 2003.

———. "The Kansas City Royals' Baseball Academy." *The National Pastime* 24 (2004): 3–14.

Queenan, Joe. *True Believers: The Tragic Inner Life of Sports Fans*. New York: Henry Holt, 2003.

Quirk, James, and Rodney D. Fort. *Had Ball: The Abuse of Power in Pro Team Sports*. Princeton, NJ: Princeton University Press, 1999.

———. *Pay Dirt: The Business of Professional Team Sports*. Princeton, NJ: Princeton University Press, 1992.

Rader, Benjamin G. *Baseball: A History of America's Game.* 2nd ed. Urbana: University of Illinois Press, 2002.

Rampersad, Arnold. *Jackie Robinson: A Biography.* New York: Knopf, 1997.

Ranker, Ryan Donald. "A Car Salesman and a White Elephant: Brewing Up Trouble in Milwaukee; The Mythical Promises of Publicly Subsidized Major League Baseball Stadium and the Reality." Master's thesis, University of Wisconsin–Milwaukee, 2001.

Ray, Edgar W. *The Grand Huckster: Houston's Judge Roy Hofheinz, Genius of the Astrodome.* Memphis: Memphis State University Press, 1980.

Reed, Robert. *Colt .45s: A Six-Gun Salute.* Houston: Lone Star Books, 1999.

Regalado, Samuel O. *Viva Baseball: Latin Major Leaguers and Their Special Hunger* Urbana: University of Illinois Press, 1998.

Reisler, Jim. *Babe Ruth: Launching the Legend.* New York: McGraw-Hill, 2004.

———. *Before They Were the Bombers: The New York Yankees' Early Years, 1903–1919.* Jefferson, NC: McFarland, 2002.

Reston, James. *Collision at Home Plate: The Lives of Pete Rose and Bart Giamatti.* New York: HarperCollins, 1991.

Rhodes, Greg, and John Snyder. *Redleg Journal: Year by Year and Day by Day with the Cincinnati Reds since 1866.* Cincinnati, OH: Road West Publishing, 2000.

Rich, Wilbur C., ed. *The Economics and Politics of Sports Facilities.* Westport, CT: Quorum Books, 2000.

Richmond, Peter. *Ballpark: Camden Yards and the Building of a Dream.* New York: Simon and Schuster, 1999.

Richter, Ed. *The View from the Dugout: A Season with Baseball's Amazing Gene Mauch.* Philadelphia: Chilton Books, 1964.

Rielly, Edward J., ed. *Baseball and American Culture: Across the Diamond.* New York: Haworth Press, 2003.

———. *An Encyclopedia of Popular Culture.* Santa Barbara, CA: ABC-CLIO, 2000.

Riess, Steven A. *City Games: The Evolution of American Urban Society and the Rise of Sports.* Urbana: University of Illinois Press, 1989.

———. *Sport in Industrial America, 1850–1920.* American History Series. Wheeling, IL: Harlan Davidson, 1995.

———. *Touching Base: Professional Baseball and American Culture in the Progressive Era.* Rev. ed. Urbana: University of Illinois Press, 1999.

Riley, Dan, ed. *The Red Sox Reader.* Boston: Houghton Mifflin, 1991.

Roberts, Randy, ed. *Pittsburgh Sports: Stories from the Steel City.* Pittsburgh: University of Pittsburgh Press, 2000.

Roberts, Robin, and C. Paul Rogers III. *The Whiz Kids and the 1950 Pennant.* Philadelphia: Temple University Press, 1996.

Robinson, Jackie, and Alfred Duckett. *I Never Had It Made.* New York: Putnam, 1972.

Robinson, Ray. *Iron Horse: Lou Gehrig in His Time.* New York: Norton, 1990.

Rose, Pete. *My Prison without Bars.* Emmaus, PA: Rodale.

Rosenbaum, Art, and Bob Stevens. *The Giants of San Francisco*. New York: Coward-McCann, 1963.

Rosenbaum, Dave. *If They Don't Win It's a Shame: The Year the Marlins Bought the World Series*. Tampa, FL: McGregor, 1998.

Rosentraub, Mark S. *Major League Losers: The Real Costs of Sports and Who's Paying for It*. New York: Basic Books, 1997.

Rosentraub, Mark S., and S. R. Nunn. "Suburban City Investment in Professional Sport—Estimating Fiscal Returns of the Dallas Cowboys and Texas Rangers to Investor Communities." *American Behavioral Scientist* 21 (1978): 393–414.

Rossi, John P. *The National Game: Baseball and Culture*. Chicago: Ivan Dee, 2000.

———. *The 1964 Phillies: The Story of Baseball's Most Memorable Collapse*. Jefferson, NC: McFarland, 2005.

Sands, Jack, and Peter Gammons. *Coming Apart at the Seams: How Owners, Players and Television Executives Have Led Our National Pastime to the Brink of Disaster*. New York: Macmillan, 1993.

Sarault, Jean-Paul. *Les Expos, cinq ans après (The Expos: Five Years Later)*. Montreal: Editions de l'Homme, 1974.

Schneider, Russell. *The Cleveland Indians Encyclopedia*. Philadelphia: Temple University Press, 1996.

Schott, Tom, and Nick Peters. *The Giants Encyclopedia*. Champaign, IL: Sports Publishing, 1999.

Scully, Gerald W. *The Business of Major League Baseball*. Chicago: University of Chicago Press, 1989.

Seidel, Michael. *Streak: Joe DiMaggio and the Summer of '41*. New York: Penguin, 1989.

———. *Ted Williams: A Baseball Life*. Lincoln: University of Nebraska Press, 2000.

Selko, Jamie. "Harry Who? The Story of Harry Heilmann's Four Batting Titles." *The National Pastime* 15 (1995): 45–50.

Seymour, Harold. *Baseball, Vol. 1: The Early Years*. New York: Oxford University Press, 1960.

———. *Baseball, Vol. 2: The Golden Age*. New York: Oxford University Press, 1971.

———. *Baseball, Vol. 3: The People's Game*. New York: Oxford University Press, 1991.

Shapiro, Michael. *The Last Good Season: Brooklyn, the Dodgers, and Their Final Pennant Race Together*. New York: Doubleday, 2003.

Shaughnessy, Dan. *At Fenway: Dispatches from Red Sox Nation*. New York: Crown Publishers, 1996.

———. *The Curse of the Bambino*. New York: Dutton, 1990.

Shecter, Leonard. *Once Upon the Polo Grounds: The Mets That Were*. New York: Dial Press, 1970.

Sherman, Len. *Big League, Big Time: The Birth of the Arizona Diamondbacks, the Billion-Dollar Business of Sports, and the Power of the Media in America.* New York: Pocket Books, 1998.

Shropshire, Mike. *Seasons in Hell: With Billy Martin, Whitey Herzog and "The Worst Baseball Team in History"—The 1973–1975 Texas Rangers.* New York: Donald I. Fine Books, 1996.

Sickels, John. *Bob Feller: Ace of the Greatest Generation.* Washington, DC: Brasseys, 2004.

Singletary, Wes. *Al Lopez: The Life of Baseball's El Senor.* Jefferson, NC: McFarland, 1999.

Skipper, John C. *Take Me Out to the Cubs Game.* Jefferson, NC: McFarland, 2000.

Slaughter, Enos, with Kevin Reid. *Country Hardball: The Autobiography of Enos "Country" Slaughter.* Greensboro, NC: Tudor Publishers, 1991.

Smelser, Marshall. *The Life That Ruth Built: A Biography.* New York: Quadrangle/ New York Times Book Co., 1975.

Snyder, Brad. *Beyond the Shadow of the Senators: The Untold Story of the Homestead Grays and the Integration of Baseball.* Chicago: Contemporary Books, 2003.

Solomon, Burt. *Where They Ain't: The Failed Life and Untimely Death of the Original Baltimore Orioles, the Team That Gave Birth to Modern Baseball.* New York: Free Press, 1999.

Spink, Alfred H. *The National Game.* St. Louis: National Game Publishing Company, 1911.

Spirou, Costas, and Larry Bennett. *It's Hardly Sportin': Stadiums, Neighborhoods, and the New Chicago.* DeKalb: Northern Illinois University Press, 2003.

Stanton, Tom. *The Final Season: Fathers, Sons, and One Last Season in a Classic American Ballpark.* New York: St. Martin's Press, 2001.

Staurowsky, Ellen J. "Sockalexis and the Making of the Myth at the Core of Cleveland's 'Indian' Image." In *Team Spirits: The Native American Mascot Controversy,* ed. C. Richard King and Charles Frueling, 82–106. Lincoln: University of Nebraska Press, 2001.

Stein, Fred, and Nick Peters. *Giants Diary: A Century of Giants Baseball in New York and San Francisco.* Berkeley, CA: North Atlantic Books, 1987.

Stein, Irving. *The Ginger Kid: The Buck Weaver Story.* Dubuque, IA: Elysian Fields Press, 1992.

Stevens, David. *Baseball's Radical for All Seasons.* Lanham, MD: Scarecrow Press, 1998.

Stockton, J. Roy. "The St. Louis Cardinals." In *The National League,* ed. Ed Fitzgerald, 170–209, New York: Grosset and Dunlap, 1959.

Stout, Glenn. *The Dodgers: 120 Years of Dodgers Baseball.* Boston: Houghton Mifflin, 2004.

———. *Yankees Century: 100 Years of New York Yankees Baseball.* Boston: Houghton Mifflin, 2002.

Stout, Glenn, and Richard A. Johnson, eds. *Red Sox Century: One Hundred Years of Red Sox Baseball.* Boston: Houghton Mifflin, 2000.

Stuart, Jeffrey Saint John. *Twilight Teams.* Gaithersburg, MD: Sark Publishing, 2000.

Suchma, Philip C. "From the Best of Times to the Worst Times: Professional Sport and Urban Decline in a Tale of Two Clevelands, 1945–1978." PhD diss., Ohio State University, 2006.

———. "The Selling of Cleveland Municipal Stadium: The Linking of Progressive Era Ideals with the Emerging Consumer Culture." *Sport History Review* 31 (November 2000): 100–19.

Sullivan, Dean A., ed. *Early Innings: A Documentary History of Baseball, 1825–1908.* Lincoln: University of Nebraska Press, 1995.

———. "Faces in the Crowd: A Statistical Portrait of Baseball Spectators in Cincinnati, 1886–1888." *Journal of Sport History* 17 (1990): 354–65.

Sullivan, Neil J. *The Diamond in the Bronx: Yankee Stadium and the Politics of New York.* New York: Oxford University Press, 2001.

———. *The Dodgers Move West.* New York: Oxford University Press, 1987.

Sumner, Jan. *Fat Pitch: My Six Seasons with the Rockies.* Denver: JaDan, 2000.

Terry, James L. *Long Before the Dodgers: Baseball in Brooklyn, 1855–1884.* Jefferson, NC: McFarland, 2002.

Thiel, Art. *Out of Left Field: How the Mariners Made Baseball Fly in Seattle.* Seattle: Sasquatch Books, 2003.

Thielman, Jim. *Cool of the Evening: The 1965 Minnesota Twins.* Minneapolis: Kirk House, 2005.

Thomas, Henry W. *Walter Johnson: Baseball's Big Train.* Lincoln, NE: Bison Books, 1995.

Thomson, Bobby, with Lee Heiman and Bill Gutman. *The Giants Win the Pennant! The Giants Win the Pennant!* New York: Kensington, 1991.

Thorn, John. *Total Baseball: The Ultimate Baseball Encyclopedia.* 8th ed. Wilmington: Sport Media, 2004.

Thorn, John, Pete Palmer, Michael Gershman, David Pietrusza, and Dan Schlossberg, eds. *Total Braves.* New York: Penguin USA, 1996.

Thornley, Stew. *Land of the Giants: New York's Polo Grounds.* Philadelphia: Temple University Press, 2000.

Threshton, Christopher. *The Integration of Baseball in Philadelphia.* Jefferson, NC: McFarland, 2003.

Titchener, Campbell B. *The George Kirksey Story: Bringing Major League Baseball to Houston.* Austin: Eakin Press, 1989.

Tofel, Richard J. *A Legend in the Making: The New York Yankees in 1939.* Chicago: Ivan Dee, 2002.

Treder, Steve. "A Legacy of What-Ifs: Horace Stoneham and the Integration of the Giants." *Nine* 10, no. 2 (2002): 71–101.

Tygiel, Jules. *Baseball's Great Experiment: Jackie Robinson and His Legacy.* New York: Vintage Books, 1984.

———. *Past Time: Baseball as History*. New York: Oxford University Press, 2000.

Unbelievable! The 2003 World Series Champion Florida Marlins. Chicago: Triumph Books, 2003.

Vanderberg, Robert. *'59 Summer of the Sox*. Champaign, IL: Sports Publishing, 1999.

———. *From Lane and Fain to Zisk and Fisk*. Chicago: Chicago Review Press, 1982.

———. *Minnie and the Mick: The Go-Go White Sox Challenge the Fabled Yankee Dynasty, 1951–1964*. South Bend, IN: Diamond, 1996.

Vecsey, George. *Joy in Mudville: Being a Complete Account of the Unparalleled History of the New York Mets from Their Most Perturbed Beginnings to Their Amazing Rise to Glory and Renown*. New York: McCall. 1970.

———. *Subway 2000: The Dramatic Story of the First Subway Series Since 1956*. London: Carlton, 2002.

Veeck, William, with Ed Linn. *The Hustler's Handbook*. New York: G. P. Putnam's Sons, 1965.

———. *Veeck—as in Wreck: The Autobiography of Bill Veeck*. New York: Putnam, 1962.

Voigt, David Quentin. *American Baseball, Vol. 1: From the Gentleman's Sport to the Commissioner System*. Norman: University of Oklahoma Press, 1966.

———. *American Baseball, Vol. 2: From the Commissioners to Continental Expansion*. Norman: University of Oklahoma Press, 1970.

———. *American Baseball, Vol. 3: From Postwar Expansion to the Electronic Age*. University Park: Pennsylvania State University Press, 1983.

Wagenheim, Kal. *Clemente!* New York: Praeger, 1973.

Walker, Robert Harris. *Cincinnati and the Big Red Machine*. Bloomington: Indiana University Press, 1988.

Walton, Ed. *Red Sox Triumphs and Tragedies*. New York: Stein and Day, 1980.

Ward, Arch. *The New Chicago White Sox*. Chicago: Henry Regnery, 1951.

Ward, Geoffrey, and Kenneth Burns. *Baseball: An Illustrated History*. New York: Knopf, 1994.

Warfield, Don. *The Roaring Redhead: Larry MacPhail, Baseball's Great Innovator*. South Bend, IN: Diamond, 1987.

Weiner, Jay. *Stadium Games: Fifty Years of Big League Greed and Bush League Boondoggles*. Minneapolis: University of Minnesota Press, 2000.

Westcott, Rich. *A Century of Philadelphia Sports*. Philadelphia: Temple University Press, 2001.

———. *Philadelphia's Old Ballparks*. Philadelphia: Temple University Press, 1996.

Westcott, Rich, and Frank Bilovsky. *The New Phillies Encyclopedia*. Philadelphia: Temple University Press, 1993.

White, G. Edward. *Creating the National Pastime: Baseball Transforms Itself, 1903–1953*. Princeton, NJ: Princeton University Press, 1996.

Whitfield, Shelby. *Kiss It Goodbye.* New York: Abelard-Schuman, 1973.

Whitford, David. *Playing Hardball: The High-Stakes Battle for Baseball's New Franchises.* New York: Doubleday, 1993.

Winfield, Dave, and Tom Parker. *A Player's Life.* New York: Avon Books, 1989.

Witt, Leonard, ed. *Magic! The 1987 Twins' Enchanted Season.* Minneapolis: Star Tribune, 1987.

Wolff, Rick. *Brooks Robinson.* New York: Chelsea House, 1991.

Zimbalist, Andrew. *Baseball and Billions: A Probing Look Inside the Big Business of Our National Pastime.* New York: Basic Books, 1994.

———. "A Miami Fish Story." *New York Times Magazine,* October 26, 1998, 26–30.

Zingg, Paul J. *Harry Hooper: An American Baseball Life.* Urbana: University of Illinois Press, 1993.

SELECTED MAJOR COURT CASES

Federal Baseball Club of Baltimore v. National League of Professional Baseball Clubs. 259 U.S. 200 (1922).

Martin v. Chandler. 174 F.2d 917 (2d Cir. 1949).

Gardella v. Chandler. 174 F.2d 198 (9th Cir. 1952), 346 U.S. 3546 (1953).

Toolson v. New York Yankees. 346 U.S. 356 (1953).

Flood v. Kuhn, 407 U.S. 258 (1972).

SELECTED MAJOR CONGRESSIONAL INVESTIGATIONS

U.S. Congress. House. Committee on the Judiciary. *Study of Monopoly Power: Hearings before the Subcommittee on Study of Monopoly Power.* Serial no. 1, pt. 6, *Organized Baseball.* 82nd Cong., 1st sess., July 30–October 2, 1951.

———. House. Committee on the Judiciary. *Organized Professional Team Sports: Hearings before the Antitrust Subcommittee.* 85th Cong., 2nd sess., June 17, 19, 20, 24–26, July 17–19, 24, 25, 31, August 1, 7, 8, 1957.

———. Senate. Committee on the Judiciary. *Organized Professional Team Sports: Hearings before the Subcommittee on Antitrust and Monopoly.* 85th Cong., 2nd sess., July 9, 15–18, 22–24, 28–31, 1958.

———. Senate. Committee on the Judiciary. *Professional Sports Antitrust Bill, 1964: Hearings before the Subcommittee on Antitrust and Monopoly.* 88th Cong., 2nd sess., January 30, 31, February 17, 18, 1964.

———. House. Committee on the Judiciary. *Antitrust Policy and Professional Sports: Oversight Hearings before the Subcommittee on Monopolies and Commercial Law.* 97th Cong., 1st and 2nd sess., February 10, 24, July 14–16, September 30, December 10, 1982.

———. Senate. Committee on the Judiciary. *Professional Sports Antitrust Immunity: Hearings before the Committee on the Judiciary.* 99th Cong., 1st sess., February 6, March 6, June 12, 1985.

————. Senate. Committee on the Judiciary. *Sports Programming and Cable Television: Hearing before the Subcommittee on Antitrust, Monopolies, and Business Rights.* 101st Cong., 1st sess., November 14, 1989.

————. Senate. Committee on the Judiciary. *Baseball's Antitrust Immunity: Hearing before the Subcommittee on Antitrust, Monopolies, and Business Rights.* 102nd Cong., 2nd sess., December 10, 1992.

————. House. Committee on the Judiciary. *Baseball's Antitrust Exemption: Hearing before the Subcommittee on Economic and Commercial Law.* 103rd Cong., 1st sess., March 31, 1993.

————. Senate. Committee on the Judiciary. *Stadium Financing and Franchise Relocation Act of 1999: Hearing before the Committee on the Judiciary.* 106th Cong., 1st sess., June 15, 22, September 13, 1999.

Index

Los Angeles Angels and, 659; New York Mets and, 243; no-hitter by, 176, 667, 838; as strikeout champion, 176, 667, 838; Texas Rangers and, 833–34

Saberhagen, Bret, 254, 650, 653; Colorado Rockies and, 146; Cy Young Awards by, 651; Kansas City Royals and, 646; as MVP, 647; New York Mets and, 248; no-hitter by, 651
Sain, Johnny, 584; Atlanta Braves and, 24, 32; New York Yankees and, 722
Salary cap, 433
Sandberg, Ryne, 86, 92; Chicago Cubs and, 82; as home-run champion, 92; as MVP, 90; Philadelphia Phillies and, 284
Sanders, Deion: Atlanta Braves and, 37; football and, 39
San Diego Padres: Alou and, 343; batting champions by, 349; Bowa and, 345; Brown, K. and, 347; Caminiti and, 347; Cy Young Awards by, 349; Dark and, 343; Garvey and, 345; Gossage and, 345; Gwynn and, 344; home-run champions by, 349; Kroc and, 342, 343, 344; managers of, 350; McCovey and, 343; McGriff and, 346; Morgan and, 343; MVPs by, 349; origins of, 339–40; Perry, G. and, 343; pitching leaders of, 351; postseason appearances by, 350; Rookies of the Year by, 349; scandal and, 343; Sheffield and, 346; Smith and, 343, 344; strikeout champions by, 350; team records of, 351; Valenzuela and, 347; Vaughn, G. and, 347; Winfield and, 343, 344
San Francisco Giants: Alou, F. and, 379; batting champions by, 392; Blue and, 384; Bonds and, 361; Cepeda and, 379; Clark W. and, 384; Cy Young Awards by, 392; Durocher and, 374; ERA champions by, 393–94; Ewing and, 356; Freedman and, 358–60; Frisch and, 367; Greenberg and, 369; home-run champions by, 393; Hubbell and, 370; Lurie and, 383–86; managers of, 396–97; Marichal and, 379; Mathewson and, 361, 364; Mays, W. and, 375; McCovey and, 379; McGinnity and, 361; McGraw, J. and, 306, 360–64; Mitchell and, 384; MVPs by, 392; night baseball and, 371, 372; no-hitters by, 394–95;

origins of, 355–57; Ott and, 370, 397; Perry, G. and, 381; pitching leaders of, 398; postseason appearances by, 395–96; Robinson, F. and, 384; Rookies of the Year by, 392; Rusie and, 361, 394; to San Francisco, 375–79; Stengel and, 368; Stoneham and, 367–69, 369, 371–72; strikeout champions by, 394–95; team records of, 397–98; Thompson and, 373–74; Thomson and, 375
Santana, Johan, 703; Cy Young Award and, 699; as ERA champion, 700; Minnesota Twins and, 698; as strikeout champion, 701
Santo, Ron: Chicago Cubs and, 80
Sasaki, Kazuhiro, 813; as Rookie of the Year, 811; Seattle Mariners and, 809
Sauer, Hank, 91; Chicago Cubs and, 78; as MVP, 90
Scandals, 326, 343, 368; Chicago White Sox and, 114, 535, 542–44; Cincinnati Reds and, 113; Kansas City Royals and, 646; McLain and, 625; New York Yankees and, 726; Rose and, 130–32
Schilling, Curt, 8, 11; Arizona Diamondbacks and, 5–6, 744; Boston Red Sox and, 525; as MVP, 7, 10; Philadelphia Phillies and, 288; as strikeout champion, 294
Schmidt, Mike, 280, 281, 283, 285, 286, 296; as home-run champion, 293; as MVP, 291, 295; Philadelphia Phillies and, 279
Schoendienst, Red, 424, 441; as manager, 427; St. Louis Cardinals and, 422
Schott, Marge: controversy with, 130–31
Scientific play, 16
Scoreboard: innovations to, 75, 112, 123
Scott, Mike, 171
Scully, Vin: Los Angeles Dodgers and, 656–57
Seattle Mariners: batting champions by, 811; Boone and, 809; Buhner and, 807; Cy Young Awards by, 811; ERA champions by, 811; Griffey, Ken, Jr. and, 801; Griffey, Ken, Sr. and, 804; home-run champions by, 811; Johnson, R. and, 801; managers of, 812; Martinez, E. and, 801; Moyer and, 809; MVPs by, 810; no-hitters by, 812; origins of, 801–3; Piniella and, 807; pitching leaders of, 813; postseason appearances by, 812; Rookies of the Year by, 811; Sasaki and, 809; strike-

About the Editor
and Contributors

Thomas L. Altherr is a professor of history and American studies at Metropolitan State College of Denver, where he has taught American baseball history since 1991. Together with Charlie Metro he wrote *Safe by a Mile* (2001). He has also edited a collection of pre-1820 North American primary-source sports documents and written several articles on baseball history, including "'A Place Level Enough to Play Ball': Baseball and Baseball-Type Games in Colonial America, the Revolutionary War, and the Early Republic," which won the 2001 McFarland/SABR Research Award. He is currently at work on a book about pre-1840 North American ball games. He has been playing senior baseball since 1999.

Kristin M. Anderson is the chair of the Art Department at Augsburg College in Minneapolis. She teaches courses in art and architectural history. A graduate of Oberlin College, she holds graduate degrees from Luther Seminary and the University of Minnesota. Her current research is focused on the intersections of baseball with art and architecture. She has written articles and papers on ballpark architecture with coauthor Chris Kimball, and they are working on a book-length history of Twin Cities ballparks. She first moved to the Twin Cities in 1961, shortly after the Twins arrived.

As third graders, **Robert K. Barney** and **David E. Barney**, twin brothers and native New Englanders, began to follow Red Sox (mis)fortunes in 1939, the year Ted Williams first arrived in Boston. Three-sport athletes at the University of New Mexico in the 1950s, they were later inducted into their university's Sports

Hall of Fame. Bob is professor emeritus at the University of Western Ontario and founding director of the International Centre for Olympic Studies. A former president of the North American Society for Sport History (1990–92), he was awarded the Olympic Order by the IOC in 1997. Among over 200 published works on the Olympics, baseball, and general sports history is his award-winning book *Selling the Five Rings: The IOC and the Rise of Olympic Commercialism* (2002). Dave is master emeritus at the Albuquerque Academy in New Mexico. A published author of both poetry and prose, including pieces written on baseball, he is also one of the nation's most experienced and respected swim coaches, having won 25 state championships while coaching more than 200 All-American swimmers and divers. He was named the National Federation of High School Athletics' inaugural Swimming Coach of the Year in 1995.

William A. Borst holds a PhD from St. Louis University (1972). Known widely as "the Baseball Professor," he taught what has been purported to be the first accredited baseball-history course in the Midwest from 1973 to 1974 at Maryville University. In 1984 he started the St. Louis Browns Historical Society and has written several books on the franchise, including *Still Last in the America League* (1992) and *The Best of Seasons: The 1944 St. Louis Browns and Cardinals* (1995). Sometimes called "the George Will of St. Louis," he has hosted his own talk show on WGNU radio since 1984 and has authored other nonfiction books such as *Liberalism: Fatal Consequences* (1999) and *The Scorpion and the Frog: A Natural Conspiracy* (2005). Since 2003 he has been the main contributing editor to the *Mindszenty Report.*

Jon David Cash is the author of *Before They Were Cardinals: Major League Baseball in Nineteenth-Century St. Louis* (2002), a 2003 finalist for the Seymour Medal that the Society for American Baseball Research (SABR) awards annually to the best book of baseball history or biography. He earned a PhD degree in American history at the University of Oregon, has taught for four different colleges, and currently lives in his hometown of Crossett, Arkansas.

Russell Field is a doctoral candidate in the Faculty of Physical Education and Health at the University of Toronto. His work focuses on the history of Canadian sport in the twentieth century.

John E. Findling is professor emeritus of history at Indiana University Southeast in New Albany. He taught sport history for more than 20 years, has done research on early baseball in Louisville and women's tennis, and with Kimberly Pelle edited *The Encyclopedia of the Modern Olympic Movement* (2004). He has also done extensive research and publishing in the area of world's fairs and exhibitions, authoring *Chicago's Great World's Fairs* (1994), and in diplomatic history, including *Close Neighbors, Distant Friends: United States–Central American Relations* (1987) and *The Dictionary of American Diplomatic History*

(2nd ed., 1989). In retirement, he manages a stamp and postcard business in Louisville, Kentucky, and frets constantly about the inability of the Chicago Cubs to reach the World Series.

Joel S. Franks teaches Asian American studies and American studies at San Jose State University. Possessing a PhD from the Program in Comparative Culture at the University of California, he has published substantially in sport history. His publications include *Crossing Sidelines, Crossing Cultures: Sport and Asian Pacific American Cultural Citizenship* (2000), *Whose Baseball? The National Pastime and Cultural Diversity in California, 1859–1941* (2001), and *Hawaiian Sporting Experiences in the Twentieth Century* (2002).

Steven P. Gietschier is senior managing editor for research for the *Sporting News*. He previously worked for the Ohio Historical Society and the South Carolina Department of Archives and History. A native of New York, he got his undergraduate degree from the School of Foreign Service at Georgetown University and his graduate degrees in history from Ohio State University. Gietschier is active in several professional associations, including the North American Society for Sport History, and he is a member of the Missouri State Historical Records Advisory Board.

Andrew Goldblatt, an administrative specialist in the Office of Risk Management at the University of California–Berkeley, is the author of *The Giants and the Dodgers: Four Cities, Two Teams, One Rivalry* (2003).

Adam R. Hornbuckle, who holds bachelor's and master's degrees in history from the University of Tennessee–Knoxville and a master's degree in medical history and ethics from the University of Washington School of Medicine in Seattle, is an independent scholar in Alexandria, Virginia.

John H. Jordan is an attorney in New York. He has a JD from Washington and Lee University School of Law and a bachelor's degree in history from Williams College.

Christopher W. Kimball is the provost and dean at Augsburg College in Minneapolis. Prior to becoming dean, he was chair of the History Department, where he taught courses in American and urban history. He also developed a popular course in baseball history. He is a graduate of McGill University and the University of Chicago. In collaboration with Kristin Anderson, he has studied local ballparks as important forms of urban architecture and identity. A New England transplant to the Midwest, he remains loyal to the Red Sox.

Robert F. Lewis II, an avid Athletics fan, spent 35 years in "corporate America" before retiring and becoming a doctoral candidate at the University of New

Mexico. He has an AB with honors from Princeton University and an MBA from Rutgers University. His dissertation, completed in 2006, is entitled "'Soft Ball': Marketing the Myth and Managing the Reality in Major League Baseball."

Richard C. Lindberg, a noted Chicago historian, has authored 11 books about the Windy City, including *The White Sox Encyclopedia* (1997) and three other team histories. Over the years he has served in an unofficial capacity as White Sox team historian, supplying statistics and information to the media-relations department. His books include *Chicago by Gaslight: A History of the Chicago Netherworld, 1880–1920* (1995) and *To Serve and Collect: Chicago Politics and Police Corruption from the Lager Beer Riot to the Summerdale Scandal* (1998).

Benjamin D. Lisle is a doctoral student in American studies at the University of Texas–Austin. His research addresses American popular culture, sports culture, architecture and design, and cultural and historical geography.

John McCarthy grew up in a suburb of Pittsburgh, Pennsylvania, and is a lifelong Pirates fan. He adopted the Brewers while working on his graduate degrees at Marquette University in Milwaukee. McCarthy is assistant professor of history at Robert Morris University. He lives in the city of Pittsburgh, where his time is spent teaching, finishing his doctoral dissertation, working with local neighborhood organizations, and rooting for the Pirates and Brewers to avoid setting the major-league record for most consecutive losing seasons in history.

Christopher Miller is a doctoral candidate at Marquette University, studying urban and suburban history, and teaches at Cardinal Stritch University and Alverno College. His dissertation is entitled "Forging the Iron Ring: Suburban Incorporation in Milwaukee County, Wisconsin, 1870–1920." His summers are spent working as a Questec operator in Milwaukee's Miller Park and traveling to other ballparks with his coauthor, John McCarthy. Miller has lived in Milwaukee since 1996. A fan of the game as well as its history, Miller is also an avid reader of performance analysis, and names *Baseball Prospectus* as an important influence in shaping his understanding of the game of baseball.

Paul M. Pedersen is an associate professor of sport marketing and sport communication at Indiana University, with a PhD in sport management from Florida State University. He has published over 25 peer-reviewed articles in national or international academic journals and is the author of *Build It and They Will Come: The Arrival of the Tampa Bay Devil Rays* (1997) and coauthor, with R. G. Schneider, of *Bobby Bowden: Win by Win* (2003).

Richard "Pete" Peterson is professor emeritus of English at Southern Illinois University. He is the editor of the Kent State University Press Writing Sports Series and the author or editor of six books, including *Extra Innings: Writing on*

Baseball (2001) and *The Pirates Reader* (2003). Peterson has also written books on James Joyce and William Butler Yeats. His baseball writings have appeared in the *Chicago Tribune* and his hometown *Pittsburgh Post-Gazette*.

Laura A. Purcell is the collections project manager at the International Tennis Hall of Fame and Museum in Newport, Rhode Island. She worked for the Arizona Diamondbacks in the ballpark attractions department from 2000 to 2005. She has her master's degree in public history from Arizona State University and her bachelor's degree in history from Washington and Lee University, and has written articles on softball and baseball history.

Edward J. Rielly chairs the English Department at Saint Joseph's College of Maine. In addition to 10 volumes of poetry, a book on Jonathan Swift's *Gulliver's Travels,* an examination of the popular culture of the 1960s, and a biography of F. Scott Fitzgerald, he has published two books on baseball: *Baseball: An Encyclopedia of Popular Culture* (2000; reprint, 2005) and *Baseball and American Society: Across the Diamond* (2003). He is currently preparing *Baseball in the Classroom: Teaching America's National Pastime.* Rielly has also published many individual articles, poems, short stories, and book reviews, and writes a regular newspaper column, "Around the Bases".

Steven A. Riess is a professor of American history at Northeastern Illinois University in Chicago, where he has taught since 1976. He is the author of *Sports in Industrial America, 1850–1920* (1995), *City Games: The Evolution of American Society and the Rise of Sports* (1989), *Touching Base: Professional Baseball and American Culture in the Progressive Era* (1980; rev. ed., 1999), and *Sports and the American Jew* (1998). He served two terms as editor of the *Journal of Sport History* and edits the Sport and Entertainment series for Syracuse University Press.

John P. Rossi is a professor of history at La Salle University in Philadelphia. A lifelong Phillies fan, he has authored three major studies of baseball's role in American history: *A Whole New Game: Off the Field Developments in Baseball, 1946–1960* (1999), *The National Game: Baseball and American Culture* (2000), and most recently *The 1964 Phillies: The Story of Baseball's Most Memorable Collapse* (2005). An essay he coauthored with David Jordan and Larry Gerlach, "A Baseball Myth Exploded: Bill Veeck and the 1943 Sale of the Phillies," won the Macmillan Award for the best baseball historical essay in 1998.

Jarrod Schenewark, a doctoral student in sport management at the University of Texas–Austin, received his BA in history from the University of Connecticut–Storrs (1994) and his MA in human biodynamics from the University of California–Berkeley (1998). He has worked for a number of years coaching collegiate football, and has five sons that enjoy playing baseball.

Myles Schrag, a SABR member since 2000, is author of *Diamond in the Desert: The Story of the Connie Mack World Series in Farmington, New Mexico* (2000) and *Grand Junction's JUCO World Series* (2004). He was born the same year as the Royals and made frequent trips to Royals Stadium as a kid.

Maureen Smith is a professor in the Department of Kinesiology and Health Science at California State University–Sacramento. She earned her BS and MS from Ithaca College and her MA and PhD from Ohio State University. Smith was raised in upstate New York and early on chose to root for the Yankees as opposed to the Mets. Her chapter "Muhammad Speaks and Muhammad Ali: Intersections of the Nation of Islam and Sport in the 1960s" appeared in *With God on Their Side: Sport in the Service of Religion* (2002), edited by Tara Magdalinski and Tim Chandler. Her chapter "New Orleans, New Football League, and New Attitudes: The American Football League All-Star Game Boycott, January 1965" is forthcoming in *Race and Sport in America*, edited by Michael Lomax.

David Stevens is the author of *Baseball's Radical for All Seasons: A Biography of John Montgomery Ward* (1998), a runner-up for the 1999 Seymour Medal for best baseball history or biography. Dave taught American history on the college level and has degrees from the University of Maryland and DePaul University. He has written many published articles on the nexus between baseball, minorities, and labor.

Philip C. Suchma's dissertation "From the Best of Times to the Worst of Times : Professional Sport and Urban Decline in a Tale of Two Clevelands 1945–1978 (Ohio State University, 1995), examines the relationship between professional sport and the American metropolis in post–World War II Cleveland. A native Clevelander, he previously published an article on the civic policy and ideology tied to the construction of Cleveland Municipal Stadium, where he also worked a summer job from 1992 to 1995.

Sarah Trembanis graduated with a BA in history from Duke University in 1999. In 2001, she received her MA in American history from the College of William and Mary, where she is currently a PhD candidate. Sarah is completing her dissertation, entitled "They Opened the Door Too Late: African Americans and Baseball, 1900–1947."

Michel Vigneault received a PhD in history from Université Laval in 2001. He has been a part-time lecturer in sport history (*chargé de cours*) in the Département de Kinanthropologie, Université du Québec à Montréal (UQAM), since 1996. He is a member of the editorial board of the *Sport History Review*. He wrote the entry on Tip O'Neill for the *Dictionary of Canadian Biography*. In 1987 he won the Prix Jean-Aucoin for young scholars from the Baseball Writers Association in Montreal for a paper on Jackie Robinson and the Montreal Royals.

Kevin B. Witherspoon is a lecturer at Florida State University specializing in twentieth-century U.S. history and the history of sport. Originally from New Orleans, he graduated with a BA from Florida State in 1993 and an MA from the University of Maine in 1996. He earned a PhD from Florida State in 2003 with a focus on race in sport and sport and international diplomacy. His most recent work is *Mexico '68: Protest, Politics, and the Modern Olympic Movement* (2006).